W9-BXX-997

Government and Politics in the Lone Star State

Theory and Practice

L. Tucker Gibson, Jr.
Trinity University

Clay Robison
Houston Chronicle

PEARSON
Prentice Hall

Upper Saddle River, NJ 07458

Library of Congress Cataloging-in-Publication Data

Gibson, L. Tucker.
  Government and politics in the Lone Star State : theory and practice / L. Tucker
Gibson, Jr., Clay Robison.—5th ed.
    p. cm.
  Includes bibliographical references and index.
  ISBN 0-13-117453-3
  1. Texas–Politics and government—1951- I. Robison, Clay. II. Title.

JK4816.G53 2005
320.4764—dc22

2004011042

Editorial Director: Charlyce Jones Owen
Acquisitions Editor: Glenn Johnston
Editorial Assistant: Suzanne Remore
Marketing Manager: Kara Kindstrom
Marketing Assistant: Jennifer Lang
Manufacturing Buyer: Sherry Lewis
Cover Design: Kiwi Design
Cover Photo: Skip Nall/Getty Images/PhotoDisc
Image Permission Coordinator:
Production Liaison: Marianne Peters Riordan
Full-Service Project Management: John Shannon/
    Pine Tree Composition
Composition: Interactive Composition Corp.
Printer/Binder: Phoenix Color Corp.

To my wife, Jena, a New Texan.
Clay Robison

To my grandchildren—Madelyn, Jared, Emma,
Victoria, and Grace: You and all of the other children
of the world deserve leaders who are committed to
democracy, justice, and peace.
L. Tucker Gibson, Jr.

Credits and acknowledgments borrowed from other sources and reproduced, with permission, in this textbook
appear on appropriate page within.

Pearson Education LTD., London
Pearson Education Singapore, Pte. Ltd
Pearson Education, Canada, Ltd
Pearson Education–Japan
Pearson Education Australia PTY, Limited

Pearson Education North Asia Ltd
Pearson Educación de Mexico, S.A. de C.V.
Pearson Education Malaysia, Pte. Ltd
Pearson Education, Upper Saddle River, New Jersey

10 9 8 7 6 5 4 3 2 1
ISBN 0-13-117453-3

Contents

CHAPTER 6
The Party System in Texas   160

CHAPTER 7
Elections, Campaigns, and Political Behavior   193

CHAPTER 8
The Texas Legislature   226

Preface

Americans tend to be ambivalent toward their governments. On one hand, there are high expectations that garbage will be picked up regularly, that street lights will work, restaurants will be regularly inspected, Social Security checks will be sent in a timely manner, roads will be paved, and so on. But taxpayers often want something for nothing. They believe that increased services should not cost any more. Taxes should not be raised. Services shouldn't be cut even if there is a financial crisis. And there are some who have open hostility toward their governments. Cut taxes, eliminate programs, deregulate, devolve power from the national government, and just get government off our backs.

This ambivalence is projected onto politicians as well. All those officeholders in city hall, the state Capitol, or Washington can't be trusted or are in politics for their own benefit. All of them, of course, except my city council member and congressman, who are doing a wonderful job.

Ambivalence toward government and politics is not a 21st century phenomenon. It is rooted in our historical experience and emerges from our political culture. But, to two longtime observers of politics, ambivalence or hostility toward government doesn't make much sense if those who express such attitudes have no knowledge or only limited knowledge of government, politics, and the policy making process. Criticism of the actions of policy makers is a legitimate exercise of one's rights and responsibilities in a democratic society. But if one's comments are based on ignorance, how does this contribute to holding those in office accountable or to the development of good public policy?

Perhaps we are excessively cranky, reflecting the many long hours we have spent observing, studying, and writing about government and politics in Texas.

Perhaps we have more time to study the subject, and besides, we get paid for it. Perhaps we are part of that small group of policy wonks who get their grins from watching the good, the bad, and the ugly of politics.

While these may be partial explanations, the truth of the matter is that we have a passion for the democratic system in which we live. It's flawed. Public officials and other actors in the political arena often act outrageously and irresponsibly. We lament the failure of reforms that would benefit the "disconnected" or the powerless in our state. We have seen the enactment of legislation that clearly had the handprints of the special interest groups. We have watched legislative battles that were over before they even began because deals had been cut in the back rooms. We pity those citizens who had read the textbook, followed the prescription to visit, call, fax, or e-mail their legislator to express their policy concerns. Justice is often denied to those without a fat checkbook. Despite the fact that the laws and administrative procedures require payments of child support, hundreds of thousands of Texas children are impoverished, in part, because child support payments are not made. It just isn't fair.

A democratic society is not always a virtuous society. From the perspective of Thomas Hobbes, a 17th century political philosopher, people are capable of all kinds of bad things and need governments to place constraints on their excessive behaviors. We are among other commentators on political behavior who are somewhat optimistic about politics and government. We believe that individuals are capable of noble acts. They do the right things and are not solely pursuing their self-interests. The trick, then, for a democratic system is to constrain the excesses of self-interests and to encourage civic virtue.

In the chapters that follow, you will be exposed to a great deal of factual material pertaining to state and local governments. Facts are the building blocks, but they only make sense if they are organized or rooted in concepts or theories. The facts that are presented are the most recent we have been able to find. We have made a continued effort to confirm the veracity of the information that we present, but there is always the possibility that we have made some mistakes. The more important issues regarding facts is that they quickly become dated. Expenditures of governments will change from year to year. Population characteristics are always changing. And the specific political actors change.

But the theories around which we have organized facts and information are far less likely to change. We have used many of the accepted theories of political science to present and develop our analysis. We use realignment theory in the analysis of the state's party system. We use the concept of institutionalization in the chapter on the Texas legislature. These and the other concepts that we present will provide you an enduring framework through which you can assess government and politics.

Both of the authors have their biases, but we have attempted to suppress these as much as possible. Our job is not to convert you to a particular philosophical or ideological position. It is to encourage you to formulate your own views based on a careful assessment of the materials presented.

One author is trained as an academic in the theories and concepts of the discipline that apply to the analysis of state and local government. He tends to be the one who writes pedantically. Despite his academic orientation, he has been engaged in party politics for over thirty years. He has served as a consultant to more than 60 local governments. He has owned a market research firm, and he has served on the San Antonio Civil Service Commission.

The second author is a journalist. He brings to the subject a thirty-five year career in journalism. He has covered state and local politics during this time, and his long career as the Austin Bureau Chief of the *Houston Chronicle* has placed him in proximity to the state institutions and many of the political actors who have contributed to the political history of the state over the last three decades. His job is to "tell the story," crafting the analysis to engage and interest the reader. Parenthetically, he is the one who has rewritten most of the arcane words of the first author.

This is our fifth go at this book, and we hope we have gotten better with repetition. Just as athletes must practice and practice until they get it write (oops, right), so must the student of politics and government.

There is updated information throughout. There are new stories as well as ones we just couldn't let go. There are new players and some old ones. There are new issues, but most of those we deal with are a continuation of an earlier sequel. The theories have remained the same.

It is our hope that this book assists you in your lifelong journey as a citizen. If it helps you understand the institutions and politics of the governments in Texas, we will feel that we have been successful.

A special thanks goes to two individuals. Bryan Henderson, who isn't even a Texan, served as our research assistant. Arleen Harrison handled many of the logistics required to complete the manuscript. Additionally, we'd like to thank Mary E. Barnes-Tilley, Blinn College, and Jimmie F. Strain, Mt. View College, for reviewing the fourth edition of this textbook while the fifth edition was under preparation for publishing. We continue to rely on the skills of the editorial staff of Prentice Hall, who bring direction and order to our work. We are appreciative of their humor, attention to details, and assistance when we have run into problems.

The Social
and Economic Milieu
of Texas Politics

> . . . Texas is a state of mind . . . It is a mystique closely approximating religion.
>
> *John Steinbeck*[1]

> American by birth. Texan by the grace of God.

> There are two kinds of people. Those who are Texan and those who wish they were.
>
> *Bumper stickers seen on cars in San Antonio*

Texans entered the twenty-first century with considerable optimism. The state's economy appeared to be in overdrive, continuing to outpace the nation's economy as it had done throughout the 1990s. Unemployment was low, and many individuals were working who previously had difficulty finding jobs. With increased revenues, governments across the state were able to hold the line on taxes and increase services. Deregulation of the energy industry was touted as a solution to high energy costs and a guarantee of adequate supplies of power. Commercial and residential construction expanded dramatically, and increased exports, particularly to Mexico, clearly demonstrated the state's links to the global economy. Many of the historic political conflicts seemed to be moving toward resolution, and the president of the United States was one of Texas's own.

But this euphoria or exuberance was soon jolted by a number of events that will shape the politics of the state for years. Excesses in the stock market resulted in reversals of dramatic proportions. Corporations and individuals lost huge amounts of money, and many of the baby boomers who had assumed that they were adequately

1

prepared for retirement awoke to the reality of evaporating wealth. Enron Corporation, a Houston firm and major player in energy deregulation, engaged in predatory policies and fraudulent accounting that raised questions about financial practices throughout the country. Recession set in with the loss of jobs and revenues, and governments across the state found themselves facing deficits that required reductions in services and employment. Those same problems, meanwhile, continued to be compounded by illegal immigration across the Mexican border. And, finally, the terrorist attacks on the World Trade Center and the Pentagon on September 11, 2001, challenged our long-held assumptions about the basic security of our country and our state.

Increasingly, the politics and economy of Texas, often described in terms of the state's uniqueness, are now challenged by global trends. The state's population has been, and will continue to be, transformed by immigration into Texas. The mass media has the potential to produce a homogenization of information, perceptions, and language that challenges the cultures of different regions of the state. The frontier, rural society characterized by the cowboy is long gone. The "Oil Patch," where wildcatters and roughnecks once prevailed, has been replaced by what one author dubbed the "Silicon Prairie," "where venture capitalists and software engineers roam."[2]

But Texas still has a rugged, larger-than-life mystique that annoys or amuses many non-Texans. In many subtle and not-so-subtle ways, Texans continue to manifest this historical legacy in their speech, their "can-do" attitude, their celebration of their "Texan-ness," and their actions. In what other state do you find the pervasive display of the state's flag or the pilgrimage of so many to the state's holy shrine—the Alamo? Behaviors and language with which others take umbrage and often misunderstand are viewed by most Texans to be simply part of the rich culture and legacy of the state.

PERPETUATING THE MYTHS OF TEXAS: THE COWBOY PRESIDENT AND THE KILLER D'S

As the nation pursued the war on terrorism, President Bush, who has been described by some as the "cowboy president," used a number of allusions to the frontier culture. He branded former Iraqi leader Saddam Hussein an "outlaw" and declared that he wanted terrorist Osama Bin Laden "dead or alive." At a conference in Aqaba on the Red Sea, Bush said that he was going to appoint a coordinator to "ride herd" on Middle East leaders along the peace trail. Many in his audience had no idea what he was talking about, but the characterization of Bush in cartoons and articles as a cowboy continues to feed the perceptions others have of the frontier culture of Texas and its style of politics.

The distorted images that other Americans have of Texans and the state were further reinforced during the 2003 legislative sessions, when House Democrats—characterized as the "Killer Ds"—fled to Ardmore, Oklahoma, and later Senate Democrats flew to Albuquerque, N.M., to delay Republican efforts to redraw congressional districts to favor GOP candidates. The national and world press attempted to sort out these theatrics in light of the state's political culture. Needless to say, cartoonists had a heyday in their caricatures of Texas politicians.

Source: BBC News, June 6, 2003.

Texas and Texans are not immune from the host of nagging, down-to-earth problems that confront most states. Despite the sense of size and wide-open spaces, Texans are only now coming to understand that their state is urban, with more than 80 percent of the population living in urbanized areas. Three of the ten largest cities in the United States—Houston, Dallas, and San Antonio—are located in Texas. Texans now confront many of the problems that other states have faced for decades, but a legacy of individualism and limited government make it difficult to adjust to these new realities of a changing economy, a changing society, and a changing political landscape.

Citizens across our country are woefully ignorant of their governments and those who make decisions affecting their daily lives. Texans are no different. Government is seen by many to be something in Austin or the courthouse, or it comprises people who do things to us, not for us. It's often described in terms of red tape, inefficiency, and anonymous or rude bureaucrats. And political campaigns are perceived as a form of organized mud wrestling in which candidates characterize each other as despicable, immoral, incompetent, or whatever, and this perception results in large numbers of Texans tuning out politics. Many distrust government—a traditionally strong sentiment in Texas—and hope it interferes with their lives as little as possible. Most Texans don't vote in elections, leaving the selection of public leaders to others.

There is irony in all of this. Like most Americans, Texans assume there will be potable water flowing through their kitchen taps, protection from epidemics, streets and highways on which to drive their cars, quality public schools to which they can send their children, parks for family outings, and police officers to help protect their lives and property. Moreover, many have come to believe that you can have all of this without raising taxes.

It should be obvious that we all have a stake in what governments do, because these institutions have a daily impact on our livelihoods and our quality of life. We pay taxes for a multitude of programs and services and would like to feel that the benefits we receive are worth what we are paying. People generally don't get excited or concerned about government, however, until it fails to meet their demands or expectations. Many Texans don't know much about their state and local governments— the governments directly responsible for essential daily services. Such indifference and ignorance can be harmful to the people's interests, particularly today, when Texas is in a critical period of change that will determine what kind of state it will be for years to come and, consequently, how well or how poorly the public's needs will be met. Our past, which has been marked by good times as well as bad times, is a prelude to our future, and decisions that we make about our politics, governments and public policies will determine how we can adapt to change.

CHALLENGES OF THE 21ST CENTURY

Sustained population growth; the continued transformation of the state's economy; environmental, transportation and water problems; and increased demands for governmental services pose tremendous challenges to the resources and capabilities of governments in the state. These policy issues also raise fundamental questions about the structures of our governmental institutions. The demographic characteristics of the state's population are also changing, as racial and ethnic minority groups increase in size and the population ages. Wealthy school districts have been forced to share revenue with their poor neighbors, but inequities in public education still persist and pose a significant challenge for developing a workforce that can compete in the global economy. Despite an unprecedented prison construction program and a decline in crime rates, many Texans still live in fear of crime. With the largest prison population in the nation, Texas now has concerns about how to reintegrate tens of thousands of ex-prisoners into the social system as productive citizens. Reduction in federal funds, new mandates, a decline in state and local revenues, high rates of unemployment or underemployment in various areas of the state, the influx of immigrants from Mexico and other countries, an aging population that requires long-term nursing care, large numbers of people who have no health care insurance, and changes in welfare laws have forced governments across the state to scramble to develop more effective and efficient means for assisting low-income populations. Intense battles over water and its use are affecting every area of the state. Finally, the state's growth has aggravated environmental problems that affect the health and well-being of everyone.

These problems and issues are the ingredients of contemporary Texas politics. They reflect the fundamental conflicts between competing interests and the way Texans decide "who gets what, when, and how."[3] Government and our form of politics are the systems that we have developed to structure conflict, develop an orderly and stable process by which competing interests can be expressed, and, finally, decide who will benefit and who will pay the bill.

As we begin our analysis of Texas government and politics, we ask why Texans and their public officials make the political choices they do. Why, for example, do expenditures for public education rank low in comparison to other states? How do we account for Texas's highly regressive tax system, which requires low-income citizens to pay a higher proportion of their income in state and local taxes than do the wealthy? Why are Texans so willing to fund the construction of highways, roads and prisons while letting their state rank near the bottom of all the states in expenditures for public welfare?[4]

These policy issues are directly linked to a variety of other questions about government and the political system. Texas functions under a state constitution that most scholars agree is obsolete, but when Texans had an opportunity in 1975 to adopt a modern constitution, they refused to do so. Why are Texans content to amend the present charter on a piecemeal basis, as they again did in 2003 when twenty-two constitutional amendments were submitted by the legislature to the voters? Why, until recently, was Texas a one-party Democratic state, and what explanations can be given for the transformation of state politics to a Republican dominant party system? And how are relationships among the state's ethnic and racial groups changing? Does a small group of powerful individuals make the primary policy decisions of the state, or are there various competitive centers of power? Many argue that special interests dominate state and local government, subordinating the public interest. Is this true? Have bitter, mudslinging political campaigns contributed to the public's loss of confidence in government and elected officials? Do Texans feel they are paying more but getting less for their tax dollars?

Most of these issues personally affect Texans. They pay the costs, even though they may not receive the benefits of every policy decision. The actions and decisions of governmental leaders can have an immediate and direct effect on people's lives, and, from time to time, those holding positions of power have made decisions that have cost Texans dearly. For example, the Enron debacle and the manipulation of energy markets were the result, in large part, of the failure of state and federal governments to regulate the energy industry adequately. And major cuts in governmental services in 2003 were the direct result of the refusal of the state legislature to increase taxes to offset the loss of revenues caused by the downturn in the state's economy.

Each generation has to address fundamental questions of the role of government, the relationship of the people to that government, and what can be done to make government more responsive and responsible. When one hears or reads of many of the contemporary policy debates or policy failures, there is a real sense of déjà vu—we have seen these problems and issues before. Funding of public education, a major problem now, was also an issue during the Texas revolution of 1836, the Reconstruction era after the Civil War, and throughout much of the state's history. There are also new issues, such as the regulation of genetic engineering, the changing international economy, the environment, the health and social problems posed by AIDS, and an aging population. But many of today's issues are enduring issues of government and politics.

The fundamental changes in the social, economic, and political structure of the state have required new solutions. Funding public education in the days of the one-room schoolhouse was one thing. Funding today's educational system in a way that provides equity among the state's 1,000-plus school districts is of an entirely different level of complexity.

The demographics, or population characteristics, of the state have changed dramatically since the 1940s, when Texas was still predominantly rural. Texas is now an urban state with urban problems. With a population of approximately 22 million, Texas is now the nation's second most populous state. Its ethnic and racial composition has changed, and it is also home to a large number of individuals who were born and reared in other parts of the United States or outside the country—people who have a limited sense of Texas history and politics. Although oil and natural gas are still important to the state's economy, economic diversification is the dominant theme promoted by business leaders, government officials, and economists.

Change places heavy demands on the state's governmental institutions, and there is increasing evidence that many of these institutions are incapable of responding adequately. As Texans face an accelerating rate of change in the twenty-first century, they will need to give increased attention to modernizing and adapting government to these new realities.

This chapter will introduce you to the people of Texas, the views they have of themselves, the state's political subcultures, and its economy. We refer to these factors generally as the political environment, a concept developed by political scientist David Easton to refer to the milieu, or context, in which political institutions function.[5]

THE MYTHS OF TEXAS'S POLITICAL CULTURE

Although most Texans have only a cursory knowledge of their state's governmental institutions, political history, and contemporary public policy, they do have views—often ill defined—of the state, its people, and its culture. Key elements of these views, shared by millions of Texans, are described by some scholars as **political myths.**

In recent years, serious scholarship has focused on myths as ways to assess the views people have of their common historical and cultural experiences. A myth can be regarded as a "mode of truth . . . that codifies and preserves moral and spiritual values" for a particular culture or society.[6] Myths are stories or narratives that are used metaphorically to describe past events, explain their significance to successive generations, and provide an interpretive overview and understanding of a society and its culture.[7] Myths provide a world picture or, in this case, a picture of the state of Texas. The relevance of a myth depends, in part, on the degree to which it approximates the events it is describing and its pervasiveness in the literature and popular culture of the state.

Texas has produced its own myth of origin, which continues to be a powerful statement about the political system and the social order on which it is based. For many Texans, the battle of the Alamo clearly serves to identify the common experiences of independence and the creation of a separate, unique political order.[8] No other state was a **republic** prior to joining the Union, and several scholars argue that independence and "going at it alone" from 1836 to 1845 resulted in a cultural experience that distinguishes the Texas political system from that of other states. The state's motto—the Lone Star State—is a constant reminder of this unique history. A whole set of heroes came out of the formative period of Texas history, including many who fought and died at the Alamo or secured Texas independence on the San Jacinto battlefield. Texas schoolchildren are introduced to these heroes at a very early age with field trips, or "pilgrimages," to the Alamo in San Antonio and visits to the San Jacinto monument in Houston.

The dime novel helped create the myth of Texas individualism by popularizing and exaggerating the image of the cowboy.

The Texas Rangers played an important (but sometimes controversial) role in the taming of the Texas frontier.

The Texas mythology also includes the Texas Ranger and the cowboy. There is considerable lore of the invincible, enduring ranger defeating overwhelming odds. Newspapers and dime novels in the nineteenth century introduced readers throughout the United States to the cowboy, who was often portrayed as an honest, hardworking individual wrestling with the harsh Texas environment. The cowboy's rugged **individualism,** with strong connotations of self-help and independence, symbolizes a political culture in Texas that doesn't like to look to government as a solution to many of its problems.[9] It is the kind of individualism that continues to be exploited by political candidates in campaign ads and by the state legislature in limited appropriations for welfare, health care, and other public-assistance programs. This legacy of individualism and risk taking is further reinforced by the stories of "wildcatters" who made and lost fortunes in the early days of oil exploration in the state.

The frontier to which the Texas Ranger and the cowboy belong is part of a cultural myth of limited government and unlimited personal opportunity. The Texas frontier experience also perpetuates the myth of "land as wilderness and land as garden."[10] The hostile Chihuahuan desert of the far southwestern part of the state eventually gives way to the more edenic green of the Piney Woods of East Texas. But, space, distance, and size are pervasive in a great deal of literature on the state. Literally thousands of books written about Texas provide varied perspectives on the geography and typology of the land. One might argue that the "wide open spaces" of the frontier shaped Texans' views of their autonomy, independence, vulnerability, and interdependence. It has clearly shaped attitudes toward land and the legal rights to use land as one sees fit.

The Texas myths, however, have been primarily the myths of the white (Anglo) population and have limited relevance to the cultural and historical experiences of many African-American and Hispanic Texans. From the 1840s to the mid-1960s, these latter groups were excluded from full participation in Texas politics and the state's economic and social life. To many Hispanics, for example, the Texas Ranger is not a hero, but a symbol of ruthless suppression often expressed in folk music.

— HOW I SEE IT —
MYTHS IN TEXAS HISTORY

T. R. Fehrenbach

T. R. Fehrenbach was born in San Benito, Texas, in 1925 to a pioneer South Texas family. He received a B.A. (magna cum laude) from Princeton University in 1947. He served in World II and Korea and retired as a lieutenant colonel.

Fehrenbach, who is one of the foremost authorities on Texas history, has published eighteen nonfiction books, mainly on historical subjects. *This Kind of War* (1963, 1995, 2000) is considered the classic military history of the Korean War, and *Lone Star* (1968, new ed. 1999) is the most widely read history of Texas and the basis for the 1986 PBS miniseries. He has contributed fiction and articles to a wide range of periodicals and newspapers and is a Sunday editorial columnist for the *San Antonio Express-News.*

Fehrenbach was interviewed by one of the authors.

Q: How do you use the concept of "myth" in the analysis and interpretation of Texas history?

A: It is impossible to create events exactly as if you were there, and people see and interpret the same event differently. History and myths are often combined so that you can't tell the difference. What a myth does is to explain the beginnings. The myths of Texas history established the nineteenth century as a familiar place, and it told us who we were and where we came from. The Alamo, the Indian Wars, the oil boom—all are true events. Myths created an imagery of life and events of that period which are still with us. They serve us by giving us a sense of belonging.

Myths give you a sense of being a people. The Texas of 1820 to the 1940s, which was rural, created a common view of what it was like to be a Texan. It is not quite nationhood but a distinct regional subculture. While many in Texas did not recognize it, Europeans saw Texas as a state where Texans had a sense of "peoplehood," with a common heritage and linkage to the soil.

Q: With all the changes that have occurred in Texas since the 1960s, does the concept of myth still have use?

A: I initially thought that with the changes that were occurring since the 1940s, Texas would lose its sense of uniqueness. We would become much like the rest of the nation. However, we have a different, unique history.

Texas has experienced enormous changes since the 1940s, but we have not been able to redefine a new mythology that integrates all of the changes in race, ethnicity, gender, and economics. Even with a large influx of new individuals and the changes to a "high-tech" economy, as long as we retain our feeling for our history, the "heroic" era of our beginnings, we will retain a certain "Texan-ness." In this sense, the more Texas changes, the more it will be the same.

One of many activities celebrating Martin Luther King, Jr.'s birthday, which is now a national and a state holiday, was held outside the Texas state capitol.

Over the past twenty years, African Americans and Hispanics have made significant political and economic gains. Their share of the population has been increasing as well, and they are expected to constitute a majority of the state's population during the first quarter of the twenty-first century.

As this shift occurs, Hispanic and African-American historical experiences are likely to be incorporated into the mythology of the state, and some components of the mythology will be redefined. These revisions may already be under way, as demonstrated by heated debates over what actually took place during the battle of the Alamo. According to recent accounts, some of the Alamo's heroes surrendered to Mexican soldiers and were executed, rather than fighting to the death, as was long believed. African Americans in Texas have been successful, after several years of trying, in persuading the legislature to make Martin Luther King, Jr.'s birthday a state holiday. June 19, the day slaves in Texas learned of their emancipation in 1865, also has significant meaning for the state's African Americans and is celebrated as the Juneteenth holiday. For Hispanics, the *Cinco de Mayo* and *Diez y Seis* celebrations speak to common cultural and historical experiences.

THE POLITICAL CULTURE OF TEXAS

Texas shares the common constitutional, institutional, and legal arrangements that have developed in all fifty states, including a commitment to personal liberties, equality, justice, the rule of law, and popular sovereignty with its limitations on government. But there are differences among the states and even among regions within individual

Throughout Texas, Cinco de Mayo is celebrated by Hispanics in commemoration of Mexico's defeat of French troops at Puebla, Mexico, in 1862.

states. Texas is a highly diverse state, with racial and ethnic differences from one region to another and divergences in political attitudes and behavior that are reflected in the state's politics and public policies. Individuals who come to Texas are often more aware of these differences than Texans.

The concept of political culture helps us compare some of these differences. **Political culture** has been defined as the "set of attitudes, beliefs, and sentiments which give order and meaning to a political process and which provide the underlying assumptions and rules that govern behavior in the political system."[11] The political culture of the state includes fundamental beliefs about the proper role of government, the relationship of the government to its citizens, and who should govern.[12] These complex attitudes and behaviors are rooted in the historical experience of the nation, shaped by the groups that immigrated to the United States, and carried across the continent to Texas.

One authority on American political culture, Daniel Elazar, believes that three political subcultures have emerged over time in the United States: the individualistic, the moralistic, and the traditionalistic. While all three draw from the common historical legacy of the nation, they have produced regional political differences. Sometimes they complement each other, while at other times they produce conflict.[13]

The Individualistic Subculture

The political view of the **individualistic subculture** holds that politics and government function as a marketplace. Government does not have to be concerned with creating a good or moral society but exists for strictly "utilitarian reasons, to handle those functions demanded by the people it is created to serve."[14] Government should be limited and its intervention in the private activities of its citizens should be kept to a minimum. The primary function of government is to assure the stability of a society so that individuals can pursue their own interests.

In this view, politics is not a high calling or noble pursuit but is like any other business venture in which skill and talent prevail and the individual can expect economic and social benefits. Politics is often perceived by the general public to be a dirty business that should be left to those willing to soil their hands in the political arena. This tradition may well contribute to political corruption, and members of the electorate who share this view may not be overly concerned when government corruption is revealed. New policy initiatives are more likely to be initiated by interest groups or private individuals than by public officials, and it is assumed that those elected to public office will pursue their self-interests.[15]

The Moralistic Subculture

The **moralistic subculture** regards politics as one of the "great activities of man in his search for the good society."[16] Politics, it maintains, is the pursuit of the common good. Unlike the attitude expressed in the individualistic subculture, that governments are to be limited, the moralistic subculture considers government a positive instrument with a responsibility to promote the general welfare.[17] Politics, therefore, is not to be left to the few but is a responsibility of every individual. Politics is a duty and possibly a high calling. This cultural tradition has a strong sense of service. It requires a high moral standard for those holding public office and believes public office is not to be used for personal gain. Politics may be organized around political parties, but this tradition has produced nonpartisanship where party labels and organizations are eliminated or play a reduced role.[18] This tradition produces a large number of "amateur" or "nonprofessional" political activists and officeholders and has little toleration for political corruption. From the moralistic perspective, governments should actively intervene to enhance the social and economic interests of their citizens. Public policy initiatives can come from officeholders as well as from those outside the formal governmental structure.[19]

The Traditionalistic Subculture

The **traditionalistic** political subculture holds the view that there is a hierarchical arrangement to the political order. This hierarchy serves to limit the power and influence of the general public, while allocating authority to a few individuals who comprise a self-perpetuating elite. The elite may enact policies that benefit the general public, but that is secondary to its own interests and objectives. Public policy reflects the interests of those who exercise influence and control, and the benefits of public policy go disproportionately to the elites.

Family and social relationships form the basis for maintaining this elite structure rather than mass political participation. In fact, in many regions of the country where traditionalistic patterns existed, there were systematic efforts to reduce or eliminate the participation of the general public. Although political parties may exist in such a subculture, they have only minimal importance often subject to manipulation or control by elites. Many of the states characterized by the traditionalistic subculture were southern states in which two-party politics was replaced by factionalism within the Democratic party.[20]

Historical Origins of Political Subcultures

The historical origins of these three subcultures can be explained, in part, by the early settlement patterns of the United States and by the cultural differences among the groups of people who initially settled the eastern seaboard. In very general terms, the New England colonists, influenced by Puritan and congregational religious groups, spawned the moralistic subculture. Settlers with entrepreneurial concerns and individualistic attitudes tended to locate in the mid-Atlantic states, while the initial settlement of the South was dominated by elites who aspired, in part, to re-create a semi-feudal society.

As expansion toward the western frontiers progressed, there were identifiable migration patterns from the initial three settlement regions. Texas was settled primarily by people holding the individualistic and traditionalistic views of a political system. The blending of these two views, along with the historical experience of the Republic and the frontier, have contributed to the distinct characteristics of the Texas political culture.[21]

These two political subcultures have merged to shape Texans' general views of what government should do, who should govern, and what constitutes good public policy. Given the characteristics of these two traditions, one might well conclude, as have many scholars, that the Texas culture is conservative. Politics in Texas is designed to minimize the role of government, is hostile toward taxes—especially those that are allocated toward social services—and is potentially manipulated by the few for their own narrow advantages. During much of its history, Texas was one of the least democratic states, with restrictions on voting rights, limited party competition and low rates of voter participation.[22]

Some scholars have reservations about the concept of political subcultures because it is a complex theory that is difficult to test. Their reservations are legitimate, but we know of no other single theory that presents such a rich historical perspective on the relationship of settlement patterns in the state and the evolution of political attitudes and behavior.

THE PEOPLE OF TEXAS

The politics and government of Texas can be understood, in part, from the perspective of the people living in the state. What follows is an assessment of a select number of demographic, or population, characteristics of Texans. In subsequent chapters, we examine the relationship of race, ethnicity, and other demographic characteristics to partisan behavior, public opinion, institutional power, and public policy.

Native Americans

There are only three small Native-American groups (Alabama-Coushatta, Tigua, and Kickapoo) living on reservations in Texas, and the Native-American population is

A Tigua father prepares a meal for his children. The Tiguas are one of only three Native American groups with reservations in Texas.

less than one-half of 1 percent of the state's total population. Unlike Native Americans in Oklahoma, New Mexico, and Arizona, those in Texas have little influence on governmental institutions, politics, or public policy.

In the early nineteenth century, there were at least twenty-three different Native-American groups residing in Texas. During the period of the Republic (1836–1845), President Sam Houston attempted to follow a policy of "peace and friendship" with the Native Americans, but he was followed by President Mirabeau B. Lamar, who set out to "expel, defeat, or exterminate" them. Statehood did not improve the conditions for Native Americans, and the period between annexation in 1845 and the Civil War (1861–1865) was "one of devastation, decimation, and dislocation" for many of the state's tribes.[23] As the eastern populations expanded to lands traditionally claimed by various Native-American tribes, conflict ensued, and most of the Native-American population was eventually eliminated or displaced to other states.

Hispanics

In the eighteenth and nineteenth centuries, neither Spain nor Mexico was very successful in convincing Hispanics to settle in the Tejas territory of Mexico. The Spanish regarded it as a border province of relatively little value, except as a strategic buffer between Spanish colonies and those held by the British and the French. By the time Mexico declared its independence from Spain in 1821, the total Texas population under Spanish control was estimated to be approximately 5,000 people. With the

---

WHAT'S IN A NAME?

The Native-American legacy of Texas remains in the state's name. The word "Texas" is derived from Tejas, which means "friends" or "allies." As Spanish explorers and missionaries moved across Texas, they confronted a Native-American confederacy, the Hasinai. It was to this particular group that they applied the term, and, eventually, the Anglo form of the name became the permanent name of the region and then the state.*

In 1989, the Texas Department of Transportation proposed changing the state's vehicle license plates to include the phrase "The Friendship State." The public reaction, however, was immediate and generally hostile, and the proposal was quickly dropped. Some Texans apparently found the phrase incompatible with the state's rugged frontier image. The irony is that the common nomenclature for the state, which means friendship, is used almost every day by these same people.

———————

*Source: Rupert N. Richardson, Ernest Wallace, and Adrian Anderson, *Texas: The Lone Star State,* 5th ed. (Englewood Cliffs, N.J.: Prentice Hall, 1988), p. 1.

---

rapid expansion of Anglo-American immigration to Texas in the 1820s and 1830s, Hispanics became a small minority of the population.[24]

Some Hispanics were part of the Texas independence movement from Mexico, and, after independence in 1836, men such as Jose Antonio Navarro and Juan Seguin were part of the Republic's political establishment. But the Anglo migration rapidly overwhelmed the Hispanic population and greatly reduced its political and economic power. There was even an effort at the Constitutional Convention of 1845 to strip Hispanics of the right to vote. The attempt failed, but it was an early indication of Anglo hostility toward the Hispanic population.[25]

By 1887, the Hispanic population had declined to approximately 4 percent of the state's population. In 1930, it was 12 percent and was concentrated in the border counties from Brownsville to El Paso (Figure 1–1). Modest increases in the Hispanic population continued until it reached 18 percent of the state's population in 1970, after which it grew at a more rapid rate. By 1990, it had reached 25 percent, spurred by immigration from Mexico and other Latin American countries as well as by higher birth rates among Hispanic women. These growth patterns continued in the 1990s, and by 2000, Hispanics comprised 32 percent of the state's population. In addition to their traditional concentrations in the Rio Grande Valley and South-Central Texas, large Hispanic populations are found in most metropolitan areas. Except for the Asian population, which is still considerably smaller, the Hispanic population is growing at a significantly higher rate than other populations in Texas.

Hispanics will continue to increase at a higher rate than most other populations, and by 2010, the Hispanic population is likely to exceed 39 percent of the state's population. By 2020, this figure may have grown to 46 percent.[26] This growth in population is being translated into political power and influence. Four Hispanics have been elected to statewide office. And, after successful redistricting and legal challenges to city, county, school board, and state legislative districts, Hispanics in 2003 held approximately 1,965 elected positions in Texas, the highest number of any state.[27]

The regions of the state where Hispanics were concentrated (South Texas and along the Mexican border) before their more widespread migration to cities were

FIGURE 1–1   Ethnic and Racial Composition of Texas 1860–2000. *Sources:* Terry G. Jordan with John L. Bean, Jr., and Willima M. Holmes, Texas: *A Geography* (Boulder: Westview Press, 1984), p. 81, 83; U.S. Censuses 1860–2000; Texas State Center.
Note: Data for Asian and other populations not tabulated by the Bureau of the Census prior to 1980. Spanish total for 1970 based on "Persons of Spanish language or surname."
*White, not of Hispanic origin.

areas heavily influenced by the traditionalistic subculture. Extreme poverty, low levels of education, and local economies based on agriculture contributed to the development of political systems dominated by a few Anglos, who often considered Hispanics second-class citizens. Hispanics' increasing political clout, however, has produced major political and governmental changes in those regions.

African Americans

Some African Americans lived in Texas during the colonization period, but the modern story of African-American settlement did not begin until after independence in 1836. When Texas was part of Mexico, Mexican law restricted slavery within the territory. During the period of the Republic and early statehood prior to the U.S. Civil War, there was a significant increase in the African-American population as Americans settling in Texas brought cotton cultivation and the slavery system with them. At the time of the Civil War, 30 percent of the state's residents were African American, but that percentage declined after the war. By 1960, it had leveled off at 12 percent. In 2000, African Americans comprised 11.6 percent of the state's population (see Figure 1–1). African Americans are expected to represent between 10 and 11 percent of the state's population during the next twenty-five years.

There is a large concentration of African Americans in East Texas, where white southerners and their slaves originally settled. African Americans are also concentrated in the urban areas of Dallas, Fort Worth, Houston, and Austin. Relatively few African Americans live in the western counties or in the counties along the Mexican border. The increased number of African-American state legislators, city council members, county commissioners, and school board trustees representing urban communities is an indication of the political power of the African-American population in selected areas. In 2001, the most recent year for which data were available, there were 460 African-American elected officials in Texas. Four African Americans have been elected to statewide office.[28]

The slaveholding whites who migrated to Texas from the lower southern states brought with them the dominant values of the traditionalistic political subculture. Although slaves were freed after the Civil War, continued political and economic discrimination against African Americans was commonplace in the eastern part of Texas into the 1960s. As in South Texas, the politics of East Texas served the interests of the white elites, by reducing or eliminating African American participation in the political process through restrictive election laws and outright physical intimidation.

Anglos

In the vernacular of Texas politics, the white population is referred to as "Anglos," although there is no census designation by that name. The term includes Jews, the Irish, Germans, Poles, and just about any other individual who is designated by the Bureau of the Census as "non-Hispanic white."

Scholars have identified two distinct early patterns of Anglo migration into Texas from other states. These patterns, as well as population movements through much of the late nineteenth and early twentieth centuries, largely explain the regional locations of the state's two dominant political subcultures.

In the early nineteenth century, the first Anglos moving to Texas were from the upper South—Tennessee, Kentucky, Arkansas, and North Carolina—a region significantly influenced by the individualistic subculture that emphasized limited government. The earliest settlements were primarily in what is now northeast Texas, in the Red River Valley. After Mexican independence from Spain, there was a second wave of immigration from the upper South. Few of these early colonists were plantation slaveholders from the lower South.

After Texas gained its independence, slavery was legalized, and settlers from the lower South began arriving. By the outbreak of the Civil War, Anglos who had moved to Texas from the lower South were roughly equal in number to those from the upper South. Arrivals from the slaveholding lower South initially settled in southeastern Texas near Louisiana, but soon they began to move northward and westward.

A line between Texarkana and San Antonio in effect divides Texas subcultures. Most of those Anglos who settled north and west of this line were from the upper South and heavily influenced by the individualistic subculture. Anglos who settled south and east of the line were by and large from the lower South and shaped by the traditionalistic subculture. While the characteristics of these two subcultures were somewhat different, they merged to create a political system that was conservative, limited the scope of government, and often served the interests of elites.

This pattern of immigration and settlement continued after the Civil War. It was primarily those populations from the upper South who pushed westward to the Panhandle and West Texas. This expansion introduced into the western part of the state the cultural experience of those who resisted the notion that government existed to solve all of society's ills. To this day, West Texas is still one of the most politically conservative areas of the state.[29]

In 1860, Anglos constituted approximately 63 percent of Texas's population (see Figure 1–1). The Anglo population increased until it reached 74 percent in 1950. But by 1990, the stabilization of the African-American population and the increase in the Hispanic population had reduced the Anglo share to 60 percent. Anglos accounted for only 53 percent of Texas's population by 2000 and were expected to decline as a percentage of the total population through the first three decades of the twenty-first century.

The Anglo population is diverse, as exhibits in the Institute of Texan Cultures in San Antonio remind us. Towns throughout Texas are identified with immigrants of national origin other than Anglo-Saxon, and these national groups brought with them a rich heritage. Castroville, for example, is identified with the Alsatians; New Braunfels and Fredericksburg, the Germans; Panna Maria, the Poles; and West and Halletsville, the Czechs.

Asian Americans

In 1980, Asian Americans accounted for 0.8 percent of the state's population, but by 1990 the figure had grown to 1.9 percent. It had grown to approximately 2.7 percent of the state total by 2000 and was projected to increase to 4.2 percent by 2020. This rapid increase parallels national trends. Changes in immigration policy and the dislocation of Asians due to war and political persecution have resulted in larger numbers of Asian immigrants entering the United States and Texas since the 1970s.

The largest concentration of Asian Americans in Texas is in Houston, where several Asian Americans have been elected to major public offices. Among them, community activist Martha Wong was elected to the Houston City Council in 1993 and then to the Texas House of Representatives in 2002. Wong apparently was the second Asian American to serve in the Texas House. Tom Lee of San Antonio, who served in the 1960s, was believed to be the first. Another Houstonian, Robert Gee, became one of the first Asian Americans to hold a state office when Governor Ann Richards appointed him to the Public Utility Commission in 1991. Asian Americans hold or have held public offices in several other Texas cities as well.

POLITICS, RACE, AND ETHNICITY

Today, few Texans go running around the state wearing Ku Klux Klan robes, burning crosses or marching in support of white supremacy, but there still are occasions of extreme racial violence and cruelty, such as the murder of James Byrd, Jr., who was dragged to death in early 1999 near Jasper in East Texas. A state law barring African Americans from voting in party primaries was declared unconstitutional in the 1940s, and many other laws that were intended to reduce the political participation of African Americans and Hispanics have been eliminated. The federal Voting Rights Act, which was enacted in 1965 and extended to Texas in 1975, has also helped open up state and local electoral systems to minorities. There is still evidence of employment and housing discrimination, and opposition to the desegregation of a public housing project in Vidor received national publicity in 1993. But restrictive codes prohibiting a specific group of people from buying residential property have been declared unconstitutional, and federal and state laws have given minorities greater access to jobs. In the views of those who have studied or commented on racial and

State troopers separate members of the Ku Klux Klan and a crowd at a rally in Jasper, Texas, where James Byrd, Jr., an African American, was dragged to his death by three whites.

ethnic relationships in the state, there has been marked improvement since the era of rigorously enforced Jim Crow laws.

Nonetheless, race and ethnicity are implicit in many contemporary political and policy issues. Throughout the ongoing debate on restructuring the school finance system, the protagonists are identified as the "rich" and the "poor" school districts of the state. But, in large part, these are alternative terms for "non-minority" and "minority" school systems. There have been bitter legal battles about redistricting of political districts to increase Hispanic and African-American representation on city councils, school boards, special districts, the state legislature and the U.S. Congress. And although many poor Anglos live in Texas, the disproportionately high poverty rates among minority groups often influence discussions about social services. The budget crisis of 2003 produced a particularly contentious legislative session, when funding was reduced for many of the state's health and social programs. Many state and local elections show evidence of polarized voting along ethnic lines. Race and ethnicity also emerge in jury selection, employment patterns, contracts with state and local governments, and expenditures for public health and social service programs. Admissions policies of Texas colleges and universities resulted in a succession of legal challenges that centered on affirmative action and reverse discrimination.

More than forty years ago, V. O. Key, a Texan scholar of American politics, concluded that Texas politics was moving from issues of race to issues of class and economics. He argued that voters in Texas "divide along class lines in accord with their class interests as related to liberal and conservative candidates."[30] In part, he was correct in that unabashed racial bigotry and public demagoguery are no longer acceptable. In part, though, he was incorrect and much too optimistic. If the state divides on economic issues, this division often puts the majority of Anglos on one side and the majority of Hispanics and African Americans on the other.[31]

GROWTH AND CHANGING DEMOGRAPHICS

Over the past fifty years, the Texas population has increased much faster than the national average. According to the 2000 census, the state's population was 20,851,820, an increase of approximately 4 million people in ten years, making Texas's population second only to California. In the last decade of the twentieth century, the state's population grew by 22.8 percent, significantly higher than the national growth rate of 13.2 percent.[32] Based on the population growth between the 1990 and 2000 censuses, Texas gained two additional seats in the U.S. Congress, raising the size of its congressional delegation to thirty-two.

High birthrates explain part of the population increase, but migration from other states has also been a significant factor. In recent decades, demographers (those who study populations) have described a nationwide shift in population from the Northeast and Midwest to the South and West. For each of the censuses from 1940 to 1970, in-migration from other areas accounted for less than 10 percent of Texas's growth. But in-migration jumped to 58.5 percent of the total growth between 1970 and 1980, the period in which demographers identified massive shifts of population from the "frostbelt" to the "sunbelt." Between 1980 and 1990, new residents contributed 34.4 percent to the state's growth.[33] In-migration slowed down somewhat between 1990 and 2000, but at the beginning of this decade, approximately 23 percent of Texas residents reported other states as their place of birth.

Although it is expected to become less significant in the future, in-migration from other states has already contributed to the restructuring of Texas's traditional one-party, Democratic political system into a Republican-dominated system. Many new residents came from states with strong Republican Party traditions and brought their party affiliation with them. In the long run, in-migration is likely to affect additional elements of the state's political culture.

Texas also attracts individuals from other countries. Approximately 2.9 million, or 14 percent, of Texas residents were identified as foreign-born in the 2000 census. Between 1990 and 2000, approximately 1.4 million, or 6.4 percent, of the state's population arrived from other countries. More than 70 percent of Texans born in other countries come from Latin America. Approximately ten percent of all Texas residents are not U.S. citizens, a fact that has several implications.[34]

Citizenship is directly related to political participation, and non-citizens, while counted in the census for reapportionment of congressional seats, cannot vote. The overwhelming majority of non-citizens are Hispanic, thus reducing the number of eligible Hispanic voters in the state.

Under current federal policy, non-citizens have been denied access to some public social services that are funded in whole or in part by the national government. Needy immigrants are especially affected by such policies, and in some instances, the state has found it necessary to use its own funds to provide services to non-citizens.

Some 6 million Texans over the age of five speak languages other than English at home, and close to half of these individuals report that they don't speak English well.[35] Some states have adopted English as their official state language, but there has not been a significant English language movement in Texas. Nonetheless, language is a policy issue for Texas in terms of bilingual education, official documents and publications, translators for court proceedings, and a host of related language issues in the workplace.

The increase in population places demands on all levels of government, and many local governments throughout Texas are hard pressed to provide adequate services. Many Texas cities, for example, are running out of landfill space. Environmental laws make it difficult to obtain new licenses for garbage and waste disposal, and without additional dumpsites, new population growth cannot be serviced. The increased population has also raised questions about the adequacy of water supplies throughout the state with different cities, regions and industries competing intensely for the resources now available. These water battles will only intensify in the future. While the state has been engaged in a massive road construction program over the past decade, streets and highways in urban and suburban areas are clogged with traffic. A report released in the fall of 2003 that surveyed driving time in metropolitan areas indicated significant increases in daily commute time. This means additional gasoline consumption, pollution, and costs of time.[36]

The Aging Population

Texans, along with other Americans, are aging. The national median age in 1900 was 22.9 years. In 2000, the median age of the state's population was 32.3 years, compared to 35.3 years for the entire country.[37] Approximately 10 percent of the state's population was older than sixty-five in 2000, and that group was expected to increase to 17 percent by 2030.[38] This aging population will place unprecedented demands on the public and private sectors for goods and services, including expanded health care and long-term care. In recent years, increasing state expenditures under the Medicaid program for long-term nursing care have strained the state's budget and forced a shift in priorities in public programs.

Younger Texans will be asked to pay increased taxes to support the needs of the projected aging population. These intergenerational obligations, which are critical to a stable political system, are often overlooked in debates over funding public services. Younger Texans need older voters to support public education through their tax dollars, and older voters need younger Texans to support health care services. If push comes to shove and comity disappears, the older population has significantly more political clout than do younger voters, who are less informed about politics and who vote at rates much lower than the older population.

URBAN TEXAS

Although Texas was a rural state during the first one hundred years of its history, 83 percent of the state's population in 2000 resided in areas classified by the Bureau of the Census as urban (Table 1–1). **Urbanization** and suburban sprawl now characterize Texas's settlement patterns, and many urban corridors and suburban areas cross county boundaries. Residents of these areas often encounter problems that cut

TABLE 1–1   Urban-Rural Population of Texas

	Urban		Rural		
Year	Percentage	Population	Percentage	Population	Total
1850	4%	7,665	96%	204,927	212,592
1860	4%	26,615	96%	577,600	604,215
1870	7%	54,521	93%	764,058	818,579
1880	9%	146,795	91%	1,444,954	1,591,749
1890	16%	359,511	84%	1,886,016	2,245,527
1900	17%	520,759	83%	2,527,951	3,048,710
1910	24%	938,104	76%	2,958,438	3,896,542
1920	32%	1,512,689	68%	3,150,539	4,663,228
1930	41%	2,389,148	59%	3,435,367	5,824,715
1940	45%	2,911,389	55%	3,503,435	6,414,824
1950	63%	4,838,050	37%	2,873,134	7,711,194
1960	75%	7,187,470	25%	2,392,207	9,579,677
1970	80%	8,922,211	20%	2,274,519	11,196,730
1980	80%	11,333,017	20%	2,836,174	14,229,191
1990	80%	13,634,517	20%	3,351,993	16,986,510
2000	83%	17,204,073	17%	3,647,747	20,851,820

Sources: U.S. Bureau of the Census, *U.S. Censuses 1850–2000.*

TABLE 1–2   Ten Largest Cities, 1900–2000

City	1900	1920	1940	1960	1980	1990	2000
Houston	44,633	138,276	384,514	838,219	1,595,138	1,630,553	1,953,631
Dallas	42,638	158,976	294,734	679,684	904,078	1,006,877	1,188,580
San Antonio	53,321	161,379	253,854	587,718	785,880	935,933	1,144,646
Austin	22,258	34,876	87,960	186,545	345,496	465,622	656,562
El Paso	15,906	77,560	96,810	276,687	425,259	515,342	563,662
Fort Worth	26,688	106,482	177,662	356,268	385,164	447,619	534,694
Arlington	1,079	3,031	4,240	44,775	160,113	261,721	332,969
Corpus Christi	4,703	10,522	57,301	167,690	231,999	257,453	277,454
Plano	1,304	1,715	1,582	3,695	72,331	128,713	222,030
Garland	819	1,421	2,233	38,501	132,857	180,650	215,768

Source: U.S. Censuses, 1900–2000.

across political jurisdictions, and local governments sometimes find it difficult to resolve them.

The dramatic growth of Texas's largest cities is shown in Table 1–2. From 1960 to 2000, the population of Houston and El Paso more than doubled. Dallas increased by 74 percent and San Antonio, 94 percent. Arlington had a population of only 44,775 in 1960, but in 2000 its population was 332,969, an increase of 744 percent. During this forty-year period, Austin's population increased by 352 percent.

Three of the ten largest cities in the United States are in Texas, and, like urban areas throughout the country, Texas's largest cities are increasingly populated by minority and lower income populations. This trend results from higher birth rates among minority populations, urban migration patterns, and what is often referred to as "white flight" from the cities to suburban areas. Minority groups now account for the majority of the population in five of Texas's ten largest cities (Houston, San Antonio, Dallas, El Paso, and Corpus Christi). These minority residents include Hispanics, African Americans, and Asian Americans—groups that do not always constitute a cohesive bloc of interests. As minority growth continues, there will be areas of potential conflict among these groups.

Population density refers to the number of people per square mile in a specific political jurisdiction, and it provides another measure of urbanization. As people crowd into smaller areas living in close proximity to each other, problems are inevitable. Noise, land use, the maintenance of property, traffic patterns, and a whole host of other issues must be addressed. People disagree on all matters of rules and regulations, but through the political processes, citizens attempt to shape the rules that have a direct bearing on the quality of their lives. The 2000 census reports the greatest population density in the Dallas-Fort Worth Metroplex and in Houston. Looking to the future, demographers also detect the evolution of an extremely dense corridor along Interstate 35 running from north of Dallas to San Antonio.

There are marked differences in the population and density of Texas's 254 counties. Loving County in West Texas has a population of about 67 living in an area of 677 square miles. The most populous county is Harris County (Houston), with more than 3.4 million people living within 1,777 square miles.[39] Clearly, the problems and issues that Loving County faces are significantly different from those faced by Harris County, yet both counties function with the same form of government that was created by the state's constitution of 1876.

Conflict in Texas politics has often divided along urban-rural lines, and in recent years, suburban areas of the state have taken on more importance, further complicating policy debates. Redistricting battles and a host of other public policy issues are evidence of that. Until recently, the Texas legislature was dominated by rural lawmakers, many of whom were often insensitive to urban needs. To make matters more difficult, suburban legislators with a different constituency base and interests often pursue policies in conflict with both the central city and rural legislators. Moreover, many of urban Texas's problems are aggravated by constitutional restrictions written when Texas was still a rural state.

WEALTH AND INCOME DISTRIBUTION

There is a wide disparity in the distribution of income and wealth across the state. In 1999, the median household income was $39,927, and the median family income was $45,861, both below national income levels (see Table 1–3). Thirty-one percent of Texas households reported incomes less than $25,000 per year. These data obscure the fact that there are Texans who made millions of dollars in 1999 and had assets in the hundreds of millions or several billions of dollars. *Forbes* magazine conducts an annual survey of the 400 richest Americans. Thirty-six Texans made the list in

TABLE 1–3   U.S. and Texas Income Figures, 2000 Census

	U.S.	Texas					
	All Persons	**All Persons**	**Anglos**	**Hispanics**	**African American**	**Native American**	**Asian American**
Median Income*							
Household	$41,494	$39,927	$47,162	$29,873	$29,305	$34,926	$50,049
Families	50,046	45,861	57,194	30,840	33,276	37,503	57,103
Per Capita Income*	21,690	19,617	26,197	16,770	14,253	15,899	20,956
Percent of Persons below Poverty level	12.4%	15.4%	7.8%	25.4%	23.4%	19.3%	11.9%

*1999 dollars.

Source: Bureau of the Census, *2000 Census of the Population.*

2003, including 26 billionaires with a reported worth ranging from $1.1 billion to $20.5 billion.[40]

On all measures of income, Hispanics and African Americans fall significantly below the Anglo and Asian populations. According to the 2000 census, 32 percent of Hispanic households and 35 percent of African-American households in Texas reported incomes below $20,000, but only 21 percent of Anglo households and a similar portion of the Asian-American population reported incomes below that level. By contrast, 43 percent of Anglo households but only 25 percent of Hispanic households and 27 percent of African-American households reported incomes above $50,000.[41]

Many Texans live in severe poverty. Seven of the twenty poorest counties in the nation are in Texas. These are border counties (Dimmit, Hidalgo, Maverick, Starr, Willacy, Zapata, and Zavala) with large Hispanic populations and unemployment rates that are more than twice the state average. The per capita income (total state income divided by the population) for Texas was $19,617 in 1999. For the Anglo population, it was significantly higher, $26,197, but for African Americans, the figure was $14,253, and for Hispanics, $16,770.

In 2002, the poverty level guidelines used in Texas to establish eligibility for many federal and state programs were $18,244 for a family of four and $9,359 for one person. According to the U.S. Bureau of the Census, 15.3 percent of the state's population, or 3.3 million people, fell below the poverty level. Nationally, 12.1 percent or 34.6 million persons fell below the poverty level in 2002. The impact of poverty is felt disproportionately by children, those living in a single-parent household, Hispanics, African Americans, and Native Americans.[42]

While the state's economic growth over the past decade has reduced some poverty, scholars who look at demographic trends are concerned that poverty is likely to worsen in Texas if several policy issues are not addressed. Without significant changes in educational levels and expanded economic opportunities, it is possible that approximately 20 percent of the state's households will fall below the poverty level by 2030, and income disparity will be especially problematic for minorities.[43]

Financial resources can be translated into political power and influence through campaign contributions, funding one's own campaign for public office, access to the mass media, and active support for policy think tanks, interest groups, and lobbying activity. Wealth is not the only dimension of political power, but some Texans obviously have the potential for much greater clout than others.

EDUCATION AND LITERACY

Public education has been a dominant issue in state politics for many years. Litigation has forced the legislature to struggle with changes in the funding of public schools, and education will be a primary factor in determining whether Texas can successfully compete in the global economy.

Over the next decade, a large proportion of the new jobs created in Texas will be in service industries. Most of these jobs will require increased reading, writing and math skills, and high-school dropouts will find fewer and fewer employment opportunities. Some experts predict that 50 percent of the jobs that will be created in the United States in the next decade will require a college education, compared to only 22 percent in the mid-1990s.[44] Texas faces a crisis in public education, and the state's ability to resolve it will directly affect the financial well-being of many Texans (see Compared to What?).

According to the 2000 census, 75.7 percent of Texans age twenty-five and older had completed high school, and 23.8 percent had completed college (Table 1–4). Educational attainment improved between 1990 to 2000, and positive changes were reported for all racial or ethnic groups in the state.[45] But there continued to be wide disparities in the educational levels of the three major ethnic-racial groups. In 1990, 66 percent of the adult African Americans in Texas had completed high school, and

TABLE 1–4   Texas and United States Educational Attainment by Race and Ethnicity, 2000 (For Population 25 and Older)

	United States		Texas	
	High School Degree	College Degree	High School Degree	College Degree
Anglo*	85.4%	27.0%	87.2%	30.0%
Hispanic	52.4	10.5	49.3	8.9
African American	72.3	14.3	75.8	15.4
Native American	71.0	11.5	71.6	15.7
Asian	80.4	44.1	80.7	47.8
All Persons	80.4	24.4	75.7	23.8

*White, not of Hispanic origin.

Source: U.S. Bureau of the Census, *2000 Census of the Population.*

12 percent had completed college. Among Hispanics, 45 percent had completed high school, and approximately 7 percent had college degrees. Some 82 percent of the Anglo population age twenty-five and older had graduated from high school, and 25 percent had completed college. In 2000, 87 percent of the Anglo population reported that they had completed high school, and 30 percent had college degrees. By contrast, 49 percent of the Hispanic population had high school degrees but only 8.9 percent reported that they had a college degree. What is particularly compelling in the 2000 census data is the level of education reported for the Asian-American population. Approximately 48 percent reported college degrees.

Education not only helps determine a person's employment and income potential but also affects his or her participation in politics. Individuals with high educational levels are much more likely to be informed about politics, public officials, and the policy making process. They are more likely to vote and engage in a wide range of political behavior than those who are less educated, and they are much more likely to believe that they can influence the actions of policymakers.

THE SIZE AND GEOGRAPHIC DIVERSITY OF TEXAS

Texas is a big state. Covering 268,601 square miles, it is second only to Alaska in land mass. Although Texans appear to have adjusted to long distances—they don't seem to mind driving fifty miles for a night out—visitors from out-of-state often are overwhelmed by Texas's size and diversity. The distance from Texarkana in Northeast Texas to El Paso in far West Texas is about 800 miles, and a person living in Texarkana is closer to Chicago than to El Paso. Brownsville in South Texas is closer to Mexico City than it is to Texline in the Texas Panhandle.[46]

Many would argue that perceptions of the state's size have helped shape political attitudes and concepts, and size obviously has affected state policy. Roads and highways, for example, historically have received a significant—and, some would argue, a disproportionate—share of the state's budget. Economic development in such a large and diverse state required a commitment to highway construction because roads were regarded as essential to the development of an integrated economy.

Size also contributes to the economic diversity of the state. While some parts of the state will be experiencing economic growth, other areas may experience economic downturns.

One scholar argued that the great distances in Texas were politically important because they made it difficult for a politician to develop a statewide following, such as could be cultivated in many southern states. Size works against the organizational strategies and continued negotiations necessary to sustain a statewide political machine similar to those that developed in Virginia and Louisiana in the 1920s and 1930s. Although there have been regional or local political machines, such as the now-defunct Parr machine in South Texas, none of these was extended statewide.[47]

Size also contributes to the high costs of political campaigns. Candidates in the 2002 gubernatorial race spent more than $100 million to communicate with and mobilize Texas voters. There are twenty separate media markets in the state, and the cost of communicating with the voters on a statewide basis continues to increase.

If Texas were still an independent nation, it would be the thirty-seventh largest in geographic area. The state has one-twelfth of the total coastline of the United

States. It has 23 million acres of forest and more than 4,790 square miles of lakes and streams. A traveler driving across Texas is struck by the diversity in topography, climate, and vegetation. The state's "landforms range from offshore bars and barrier beaches to formidable mountains, from rugged canyons, gorges, and badlands to totally flat plains."[48] The western part of the state is dry and semiarid, while the east is humid and subtropical, producing extremes in precipitation. South Texas often enjoys a tropical winter, while North Texas experiences cold winters with snowfall.[49] The growing seasons in the south are virtually year round, while those in the north are approximately 180 days. East Texas is characterized by its piney woods, semiarid South Texas by its brush country.

   Geography shaped historical migration and land use in Texas. Although we are capable of partially compensating for climate and geography through modern technology, geography continues to shape the economies and population patterns of the state.

THE ECONOMY OF TEXAS

Politics, government, and economics are inextricably linked. An economy that is robust and expanding provides far more options to government policymakers than an economy in recession. A healthy tax base is dependent on an expanding economy, and when the economy goes through periods of recession, state and local governments are confronted with the harsh realities of having to increase taxes or cut back on public services, usually at a time when more people are in need of governmental assistance.

   At the beginning of the 1980s, Texas experienced a sustained period of growth, and state government adopted new policies and expanded existing services with only minimal tax increases. But by 1991, the state had experienced a decade of economic boom and bust with two severe recessions, and the legislature had been forced to reduce public services and impose a series of significant tax increases.

For much of the twentieth century, oil played a dominant role in the Texas economy, as the derricks in this photo of the town of Kilgore in the 1930s reflect. But with increased reliance on imported oil and the subsequent decline in Texas oil exploration and production, the Texas economy has become more diversified, reducing its reliance on oil and natural gas.

COMPARED TO WHAT?

If you compare Texas to other states, it ranks:

#1 in percentage of non-elderly population without health insurance in 2001 (25.9%)
#2 in total resident population in 2002 (21,779,893)
    in youngest median age in 2000 (32.3)
#3 in gross state product in 2002 ($791.3 billion in current dollars)
    in Hispanic population in 2000 (32%)
#4 in percent resident population under 18 in 2000 (28.2%)
#5 in lowest voter turnout in November 2002 (33.1%)
#6 in percentage change in food stamp participation from 1997 to 2001 (−32.8%)
#7 in crime rate in 2001 (5,153 crimes per 100,000 inhabitants)
#8 in percentage change in population, 1990–2000 (22.8%)
    in lowest cost of living in 2002
#9 in poverty rate in 2001 (14.9%)
    in sales taxes per capita in 2000 ($1,275)
#10 in percentage of households headed by married couples in 2000 (54%)
    in rate of children in poverty in 2001 (21.1%)
#11 in percentage of public elementary and secondary students eligible for free or reduced-price lunch in 2000 (44.7%)
#12 in marriage rate in 2000 (9.4 per 1,000 population)
#13 in age-adjusted death rate by AIDS in 1999 (5.4 deaths per 100,000 population)
    in violent crime rate in 2001 (572.8 per 100,000 population)
#14 in per capita state government general sales tax revenue in 2001 ($690)
#15 in per capita state and local government expenditures for elementary and secondary education in 1999 ($1,267)
    in average annual pay in 2001 ($36,039)
#16 in per capita state and local government property taxes in 1999 ($938)
#17 in rape rate in 1999 (38 rapes per 1,000 population)
#18 in per capita gross state product in 2000 ($35,598)
    in percentage change in state and local taxes from 1994 to 1999 (32.2%)
#19 in abortions in 1998 (239 per 1,000 births)
    in percentage of population subscribing to wireless telephone service in 2002 (45.7%)
#20 in per capita local government revenue from federal government in 1999 ($101)

Source: Texas Comptroller of Public Accounts, *Window on State Government,* June 2003; Kendra A. Hovey and Harold A. Hovey, *Congressional Quarterly's State Fact Finder 2003.* Washington, DC: CQ Press, 2003.

Historically, the health of the Texas economy had been linked to oil and natural gas. In 1981, for example, 27 percent of the state's economy was tied to energy-related industries. The decade started with rapid increases in the world price of oil, and there was an economic boom throughout the financial, construction, and manufacturing sectors of the state's economy.[50]

But a series of national and international events soon produced major problems. World oil prices began to drop in 1981, resulting in serious unemployment problems in the Gulf Coast and Plains regions of the state. There was a disastrous decline in the value of the Mexican peso, which had a negative impact on the economies of border cities and counties, and in 1983, a harsh freeze in South Texas and a severe drought in West Texas had serious adverse effects on the agricultural sector. Some regions of the state were insulated from these conditions, but others experienced a significant economic downturn.[51]

Economic disaster struck again in 1986, with a 60 percent drop in the price of oil and corresponding reductions in the price of natural gas. Drilling activity in the state plummeted and was followed by a loss of 84,000 energy-related jobs. The problem was confounded by a worldwide slump in the electronics industry. These events hurt the construction and real estate sectors of the economy and, in turn, manufacturing and retail trade. For sixteen straight months in 1986 and 1987, the state's employment dropped, with an estimated loss of 233,000 jobs.[52]

These economic reversals had disastrous effects on Texas's banks and savings and loan institutions. "In 1987 and 1988, more Texas financial institutions failed than at any other time since the Great Depression," the state comptroller's office reported. And the pattern of bank failures continued through 1990. The federal government developed a plan to bail out institutions that were covered by federal deposit insurance. But as the magnitude of the problem became clearer, there was a bitter debate over its causes, including the deregulation of the savings and loan and banking industries, inadequate government scrutiny of banking practices, a frenzy of speculation with questionable or unsecured loans, and outright fraud and malfeasance.[53]

State and local governments consequently suffered declines in revenues. With falling property values, local governments that depended on the property tax were particularly vulnerable. The legislature convened in special session in 1986 to pass an $875 million tax bill and cut the state budget by about $580 million in an attempt to "patch up" the widening holes in projected state revenues. In 1987, the legislature, mandated by the constitution to a "pay as you go" system of government and denied the option of deficit financing, enacted a $5.6 billion tax bill, including an increase in the sales tax, a **regressive tax** that most adversely affects low-income people.[54]

By 1988, the economy was recovering, with slow, modest growth in most of the state. Oil and natural gas, while still important to the economy, were being replaced as the driving force in economic expansion. Increased manufacturing and the expansion of service industries, in particular, were responsible for the incremental recovery the state experienced through 1990. The state's growth rate declined slightly in 1991, reflecting broad recessionary patterns of the national economy. But beginning in 1992 and continuing through the end of the decade, there was robust growth in the state's economy that outpaced the national economy at rather significant rates. Unemployment dropped throughout the state, and business expanded across most sectors of the economy. Texas created more jobs than any other state, and personal and family income increased. New industries came to the state, and foreign exports rose. Government revenues also increased, and the state and local governments were able to expand services without significant tax increases.

But in early 2001, recessionary pressures returned with a significant decline in the state's rate of growth. Unemployment inched up, and business activity slowed down in many sectors of the economy. By late 2003, many economists argued that the recession was over, but few predicted that the recovery would be anything like the robust growth of the late 1990s. When the Texas legislature convened in early 2003, state government faced a large revenue shortfall. Lawmakers, led by a new Republican majority, made major reductions in state services to balance a new budget without raising state taxes. The spending cuts affected virtually every local government across the state.

In 2003, Texas had a gross state product of $739 billion in 1996 dollars (or $827 billion in current dollars). By comparison, the gross domestic product of the United States was $9.684 trillion in 1996 dollars. The Texas economy was the third largest among the states, following California and New York. If Texas were a nation, its economy would rank eleventh in the world.[55]

Several lessons can be drawn from the state's economic history. Because of the significant economic changes, a number of experts believe that the state is now less vulnerable to the volatility of the energy industry. Oil and gas production has declined in the past two decades, and now only 10 percent of the state's economy is tied to oil- and gas-related industries.[56] **Economic diversification** has made the state less reliant on one dominant industry. So now, even in recessionary periods, not all sectors of the state's economy are affected the same way.

The state has created a significant number of jobs for its expanding population. Some 2.35 million new jobs were created in Texas, more than in any other state, during the 1990s. More than half of those were linked to services and trade. Construction and government employment also expanded during this period.[57] And, a restructured financial industry experienced a noticeable recovery by 1993.[58]

Another dimension of the state's economic success has been an ever-increasing shift to high-tech industries. Many economic and political leaders argue that the state's future must be directly tied to these developing industries, and state government and many cities have developed aggressive recruitment programs that include economic development bonds and tax breaks for high-tech companies.

The term high-tech is generally used to describe business activities that produce new technology based on highly sophisticated computer applications. Companies that make semiconductors, microprocessors, and computer hardware and software clearly fall into this category, as do companies that produce telecommunications devices, fiber optics, aerospace guidance systems, and some medical instruments.[59] These industries have been joined by new biotechnology industries that are involved in producing new medicines, vaccines, and genetic engineering of plants and animals. Houston and Dallas have emerged as centers for biotechnology, with some development also occurring in San Antonio, Austin, and Fort Worth.[60] With the cooperation and support of state universities and two major research consortia in the area, Austin has attracted a significant number of computer-related industries.

Texas and the United States also are contributing to what is often referred to as the **globalization of the economy.** Throughout the 1980s, as world oil prices directly affected the state, Texans were made keenly aware of their increased dependence on the world economy. Foreign investment in Texas has become increasingly common. Moreover, Texas exported $84.3 billion in goods and services in 1997, with approximately 37 percent going to Mexico.[61] But the flow of exports to Mexico slowed considerably due to recessionary pressures in 1999 through 2002.[62] The North American Free Trade Agreement among the United States, Mexico, and Canada (see Chapter 3) has already produced changes in the economic relationships among these countries. More economic interdependence for North America is anticipated.

ECONOMIC REGIONS OF TEXAS

The economic diversity of Texas can be described in terms of thirteen distinct economic regions (Figure 1–2). There are marked differences among these areas.[63] One may be undergoing rapid growth, while another may be experiencing a recession. Regions vary in population, economic infrastructure, economic performance, and rates of growth. One region's economy may be heavily dependent on only two or three industries. If one or two of those industries suffers an economic downturn, that region may have a more severe recession than the state overall. There also are marked differences in personal income, poverty levels and geography among the areas. All regions, meanwhile, share in one economic sector—fairly significant levels of government employment.

Houston, linked to the Gulf Coast by a ship channel, is the second largest port city in the nation. Dallas is a major transportation hub, thanks to Interstate 35, a

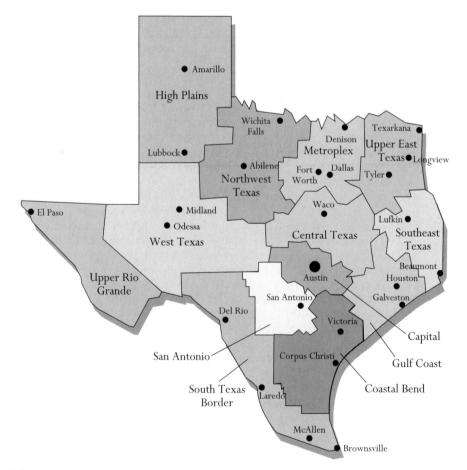

FIGURE 1–2 Economic Regions of Texas. *Source:* Texas Comptroller of Public Accounts

primary north-south highway that runs from Laredo on the Mexican border to Duluth, Minnesota, near Canada. Dallas and other cities along this route have benefited from increased trade between the United States and Mexico.

The economic factors at play in a region help shape the priorities of local governments and the priorities of state legislators elected from that area. The following descriptions of five of the thirteen regions offer a sampling of the economic differences encountered throughout Texas (see Table 1–5).

The *High Plains Region* is made up of forty-one counties and includes Amarillo, Lubbock, the XIT Ranch, and Palo Duro Canyon. Agriculture production, whose major source of water is the Ogallala Aquifer, is a dominant industry. Related businesses include agricultural services, food processing, and the manufacturing of feed, fertilizers, and farm machinery and equipment. Oil and gas production is still an important component of the region's economy, but employment in the energy industry has declined from earlier periods. While the landmass of this region is large, its 2000 population was approximately 753,000 people. From 1970 to 2000, its population grew only 13 percent. Its per capita income was higher than the state average, but it is projected to produce only 20,000 new jobs in the next few years. The High Plains had a gross regional product of $19.8 billion in 2000, which grew at an annual rate of 3.3 percent for the period from 1970 to 2000.

The *Metroplex Region* includes nineteen counties and, with the cities of Dallas, Fort Worth, Sherman, and Denison, has the greatest concentration of large and middle-sized cities in the state. The area is a major financial center, with regional offices of the Federal Reserve Bank and the Federal Home Loan Bank. It also has the Dallas Market Center (the world's largest trade complex) and the Dallas-Fort Worth International Airport. This region's manufacturing base is the most diversified in the state. The area is also home to growing and highly specialized electronics and communications industries anchored by high-tech firms. This region had a total population of 5,284,000 people in 2000, doubling in number since 1970. Its gross regional product was approximately $193 billion in 2000, and it will generate approximately 100,000 new jobs annually over the next few years. Its annual economic growth rate over the past thirty years has been 4.7 percent, significantly higher than the rest of the state.

The *Upper East Texas Region* encompasses twenty-three counties and the cities of Texarkana, Marshall, Longview, and Tyler. Historically, the region's economy has been based on oil and gas, lumber, cotton, and cattle, but it has diversified over the past few decades. The area is now more manufacturing-intensive than the state as a whole. The manufacture of lumber products was expected to grow, buoyed by home construction. Despite earlier losses, the oil and gas industry will continue to play a key role in the region's economy. Close to one million people live in this area, and it has grown by 54 percent over the past 30 years. Its gross regional product was $23.8 billion in 2000, reflecting an annual growth rate of 3.5 percent. This region is projected to produce 11,000 jobs or so over each of the next few years.

The *South Texas Border Region* includes the Lower Rio Grande Valley and runs to Val Verde County. This region includes some of the poorest counties in the United States and has high unemployment rates. Agriculture, livestock, and food processing are major industries in this region. This area has received a boost from the construction of manufacturing plants in Mexico and trading benefits from the North American Free Trade Agreement (NAFTA). Laredo is the region's primary point of imports from Mexico. The population in this area has increased by 43 percent over the past 30 years. Its per capita income—$13,000 in 1999—was the lowest in the state.

TABLE 1–5 Characteristics of the Comptroller's Thirteen Economic Districts

Economic Region of the State	Number of Counties	1970 Population	2000 Population	Percent Population Change, 1970–2000	1970 Per Capita Real Income*	2000 Per Capita Real Income*	Projected Employment 2005	Projected Average Yearly Increase in Jobs 2002–2005	1970 Gross Regional Product in Billions*	2000 Gross Regional Product in Billions*	Average Annual Growth Rate 1970–2000
Alamo	12	1,012,300	1,805,200	78%	$11,200	$20,200	1,126,600	23,100	$15.6	$44.1	3.5%
Capitol	10	450,000	1,291,600	187%	11,500	23,700	972,000	19,200	6.7	45.7	6.6%
Central Texas	20	564,300	916,300	62%	11,050	19,400	572,100	9,900	7.9	21.8	3.4%
Coastal Bend	19	564,400	749,900	33%	10,600	19,000	426,500	5,600	9.1	17.5	3.2%
Gulf Coast	13	2,320,000	4,730,000	103%	12,400	23,600	3,147,700	68,600	47.8	159.6	4.1%
High Plains	41	665,900	753,400	13%	13,000	21,800	505,000	6,900	10.4	19.8	3.3%
Metroplex	19	2,649,900	5,284,500	199%	12,600	23,800	3,961,600	97,300	49.3	193.2	4.7%
Northwest Texas	30	485,700	530,700	9%	12,000	21,600	338,900	4,800	7.5	12.8	1.8%
South Texas Border	16	535,000	1,358,700	143%	7,400	13,000	612,900	13,000	5.3	20.3	4.6%
Southeast Texas	15	564,400	731,600	30%	10,800	19,000	385,600	4,500	8.7	16.1	3.2%
Upper East Texas	23	640,900	987,200	54%	11,000	20,100	573,300	11,400	8.6	23.8	3.5%
Upper Rio Grande	6	380,400	745,700	96%	9,600	14,770	365,500	8,900	5.5	15.4	3.5%
West Texas	30	415,900	524,100	26%	12,100	20,500	325,000	4,500	9.3	14.9	1.6%

*Based on 1992 dollars.

Source: Texas Comptroller of Public Accounts, *Texas Regional Outlook, 2002.*

It is projected to generate an additional 13,000 jobs annually over the next few years, and its gross regional product was $20 billion in 2000.

The six-county *Upper Rio Grande Region* is located in the Chihuahuan Desert and includes El Paso (the oldest city in Texas) and Big Bend National Park. This area has close economic ties to Mexico. Rapid industrialization has produced impressive job gains, particularly in manufacturing, since the late 1980s. NAFTA has further stimulated economic growth in this region because Juarez, a major center of manufacturing in Mexico, is just across the border from El Paso. Economic and population growth on both sides of the border has increased concerns about clean air and water. The region's economy grew 3.5 percent annually over the past thirty years to produce a gross regional product of $15.4 billion in 2000. It had a population of approximately 750,000 and a per capita income of approximately $14,800 in 2000.

SUMMARY AND CONCLUSIONS

1. Texas is a highly diverse state with a rapidly expanding population and a rich cultural legacy.
2. The traditional, conservative politics of the state were shaped by several historical factors. They included the state's dominant political subcultures, a political ethos based on individualism and traditionalism, the aftermath of the Civil War, the systematic exclusion of minorities from the political process, one-party politics, and the dominance of conservative economic elites.
3. Expanding populations place additional burdens and responsibilities on governments, and as the state enters the twenty-first century, the decisions of leaders in both the public and private sectors will directly impact the standard of living and the quality of life for Texans.
4. Politics in Texas has been characterized as the politics of race and class, and although Hispanics and African Americans now participate in the political process, marked disparities in income and wealth related to ethnicity and race have produced political dividing lines on policy priorities.
5. Texas is now the second most populous state and has the third largest state economy. Once dependent on oil and natural gas, its economy has demonstrated a rapid diversification, structured, in part, by the dramatic expansion in service and high-tech industries and the increase in manufacturing and service exports to other countries.
6. The state's economy is, in fact, a composite of thirteen diversified regional economies, and based on the experiences of the past thirty years, these regions are affected in markedly different ways by national and international economic trends.
7. For much of the 1980s, the state's economy lagged behind the national economy, but this pattern was reversed in the early 1990s, when the state's economy outpaced national economic growth. And, it is expected to continue to do so.

KEY TERMS

Political myths	Individualistic subculture	Population density
Republic	Moralistic subculture	Regressive tax
Individualism	Traditionalistic subculture	Economic diversification
Political culture	Urbanization	Globalization of the economy

FURTHER READING

Articles

Champagne, Anthony, and Edward J. Harpham, "The Changing Political Economy of Texas," in *Texas Politics: A Reader,* eds. Anthony Champagne and Edward J. Harpham. New York: W. W. Norton, 1997, pp. 3–15.

Chilton, Stephen, "Defining Political Culture," *Western Political Quarterly* 41 (September 1988), pp. 419–45.

Fitzpatrick, Jody L., and Rodney E. Hero, "Political Culture and Political Characteristics of the American States: A Consideration of Some Old and New Questions," *Western Political Quarterly* 41 (March 1988), pp. 145–53.

Rice, Tom W., and Alexander F. Sumberg, "Civic Culture and Government Performance in the American States," *Publius* 27 (Winter 1997), pp. 99–114.

Books

Bouvier, Leon F., and Dudley L. Poston, Jr., *Thirty Million Texans?* Washington, D.C.: Center for Immigration Studies, 1993.

Buenger, Walter L., and Robert A. Calvert, eds., *Texas Through Time: Evolving Interpretations.* College Station: Texas A & M University Press, 1991.

Calvert, Robert A., and Arnoldo DeLeon, *The History of Texas.* Arlington Heights, IL: Harlan Davidson, 1990.

Elazar, Daniel J., *American Federalism: A View from the States.* New York: Thomas Y. Crowell, 1966.

————, *The American Mosaic: The Impact of Space, Time, and Culture on American Politics.* Boulder, CO: Westview Press, 1994.

Fehrenbach, T. R., *Lone Star: A History of Texas and the Texans.* New York: Collier, 1968.

Hill, Kim Quaile, *Democracy in the Fifty States.* Lincoln: University of Nebraska Press, 1994.

Jordan, Terry G., with John L. Bean Jr., and William M. Homes, *Texas: A Geography.* Boulder, CO: Westview Press, 1984.

McComb, David G., *Texas: A Modern History.* Austin: University of Texas Press, 1989.

Montejano, David, *Anglos and Mexicans in the Making of Texas, 1836–1986.* Austin: University of Texas Press, 1987.

Murdock, Steve H., Md. Nazrul Hogue, Martha Michael, Steve White, and Beverly Pecotte, *The Texas Challenge: Population Change and the Future of Texas.* College Station: Texas A & M University Press, 1997.

O'Conner, Robert F., ed., *Texas Myths.* Texas A & M University Press, 1986.

Richardson, Rupert, Ernest Wallace, and Adrian N. Anderson, *Texas: The Lone Star State,* 7th ed. Upper Saddle River, NJ: Prentice-Hall, 1988.

Wright, Bill, *The Tigua: Pueblo Indians of Texas.* El Paso: Texas Western Press, 1993.

Websites

State of Texas http://www.state.tx.us The state's web page provides links to state agencies, local and county governments, and councils of states, where a wide array of data for the state is to be found.

U.S. Bureau of the Census http://www.census.gov Population and economic data for the state are provided by the Bureau of the Census, which conducts the decennial census and a wide range of demographic studies between censuses.

Office of the Comptroller http://www.cpa.state.tx.us The comptroller's office maintains a database for the Texas economy.

Texas State Data Center http://txsdc.utsa.edu The Texas State Data Center provides "ready access to Texas census information and other information on the population of Texas."

ENDNOTES

1. John Steinbeck, *Travels with Charley: In Search of America* (New York: The Viking Press, 1967), p. 203.
2. *New York Times,* November 11, 1997.
3. Harold Lasswell, *Who Gets What, When, and How* (New York: Meridian Books, Inc., 1958).
4. Texas Comptroller of Public Accounts, *Texas: Where We Stand,* 1994 and 1996, p. 6.
5. David Easton, *A Framework for Political Analysis* (Englewood Cliffs, NJ: Prentice-Hall, 1965), Chap. 5.
6. Louise Cowan, "Myth in the Modern World," in *Texas Myths,* ed. Robert F. O'Conner (College Station: Texas A & M University Press, 1986), p. 4.

7. Joseph Campbell, *Thou Art That* (Novato, CA: New World Library, 2001), pp. 1–9.

8. Cowan, p. 14; For an excellent analysis of the concept of the "myth of origin" as integrated into the American mythology, see Robert N. Bellah, *The Broken Covenant: American Civil Religion in Time of Trial* (New York: Seabury Press, 1975).

9. T. R. Fehrenbach, "Texas Mythology: Now and Forever," in *Texas Myth*, pp. 210–17.

10. Robin Doughty, "From Wilderness to Garden: Conquering the Texas Landscape," in *Texas Myths*, p. 105.

11. Lucian W. Pye, "Political Culture," *International Encyclopedia of the Social Sciences*, Vol. 12 (New York: Crowell, Collier and Macmillan, 1968), p. 218.

12. Ellen M. Dran, Robert B. Albritton, and Mikel Wyckoff, "Surrogate Versus Direct Measures of Political Culture: Explaining Participation and Policy Attitudes in Illinois," *Publius* (Spring 1991), p. 17.

13. Daniel Elazar, *American Federalism: A View from the States* (New York: Thomas Y. Crowell, 1966), p. 86.

14. Ibid., p. 86

15. Ibid., pp. 86–89.

16. Ibid., p. 90.

17. Ibid., p. 90.

18. Ibid., p. 91.

19. Ibid., p. 92.

20. Ibid., pp. 92–94.

21. Ibid., pp. 97, 102, 108.

22. Kim Quaile Hill, *Democracy in the Fifty States* (Lincoln, NE: University of Nebraska Press, 1994), Chap. 5.

23. Ellen N. Murray, "Sorrow Whispers in the Winds," *Texas Journal 14 (Spring/Summer 1992)*, p. 16.

24. Terry G. Jordan, with John L. Bean, Jr., and William M. Holmes, *Texas: A Geography* (Boulder, CO: Westview Press, 1984), pp. 79–86.

25. David Montejano, *Anglos and Mexicans in the Making of Texas, 1836–1986* (Austin: University of Texas Press, 1987), p. 38.

26. Texas State Data Center and Office of State Demographer, Texas A & M University, *The Texas Challenge in the Twenty-first Century: Implications of Population Change for the Future of Texas*, August 2003.

27. National Association of Latino Elected and Appointed Officials, *2003 National Roster of Hispanic Elected Officials*.

28. Joint Center for Political Studies, *National Roster of Black Elected Officials, 2001*.

29. Jordan, et al., pp. 71–77.

30. V. O. Key, *Southern Politics in State and Nation* (New York: Vintage Books, 1949), p. 261.

31. For an excellent analysis of Key's projections for political change in Texas, see Chandler Davidson, *Race and Class in Texas Politics* (Princeton, NJ: Princeton University Press, 1990).

32. U.S. Bureau of the Census, *Census 2000*.

33. Office of the Governor, Texas 2000 Commission, *Texas Trends*, pp. 5–6; Office of the Governor, Texas 2000 Commission, *Texas Past and Future: A Survey*, p. 6.

34. U.S. Bureau of the Census, *Census 2000*.

35. Ibid.

36. *San Antonio Express-News*, October 1, 2003, p. 1A; Texas Transportation Institute, Texas A & M University, *2003 Urban Mobility Study*, September 2003.

37. U.S. Bureau of the Census, *Census 2000*.

38. Texas Comptroller of Public Accounts, *The Changing Face of Texas through the Year 2000*, pp. 11–12; U.S. Bureau of the Census, *Current Population Reports: Population Trends in the 1980s*, Series P-23, No. 175.

39. U.S. Bureau of the Census, *Census 2000*.

40. *Forbes*, Special Edition 2003, "The 400 Richest People in America," pp. 186–284.

41. U.S. Bureau of the Census, *Census 2000*.

42. Protor, Bernadette D., and Joseph Dulaker, U.S. Census Bureau, Current Population Reports, P60-223, *Poverty in the United States: 2002* (Washington, D.C.: U.S. Government Printing Office, 2003).

43. Steve H. Murdock, Md. Nazrul Hoque, Martha Michael, Steve White, and Beverly Pecotte, *The Texas Challenge: Population Change and the Future of Texas* (College Station: Texas A & M University Press, 1997), pp. 64–65.

44. Betsey Bishop and Terry Heller, "Education Reform: Preparing Our Children for the Future," *Fiscal Notes* (March 1991), p. 10.

45. U.S. Bureau of the Census, *Census 2000*.

46. Rupert N. Richardson, Ernest Wallace, and Adrian Anderson, *Texas: The Lone Star State*, 5th ed. (Englewood Cliffs, NJ: Prentice Hall, 1988), p. 2.

47. Key, p. 260.

48. Jordan, et al., p. 7.

49. Ibid., pp. 18–21.

50. For an expanded analysis of the Texas economy and the dominant role played by corporations, see James W. Lamare, *Texas Politics: Economics, Power and Policy*, 7th ed. (St. Paul, MN: West Publishing Company, 2001), Chap. 2.

51. "Boom, Bust and Back Again: Bullock Tenure Covers Tumultuous Era," *Fiscal Notes* (December 1990), pp. 6–7.

52. Ibid.

53. "Road to Recovery Long and Bumpy, but Positive Signs Begin to Appear," *Fiscal Notes* (March 1989), p. 4.

54. "Boom, Bust and Back Again," p. 7.

55. Texas Comptroller of Public Accounts, *Spring 2004 Economic Forecast*.

56. "Texas Economic Outlook," *Texas Economic Quarterly* (December 1996), p. 2.

57. Texas Economic Development, May 2002, www.bidc.state.tx.us/overview/2-2te.

58. Augustin Redwine, "Back in Business: Once Beleaguered Financial Industry Riding the Waves of Texas Economic Development," *Fiscal Notes* (August 1994), pp. 1, 10.

59. Harry Hurt, "Birth of a New Frontier," *Texas Monthly* (April 1984), pp. 130–35.

60. "Biotechnology: New Science Brings Jobs to Texas as Biotech-related Efforts Blossom," *Fiscal Notes* (April 1990), pp. 1–8.

61. Texas Department of Economic Development, phone interview, April 1998.

62. Census Bureau, Foreign Trade Division, Special Report, April, 2003.

63. The following discussion of the thirteen economic regions is based on a series of reports produced by the Texas Comptroller of Public Accounts. The reports are part of a series entitled *Texas Regional Outlook, 2002.*

The Texas Constitution

Humbly invoking the blessings of Almighty God, the people of the
State of Texas do ordain and establish this Constitution.

Preamble to the Texas Constitution

People like to be remembered in the Texas Constitution; but
unfortunately, not all people are remembered equally, and the sum
of those special interests protected does not necessarily add up to
the general or public interest.

Janice May[1]

The year was 1874, and unusual events marked the end of the darkest chapter in
Texas history—the Reconstruction era and the military occupation that followed the
Civil War. Texans, still smarting from some of the most oppressive laws ever imposed
on American citizens, had overwhelmingly voted their governor out of office, but
he refused to leave the Capitol and hand over his duties to his elected successor. For
several tense days, the city of Austin was divided into two armed camps of people—
those supporting the deposed governor, **Edmund J. Davis,** and those supporting the
man who defeated him at the polls, Richard Coke. Davis finally gave up only after the
Texas militia turned against him and marched on the Capitol.

That long-ago period bears little resemblance to modern Texas, but the experience still casts a long shadow over state government. The state constitution, written
by Texans at the close of Reconstruction, was designed to put strong restraints on government to guard against future abuses; and most of those restraints remain in place
today. The Texas Constitution, adopted in 1876 and amended many times since, is so
restrictive that many scholars and politicians believe it is counterproductive to effective,
modern governance. They believe the document, which is bogged down with statutory
detail, is a textbook example of what a constitution should not be. State government
functions despite its constitutional shackles: a weak chief executive, an outdated, part-
time legislature, a poorly organized judiciary, and dedicated funds that limit the state's
budgetary options. But a total rewrite of the Constitution has been elusive, thanks to
numerous special interests who find security in the present document—from holders

37

of obsolete offices to beneficiaries of dedicated funds and bureaucrats who fear change. Public ignorance and indifference to the problems created by the restrictive constitutional provisions also thwart an overhaul of the document.

It is our position, shared by others who study state governments, that one cannot develop a clear understanding of Texas government or its politics without some familiarity with and understanding of the Texas constitution.[2] Constitutions are more than the formal frameworks that define the structure, authority, and responsibilities of governmental institutions. They also reflect fundamental political, economic, and power relationships as determined by the culture, values, and interests of the people who create them and the events of the period in which they were written.[3]

The constitution of Texas is not an easy read, and one can quickly get bogged down in details that make little sense to the casual reader. But a careful study of the document will provide insights into the distribution of power among competing groups and regions within the state. The constitution outlines the powers of the state and local governments, and it also defines the limitations imposed on these governments. From the perspective of political economy, the constitution also speaks to "the relation of the state to economic activity, including both the extent of direct governmental support for enterprise and the appropriate balance between promotion and regulation of economic development."[4]

Texas has had seven constitutions, and understanding that legacy is critical to understanding contemporary Texas politics and public policy. The first constitution was adopted in 1827, when the state was still part of Mexico. The second was drafted when Texas declared its independence from Mexico in 1836 and became a republic. The third was adopted in 1845 when the state joined the Union. The fourth constitution was written when Texas joined the Confederacy in 1861, and the fifth was adopted when the state rejoined the Union in 1866. The sixth constitution was adopted in 1869 to satisfy the **radical reconstructionists'** opposition to the 1866 constitution, and the seventh constitution was adopted in 1876 after the termination of Reconstruction policies.

CONSTITUTIONALISM

The Functions of a Constitution

A **constitution** defines the principles of a society and states or suggests what political objectives that society is attempting to achieve. It outlines the specific institutions that the people will use to achieve their objectives, and it defines who can participate in collective decisions and who can hold public office. It also defines the relationship between those people who govern and those who are governed and sets limits on what each group can and cannot do. Because of the stability of the American political system and a general commitment to the rule of law, we often overlook the fact that a constitution also reflects the way a society structures conflict through its institutional arrangements.[5]

The Texas Constitution in a Comparative Perspective

Constitutions do not lend themselves to easy reading. The formal, legal language often obscures the general objectives of the document and its relevance to contemporary issues of political power and public policy. Scholars believe, first, that constitutions should be brief and should include general principles rather than specific legislative provisions. In other words, constitutions should provide a basic framework for government and leave the details to be defined in **statutory law.** Second, experts say, constitutions should grant authority to specific institutions, so as to increase the responsiveness and the accountability of individuals elected or appointed to public office. Scholars also believe that constitutions should provide for orderly change but should not be written in such a restrictive fashion that they require continual modifications to meet contemporary needs.[6]

Amended only twenty-seven times since its adoption in 1789, the U.S. Constitution is a concise, 7,000-word document that outlines broad, basic principles of authority and governance. No one would argue that the government of the 2000s is comparable to that of the 1790s, yet the flexibility of the U.S. Constitution makes it as relevant now as it was in the eighteenth century. It is often spoken of as "a living constitution" that doesn't have to be continually amended to meet society's ever-changing needs and conditions. Its reinterpretations by the courts, the Congress, and the president have produced an expansion of powers and responsibilities within the framework of the original language of the document (see Table 2–1).

By contrast, the Texas Constitution—like those of many other states—is an unwieldy, restrictive document. With more than 100,000 words, it has been on a life-support system—the piecemeal amendment process—for most of its lifetime

TABLE 2–1   Comparison of the Texas Constitution and U.S. Constitution

	U.S. Constitution	**Texas Constitution**
1. General Principles	Popular sovereignty Limited government Representative government Contract theory Separation of powers	Popular sovereignty Limited government Representative government Contract theory Separation of powers
2. Context of Adoption	Reaction to weakness of Articles of Confederation—strengthened significantly national powers	Post Reconstruction—designed to limit powers of government
3. Style	General principles stated in broad terms	Detailed provisions
4. Length	7,000 words	100,000 words
5. Date of Implementation	1789	1876
6. Amendments	27	432
7. Amendment Process	Difficult	Relatively easy
8. Adaptation to Change	Moderately easy through interpretation	Difficult and often requires constitutional amendments
9. Bill of Rights	Amendments to the Constitution—adopted in 1791	Article 1 of the Constitution of 1876
10. Structure of Government	Separation of powers with a unified executive based on provisions of Articles I, II, III	Separation of powers with plural executive defined by Article 2
11. Legislature	Bicameral	Bicameral
12. Judiciary	Creation of one Supreme Court and other courts to be created by the Congress	Detailed provisions creating two appellate courts and other state courts
13. Distribution of Powers	Federal	Unitary
14. Public Policy	Little reference to policy	Detailed policy provisions

TABLE 2–2   Ten Shortest and Ten Longest State Constitutions (As of January 1, 2003)

State	Number of Constitutions	Effective Date of Current Constitution	Estimated Number of Words	Amendments Submitted to Voters	Amendments Adopted
Ten Shortest State Constitutions					
New Hampshire	2	1784	9,200	283	143
Vermont	3	1793	10,286	211	53
Indiana	2	1851	10,315	75	43
Rhode Island	3	1843	10,908	105	59
North Carolina	3	1971	11,000	39	31
Utah	1	1896	11,000	154	103
Minnesota	1	1858	11,547	213	118
Kansas	1	1861	12,246	122	92
Iowa	2	1857	12,616	57	52
Montana	2	1973	13,145	49	27
Ten Longest State Constitutions					
New York	4	1895	51,700	288	215
Florida	6	1969	52,421	127	96
Louisiana	11	1975	54,112	169	113
California	2	1879	54,645	846	507
Colorado	1	1876	56,944	297	143
Arkansas	5	1874	59,500	186	89
Oregon	1	1859	63,372	468	234
Oklahoma	1	1907	74,075	329	165
Texas	7	1876	100,000	605	432
Alabama	6	1901	340,136	1024	743

Source: *The Book of the States,* 2003 Edition, Volume 35 (Lexington, KY: The Council of State Governments, 2003).

(Table 2–2). It is less a set of basic governmental principles than a compilation of detailed statutory language reflecting the distrust of government that was widespread in Texas when it was written. In effect, it attempts to diffuse political power among many different institutions. As drafted in 1875, it also included restrictions on elections and civil rights that were later invalidated by the U.S. Supreme Court. Those early provisions were efforts to limit the power of minority groups to fully participate in state government.[7]

The historical constitutional experiences of Texas parallel those of many southern states that have had multiple constitutions in the post–Civil War era. The former Confederate states, Texas included, are the only states whose constitutions formally acknowledge the supremacy of the U.S. Constitution, a provision required by the Radical Reconstructionists for readmission to the Union.

THE CONSTITUTIONAL LEGACY

Each of Texas's seven constitutions was written in a distinct historical setting. And while there are significant differences—as well as similarities—among these documents, each contributed to the state and local governments that we know today.

The Constitution of Coahuila y Tejas (1827)

Sparsely populated Texas was part of Mexico when that country secured its independence from Spain in 1821, about the same time that Stephen F. Austin and others initiated Anglo colonization of Texas. Initially, Anglo Texans appeared to be willing to be incorporated into the Mexican political system as long as there was limited intrusion by the Mexican government into their daily affairs. In 1824, the new Republic of Mexico adopted a constitution for a federal system of government that recognized Texas (Tejas) as a single state with Coahuila, its neighbor south of the Rio Grande. Saltillo, Mexico, was the state capital.

TEXAS'S SEVEN CONSTITUTIONS

1827: Constitution of Coahuila y Tejas

The first Texas constitution, adopted in 1827. It recognized Texas as a Mexican state, along with Coahuila.

1836: Constitution of the Republic

The constitution, adopted March 16, 1836, by Texas colonists declaring independence from Mexico. Texas functioned as an independent republic for nine years under this constitution.

1845: Constitution of 1845

The constitution under which Texas was admitted into the United States.

1861: Civil War Constitution

The constitution adopted by Texans after the state seceded from the Union and joined the Confederacy in 1861.

1866: Constitution of 1866

The short-lived constitution under which Texas sought to be readmitted to the Union after the Civil War and before the Radical Reconstructionists took control of the U.S. Congress.

1869: Reconstruction Constitution

The constitution centralizing power in state government and weakening local governments. It reflected the sentiments of Radical Reconstructionists, not of most Texans.

1876: Texas Constitution

The constitution adopted at the end of Reconstruction, amended many times since, and still in effect. Highly restrictive and antigovernment, this constitution places strict limitations on the powers of the governor, the legislature, and other state officials.

Each state was authorized to develop a constitution, and the state constitution for Coahuila y Tejas was completed in 1827. This document provided for a **unicameral** congress of twelve deputies, including two from Texas, elected by the people. Most of the legislators were from the more populous and Spanish-speaking Coahuila, and the laws were published in Spanish, which few Texas colonists understood. The executive department included a governor and a vice governor. The governor enforced the law, led the state militia, and granted pardons. The constitution made Catholicism the state religion, although that requirement was not enforced among Texas's Anglo settlers. Additionally, Anglo Texans were not subject to military service, taxes, or custom duties. In effect, Texas served as a buffer between Mexico and various Native American tribes and the United States.

But with increased Anglo immigration and the perceived threat of U.S. imperial or expansionary policies, Mexico soon attempted to extend its control over Texas. This effort reinforced cultural differences between the Anglo and Spanish populations and would eventually lead to revolution by Anglo Texans.[8]

This formative period produced some enduring contributions to the Texas constitutional tradition. Elements of the Mexican legal system are still to be found in property and land laws, water laws and water rights, and community property laws. One justification for the revolution of 1836 was the failure of the Mexican government to provide for sufficient funding for public education. But while there were expectations of funding by the central government, a "concept of local control over school development was firmly established."[9] This issue of local control has been a continuing constitutional question and is central to the current issue of funding public education.

The Constitution of the Republic of Texas (1836)

During the late 1820s and the early 1830s, increased immigration from the United States into the territory of Texas heightened the tension and conflict between the Anglo settlers and the Mexican government. Mexico's efforts to enforce its laws within Texas produced conflicts between cultures, legal traditions, and economic interests that resulted in open rebellion by the colonists.

At the same time, Mexico was embroiled in its own internal dissension. It struggled to stabilize its political system but didn't have the legacy and social and political institutions to assure a successful democratic system. In many respects, the events in Texas were a footnote to the power politics in Mexico. Had the autonomy of Texas that was mandated in the Mexican Constitution of 1824 been maintained, the history of this region might well have been different.

Increased internal conflict among competing Mexican interests resulted in the seizure of power by the popular general, Antonio Lopez de Santa Anna Perez de Lebron. Santa Anna began to systematically suspend the powers of the Mexican Congress and local governments and, in October 1835, the national Constitution of 1824 was voided. Mexico adopted a new constitution providing for a **unitary system** with power centralized in the national congress and the presidency. The principle of **federalism,** which divided power and authority between the national government and the states, was repudiated. This major change intensified conflict between the national government and the Mexican states. Texas was not the only area of Mexico where the principles of federalism were highly regarded, and although Texas was eventually successful in establishing its autonomy, several other Mexican states were subjected to harsh military retaliation.

As the Mexican government under Santa Anna attempted to regain control over Texas, colonists who initially supported the national government and those who expressed ambivalence were only slowly converted to the cause of independence. Stephen F. Austin had consistently supported the position that Texas was a Mexican state, and he represented a large part of the Anglo population living in Texas. But when Mexican troops moved across the Rio Grande into Texas in the fall of 1835, Austin sent out a call for resistance.

The numerous special interests that later were to obstruct the course of constitutional development in Texas were missing at the small settlement of Washington-on-the-Brazos in 1836. The fifty-nine male colonists who convened to declare Texas's independence from Mexico on March 2 and to adopt a constitution for the new republic two weeks later had two overriding interests: the preservation of their fledgling nation and the preservation of their own lives. By the time they had completed their work, the Alamo—only 150 miles away—had fallen to a large Mexican army under Santa Anna, and a second Mexican force was also north of the Rio Grande. Accordingly, the constitution writers wasted little time on speechmaking.

Faced with the advancing Mexican armies, Texans hastily met in the small settlement of Washington-on-the-Brazos, declared their independence on March 2, 1836, and wrote the Constitution of the Republic, which was adopted on March 16, 1836.

Consequently, the constitution adopted on March 16, 1836, was not cluttered with the details that weaken the present Texas Constitution. It drew heavily from the U.S. Constitution, and since forty-four of the fifty-nine delegates were from the South, from the constitutions of several southern states. The document created an elected **bicameral** Congress and provided for an elected president. Members of the clergy were prohibited from serving as president or in Congress, and there was no official, state-preferred religion. Slavery was legal, but importation of slaves from any country other than the United States was illegal. Free African Americans had to have the Congress' permission to leave Texas.

Approximately six weeks after the disastrous defeat at the Alamo, the Texas army, under the command of Sam Houston, defeated Santa Anna's army at the battle of San Jacinto on April 21, 1836. The war of independence had been relatively short and involved limited casualties, but the problems of creating a stable, political system under the new constitution were formidable. There was no viable government in place, no money for paying the costs of government, and no party system.[10] And, although defeated, Mexico did not relinquish its claims to Texas and was to demonstrate in subsequent actions that it wanted to regain this lost territory. Nevertheless, the "transition from colony to constitutional republic was accomplished quickly and with a minimum of disorganization."[11]

The experience of independence and national autonomy from 1836 to 1845 contributed significantly to the development of a sense of historical uniqueness among Texans. While the effects on the state's political psyche may be difficult to measure, the "Lone Star" experience has been kept alive through school history texts, the celebration of key events, and the development of a mythology of the independence period.

The Constitution of 1845

During the independence movement and immediately thereafter, there were overtures by some Texans to the United States to annex Texas, but they were initially blocked by the issue of slavery and its relationship to economic and regional influence in U.S. politics. Increased immigration to Texas in the late 1830s and early 1840s, more interest among Texans in joining the Union, and expansionist policies of the U.S. government stepped up pressures for annexation. It was a major issue in the U.S. presidential campaign of 1844, and the election of James K. Polk accelerated the move toward Texas's admission to the United States in 1845.

The annexation bill approved by the U.S. Congress included a compromise that allowed slavery to continue in Texas.[12] Racial issues that emerged from this period continue to shape contemporary politics and public policy in the state. Texas still struggles with voting rights issues, inequities in funding of education, and the maldistribution of economic resources that directly affect the quality of life for many minorities.

The Constitution of 1845, which was drafted to allow Texas's annexation, was about twice as long as the Constitution of 1836. It borrowed not only from its predecessor but also from the constitutions of other southern states, particularly from Louisiana.

The Constitution of 1845 created an elected legislature that met biennially and included a house of representatives and a senate. It provided for an elected

---

FIVE "LONE" STARS?

The terms of Texas's admission into the Union provided that Texas could divide itself into as many as five states, a provision largely forgotten until state Representative David Swinford, a Republican from Dumas, made such a proposal in 1991. The idea attracted some newspaper headlines and some interest in the Panhandle, which is geographically isolated from most of Texas, but wasn't given serious consideration.

---

governor and an elected lieutenant governor, and it empowered the governor to appoint a secretary of state, attorney general, and state judges, subject to senate confirmation. The legislature chose a comptroller, treasurer, and land commissioner. But in 1850, Texas voters amended the constitution to make most state offices elective. In this respect, Texas was following a national pattern of fragmenting the powers of the executive branch of state government. Today, Texas still has a plural executive system under which practically all statewide officeholders are elected independently of the governor, a system that contrasts sharply with the appointive cabinet system of executive government enjoyed by the president of the United States.

The 1845 Constitution protected private homesteads from foreclosure, guaranteed separate property rights for married women, and established a permanent fund for the support of public schools—provisions also found in the present constitution. The 1845 charter also recognized slavery, prohibited anyone who had ever participated in a duel from holding public office, and prohibited state-chartered banks. This constitution "worked so well that after several intervening constitutions, the people of Texas recopied it almost *in toto* as the Constitution of 1876."[13]

The Civil War Constitution (1861)

When Texas seceded from the Union in 1861, just before the outbreak of the Civil War, the state constitution was again revised. Although most of the provisions of the 1845 document were retained, significant changes were made in line with Texas's new membership in the Confederacy. Public officials were required to pledge their support of the Confederate constitution, greater protection was given to slavery, and the freeing of slaves was prohibited.

Any semblance of a two-party system had been destroyed by the issues of slavery and secession during the 1850s, and state politics was dominated by personalities, factions, and war-related issues. Factionalism within the Democratic party persisted for more than 100 years, until the emergence of a two-party system in the 1980s.

The Civil War era also contributed to a legacy of states' rights, which was to persist well into the next century and spark an extended struggle for desegregation. Theoretically, the constitutional issue of the Civil War was whether a state, once having joined the Union, could leave the Union. The southern states subscribed to a view of the national government as a **confederacy,** and it was their position that a state could withdraw, or secede. Although the northern victory dispelled this interpretation, Texas, along with other southern states, found ways to thwart national policy through the 1960s. Their efforts were based, in part, on their continued arguments for states' rights.

The Constitution of 1866

After the Civil War, Texas government was subject to national control, first through a military government, and then a provisional government headed by A. J. Hamilton, a former U.S. congressman who had remained loyal to the Union. These were dark days for Texans. Although the state had witnessed relatively few battles and had not suffered from the scorched-earth tactics used by Union generals elsewhere, the economy was in disarray. Many Texas families had lost loved ones, and many surviving Confederate veterans had been wounded physically or psychologically. Although the national government developed policies to assist the newly freed slaves, these policies were never fully funded and were halfheartedly—and often dishonestly—carried out. And the presence of an occupation army heightened tensions and shaped subsequent political attitudes.

The Reconstruction plan initiated by President Abraham Lincoln but never fully implemented envisioned a rapid return to civilian government for the southern states and their quick reintegration as equals in the national political system. Requirements were modest: the abolition of slavery, the repudiation of the Secession Ordinance of 1861, and the repudiation of all debts and obligations incurred under the Confederacy.[14]

Texas voters revived the Constitution of 1845 and amended it to include the stipulations required by the national government. But while slavery was eliminated and the freed slaves were given the right to hold property and were accorded legal rights before a jury, no black people could testify in any court case involving whites. And African Americans were denied the right to vote.[15] The new constitution was adopted in June 1866, a new government was elected, and on August 20, 1866, President Andrew Johnson "declared the rebellion in Texas at an end."[16]

In short order, however, the mild Reconstruction policies of Johnson were replaced by the severe policies of the Radical Reconstructionists who captured control of Congress in 1866. The new Texas constitution was invalidated by Congress, which passed, over the president's veto, the Reconstruction Acts, which established military governments throughout the South. The civilian government initiated by the state constitution of 1866 was short-lived, and Texas functioned for two years under a reinstituted military government.

This period had an enduring impact on Texas constitutional law and politics. In a broad sense, it prolonged the full reintegration of Texas into the national political system. In specific terms, it transformed the constitutional tradition of Texas into one of hostility and suspicion toward government.

The Constitution of Reconstruction (1869)

The Reconstruction Acts required a Texas constitution that would grant African Americans the right to vote and include other provisions acceptable to Congress. A Republican slate of delegates to a new constitutional convention produced a new charter in 1869. It did not reflect the majority Texas sentiment of the time, but it conformed to Republican wishes. Centralizing more powers in state government while weakening local government, the charter gave the governor a four-year term and the power to appoint other top state officials, including members of the judiciary. It provided for annual legislative sessions, gave African Americans the right to vote, and, for the first time, provided for a centralized, state-wide system of public schools.

Texans were unhappy enough with their new constitution, but the widespread abuses of the document that followed under the oppressive and corrupt administration of Radical Republican Governor Edmund J. Davis would soon produce shackles on state government that are still in place today.

In the 1869 election, the first under the new constitution, large numbers of former slaves voted, while Anglos who had volunteered during the war to fight for the Confederacy were not allowed to cast ballots. The entire process was supervised by Radical supporters of Davis, a former Union Army officer. The military governor certified that Davis beat Conservative Republican A. J. Hamilton by 39,901 to 39,092 votes. This outcome was allowed despite widespread, flagrant incidents of voter fraud, which also were ignored by President Ulysses S. Grant and Congress. A radical majority in the new Texas legislature then approved a series of authoritarian—and, in some respects, unconstitutional—laws proposed by Davis. They gave the governor the power to declare martial law and suspend the laws in any county and created a state police force under the governor's control that could deprive citizens of constitutional protections. The governor also was empowered to appoint mayors, district attorneys, and hundreds of other local officials. Another law that designated newspapers as official printers of state documents in effect put much of the press under government control.

Davis exercised some of the most repressive powers ever imposed on United States citizens. And Texans responded. First, in 1872, they elected a Democratic majority to the legislature that abolished the state police and repealed other oppressive laws. Then, in 1873, they elected a Confederate veteran, Democrat Richard Coke, governor by more than a 2–1 margin over Davis. Like the Radical Republicans in the previous gubernatorial election, the Democrats were not above abusing the democratic process, and once again, voting fraud was rampant.

A Union general and later governor of Texas (1870–74), Edmund J. Davis conducted one of the most oppressive administrations in U.S. history. Texans reacted to such practices with restrictions built into the Constitution of 1876.

"Democrat politicos bluntly indicated that power would be won depending on who outfrauded whom. No practice was ignored. . . . There was terror, intimidation, and some murders on both sides," wrote historian T. R. Fehrenbach.[17]

As was described earlier in this chapter, Davis initially refused to leave office and appealed to President Grant for federal troops to help him retain power. Grant refused, and Davis finally gave up after the Texas militia turned against him and marched on the capitol in January 1874. Bloodshed was avoided, Reconstruction was ending, and the Constitution of 1869 was doomed.

The Constitution of 1876: Retrenchment and Reform

The restored Democratic majority promptly took steps to assemble a new constitutional convention, which convened in Austin on September 6, 1875. The delegates were all men. Most were products of a rural and frontier South, and still smarting from Reconstruction abuses, they considered government a necessary evil that had to be heavily restricted. Many, however, had previous governmental experience. Initially, seventy-five Democrats and fifteen Republicans were elected delegates, but one Republican resigned after only limited service and was replaced by a Democrat.[18]

The vast majority of the delegates were white, and some disagreement remains over how many African Americans served in the convention. Some historians say there were six. According to one account, however, six African Americans were elected but one resigned after only one day of service and was replaced in a special election by a white delegate. All of the African American delegates were Republicans.[19]

Only four of the delegates were native Texans. Most had immigrated to Texas from other southern states, including nineteen—the largest single group—from Tennessee, which one author called the "breeding ground" of Texas delegates. Their average age was forty-five. The oldest was sixty-eight; the youngest was twenty-three.[20] Eleven of the delegates had been members of previous constitutional conventions in Texas, but there is disagreement over whether any had participated in drafting the Reconstruction Constitution of 1869. In any event, the influences of the 1869 constitution were negative, not positive.

At least thirty of the delegates had served in the Texas legislature, two others had served in the Tennessee and Mississippi legislatures, two had represented Texas in the U.S. Congress, and two others had represented Texas in the Confederate Congress. Delegates also included a former attorney general, a former lieutenant governor, and a former secretary of state of Texas; and at least eight delegates had judicial experience. Many delegates had been high-ranking Confederate military officers. One, John H. Reagan, had been postmaster general of the Confederacy.[21] Reagan later would become a U.S. senator from Texas and the first chairman of the Texas Railroad Commission.

Another delegate who epitomized the independent, frontier spirit of the time was John S. "Rip" Ford, a native of South Carolina who had come to Texas in 1836 as a physician. He later became a lawyer, journalist, state senator, mayor of Austin, and Texas Ranger captain. In 1874, he was a leader of the militia that marched on the Capitol and forced Edmund J. Davis to relinquish the governor's office to his elected successor. Ford had been a secessionist delegate to the 1861 convention and, during the Civil War, had commanded a makeshift cavalry regiment that fought Union soldiers along the Texas-Mexico border.[22]

Six recently emancipated African Americans, all Republicans, were elected to the 1875 Constitutional Convention.

According to one account, delegates to the 1875 convention included thirty-three lawyers, twenty-eight farmers, three physicians, three merchants, two teachers, two editors, and one minister. At least eleven other delegates were part-time farmers who also pursued other occupations.[23] Other historians have suggested slightly different breakdowns, but all agree that the influence of agricultural interests was substantial in the writing of the new Texas charter.

About half the delegates were members of the Society of the Patrons of Husbandry, or the **Grange.** An organization formed to improve the lot of farmers, the Grange became politically active in the wake of national scandals involving abuses by big business and government. The Grange started organizing in Texas in 1873, and its influence was directly felt in constitutional provisions limiting taxes and governmental expenditures and restricting banks, railroads, and other corporations.

The delegates did not try to produce a document that would be lauded as a model of constitutional perfection or mistaken for a literary classic. They faced the reality of addressing serious, pressing problems—an immediate crisis that did not encourage debate over the finer points of academic or political theory or produce any prophetic visions of the next century.

The Civil War, Reconstruction, and the Radical Republican administration had plunged the state into economic ruin and state government into deep debt, despite the heavy taxation of Texas citizens, particularly property owners. The bottom had fallen out of land prices, a disaster for what was still an agricultural state. Governmental corruption had been pervasive under the Davis administration, and the dictatorial powers that Davis had exercised, particularly the abuses of his hated state police, had left deep scars. Moreover, the national political scene under President

---

ARTICLES OF THE 1876 TEXAS CONSTITUTION

Preamble
Article I   Bill of Rights
II   The Powers of Government
III   Legislative Department
IV   Executive Department
V   Judicial Department
VI   Suffrage
VII   Education
VIII   Taxation and Revenue
IX   Counties
X   Railroads
XI   Municipal Corporations
XII   Private Corporations
XIII   Spanish and Mexican Land Titles (repealed August 6, 1969)
XIV   Public Lands and Land Office
XV   Impeachment
XVI   General Provisions
XVII   Mode of Amending the Constitution

Grant's two administrations (1869–1877) had also been plagued by corruption and scandal.

The framers of the Texas Constitution of 1876 reacted accordingly. In seeking to restore control of their state government to the people and restore economic stability, they fashioned what was essentially an antigovernment charter. Centralization was replaced with more local control, strict limits were placed on taxation, and short leashes were put on the legislature, the courts, and especially the governor.[24]

Texas's traditional agricultural interests, which had been called upon to finance industrial development and new social services during Reconstruction, were once again protected from onerous governmental intrusion and taxation. The retrenchment and reform embodied in the new charter soon would hamper the state's commercial and economic development. But the post-Reconstruction Texans applauded the multitude of restrictive details that the new constitution carried. They ratified the new document in February 1876 by a vote of 136,606 to 56,052.

GENERAL PRINCIPLES OF THE TEXAS CONSTITUTION

A relatively short preamble and the first two sections of the Bill of Rights express the underlying principle of the Texas Constitution of 1876. It is a social compact, formed by free men (no women participated in its drafting), in which "all political power is inherent in the people . . . founded on their authority, and instituted for their benefit."[25] These brief sections are based on the principles of **popular sovereignty** and **compact theory,** both of which were part of a legacy of constitutional law in the United States. While the language articulates the noble aspirations of a free and just society, it was limited in scope and application. Women and minorities were initially denied full citizenship rights. And although women gained the right to vote in 1920, it has taken years for African Americans and Hispanics to receive the full protection implicit in these statements.

A third major principle is **limited government.** The Bill of Rights and other provisions throughout the constitution place limits on governmental authority and power. The constitution spells out the traditional rights of religious freedom, procedural due process of law, and other rights of the citizen in relation to the government.

A fourth major principle is **separation of powers.** Unlike the U.S. Constitution, in which this principle emerges through powers defined in the three articles related to Congress, the president, and the judiciary, Article 2 of the Texas Constitution specifically provides for it.

The Constitution of 1876 created three branches of government—legislative, executive, and judicial—and provided for a system of checks and balances that assured that no single branch would dominate the others. This principle originated with the U.S. Constitution, whose drafters were concerned about the so-called "mischief of factions." They feared that groups or special interests would be able to capture governmental institutions and pursue policies that were not in the national interest. So institutional power was fragmented to guard against that potential problem. In some respects, this was an issue of even greater concern to the framers of the Texas Constitution. Reacting to the highly centralized authority and abuses of the Davis administration, they took the separation of powers principle to its extreme.

Lawmaking authority is vested in an elected legislature that includes a 150-member House of Representatives and a 31-member Senate and meets in regular sessions in odd-numbered years and in special sessions of limited scope and duration when called by the governor. The sixty-five sections of Article 3 spell out in detail the powers granted and the restrictions imposed on the legislature.

An elected governor shares authority over the executive branch with several other independently elected, statewide officeholders. The governor can veto bills approved by the legislature, and a veto can be overridden only by a two-thirds vote of the house and the senate.

Also elected are members of the judiciary—from justices of the peace, with limited jurisdiction at the county level, to the highest statewide appellate courts. This provision reflects the strong sentiment of post-Reconstruction Texans for an independent judiciary and is a major difference from the federal government, in which judges are appointed by the president. Also unlike the federal system, in which the U.S. Supreme Court is the court of last resort in both civil and criminal appeals, Texas has two courts of last resort. The Texas Supreme Court has jurisdiction over civil matters, and the Texas Court of Criminal Appeals has final review of criminal cases.

WEAKNESSES AND CRITICISMS OF THE CONSTITUTION OF 1876

Executive Branch

Many experts believe that the Texas Constitution excessively fragments governmental authority and responsibility, particularly in the executive branch. Although there is a natural disposition for the public to look to the governor to establish policy priorities, the governor does not have control over other elected state executives, but rather shares both authority and responsibility for policy with them. This situation can be problematic, as when former Republican Governor Bill Clements, for example, shared executive responsibilities with Democrats who sharply disagreed with his priorities. Even when the governor and other elected officials are of the same party, differences in personality, political philosophy, and policy objectives can produce tension and sometimes deadlock.

The governor's power has been further diffused by the creation over the years of numerous boards and commissions that set policy for executive agencies not headed by elected officials. Although the governor appoints most of those board members, they serve staggered six-year terms that are longer than a governor's term. And a newly elected governor—who cannot fire a predecessor's appointees—usually has to wait through most of his or her first term to gain a majority of appointees to most boards.

Fragmented authority and responsibility also are found in county governments, which are administrative agents of the state (see Chapter 12). Various elected county officials often clash over public policy, producing inefficiencies or failing to meet public needs. And just as the voters are faced with a long ballot for statewide offices, they also must choose among a long, often confusing list of county officers. Because a long ballot discourages many people from voting, this obstacle reduces public accountability, an end result that the framers of the Constitution of 1876 certainly never intended.

Legislative Branch

The constitution created a low-paid, part-time legislature to ensure the election of citizen-lawmakers who would be sensitive to the needs of their constituents, not of professional politicians who would live off the taxpayers. Unwittingly, however, the constitution writers also produced a lawmaking body easily influenced by special interest groups. And the strict limitations placed on the legislature's operations and powers slow its ability to meet the increasingly complex needs of a growing, modern Texas.

In 1972, voters approved a constitutional change to lengthen the terms of the governor and other executive officeholders from two to four years. This change gave the governor more time to develop public policies with the prospect of seeing them implemented. But voters repeatedly have rejected proposals to provide for annual legislative sessions, and legislative pay remains among the lowest in the country.

Judicial Branch

The Texas Constitution also created numerous locally elected judicial offices, including justice of the peace and county and district courts. Although there are appeal procedures, these judges derive a great deal of autonomy, power, and influence through their local constituencies.

Public Education

Another example of decentralization is the public school system. The centralized school system authorized under the Constitution of 1869 was abolished, and local authorities were given the primary responsibility of supervising public education. The concept of "local control" over their schools is important to many Texans, but decentralization and wide disparities in local tax bases have produced an inequitable public education system.

Budgeting and Finances

The Texas Constitution, including key amendments adopted after 1876, requires a balanced state budget, but also heavily restricts the legislature's choices over state spending. The dedication of large amounts of revenue to specific purposes has made it increasingly difficult for lawmakers to address changing state needs (see Chapter 13).

Individual Rights

Although articulating a general commitment to democracy and individual rights, the constitution initially retarded democratic development in Texas.[26] Like many other southern states, Texas had restrictive laws on voter participation. It levied a poll tax, which reduced the voting of minorities and poor whites until 1966, when an amendment to the U.S. Constitution and a decision by the U.S. Supreme Court outlawed poll taxes. Federal courts struck down a Texas election system that excluded African Americans from voting in the Democratic primary, which was where elections were decided when Texas was a one-party state. The elimination of significant numbers of people from participating in elections helped perpetuate the one-party political system for approximately 100 years.[27]

Excessive Details

The Texas Constitution is also burdened with excessive detail. Although few individuals are disposed to read the 100,000-plus-word document, a person casually perusing it can find language, for example, governing the operation of hospital districts in Ochiltree, Castro, Hansford, and Hopkins counties and a provision dealing with expenditures for relocation or replacement of sanitation sewer laterals on private property. Whereas the 7,000-word U.S. Constitution leaves the details for implementation to congressional legislation, the Texas Constitution often spells out the authority and power of a governmental agency in specific detail. Most experts would argue that many constitutional articles are of a legislative nature and have no business in a constitution.[28] The excessive detail limits the adaptability of the constitution to changing circumstances and places undue restrictions on state and local governments.

Consequently, there are obsolete and contradictory provisions in the constitution that create confusion in its interpretation and application. Constitutional

---

WHO NEEDS ALL THE TROUBLE?

Roberts County Judge Vernon H. Cook was convinced that his rural county near the top of the Texas Panhandle did not need a constable. He believed the sheriff provided enough law enforcement for the county's 1,500 residents. For years, the county had not had a constable, but the office, which was created in the Texas Constitution, remained on the books. Unexpectedly, in 1992, a write-in candidate ran for constable and was elected. The office then became an extra expense for county taxpayers, as county commissioners felt obliged to pay the new officeholder a $600-a-month salary plus a $200-a-month car allowance and health insurance benefits.

Convinced they were not getting their money's worth—"As near as we can tell, he served two official papers in his first year in office," Cook complained—commissioners later reduced his salary, and the constable left town. To avoid a recurrence of the problem, commissioners had to ask the state legislature to put a constitutional amendment abolishing the Roberts County constable's office on a statewide ballot so all the state's voters could decide the issue. Thus voters in Houston—600 miles away—would have a greater say in abolishing the office than Roberts County's own taxpayers, because Houston's 1.6 million residents cast many more votes. Although that may not seem fair—Houston taxpayers, after all, did not pay the Roberts County constable's salary—it is just one of many obstacles and inconveniences imposed on modern government by a nineteenth-century constitution. Most amendments abolishing obsolete county offices, however, are approved by Texas voters, including amendments abolishing the constables' offices in Roberts County and two other rural counties in 1995.

Source: Houston Chronicle, November 6, 1995.

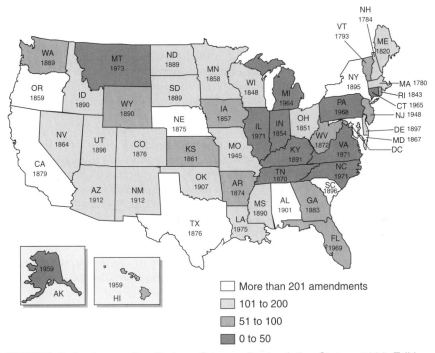

More than 201 amendments

101 to 200

51 to 100

0 to 50

FIGURE 2–1 Across the States. *Source: Book of the States, 2003 Edition* (Lexington, KY: The Council of State Governments, 2003).

amendments have been periodically approved to "clean up" such deadwood, but the problem persists.[29]

Another important criticism of the Texas Constitution focuses on amendments and the amendment process. Alabama has had more constitutional amendments than any other state (see Figure 2–1), but Texas ranked fourth, with 432 amendments from 1876 through 2003. In contrast, the U.S. Constitution has been amended only twenty-seven times since 1789, and ten of those amendments were adopted as the Bill of Rights immediately after the government organized. The numerous restrictions and prohibitions in the Texas Constitution require excessive amendments to enable state government to adapt to social, economic, and political changes.

CONSTITUTIONAL CHANGE AND ADAPTATION

Amendments

Although the drafters filled the constitution with a multitude of restrictive provisions, they also provided a relatively easy method of amending it. This piecemeal amendment process has enabled state government to meet some changing needs, but it has also added thousands of words to the document.

Proposed constitutional amendments can be submitted only by the legislature. Approval by two-thirds of the house and the senate puts them on the ballot, where adoption requires a majority vote. While voters had approved 432 amendments through 2003, they had rejected 173 others. The first amendment was adopted on September 2, 1879. A record twenty-five amendments were on the November 3, 1987, ballot. Seventeen were adopted, and eight were defeated.

Some amendments are of major statewide importance, but many have affected only a single county or a handful of counties or have been offered simply to rid the constitution of obsolete language. One amendment approved by voters in 1993 affected only about 140 families, two church congregations, and one school district in Fort Bend and Austin counties. It cleared up a title defect to their land.

Unlike voters in many other states, Texas citizens cannot force the placement of constitutional amendments or binding referenda on the ballot because Texas does not have **initiative** or **referendum** on a statewide level. On taking office in January 1979 as Texas's first Republican governor since Reconstruction, Governor Bill Clements made the adoption of initiative and referendum a priority. But the process could not be provided without a constitutional amendment, and the legislature—which did not want to give up such a significant policy prerogative to the electorate—ignored Clements.

In recent years, however, the legislature has demonstrated a tendency to seek political cover by selectively letting the voters decide particularly controversial issues, such as a binding referendum in 1987 on the legalization of parimutuel betting on horse and dog racing. In 1993, the legislature proposed a constitutional amendment, which voters overwhelmingly endorsed, to prohibit a personal income tax in Texas without voter approval.

Constitutional Convention

The constitution also provides for revision by constitutional convention, which the legislature can call with the approval of the voters. Delegates to such a convention have to be elected and their terms subject to voter approval. Proposed changes adopted by a constitutional convention must also be approved by the voters. In 1919, voters overwhelmingly rejected a proposal for a constitutional convention.[30] There were subsequent efforts, including an attempt by Governor John Connally in 1967, to initiate reforms using a constitutional convention, but they also were defeated.[31] Connally's efforts, however, did result in adoption of a "cleanup" amendment in 1969 that removed many obsolete provisions from the constitution, and it laid the groundwork for a constitutional convention in 1974. The 1974 convention, the only one ever held under the present 1876 charter, ended in failure. Its delegates were the 181 members of the legislature.

The Constitutional Reform Efforts of 1971 to 1975

The **constitutional convention of 1974** had its beginning in 1971, when state Representative Nelson Wolff of San Antonio and several other first-term legislators won the leadership's backing for a full-scale revision effort. In 1972, voters approved the necessary constitutional amendment that specified that the convention would comprise house members and senators elected the same year.

In 1973, the legislature created a thirty-seven-member Constitutional Revision Commission to hold public hearings around the state and make recommendations to the convention. Members of the commission, chaired by former Texas Supreme Court Chief Justice Robert W. Calvert, were appointed by Governor Dolph Briscoe and other top state officials.

The constitutional convention, or "con-con," as it came to be called by legislators and members of the media, convened on January 8, 1974. House Speaker Price Daniel, Jr., was elected president, and Lieutenant Governor Bill Hobby, in an address to delegates, offered a prophetic warning: "The special interests of today will be replaced by new and different special interests tomorrow, and any attempt to draft a constitution to serve such interests would be futile and also dishonorable."[32]

Hobby's plea was ignored. Special interests dominated the convention, which finally adjourned in bitter failure on July 30, failing by three votes to get the two-thirds vote necessary to send a new constitution to Texas voters for ratification.

The crucial fight was over a business-backed attempt to lock the state's **right-to-work law** into the constitution. The right-to-work law prohibits union membership as a condition of employment, so the effort was bitterly fought by organized labor. Then as now, business was politically stronger than labor in Texas, but the two-thirds vote necessary to put a new constitution on the ballot was too high an obstacle.

After three years of preparation and deliberations, the proposed constitution of 1974 failed by three votes in the final hectic session of the constitutional convention, when the gallery was filled with interested onlookers, including many representatives of labor.

The gallery in the House of Representatives chamber, which served as the convention hall, was packed with labor representatives and other spectators when the final vote was taken, about one-half hour before the convention's midnight adjournment deadline. Daniel held the electronic voting board open for twenty-eight minutes, hoping three delegates could be persuaded to switch their votes, but time ran out. Tension and emotions were running so high that, at one point, state Representative Jim Mattox of Dallas, who later would become attorney general, challenged Daniel's delay in announcing the vote and publicly called the convention president a "liar."[33]

Although the right-to-work dispute took the brunt of the blame for the convention's failure, there also were other factors working against the revision effort. One was Governor Briscoe's refusal to exercise any significant leadership on behalf of a new state charter. Except for opposing proposals that he thought would further weaken the authority of the governor, he provided little input to the convention and did not attempt to twist delegates' arms to get enough votes to send the document to the electorate. Louisiana voters approved a new state constitution in 1974, and Governor Edwin Edwards' strong support had been considered instrumental. Gubernatorial leadership in other states also appears to have been critical to successful constitutional conventions.

Another major obstacle was the convention's makeup. The 181 members of the legislature constituted the constitutional convention. Soon after the convention began its work, many of them were facing reelection campaigns in the party primaries that diverted their attention from the business of the convention.

Additionally, a minority of legislators—dubbed "cockroaches" by President Daniel—did not want a new constitution and attempted to delay or obstruct the convention's work at every opportunity. Most legislators, even those who wanted a new constitution, reacted to their own political fears and ambitions. They were very susceptible to the influence of special interests, far more susceptible than most private-citizen delegates likely would have been. And special interests were legion at the convention. In addition to various business and professional groups and organized labor, many county officeholders whose jobs—protected by the Constitution of 1876—were suddenly in jeopardy put pressure on the delegates.

Some county judges lobbied against a proposal to streamline the judiciary because they feared it would relieve them of judicial duties. Under the present constitution, county judges are primarily administrative officers and do not have to be lawyers, but they do have limited judicial responsibilities. So persistent was their lobbying that Daniel referred to some of them as a "wrecking crew."[34] Representative DeWitt Hale of Corpus Christi, chair of the Committee on the Judiciary, was "disgusted because a handful of judges could be so disruptive to the convention."[35]

Influential regents, lobbyists, and alumni of the University of Texas and Texas A&M University systems guarded the Permanent University Fund, their rich constitutional endowment. Further, highway lobbyists, backed by thousands of contractors and businesspeople from throughout the state, fought any attempt to raid the Highway Trust Fund, the constitutional provision that dedicates three-fourths of the revenue from the state gasoline tax to highway projects.

Delegates tried to walk a tightrope over the emotionally charged issue of gambling. They yielded to the wishes of charitable and fraternal organizations and tentatively approved a provision to allow bingo and raffles to be conducted for charity, receiving some public ridicule for giving constitutional status to a game of chance.

But delegates voted to retain the general constitutional prohibition against lotteries. In a letter to Robert W. Calvert, the chair of the Constitutional Revision Commission, Baylor University President Abner McCall had warned of considerable public opposition to any new constitution that legalized gambling: "The commission may adopt proposals to make the machinery of Texas government more efficient, but many of us will not trade a little more efficiency for a greater danger of corruption of government by state sponsored gambling."[36] The ban on lotteries was to remain in the constitution for another seventeen years until Governor Ann Richards successfully promoted the creation of a state lottery as a new revenue source for state government in 1991 (see Chapter 13).

During its next regular session in 1975, the legislature, with the strong support of House Speaker Bill Clayton and Lieutenant Governor Bill Hobby, resurrected the constitutional revision effort. Lawmakers voted to present to Texans the basic document that the convention had barely rejected the previous summer in the form of eight separate constitutional amendments. The first three articles dealing with the separation of powers and the legislative and executive branches were combined into one ballot proposition. Each of the remaining seven propositions was a separate article, each to be independently approved or rejected by the voters. The most controversial issues that the 1974 convention had debated, such as right-to-work, were excluded. The streamlined amendments would have considerably shortened the constitution and provided some major changes, including annual legislative sessions, a unified judicial system, and more flexibility in county government. It would have been a much more flexible, modern constitution than the 1876 document and had cost several million tax dollars and countless hours to produce. But voters rejected all eight propositions on November 4, 1975, some by margins of more than 2 to 1.

The legislature's stock fraud scandal of 1971 (see Chapter 8) and the Watergate scandal that forced the resignation of President Richard Nixon in 1974 had raised Texans' distrust of government, and the proposed new constitution had been drafted by state officials, not by private citizens.

Nelson Wolff, who years later would be elected mayor of San Antonio and then county judge of Bexar County, also had noted an earlier, general lack of citizen interest in the work of the constitutional convention. In his book, *Challenge of Change,* he wrote: "The constitutional revision effort in Texas had attempted to use every means known to get citizen participation in the process. A toll-free telephone had been set up for the convention. Committees of the convention met at night and on weekends to provide working people an opportunity to testify. We provided to the best of our ability optimum conditions for testimony. Yet many people avoided participation in the revision process."[37]

Most people are not attentive to the details and nuances of constitutional revisions, and it is a difficult task translating these complexities into arguments that make sense to the average voter.[38] The voter distrust and apathy played right into the hands of numerous special interests, who did not want to give up the protections that the old constitution afforded them.

Efforts to enact these proposals were further thwarted by Governor Dolph Briscoe. While he had never taken an active role in the revision effort, three weeks before the 1975 election, he openly opposed the eight propositions and suggested that the existing constitution had served the state well and would continue to be adequate for the future.[39]

Further Piecemeal Reforms

So it was back to piecemeal constitutional changes. Between 1975 and 2003, 212 amendments were approved by Texas voters, and 37 were rejected. Besides the lottery, amendments winning approval included the 1993 amendment to ban a personal income tax without voter approval and a series of propositions authorizing $3 billion in tax-backed bonds for a huge prison expansion program (see Chapter 13). In 1985, voters approved an amendment to give the governor and legislative leaders authority to deal with budgetary emergencies between legislative sessions. In 1995, they approved an amendment to abolish the state treasurer's office and transfer its duties to the comptroller. And in 1997, Texas voters by a wide margin approved a constitutional amendment to increase homeowners' $5,000 exemptions from school property taxes to $15,000. The measure, part of a property tax relief initiative promoted by then-Governor George W. Bush, saved the average homeowner about $140 a year in local school taxes (see Chapter 13). In 1999, voters approved an amendment—prompted by Governor Bush's presidential campaign—to make it clear that a lieutenant governor who was promoted to fill out an elected governor's unexpired term would have to give up the lieutenant governor's job to take the higher office. During its 1999 session, the Legislature rejected a proposal—the first of its kind in more than twenty years—to rewrite the constitution. But legislators approved an amendment, which voters also approved, to remove more obsolete language from the document. One of the more controversial amendments in recent years, Proposition 12, ratified new limits on some monetary damages in medical malpractice lawsuits. It was narrowly approved by voters in 2003 (see "High Stakes over Lawsuits").

Constitutional Provisions, Interest Groups, and Elites

Only a small percentage of registered voters—often less than 10 percent—participate in elections when constitutional amendments are the only issues on the ballot (Table 2–3). When amendments are submitted to the voters along with gubernatorial or presidential elections, the turnout is much higher. But in many instances, a relative handful of Texans ultimately decide on fundamental changes in government, which enhances their influence over the constitutional revision process.

Interest groups, which historically have been strong in Texas, work diligently to protect their concerns and objectives. They develop strategies to get provisions into the constitution that would benefit them or to keep provisions out that they fear

TABLE 2–3   Turnout for Constitutional Amendments 1970–2003

Type of Election	Number of Elections	Percent of Registered Voters	Percent of Voting Age Population
Special*	15	12.7	8.5
General (Gubernatorial)	9	43.7	28.4
General (Presidential)	8	66.9	45.2

*Only constitutional amendments on the ballot.

Source: Texas Secretary of State, Elections Division.

HIGH STAKES OVER LAWSUITS

The constitutional amendment concerning civil lawsuits against doctors and health care providers, and other actions, authorizing the legislature to determine limitations on non-economic damages.

Proposition 12, Special Constitutional Amendments Election, September 2003

Supporters said Proposition 12 was a cure for high medical malpractice insurance premiums that were forcing some doctors, particularly in rural areas, to close their practices. Opponents argued that medical malpractice coverage was high because state regulators weren't effectively clamping down on bad doctors, and they warned that Proposition 12 was instead an effort by business and insurance interests to further restrict access to the courts for injured or aggrieved consumers. In any event, Texas voters narrowly approved the constitutional amendment in 2003 after a multimillion-dollar advertising war. Doctors, hospitals, nursing homes and other business interests primarily financed the campaign promoting the amendment. Plaintiffs' lawyers—who make their living suing doctors, hospitals and businesses on behalf of injured consumers—picked up most of the tab for the media campaign against it, although numerous consumer advocacy groups also opposed the proposal.

The amendment did two things. First, it ratified a 2003 law enacted by the Legislature to put new limits on non-economic damages—money awarded for such things as pain, suffering and disfigurement—in medical malpractice suits. Such damages, which are in addition to medical costs and other actual economic losses that could be awarded a patient who suffered from a botched medical procedure, were capped at $750,000 for each case. Of that amount, only $250,000 can be recovered from physicians or other medical personnel. The remainder would come from hospitals, nursing homes or other health care facilities that may be involved. Additionally—and potentially more far-reaching—Proposition 12 included language clearing the way for future sessions of the Legislature to enact new limits on damages in other civil lawsuits.

Legislative sponsors of Proposition 12 also were accused of trying to sneak the proposal past the voters by scheduling the constitutional amendments election for September 13, rather than November 4, the general election date on which constitutional amendments were traditionally set for voter review. Supporters of the amendment said it was important to win voter approval earlier than normal to remove any legal uncertainty over the new malpractice limits. But opponents argued that the early election, with no other issues to attract voters, was designed to avoid the higher voter turnout that would be generated by a hotly contested mayoral race in Houston on November 4. Voters in Houston, the state's largest city, usually are a major factor in determining statewide elections, and a high voter turnout there could prove to be pivotal in determining the fate of Proposition 12. According to this argument, the higher the voter turnout in Houston, the higher the likelihood that the amendment would be defeated, because Democrats and plaintiffs' lawyers still had some clout over elections in that city. Opponents of Proposition 12, as it turned out, had reason to fear the early election date. The proposal narrowly passed statewide, but 58 percent of Houston voters—turning out in far fewer numbers than would vote two months later in the mayor's race—cast ballots against it. "It (the statewide result) would have been a real horse race if it had been held in conjunction with the Houston mayor's race," said University of Houston political scientist Richard Murray.

Source: Houston Chronicle, September 16, 2003, p. 13A.

GOVERNMENT BY AMENDMENT

The nonpartisan League of Women Voters of Texas has been a long-suffering advocate of a total rewrite of the Texas Constitution. Nevertheless, before each constitutional amendments election, it normally announces which propositions it endorses for the sake of good government and which it opposes. But league leaders lost their patience in 1987 with the placement of a record 25 amendments on the same ballot. They announced they would neither support nor oppose any amendment that year. Instead, they urged voters to examine the propositions carefully and to complain to their legislators about the length of the ballot. "Enough is enough. Let us work together to halt this ridiculous system of running the government by means of the constitution," the league said.

But without a new constitution, the only way state government can prepare for the challenges of the twenty-first century under a highly restrictive constitution written in the nineteenth is to continue this pattern of "amendomania."

Source: The term "amendomania" came from "California's Constitutional Amendomania," *Stanford Law Review,* 1 (1949), 279–288.

ADDING A LITTLE FLAVOR TO THE CONSTITUTION

Many people may enjoy a cup of coffee with a chocolate dessert. But do such treats belong in the state constitution? Most Texas voters said they did. One of nineteen propositions approved on the 2001 ballot exempted raw coffee beans and cocoa imported through the Port of Houston from property taxes. The proposal was promoted by business people seeking to increase imports of those commodities through Houston. More imports, they hoped, would increase the need for more warehouses, create more jobs, and boost business profits. The tax exemption met a condition necessary for the New York Board of Trade to award "exchange port" status to the Port of Houston, a key requirement for import growth.

There was no organized opposition to the amendment, which also was endorsed by city and county officials in Houston, who believed it offered a potential boost to the area's overall economy. But the proposal was approved by a relatively close margin—52 percent—perhaps because many non-Houstonians viewed it as a special-interest favor for the state's largest city and didn't like the way it tasted.

---

would hurt them (see "Government by Amendment"). Because most amendments represent nonpartisan issues, a well-financed public relations campaign is likely to produce public support for an amendment.[40]

Many recent constitutional changes have reflected a pro-industry and economic development push that contrasts sharply with the antibusiness sentiment of the original constitutional framers (see "Adding a Little Flavor to the Constitution"). Recent amendments also have helped build up a public-bonded indebtedness that the nineteenth-century writers would have been unable to comprehend. Texas was rural then. It is now the country's second most populous state, is largely urban, and is working to diversify and expand its economy as well as provide the infrastructure required to support the large increases in population. Business has repeatedly turned to state government for tax breaks and other economic incentives and has found receptive ears in the legislature and the governor's office.

Nine of the record twenty-five amendments on the November 1987 ballot were actively promoted as an economic development package by the Build Texas Committee, a bipartisan group of business and civic leaders. Voters approved most of the amendments, including bonds for new water projects and prisons.

Industry, with the unusual support of organized labor and environmental groups, won a major tax break through a constitutional amendment approved by Texas voters in November 1993. It requires local governments to grant property-tax exemptions for expensive pollution-control equipment that businesses are required by state or federal law to install in their plants and other facilities. The business community supported the amendment because it represented untold millions in potential tax savings. Labor supported it because money not spent on taxes could mean more money spent on jobs. And environmentalists viewed it as an antipollution measure. Some local officials were fearful of the potential loss of huge amounts of revenue to counties, school districts, and other local governments, but they were clearly overpowered. Sometimes, however, relief can turn into heartburn, as it did in 2001 when lawmakers and Texas voters accidentally put a new tax law into the constitution when they thought they were repealing one (see "Oops! How Did That Happen?").

It has been argued that the Texas Constitution serves the interests of a small number of elites—those individuals who control businesses and other dominant institutions in the state. This argument suggests that the severe constraints built into the constitution limit the policy options of state government and have historically thwarted the efforts of public interest groups to restructure or improve the tax system, education, social services, health care, and other policies that would benefit low- and middle-income Texans. Power is so fragmented that these groups have had to turn to the courts to force change. This same argument, incidentally, has often been made about the U.S. Constitution.

If this interpretation is accurate, it is ironic that those who framed the Texas constitution of 1876 directed much of their wrath against railroads, banks, and other institutions that are today considered elitist. The tumultuous last quarter of the nineteenth century witnessed high levels of class and economic conflict with the emergence of the Greenback and the Populist political parties, which articulated the interests of the lower income groups. But monied business interests eventually were able to use the state constitution and subsequent legislation to reestablish their dominance over Texas government. Although the elite structure of the state has changed since 1876, some scholars argue that there has been a gradual transfer of power and control to new elites, who continue to exercise enormous influence over public policy.

Change through Court Interpretation

Some evidence indicates that Texas courts are now prepared to play a more expansive role in interpreting the constitution and, in turn, effect major changes in state policy. The best-known example is the Edgewood school-finance case, in which the courts invalidated the system of funding public education and ordered the legislature to provide more equity in tax resources among the state's 1,000-plus school districts. Wide disparities in spending on students between rich and poor districts—the result of wide disparities in local property values—violated the state constitution's requirement for an "efficient" system of public schools, the Texas Supreme Court ruled.

Prospects for Future Change

Experts can point out the many flaws of the Texas Constitution, but attempts at whole-sale revision have not been successful. Numerous piecemeal changes have been made, but they have not addressed the fundamental criticisms of the charter. What is to be made of all this?

First, Texas has a long history of suspicion of government, and this tradition continues. Most people fear governmental abuses and excesses more than they worry about government's inability to respond quickly and efficiently to the needs of its citizens. In the vernacular of the layperson, "If it ain't broke, don't fix it." And it is not clear that the layperson regards the constitution to be "broke."

Second, many groups and interests benefit from the existing constitution, and they have demonstrated a collective resolve to minimize change.

Finally, most Texans give little thought to changing the constitution because they are ill prepared to deal with the complexities of the document. Enormous problems must be overcome if citizens are to be educated and motivated to press for constitutional revision.

OOPS! HOW DID THAT HAPPEN?

People who have any doubts that an election ballot loaded with constitutional amendments is an accident waiting to happen need only consider Proposition 14, one of the nineteen amendments on the November 2001 ballot, all of which were approved by voters. The proposal was promoted as a means of allowing local governments, except for school districts, to exempt registered, non–income-producing travel trailers from local property taxes. Supporters said the tax break was needed to encourage the so-called "winter Texans" to continue making their seaonal homes in the Rio Grande Valley. These people, who travel south to escape the cold winters up north, have become an important part of the South Texas economy and represent an important financial boost to some of Texas's poorest counties. Many of the winter visitors are senior citizens who live in recreational vehicles.

Everybody was sure the amendment did what it was intended to do. No one—legislative sponsors, legislative analysts, local officials, the media—noticed a problem, until after the amendment was approved and then became part of the constitution. Only then did someone discover that the amendment had inadvertently imposed a new tax on travel trailers rather than removed one. The new provision labeled trailers as taxable, while the constitution previously said nothing about them. And because the exemption didn't apply to school districts, legal experts believed that travel trailers had been made subject to school taxes.

The goof prompted Governor Rick Perry and legislative sponsors to start scrambling. Perry asked school districts to refrain from taxing travel trailers before the legislature had a chance to correct the mistake during the 2003 session. But other officials questioned whether the governor had the legal authority to make such a request.

"I guess it moved through the process and went and went and went," the amendment's sponsor, state Representative Kino Flores of Mission, said of the blunder.

Source: Associated Press, March 8, 2002.

SUMMARY AND CONCLUSIONS

1. In addition to defining the formal institutional structure of governments, constitutions reflect the primary values and political objectives of a state. A constitution defines the relationships between those who govern and the general population and ultimately structures political power. A constitution limits the power and authority of government and provides basic protection for the citizen from excesses and abuses of those who hold power.

2. A constitution should spell out broad powers and general principles and leave it to the legislature and state agencies to fill in the details with statutory laws and regulations.

3. Texas, like most other states, has functioned under a series of constitutions. Each is appropriately understood from the perspective of the period in which it was adopted.

4. Texas currently operates under a constitution that was adopted following the Civil War and the Radical Reconstruction era. Events of that period left an enduring legacy of suspicion of government, limited government, and fragmented governmental institutions. The 1876 Constitution was predicated on the theory that governmental excesses could be minimized by carefully defining what governments could or could not do.

5. The framers failed to anticipate that the limitations they imposed on governmental institutions would ultimately allow major economic interests within the state to dominate the policymaking process, often to the detriment of the lower socioeconomic groups.

6. What the delegates to the Constitutional Convention of 1875 regarded as the strengths of the constitution—fragmented authority, detailed limitations on the power of governmental institutions, and decentralization—have served to limit the ability of state and local governments to adapt effectively to economic and demographic changes. The perceived solutions to many of the problems of 1875 have compounded the problems of state and local governments in the 2000s.

7. Efforts to overhaul the Texas Constitution have failed. Consequently, the state has been forced to amend the document continually on a piecemeal basis. This process has produced some success in modernizing the charter, but many structural problems of state government require major institutional changes that cannot be resolved through this amendment process.

8. In many ways, the Texas Constitution reflects the values of the state's conservative political culture, which continues to be suspicious of far-reaching constitutional changes. Moreover, constitutions and the debates that surround them are complex, and most people pay little attention to these issues. Consequently, it is much easier to mobilize public opinion against rather than for wholesale change.

9. Over the years, numerous groups have attempted to protect their interests through constitutional amendments. But the same groups usually oppose any proposed changes that threaten their influence, power, or benefits. Consequently, the interests of small segments of the state's population often prevail over the interests of the majority.

KEY TERMS

Edmund J. Davis	Bicameral	Initiative
Radical Reconstructionists	Confederacy	Referendum
Constitution	Grange	Constitutional convention
Statutory law	Popular sovereignty	of 1974
Unicameral	Compact theory	Right-to-work law
Unitary system	Limited government	
Federalism	Separation of powers	

FURTHER READING

Articles

Bruff, Harold H., "Separation of Powers under the Texas Constitution," *Texas Law Review* 68 (June 1990), 1337–67.

Harrington, James C., "Free Speech, Press, and Assembly Liberties under the Texas Bill of Rights," *Texas Law Review* 68 (June 1990), 1435–67.

Hirczy, Wolfgan, "Texas Equal Rights Amendment: Twenty Years and a Few Surprises Later," *Texas Journal of Political Studies* 16 (Fall 1993), 22–46.

Keyser, David R., "State Constitutions and Theories of Judicial Review: Some Variations on a Theme, *Texas Law Review* 63 (March–April 1985), 1051–80.

Lutz, Donald S., "The Purposes of American State Constitutions," *Publius* 12 (Winter 1982), 27–44.

Maltz, Earl M., "The Dark Side of State Court Activism," *Texas Law Review* 63 (March–April 1985), 995–1023.

Mauer, John Walker, "State Constitutions in a Time of Crisis: The Case of the Texas Constitution of 1876," *Texas Law Review* 68 (June 1990), 1615–47.

Parker, Allan E., "Public Free Schools: A Constitutional Right to Educational Choice in Texas," *Southwestern Law Journal* 45 (Fall 1991), 825–976.

Watts, Mikal, and Brad Rockwell, "The Original Intent of the Educational Article of the Texas Constitution," *St. Mary's Law Journal* 21 (1990), 771–821.

Books

Braden, George D., et al., *The Constitution of the State of Texas: An Annotated and Comparative Analysis.* 2 vols. Austin: Texas Advisory Commission on Intergovernmental Relations, 1977.

Braden, George D., *Citizens' Guide to the Texas Constitution.* Austin: Texas Advisory Commission on Intergovernmental Relations and the Institute for Urban Studies, University of Houston, 1972.

Cnudde, Charles F., and Robert E. Crew, Jr., *Constitutional Democracy in Texas.* St. Paul, MN: West Publishing Company, 1989.

Lutz, Donald S., "The Texas Constitution," in *Perspective on American and Texas Politics: A Collection of Essays,* eds. Donald S. Lutz and Kent L. Tedin. Dubuque, IA: Kendall/Hunt, 1987.

May, Janice C., *The Texas Constitution Revision Experience in the 70s.* Austin: Sterling Swift, 1975.

———, *The Texas State Constitution: A Reference Guide.* Westport, Conn.: Greenwood Press, 1996.

McKay, Seth Shepard, *Debates in the Texas Constitutional Convention of 1875.* Austin: University of Texas Press, 1930.

McKay, Seth Shepard, *Seven Decades of the Texas Constitution of 1876.* Lubbock: Texas Tech College, 1943.

Tarr, G. Alan, *Understanding State Constitutions.* Princeton, NJ: Princeton University Press, 1998.

Wolff, Nelson, *Challenge of Change.* San Antonio: The Naylor Co., 1975.

Websites

Texas Legislative Council   http://www.capitol.state.tx.us/txconst/toc.html   The entire text of the Texas Constitution can be downloaded from this site. It also provides an index to the constitution and allows the text of the constitution to be searched using key words.

Texas Legislature On-Line   http://www.capitol.state.tx.us   Access to legislative resolutions providing for constitutional amendments can be found here. Legislative intent and legislative histories of proposed constitutional amendments are also available.

Secretary of State   http://www.sos.state.tx.us   This office is responsible for compiling state election returns, including constitutional amendments. County-level returns for constitutional amendments since 1993 can be accessed from this site.

League of Women Voters   http://www.lwvtexas.org   The Texas League of Women Voters is a nonpartisan organization committed to increasing political participation, improving state and local government, and increasing public understanding of major policy issues. When constitutional amendments are submitted to voters, the league usually publishes information about the purpose and effects of the amendments.

Indiana University Law   http://www.iulaw.indy.indiana.edu/library/State_Constitutions.htm   If you are interested in the constitutions of other states, this is one of several sites that provide you access to these documents.

ENDNOTES

1. Janice May, "Constitutional Revision in Texas," in *Texas: Readings in Politics, Government and Public Policy,* eds. Richard H. Kramer and Philip W. Barnes (San Francisco: Chandler Publishing Company, 1971), p. 317.
2. G. Allan Tarr, *Understanding State Constitutions* (Princeton, NJ: Princeton University Press, 1998), p. 3.
3. Daniel Elazar, "The Principles and Traditions Underlying American State Constitutions," *Publius* 12 (Winter 1982), p. 23.
4. Tarr, pp. 4–5.
5. Donald S. Lutz, "The Purposes of American State Constitutions," *Publius* 12 (Winter 1982), 31–36.
6. David Saffell, *State Politics* (Reading, MA: Addison-Wesley Publishing Company, 1984), pp. 23–24.
7. Elazar, pp. 20–21.
8. T. R. Fehrenbach, *Lone Star: A History of Texas and Texans* (New York: The Macmillan Company, 1968), pp. 152–73.
9. Richard Gambitta, Robert A. Milne, and Carol R. Davis, "The Politics of Unequal Educational Opportunity," in *The Politics of San Antonio*, eds. David R. Johnson, John A. Booth, and Richard J. Harris (Lincoln: University of Nebraska Press, 1983), p. 135.
10. Joe B. Frantz, *Texas: A Bicentennial History* (New York: W. W. Norton & Company, Inc., 1976), p. 73.
11. Ibid., p. 76.
12. Fehrenbach, *Lone Star,* p. 265.
13. Frantz, *Texas,* p. 92.
14. Fehrenbach, *Lone Star,* p. 396.
15. Ibid., pp. 398–99.
16. Ibid., p. 401.
17. Ibid, p. 429.
18. J. E. Ericson, "The Delegates to the Convention of 1875: A Reappraisal," *Southwestern Historical Quarterly* 67 (July 1963), p. 22.
19. Ibid., p. 23.
20. Ibid., p. 23.
21. Ibid., pp. 25–26.
22. Fehrenbach, *Lone Star,* pp. 374, 431, 434.
23. Ericson, "The Delegates to the Convention of 1875: A Reappraisal," pp. 24–25.
24. Fehrenbach, *Lone Star,* p. 435.
25. Texas Constitution, Art. 1, Sec. 2 and 3.
26. Janice May, "Constitutional Revision in Texas," in *The Texas Constitution: Problems and Prospects for Revision* (Arlington: Texas Urban Development Commission, 1971), p. 82.
27. Ibid., p. 82.
28. David Berman, *State and Local Politics,* 6th ed. (Dubuque, IA: Wm. C. Brown Publishers, 1991), p. 61.
29. May, p. 76.
30. John E. Bebout, "The Problem of the Texas Constitution," in *The Texas Constitution: Problems and Prospect for Revision,* p. 9.
31. Ibid., p. 11.
32. *Houston Chronicle,* Jan. 8, 1974.
33. Houston Chronicle, July 31, 1974.
34. Nelson Wolff, *Challenge of Change* (San Antonio: The Naylor Co., 1975), p. 170.
35. *Houston Chronicle,* July 31, 1974.
36. *Houston Chronicle,* Sept. 20, 1973.
37. Wolff, *Challenge of Change,* pp. 45–46.
38. Bebout, "The Problem of the Texas Constitution," pp. 45–46.
39. *Houston Chronicle,* Oct. 15, 1975.
40. Lewis A. Froman, Jr., "Some Effects of Interest Group Strength in State Politics," *American Political Science Review* 60 (December 1966), pp. 952–63.

CHAPTER 3

Intergovernmental Relationships

> The question of the relation of the States to the Federal Government is the cardinal question of our constitutional system. It cannot be settled by one generation, because it is a question of growth, and every new successive stage of our political and economic development gives it a new aspect, makes it a new question.
>
> *Woodrow Wilson*[1]

Texans, like most American citizens, are subject to the authority of an array of governments. If you live in a large metropolitan area in Texas, you may be under the jurisdiction of as many as ten or more different governments or taxing authorities. A person living within the corporate limits of San Antonio is subject to the laws, regulations, and/or taxes of the federal government, the state of Texas, Bexar County, the city of San Antonio, the Alamo Community College District, one of sixteen independent school districts, the Edwards Aquifer Authority, the San Antonio River Authority, the Bexar County Hospital District, and a public transportation authority.

There are more than 87,000 governmental units in the United States, with approximately 500,000 persons serving on their governing bodies. According to a 2002 census of governments (Table 3–1), Texas had 4,784 individual governments, including 254 counties, 1,196 municipalities, and 3,334 school districts and other special districts. What's more, the total number of governments in Texas increased by more than 1,000 between 1972 and 2002.

The jurisdictional structure of governments in this country is complex and confusing, and people are often frustrated when they try to identify the government that has the authority or responsibility to address one of their specific needs or concerns. Governments share many responsibilities, and it is quite possible for an individual to get caught between agencies of different governments.

From our very beginnings, Americans have been leery of highly centralized government. So these diverse and complex jurisdictional arrangements were created

TABLE 3–1   Governments in the U.S. and Texas, 2002

	U.S.	Texas
U.S. Government	1	—
State Government	50	1
Counties	3,034	254
Municipalities	19,429	1,196
Townships and Towns	16,504	—
School Districts	13,506	1,089
Special Districts	35,052	2,245
TOTAL	87,576	4,785

Source: U.S. Department of Commerce, Bureau of the Census, *2002 Census of Governments,* Vol. 1, Government Organizations, Table 3.

to limit government, especially the federal government. Moreover, the enormous size of the country and the great distances between settlements during the nation's formative period made it extremely difficult for a centralized government at either the national or state level to serve and control political subdivisions. This contributed to the proliferation of smaller governmental units. Regional differences in religion, economics, and political cultures also encouraged decentralization and the development of local governments.

STRUCTURING REGIONAL AND NATIONAL INTERESTS

Governments around the world are struggling to find ways to coordinate local and regional interests with national interests. The former Soviet bloc, for example, has struggled with institutional arrangements to integrate diverse racial, cultural, and ethnic groups within a single political system. Canada, which already has a stable political system, continues to seek political and institutional solutions to the movement for French separatism. In the effort to rebuild Iraq, there is extensive debate over the geographical distribution of power and authority among the Sunnis, Shiites, Arabs, and Kurds. Many of the same issues confronted the constitutional framers during the United States' formative period, and their solution was to structure federal–state relationships on the federal principle.

There are three fundamental systems—unitary, confederal, and federal—used in designing the relationship of a central government to its constituent parts.

In some countries, democratic as well as authoritarian, ultimate power is vested in a national or central government. Under such a **unitary system,** local or regional governments are created by the national government, have only the power and authority granted to them by the national government, and serve "only to implement policies established by the national government."[2]

A **confederation** is based on the principle that each component government is sovereign in its own right, and the powers of the national government are limited to those powers delegated to it by the member governments. The United States experimented with a confederal system prior to the adoption of the present Constitution in 1789, and the southern states used the confederal principle during the Civil War. There are inherent weaknesses in such a system, including the ability of member governments to nullify the acts of the national government and withdraw from the relationship. Citizenship and loyalty to the component parts precedes citizenship in and loyalty to the central power.

Delegates to the U.S. Constitutional Convention of 1787 rejected the confederal principle in favor of **federalism,** which balances the power and sovereignty of the state governments with that of the national government. Both the states and the national government derive their authority directly from the people, and the states have considerable latitude and autonomy within their areas of defined power and responsibility. In many respects, federalism is a middle ground between a confederal system and a unitary system of government.

The unitary principle, however, is the basis for the relationship between state and local governments under the Texas Constitution and state laws (see Chapter 12). Counties, cities, and special districts have only those powers granted to them by the state. There is no such thing as the sovereignty of local government in Texas. Local governments are primarily administrative subdivisions of the state. The prevailing constitutional theory regarding local governments in the United States, which has been incorporated into Texas law, was articulated in the Dillon rule, which held that if a state could create local governments, it could also destroy or eliminate them.[3] Political and practical considerations, however, usually preclude the elimination of local governments.

DEFINING FEDERALISM

While the U.S. Constitution outlines federalism in broad terms, it does not clearly specify the governmental relationships that should be established. For more than 200 years, scholars, politicians, judges, and bureaucrats not only have been debating the complexities of the federal system, they also have been trying to figure out how to define federalism.[4] One scholar has identified 267 concepts relating to the term.[5] The problem is compounded by the fact that the relationships among federal, state, and local governments have changed over the past two centuries.

Federal-State Relationships

We tend to think of federalism as a division of power between the states and the national government, and we look to the U.S. Constitution to specify the powers and responsibilities of each. However, the Constitution is vague on these points, and "all efforts to define the distribution of authority among governments have been unsuccessful."[6] The structure and operation of our federal system of government confuse many individuals. It is a system of many shared functions and responsibilities that often make it difficult to identify a single person or institution as having the ultimate responsibility for addressing a specific issue or problem.

Ambiguous constitutional provisions have helped produce jurisdictional conflicts throughout the nation's history. We even fought a war among ourselves to determine what were the powers and authority of the states and national government. While the Civil War resolved the issue that a state could not withdraw from the federal union, a large number of other questions continue to be debated. These

GET OFF OUR LAND, YOU VARMINTS!

During the contentious 2003 sessions of the Texas Legislature, one had to look for humor wherever it could be found. For a few days, the atmosphere at the Capitol in Austin was provided limited relief with news that a New Mexico legislator had filed a bill in that state's senate to recover some 603,485 acres—a three-mile strip along the Texas-New Mexico border—which had been wrongly assigned to Texas in 1859 as a result of a surveyor's error. For whatever reason, the issue periodically has been resurrected over the years by New Mexican officials.

No one in Texas expected the latest claim to go anywhere, and it didn't. But as the issue churned around in the corridors of the New Mexico Legislature and the newsrooms of state papers, an element of absurdity emerged. New Mexico papers began to pick up on the potential humor and demanded that Texans vacate the disputed area. An *Albuquerque Tribune* headline ordered: "Waltz off our land, you Texas varmints."

About the same time, Texas Land Commissioner Jerry Patterson challenged his New Mexican counterpart, Patrick H. Lyons, to a duel. The last we heard—the information is quite sketchy—the duel took place in early 2004 in Austin. The weapons of choice were vintage flintlocks. We don't know if shots were fired, but both claimed the honor of their respective states had been served.

_____

Source: Patrick H. Lyons, New Mexico State Land Office, press release, March 14, 2003; Ray Cooklis, "Border Dispute: Texas Strip Stake," *Cincinnati Enquirer,* March 14, 2003; Texas General Land Office, Press Release, January 7, 2004.

ambiguities and changes in political and economic conditions make the relationships among governments subject to further change in the future. Currently, there is a great deal of debate over **devolution,** or the return of power to the states, at all levels of government. But any action in response to this debate has been put on hold due, in large part, to the responses to the terrorist attacks on the Pentagon and the World Trade Center in 2001.

The enumerated, or **delegated powers,** of the national government are outlined primarily in Article 1, Section 8, of the U.S. Constitution. They include the powers to tax, to borrow and coin money, to declare war, and to regulate interstate and foreign commerce.

The first seventeen paragraphs of Section 8 are rather specific, apparently because the constitutional framers, who were apprehensive about potential abuses, intended to limit the powers of the national government. But they did not close the door to unforeseen events. In paragraph 18 of Section 8, they further provided that Congress shall have the power "to make all Laws which shall be necessary and proper for carrying into Execution the foregoing Powers."[7] This is the **implied powers** clause, which has been used to justify the subsequent expansion of the federal government's powers.

To further compound the jurisdictional question, Article 6 states that the U.S. Constitution and the laws made in pursuance "shall be the supreme Law of the Land."[8] This **supremacy clause** suggests that when a conflict develops between the powers of the states and the national government, the federal law prevails.

But the Constitution also provides that the states shall have certain powers. The Tenth Amendment, adopted in 1789 by Congress and ratified by the states in 1791, was intended to address the concerns of state governments. This **reserved powers** clause states, "The powers not delegated to the United States by the Constitution, nor prohibited by it to the States, are reserved to the States respectively or to the people."[9] Although the Constitution does not spell out the authority of the states and their subdivisions in detail, the states have assumed a formidable array of powers and responsibilities in domestic affairs. Most governmental actions affecting our daily lives are taken by state or local governments. The police, regulatory, and taxing powers of the state affect us daily. Also, more than 95 percent of all litigation in the country takes place in state or local courts, not in federal courts.

There are also certain constitutional guarantees to the states. Texas is assured a republican form of government, protection against invasion and domestic violence, and the power to maintain a militia. If a person is accused of a federal crime in Texas, the trial is to be held in Texas. Texas cannot be divided into another state without its permission and is assured two members of the U.S. Senate and membership in the U.S. House of Representatives based on its population in relation to the other states. After the 1990 census, Texas had thirty members of the U.S. House but gained two seats after the 2000 census. The state also has a role in ratifying amendments to the U.S. Constitution and controls many aspects of federal elections.[10]

Nevertheless, the U.S. Constitution's language lends itself to controversy and interpretation, and over the years, Congress, the states, and the courts have attempted to resolve conflicts over powers and jurisdiction. In many instances, the Supreme Court has played an instrumental role in redefining the relationship between the states and the federal government.

Reflecting its drafters' concerns about governmental excesses, the Constitution also limits the powers of both the states and the national government. These prohibitions, or **denied powers,** are interspersed throughout the document and are enumerated, in particular, in the first ten amendments—the Bill of Rights. The original intent of the Bill of Rights was to limit the powers of the national government. But since the Civil War, the federal courts have gradually incorporated the Bill of Rights into the Fourteenth Amendment, which was intended to restrict the powers of the state governments. This expansion of the Bill of Rights to the states has been described by some as the nationalization of the Bill of Rights.

Relationships among the States

The federal system is not limited to the relationship between the states and the national government (vertical federalism). It also includes the relationship of the states to each other (horizontal federalism). Many of these constitutional-legal obligations were included in the Articles of Confederation, which established the first system of national government in the United States. Conflict as well as cooperation among the states during that period provided the rationale for defining the obligations and responsibilities of the states to each other.

The Constitution states, "Full Faith and Credit shall be given in each State to the public Acts, Records, and judicial Proceedings of every other state."[11] To eliminate chaos and to stimulate cooperation, this **full faith and credit** clause assures that official governmental actions of one state are accepted by other states. A marriage of a heterosexual couple in Texas is recognized as legal in other states. So are business contracts. This also means that a person cannot flee to another state to avoid an adverse court judgment. But this obligation is not absolute, as demonstrated by the enactment of the federal Defense of Marriage Act (1996). This law, which denies federal recognition of marriages or civil unions between homosexuals, has allowed states to refuse to recognize civil unions of same-sex couples performed in other states. And, it has generated considerable political controversy.

As a person travels from one state to another, the Constitution entitles that person to the **privileges and immunities** of the states where he or she is going. A person can acquire property in another state, establish residency and eventually citizenship, and be assured of access to the legal system of that state. But there are certain exceptions that have been established by court interpretation. States, for example, can charge non-residents higher college tuition or higher fees for hunting and fishing licenses.

The Constitution also provides for the return of a person accused of a crime. If a person who has been charged with manslaughter or another offense in Texas attempts to avoid trial by fleeing to Oklahoma, he or she can be returned to Texas by a process called **extradition.** States routinely handle hundreds of these cases each year. Once the accused has been located, the state seeking the individual will request that the second state arrest and return him. The governor is responsible for granting extradition requests.

Until fairly recently, governors used an 1861 court decision to maintain that they had the discretion to refuse another state's extradition request.[12] This was the prevailing view for 125 years, until Puerto Rico challenged the discretionary powers of the governor in a 1987 case.[13] The Supreme Court held that the "duty to extradite is mandatory, and the federal courts are available to enforce that duty."[14]

The Constitution writers also anticipated the need for structuring more formal, long-term, cooperative relationships among the states. Article I, Section 10 allows the states, with the approval of Congress, to enter into **interstate compacts.** There are more than one hundred of these, some affecting only two states, while others include all fifty states. Texas now belongs to several interstate compacts, including the Interstate Oil and Gas Compact, the Interstate Mining Compact, and the Low Level Radioactive Waste Compact.

FEDERALISM WITHOUT WASHINGTON

In addition to interstate compacts, joint action among the states has included the enactment of uniform state laws, reciprocal or contingent legislation, and interstate administrative cooperation. These actions permit the states to work together in dealing with common issues or problems, such as water pollution, drug abuse, radioactive waste, economic development, and higher education. And, it is believed that the use of these resources has been expanded. To achieve what Morton Grodzins, an authority on American federalism, termed "federalism without Washington," the states have organized a number of cooperative organizations, including the Council of State Governments and a variety of groups of state elected officials.

Source: Morton Grodzins, *The American System,* ed. Daniel J. Elazar (Chicago: Rand McNally & Company, 1966), pp. 151–53.

While cooperation is desired, states often find themselves involved in disagreements that only lawsuits can resolve. Boundary disputes, control or use of water resources, and licensing fees that affect interstate shipping are among issues that are litigated in the federal judiciary, where the Supreme Court has original jurisdiction in all "controversies between two or more states."[15]

CHANGING PATTERNS IN FEDERAL RELATIONSHIPS

The constitutional-legal descriptions of federalism can leave one with the idea that the federal, state, and local levels of government are autonomous and function independently, a view often linked to dual federalism. Morton Grodzins, an authority on federalism, has argued that this perspective, which is now inaccurate, was analogous to a "layer-cake" theory of intergovernmental relations.

Grodzins suggested that intergovernmental relations can be more accurately symbolized by a "marble cake." Rather than possessing distinct and separate powers and responsibilities, governments have shared responsibilities. In describing federalism, Grodzins wrote:

> Whenever you slice through it [the marble cake] you reveal an inseparable mixture of differently colored ingredients. There is no neat horizontal stratification. Vertical and diagonal lines almost obliterate the horizontal ones, and in some places there are unexpected whirls and imperceptible merging of colors, so that it is difficult to tell where one ends and the other begins. So it is with federal, state, and local responsibilities in the chaotic marble cake of American Government.[16]

Public functions are not neatly divided among the different levels of government. In virtually every area of public policy, governments coordinate, collaborate, and cooperate to meet shared goals and objectives. This view reflects, in large measure, governmental relationships associated with **cooperative federalism,** which we will discuss later in this chapter.

A third metaphor, the "picket-fence" theory of federalism, builds on Grodzins's notions of shared powers and responsibilities but focuses on specific policy areas that cut across each level of government. This metaphor suggests that we look at a specific policy arena (for example, highways, education, or welfare), identify the primary participants at each level of government, and map out their patterns of interaction. While the concept is an oversimplification, it does suggest complex institutional and political relationships that cut across all levels of government.[17]

As might be expected, the complexity of federalism has generated much discussion about how to best describe and assess the relationships among governments. The problem, of course, is compounded by the fact that governmental relationships change over time with changes in the political parties, presidents, prevailing economic and social conditions, and general expectations and demands of governments.

Dual Federalism

In both theory and practice, federal relationships from 1790 to the 1930s usually are defined in terms of dual federalism. Both the national and state governments were continually engaged in legal and policy issues that attempted to define the lines of demarcation between their respective powers. There was a continued saga of "sorting out roles and specifying clear boundaries."[18] Conflicts usually were resolved through court cases and statutory laws, but the federal-state issues centering on slavery erupted into the Civil War. The dual federalism of this era was marked by adversarial, if not antagonistic, relationships at various levels of government.

One of the first instances when the U.S. Supreme Court addressed the issue of state-federal relationships was in 1819 in the case of *McCulloch v. Maryland*.[19] The state of Maryland had levied a tax on the Baltimore branch of the Bank of the United States. McCulloch, the bank's cashier, refused to pay the tax, thus precipitating a lawsuit. The case raised a fundamental issue regarding federalism. Did the national government have the power to create a bank that, in fact, would compete with state banks? The Supreme Court, then headed by Chief Justice John Marshall, an advocate of central power, ruled that the implied powers clause of the Constitution, linked to the delegated or enumerated powers, gave the federal government this authority.

A second issue was whether a state could tax the branch bank, an institution of the national government. The court again ruled in favor of the U.S. government. It held that the states do not have the power to tax the national government because, if this were to be permitted, the states could destroy national institutions, and federal laws would be subordinate to those of the states, thus undermining the supremacy clause of the Constitution.

Hundreds of federal-state issues have been litigated in the federal courts since McCulloch, and those cases making it to the Supreme Court demonstrate the role of the court to arbitrate disputes between state and federal authority.[20] Along with political and economic changes, these cases have been central to redefining federal-state relationships over the past 200 years, although the principles outlined in *McCulloch* remain intact.

Cooperative Federalism

The economic hardships produced by the Great Depression of the 1930s resulted in demands for a greater role of the federal government in domestic policy. States and cities simply were unable to provide many basic services or address the personal needs of large numbers of people who were unemployed. The states did not have the economic resources to deal with problems that extended beyond their borders, and many lacked the political or institutional will to implement new policies. Moreover, the increased economic interdependency of the states and the national scope of economic problems were compelling arguments for federal intervention. While there were precedents for greater federal-state cooperation prior to the 1930s, the New Deal expanded dramatically the role of the federal government in relation to the states and local governments.[21] V. O. Key, who wrote extensively on state government, summarized the extent of these changes:

> The federal government underwent a radical transformation after . . . 1932. It had been a remote authority with a limited range of activity. It operated the postal system, improved rivers and harbors, maintained armed forces on a scale fearsome only to banana republics, and performed other functions of which the average citizen was hardly aware. Within a brief time, it became an institution that affected intimately the lives and fortunes of most, if not all, citizens.[22]

Those supporting the development of cooperative federalism rejected the notion of dual federalism, where each level of government had virtual or exclusive authority in select areas of domestic policy. The commerce and the supremacy clauses of the Constitution were used to support an expanded role of the federal government. Many of the new programs engaged local, state, and federal policymakers in cooperative efforts—from program development to program implementation. Cooperative federalism assures that all three levels of government share the responsibility for domestic programs "by making the larger governments primarily responsible for raising revenues and setting standards, and the smaller ones primarily responsible for administering the programs."[23]

Over the past fifty years, the federal government has used various devices to shape and implement domestic programs, but the primary vehicle has been the provision of federal funds for public programs through **categorical grants-in-aid.** There are more than 400 of these grant programs, through which approximately 80 percent of federal aid to states and local governments is allocated. Money allocated under a specific program can be spent only for that purpose or category. Federal laws also include specific standards or requirements that recipients must meet, such as prohibitions against racial or sex discrimination or prohibitions against non-union pay scales.

There are two types of categorical grants. The first is the **project grant,** which requires a state or local government to apply for a grant to the appropriate federal agency and compete against other state or local governments for the funds. The money is awarded on the merits of an application. The second type of categorical grant is the **formula grant.** As the name implies, federal funds are allocated to states and local governments on the basis of a prescribed formula. These formulas vary from program to program, but might include income or poverty levels of a state's residents or its population figures. Congress determines the formulas for specific programs, and the federal dollars are then distributed on the basis of the statutory criteria. Many of these federal grants require **matching funds** from the governments that receive the money. The percentage of costs borne by the federal government varies from program to program, with the state or local governments picking up the balance. One reason for requiring such matches is to encourage state and local governments to have a strong commitment to the funded program and its policy objectives.

Centralized Federalism

The domestic programs initiated by President John F. Kennedy (1961–1963) and subsequently expanded by President Lyndon B. Johnson in the Great Society programs resulted in a dramatic expansion of the federal government's role to virtually every area of domestic policy. The number of identifiable grant programs increased in eight years from 132 to 379; federal funding for grant programs more than tripled within ten years, and the federal share of state and local budgets increased from 17 percent in 1960 to 23 percent in 1970. Many of these programs targeted specific populations for assistance and were intended to redistribute resources primarily to lower income groups. Moreover, there were several federal programs that virtually bypassed state governments and went directly to local governments, thus eroding the legal relationship of local governments to the states.[24] Some scholars suggest that this massive extension of federal initiatives in domestic policy transformed cooperative federalism into coercive federalism, a relationship in which state power was subordinated to federal power in a wide range of policy arenas.[25]

The Multiple Phases of New Federalism

Organized opposition to cooperative federalism can be detected from its origins in the 1930s. As federalism was transformed to the more centralized programs of the 1960s during the Democratic administrations of Kennedy and Johnson, conservatives, who are often Republicans, intensified their criticism of this shift of power to the national government, and the Republican party began to stake out what has become a rather consistent theme of decentralizaton and devolution.

Opposition to the increased role of the national government in domestic policy is based on many factors. Some argue that the Constitution never provided for the expanded powers claimed by the national government. The new programs, coupled with mandates and preemptions, placed a heavy financial burden on states and local governments. Moreover, these policies often encouraged governments to pursue federal dollars even when funded programs were not their most pressing issues. The expansion of the federal bureaucracy was deemed to be directly related to the new programs. Inefficiencies were built into the programs, and some were mismanaged. Finally, federal programs placed restrictions on how monies could be spent, and it was argued that no one size fit all of the local conditions or needs.

For the Republican party, there was a subtle political issue. As grant programs had evolved, various groups and individuals—or stakeholders—developed vested interests in maintaining them. Members of Congress viewed many of these programs as "pork" for the folks back home, and administrators at all levels of government justified their jobs and their agencies' existence on the basis of these programs. Many of the constituencies that benefited from federal grants traditionally supported the Democratic party, and if the Republican party were to become the majority party, it would have to break up the implicit alliances built on federal funding of state and local programs.

The Nixon Years (1969–1974)

Republicans, beginning with President Richard Nixon (1969–1974), defined their views of federal-state relationships using the term "new federalism." In fact, there have been several iterations of "new federalism," reflecting the philosophical differences among Republican presidents. The details of presidential proposals varied, but the general objective was to return responsibilities for many domestic policies to the state and local governments. Presidential proposals were also based on a desire to reduce federal spending for many domestic programs and reduce the federal budget, a policy that had widespread appeal among many of the Republican constituencies.

When Richard Nixon was elected president in 1968, he, like many other conservatives, criticized the expanded role of the federal government and advocated a reversion of program responsibilities to the states. Nixon argued that his **"new federalism"** was designed to "rationalize the intergovernmental system by restructuring the roles and responsibilities of governments at all levels."[26] At the same time, Nixon wanted to reduce the role of the federal government and largely decentralize federal programs. His strategy included four key components. He proposed management changes to expedite and coordinate the grant application process and the consolidation of many categorical grants into a few large **block grants,** which would give state and local governments greater discretion over the use of funds. He also proposed the replacement of many categorical grants with **revenue sharing** dollars, which could be used by the recipient government for virtually any purpose—with "no strings attached." Finally, Nixon advocated a restructuring of the nation's welfare system. He unsuccessfully proposed replacing Aid to Families with Dependent Children (AFDC), the existing grant program, with the Family Assistance Plan, a federal income payment based on family size.[27]

After almost six years of program initiatives and changes that were supposed to increase state and local powers, policies enacted during Nixon's administration produced results that appeared to be just the opposite. Many believe that "Nixon left behind what was probably a more centralized federal system than the one he inherited."[28] Federal expenditures for many domestic programs had increased dramatically, and the regulatory powers of the federal government had been expanded.

The Ford (1974–1977) and Carter (1977–1981) Years

Nixon was followed by Presidents Gerald Ford (1974–1977) and Jimmy Carter (1977–1981). President Ford, who took over the White House after Nixon's humiliating resignation, also called for a greater balance between the national and state governments, and initiatives enacted during his administration were similar to that of his predecessor. There was an extension of revenue sharing and two block grants—community development and manpower programs—during his short time in office.[29]

President Carter, a Democrat who had served as governor of Georgia, attempted to expand the federal role to assist local governments. His budgets reduced revenue sharing dollars to the states, and he attempted to redirect those funds to cities with several new policy initiatives. There was a great deal of planning and consultation with mayors and other local officials during his administration, but little of his urban program made its way through Congress.[30]

The Reagan (1981–1989) and Bush (1989–1993) Years

President Ronald Reagan (1981–1989), a Republican who is often given credit for initiating what some call the "Reagan Revolution," also expressed a commitment to reducing federal programs—especially welfare programs—and the revitalization of the powers of state and local governments. While he used some of the same tactics and resources as Nixon, he clearly had a different agenda. Reagan was particularly critical of welfare assistance, and beginning with his 1981 legislative agenda, he attempted to reduce federal support of social programs and eliminate categorical grants through their consolidation into block grants. In 1981, Reagan "convinced Congress to consolidate seventy-six categorical grant-in-aid programs and a block grant program into nine new or reconstituted block grants."[31] He also attempted to consolidate additional grant programs during subsequent congressional sessions, but had little success.

Reagan also opposed revenue sharing, which the federal government ended in 1986. The program was attacked for contributing to the federal budget deficit, funding governments that did not need the money, funding programs of questionable merit, and producing a reliance on revenue-sharing dollars for the operating budgets of many governments.

Reagan's efforts to reduce federal funding of social services was particularly harsh on state and local governments, which had taken on many of the responsibilities for the administration of public assistance. One strategy initiated by the Reagan administration in 1982 was to turn back welfare (Aid to Families with Dependent Children) and the food stamp programs to the states in return for the federal government assuming responsibility for the Medicaid program, which provided health care for many low-income individuals. Although this proposal was rejected by Congress, Reagan, as well as his successor, George Bush (1989–1993), attempted on numerous occasions to return programs to state governments.[32]

Presidential and congressional rhetoric about reducing federal powers and returning authority to the states, however, often does not correspond to what actually takes place. During the Reagan and first Bush administrations, there was no restructuring of the federal system in the direction of dual federalism. While some efforts were made, primarily through executive orders and administrative initiatives, to increase the discretionary powers of the states, the **mandates** and **preemptions** enacted by Congress as well as court decisions affecting federal relations during this period (1981–1993) worked against the transfer of power to the states. Moreover, some argue that Reagan's "New Federalism was a general philosophy favoring a smaller federal role but not necessarily a larger state and local role in the governance system."[33]

From 1789 to 1991, Congress enacted more than 470 laws preempting state or local authority. Approximately 250, or more than half, were enacted after 1970. Only thirty-four laws in this period provided relief from federal preemptions.[34] Many preemptive restrictions were adopted with Reagan's approval and appear to reflect Reagan's commitment to marketplace economics and a reduced role for all government.[35]

Under constitutional law, statutory law, or federal regulations, the federal government also can require states or local governments "to undertake a specific activity or provide a service meeting minimum national standards."[36] Throughout the 1980s, while decentralization and return of power to the states were major themes of the Reagan and first Bush administrations, Congress enacted numerous statutes that imposed additional mandates and regulations on the states.[37] There is no question that the costs imposed by federal "mandates and restraints on state and local governments total in the billions of dollars and force these governments to divert funds from many worthy projects to finance the national policies."[38] According to data from the Congressional Budget Office, federal regulations adopted between 1983 and 1990 imposed cumulative estimated costs of between $8.9 billion and $12.7 billion on states and localities, depending on how mandates are defined. These costs increased at a pace faster than overall federal aid.[39] In 1994, the Texas Legislative Budget Board reported that increases in mandates and other federal programs had accounted for $13 billion, or 65 percent, of a $20 billion increase in the Texas budget since 1990–1991.[40]

President George Bush was perceived as sensitive to state and local problems during his administration (1989–1993), but the huge federal deficit and agreements to cap federal expenditures provided no prospects for additional financial assistance to the states. Congress, with his approval, continued to impose mandates that added to the financial burdens of states and cities while preempting more and more authority over programs from the states.[41] During Bush's administration, Congress passed the Americans with Disabilities Act in 1990. The act prohibits discrimination against persons with disabilities and requires governments to make extensive and costly changes in public facilities to accommodate disabled individuals.[42] During 1990, Congress also passed three other major pieces of legislation (the Clean Air Act Amendments, the Education of the Handicapped Act Amendments, and the Fiscal 1991 Budget Reconciliation Act) which imposed additional requirements on the states and local governments.

The Clinton (1993–2001) Years

Democrat Bill Clinton assumed the presidency in 1993 after serving six terms as governor of Arkansas, and many expected him to be more understanding of the impact of mandates. But, like his predecessor, Clinton failed to provide a coherent theory of federalism in the wide range of proposals he initially submitted to Congress. Committed to deficit reduction, Clinton and Congress left little leeway to provide financial relief or expand funding to states and local governments. The enactment of the MotorVoter bill in 1993, which encouraged the registration of more voters, also expanded federal authority in the administration of state elections. The Family and Medical Leave Act, enacted the same year, requires firms with fifty or more employees and state and local governments to provide up to twelve weeks of unpaid personal leave to employees. In 1994, Congress passed the Goals 2000: Educate America Act, which potentially expands the federal role in public education through the development of national curriculum content and student performance standards.

Republicans gained control of both houses of Congress in 1994, and their "contract with America" raised several issues that had a potential impact on federal relationships. These included term limits for elected officials, a balanced budget, restrictions on punitive damages in civil lawsuits, the line-item veto for the president, regulatory relief, and welfare reform. Many of the newly elected Republicans were clearly committed to restricting the powers of the national government. And, in response to state demands, Congress enacted the Unfunded Mandates Reform Act (1995). Any legislation that would impose $50 million or more in costs to state and local governments would be subject to a parliamentary procedure that requires a vote to waive the prohibition on unfunded mandates. In effect, it requires members of Congress to go on record that they are voting to impose more costs on the state and local governments. The act did nothing to remedy mandates that were already on the books, and since its enactment, it has had very little effect on reducing costs to the other governments in the federal system.[43]

Deficit reduction in 1995 was directly linked to devolution of powers to the states. Debate over spending limits for Medicare and Medicaid, tax reductions, and a cash assistance program for the poor demonstrated the intentions of Republicans to shrink the national budget and give states additional control over domestic programs.[44]

Congress enacted a major welfare reform bill in 1996 that eliminated the entitlements under the sixty-one-year-old Aid to Families with Dependent Children program. It was replaced by a new program, Temporary Assistance for Needy Families, which is funded by block grants to the states and gives the states a wide range of options for establishing their own welfare programs.[45] Under waivers permitted by federal law, states also are experimenting with a variety of managed health care reforms in the Medicaid program, which serves low-income people. States, supported by new federal funds, expanded the medical insurance coverage of low-income children in 1997 and obtained relief from some of the regulations of the Environmental Protection Agency. In 1998, Congress enacted a $216 billion public works program which was designed to help states and local governments build roads, bridges, and mass transit systems.[46] Despite the Unfunded Mandates Act of 1995, additional requirements and preemptions in health care, telecommunications, immigration reform, securities reform, and minimum wages were enacted by Congress in 1997.[47]

In 1996, Congress passed the Defense of Marriage Act, which was a response to the state Supreme Court in Hawaii upholding the legality of gay marriages. For fear that the "full faith and credit clause" of the U.S. Constitution would require other states to recognize gay marriages, Congress, with Clinton's encouragement, defined marriages as heterosexual unions and permitted states to refuse to recognize homosexual marriages.[48]

Some have argued that the "devolution revolution" of 1996 has been transformed into a "new federal order," in which the "federal government intrudes less into the affairs of states and also offers less financial assistance."[49] Additionally, others believe that recent congressional action gives states and local governments greater "flexibility" in carrying out federally funded programs.

But there are skeptics. John Kincaid, a specialist in federalism, argues that "devolution (is) plodding along at a turtle's pace while centralization is still racing ahead at a rabbit's pace."[50] While there has been considerable symbolic rhetoric and some federal legislation that point to greater state and local responsibility and authority, a closer assessment suggests minimal changes in federal relationships. There is also some evidence of the national government actually increasing its influence in select policy areas.[51] In the early years of the 21st century, "the federal government provides about 25 percent of the states' general-fund revenues through its approximately 608 categorical grants and 17 block grants."[52]

Bush and Post 9/11 Federal Relationships

The attacks on the World Trade Center and the Pentagon on September 11, 2001, sent shockwaves through the nation as Americans were immediately awakened to their vulnerability to attacks by small but well-organized groups of terrorists. As people were still struggling to make sense out of these attacks and re-establish their sense of security, there was an unrelated, 21-day period the next year of random sniper attacks on people in the Washington, D.C. area. National unease was further compounded by American military attacks in Afghanistan and later Iraq, the breaking of the stock market bubble in 2001, a sluggish economy, the collapse of Enron Corporation and other corporate abuses, and massive budget deficits that confronted most states as well as the federal government by the end of 2002.

In the initial months of his administration, President George W. Bush (2001–) gave few clues of how his policy objectives would affect state-federal relationships. Some government watchers expected him to outline and pursue policies similar to his Republican predecessors, but the September 11 terrorist attacks retarded the development of many initiatives. Homeland security took priority.

Historically, the federal government had played a very limited role in police functions or domestic security. America has never had a national police force because that responsibility was—and still is—allocated to the states and local governments. But the magnitude of the terrorist threat to domestic security prompted President Bush to call for the creation of a new national agency charged with coordinating security programs of federal, state, and local agencies. The Department of Homeland Security, created by Congress in November 2002, represented a comprehensive re-alignment of federal agencies with functions relating to security, including everything from commercial air travel to patrols along U.S. borders. The new department also developed collaborative programs with states and local governments. It is premature to predict all the implications of these changes, but few experts doubt that it will have "immense and compelling implications for federalism and intergovernmental relations."[53]

Controversy over the time it was taking to carry out the reorganization, inade-quate financial assistance to state and local governments to upgrade their policing capabilities, and evidence of continued vulnerability to terrorist attacks continued through 2003. But as the federal government and state governments tried to work out their individual and combined responsibilities, it was clear that the Homeland Security Act was leading the country

> "... toward greatly enlarging national control of domestic security and other functions traditionally controlled at the state and local level. This imperative has the potential to significantly tip the federal system—in matters of politics, police functions, and the law—towards Washington to an unprecedented degree."[54]

With President Bush's support, Congress also enacted the USA Patriot Act soon after the September 11 attacks. That measure increased government surveillance powers in investigations of espionage or terrorism. Supporters contended the legis-lation was essential in combating terrorists. But civil libertarians, among other critics, feared that the changes it made in federal law enforcement tactics could be abused. By the end of 2003, more than 170 cities and counties around the country had passed resolutions criticizing the law.[55]

A significant piece of legislation passed during the second Bush presidency, which was unrelated to the fight against terrorism, was the "No Child Left Behind Act" of 2002. As governor of Texas, Bush had prided his record on education, which was intended to bring accountability into the public schools while expanding state sup-port for local school districts. Education reform was a cornerstone of his presiden-tial campaign and his legislative agenda. His education initiatives as president were significant to state-federal relationships because, historically, education had been primarily a function of state and local governments. Federal aid to public education had been limited and often targeted toward specific groups of students, such as the disabled or those from low-income families. The potential impact of the "No Child Left Behind Act" was enormous because it included new federal mandates for read-ing and math proficiency, based on testing. Test scores were to be used to evaluate the progress of a school or a school district. If schools failed to meet specified stan-dards, they would suffer repercussions, including loss of funding and loss of students, who would be allowed to transfer to better performing schools.[56]

The education reform law, the increased federal control over security, and other recent policy changes have the potential to tilt the federal system significantly toward the national government, especially if the new laws lay the predicate for additional centralizing legislation. It is ironic that conservative Republicans, who have long decried centralization, are helping to lead the country in that direction. It is critical that the student of politics does not simply listen to the rhetoric or sym-bolism of policy initiatives. The reality is in the details, which may not correspond to the rhetoric.

The Role of the U.S. Supreme Court in Defining Federalism

The federal courts have played a central role in defining power, authority, and jurisdiction in the federal system. In looking to the courts to provide the definitive theory of federalism, we might expect a conservative Supreme Court to be more concerned with states' rights and to reconsider the doctrines underlying mandates and preemptions. But this has not always been the case.

In a 1985 Texas case, *Garcia v. San Antonio Metropolitan Transit Authority*, the U.S. Supreme Court held 5–4 that states could not claim immunity from federal regulation over functions that have been defined as "integral" or "traditional."[57] This case, which involved municipal employees and their coverage by the Fair Labor Standards Act, had far-reaching implications for federal-state relationships.[58] In the extreme, the case suggested that Congress, not the courts interpreting the Constitution, would define federalism. The case also suggested that there were no "discrete limitations on the objects of federal authority" other than those provisions of the Constitution that give the states a role in the selection of the president and members of Congress.[59]

By 1995 the Court, under the leadership of Chief Justice William Rehnquist, had become much more concerned with the expansion of federal powers and was re-asserting itself in cases that involved federal issues. The Court ruled 5–4 in the case of *United States v. Lopez* that "the Congress had overreached its constitutional power to regulate interstate commerce when it passed the Gun-Free School Zones Act of 1990."[60] In *Bush v. Vera* the Court struck down a Texas political redistricting plan, suggesting that it was less likely to support redistricting that was designed primarily to benefit minority groups. Other cases soon followed challenging race and ethnicity as criteria for redistricting, and the court's position was clarified somewhat in a 2001 decision (*Easley v. Cromartie*) in which it held that race is not an unconstitutional consideration in redistricting as long as it is not the "dominant and controlling" factor.[61] In another case, the Court held that federal laws did not preempt state laws that penalized negligent manufacturers.[62]

A Texas case, *City of Boerne, Texas v. Flores* (1997), also demonstrated the Supreme Court's disposition to place limits on congressional powers.[63] In this case, the high Court ruled that the Religious Freedom Restoration Act of 1993 was unconstitutional because it was too broad in its protection of religious freedom. The Court ruled that provisions of the act infringed on state powers and also threatened "the authority of the Court to determine the constitutionality of federal and state laws."[64] The ruling was handed down after a Roman Catholic parish in Boerne used the law to challenge the city's decision to deny it a permit to enlarge a church in a historic district. The Court also struck down provisions of the Brady Handgun Violence Prevention Act, which required background checks on gun purchasers, in *Printz v. United States*.[65]

The Court has not been single-minded in its efforts to restrain the powers of the national government.[66] In 1996, the Court handed down several civil rights decisions that imposed limits on state powers. It also struck down a 1992 Colorado constitutional amendment that prohibited governments from defining homosexuals as a protected class. In another case, Virginia, on the basis of the Fourteenth Amendment, was required to permit women to attend Virginia Military Institute, which had been an all-male school.[67] In the *Seminole Tribe v. Florida* case, the Supreme Court concluded that Congress had virtually all "authority to legislate in the area of Indian affairs and states had none."[68]

In more recent terms, the Supreme Court has continued to receive a number of cases involving federal issues, and many more cases have been filed in federal district courts. Although not all of the Court's recent decisions reflect a pro-state position, the Supreme Court does appear to have pursued an agenda of redefining or clarifying federal-state relationships, and through its decisions the "allocation of powers in the federal system are still evolving."[69]

THE IMPACT OF FEDERALISM ON STATE FINANCES

Federal taxes paid into the national treasury from Texas in 2002 totalled approximately $126.3 billion, or approximately $5,824 per person. Federal expenditures in the state were $116.7 billion. For each federal tax dollar paid, the state received only about 92 cents in federal expenditures in return, including government payroll, defense and other procurement, direct payments to residents under programs such as Social Security, and grants to the state and local governments.[70]

The state's return is significantly smaller when only government grants are counted. In 1990, the state comptroller's office determined that Texas ranked near the bottom of the fifty states in per capita distribution of federal grants to state and local governments. The state attempted through its congressional delegation to obtain more equitable formulas as Congress amended or reauthorized these grant programs in the 1990s.[71]

Federal funds accounted for $39.2 billion, or about one-third, of the $118 billion state budget for 2004–2005. The 2002–2003 budget included $34.8 billion in federal funds, or about 29 percent of the total (Table 3–2). Health and human services, which include a wide range of social services for millions of low-income Texans, received about 60 percent of all federal funds to the state during 2002–2003. Business and economic development programs received 20 percent, and education programs received 16 percent.[72]

State government, through the Office of State-Federal Relations, and many of the larger cities in Texas have full-time staffers dedicated to obtaining additional federal dollars. Like other states, Texas also lobbies the federal government for additional programs, changes in existing programs, relief from mandates and preemptions, and adjustments in funding formulas that adversely affect the state.

TABLE 3–2   Federal Funds for the 2002–2003 Biennium (In millions)

General Government	$ 614.8
Health and Human Services	21,025.9
Agencies of Education	5,635.7
Public Safety and Criminal Justice	262.5
Natural Resources	213.3
Business and Economic Development	6,963.5
Regulatory	4.8
General Provisions	87.4
TOTAL	$34,807.9

Source: Texas Legislative Budget Board, *Fiscal Size Up 2002–2003,* Table 17.

Some counties, cities, and school districts are aggressive and successful in obtaining federal grants, but others are not. Some local governments apparently have difficulty mastering the complexities of the grant application process. As noted earlier, many federal programs are competitive. Available programs must be identified through publications such as the *Federal Register,* and applications must be submitted in a timely manner. Many small cities across Texas may have only a handful of employees performing everything from garbage collection to tax collection. These communities may not have the resources or employees with skills to apply for federal grants, and other communities may be disinterested. The state is organized into regional councils of government, which can assist local governments in this process.

State agencies are required to look at their specific programs and aggressively pursue relevant federal grants. Within the governor's office, there is a State Grants Team whose "mission is to alert entities throughout Texas about funding opportunities." This agency helps in the identification of grant programs, informs other state and local agencies of grant availability, assists in the writing of grant applications, and monitors agency activities in pursuing grants.[73]

REACTIONS TO THE EXPANDED ROLE OF THE FEDERAL GOVERNMENT

Many citizens argue that economic, environmental, and social issues are national in scope, and it is impossible for states, singularly or collectively, to address these problems adequately. The complexity of these problems requires a coordinated national effort with common standards and objectives. Not all governments have the financial resources to deal with many of these problems, and without federal assistance, some significant segments of our society would simply do without or suffer. From a philosophical perspective, these individuals are inclined to ask why some parts of our population should be neglected. Others have taken the view that many governments would not address such issues if they were not required to do so by federal mandates. Others argue the federal system potentially brings expertise and support to those governments that don't have adequate resources. Still others look at the long history of discrimination in the United States and argue that changes would not have occurred if the federal government had not taken the lead through legislation and public policy.

And, finally, the expanded role of the national government comes with some high costs and "strings" attached. Some state agencies and communities across Texas have even resisted taking federal dollars because of the conditions attached to the grant programs. A recipient of money from the federal government is obligated to comply with the regulations covering its use. This is something like a "carrot-and-stick" approach, enticing state and local governments to comply with the agenda of the national government in exchange for funding of public programs.

Regulations tied to a specific grant can cross over to a totally different policy arena, thus further coercing states and local governments to comply with federal policy objectives. For example, the Texas legislature raised the minimum legal drinking age from eighteen to twenty-one in 1986. Although some Texans had lobbied for the older drinking age, a major impetus for the change came from federal legislation that linked the drinking age to federal grants for road construction. Texas could have refused to adopt the higher age, but it would have lost 10 percent of its federal highway dollars after 1988. Federal law also makes a similar link between highway speed limits and federal highway construction funds.

Many of the federal assistance programs were designed to redistribute resources from the wealthier segments of the population to lower income groups, a practice that some people oppose. Moreover, this redistribution is linked in Texas to issues of race and ethnicity because minority groups constitute a disproportionate segment of the state's low-income population. Some political leaders have resisted federal grant programs for fear that funding projects would enhance the political position of minority groups.

Federal grants also have been criticized and resisted by some groups and officeholders in Texas on the grounds that they force governments to rearrange their priorities. The funds for specific programs may not meet the primary needs of a state or a community, but it is very difficult for most public officeholders to pass up these available dollars.

Some suggest that the increased use of fiscal federalism (federal grants linked to preemptions and mandates) has produced a mindset that the federal government should assume more responsibility for domestic programs, both in terms of program development and funding.[74] They fear that federal dominance undermines the creative capacity of states and local governments to deal with many local and regional problems. Moreover, many would argue that the states are now much more innovative than the federal government in policy implementation and streamlining the administrative processes.

TRANSNATIONAL REGIONALISM

Texas shares a 1,200-mile border with Mexico, and common problems and interests that bond the two neighbors, called **transnational regionalism,** have taken on increased importance since the mid-1980s. Historically, relations between the United States and Mexico were often strained. The United States fought a war against Mexico from 1846 to 1848, and on subsequent occasions, American troops entered Mexican territory, ostensibly to protect U.S. economic and national security interests. Apprehension about U.S. objectives resulted in Mexican policies on trade, commerce, and foreign ownership of property that were designed to insulate the country from excessive foreign influence and domination. Nevertheless, the interests of the two countries have long been bound by geopolitical factors, economics, and demographics. One Mexican author has compared the interdependence of the two countries to Siamese twins, warning that "if one becomes gangrenous, the other twin will also be afflicted."[75]

Maquiladoras

Changes in the economic relationship between Mexico and the United States began with the **maquiladora program,** an initiative under Mexico's 1964 Border Industrialization Program to boost employment, foreign exchange, and industrial development. It was also designed to transfer technology to Mexico, help train workers, and develop managerial skills among Mexican nationals.[76]

The concept was to develop twin plants, one in the United States and one in Mexico, under a single management. The plant in the United States would manufacture parts, and its Mexican counterpart would assemble them into a product, which, in turn, would be sent back to the United States for further processing or for shipping to customers.[77] Parts shipped into Mexico would not be subject to the normal tariffs, and the tax imposed on the assembled product would be minimal. In 1984, Mexico changed its laws to permit the United States and other foreign countries to establish these relationships throughout Mexico, rather than just on the border, and to permit 100 percent foreign ownership of the assembly plants in Mexico. The latter step was a radical departure from previous Mexican law, which prohibited such foreign ownership.[78]

The maquiladora program has not resulted in the construction of a significant number of manufacturing plants on the Texas side of the border, however, because American companies have used existing plants throughout the United States to produce parts to be assembled in Mexico. Nevertheless, Texas's border counties have benefited through the creation of thousands of support jobs in transportation, warehousing, and services.[79]

With Mexico's membership (since 1986) in the international General Agreement on Tariffs and Trade (GATT), which later became the World Trade Organization, and the implementation of the North American Free Trade Agreement, the maquiladora program will continue to play a major role in transnational economic development. American organized labor opposes the program, arguing that the maquiladoras drain jobs from the United States. But the program provides a source of inexpensive labor for American businesses, which have complained for years that they cannot compete against cheap foreign labor costs.

The North American Free Trade Agreement (NAFTA)

Negotiations on a free trade agreement in 1991 marked a significant change in the relationship between Mexico and the United States. The negotiations were precipitated, in part, by world economics and the emergence of regional trading zones. But the administration of Mexican President Carlos Salinas de Gortari was also reacting to the failure of Mexico's economic policies of the 1980s and a fear of economic isolation. The end of the Cold War, a reduction in Central American conflicts, and internal population pressures also were factors.[80]

The convergence of interests of the United States, Mexico, and Canada produced the **North American Free Trade Agreement (NAFTA)** to reduce tariffs and increase trade among the three countries. It created the world's largest trading bloc, with a combined population of approximately 400 million and a combined gross national product of more than $8 trillion in 1997.[81] Approved by the U.S. Congress in late 1993, the agreement had the strong support of the Texas business community, Governor Ann Richards, both U.S. senators from Texas, and twenty-four of the state's thirty members of the U.S. House of Representatives.

The treaty has increased trade among the three countries, strengthening previous economic ties and creating new ones. Texas has experienced significant economic changes from these new relationships, but the benefits have not been uniformly distributed throughout the state. The regions expected to benefit most in terms of new manufacturing jobs are the Dallas-Fort Worth area and Houston because of their concentrations of chemical and electronics industries.[82]

Some people on both sides of the U.S.-Mexico border believe that NAFTA is harming their respective countries. Labor unions in the United States are particularly concerned that cheap labor costs in Mexico have moved jobs from the United States. Some manufacturers argue that labor and capital costs in Mexico threaten their American markets. Some Texas officials and many Texas residents fear that opening up the state's highways to Mexican trucks will create safety problems, and American trucking interests, including owners and drivers, oppose competition from Mexican trucks. Mexican trucks still were not allowed unlimited movement in all fifty states, despite treaty provisions to the contrary. There were indications in early 2001 that the Bush administration was prepared to carry out the free access provisions of the treaty, but progress has been slow. In Mexico, there is concern that American corporations will dominate and reduce Mexico's control over its own economy. And, finally, environmentalists have argued that increased commerce compounds air and water pollution problems.

A number of American critics of NAFTA also have raised questions about Mexican political corruption and human rights violations, the longtime domination of Mexican politics by the Revolutionary Institutional Party (PRI), and increased drug smuggling into the United States. Drug-related violence and alleged collusion between high-ranking Mexican officials and drug smugglers have raised questions about Mexico's ability to fight the drug problem. In recent years, there has been considerable violence among the competing drug cartels in Mexico, and several Mexican government officials responsible for enforcing drug laws have been murdered. Efforts to control drug smuggling along the border have had only limited success because the border is simply too long and cross-border traffic too heavy. Thousands of trucks cross from Mexico into the United States each day. The flood of illegal immigration into the United States from Mexico also is an issue, which will be discussed in more detail later in this chapter.

The Free Trade Commission, based in Mexico City, is the central agency responsible for implementing NAFTA. Assisted by twenty-one committees, subcommittees, and advisory groups, it is charged with resolving disputes and developing and administering procedures, measures, and standards authorized by the agreement.[83]

Three agencies were created under auxiliary agreements to NAFTA to help address common problems arising under the treaty. The Border Environmental Cooperation Commission is responsible for tackling international environmental issues that face the three nations. Working with states and local communities along the U.S.-Mexican border, the agency is charged with developing plans to improve such things as water supplies, wastewater treatment, and garbage disposal. It is responsible for certifying infrastructure projects for funding by the North American Development Bank, or NADBank, or other financial agencies. By the fall of 2003, it had certified 91 projects with a total cost of $1.9 billion.[84]

The Commission for Labor Cooperation is charged with improving working conditions and living standards and strengthening the enforcement of domestic labor laws with trade sanctions and other penalties. It takes complaints from interested parties and conducts quasi-judicial proceedings with recommendations based on the labor laws of the three treaty participants.[85] The Working Group on Emergency Action addresses import surges that may adversely affect industries in the three countries.

In addition, the North American Development Bank, which is located in San Antonio, was created by the United States and Mexico to fund infrastructure and environmental projects along the U.S.-Mexico border.[86] NADBank was criticized for a slow start, and many wondered if it would accomplish its objectives. By the fall of 2003, it had made $628 million in loans for 68 infrastructure projects along the border. The total costs of these projects will be $2.17 billion, and they will affect six million people.[87]

The Impact of Recent Political Events on U.S.–Mexican Relationships

The potential for political instability in Mexico surfaced dramatically with the uprising on January 1, 1994, of the Zapatistas, a peasant-based guerrilla movement centered in Chiapas. Although some efforts were made to address the Zapatistas' grievances, the massacre of forty-five people in late December of 1997 by gunmen with alleged links to the ruling party cast more shadows on Mexico's political system.

Mexico's national government tried in early 2001 to defuse the issues surrounding the Zapatista conflict. Some federal troops were withdrawn from the area. Leaders of the Zapatistas were invited to travel from Chiapas to Mexico City to address the congress, and the leader of the organization met with the president. But progress has been limited.

The devaluation of the peso in late 1994 and the beginning of a serious Mexican recession in 1995 increased concerns that the troubled Mexican economy would further destabilize the Mexican political system. President Bill Clinton responded with an economic rescue plan for Mexico. Clinton maintained that the collapse of the Mexican economy threatened to weaken the U.S. dollar, hurt exports, and generate disruption in other Latin American countries. It also was feared that social unrest could spill over into the United States, with even more illegal immigration.[88] The Mexican government responded with austere economic measures and repaid its guaranteed loans before they were due. By early 1997, the Mexican economy was showing signs of a slow recovery, but the economic troubles south of the border and the U.S. recession that began in 2001 contributed to cool relations between the two countries.

Vicente Fox Quesada of the Partido Accion Nacional (PAN) was elected president of Mexico in 2000, promising a concerted attack on drug smuggling and governmental corruption. It was the first time that PRI, the long-time ruling party, had lost a presidential election since its inception 70 years earlier. President Fox and President Bush had developed a cooperative relationship when they served as governors of their respective states, and most observers assumed that this cooperation would extend into their presidencies. Initially, it did, but their relationship soured in 2003 when Mexico, along with most other members of the United Nations, refused to endorse America's military action against Iraq. Relations between the two countries further eroded because of a dispute over water allocations from the Rio Grande under a 1944 treaty and the sense that the Bush administration was giving little attention to the interests of Mexico and other Latin American countries.

Trade Patterns between Texas and Mexico

The United States and Texas clearly profit from Mexico's prosperity. U.S. exports to Mexico were $12.4 billion in 1986 and $97.5 billion in 2002 (Table 3–3). Imports from Mexico, now the United States' second largest trading partner, were $134 billion in 2002. Texas exported more than $41 billion worth of goods, comprising close to six percent of the state's gross domestic economy, to Mexico in 2002. Texas's exports to Mexico had increased dramatically from the $8.8 billion exported in 1987. These exports create hundreds of thousands of jobs in Texas.

The sheer volume of the movement of goods, services, and people is obvious on the highways leading into Mexico and the long lines of autos and trucks at border crossings in Brownsville, Laredo, and El Paso. Anyone traveling down Interstate 35

TABLE 3–3   Texas and U.S. Exports to Mexico, 1993–2002

Year	Texas Exports to Mexico	U.S. Exports to Mexico	Texas as a Percent of U.S.
1993	$20,379,583,586	$41,581,100,000	49.01%
1994	$23,849,512,126	$50,843,500,000	46.91
1995	$21,863,455,716	$46,292,100,000	47.23
1996	$27,036,930,968	$56,791,500,000	47.61
1997	$31,172,597,636	$71,388,400,000	43.67
1998*	$36,328,363,149	$78,772,500,000	46.12
1999	$37,860,871,019	$87,044,038,183	43.50
2000	$47,761,021,704	$111,720,877,976	42.75
2001	$41,647,797,064	$101,503,075,013	41.03
2002	$41,647,027,169	$97,530,612,979	42.70

*Note: The Massachusetts Institute for Social and Economic Research applied a more advanced algorithm to data beginning in 1999. Thus, the post-1998 export figures more accurately account for unreported exports by states and therefore more accurately reflect actual export revenue than do pre-1999 figures.
Source: Massachusetts Institute of Social and Economic Research and the U.S. Census Bureau (based on "origin of movement to port" state-level data series); Texas Department of Economic Development, April 2000.

from Dallas to Laredo experiences the effects of these changes with bumper-to-bumper traffic. There are an estimated 100 million legal crossings of the border between Texas and Mexico each year. Many people move back and forth daily. Some people from Mexico, for example, do most of their shopping in the United States, and many American citizens make frequent visits to Mexico for any number of reasons. Some walk, some drive, and some fly, creating an enormous amount of transnational movement. Billions of dollars are required to upgrade and expand the roads, highways, bridges, water and sanitation systems, and other facilities on both sides of the border. Some initiatives have been taken by both countries, but many of these facilities will not be completed for years, contributing to delays and gridlock in both countries. As noted above, the North American Development Bank was created to help address these needs.

The American government's response to the terrorist attacks of September 11, 2001, will further impede traffic across the border. The new "U.S. Visit" program, to be carried out by the Department of Homeland Security in an effort to interdict potential terrorists at the border, will increase the number of checks of American citizens and foreign visitors at border crossings. As initially planned, foreign visitors will be fingerprinted and photographed at each port of entry. If a person overstays his or her visa, their Mexican visa, which can be electronically read, will be confiscated. Foreigners who violate the time period of the visa will not be permitted to re-enter the United States for a year, and repeat offenders will be denied admittance for life. Some of these provisions do not apply to Canadians and other visitors, primarily those from European nations. Questions have been raised about the costs and effectiveness of these proposals and also about why the policies single out visitors from south of the U.S. border.[89] Some experts doubt the new border security program will deter entry by terrorists. It will, though, increase transportation and shipping costs, impede the free flow of goods, cost individuals an untold amount of time waiting in long lines, and generate a great deal of hostility from Mexican citizens.

Common Borders, Common Problems

To anyone living on the border, the economic interdependence of the United States and Mexico is evident every day. Thousands of pedestrians, cars, and trucks move across the international bridges, to and from the commercial centers on both sides of the Rio Grande. When the Mexican economy suffered a precipitous decline in 1982, the peso devaluation severely disrupted the Texas border economy, causing unemployment to skyrocket and a considerable number of U.S. businesses to fail.

While much of the effort toward improving relations between the United States and Mexico has focused on potential economic benefits, other complex problems confronting both countries also merit attention. One is health care. On both sides of the border, many children have not been immunized against basic childhood diseases. On the Texas side are more than 1,200 *colonias*—rural, unincorporated slums that have substandard housing, roads, and drainage and, in many cases, lack water and sewage systems. These conditions have contributed to severe health problems, including hepatitis, dysentery, and tuberculosis. Higher than normal numbers of both Texan and Mexican children along the border also have been born with serious birth defects. Public health facilities in Texas report that Mexican women come across the border to give birth to their children in American facilities. This practice, which has the effect of creating "binational families," increases the burden on public hospitals—and taxpayers—in Texas. Children born in the United States are U.S. citizens and are entitled to various public services.[90]

Industrial development and population growth along the border also increase environmental problems. U.S. antipollution laws have been more stringent than those of Mexico, but air and water pollution generated in Mexico does not stop at the border. The side agreements to NAFTA provide a basic framework for addressing these problems, but some have argued that a country such as Mexico, under enormous pressure to industrialize rapidly, is less likely to be concerned with environmental issues. In addition, U.S. efforts to impose its environmental standards on Mexico could be interpreted as another American effort to dominate the country.[91] In June 1994, several maquiladora plants in Matamoros, across the border from Brownsville, settled lawsuits alleging that pollution caused rare birth defects in children born in Texas. A report published by Public Citizen, a public interest group organized by Ralph Nader, concluded in late 1995 that public health and the environment on the U.S.-Mexico border had worsened since NAFTA was approved in 1993.[92]

Regional interdependence, while perhaps not recognized by most people on both sides of the border, has taken on greater importance in the press and in academic, business, and labor communities in the United States. Transnational public policies are emerging, creating legal issues in product liability, insurance, copyrights, and patents that must still be resolved. The governors of Mexican and U.S. border states have their own association, the Border Governors Conference, which meets regularly to discuss such issues as free trade, the environment, education, and tourism. Recent Texas governors have supported efforts to improve relations with Mexico,

---

THE NUMBERS KEEP INCREASING

Those who predicted that NAFTA would increase border crossings between Mexico and the United States were correct. During the 1997 fiscal year, the U.S. Customs Service reported that more pedestrians, trucks, and cars cleared the eleven ports of entry along the Texas-Mexico border than in the previous year. Some 17.8 million people walked across the border, and 2.4 million trucks and 43.1 million cars were driven across. Approximately 15.2 million cars crossed the border at El Paso, and 1.2 million trucks crossed the border at Laredo.

Source: "Border Entries in South Texas No. 1 in Nation," *San Antonio Express-News,* June 19, 1998, p. 7B.

---

and Texas state agencies have been given increased authority to work in cooperative efforts with Mexican officials.[93] Although the Border Governors Conference has no regulatory powers, it has taken recent initiatives in collaboration with governments on both sides of the border to address animal and plant disease prevention and eradication, border crossing issues, and economic development.[94] Private groups have also organized to address transnational issues and to pressure governments in the United States and Mexico to develop policies and allocate resources to resolve problems.

Illegal Immigration

Population growth in Texas has always been affected by migration from other states and foreign countries. But the proximity of Texas to Mexico has put the state in the center of a long-running dispute over the illegal immigration of large numbers of Mexicans and other Latin Americans. In 2002, there were an estimated 7.9 million people, mostly from Mexico and Central America, living in the United States illegally.[95] Many enter through Texas and continue on to other areas of the country, but others remain in the state. The actual number of illegal immigrants in Texas will never be known because these people do not go out of their way to participate in studies or report their status, but the most recent estimates are 600,000 to one million.[96]

The failure of the Mexican economy and the attraction of employment opportunities north of the border have been major reasons for this migration, although political instability and persecutions in Central America have also been significant factors. Large portions of the Texas and American economies were built on the availability of cheap, low-skilled Mexican labor.[97] If arrested, illegal workers are returned to Mexico, but until 1986, it was not illegal for American employers to hire them.[98]

In 1986, the U.S. Congress enacted the Immigration Reform and Control Act, which imposed fines on employers who hired illegal aliens and provided jail sentences for flagrant violators. Potential employees had to provide documentation, and employers had to verify their employees' citizenship. The new law also provided a means for giving legal status, or amnesty, to hundreds of thousands of illegal immigrants who had moved to the United States prior to January 1, 1982. It also provided for temporary status for agricultural workers who could satisfy specific residency requirements.[99]

DID WELFARE CHANGES DETER ILLEGAL IMMIGRATION?

The U.S. Congress passed major changes in welfare laws in 1996, cutting off most public assistance to both legal and illegal immigrants in the United States.

Critics of the previous welfare system had argued that the accessibility of public funds and services was a strong attraction to immigrants. They argued that American taxpayers had no obligation to support anyone who entered the country illegally or even legal immigrants who couldn't support themselves.

With some exceptions for medical emergencies, the 1996 welfare law barred illegal immigrants from receiving benefits provided by a federal agency or by federal funds, including welfare, retirement, health, disability, food assistance, or unemployment benefits. States are also prohibited from providing state or local benefits to illegal immigrants unless state officials pass specific laws making immigrants eligible for aid from state or local funds.

Although there are some exceptions for emergency medical care and education, most legal immigrants, even those already in the country when the law was changed, are now ineligible for federal supplemental security income and food stamps until they become citizens. Those who have come to the United States legally since the law was passed will be denied most federal welfare benefits for five years. States, however, can assist legal immigrants with benefits funded entirely by state or local funds. The law also places additional financial responsibilities on people who sponsor immigrants.

These welfare changes were designed to discourage persons who are unable to support themselves and perceive the possibility of easy access to public assistance from immigrating to the United States. But would these changes deter immigrants who come to the United States to escape desperate economic, political, or social conditions in their own countries? Several years have now passed, and there is considerable evidence that these welfare restrictions are not deterring immigration.

Major welfare programs in the United States are usually identified as Temporary Assistance to Needy Families (TANF), food stamps, Supplemental Security Income (SSI), and Medicaid. In the first few years after the enactment of the welfare changes, it appeared that there was a decrease in the use of services by legal and illegal immigrants. But by 2002, participation rates in welfare programs just about matched the figures for 1996. Native-born Americans use the welfare system much less than immigrants. There were reductions in the use of the TANF and food stamp programs by illegal immigrants, but they were offset by a dramatic increase in participation in Medicaid. The average support for low-income immigrant households in 2001 was approximately $2,000. For the illegal immigrant household, the figure was $1,000.

Source: Jeffrey L. Katz, "Welfare Overhaul Law," *Congressional Quarterly Weekly Report* 54 (September 21, 1996), pp. 2696–2705; Stephen A. Camarota, "Back Where We Started: An Examination of Trends in Immigrant Welfare Use Since Welfare Reform," Center for Immigration Studies, March 2003.

By 1996, it was clear that this law had not stemmed the tide of illegal immigration, because Mexicans were still drawn to the economic opportunities available in the United States. Throughout the Southwest, hundreds of thousands of illegal aliens are still being arrested and detained before being returned home, and the movement of Mexican workers into Texas and the rest of the United States remains a controversial political issue.

Children of illegal immigrants represent a heavy financial burden for many school districts and taxpayers along the border. Undocumented workers also increase demands on public health care programs. Some citizens, particularly unskilled workers, view the illegal arrivals as a threat to their jobs and standard of living.[100]

There is a widespread complaint in Texas that the state's citizens carry the burden for the failure of the federal government to develop policies to stem the illegal flow. In 1994, Texas joined several other states in filing lawsuits seeking reimbursement from the federal government for billions of dollars in state and local expenditures attributed to illegal immigration.

In 1995 and 1996, some members of the U.S. Congress attempted to enact comprehensive immigration reforms to restrict both legal and illegal immigration. A coalition of immigrant advocacy groups and business interests was able to block key provisions of the original proposal, and by the time the final measure was enacted in late 1996, its provisions were directed primarily against illegal immigrants. The new law authorized funds for improvements to a border fence in California and additional Immigration and Naturalization Service border guards and inspectors. The measure also increased the penalties for smuggling illegal immigrants and using fraudulent documents and made it easier to detain illegal immigrants or deport them after their arrival in the United States.[101]

One of the unspoken realities of illegal immigration in Texas is that there are many native Texans who have no desire to curtail the flow of people from the south. Within blocks of where one of the authors works, there are household domestics, nannies, and yardmen who are "illegals," and neighbors know their status. Numerous businesses throughout the state hire illegal immigrants for low-wage labor, despite the legal and financial risks. Good, law-abiding citizens have hired undocumented workers for temporary, contract jobs and never asked their status, as required by law. There are so many "illegals" in Texas that the responsible federal agencies simply cannot always enforce the law. As a source of cheap labor, the illegal immigrant is, in effect, subsidizing business interests and others throughout the state. The state funds that are spent for social services for the immigrants are also a subsidy.

SUMMARY AND CONCLUSIONS

1. Government and politics in Texas cannot be understood in a vacuum, but as part of the federal system. Federalism is a complex structure of overlapping authority and shared responsibilities among different levels of government. These relationships have changed over the country's history through policy initiatives by Congress, the president, the federal courts, and state and local governments.

2. Many have argued that the federal government has encroached on the powers of the state and local governments through mandates and preemptions.

3. State and local governments aggressively lobby the national government to address their needs and interests. Members of Congress, who have close relationships with the communities within their districts and states, make continuous efforts to obtain funding for local projects or changes in federal policies or regulations that adversely affect community interests. Cooperative federalism best describes most of these relationships.

4. The expanded debate over devolution, or the return of powers to the states, was manifested in legislative initiatives after Republicans gained

control of Congress in 1994. It also was prominent in several U.S. Supreme Court cases, suggesting a disposition of the court to limit the powers of the national government.

5. In addition to the relationships between states and the federal government (vertical federalism), the U.S. Constitution defines the obligations that states have to each other (horizontal federalism). Issues and problems facing states do not stop at their borders, and states have joined numerous cooperative efforts, including interstate compacts, uniform laws, and collaboration on shared problems.

6. The politics and economy of Texas are now inextricably linked to Mexico, and the adoption of the North American Free Trade Agreement in 1993 confirmed the complex interrelationships we have defined as transnational regionalism.

7. The stability of the Mexican government and its ability to promote economic development have direct consequences for Texas and the United States. Trade between the United States and Mexico has expanded dramatically since the mid-1980s.

8. The massive movement of people and merchandise across the border is redefining a whole range of social, economic, and political relationships as well as American attitudes toward Mexico.

9. The increased economic integration is also having an impact on such concerns as immigration, infrastructure requirements, air and water pollution, and health care.

10. While many people expect the North American Free Trade Agreement to produce tremendous benefits, the success of this collaborative effort will depend directly on the policy initiatives of governments on both sides of the U.S.-Mexican border and the abilities of the economies of both countries to expand and meet the needs and expectations of their citizens.

KEY TERMS

Unitary system	Full faith and credit	New federalism
Confederation	Privileges and immunities	Block grants
Federalism	Extradition	Revenue sharing
Devolution	Interstate compacts	Mandates
Delegated powers	Cooperative federalism	Preemptions
Implied powers	Categorical grants-in-aid	Transnational regionalism
Supremacy clause	Project grant	Maquiladora program
Reserved powers	Formula grant	North American Free Trade
Denied powers	Matching funds	Agreement (NAFTA)

FURTHER READINGS

Articles

Center for the Study of Federalism, *Publius*. This journal is an excellent source of information on a wide variety of topics centered on federalism and federal relationships.

Cole, Richard L., Rodney V. Hissong, and Enid Arvidson, "Devolution: Where's the Revolution?" *Publius* 29 (Fall 1999), pp. 99–112.

Hanson, Russell L., "Intergovernmental Relations," in *Politics in the American States: A Comparative Analysis,*

6th ed., eds. Virginia Gray and Herbert Jacob. Washington, DC: CQ Press, 1996, pp. 35–77.

Posner, Paul L., "Unfunded Mandates Reform Act: 1996 and Beyond," *Publius* 27 (Spring 1997), pp. 53–71.

Krane, Dale A., "The State of American Federalism, 2001–2002," *Publius* 32 (Fall 2002), pp. 1–28.

Books

Dye, Thomas R., *Politics in States and Communities*, 11th ed. Upper Saddle River, NJ: Prentice Hall, 2003.

Graves, W. Brooke, *American Intergovernmental Relations: Their Development and Current Status.* New York: Charles Scribner's Sons, 1964.

Grodzins, Morton, *The American System,* ed. Daniel J. Elazar. Chicago: Rand McNally & Company, 1966.

Hanson, Russell L., ed., *Governing Partners: State-Local Relations in the United States.* Boulder, CO: Westview Press, 1998.

Henig, Jeffrey R., *Public Policy and Federalism.* New York: St. Martin's Press, 1985.

Langley, Lester D., *MexAmerican: Two Countries, One Future.* New York: Crown Publishers, 1988.

Martin, Roscoe C., *The Cities and the Federal System.* New York: Atherton Press, 1965.

Martinez, Oscar J., *Troublesome Border.* Tucson: University of Arizona Press, 1988.

Metz, Leon C., *Border: The U.S.-Mexico Line.* El Paso, TX: Mangan Books, 1989.

Weintraub, Sidney, *A Marriage of Convenience: Relations between Mexico and the United States.* New York: Oxford University Press, 1990.

Wright, Deil S., *Understanding Intergovernmental Relations,* 2nd ed. Monterey, CA: Brooks/Cole Publishing Company, 1982.

Websites

Council of State Governments   http://www.csg.org This site provides links to other organizations of state officials as well as information on policies affecting states, publications, suggested legislation, and state information centers.

Nelson A. Rockefeller Institute of Government http://www.rockinst.org   This institute is located at the State University of New York and is actively involved nationally in research and special projects on the role of state governments in American federalism. In addition to providing a link to other public policy websites, this site references numerous studies related to federalism.

Urban Institute   http://www.urban.org   The Urban Institute focuses on a range of social policies. It has developed a multiyear research project entitled "Assessing the New Federalism."

Federal Web Locator   http://www.infoctr.edu/fwl/ This site provides the Federal Web Locator, which accesses a wide range of federal agencies whose activities directly impact state and local governments.

ENDNOTES

1. Woodrow Wilson, *Constitutional Government in the United States* (New York: Columbia University Press, 1921), p. 173.
2. David C. Nice, "The Intergovernmental Setting of State-Local Relations," in *Governing Partners: State-Local Relations in the United States,* ed. Russell L. Hanson (Boulder, CO.: Westview Press, 1998), p. 17.
3. For a discussion of the Dillon Rule, see Anwar Syed, *The Political Theory of American Local Government* (New York: Random House, 1966), Chap. 3.
4. Thomas J. Anton, *American Federalism and Public Policy* (New York: Random House, 1989), p. 3.
5. See William H. Stewart, "Metaphors, Models, and the Development of Federal Theory," *Publius* 12 (Winter 1982), pp. 5–24; and William H. Stewart, *Concepts of Federalism* (Lanham, MD: Center for the Study of Federalism and University Press of America, 1984).
6. Anton, *American Federalism and Public Policy,* p. 19.
7. U.S. Constitution, Article I, Section 8, Paragraph 18.
8. U.S. Constitution, Article VI.
9. U.S. Constitution, Amendment X.
10. For an excellent summary of the guarantees to and limitations on state governments defined by the U.S. Constitution, see Thomas Dye, *American Federalism* (Lexington, KY: D. C. Heath and Company, 1990), pp. 9–11.
11. U.S. Constitution, Article IV, Section 1.
12. *Commonwealth of Kentucky v. Denison, Governor,* 65 U.S. (24 How.) 66 (1861).
13. *Puerto Rico v. Branstad,* 483 U.S. 219 (1987).
14. Kenyon Bunch and Richard J. Hardy, "Continuity or Change in Interstate Extradition? Assessing *Puerto Rico v. Branstad,*" *Publius* 21 (Winter 1991), p. 59.
15. U.S. Constitution, Article III, Section 2.
16. Morton Grodzins and Daniel Elazar, "Centralization and Decentralization in the American Federal System," in *A Nation of States,* 2nd ed., ed. Robert A. Goldwin (Chicago: Rand McNally College Publishing Company, 1974), p. 4.
17. Deil S. Wright, *Understanding Intergovernmental Relations,* 2nd ed. (Monterey, CA: Brooks/Cole Publishing Company, 1982), pp. 60–68.
18. Ibid., p. 46.
19. *McCulloch v. Maryland,* 4 Wheaton 316 (1819).
20. Thomas R. Dye, *Politics in States and Communities,* 8th ed. (Englewood Cliffs, NJ: Prentice Hall, 1994), p. 67.
21. Timothy Conlan, with an introduction by Samuel H. Beer, *New Federalism* (Washington, DC: The Brookings Institution, 1988), p. 5.
22. V. O. Key, *The Responsible Electorate* (Cambridge, MA: Harvard University Press, 1966), p. 31.
23. Daniel J. Elazar, *American Federalism: A View from the States,* 2nd ed. (New York: Harper & Row Publishers, 1972), p. 47.

24. Conlan, New Federalism, p. 6.
25. Dye, *Politics in States and Communities,* p. 83.
26. Conlan, *New Federalism,* p. 3.
27. Ibid., pp. 3, 19–30, 77–81.
28. Ibid., p. 90.
29. Richard P. Nathan, Thomas L. Gais, and James W. Fossett, "Bush Federalism: Is There One, What is It, and How Does It Differ?" Paper presented at the Annual Research Conference Association for Public Policy Analysis and Management, Nov. 7, 2003, Washington, DC, p. 5.
30. Ibid., p.6.
31. Joseph F. Zimmerman, "Federal Preemption Under Reagan's New Federalism," *Publius* 21 (Winter 1991), p. 11.
32. Michael A. Pagano, Ann O'M. Bowman, and John Kincaid, "The State of American Federalism, 1990–1991," *Publius* 21 (Summer 1991), p. 1.
33. Zimmerman, "Federal Preemption Under Reagan's New Federalism," p. 26.
34. Robert B. Hawkins, "Pre-Emption: The Dramatic Rise of Federal Supremacy," *The Journal of State Government* 63 (January–March 1990), p. 10.
35. Zimmerman, "Federal Preemption Under Reagan's New Federalism," p. 26.
36. Ibid., p. 27.
37. Timothy J. Conlan, "And the Beat Goes On: Intergovernmental Mandates and Preemption in an Era of Deregulation," *Publius* 21 (Summer 1991), p. 52.
38. Joseph F. Zimmerman, "Preemption in the U.S. Federal System," *Publius* 23 (Fall 1993), p. 9.
39. Timothy J. Conlan and David R. Beam, "Federal Mandates: The Record of Reform and Future Prospects," *Intergovernmental Perspective* 18 (Fall 1992), p. 9.
40. State of Texas, Legislative Budget Board, *Analysis of Federal Initiatives and State Expenditures,* June 15, 1994.
41. Pagano, et al., "The State of American Federalism, 1990–1991," p. 1.
42. Conlan, "And the Beat Goes On: Intergovernmental Mandates and Preemption in an Era of Deregulation," pp. 44–46.
43. Paul L. Posner, "Unfunded Mandates Reform Act: 1996 and Beyond," *Publius* 27 (Spring, 1997), p. 53.
44. Carol S. Weissert and Sanford F. Schram, "The State of American Federalism, 1995–1996," *Publius* 26 (Summer 1996), p. 6.
45. Sanford F. Schram and Carol S. Weissert, "The State of American Federalism, 1996–1997," *Publius* 27 (Spring, 1997), pp. 5–8.
46. Alan K. Ota, "Highway Law Benefits Those Who Held Purse Strings," *Congressional Quarterly Weekly* 56 (June 13, 1998), pp. 1595–1596.
47. Schram and Weissert, "The State of American Federalism, 1996–1997," p. 8.
48. Weissert and Schram, "The State of American Federalism, 1995–1996," p. 14.
49. Schram and Weissert, "The State of American Federalism, 1996–1997," p 1.
50. John Kincaid, "The Devolution Tortoise and the Centralization Hare," *New England Economic Review* (May, June 1998), pp. 36, 38.
51. Richard L. Cole, Rodney V. Hissong, and Enid Arvidson, "Devolution: Where's the Revolution?" *Publius* 29 (Fall 1999), pp. 99–112.
52. John Kincaid, "Trends in Federalism: Is Fiscal Federalism Fizzling?" *The Book of the States 2003,* vol. 35 (Lexington, KY: The Council of State Governments, 2003), p. 27.
53. Deil S. Wright, "Federalism and Intergovernmental Relations: Traumas, Tensions and Trends, *The Book of the States, 2003* (Lexington, KY: The Council of State Governments, 2003), p. 22.
54. Daniel Henniger, "Homeland Security Will Reshape the Homeland," *Wall Street Journal,* November 22, 2002, p. 16.
55. *Austin American-Statesman,* September 26, 2003, p. B1.
56. Wright, p. 23.
57. *Garcia* v. *San Antonio Metropolitan Transit Authority,* 105 S. Ct. 1005.
58. Anton, *American Federalism and Public Policy,* pp. 14–16.
59. Dye, *American Federalism,* pp. 8–12.
60. *U.S. v. Lopez,* 115 S. Ct. 1624 (1995); Schram and Weissert, "The State of American Federalism, 1996–1997," p. 10
61. *Bush v. Vera,* 135 L. Ed. 2d 248 (1996); *Easley v. Cromartie,* 532 U.S. 284 (2001); *New York Times,* April 19, 2001, p. 1.
62. Weissert and Schram, "The State of American Federalism, 1995–1996," p. 12; *Metronic, Inc. v. Lohr et vir.,* 135 L.ED. 2d 700 (1996).
63. City of Boerne, *Texas v. Flores,* 117 S.Ct. 2157 (1997).
64. Schram and Weissert, "The State of American Federalism, 1996–1997," p. 26.
65. *Printz v. U.S.,* 117 S.Ct. 2365 (1997).
66. Weissert and Schram, "The State of American Federalism, 1995–1996," p. 13.
67. Ibid., p. 10; *Roemer et al. v. Evans, et al.,* 1996 U.S. LEXIS 3245, 64 U.S. LW (4353); *U.S. v. Virginia et al.,* 135 L Ed 2d 735 (1996).
68. Ibid.; *Seminole Tribe v. Florida,* 1996 U.S. LEXIS 2165.
69. Sanford F. Schram and Carol S. Weissert, "The State of U.S. Federalism: 1998–1999," *Publius* 29 (Spring 1999), p. 34.
70. Tax Foundation, "Federal Tax Burdens and Expenditures by State," No. 124, July 2003.
71. See Texas Comptroller of Public Accounts, *Dollars We Deserve* (Austin: Texas Comptroller of Public Accounts, 1990).
72. Legislative Budget Board, *Fiscal Size Up, 2002–2003* (Austin: Legislative Budget Board, 2000), Table 17.
73. Telephone interview with Tara Russell, Office of State-Federal Relations, Austin, Texas, November 22, 1991.
74. Hawkins, "Pre-emption: The Dramatic Rise of Federal Supremacy," p. 12.

75. M. Delal Baer, "North American Free Trade," *Foreign Affairs* 70 (Fall 1991), p. 138.

76. Joan B. Anderson, "Maquiladoras and Border Industrialization: Impact on Economic Development in Mexico," *Journal of Borderland Studies*, V (Spring 1990), p. 5.

77. Michael Patrick, "Maquiladoras and South Texas Border Economic Development," *Journal of Borderland Studies*, IV (Spring, 1989), p. 90.

78. Martin E. Rosenfeldt, "Mexico's In Bond Export Industries and U.S. Legislation: Conflictive Issues," *Journal of Borderland Studies*, V (Spring 1990), p. 57.

79. Patrick, "Maquiladoras and South Texas Border Economic Development," p. 90.

80. Baer, "North American Free Trade," pp. 132–49.

81. Central Intelligence Agency, *The World Factbook* (Washington, DC: CIA, 1997).

82. Chandler Stolp and Jon Hockenyos, "Free Trade Over Texas," *San Antonio Light,* September 15, 1991, p. E–1.

83. Augustin Redwine, "A Bureaucracy Is Born: International Departments Being Organized to Oversee NAFTA," *Fiscal Notes* (April 1994), p. 12.

84. Border Environmental Cooperation Commission, Operations Department, "Certified Projects Report," October 2003.

85. Commission for Labor Cooperation. Internet site—www.NAALC.org—April 2003.

86. Redwine, "A Bureaucracy is Born: International Departments Being Organized to Oversee NAFTA," *Fiscal Notes* (April 1994), p. 12.

87. North American Development Bank, press release, Oct. 29, 2003.

88. Robert S. Chose, Emily B. Hill, and Paul Kennedy, "Pivotal States and U.S. Strategy," *Foreign Affairs* 75 (January/February 1996), p. 39.

89. David Hendricks, "Security Change Will Discriminate Against Mexico, South Texas," *San Antonio Express-News,* October 25, 2003, D1.

90. Joan Anderson and Martin de la Rosa, "Economic Survival Strategies of Poor Families on the Mexican Border," *Journal of Borderland Studies* VI (Spring 1991), p. 51.

91. Howard G. Applegate, C. Richard Bath, and Jeffery T. Trannon, "Binational Emissions Trading in an International Air Shed: The Case of El Paso, Texas and Ciudad Juarez," *Journal of Borderland Studies* IV (Fall 1989), pp. 1–25.

92. *San Antonio Express-News,* January 26, 1996, p. A-9.

93. *San Antonio Express-News,* February 18, 1991, p. A-1.

94. United States-Mexico Border Governors Conference, Phoenix, Arizona, June 2002.

95. Stephen A. Camarota, "Back Where We Started: An Examination of Trends in Immigrant Welfare Use Since Reform," Center for Immigration Studies, March 2003, p. 5 for 2002 figure.

96. Migration Policy Institute, "Immigration Facts," 2003; Immigration and Naturalization Service.

97. James F. Pearce and Jeffery W. Gunther, "Illegal Immigration from Mexico: Effects on the Texas Economy," *Federal Reserve Bank of Dallas Economic Review* (September 1985), p. 4.

98. Robert W. Gardner and Leon F. Bouvier, "The United States," in *Handbook on International Migration,* eds. William J. Serow, Charles B. Nam, David F. Sly, and Robert H. Weller (New York: Greenwood Press, 1990), p. 342.

99. "Congress Clears Overhaul of Immigration Law," *Congressional Quarterly Almanac, 1986* (Washington, DC: Congressional Quarterly, 1987), pp. 61–67.

100. Pearce and Gunther, "Illegal Immigration from Mexico: Effects on the Texas Economy," p. 2.

101. Dan Carney, "Law Restricts Illegal Immigration," *Congressional Quarterly Weekly Report* 54 (November 16, 1996), p. 3287.

4

Interest Groups and Political Power in Texas

> The Citizens shall have the right, in a peaceable manner, to assemble for their common Good, and apply to those invested with the powers of government for redress of grievances or other purposes by petition, address or remonstrance.
>
> *Texas Constitution, Article 1, Section 27*

> In America there is no limit to freedom of association for political ends.
>
> *Alexis de Tocqueville*[1]

The business community, through endorsements and political contributions, was influential in Republicans capturing a majority of Texas House of Representative seats in 2002, giving the GOP control of that body for the first time since Reconstruction and leading to the election of the first Republican House speaker of modern times. The Texas Association of Business, or TAB, an umbrella group representing many businesses, was one of the most visible backers of Republican candidates who supported business priorities, including more restrictions on civil lawsuits, fewer governmental regulations and holding the line on state taxes. In pursuit of its policy agenda, TAB took the unusual—and controversial—step of spending $2 million in corporate contributions on political advertising in twenty-four legislative races. Most of the candidates supported by TAB won, but the tactic prompted a criminal investigation of the business group and precipitated a debate over free speech versus undue corporate influence over elections.

State law allows officers and employees of corporations to make personal contributions to political candidates or to contribute through political action committees established for that purpose. But it is illegal for corporate funds to be given directly to a candidate, and soon after the election, Travis County District Attorney Ronnie Earle began investigating the Texas Association of Business' contributions. TAB argued that the corporate donations were legal because they weren't given directly to candidates but were used to purchase advertising that educated voters on issues important to the group. The ads didn't directly advocate the election or defeat of any candidates, although they obviously influenced election results.

Almost a year after it had begun, the criminal investigation was still incomplete, because TAB fought it with a series of legal maneuvers, arguing that the ads amounted to constitutionally protected free speech. National business groups also rallied to TAB's defense, claiming that Earle, a Democrat, was letting politics influence his investigation. But Earle argued that he was merely investigating "allegations of crime."[2]

The Texas Association of Business' ad campaign was one of the more visible examples of lobby influence in Austin in recent years. The objectives of the association were clear and unambiguous—defeat Democratic candidates who were deemed hostile to the members' interests. But much of the influence of interest groups and their lobbyists is subtle, elusive to public scrutiny, and reflects complex relationships among interest groups, elected public officials, and those who administer the law.

To many Texans, lobbying is an unsavory business that puts the interests of the few ahead of the general welfare or needs of the state. Sensing this underlying disdain or contempt, political candidates often claim to be running against "the special interests" and promise to be responsive to all the people rather than to a few well-financed business, trade, or union groups. But most successful candidates freely accept campaign contributions from interest groups, and many Texans, along with Americans nationwide, feel that governments are dominated by a few big interests looking out for themselves. National election surveys conducted by the University of Michigan for more than thirty years indicate a clear pattern of increased public distrust of government. In 1964, 28 percent of those surveyed felt that government was run by a few big interests, but during most of the years since 1974, more than 60 percent of Americans expressed this sentiment.[3]

Two other studies, conducted more than thirty years apart, placed Texas among states with strong pressure-group systems.[4] Powerful pressure groups usually evolve in states with weak political parties, which characterized Texas during most of this century.[5] During the many years that Texas was a one-party state, the Republican party posed no serious challenge to the Democratic monopoly, and the Democratic party was marked by intense factionalism. Although the conservative Democratic wing generally dominated state politics through the 1970s, interest groups often played a greater role in the policymaking process. Subsequent Republican growth has changed Texas's party system (see Chapter 6), but interest groups remain strong in the state and spend millions of dollars trying to elect favored candidates or influence governmental decisions. More often than not, these interest groups still have a greater impact on the policy than do the political parties.

Lobbyists' footprints can be found throughout the legislative process. In 1991, for example, then-Lieutenant Governor Bob Bullock, through a coordinated strategy, enlisted the support of business lobbyists to sell the legislature on a tax increase to help close a budgetary shortfall. Bullock made not-so-subtle suggestions that failure to assist mobilizing support would have consequences for those groups that did not support his legislative maneuverings. But lobbyists in 1997 helped defeat a tax overhaul sought by then-Governor George W. Bush. Bush had asked the legislature

Lobbyists and visitors, who are denied access to the floor of the senate while it is in session, are seen mingling outside the chamber during a tax debate.

to enact higher state taxes as a partial tradeoff for lowering local school property taxes. But the proposed swap failed after the Senate refused to join the House in passing a large tax bill. One reason the Senate balked was because, unlike 1991, the legislature in 1997 didn't face a budgetary crunch that required higher state taxes.

INTEREST GROUPS DEFINED

Theorists have spent considerable effort distinguishing interest groups from other social organizations, and while differences in definition remain, an interest group may be defined as "an organized collection of individuals who are bound together by shared attitudes or concerns and who make demands on political institutions in order to realize goals which they are unable to achieve on their own."[6] Members of an interest group share common interests or goals, organize to pursue those goals collectively because they cannot achieve them individually, and focus some of their efforts on influencing governmental decisions.[7] These characteristics, particularly the political and policy objectives of the interest group, distinguish these groups from other organizations.

We do not know exactly how many groups or organizations there are in the United States or even in Texas. Nationally, the *Encyclopedia of Associations* has identified approximately 23,000 national, nonprofit organizations. Comparing these totals with earlier estimates, it is clear that there has been an "explosion" of group activity over the past thirty years.[8] Across the country at the state and local level, it has been estimated that there are 200,000 different groups or organizations.[9] We have no comprehensive directory of groups or organizations in Texas, but a casual review of the list of associations and organizations in metropolitan phone books leads to the conclusion that there are thousands. Some have long histories, while others are formed to address a specific need, interest, or problem and disappear after a relatively short period. While most organizations have the potential to participate in the policymaking process, many will not. In our attempt to define the pressure-group system in Texas, we place considerable emphasis on those groups that can be identified as continuous active players.

Most organizations are not formed for political purposes. One scholar has suggested that only 10 percent of the people participate in organizations active in the pressure group system.[10] People usually don't join a chess club or a fraternal order, for example, to have an impact on public policy. Participation in church-related activities is usually based on spiritual or personal needs, although church groups can become involved in the political process (see Chapter 6).

We also should distinguish between categorical groups and interest or pressure groups. Women collectively constitute a categorical grouping of the female population; and senior citizens, African Americans, and Hispanics also comprise categorical groups. While these are often spoken of as groups of people with similar political objectives, individuals within each group hold a wide diversity of interests, concerns, and goals. By contrast, an interest group is a segment of the population that organizes for specific purposes and objectives in the policymaking process. The San Antonio Chapter of the National Association of Hispanic Nurses is an interest group representing a segment of the nurses in Bexar County.

Group Membership

It has been estimated that 75 percent of Americans belong to some type of organization. Church membership is clearly the single largest category, with approximately 42 percent of the total population listing church affiliation. Americans also join a wide array of civic, sports, service, fraternal, hobby, economic, and professional groups and organizations. Close to 50 percent of the country's population reported membership in two or more groups.[11]

At first glance, it would appear that the overwhelming majority of Americans have potential access to the policymaking process by way of their group memberships. Closer inspection, however, raises serious questions as to the distribution of political power and resources in this country and Texas. The argument that the policy playing field is tilted to benefit some groups or interests to the exclusion of others has some validity.[12] And, if parts of the population have limited potential to affect the decisions of government, this raises serious questions about the very nature of a democratic society and the role of groups within this political structure.

Those who study organizations generally agree that persons with higher incomes, better educations, higher status occupations, and higher standards of living are more likely than other people to belong to groups.[13] Historically, men have joined at a higher rate than have women; older people join at higher rates than do younger people; Anglos are more likely to be members than are Hispanics or African Americans; and people with established community ties are more likely to participate. Not only do these people join more groups, but they also are more likely to be active participants. These findings suggest that there is a class bias in the interest group system in Texas. People from higher socioeconomic classes are more easily organized and are more likely to maintain their support for these organizations.[14] Lower socioeconomic groups, minorities, and diffused constituencies, such as consumers, find it very difficult to compete on an equal footing with business, industrial, and professional groups, who also can better afford lobbying expenses and the financial contributions to political campaigns that usually guarantee access to officeholders.

Why People Join Interest Groups

Individuals join groups for a variety of reasons, which may change over time. One is the number of personal and material benefits that can be derived from interest groups.[15] A teacher, for example, may join the Texas State Teachers Association because it lobbies for higher teacher salaries, better fringe benefits and working conditions, and general educational issues. But TSTA also offers its members publications, insurance programs, potential legal assistance, discounts for travel, and valuable professional information.

People also realize social benefits from joining groups. Membership and participation provide them with a sense of personal identification with larger organizations and institutions that are likely to be more visible and potentially effective in the policymaking process than an individual would be if acting alone.[16] They may believe their personal status and prestige also are enhanced by group membership.[17]

Finally, there is the personal satisfaction or sense of purpose that a person receives from belonging to a group that he or she believes has a worthwhile cause or objective. There are people who join groups to try to make the world a better place.[18] One motivation for joining such groups as Common Cause or the League of Women Voters, for example, may be a commitment to improving the election system in Texas. For many people, reform of the election system provides broad, but intangible, benefits that go well beyond the group or organization.

INTEREST GROUPS, PLURALISM, AND DEMOCRATIC THEORY

The issue of **interest groups** and political power in American politics has been debated since the Constitutional Convention of 1787. Writing in the *Federalist Papers* at a time when there were no political parties or interest groups as we know today, James Madison argued that it was inevitable that people would organize into groups, or "factions," and attempt to impose their will on others and use governments for their specific purposes. Madison also recognized two basic problems: there was a potential for the majority to tyrannize or impose its will on others, and a potential for the majority, in its pursuit of narrow self-interests, to harm the long-term interests of society as a whole.[19]

The cure for this **mischief of factions** was both institutional and socioeconomic. If the number of factions or groups increased, there would be greater competition and less likelihood that any one group could dominate the policymaking process. Competitors would have to find compromises. And, institutional power would be fragmented among three branches of government and a federal system, where powers would be further divided between the national government and the states. Elections for different offices are staggered in different years, and there are significant variations in electoral constituencies. The effect of the variations in national, state, and local election systems is to make it even more difficult to construct large, permanent coalitions that could exercise absolute control over all institutions and subsequently dominate all policies.

Drawing in part on this tradition established by Madison, David Truman, an American political scientist, argued in his classic study, *The Governmental Process,* that American politics can be understood primarily in terms of the way groups interact with each other.[20] Expanding on Truman's theories, other scholars have attempted to develop a general understanding of politics organized around groups. These scholars often are referred to as pluralists and their theories as **pluralism.** They believe that significant numbers of diverse and competing interest groups share political influence in a way that limits the power of any single group.

While there are differences in emphasis among the pluralists, they have established the following general characteristics of a pluralistic society:

- Groups are the primary actors in the policymaking process. They provide the individual with political resources and link a person to governmental institutions.
- Politics is basically group interaction, where groups come into conflict with each other over the limited resources of society, and public policy is ultimately the resolution of group conflict and differences.
- There are so many groups that no one group can dominate the political process. While some groups have more resources than others, a group always has the potential to influence policy. If there is no group to address a particular concern or problem, one can be organized.
- While most people do not actively participate in the policymaking process, they have access to the process through the leaders of the groups to which they belong. There are numerous leadership opportunities within groups for individuals who want active roles.
- Most group leaders are committed to democratic values, and competition makes them responsive to other members and serves to check or constrain their actions.[21]

Pluralism is appealing because it gives credence to our general views of a democratic society and offers potential solutions, or at least hope, for those people who are excluded from full political participation or benefits.

One can find evidence in Texas to support the pluralist view. There are thousands of different groups organized on a statewide or community level. Hundreds of lobbyists are registered in Austin to represent a wide variety of economic, social, civic, and cultural organizations. A growing state population and a diversifying economy have significantly increased the number of interest groups over the past three decades.

David Truman has suggested that there are periods, or "waves," in American political history in which there are rapid proliferations of groups in response to economic, social, or political change.[22] To compensate for imbalances in the political system, additional groups will be organized and attempt to reestablish an equilibrium.

Groups can be formed for any number of reasons. Concerns over economic changes, public school funding, environmental protection, medical care for low-income Texans, and other pressing issues have generated additional interest groups in Texas in recent years. So have movements focusing on the interests of Hispanics, African Americans, women, and homosexuals. Still other organizations have emerged to protect existing interests, or the status quo, and some groups have been formed in response to new governmental policies and regulations.[23]

With the elimination of historic discriminatory practices, minority Texans have made significant economic, social, and political gains. In addition to having increased access to mainstream groups, minorities have formed their own professional and economic organizations. It is not uncommon to find Hispanic chambers of commerce or African-American bar associations in many Texas cities.

Advocates of pluralism use the foregoing arguments and examples to support their view. Despite the earlier periods in Texas history, when large segments of the population were excluded from the political and policymaking processes, they argue that the political system is now open and accessible to new groups. They believe that those holding public office are responsive to the needs and interests of a greater diversity of Texans than ever before.

THE ELITIST ALTERNATIVE

Other political scientists, however, insist that the pluralist theories simply do not describe the realities of power and policymaking in Texas or the United States. They say the pluralists have not given enough attention to the fact that a few individuals still control enormous resources. Although there are thousands of groups, they are not equal in political resources nor can they equally translate their interests or demands into public policy. These scholars believe the political system in Texas can be more accurately described in terms of **elitism.**

According to this view, the ability to influence the most important policy decisions is monopolized by a few individuals who derive power from their leadership positions in large organizations or institutions, particularly those with great financial resources. From the elitist perspective, power is not an individual commodity or resource but an attribute of social organizations.[24]

People who subscribe to this theory also believe that the existence of elites within any society is inevitable. Robert Michels, a European social scientist writing during the first part of the twentieth century, argued that any organization, no matter how structured, will eventually produce an "oligarchy," or rule by a few individuals. Michels' **iron rule of oligarchy** was applicable to any organization and was a universal law applied to all social systems.[25]

Beginning with C. Wright Mills in his book, *The Power Elite,* many American scholars have been proponents of the elitist theory.[26] Although there has been rigorous intellectual debate between elitist and pluralist theorists, a number of generalizations can be derived from the elitist school of thought:

- Power is held by a few individuals and is derived from their positions in large institutions. In addition to economic institutions, these include the government, the mass media, and civic organizations.
- Historically, political elites constituted a homogeneous group drawn primarily from the upper and upper-middle classes. They were older, well-educated, primarily white, Anglo-Saxon males.

- While there is competition among elites and the institutions they represent, there is considerable consensus and cohesion among elites on primary values, interests, and the rules of the game.
- Elites are linked by a complex network of interlocking memberships on the governing bodies of corporations, financial institutions, foundations, and civic and cultural organizations.
- Policy decisions are made by a few individuals and primarily reflect the interests of the dominant institutions. The interests of the dominant elites are not necessarily opposed to those of other classes of society.
- The vast majority of people are passive spectators to the policymaking process. Voting has been the primary means by which the masses can participate in governmental decisions, but other than selecting governmental officials, elections have limited effects on policy decisions.[27]

A number of students of Texas government and politics have argued from the elitist perspective. George Norris Green, writing about the period from 1938 to 1957, concluded that Texas was "governed by conservatives, collectively dubbed **the Establishment.**"[28] This was a "loosely knit plutocracy comprised mostly of Anglo businessmen, oilmen, bankers and lawyers" that emerged in the late 1930s, in part as a response to the liberal policies of the New Deal.[29] They were extremely conservative, producing a "virulent" strain of conservatism marked by "Texanism" and "super-Americanism."[30]

The "traditionalistic-individualistic" political culture described in Chapter 1 was especially conducive to the dominance of the conservative establishment, which had little interest in the needs of the lower socioeconomic groups within the state. The exclusion of minorities from participation in elections and the low rates of voter turnout resulted in the election of public officials who were sympathetic to the views of the conservative elites. In addition, public opinion was manipulated by "unprincipled public relations men" and "the rise of reactionary newspapers."[31]

In a more recent study of Texas politics, Chandler Davidson argues that there is a group of Texans, extraordinarily wealthy or linked to large corporations, who constitute "an upper class in the precise meaning of the term: a social group whose common background and effective control of wealth bring them together politically."[32] While warning against a hasty conclusion that an upper class is a ruling class, Davidson describes their shared values, group cohesiveness, and interlocking relationships.[33] The upper class has enormous political power. When united on specific policy objectives, its members usually have prevailed against "their liberal enemies concentrated in the working class."[34] Moreover, the institutional arrangements of the state's economic and political structure work to produce an upper-class unity that contributes to their successes in public policy.[35]

The sharply contrasting views of political power in Texas have produced an ongoing debate. To a large extent, the issue of who controls Texas politics has not been resolved because of insufficient data to support one position over the other. There also is evidence suggesting that power relationships have changed over time. Historically, Texas government and public policy were dominated by an upper class or a conservative establishment. But with the enormous social, economic, and political changes that have taken place over the past twenty years, Texans may well be moving from an elitist system to some variation of pluralism.

HYPERPLURALISM, POLICY SUBSYSTEMS, AND SINGLE-ISSUE INTEREST GROUPS

Some scholars believe that the rapid expansion of interest groups in Texas and the nation has produced a system of **hyperpluralism.** In effect, hyperpluralism is the interest group system out of control.[36] Historically, political stability was achieved by competition and bargaining among interest groups. Public policy that had some degree of coherence and reflected shared views of the general interest was developed.

But, as groups proliferate, there is a potential for the policy process to degenerate into a series of subsystems. This problem has been compounded by the notion that the demands of all interest groups are legitimate and governments should attempt to respond to as many groups as possible. This theory of interest group liberalism is developed at length by Theodore Lowi in *The End of Liberalism.*[37]

Governments respond to the demands of various groups by enacting laws and regulations or appropriating funds to address their priorities. In many cases, additional governmental agencies may be created to carry out the new laws. Legislative committees also may be given control over new programs. Eventually, the interactions among the interest groups, the administrative agencies, and the legislative committees produce permanent relationships that have been described as the **iron triangles** of government (see Chapter 13).

Lowi's concerns about the excesses of pluralism may be valid. Some state agencies are closely tied to the industries they regulate. Sometimes, interest groups even lobby for dedicated sources of funding for their programs, thus assuring they will benefit from specific taxes year after year, regardless of other state needs.

Hyperpluralism can also lead to deadlock. As each group expands its demands on government, some interests or groups may be neglected. Also, established groups with significant financial and organizational resources can block changes in public policies that would adversely affect them. This can serve to almost immobilize government and maintain the status quo, despite pressing needs for change.

In recent years, a number of scholars have identified another threat to the stability of the political system—the **single-issue groups.** These are highly ideological groups that attempt to push on the public agenda a single issue or cause without regard for the views or attitudes of other groups. These groups often are reluctant to compromise and often engage in tactics and strategies designed to extract concessions upon threat of policy deadlock. The National Rifle Association, for example, is single-minded in its opposition to any efforts to regulate or control firearms. Some of the groups involved in the abortion issue also demonstrate similar characteristics. Their definition of an issue leaves no grounds for accommodation or compromise.

RESOURCES OF INTEREST GROUPS

Some interest groups are extremely powerful and exercise considerable influence over the formation of public policy, while others are ineffectual and weak. The differences can be explained by a number of factors.

One is the size of a group, the number of members and voters it can potentially influence. There are numerous teachers' and educational groups within the state, for example, representing a significant number of people. The promise of support or the threat of retaliation by such groups will be assessed by a legislator as he or she decides to support or oppose the groups' policy proposals. As will be discussed later in this chapter, individual educational groups don't always agree on legislation, but their numbers are difficult to ignore. Teachers who had been instrumental in the 1982 election of Governor Mark White withdrew that support in 1986 in a dispute over some of White's education reforms; the loss of that support contributed to his defeat.

The size of a group alone, however, does not guarantee power or influence. A large group internally divided, with no clear policy focus, is less likely to be successful than a smaller group with a fixed goal. Other major factors in a group's success are its cohesiveness and the ability of its leaders to mobilize its membership in support of policy objectives.

Another key factor is the distribution of a group's membership across the state. A group concentrated in one geographic area has less potential impact on the election of a large number of legislators than does a group with members distributed across the state. Organized labor, for example, has its greatest membership strength in the Houston and Beaumont areas in Southeast Texas. On the other hand, teachers and small business owners are plentiful throughout the state and have the potential to affect more local and district elections.

A group's power is also determined by its financial resources. Groups that represent low-income people have difficulty raising the dollars necessary to mount effective lobbying or public relations campaigns. By contrast, organizations representing large corporations or high-income professional groups are in a much better position to raise funds for the campaign contributions and lobbying expenditures necessary to assure access to policymakers.

A group's influence is also affected by its reputation. A major function of interest groups is to provide information to policymakers, and the reliability and accuracy of this information are critical. If a group lies, unduly distorts information, or is less than forthright in its dealings with other actors in the policymaking process, its reputation can be irreparably damaged.[38]

The leadership of a group and its hired staff also contribute to its success. As policy issues develop, a competent staff will conduct research, provide position papers, draft specific proposals, contact key decisionmakers and the press, maintain communication with the membership, and develop public relations strategies to mobilize the membership to bring pressure on policymakers.

THE DOMINANT INTEREST GROUPS IN TEXAS

Throughout much of our history, state government was dominated by large corporations and banks, oil companies, and agricultural interests that backed the conservative Democratic officeholders who had a stranglehold on the legislature, the courts, and the executive branch.[39] Big business still carries a lot of weight in Austin and can purchase a lot of influence with major political contributions and the sophisticated skills of public affairs strategists. That's why, for example, Lieutenant Governor Bob Bullock enlisted the lobby's help in getting the 1991 tax bill passed. State officials who want to build public support for new policy proposals usually solicit the support of the business community first.

Beginning in the 1970s, however, influence began to be more diffused. Single-member districts (see Chapter 8) increased the number of minorities, Republicans, and liberal Democrats elected to the legislature. Consumer, environmental, and other public advocacy groups emerged. Organized labor, which had been shut out by the corporate establishment, found some common interests with the trial lawyers, who earn fees suing businesses on behalf of consumers and other plaintiffs claiming damages or injuries caused by various companies or products. The decline of oil and gas production and the emergence of high-tech service industries also helped diffuse the business lobby into more competitive factions.

Business

The diverse business interests in Texas organize in several ways to influence the policymaking process. First, broad-based associations represent business and industry in general, including the Texas Association of Business and the Texas Taxpayers and Research Association. Their overall goal is to maintain and improve upon a favorable business climate.

The business community also organizes through trade associations that represent and seek to advance the interests of specific industries. Some of the more visible and active associations are the Texas Bankers Association, the Wholesale Beer Distributors of Texas, the Texas Motor Transportation Association, the Texas Independent Producers & Royalty Owners Association, the Texas Chemical Council, the Texas Automobile Dealers Association, the Texas Restaurant Association, the Association of Fire and Casualty Companies in Texas, and the Associated General Contractors of Texas. The contractors' group has two branches, including one to which most highway contractors belong. Many highway contractors also belong to the Texas Good Roads and Transportation Association, which lobbies for highway construction funding. This group, which is quite effective in Austin, also includes representatives of other businesses and individuals interested in the maintenance of a strong highway network.

Many individual companies also retain their own lobbyists to represent them before the legislature and administrative agencies. A lobbyist may be a salaried employee of a company or a professional, freelance lobbyist—or "hired gun"—who is retained by several clients. Some wealthy individuals, such as Ross Perot, the Dallas billionaire computer magnate and former presidential candidate, even hire their own lobbyists.

And, finally, a group representing a broad range of business members can be organized to pursue a single issue. Perhaps the best-known example of this is Texans for Lawsuit Reform, which for several years has doggedly lobbied for a series of limitations on civil lawsuits and court-ordered damage awards against businesses and their insurance companies.

Most business groups band together against organized labor, consumer advocates, and trial lawyers on major political and philosophical issues, such as limits on consumer lawsuits. But the business lobby is far from monolithic. There are numerous issues, including tax policy and utility regulation, on which different companies or trade associations differ. During the 1999 legislative session, for example, lawmakers had to perform a delicate balancing act to put together an electric deregulation bill allowing petrochemical plants and other heavy industrial users of electricity to generate and sell power in competition with utility companies. And government has been frequently confronted in recent years with rivalries in the expanding telecommunications industry.

For many years, the interest groups associated with oil and natural gas played a dominant role among the business and industry lobbies. At one time, oil and gas accounted for 30 percent of the state's economic output. But this contribution has sharply declined since the 1980s recession, and the oil and gas lobby, though still effective, now has to work with political leaders who are focused on economic diversification. Other sources of traditional political power in Texas—the financial and real estate industries—also were at the center of Texas's economic downturn in the 1980s, but have recovered and remain an effective lobbying force.

Professional Groups

A number of professional groups have played dominant roles in Texas politics and the policymaking process. One of the better known is the Texas Medical Association (TMA), which in recent years has joined forces with business against trial lawyers to push for laws putting limits on malpractice suits and other damage claims against physicians and the business community. The TMA's political action committee (TEXPAC) is a major contributor of campaign dollars to candidates for the legislature, the Texas Supreme Court, and other state offices.

Litigation over medical malpractice, product liability, and workers' compensation also has expanded the influence of trial lawyers, who make their living representing injured persons, or plaintiffs. Trial lawyers are compensated with a share of the damages awarded their clients by a court or negotiated in a settlement with the defendant or the defendant's insurance company. A defendant can be a doctor accused of malpractice in the handling of an individual's care, a manufacturer accused of making a faulty product that caused an injury, a city whose truck was involved in an auto accident, an employer whose worker suffered an injury on the job, or just about any legal entity deemed responsible for causing harm to someone. Individually and through their political action committee, trial lawyers have contributed millions of dollars to judicial, legislative, and other selected candidates since the 1970s, when they became a major political factor in Texas. In the early 1980s, they succeeded in electing several Texas Supreme Court justices who shared their viewpoint, and the court issued precedent-setting opinions making it easier for plaintiffs to win large damage awards. The business and medical communities retaliated by boosting their own political contributions and lobbying efforts and, by 1990, had succeeded in tipping the state Supreme Court's philosophical scale back to its traditional business-oriented viewpoint (see Chapter 11).

But the war over tort law, as these types of damage suits are called, continued to rage—before the courts and in the legislature. Trial lawyers have lost significant battles on both fronts in recent years, mainly because of continued Republican growth. In 1995, the legislature enacted several laws backed by then-Governor George W. Bush to put significant restrictions on damage lawsuits. Lawmakers enacted additional restrictions in 2003 that were protected by a constitutional amendment approved by voters (see Chapter 2).

Education

Educational interests are very visible in the policymaking process in Austin, and lobbying for higher education can be particularly effective. The changing global economy has enhanced the role of higher education in developing the state's future, and there is widespread public support for expanded access to colleges and universities.

Most university regents, chancellors, and presidents are well connected politically. Universities also are capable—through the use of donations and other nontax funds—of hiring a well-paid cadre of legislative liaisons, or lobbyists. Another effective lobbying source for universities, particularly the larger ones, are the armies of alumni, many of them politically influential, ready to make phone calls or write letters on behalf of their alma maters when the need arises. The business community also is a strong supporter of higher education.

The struggle for equity and quality in public elementary and secondary education in Texas, a major issue for many years, has been complicated by more than two dozen groups representing various—and often conflicting—interests within the educational community. There are at least four different teachers' associations, one for school boards, a separate lobby group for school administrators, and still others for elementary school principals and secondary school principals. Separate groups also have been formed for urban school districts, suburban districts, rural districts, and districts with large numbers of special-needs students. Many of the associations are well financed, and some indirectly receive taxpayer money through dues paid by member school districts. Virtually all the groups have paid lobbyists, and while all claim to support educational quality, their primary goals are to protect the specific interests of their members.

Public Interest Groups

Most of the **public interest groups** represented in Austin are concerned primarily with protecting consumers and the environment from big business, promoting stronger ethical standards for public officials, and increasing funding for health and human services programs for the poor, the elderly, the young, and the disabled. Many have full-time lobbyists, but grassroots volunteer efforts and the effective use of the mass media are crucial to their success. Among the most active are Common Cause, the Sierra Club, Consumers Union, Texas Citizen Action, Texas Watch, the Gray Panthers, the Children's Defense Fund, Americans Disabled for Attendant Programs Today (ADAPT), and Public Citizen, a Texas affiliate of the national public interest group founded by consumer advocate Ralph Nader.

Although public interest lobbyists concentrate most of their attention on the legislature, some consumer groups are also active before state regulatory agencies, particularly the Public Utility Commission, which has oversight over telephone and electric utilities, and the Department of Insurance, which regulates insurance rates and practices. Among the more militant groups is ADAPT, which has staged highly visible demonstrations by wheelchair-bound Texans—including an overnight occupation of the governor's reception room—to demand more money for community-based facilities and attendant services for the disabled.[40]

Public interest advocates usually play more defense—trying to keep anticonsumer legislation from becoming law—than they do offense whenever lawmakers meet. But they scored a rare, significant victory during the 2003 regular session, when lawmakers enacted one of their priorities—a strengthened ethics law for public officials and political candidates. Among other things, the new law required officeholders to list the occupations and employers of their political contributors and imposed new, financial reporting requirements on mayors and city council members.[41]

Minorities

The advent of single-member, urban legislative districts in the 1970s significantly increased the number of African-American and Hispanic lawmakers and strengthened the influence of minority interest groups. These groups have often found that the courthouse can still be a shorter route to success than the statehouse, but the legislature has become increasingly attentive to their voices.

The League of United Latin American Citizens (LULAC) and the Mexican American Legal Defense and Educational Fund (MALDEF) are two of the better-known Hispanic organizations. LULAC, founded in 1929, is the oldest and largest Hispanic organization in the United States and continues to be particularly influential in causes such as education and election reform in Texas. It was a plaintiff in a federal lawsuit that sought to replace the countywide system of electing urban trial judges in Texas with district elections so as to boost the election of minorities to the bench. LULAC lost the suit but focused much public attention on an important policy issue (see Chapter 11).

MALDEF, formed in San Antonio in 1968, fights in the courtroom for the civil rights of Hispanics. It has been successful in numerous battles over the drawing of political boundaries for governmental bodies in Texas and in lengthy litigation over public school finance. MALDEF represented the property-poor school districts that won a unanimous landmark Texas Supreme Court order (*Edgewood v. Kirby*) in 1989 for a more equitable distribution of education aid between rich and poor districts. The victory eventually led to major legislative changes in the school finance system (see Chapter 13).

The National Association for the Advancement of Colored People (NAACP) is a leader in promoting and protecting the interests of African Americans. The NAACP initiated many of the early court attacks on educational inequality and the disfranchisement of minorities. More recently, this group has worked hard to increase employment opportunities for African Americans in state agencies, particularly in higher paying administrative jobs. Publicity and pressure generated by the NAACP doubtlessly contributed to the Texas Department of Public Safety's decision in 1988 to promote the first African-American trooper, at least in this century, to the elite Texas Rangers crime-fighting force. Lee Roy Young Jr., a fourteen-year DPS veteran, became a Ranger on September 1 of that year. The DPS also began work on a new affirmative action plan and developed racial-sensitivity training. After taking office in 1991, Governor Ann Richards encouraged the recruitment of more minorities and women for the Texas Rangers and other DPS positions.

About that same time, the legislature encouraged all state agencies to make a "good faith effort" to improve minority contracting by establishing a program under which historically underutilized businesses (HUBs)—companies owned by minorities or women—received special notification of contracts and work available from the state. The HUBs, however, had to compete with other companies for the contracts. By 1996, women- and minority-owned businesses received $936 million in contracts from the state, or about 16 percent of the total contracts the state awarded that year.[42] But the share began steadily dropping after that year, slipping to 9.7 percent in 2002, much to the concern of minority groups and minority legislators.[43]

In recent years, the Industrial Areas Foundation (IAF), a collection of well-organized, church-supported community groups, also has been a strong and effective voice for low-income minorities. Member groups include Valley Interfaith in South Texas, Communities Organized for Public Service (COPS) in San Antonio, The Metropolitan Organization (TMO) and the Fort Bend Interfaith Council in the Houston area and the El Paso Interreligious Sponsoring Organization (EPISO).

The first IAF chapter in Texas, San Antonio's COPS, developed an early reputation for being confrontational and raucous in demanding better drainage facilities and other improvements for the city's impoverished neighborhoods. COPS members would surround city council members in city hall offices and hallways, yell their demands, and refuse to take "no" or "maybe" for an answer. The group began to moderate its tactics as it matured politically and developed influential friends. At the state level, it has lobbied for health care for the poor, more equity in school funding, and water and sewer service for the *colonias,* or unincorporated slums, along the Texas-Mexico border.

Minority groups were confronted with perhaps their biggest challenge in decades when then-Attorney General Dan Morales, interpreting a federal court order in 1997, banned universities in Texas from using racial preferences in deciding admissions and granting student aid. Supporters of affirmative action had considered those preferences crucial to reversing the effects of historic discrimination against African Americans and Hispanics. The ban was lifted after the U.S. Supreme Court, ruling in a case from Michigan in 2003, held that affirmative action could be a factor in university admissions (see Chapter 13).

Labor

Organized labor has traditionally taken a back seat to business in Texas, a strong "right-to-work" state in which union membership cannot be required as a condition of employment. Anti-labor sentiment ran particularly high in the 1940s and 1950s, at the height of the conservative Democratic establishment's control of Texas politics. Labor-baiting campaigns in which unions were portrayed as evil communist sympathizers were not uncommon then.[44]

Today, about 500,000 Texans are members of labor unions. Among the largest unions in the state are the Communications Workers of America, the International Brotherhood of Electrical Workers, the International Association of Machinists and Aerospace Workers, the United Food and Commercial Workers International Union and the American Federation of State, County and Municipal Employees.

Unions can provide grassroots support for political candidates through endorsement cards, phone banks, and other get-out-the-vote efforts, and this support has historically gone to Democratic candidates. With Republican and conservative gains in recent years, many labor-backed candidates have not fared well in Texas, especially in statewide elections.

In 1994, the Texas AFL-CIO, the state's umbrella labor organization, endorsed Democratic Governor Ann Richards in her unsuccessful reelection bid against Republican George W. Bush, even though Richards was the main proponent in Texas of the North American Free Trade Agreement, which labor strongly opposed. Labor feared NAFTA would prompt businesses to replace union jobs with less expensive labor in Mexico.

Labor generally sides with the trial lawyers on such issues as workers' compensation, worker safety, and business liability for faulty products. One of labor's major victories in Texas politics was the defeat of a proposal to lock the right-to-work law into the state constitution. That dispute helped scuttle the Constitutional Convention of 1974, and labor prevailed only because of a convention rule that required proposals to receive a two-thirds vote (see Chapter 2).

Governmental Lobbyists

Local governments are significantly affected by state laws and budgetary decisions. The stakes are particularly high now because governments are finding revenue harder to raise—especially with the federal government passing the cost of numerous programs on to the state, and the state issuing similar mandates to local governments. As a result, counties, cities, prosecutors, metropolitan transit authorities, and various special districts are represented by lobbyists in Austin.

Many local governments belong to umbrella organizations such as the Texas Municipal League, the Texas Association of Counties, and the Texas District and County Attorneys Association, which have full-time lobbyists. Several of the larger cities and counties also retain their own lobbyists, and mayors, city council members, and county judges frequently travel to Austin to visit with legislators and testify for or against bills.

Some legislators complain that Houston and Harris County, the state's largest city and county, take up a disproportionate amount of the legislature's time with perennial fights over fire and police civil service regulations, mass transportation, and other local issues. One reason is because political unanimity is seldom achieved among Harris County's large, diverse legislative delegation. Another reason is restrictive state laws, such as those governing fire and police civil service, which may better be left to local discretion.

Agricultural Groups

Although Texas is now predominantly urban, agriculture is still an important part of the state's economy, and a number of agricultural groups are represented in Austin. Their influence is obviously strongest among rural legislators. But the Texas Farm Bureau, the largest such group, was instrumental in the 1990 electoral defeat of liberal Democratic Agriculture Commissioner Jim Hightower, who had angered many agricultural producers and the chemical industry with tough stands on farm worker rights and pesticide regulation.

Other producer groups include the Texas and Southwestern Cattle Raisers Association, the Texas Nurseryman's Association, and the Texas Corn Producers Board.

The United Farm Workers Union has been a strong advocate of better conditions for workers and has frequently been at odds with agricultural producers. Represented in court by the Texas Civil Liberties Union and Texas Rural Legal Aid attorneys, farm workers won major lawsuits and legislation in the 1980s on such issues as unemployment compensation, picketing rights, the right to be informed about dangerous pesticides used in fields, and a higher minimum wage.

Religious Groups

Influenced in part by their views of separation of church and state, many people think religious groups have little or no legitimate role in the political process. Nevertheless, religious groups have helped influence policy in Texas, and the abortion issue and other social and economic issues have increased the presence of religious groups in Austin.

A number of religious groups have emerged since the 1940s with an identifiable right-wing orientation. These groups, predecessors of what is now known as the Religious Right, combined Christian rhetoric and symbols with anticommunism, antilabor, anticivil rights, antiliberal, or anti–New Deal themes. Although these groups were often very small, they were linked to the extreme right wing of the Texas establishment, and they were the precursors to many of the conservative ideological groups that have emerged in American politics in the past twenty years.[45] Many of these organizations have gravitated toward the Republican party.[46] With a strong organizational effort, religious conservatives were influential in a right-wing takeover of leadership positions in the Texas Republican party in 1994 (see Chapter 6).

Many religious denominations have boards or commissions responsible for monitoring governmental action. One well-known religious interest group is the Christian Life Commission of the Baptist General Convention of Texas, a strong advocate of human services programs and an outspoken opponent of gambling.

Churches across the state, particularly the Catholic church, whose policies on social action have been shaped by papal encyclicals and Vatican II, have established links to community-based organizations that address the social and economic needs of the poor. In many regards, this is a redefinition of the Social Gospel, a church-based political movement of the late-nineteenth and early twentieth centuries.

WHO ARE THE LOBBYISTS?

During the 2003 regular and special sessions of the Texas legislature, about 1,600 individuals representing hundreds of businesses, trade associations, and other interests registered as lobbyists with the Texas Ethics Commission. They ran the gamut from well-dressed corporate lobbyists with generous expense accounts to volunteer consumer and environmental advocates in blue jeans and sneakers. Most were male, although the number of female lobbyists has increased in recent years, and many women now hold major lobbying positions. Most lobbyists came to their careers by way of other occupations and jobs, but they have, on the whole, an acute understanding of the policymaking process and the points of access and influence in that process.

Many lobbyists are former legislators. They bring to the process their legislative skills, personal relationships with former legislative colleagues, and expertise in substantive policy areas. A number of other lobbyists are former legislative staffers.

Many of the trade and professional associations, labor unions, and public interest groups have full-time staffs in Austin who function as their lobbyists. Many corporations also use their own employees to lobby. Some companies have governmental affairs departments or offices staffed by employees with experience in government or public affairs. In large corporations that do business across the country, the governmental affairs staffs may be rather large because such companies will attempt to follow the actions of numerous state legislatures, city councils, and the U.S. Congress.

A number of lawyers have developed very successful lobby practices. Some of these professional freelancers, or "hired guns," specialize in specific policy areas, while others represent a wide array of clients. Some may be identified as "super lobbyists" because of their ability to exercise considerable influence in the policymaking process. Many work for the state's largest law firms, which have established permanent offices in Austin. Some of the topnotch freelancers aren't attorneys, but they have a strong knowledge of the governmental process.

Some public relations firms also offer their services to interest groups. These companies specialize in "image creation" or "image modification."[47] Although they may not handle direct lobbying efforts, they often are retained to assist in indirect lobbying campaigns. They are responsible for developing relationships with the press, developing media campaigns, and assisting in political campaigns.

The number of registered lobbyists has increased significantly since 1991, when the legislature, in an ethics reform bill, adopted stricter reporting requirements.

INTEREST GROUPS AND THE POLICYMAKING PROCESS

For many people, the term **lobbying** may suggest shady characters lurking in the halls of the state Capitol, attempting to bribe legislators with money, sex, or booze. That perception was reinforced, especially before the new ethics law in 1991, by published reports of legislators being treated to trips, golf tournaments, and concerts by lobbyists (see Chapter 8). While such tactics are questionable, they are only part of the complex relationships between interest groups and policymakers. Lobbying is central to a pluralistic society, and the legal foundations of lobbying activity are found in the U.S. and Texas constitutions, which provide for the right to petition "the governments for a redress of grievances."[48]

In the broadest sense, lobbying is "simply the practice of attempting to influence the decisions of government."[49] Most scholars take this view. Lobbying is both indirect and direct and includes, but is not limited to, electoral activities, public relations campaigns, protests and demonstrations, and direct contact with policymakers (Table 4–1). According to political scientist Carol Greenwald, "Lobbying may thus be defined as any form of communication, made on another's behalf, and intended to influence a governmental decision."[50]

Indirect Lobbying

Effective lobbying starts with the election of officeholders supportive of a group's viewpoint on key issues and the building of general public support for a group and its objectives.

Electoral Activities.   Although the electoral activities of interest groups are similar to those of political parties, there are some significant differences. Political parties are broad coalitions of voters concerned with a wide range of issues, while most interest groups are focused on only a limited set of issues. Parties function not only to contest elections but also to govern once elected. Interest groups primarily are concerned

TABLE 4–1   Techniques of Exercising Influence in the Policymaking Process

1. Testifying at hearings
2. Contacting government officials directly to present organization's point of view
3. Engaging in informal contacts with legislators and other officials—at conventions, over lunch, and so on
4. Presenting research results or technical information
5. Sending letters to members of the organization to inform them about organizational activities
6. Entering into coalitions with other organizations
7. Making media contacts
8. Consulting with government officials to plan legislative strategy
9. Helping to draft legislation
10. Inspiring letter writing or e-mail campaigns
11. Mounting grass roots lobbying efforts
12. Having influential constituents contact their representatives' offices
13. Helping draft regulations, rules, or guidelines
14. Serving on advisory commissions and boards
15. Alerting legislators to the effects of a bill on their districts
16. Filing suit or otherwise engaging in litigation
17. Making financial contributions to political candidates
18. Doing favors for officials who need assistance
19. Attempting to influence appointments to public office
20. Publicizing candidates' voting records
21. Engaging in direct-mail fundraising for the organization
22. Running advertisements in the media about the organization's position on issues
23. Contributing work or personnel to electoral campaigns
24. Making public endorsements of candidates for office
25. Engaging in protests or demonstrations

Source: From Kay Lehman Scholzman and John T. Tierney, *Organized Interests and American Democracy.* New York: Harper and Row, 1986.

with influencing and shaping only those policies that directly affect them. Most interest groups also cross party lines in supporting candidates.

Interest groups must decide which candidates they will back through campaign contributions, organizational support, and public endorsements. Most groups are not interested in political ideology or philosophy but primarily are concerned with electing their "friends" and defeating their "enemies."

Most interest groups spend their money selectively, contributing to those legislators who serve on the committees that have jurisdiction over their industry or areas of concern. (See the discussion of the "iron triangles" of government earlier in this chapter and in Chapter 13.) The Texas legislature's highly centralized leadership encourages groups to concentrate their resources on a small number of key lawmakers.

— HOW I SEE IT —
LONG-TERM SURVIVAL ASSESSMENTS FOR LOBBYIST-TO-BE

Jack W. Gullahorn

Jack Gullahorn, who operates his own public issues consulting firm, has a wealth of experience as a lobbyist and governmental insider. His current activities include serving as president and general counsel to the Professional Advocacy Association of Texas (www.texasadvocacy.com), a trade association for contract lobbyists in Texas, which Gullahorn founded in 2002. He is a former senior vice president of Public Strategies, an Austin-based national public affairs and policy development firm, and is a former partner with the national law firm of Akin, Gump, Strauss, Hauer and Feld, L.L.P, where he headed the firm's Texas public law and policy section, overseeing governmental affairs.

Prior to his association with Akin, Gump, Gullahorn was both an independent attorney and lobbyist in Austin. In 1978, he cofounded the firm of Roan & Gullahorn, P.C. Through his appointment to the Public Servants Standards of Conduct Advisory Committee, he was involved in the recommendations that ultimately led to the creation of the Texas Ethics Commission. He maintains an expertise in Texas ethics and campaign law.

Gullahorn began his career in government service in 1973, serving in the office of Texas State Representative Bill Clayton. When Clayton was elected speaker of the Texas House in 1975, he became his executive assistant.

A native Texan, Gullahorn graduated from Trinity University with a degree in political science. He received his Doctor of Jurisprudence degree from the University of Texas Law School.

Lobbying IS a career.

It seems, however, that most people accept it as a vocational choice somewhat akin to prostitution, deciding to engage in the activity after acknowledging that selling your body for immoral purposes is the prevalent public view of the lobbyist's job description.

It doesn't have to be that way. Those who choose the profession can either change the perception or fulfill the public's low expectations. What follows is a suggested template for what could become a career type. How well suited are you to the key elements of the profession that could allow you to survive and at the same time enhance the image of a lobbyist to the public?

1. ***Ego Subjugation***

How impressed are you with yourself? Nothing wrong with that (as a matter of fact, you shouldn't be considering this as a lifestyle if you don't think that you were pretty much able to handle any situation extemporaneously). But if you want to succeed at this game, be prepared to mask that superior intellect and ability. Most policymakers actually believe that they are there as a fulfillment of a mission. Your role is to make them feel as if you are there to help them fulfill that destiny, not to mold the world through your brilliance, using them as your tool. One of the reasons that the majority of former legislators and officeholders make such lousy lobbyists is that they just aren't able to make the ego transition—from imperious to supplicant.

2. *Political Addiction*

If you don't love politics, go do something else. A disdain for the system will show through. As your cynicism grows, unless you have a real passion for the game, your patience and willingness to play the part (see #1) won't cut it. This means staying current, knowing the players as well as understanding the system. And it means that you are always thinking further ahead of the political consequences of every action than is the policymaker with whom you are dealing.

3. *Ethics*

Don't leave home without it. Knowing the law is a big part of it, but your personal morality in how you handle your business is what will show through to your audience. Assume that every phone conversation, every e-mail, every memo will be on the front page of the *New York Times*. Overreport when in doubt—no one ever got in trouble for disclosing too much.

4. *Truth or Consequences*

Never, never lie to a policymaker. Know that if you are going to be doing this job for a while, you will be back in front of that policymaker again, and your reputation for shooting straight (or not) will precede you. Once you develop the reputation for bending the facts, start preparing for mediocrity.

5. *Relationships*

It's not who you know, it's how you know them. The key maxim of lobbying is the realization that policymakers come and go, but lobbyists stay around a lot longer and, as a result, meeting and learning about those you seek to convince is a continuing art form. If you are an introvert, focus on one-on-one opportunities. If you like receptions, bars, and crowds, great, but don't lose sight of the fact that building trust requires a substantive relationship beyond the "friendship" veneer of the "social lobbyist." Relationships build trust. Trust inspires action. Action is what you get paid for.

6. *Pay Your Dues*

Don't expect to walk into the lifestyle of a successful lobbyist without earning the right to be there. Government is a great training ground for lobbyists because it allows you to experience firsthand the system and the ego glorification of the process. So are campaigns, because the same lessons are taught: fidelity, loyalty, friendship, and the importance of relationships. Also, you make acquaintances that will survive a lifetime. Both of these are better done when young—when you can afford it, monetarily and physically, especially the wear and tear on your mind, body, and soul.

7. *Staying Fresh*

You are only going to be as good as your last creative strategy. Tomorrow, everyone else will be doing the same thing, and you better be figuring out a new and improved way to move your message so it will stand out from the masses. Read and reserve a special time for yourself dedicated to shutting your eyes and actually thinking. On top of all that, learn who are the best thinkers on substance and process and study them.

8. *Ideas Have Consequences*

Subscribe to the belief that for every action there *will* be a reaction, a consequence. That can be either positive or negative, but count on the fact that you should be prepared to deal with whichever consequence you are dealt so you can make the most of every situation. As you think, plan for the consequences. Most people act, then realize that something will happen from that action, then decide how to react, continuing the cycle and never getting ahead of the curve.

9. ***Life Is Easier if You Believe Your Own BS.***
To thine own self be true. Sometimes the engagement may be tempting: the profile, the money, the players. But if you can't believe in the issue, pass on the opportunity. If your standard is to at least not represent issues and clients with which/whom you disagree personally, your credibility will be much easier to maintain. Think about it: You are trying to convince a decisionmaker to act based on the wisdom of following your advice. If you don't believe it, it will show, eventually. Same song for representing different sides of the same issue, because your client has changed.

Bottom line, remember that how you spend your days is how you spend your life.

In some cases, interest groups will use promises of financial campaign support to recruit opponents for incumbent legislators who consistently vote against them. In other instances, incumbents and potential challengers will approach interest groups for support. Although this process has become a permanent fixture of contemporary elections, it still can present an unsavory image of a mutual shakedown. Although a candidate cannot legally promise a specific vote for financial or other campaign support, an interest group will make every effort to assure that a potential recipient of campaign contributions is "sympathetic" and will be "accessible" to the group.

Under state and federal laws, interest groups and many corporations are able to form political action committees (PACs) for raising and distributing campaign funds. Money is contributed to a PAC by individual members of a group or employees of a corporation and then distributed among selected candidates. In most instances, a PAC is managed by the professional staff of the interest group, and the campaign contributions are a key part of the organization's overall lobbying strategy.

Federal campaign finance restrictions and reporting requirements are stricter than the state's. Federal law limits individual contributions to $2,000 per candidate for each election and PAC contributions by corporations, labor unions, trade associations, and other organizations to $5,000 per candidate per election. After several years of debate, the U.S. Congress in 2002 enacted the Bipartisan Campaign Reform Act, which banned the previously unlimited "soft money" contributions that businesses and special interest groups had been increasingly making to political parties to support candidates and campaign activities. The new federal law also restricted political television advertising by corporations and labor unions. The law was challenged in court by a diverse array of groups, including the United States Chamber of Commerce, the National Rifle Association and the American Civil Liberties Union, who contended it unconstitutionally restricted free speech. A three-judge federal district court in Washington struck down parts of the law in 2003, putting the issue in the hands of the United States Supreme Court, which upheld its constitutionality during its 2003–2004 term.[51]

Texas law prohibits corporations or labor unions from making direct contributions to state and local political candidates, but sets no limits on the amount of money a PAC or an individual can give to candidates. There have been instances in which a PAC has contributed more than $100,000 to a single candidate.

Interest groups sometimes provide in-kind support for political candidates. A group may make its phone banks available to a candidate, it may conduct a poll and provide the candidate with the results, or it may provide office space and equipment to a candidate's campaign. Some organizations may even "loan" the services of its staffers to a campaign or provide postage, cars for travel, printing services, and other types of assistance. State law requires such in-kind contributions to be publicly reported to the Texas Ethics Commission, just as financial donations are. Some groups, depending on how they are organized under federal tax laws, cannot make in-kind contributions directly, but can do so through their political action committees.

Groups also endorse candidates and publicize their endorsements in newsletters, news releases, press conferences, or conventions. Some groups maintain phone banks during election campaigns to inform their members of their endorsements and encourage them to get out and vote for their chosen candidates. Public endorsements often are sought by candidates when a group's size, prestige, and influence are considered valuable, and candidates use these endorsements in their advertising campaigns.

Public Opinion. Interest groups also may try to cultivate favorable public opinion about themselves through media campaigns. One objective is to "develop a reservoir of good will in the minds of the citizenry that can be drawn upon when political battles over specific issues occur."[52] Although this practice is more pronounced at the national level, state organizations in Texas that are associated with national interest groups often participate in national campaigns.

Public relations campaigns also are used to mobilize public support for a group's position on a specific issue being debated in Austin.[53] Voters may be encouraged to write, call, fax, or send e-mail to their legislators. The Texas Medical Association, for example, has sought public support for restrictions on medical malpractice awards by distributing cards to doctors' waiting rooms that attempt to explain how the high cost of malpractice insurance can affect the costs and quality of health care.

Interest groups may sponsor advertising campaigns featuring emotional language and imagery. They may use press conferences and informal media contacts to encourage favorable editorials or put their "spin," or viewpoint, on news coverage. For years, Texas legislators resisted pari-mutuel horserace betting and the lottery. But groups supporting those proposals continued to wage strong media campaigns, insisting that gambling would boost state revenue. Eventually, during economic downturns when the legislature was struggling to find new sources of revenue, they won the fight.

Public interest advocates, in their efforts to protect consumers and the environment, cannot match the financial firepower that utilities, insurance companies, and other big industries can muster. Their success depends on their ability to stir up public concern—or outrage—over pocketbook issues and the relationships between monied special interests and government. Quality research that focuses on political issues such as campaign contributions or policy issues is one of the more effective resources available to public interest groups. Using this research, they avidly work the news media, which are crucial to their ability to spread their message. They seldom can afford paid advertising campaigns, but they hold frequent news conferences, issue a stream of press releases, and readily return reporters' phone calls. They also recognize strength and efficiency in numbers and sometimes issue joint statements or hold joint news conferences on issues of mutual concern.

Protests and Marches.   Staged demonstrations against governmental decisions or in-action have long been used by individuals or groups attempting to influence public policy. Although many people have mixed feelings about such tactics, protests and marches can be effective in capturing public attention. Television coverage of such events, in particular, can convey powerful and intense images. The civil rights move-ment capitalized on this resource, and that movement's success, in large measure, turned on the ability of minority leaders to show the nation that discriminatory poli-cies were incompatible with the values of a democratic society.

In recent years, both antiabortion groups and abortion rights activists in Texas have marched in support of their positions. Animal rights groups have picketed stores that sell fur coats. Gay and lesbian groups have held vigils to protest incidents of "gay bashing," and a variety of other groups have used public demonstrations to drama-tize their particular issues or concerns. It is not clear what effects these tactics have. But many groups that use them have limited resources and recognize their value in gaining free media attention.

Direct Lobbying

Although interest groups may spend much time and money electing "friendly" can-didates and building public support for their objectives, their work has only begun. The next crucial step is direct lobbying, or the communication of information and policy preferences directly to policymakers. Lobbying is often associated with legis-latures, but it is directed to other governmental institutions as well. Public officials depend on the information provided by interest groups, and many policy initiatives, including proposed legislation, come from lobbyists. Interest groups also attempt to use the courts to advance their policy goals. They file lawsuits to challenge existing laws or regulations—and force changes—or file briefs supporting or opposing other groups' positions in pending litigation.[54]

Lobbyists engage in a wide range of activities. Most groups understand the necessity of pursuing their legislative agendas at every conceivable opportunity, and they also realize it usually is easier to block policy initiatives than to enact new policies.[55]

Drafting Legislation.   Interest groups often will draft proposed laws for formal in-troduction into the legislature. In any given legislative session, hundreds of bills are drafted by the legal or technical staffs of interest groups. The groups usually work closely with legislative sponsors or their staffs in the drafting process, and they may consult staffers from the agencies that would be affected by the legislation.

Planning and Implementing a Legislative Strategy.   Interest groups supporting a bill will usually work closely with the bill's sponsor, committee chairs, and other legislative leaders at every stage of the process. Strategy will be planned from the introduction of the legislation through committee hearings and then through final action by the House and the Senate. Potential opposition will be assessed, and ways of diffusing that opposition and building support for the bill will be mapped out.

Personal Contacts and Communications.   If one were to ask most interest groups why they contribute to political candidates and what they expected in return, the over-whelming response would be "access." The interest group system revolves around communication and the exchange of ideas and information with policymakers. To have some prospects of success, a group must have access to lawmakers, something that often is no small task to achieve.

With thousands of bills considered during each regular legislative session, interest groups have to compete for the opportunity to discuss their programs with lawmakers. Lobbyists are denied direct access to legislators on the floor of the House and the Senate while legislators are in session, but there are numerous other opportunities for direct or indirect contact.

During House and Senate sessions, many lobbyists will wait outside the chambers to stop legislators who pass by. Or they will have the doorkeepers send messages asking individual lawmakers to step outside the chambers for brief meetings in the lobby—hence the term, "lobbyists." It is not unusual for several dozen lobbyists to be gathered at one time outside the House or the Senate chamber on the second floor of the Capitol, particularly on days when major bills are being debated. Lobbyists also sit in the House and Senate galleries. In some instances, a lobbyist's presence in the gallery is simply a matter of minor interest or a way to kill some time before a committee meeting. But sometimes special interest groups will pack the gallery in a show of force to threaten recrimination against lawmakers who don't vote their way.

SUMMER SCHOOL (OR RECESS) FOR LEGISLATORS

Lobbyists for numerous special interest groups spend thousands of dollars entertaining and influencing Texas lawmakers during the state's biennial, regular legislative sessions, and they don't stop there. Only a few weeks after their work in Austin ends, many lobbyists and legislators head to summer conferences, where the lawmakers are wined and dined some more. Such conferences offer Texas lawmakers the opportunity to discuss problems and exchange ideas with legislators from other states and to hear experts speak about a variety of important issues. They also offer special interests additional opportunities to buy access to policymakers. The meeting schedules are usually crammed with opportunities for play as well as work. And most of the social events—dinners, golf games, tourist excursions, and other attractions—are sponsored by corporations and special interest groups. Texas taxpayers, meanwhile, pick up the tab for the legislators' air fare and hotel rooms. According to research by the *Austin American-Statesman,* taxpayers spent more than $265,000 on travel expenses for lawmakers attending three major, out-of-state conferences in 1995 and 1996.

As many as half of Texas's lawmakers may attend one or more of these conferences in any given year. Some legislators conscientiously attend as many work sessions as they can. State Representative Bob Hunter of Abilene told the *Austin American-Statesman* that he brought an empty suitcase to carry home the stacks of reports that were distributed so that he could share them with colleagues. "You glean some tremendous ideas," he said. Many other lawmakers, however, view the conferences more as social opportunities. "What did I do today? I played golf," state Representative Pat Haggerty of El Paso told a reporter after skipping an afternoon's work session. "This (the golf course) is where you make the connections that are good for business, that are good for government, that are good for whatever," Haggerty said.

Source: Austin American-Statesman, November 2, 1997.

Effective lobbyists, however, do most of their work long before a bill reaches the House or the Senate floor for a vote. They will stop by legislators' offices to present information and solicit support for or against specific legislation. If they can't meet personally with a legislator, they will meet with his or her staff. In many cases, lobbyists will provide lawmakers with written reports, summarizing the highlights of an issue and their position on it. Many interest groups will back up the personal efforts of their lobbyists with letter-writing, e-mail or telephone campaigns directed at legislators by the groups' members.

Much of the personal lobbying is done away from the Capitol, sometimes far away—over lunch and dinner tables, at cocktail parties, and on golf courses. While these occasions involve a great deal of socializing, they also provide lobbyists with golden opportunities to solidify friendships with lawmakers and make pitches for or against specific legislative proposals. A five- or ten-minute business conversation reinforced with a few hours of social camaraderie can work wonders, as many interest groups and their lobbyists very well know. Such entertainment, however, is expensive—lobbyists have spent well in excess of $1 million during a regular legislative session entertaining lawmakers—and it can easily be used to abuse the policy-setting process. Repeated news accounts of extravagant and questionable lobby spending finally convinced the legislature in 1991 to ban many lobby-paid trips for lawmakers and to limit lobby expenditures on entertainment to $500 per year per legislator (see Chapter 8).

Many lobbyists and legislators were concerned that the 1991 ethics law also may have outlawed that most sacred and basic of lobby handouts—the free lunch. Their uncertainty prompted the legislature to pass a bill in 1993 to make sure that it remained legal for lawmakers to dine at lobbyists' expense.

Testifying at Hearings.   During each regular legislative session, House and Senate committees and subcommittees hold hundreds of hearings on bills that have to win committee approval before they can be considered by the full House and Senate. Interest groups can use committee hearings to present information formally to legislators or to help mobilize public support for or against a bill. Testifying at public hearings is often symbolic and secondary to the personal communications with legislators and their staffs.

Coalitions of Interest Groups.   Sometimes, a group will not have sufficient resources to influence the outcome of a contested issue, or a legislative or regulatory proposal may affect many different groups. Groups thus sometimes find it advantageous to form coalitions to coordinate their electoral and direct lobbying activities. These coalitions are informal, tenuous, or short-lived, based on current common interests or objectives and a desire to maximize resources and share costs and expenses.[56]

In 1991, some consumer advocates teamed up with the Texas Trial Lawyers Association to defeat a products-liability bill that would have made it more difficult for consumers injured by defective products to sue manufacturers and retailers. But two years later, consumers learned how tenuous that alliance was when trial lawyers and key legislators negotiated a products-liability compromise with the business community. Consumer groups, who opposed the legislation, were excluded from the negotiations.

SUMMARY AND CONCLUSIONS

1. Political power in Texas is essentially structured around organizations, whether they be corporations, professional associations, or interest groups. The interaction and conflict among these groups in the policymaking process help decide who gets what, when, and how. The great disparity in the distribution of resources among these institutions raises a fundamental question: Does everyone in the political system have equal access and influence in the decisionmaking process?

2. Pluralists, while recognizing the inequities in political resources, argue that individual interests are adequately represented through membership in interest groups. They contend that with thousands of groups competing, no one group can dominate the policy process. New groups are constantly being formed to provide new leadership opportunities and greater access to the decisionmaking process for people who have been historically denied influence. With the political mobilization of minorities and public interest groups, the decline of the oil and gas industry, and the emergence of new economic interests, the interest group structure in Texas now bears little resemblance to the restricted interest group system of the 1950s. Moreover, pluralists believe that leaders of groups are generally committed to democratic values and faithfully represent the concerns, needs, and expectations of their membership.

3. The elitist theory emphasizes the marked differences in the resources and subsequent political influence of groups and contends that relatively few corporations and other institutions with great financial resources dominate the policy process in Texas. Over much of the state's political history, the most influential institutions have been dominated by white, Anglo-Saxon men from Texas's higher socioeconomic levels. Although there is some competition among these leaders, they agree on most public policy issues and the underlying functions of government. Historically, this Texas "establishment" has expressed indifference, if not hostility, toward the interests of labor, minorities, and the lower socioeconomic groups. These wealthy institutions are tied together through complex interlocking relationships, and access to leadership positions in them is limited.

4. There is evidence suggesting that the source of political power and influence lies somewhere between the elitist and pluralist positions. Sometimes, the narrow, limited interests of a few groups prevail, but public policy at other times is responsive to the needs and interests of broad segments of the population.

5. The effectiveness of an interest group in the policymaking process is determined by its size, the geographical distribution of its membership, its economic resources, its reputation, and its leadership and staff.

6. Interest groups and other organizations use a variety of techniques to communicate their wants and needs to policymakers. Although lobbying has a negative connotation for many Texans, it is essential to elected and appointed policymakers, who depend on the information, coalition building, and public support of groups for their decisions and actions.

7. Interest groups engage in indirect and direct lobbying. Indirect lobbying includes campaign financing and other efforts to elect candidates who share a group's views. It also includes efforts to shape public opinion to favor the group's objectives. Direct lobbying involves a variety of strategies and techniques to shape the decisions of policymakers. Effective lobbyists know how to gain access to legislators and other policymakers, to build and maintain coalitions with other interests, and to follow policy decisions at every step of the process.

8. Interest groups are the fundamental building blocks of the Texas political system. Policymakers must resolve the fundamental conflicts among these competing interests with sound public policy that serves specific and general interests. But the excessive influence that comes through large campaign contributions and the limited resources of many groups challenge the concept of equity and fairness.

KEY TERMS

Interest group	Iron rule of oligarchy	Single-issue group
Mischief of factions	Establishment	Public interest groups
Pluralism	Hyperpluralism	Lobbying
Elitism	Iron triangles	

FURTHER READINGS

Articles

Coombs, Kathryn, Mark Reilly, and Robert Stone, "Grassroots Lobbying and the Internet Explosion," *Campaigns & Elections,* February 1999, pp. 26–33.

Garcia, John A., and Rodolfo de la Garza, "Mobilizing the Mexican Immigrant: The Role of Mexican-American Organizations," *Western Political Quarterly* 38 (December 1985), pp. 551–564.

Thomas, Clive S., and Ronald J. Hrebenar, "Who's Got Clout? Interest Group Power in the States," *State Legislatures* (April 1999), pp. 30–34.

Books

Bachrach, Peter, *The Theory of Democratic Elitism: A Critique.* Boston: Little, Brown, 1967.

Berry, Jeffrey M., *The Interest Group Society,* 3rd ed. New York: Longman, 1997.

Davidson, Chandler, *Race and Class in Texas Politics.* Princeton: Princeton University Press, 1990.

Domhoff, G. William, *Who Really Rules?* Santa Monica, CA: Goodyear Publishing Company, Inc., 1978.

Domhoff, G. William, *Who Rules America Now?* Englewood Cliffs, NJ: Prentice Hall, Inc., 1983.

Dye, Thomas R., *Who's Running America? The Bush Era,* 5th ed. Englewood Cliffs, NJ: Prentice Hall, Inc., 1990.

Green, George Norris, *The Establishment in Texas Politics, 1938–1957.* Westport, CT.: Greenwood Press, 1979.

Greenwald, Carol S., *Group Power: Lobbying and Public Policy.* New York: Praeger Publishers, 1977.

Hrebenar, Robert J., and Clive S. Thomas, eds., *Interest Group Politics in Southern States.* Tuscaloosa: University of Alabama Press, 1992.

Hrebenar, Robert J., and Ruth K. Scott, *Interest Group Politics in America,* 2nd. ed. Englewood Cliffs, NJ: Prentice Hall, Inc., 1990.

Lowi, Theodore J., *The End of Liberalism,* 2nd ed. New York: W. W. Norton & Company, 1979.

Morehouse, Sarah McCally, *State Politics, Parties, and Policy.* New York: Holt, Rinehart and Winston, 1981.

Pittman, H. C., *Inside the Third House.* Austin: Eakin Press, 1992.

Rogers, Mary Beth, *Cold Anger: A Story of Faith and Power Politics.* Denton, TX: University of North Texas Press, 1990.

Rosenthal, Alan, *The Third House: Lobbyists and Lobbying in the States.* Washington, DC: Congressional Quarterly Press, 1993.

Rosenthal, Alan, *The Decline of Representative Democracy: Process, Participation, and Power in the State Legislatures.* Washington, DC: Congressional Quarterly Press, 1998.

Sabato, Larry J., *PAC Power.* New York: W. W. Norton & Company, 1985.

San Miguel, Guadalupe, Jr., *Let Them Take Heed: Mexican Americans and the Campaign for Educational Equality in Texas, 1910–1981.* Austin: University of Texas Press, 1987.

Schlozman, Kay Lehman, and John T. Tierney, *Organized Interests and American Democracy.* New York: Harper & Row, Publishers, 1986.

Thomas, Clive S., and Ronald J. Hrebenar, "Interest Groups in the States," in *Politics in the American States: A Comparative Analysis,* eds. Virginia Gray and Herbert Jacob. Washington, DC: Congressional Quarterly Press, 1996.

Websites

Texas Ethics Commission   http://www.ethics.state.tx.us   Under Texas law, organizations that lobby the legislature are required to file with the Ethics Commission. This source provides names of registered lobbyists and their clients, as well as lobbyists organized by legislative subject matter. Candidates and political action committees are also required to file their financial statements with this agency.

ENDNOTES

1. Alex de Tocqueville, *Democracy in American: A New Translation* by George Lawrence, J. P. Mayer, ed. (Garden City, NY: Anchor Books, 1969, copyright in the English translation by Harper & Row, Publishers, 1966), p. 191.
2. *Houston Chronicle,* October 2, 2003, p. 19A.
3. See Robert S. Erikson, Norman R. Luttbeg, and Kent L. Tedin, *American Public Opinion,* 3rd ed. (New York: Macmillan Publishing Company, 1988), p. 118; and Robert L. Lineberry, George C. Edwards, III, and Martin P. Wattenberg, *Government in America,* 5th ed. (New York: HarperCollins Publishers, 1991), p. 341.
4. Belle Zeller, *American State Legislatures* (New York: Thomas Y. Crowell, 1954) and Clive S. Thomas and Ronald J. Hrebenar, "Interest Groups in the States," in *Politics in the American States,* 6th ed., Virginia Gray and Herbert Jacob, eds. (Washington, DC: Congressional Quarterly Press, 1996), p. 152.
5. Harmon L. Zeigler and Hendrik van Dalen, "Interest Groups in State Politics," in *Politics in the American States,* 3rd ed., Herbert Jacob and Kenneth N. Vines, eds. (Boston: Little, Brown, 1976).
6. Dennis S. Ippolito and Thomas G. Walker, *Political Parties, Interest Groups, and Public Policy* (Englewood Cliffs, NJ: Prentice Hall, Inc., 1990), p. 271.
7. Ibid., pp. 270–71.
8. Kay Lehman Schlozman and John T. Tierney, *Organized Interests and American Democracy* (New York: Harper & Row, Publishers, 1986), p. 75.
9. Ronald J. Hrebenar and Ruth K. Scott, *Interest Group Politics in America,* 2nd ed. (Englewood Cliffs, NJ: Prentice Hall, Inc., 1990), p. 13.
10. See E. E. Schattschneider, *The Semi-Sovereign People* (Hinsdale, IL: Dryden Press, 1975) and Hrebenar and Scott, *Interest Group Politics in America,* p. 29.
11. Robert Salisbury, "Overlapping Memberships, Organizational Interactions, and Interest Group Theory." Unpublished paper presented at the annual meeting of the American Political Science Association, Chicago, 1976. See also Carol S. Greenwald, *Group Power* (New York: Praeger Publishers, 1977), pp. 38–40.
12. Schlozman and Tierney, Organized Interests and American Democracy, pp. 73–74.
13. Hrebenar and Scott, *Interest Group Politics in America,* p. 29.
14. Ippolito and Walker, *Political Parties, Interest Groups, and Public Policy,* p. 278.
15. For an extended summary of these incentives, see Jeffrey M. Berry, *The Interest Group Society,* 3rd ed. (New York: Longman, 1997), pp. 70–77. See also Robert H. Salisbury, "An Exchange Theory of Interest Groups," *Midwest Journal of Political Science* 13 (February 1969), pp. 1–32.
16. Greenwald, *Group Power,* pp. 32–35.

17. Ippolito and Walker, *Political Parties, Interest Groups, and Public Policy,* pp. 279–80.
18. Berry, *The Interest Group Society,* p. 73.
19. Lawrence J. R. Herson, *The Politics of Ideas* (Prospect Heights, IL: Waveland Press, Inc., 1990), p. 68.
20. David B. Truman, *The Governmental Process,* 2nd ed. (New York: Alfred A. Knopf, 1971).
21. For a succinct summary of the elitist-pluralist debate, see Thomas R. Dye and Harmon Zeigler, *The Irony of Democracy,* 7th ed. (Monterey, CA: Brooks/Cole Publishing Company, 1987), Chap. 1.
22. David Truman, *The Governmental Process,* Chap. 4.
23. Ippolito and Walker, *Political Parties, Interest Groups, and Public Policy,* pp. 275–76.
24. Thomas R. Dye, *Who's Running America: The Bush Era,* 5th ed. (Englewood Cliffs, NJ: Prentice Hall, Inc., 1990), p. 4.
25. Robert Michels, *Political Parties: A Sociological Study of the Oligarchical Tendencies of Modern Democracy* 1915 (New York: Free Press, 1962), p. 70.
26. C. Wright Mills, *The Power Elite* (New York: Oxford University Press, 1956).
27. See Dye and Zeigler, *The Irony of Democracy,* Chap. 1.
28. George Norris Green, *The Establishment in Texas Politics: 1938–1957* (Westport, CT: Greenwood Press, 1979), p. 1.
29. Ibid., p. 17.
30. Ibid., p. 1.
31. Ibid., p. 10.
32. Chandler Davidson, *Race and Class in Texas Politics* (Princeton: Princeton University Press, 1990), p. 54.
33. Ibid., Chap. 4 and 5.
34. Ibid., p. 83.
35. Ibid., p. 108.
36. Lineberry, et al., *Government in America,* p. 342.
37. See Theodore J. Lowi, *The End of Liberalism,* 2nd ed. (New York: W. W. Norton & Company, 1979).
38. Schlozman and Tierney, *Organized Interests and American Democracy,* p. 103.
39. See Green, *The Establishment in Texas Politics,* Chap. 1.
40. *Houston Chronicle,* September 15, 1991.
41. *Houston Chronicle,* June 20, 2003, page 29A.
42. *Austin American-Statesman,* November 4, 1997.
43. *El Paso Times,* February 18, 2003, page 7B.
44. See George Norris Green, *The Establishment in Texas Politics,* for an excellent analysis of the labor-bashing techniques used by Texas business in the 1940s and 1950s.
45. See Green, *The Establishment in Texas Politics,* Chap. 5.
46. See Davidson, *Race and Class in Texas Politics,* Chap. 10.
47. Hrebenar and Scott, *Interest Group Politics in America,* p. 83.
48. U.S. Constitution, First Amendment; Texas Constitution, Article 1, Section 27.

49. Alan Rosenthal, *Third House: Lobbyists and Lobbying in the States* (Washington, DC: Congressional Quarterly Press, 1993), p. 1.

50. Greenwald, *Group Power*, pp. 61–62.

51. *The New York Times*, September 9, 2003, page 1A.

52. Ippolito and Walker, *Political Parties, Interest Groups, and Public Policy*, p. 323.

53. Hrebenar and Scott, *Interest Group Politics in America*, pp. 114–15.

54. Ippolito and Walker, *Political Parties, Interest Groups, and Public Policy*, pp. 364–65.

55. The following section draws from the research of Scholzman and Tierney, *Organized Interests and American Democracy*, Chap. 7.

56. Hrebenar and Scott, *Interest Group Politics in America*, pp. 148–53.

5

The Mass Media in Texas Politics

> The people, in delegating authority, do not give their public servants the right to decide what is good for the people to know and what is not good for them to know.
>
> *Texas Legislature, 1973*

The news media and any number of state officials have been expressing misgivings for years about each other and their adversarial, yet symbiotic, relationship. The Capitol press corps obviously wouldn't exist without a state government to cover. Some governors, legislators, and bureaucrats believe they could do their jobs very well without the media looking over their shoulders, but they know where to turn when they have a message or an image they want to convey to the public.

Officeholders can communicate directly with their constituents, relaying their own subjective accounts of their accomplishments through personal contact, public speeches, newsletters, websites on the Internet, or paid television commercials. Political parties and special interest groups regularly disseminate governmental information through their membership networks. But most of the information that people have about their government—particularly on the state and federal levels—comes directly or indirectly through the mass media. An individual reads a newspaper or magazine article, sees a television newscast, hears a radio summary of a particular event, receives an e-mail on a particular news media story or otherwise hears the news from a newspaper or magazine reader, television viewer, or radio listener.

In adopting First Amendment guarantees of press freedom more than 200 years ago, the framers of the U.S. Constitution recognized that a free press was an independent conduit of information essential to making a representative democracy work. It was to provide a public forum for the exchange of ideas and a means of scrutinizing the actions of public officials so as to establish accountability. The mass media has not always been impartial, and in many cases, it has not been as independent as the Constitution's drafters probably envisioned. But the unofficial fourth branch of government, for all its flaws, has served—and continues to serve—as a check and balance on the legislative, executive, and judicial branches.

The media plays a significant role in setting public policy by influencing the outcome of elections in which policymakers are chosen and by contributing to the public debate over policy alternatives. The media also is a watchdog over officialdom, evaluating the competency of public officials and attacking their ethical lapses. The media informs, educates, and often angers its audience and, like the political figures and issues it covers, is itself constantly subjected to public scrutiny and questions of fairness.

Subjective decisions by a newspaper editor or television news producer can affect the final news product and determine whether it is perceived as fair. Should a paper, for example, publish a story about a minor indiscretion by a political candidate? Or a story suggesting a major indiscretion that is based on circumstantial, largely undocumented evidence? Or a story about a suggestive joke that a political candidate utters in an informal setting? If any of these stories are published or broadcast, should they be on the front page or used to lead the evening newscast? How much space or time should be given to a particular issue, event, or personality? Editors' and producers' answers to these questions, which can help determine who is elected to public office and influence government policymaking, are influenced by the highly competitive nature of the news business.

The media has become a major institution linking governments to their constituents. Ironically, however, in the current, so-called **information age**—when it has become easier than ever before to be informed—millions of Americans, particularly young adults, are ill-informed and indifferent to the actions and decisions of their leaders and governmental institutions. This disturbing development threatens the foundations of a democratic society, because democracy depends on an informed and involved public.

THE MASS MEDIA AND THE POLICY AGENDA

The media has an impact on public policy, although it doesn't dictate policy to elected officials. Some scholars and media experts believe one of the major contributions of the media to politics is **agenda setting.** By choosing which events and issues to cover and how extensively to cover them, they say, the media helps define what is important for the public and, by omission, what is not important. Maxwell McCombs and Donald Shaw, recognized authorities on the mass media, argue that "the idea of agenda-setting asserts that the priorities of the press to some degree become the priorities of the public. What the press emphasizes is in turn emphasized privately and publicly by the audiences of the press."[1]

The media uses five basic criteria to select what events and subjects to cover. First, a story must have a significant impact on its audience, such as a legislative proposal to increase taxes or change the public education system. Second, it needs to be something that generates considerable interest. That may be an act of violence or conflict, a natural disaster, a political scandal, or legislation to ban assault rifles. A third component is familiarity—the public identifies with well-known individuals or familiar situations. A reported event also should occur in some proximity to readers and viewers, and, finally, a news story should be timely. Conflict, proximity, and timeliness often appear to be the more critical elements of a story's newsworthiness.[2] Yet, public policymaking is complex and often highly technical and doesn't always produce the kinds of stories necessary to sustain general public interest.

In cases in which the public interest is aroused, some experts extend the agenda-setting role of the media to **agenda building.** The media's coverage of specific issues creates a climate for political action by shaping the atmosphere in which these issues will be debated and their solutions developed.[3] By helping to make an issue relevant, the media gives people reasons for taking sides and converting the problem into a serious political issue. From this perspective, "the public agenda is not so much set by the media as built up through a cycle of media activity that transforms an elite issue into a public controversy."[4] Issues and concerns of a few individuals now become the concerns of many, and the dynamics of the policymaking process are changed.[5]

The most consistent readers and viewers of governmental and political news are the business, community, and political leaders who actively influence and work on policy formation. Most key public officials and their staffs spend a lot of time keeping up with media coverage of public issues. Clipping and filing news stories and checking newspaper websites on the Internet are important parts of the routine in many state offices. A number of independent clipping services also compile newspaper articles daily for influential clients, and some firms provide video clips of news stories carried on television.

But some people familiar with the workings of Texas government believe that the policy-building role of the press is overstated. Bo Byers, who spent almost forty years covering state government and politics for the *Houston Chronicle* and the Associated Press, said he found the media's role primarily reactive. "In most cases, the media is kind of like the politicians. They see public sentiment developing for something, and they get behind it. Then you see the editorials start appearing."[6] This view suggests a less intrusive role of the mass media in the policy process and is similar to the notion that the press merely mirrors what others think about public issues.

This passive view is supported by the argument that the Texas press was largely reactive in reporting some of the most crucial issues facing Texans in recent memory, including educational equality, criminal justice, and care of the mentally ill and the mentally retarded. Although newspapers were influential in prompting the legislature to make improvements in all three of these areas in the years following World War II, deterioration set in, and the media and the legislature of the next generation took back seats to the judiciary. The media had largely ignored a recurrence of substandard conditions in state prisons and Department of Mental Health and Mental Retardation facilities—and, consequently, so had the legislature—until after the federal courts had stepped in with landmark reform orders. Disparities in property wealth and educational opportunities between rich and poor school districts had been growing wider for years, worsening a dropout problem that, in turn, helped keep the prisons crowded. But educational disparities received only occasional attention from news reporters until after the Mexican American Legal Defense and Educational Fund had won a state court judgment declaring the school finance system unconstitutional. Once the courts had forced the issues, however, the media devoted extensive coverage to them, keeping the problems, their causes, and potential solutions in the public eye.

The media's attention to public problems and officialdom's response form something of a never-ending cycle. In the early 1980s, for example, the deaths of several elderly patients at the Autumn Hills Nursing Home in Galveston prompted changes in state law designed to tighten oversight of such facilities. By the early 1990s, however, the *Houston Chronicle* and other newspapers again were reporting widespread deficiencies in state regulation of the nursing home industry. Those reports and a hard-hitting, national network television exposé of abuse and neglect at Texas nursing homes—complete with nauseating glimpses shot by a hidden camera—put pressure on Governor Ann Richards, the legislature, and the Texas Department of Health to address the problem again. The media reports suggested that the lax attitudes of some state regulators may have been partly to blame, but inadequate funding of nursing home regulation also may have been a factor. If so, it was an all-too-typical conflict of two governmental policies: a policy to protect vulnerable members of society, but to do so within the confines of a broader policy to limit costs and taxes.

Anthony Downs describes these phases of news coverage and public interest in terms of an **issue-attention cycle.**[7] There is a pre-public phase in which a problem, such as poor nursing home conditions, quietly affects numerous individuals. Someone, perhaps a relative of a nursing home resident, then attempts to transform the issue into a public concern through the media. Press coverage starts slowly but rapidly intensifies, prompting more and more outraged citizens to discuss the problem. But initial enthusiasm for solutions gives way to the "realization that significant progress will be costly not only in terms of money but social stability," and many people begin to lose interest. After the enactment of policies to address some of the problems, governmental responses tend to become institutionalized, and many of the initial changes are ignored or become ineffective. Although press coverage may continue intermittently, it has limited effect in renewing public opinion or prompting further governmental action—until someone, usually several years later, restarts the cycle.[8]

The media's degree of influence over specific governmental actions can vary considerably, depending on the media's own interest in an issue and the public's reaction to what they read and hear. All too often, an apathetic public and indifferent public officials—or strong differences in opinions between the media and policymakers—minimize the media's role in agenda setting or agenda building. During the 2003 regular legislative session, for example, when the state faced a $10 billion revenue shortfall, most of the state's newspapers repeatedly wrote editorials urging Gov. Rick Perry and lawmakers to minimize budget cuts—particularly for health and human services programs—with a modest increase in state taxes. But Perry and the Republicans in control of the legislature ignored the pleas and chose deep cuts over any tax increase. They insisted that most Texans didn't want higher taxes. They also may have been influenced by the fact that Hispanics, who benefit disproportionately from health and human services programs, weren't a significant factor in the 2002 election, when Perry defeated a Hispanic Democratic challenger.

THE MASS MEDIA AND THE ELECTORAL PROCESS

Candidates for public office in Texas still attend rallies in the park and salute the flag at Fourth of July parades. Some legislative and local candidates, particularly those with more shoe leather than money, still rely heavily on door-to-door campaigning. But in races for statewide offices, and many local and district offices as well, the campaign stump has long since been replaced by the **sound bite,** the press conference, and the contrived pseudo-event developed by the campaign consultant. Campaigning is now constructed around the mass media, particularly television, and the media, in effect, has displaced the political party as the major information link between the voters and those in government (see Chapter 6).

Journalists and political scientists repeatedly debate the effects of news coverage on elections. Most journalists believe their job is to be as objective as possible in outlining the issues and reporting and evaluating the backgrounds, philosophies, activities, and policy proposals of candidates. The news media tries to determine what issues should be important in a campaign, although journalists are being increasingly challenged by television advertising with which the candidates themselves seek to dictate what the electorate should consider important.

News media reports and paid political advertising obviously play major roles in shaping voters' decisions. Studies have indicated that party identification helps determine voters' choices in general elections—there is a lot of straight-ticket, one-party voting—but long ballots in primaries and general elections force many voters to seek other sources of information about the candidates as well. These voters may rely on news reports and television advertising to clarify the candidates' characteristics, campaign issues, policy positions, and electoral prospects. Newspaper editorial endorsements of candidates also provide additional cues to many voters. Candidates, of course, welcome editorial endorsements and often feature them in political advertising. But favorable exposure on the news pages and on television screens often is more crucial to a candidate's electoral success.

Covering the "Horserace"

The media has been criticized for covering campaigns much as it would a horserace. Some critics argue that reporters often neglect candidates' positions on substantive policy issues in favor of stories about campaign strategies, tactics, and personalities, which usually are easier to develop. Numerous national studies indicate that policy issues receive only a small part of campaign coverage, and a cursory review of campaign reporting in Texas leads to a similar conclusion.

The "horserace" approach includes the publication of poll stories indicating candidate voter strength in trial heats at different stages of a campaign. Some polls are leaked to the press by the candidates who commission them—if the polls make a candidate look strong or his opponent appear weak. Other polls are conducted periodically by media organizations and other independent groups. While some of these surveys also attempt to measure public opinion on selected issues, their primary focus is on who is winning and who is losing.

Campaigning for Television

Most candidates for major offices plan their daily campaign appearances with television newscasts in mind. They participate in activities—such as visits to schools or high-tech plants—that look good in a thirty-second news segment. Unfortunately for the viewers, however, such superficial coverage doesn't even begin to shed light on the complex issues in a race or the candidate's position on them. Neither does a candidate's paid television advertising.

During campaigns, reporters in Austin are frequently given videotapes or computer discs of a candidate's latest television advertisement. It may be a positive, "feel good" spot, portraying the candidate in the best possible light—playing with children, visiting a hospital, or shaking hands with the president of the United States. Or it may be a negative, "attack" advertisement, charging an opponent with a weakness or an indiscretion unworthy of the public trust, or deliberately misrepresenting the opponent's record or position on an issue. Reporters often write reviews of the ads, usually getting reaction from the candidate's opponent or the opponent's campaign consultant.

Several media organizations analyze paid television spots for accuracy and report their findings. Major Texas newspapers—while often preoccupied with the horserace—also devote considerable resources to coverage of candidates and issues, attempting to provide the in-depth perspective missing in the electronic media. Most Texas voters, though, become acquainted with a candidate through televised images, and television has come to dominate the political process.

Television has allowed a candidate with enough money to "buy" an election legally. Bill Clements, who had never previously held elective office and was a stranger to most Texans, spent millions of dollars of his own fortune on television advertisements in 1978 to become the first Republican to capture the governor's office in modern times. But not every multimillionaire candidate has been so successful. In 1990, Clayton Williams, another wealthy businessman and political neophyte, spent more than $21 million, including $8.4 million from his own pocket, to create an attractive, thirty-second television image but lost by a whisker to Democrat Ann Richards. And Laredo businessman Tony Sanchez, a Democrat making his first statewide race, spent $59 million of his own fortune on a 2002 gubernatorial campaign, only to lose to Republican Rick Perry.

Political scientists, reporters, many voters, and even some candidates loudly criticize what television has done to campaigns for public office, putting style over substance and orchestrated events over thoughtful debate of the issues. But the creators of superficial television ads know they have a large audience. Since candidates are in the race to win office and not to reform the system, they spend millions of dollars perpetuating the political problem, which is actually part of a larger social problem.

Particularly susceptible to the image creators and media manipulators are the young adults who, according to recent studies, are less likely to read newspapers, watch television news programs, and otherwise keep up with current events than their parents or grandparents. "The 30-second commercial spot is a particularly appropriate medium for the MTV generation," noted one study. "Sound bites and symbolism, the principal fuel of modern political campaigns, are well-suited to young voters who know less and have limited interest in politics and public policy. Their limited appetites and aptitudes are shaping the practice of politics and the nature of our democracy."[9] It isn't just curiosity, after all, that prompts presidential candidates to campaign on MTV and the late-night television circuit. But the long-term implications of the superficial, image-oriented campaign and an increasingly indifferent electorate are no less disturbing.

Television is now the main source of news for most Americans, but nationwide, more and more objective television coverage of political campaigns has given way in recent years to paid commercials and soft news. Many opinion leaders fear the trend is further destroying Americans' interest in politics and urge the major television networks to voluntarily give free air time to presidential candidates. "Politics isn't going very well on television these days. . . . Campaigns unfold on all commercial television as a bread-and-circus blur of thirty-second attack ads and eight-second sound bites. Citizens feel cheated. They grow cynical," wrote former longtime CBS News anchor Walter Cronkite.[10]

In 1996, the TV networks agreed to give major presidential candidates several minutes of free, uninterrupted time during news programs to speak directly to voters. But the problem hasn't been resolved.

An estimated $1 billion was spent on paid political advertising on television during the 2000 campaign cycle, including the presidential race, with special interest contributions to candidates picking up most of the tab. But most local television stations and the national networks each broadcast an average of fewer than forty seconds a night of discussion or debate by candidates, according to reports by the University of Southern California and the Annenberg Public Policy Center. "Citizens are trapped in a system controlled by big-money candidates, special-interest donors and profit-hungry broadcasters," said Paul Taylor, chairman of the Alliance for Better Campaigns, which encourages broadcasters to offer candidates more free air time. "Increasingly, political campaigns have become a transfer of income from wealthy donors to wealthy broadcasters. Meantime, substantive issue discussion is disappearing from the public square of broadcast television."[11]

The 2003 gubernatorial recall election in California also generated much paid TV advertising, but unlike most campaigns it also received considerable coverage—in California and nationally—on TV news segments, thanks to the starring role played by action actor Arnold Schwarzenegger. According to an analysis by the Tyndall Report, which tracks national TV coverage, three major networks—ABC, CBS and NBC—aired 169 minutes of stories about the October 7 recall between August 1 and October 3. That compared to only 40 minutes of news coverage on the same networks for all 36 gubernatorial races, including the one in Texas, in 2002. Moreover, more than one-third of the California recall stories, or 69 minutes' worth, focused exclusively on the candidacy of Schwarzenegger, a Republican who unseated Democratic Gov. Gray Davis. "It's a shame that it takes a movie star candidate to get the media to pay attention to campaigns," said Meredith McGehee, president and executive director of the Alliance for Better Campaigns. "When it comes to covering elections, most broadcasters are AWOL. The 2002 gubernatorial campaigns were no less important to our democracy than this recall election. If money is the mother's milk of American politics, then celebrity must be its crack cocaine." McGehee also noted that most of the TV coverage of the recall focused on voter opinion polls or on "the circus-type atmosphere of the race," rather than on substantive issues. "That type of news does little to help citizens become informed, engaged voters," she said.[12]

Despite the national criticism, Ann Arnold, executive director of the Texas Association of Broadcasters, said that a "substantial number" of television and radio stations in Texas offered free air time to candidates. But many candidates don't accept the offers, she said. Arnold said the broadcasters' group also has sponsored seminars to help TV and radio stations find ways to make political news coverage more interesting and encourage more people to vote.[13]

Media Coverage of Recent Gubernatorial Campaigns in Texas

Some of the worst aspects of contemporary political campaigning occurred in the 2002 and 1990 Texas gubernatorial elections, which were characterized by **negative television ads,** personal attacks on the character and integrity of the candidates, and distortions of their public records. The races also demonstrated the dominance of well-financed campaigns and political advertising.

The news media's performance in covering both campaigns was mixed. The voters who followed the campaigns through the state's major daily newspapers—if they periodically wiped off the mud—were given more than enough information to compare the candidates' qualifications and personalities and evaluate their proposed solutions—or lack thereof—to the state's major problems. But many voters never got past the paid TV commercials.

Kicking off the 2002 political season with a large investment in a TV media campaign, multimillionaire Laredo businessman Tony Sanchez beat former Texas Attorney General Dan Morales in a mud-splattered fight for the Democratic gubernatorial nomination. Gov. Rick Perry, who had succeeded former Gov. George W. Bush in mid-term after Bush was elected president, was unopposed in the Republican primary for his first full term as governor.

Perry later defeated Sanchez in the general election after both campaigns had spent almost $100 million combined, much of it on negative TV advertising that became almost vicious. In one spot, Perry even tried to link Sanchez to the murder of a federal law-enforcement officer. That ad was one of a series of commercials in which the Perry campaign attacked Sanchez over his previous ownership of Tesoro Savings & Loan, a thrift in Laredo that had failed during the recession of the 1980s. In his advertising and campaign statements, Perry repeatedly attacked Sanchez over $25 million in drug money that had been laundered through Tesoro. The deposits, made in 1983 and 1984, had been investigated by federal authorities, but no one at the financial institution was ever charged with a crime. Sanchez and other former Tesoro officials said they hadn't known the money belonged to drug dealers. Perry's Tesoro ads, nevertheless, continued, culminating in a commercial in which two former Drug Enforcement Agency agents blamed the drug lords who had laundered the money through Tesoro for the torture and slaying of a DEA agent. Sanchez called the attack sleazy, and his supporters said it was racist. Sanchez ran television commercials blaming Perry for high consumer electric bills. The Democratic nominee also sponsored a TV spot that featured video from a police camera, which had recorded Perry, then lieutenant governor, in a confrontation with a state trooper who had pulled over Perry's driver for speeding. But Sanchez couldn't counter the devastating effect of Perry's attack. Perry's Tesoro ads assured the Republican governor's election, said University of Houston political scientist Richard Murray. He said the ads were influential because Sanchez had never held elective office and many voters already were uncertain of his abilities.[14]

The Democratic gubernatorial primary of 1990 may have been even muddier than the 2002 campaign, and the media was in the middle of the fray. Before Ann Richards defeated then–Attorney General Jim Mattox in a runoff for the Democratic nomination, some media outlets even ran uncorroborated reports about Richards and Mattox using illegal drugs. Fearful of being beaten by a competitor in what had become a virtual feeding frenzy, some news people threw basic journalistic standards of substantiation and fairness out the window.

Businessman Clayton Williams, meanwhile, easily won the Republican gubernatorial nomination that year over three opponents, thanks to an effective television advertising campaign financed mainly by his own wealth. Williams received little critical media attention during his primary race. But almost immediately after he was nominated, he found himself thrust into the spotlight, beginning with negative news stories about a rape joke that he told several reporters in what he thought was an informal, off-the-record setting (see "Telling a Bad Joke").

Williams's campaign operatives then tried to restrict the media's access to him and to manage his public appearances more carefully. But Williams saw a gradual erosion of an early lead, with costly losses among Texas women. He also committed other major gaffes late in the campaign.

Only a few days before the November election, he admitted that he had paid no federal income tax in 1986 because of business losses, an admission that angered tax-weary voters of more modest means. In the fall, the *Houston Chronicle* also reported allegations that a bank of which Williams was a director had illegally required high-risk auto loan customers to purchase credit life insurance.[15]

The 1994 governor's race between Richards and her successful Republican challenger, George W. Bush, was much tamer, and the media's coverage reflected the difference. Richards received some criticism for referring to Bush as a "jerk" early in the campaign and for running television commercials attacking Bush's record as a businessman. Bush contended the attacks on his business record were a "personal" assault. But Richards's supporters said they were fair because Bush, who had never held public office, had touted his business experience as proof of his leadership ability.

Reporters' access to both candidates was tightly controlled by their respective campaign organizations, while Bush and Richards both relied heavily on television advertising to carry their carefully crafted messages to the public. More than ever before, major newspapers, television stations, and the Associated Press analyzed the truthfulness of campaign advertising for their readers and viewers, a process requiring considerable time and research. But a *Texas Poll* published late in the campaign indicated that more people believed the TV ads than the news media's "fact checks." Fifty-four percent of the survey's respondents said they trusted what they saw and heard in both Bush's and Richards's commercials, while only 48 percent said they trusted the media's independent analyses of them. Forty-one percent of the respondents indicated the impressions they formed of the candidates from televised images affected how they voted more than published news accounts or the candidates' stands on the issues.

Coverage of Down-ballot Races

Although presidential, gubernatorial and United States Senate races receive heavy media coverage by Texas news organizations, most races for down-ballot statewide offices in Texas are traditionally under-covered. Recent exceptions were races for lieutenant governor and attorney general in 1998. They received more media attention than usual because they were wide-open races for offices being vacated by the retirement of incumbents and were crucial to both major parties in the wake of recent, strong Republican gains in Texas. The 1998 lieutenant governor's race, in which Republican Rick Perry defeated Democrat John Sharp, took on even more importance because of then-Gov. George W. Bush's anticipated race for president two years later. Most voters realized that the winner of the lieutenant governor's race would succeed Bush as governor in mid-term if Bush were promoted to the White House, which is what happened in 2000.

Newspapers and television stations usually don't have sufficient staff, news columns, or air time to provide the in-depth coverage that many races for other executive offices and the statewide courts deserve. Spotty news coverage, in turn, has

---

TELLING A BAD JOKE

Clayton Williams, a rancher-oilman from Midland, took full advantage of Texas's television markets to swamp three opponents and win the 1990 Republican nomination for governor. Bankrolling his own campaign to the tune of $6 million for the March primary, Williams literally galloped to the nomination across the small screen. With paid television spots of himself riding horseback in cowboy duds across his ranch, he cultivated an image as an independent, successful businessman and governmental outsider with strong traditional roots who would mount a no-nonsense attack on the problems in Austin.

After the primary, however, Williams began to be subjected to closer and more critical scrutiny. His first encounter with increased media attention occurred in spectacular fashion when he invited reporters to his West Texas ranch for spring roundup. Sharing a cup of coffee around an early morning campfire with cowhands, campaign staffers, and three male reporters—R. G. Ratcliffe of the *Houston Chronicle,* Sam Attlesey of the *Dallas Morning News,* and John Gravois of the *Houston Post*—Williams saw no reason for caution. When he told an old joke comparing the morning's foggy weather to rape—"if it's inevitable, just relax and enjoy it"—he certainly had no idea it would become page one headlines in the next day's newspapers and an issue in the remainder of the campaign. But it did.

In the not-too-distant past, such remarks in an informal setting, where the candidate was hosting reporters, would have been treated as off-the-record and not been reported. But now every aspect of a public official's or candidate's life is subject to public scrutiny, as demonstrated on the national scene by the widespread reporting of sexual misconduct by President Bill Clinton. Reporters are making greater efforts to present voters with a candid view of a candidate, "warts" and all, something that viewers aren't going to see in the candidate's television commercials.

In reporting Williams's rape joke, the media also took into consideration society's increasing sensitivity to sexual abuse and harassment, the fact that a violent crime is no laughing matter, and the question of whether Williams, as governor, would be sensitive to issues of particular concern to half of Texas's population—women.

---

increased the likelihood that candidates can win election almost solely on the basis of straight-party voting or effective television advertising campaigns. Television certainly was a key factor, for example, in Rick Perry's narrow victory over Democratic Agriculture Commissioner Jim Hightower in 1990.

Some reporters believed that Hightower, who had used no paid television, had underestimated his opponent. But Hightower sharply criticized the media for ignoring foreign trade and other issues that he had discussed in numerous personal appearances throughout Texas. "Frankly there's just a lot of stupidity in the press," he said in a post-election interview in the *Texas Observer.* "I mean there are people who just aren't very bright. They don't get it. I mean, you can talk issues all day long, and they just don't follow you."[16]

To receive any appreciable press coverage, a candidate for statewide office has to establish himself or herself as a serious, viable contender. And one of the standards by which such viability is measured is a candidate's ability to finance a campaign adequately—either through personal wealth or a broad base of financial contributors. That is an insurmountable obstacle for many would-be officeholders.

THE MASS MEDIA AND PUBLIC ETHICS

Perhaps the greatest potential for media influence in Austin is over the ethical conduct of legislators and other public officials, simply because of the potential embarrassment and political damage that can befall an elected official caught in an impropriety. But even that influence is sporadic, because memories are short and, sooner or later, there will be another scandal. And seldom is the relationship between reporters and governmental officials more adversarial than when the media is questioning the ethical behavior of officeholders or reporting on a prosecutor who is doing so.

Tension was particularly high in 1990 and 1991 when then–House Speaker Gib Lewis was fighting two misdemeanor ethics charges stemming from a grand jury investigation of his relationship with a tax-collection law firm. After Lewis was indicted on December 28, 1990—twelve days before the 1991 legislative session was to convene—the speaker mailed letters to newspapers across the state, urging editors to avoid a "rush to judgment" about his case. Maintaining his innocence, Lewis said, "All I ask is basic fairness—that I be given the time and opportunity to gather the facts and present my case before you judge me." The *Houston Chronicle* ran the letter at the top of its "Viewpoints," or letters-to-the-editor, column, accompanied by the mug shots, front and side views, taken of Lewis when he surrendered to law enforcement officers at the Travis County jail.[17]

Lewis was easily reelected speaker when the legislature convened, and he maintained a reasonable working relationship with the news media throughout the 1991 session. He had always been personable, but there were some rough spots. He accused the media of manufacturing the ethics issue and suggested news people should monitor their own behavior first. The day before the session convened, he told a group of Capitol reporters, in a seemingly jocular vein: "You guys ought to be lucky I am close-mouthed. I know who every one of you is sleeping with. I now understand where you get some of your leads. My phone has been ringing off the wall the last couple of weeks. . . . So you better be nice to me."[18]

The controversy over Lewis's legal troubles, however, was tame compared to the furor that erupted two years later when Travis County District Attorney Ronnie Earle, a Democrat, began investigating newly elected U.S. Senator Kay Bailey Hutchison, a Republican, for allegedly using state employees for political and personal chores while Hutchison was state treasurer. Hutchison, whose conduct had been questioned months earlier in a story in the *Houston Post,* was indicted by a Travis County grand jury in 1993. She was acquitted, however, in February 1994. Republican leaders had bombarded reporters with press releases and telephone calls accusing Earle of prosecuting the senator for political purposes. Republicans repeatedly pointed out that Earle had neglected to prosecute Land Commissioner Garry Mauro, a Democrat, for using state telephones and employees to campaign for then–presidential candidate Bill Clinton in 1992. Mauro, who had chaired Clinton's campaign in Texas, reimbursed the state after the *Houston Chronicle* reported the extent of the land office's political activity. Republicans also complained that Earle seemed reluctant to investigate Democratic Governor Ann Richards after her office had prematurely destroyed some state telephone records.

Although the Republicans' public relations campaign didn't influence Hutchison's acquittal, GOP officials said they were forced to attack Earle and try to influence public opinion in order to repair any political damage to the senator and other Republican candidates. Hutchison supporters met with newspaper editorial boards and spoke on radio talk shows. Her attorneys even sent grand jury members packets of news clippings about the case. Dr. John Todd, an associate professor of political science at the University of North Texas, told the *Dallas Morning News* that the Republicans had "surprising success in planting the idea that this has all been just a political enterprise undertaken against her [Hutchison]."[19]

GUARDIANS OF OPEN GOVERNMENT

Since the soundness of any governmental policy or program is affected by the motives and capabilities of those officials who design and administer it, most members of the Capitol press corps take very seriously their role as watchdogs over the behavior and performance of elected officials and bureaucrats. Consequently, news people are persistent guardians of the public's access to governmental business

---

— HOW I SEE IT —
OPEN RECORDS AND OPEN MEETINGS

Jack D. Loftis

Jack D. Loftis is editor emeritus of the *Houston Chronicle* and past president of the Freedom of Information Foundation of Texas, which promotes openness in government. He also is past president of the Newspaper Features Council, founding director of Crime Stoppers of Houston, and a Distinguished Alumnus of Baylor University. A native of Hillsboro, Texas, Loftis began his newspaper career at the Hillsboro *Daily Mirror* while he attended Baylor.

Hugh Powers, the late, former editor of the *Houston Chronicle*'s editorial page and a wise man on any number of topics, used to delight in stating the following: "Government, given the choice, will most often choose to conduct its business in secret."

What an indictment of our elected and appointed leaders—all of whom, I am certain, see themselves as upstanding citizens and dedicated guardians of the public trust.

But Powers' critical appraisal of government's unwillingness to fully share business with its constituents is closer to the truth than most of us would care to believe. Otherwise, why all the fuss during every legislative session over what is a public record and what is not?

And even as public information laws get written and rewritten, elected and appointed officials at every level of government appear willing—in degrees ranging from casual to arrogant—to ignore legislation that grants public access.

I have always suspected the public has come to accept the belief that legislation promoting openness in government is on the books for the sake of the media. Many public officials through the state's **Open Meetings and Public Information acts.** These laws, which apply to state and local governments, basically provide that the public's business is to be conducted in public and that most records produced in the conduct of the public's business are to be made available to the public on demand. Each law provides for certain exceptions. Governmental bodies, for example, are allowed to hold closed-door meetings to consider personnel matters, to discuss lawsuits in which they are involved, and to consider real estate purchases, although all formal actions are to be taken in public. The Open Meetings Act requires a governmental body to post advance notices of all its meetings, even closed-door, executive sessions, and the Public Information Act establishes a procedure whereby the state attorney general's office decides disputes over whether specific governmental records can be kept confidential. But media representatives are engaged in a constant struggle against abuses and outright violations of the laws and attempts by school boards, city councils, and other governments to expand the list of exceptions that allow them to discuss business in private.

---

probably share the same view. This widespread misconception is strengthened because news outlets go to court to challenge abuses in open records/meetings laws more often than any other group. The reason for this is quite simple. Media companies usually have the resources to move the disputes into the courtroom, while many citizens who feel equally offended do not.

The hope that prosecuting attorneys across the state of Texas will someday unleash their power and authority at local levels to remedy open-government misconduct is a long shot, but it could happen. It depends on how informed the public becomes on its right to information and how soon citizens demand that these rights be respected by governmental bodies acting responsibly.

As to why public access to the actions of governmental bodies is important, one only has to imagine living under a totalitarian regime in which individuals are penalized for violating laws imposed on the people without their knowledge or approval.

Is a tax an unfair tax if levied in silence? Do public officials owe their constituents information regarding their votes on issues? Do communities have a right to know why their neighbors are accused of crimes? Should regulatory agencies be expected to explain their rules and procedures?

I believe most people would answer in the affirmative.

Those individuals who oppose the release of public documents most often cite a citizen's right to privacy as their fundamental defense against the public's right to know. There is no question that privacy is a factor in some situations. But reasonable people should be able to sort out information that, if released, could prove damaging from information that might only embarrass or cause inconvenience. The test should be as simple as this: Is the information being shared of substantial benefit to the public in general?

In closing, perhaps the most alarming rationale for suppressing information from the public was expressed by one bureaucrat in testimony before a state Senate Interim Committee on Public Information. The reason stated was that gathering and preparing the data are a whole lot of trouble.

That statement should prepare even the most timid proponents of open government to rest their case.

In one glaring case of abuse, the Houston Independent School District used a variety of legal maneuvers to circumvent a request by the *Houston Chronicle* for access to the educational records of some HISD administrators. The newspaper was trying to determine how many administrators held degrees from a non-accredited college, something of likely concern to many parents and taxpayers. But the school district continued to resist even after rulings from the attorney general and the Texas Supreme Court that the information the newspaper sought was public.

Several media organizations monitor and promote open government issues. The Freedom of Information Foundation of Texas, a nonprofit corporation that includes journalists, educators, and attorneys among its directors, maintains a telephone hotline to advise news people on open meetings and open-records rights and procedures and generally promotes openness in government. The Texas Daily Newspaper Association, the Texas Press Association, and the Texas Association of Broadcasters also lobby the legislature on open government issues. It's a difficult struggle because many public officials throughout Texas prefer to conduct the public's business in private. Numerous attempts usually are made each legislative session to weaken the open meetings and public information laws.

Media organizations are obviously in the business of disseminating information. But it is important to remember that they are not the only ones with a stake in strong open-government laws. Every Texan also has a right to know what his or her government is doing, to find open doors in city council chambers and school board meeting rooms, and to have ready access to public documents.

MEDIA BIAS

Most public officials are sensitive about what is written and broadcast about them, particularly if a controversial issue has thrust them into the spotlight. Consequently, they will often consider news stories slanted against them or their viewpoints. Complaints about alleged **media bias** are also made by readers and viewers, and the issue has sparked considerable debate and research. National studies have indicated that most reporters are more liberal than the general population in personal ideology and on many public policy issues, and conservatives have exploited these findings to support their contention of a liberal media bias.[20] But other people, including many liberals, have pointed to corporate media ownership and concluded that those who make the final decisions as to what news is covered and how it is covered reflect more conservative biases.

State Capitol reporters in Texas normally attempt to present all sides of an issue. Most believe they are objective, dedicated to principles of fairness and balance, and report events as they happen. This view of the press as a mirror was summarized by Frank Stanton, former president of CBS, when he testified before a congressional committee that "what the media do is to hold a mirror up to society and try to report it as faithfully as possible." But news people and the organizations they represent sometimes have strong personal or corporate opinions about the issues or individuals they cover, and bias and the perception of bias are problems the media constantly has to fight.[21]

Subjective decisions—such as a reporter's own strong interest in an issue—may determine which news events are covered on a particular day or which angle is emphasized in a particular story. Unless they are personal friends, reporters seldom discuss their political preferences with each other, but their personal politics doubtlessly cover the spectrum—Democrats, Republicans, and independents; conservatives, moderates, and liberals.

More often than not, however, reporters eagerly provide a forum for the viewpoints of consumer advocates, environmentalists, and other individuals purporting to promote the public interest. One reason is that spokespersons for these groups are readily accessible, hold frequent news conferences, and actively cultivate media contacts. They depend on free media exposure to compensate for limited budgets in their battles against the business lobby for the tougher regulations and higher taxes that progressive programs often require. Another reason is that stories about the age-old struggle between the powerful and the powerless, the rich and the poor, attract considerable reader and viewer interest, centering as they do on controversy and conflict.

The prominence with which editors or news directors "play" stories—page one versus inside the paper, the lead item on the 10 o'clock news versus minor air

---

A REPORTER'S SHIELD?

Some reporters and news organizations in Texas, particularly in the broadcast media, have advocated a so-called reporter's **shield law** to protect journalists from having to reveal the names of confidential news sources when they are subpoenaed to appear in court. Often, the only way a reporter can learn of and develop stories of governmental corruption is through confidential sources, who in many cases are government employees or contractors who would lose their jobs if their names were made public. Without the protection of confidentiality, news organizations fear their sources would dry up and deprive the public of stories it needs to know.

About half of the other states have similar laws. But even though a number of reporters have been sent to jail by judges for refusing to reveal confidential sources, many Texas reporters and editors still oppose a shield law. They don't like the idea of the legislature trying to define what constitutes a news organization or a reporter or trying to determine how broad or how narrow the protection should be. They prefer to rely on First Amendment guarantees of a free press and the courts' interpretations of it. The Fifth U.S. Circuit Court of Appeals in New Orleans, which has appellate jurisdiction over cases originating in federal courts in Texas, has ruled in favor of confidentiality protections for news sources.

But in a criminal case originating in state court, the Texas Court of Criminal Appeals, Texas's highest criminal court, ruled in 1994 that there is no reporter's privilege to protect news organizations from subpoenas. The decision was prompted by a Fort Bend County case in which a funeral home operator was charged with abuse of a corpse after allegedly dumping a man's body at his son's apartment in a dispute over cremation fees. The district attorney had subpoenaed employees of Houston television stations who had shot videotape of the defendant. Many television and radio news people complain that prosecutors and other lawyers are increasingly issuing subpoenas for video and audiotapes of news events instead of independently trying to develop their own information, which is often readily available from other sources.

A shield bill died in the 1993 legislative session, partly because the media was divided over the issue. But the issue periodically resurfaces.

treatment—is usually determined by the newsperson's perception of the public's interest in a given story. But an editor's or publisher's own opinion of an issue may also be a factor. Newspapers and broadcast stations often disagree with each other—and with their own reporters—on how stories should be played. Ultimately, a relatively few individuals decide which stories will be reported, how prominently they will be presented, and how much space or time will be allotted to them. And people alleging media bias will point out that fact.[22] Michael Parenti, a critic of institutional elites in the United States, concludes that "the very process of selection allows the cultural and political biases and class interests of the selector to operate as censor."[23] Other media watchers argue, however, that the media "gatekeepers"—those who decide what news to publish or broadcast—are constrained, at least in part, by their readers' or viewers' preferences, as determined through market research.

Stories about governmental scandals and political corruption are often displayed on page one of newspapers and at the top of evening television newscasts. Attempting to follow in the footsteps of the early muckrakers of American journalism, some Texas news people view themselves as crusaders and are determined to "clean up" government. In their eagerness, however, they can become susceptible to charges of unfair, personal bias against the public officials they are targeting. This is particularly true when haste to be the first with the latest development in an ongoing scandal produces reporting or editing mistakes.

Newspapers and radio and television stations in Texas are big businesses and, as such, sometimes have their own special interests to protect. Media opposition, for example, has played a major role in killing periodic attempts by legislators to put a sales tax on advertising. An advertising tax could raise millions of dollars for education, human services, and other programs that media outlets generally support, but media owners fear it would reduce advertising volume and deprive them of critical revenue.

THE DEVELOPMENT OF THE PRESS IN TEXAS

Frontier Newspapers

Frontier Texans, isolated in their farmhouses and small settlements, lacked many creature comforts, but most had the opportunity to keep informed about the political sentiment of the day. The short-lived *Graceta de Tejas*, or the *Texas Gazette*, was established in Nacogdoches in 1812 long before Texas won its independence in 1836.[24] By 1860, according to historian T. R. Fehrenbach, there were seventy-one daily and weekly newspapers in Texas, with a total circulation of about 100,000. "Ninety-five percent of the white population could read and write and some publication reached virtually every family."[25] Like other early American newspapers, these publications were often highly partisan and primarily devoted to commentary on public issues—the local, state, and national political events of that turbulent period. Social calendars and stories about floods, fires, murders, and other everyday disasters were not yet standard journalistic fare. Editorial writing, however, had already developed into a backwoods art form. "This writing was often irate, biased, and misinformed—but much of it was clear and sound. It kept the freeholders of Texas fully aware of events; many farmers could quote Senator Stephen Douglas or Sam Houston at length. Texans were already keen political animals."[26]

Newspapers and "The Establishment"

Throughout much of the twentieth century, Texas's major newspapers were active members of the conservative, big-business, big-oil establishment that ran the state-house and the state. During the pre-television years of the 1940s and 1950s, in particular, publishers of some of the state's major newspapers, such as Amon Carter in Fort Worth and Jesse Jones in Houston, were oilmen and financiers who helped control local and state politics for the dominant conservative wing of the Texas Democratic Party. Another strong voice for the establishment was the *Dallas Morning News,* a tireless anticommunist, antilabor, antiliberal crusader. At various times, the *News* editorialized that "the presidency of Franklin Roosevelt was actually destructive of the Republic, the Senate's censure of Joe McCarthy [was] 'a happy day for Communists,' and the Supreme Court [was] 'a threat to state sovereignty second only to Communism itself.' "[27] There was little pretense of detached, neutral reporting, as the newspapers actively participated in the political process.

The establishment's close relationship with the Texas press was convincingly demonstrated in numerous election campaigns, including the 1954 Democratic gubernatorial runoff between Governor Allan Shivers, who had led conservative Texas Democrats in supporting Republican Dwight Eisenhower in the 1952 presidential race, and liberal challenger Ralph Yarborough, a party loyalist and strong supporter of organized labor. In the closing weeks of the campaign, ninety-five of the state's one hundred daily newspapers carried editorials endorsing Shivers, who won the runoff. Yarborough would later win election to the U.S. Senate, but the establishment's opposition to him was rabid. In its editorial endorsement of Shivers in 1954, the *Dallas Morning News,* however, was kind enough to concede that some of Yarborough's Texas supporters were not "reds . . . radicals or goon squad supporters."[28]

Evolution of Texas Newspapers

News coverage has changed significantly during the past forty years, and readers now will almost never find the kind of inflammatory, racist, demagogic writing that characterized much of the earlier Texas press. The media today is much more disposed to cover issues affecting the lower income populations, minorities, and others struggling against the power structure. Texas is still largely a conservative state, and a restructured business community is still influential in the setting of state policy. But the media—particularly the large newspapers and television stations—is much more eager to challenge the political and business establishment today.

For one reason, there is a high level of distrust of government now. A turning point in Texas was the Sharpstown stock fraud scandal that broke in 1971. It revealed that the legislature had given quick passage in 1969 to two banking regulation bills sought by Houston financier Frank Sharp and that high-ranking state officials had profited from insurance stock purchases financed with loans from Sharp's bank (see Chapter 8). That was soon to be followed by the Watergate scandal, which would force the resignation of President Richard Nixon and shake public confidence in government throughout the country, much as the bitter experience of the Vietnam War already had begun to do.

News people still depend on government officials for much of their information. But now they more readily question the motives of the governor, legislators, and other public officeholders and political candidates. The ethical behavior of officeholders and their relationship to the special interests that spend millions of dollars trying to influence state government came under closer scrutiny after the Sharpstown and Watergate scandals. The media also reexamined its own ethics. Most news organizations, for example, adopted policies prohibiting their reporters from accepting free airplane rides, junkets, and other "freebies" from state officials or candidates, practices that had been fairly common in Texas in the past.

Another significant factor in the evolution of the Texas press was the passing of the high-profile publishers who had been part of the conservative establishment. Many of their newspapers were subsequently sold to large national conglomerates with newspapers and broadcast holdings in many cities. Such purchases of major, once independently owned newspapers like the *Houston Chronicle,* the *Fort Worth Star-Telegram,* and the *Austin American-Statesman* are part of a consolidation of media ownership across the country, a development regarded as unhealthy by many within and outside the industry.

Such consolidations raise concerns that national owners, who have no personal ties to the local communities, may be more concerned about profits and losses than the quality of news coverage—or diversity of editorial viewpoints—in their local outlets. And those concerns have been renewed in the wake of recent technological advances and corporate mergers.

But, perhaps paradoxically, national ownership can offer Texas newspapers a greater degree of independence than was true in the past. Absentee corporate owners don't have sacred cows to protect in the Texas statehouse, the local courthouse, or city hall, and don't feel compelled to defend old provincial prejudices. If the *Austin American-Statesman,* for example, still had Texas owners, it may not have been so bold as to editorialize in the early 1990s for a state income tax when that proposal was still highly unpopular in Texas and opposed by most elected officials and business people. The *American-Statesman,* owned by Atlanta-based Cox Enterprises, helped provoke a public debate over a critical issue that is becoming more and more difficult for the legislature to avoid. For the most part, Texas newspapers have maintained considerable **editorial autonomy** under national owners.

The *Dallas Morning News* is the only major metropolitan newspaper in the state still owned by a Texas-based corporation. It also still presents one of the most conservative editorial viewpoints on its opinion pages, but it aggressively covers governmental and political institutions on its news pages.

The 1970s and 1980s were turning points for many Texas newspapers. Many changed owners during this period, and the overall quality of Texas journalism began to improve noticeably. The most dramatic and most influential change occurred in Dallas, and it was brought about by the brief entry of one of the nation's media giants, the Times Mirror Company, into the Dallas newspaper market.

Times Mirror, publisher of the *Los Angeles Times,* one of the country's most respected newspapers, purchased the *Dallas Times Herald* from local owners in 1970. Within a few years, it precipitated a major newspaper war with its dominant competitor, the *Morning News.* Times Mirror brought in new editors, recruited reporters from all over the country, improved the quality and aggressiveness of its news coverage—"The Only Sacred Cow Here Is Hamburger," read a sign on the newsroom wall—and awakened the *Morning News* from what many media watchers had considered a long, provincial slumber. At one point, the *Times Herald* briefly passed the *Morning News* in Sunday circulation. But the *Morning News* responded by bringing in new editors of its own, expanding its news staff, and vastly improving its own product. During this period, both newspapers became major national award winners.

Initially, Times Mirror's foray into Dallas was extremely profitable, but with the precipitous decline in the Texas economy during the 1980s, the *Times Herald* began to lose money and was still second in advertising and circulation. The paper was sold in 1986 to a Texan, who was unable to reverse its financial position. It changed hands one more time before the *Morning News* purchased the struggling property and closed it in 1991. The *Morning News* remains one of the state's and nation's premier newspapers, thanks in large part to the swift kick administered by Times Mirror. Moreover, the higher journalistic standards that emerged in Dallas had positive effects on some of the state's other newspapers, which soon began undergoing transformations of their own.

Modern Newspapers, Modern Problems

Hundreds of newspapers in the United States have ceased publication since 1900, a reflection of changing reader habits, corporate consolidations, the emergence of television, the proliferation of radio stations with targeted audiences, the development of specialized magazines, and other factors. The folding of the *Dallas Times Herald* was followed by the closing of the *San Antonio Light* in 1993, the *Houston Post* in 1995, and the *El Paso Herald-Post* in 1997, leaving all of the large cities in Texas with only one daily newspaper each.

Hearst, the *San Antonio Light*'s long-time owner, closed the paper after purchasing the rival *San Antonio Express-News*, which had gained the circulation lead in San Antonio. The *Light* had been published in San Antonio for 112 years, but lost a reported $60 million during its last six years of operation.[29] During its final years, the *Houston Post* also lost millions of dollars as it went through a succession of owners. Texas now has about ninety daily newspapers and about 450 weekly, biweekly, or monthly newspapers.

Local newspaper competition can help improve the quality of news coverage, provide alternative views and interpretations of events, and reduce the potential for cozy relationships between the media and the community's establishment. But it is increasingly difficult for a city to support two daily newspapers. For many years, the *El Paso Herald-Post* survived because of a federal law designed to protect struggling newspapers. Owned by E. W. Scripps Co., it was published under a joint operating agreement with the larger *El Paso Times,* owned by Gannett Co. The joint operating agreement allowed the two papers to maintain separate, competitive news staffs but save money by sharing advertising and circulation staffs, the same building, and the same presses. But by 1997, with its daily circulation having fallen from more than 31,000 to 18,000 in ten years, even that wasn't enough to save the *Herald-Post.*

Most small-town weekly newspapers are oriented primarily to their local communities and carry little news of state government or politics. But most of the small towns served by weeklies also are in the circulation areas of daily newspapers. There are also a number of African-American-oriented and Spanish-language papers in Texas, but they have limited circulations. The demise of major daily newspapers has raised the profiles of aggressive, alternative weeklies in some Texas cities. Two of the better known are the *Houston Press* and the *Dallas Observer.*

Newspapers can more thoroughly explain a pending issue, its history, and possible options for its resolution than can the electronic media. But newspapers also have their limits, primarily in the amount of space they can or will devote to governmental news. Responding to the popularity of television and its drain on available advertising revenue, newspapers in recent years generally have reduced the proportion of space allocated to so-called "hard news." "Newspaper editors, like TV producers, have discovered the American public's insatiable hunger for 'fluff,' " one critic wrote.[30]

The larger Texas papers, nevertheless, still set aside a respectable amount of space for national, state, and local government news, alongside the travel and lifestyle stories and gourmet recipes. A modern daily newspaper is much like a cafeteria. It has a variety of offerings for a variety of tastes and expects its readers to scan the headlines, choosing what they want to try to digest.

The Electronic Media

Dramatic changes in mass communications over the past forty years, primarily the emergence of television, have had a major impact on the role of the media in government and politics. An estimated 98 percent of American homes have at least one television set, and most are linked to cable television systems. Television has replaced the newspaper as the public's primary source of news.

Sixty-one percent of Texans responding to a 1999 edition of the Scripps Howard *Texas Poll* said that television was their primary source of local news. Seventy-one percent said TV was their primary source of national news, and 70 percent said it was their main source of world news. Only 22 percent said newspapers were their primary source of local news. Only 11 percent and 12 percent identified newspapers as their main sources of national and world news, respectively. There was no category for "state news." Moreover, 41 percent of the respondents identified television as the "most credible or believable" news medium, compared to 23 percent for newspapers. And 50 percent of the respondents said they would be relying more on television for news in the future, compared to 18 percent who chose newspapers.[31]

With these changes, there has been increased concern about the role of television in shaping our view of politics and setting the agenda for public policies. This concern is compounded by declining levels of news literacy among Americans, particularly the young. Although there has been a proliferation of news sources, a 1990 national survey concluded that "those under 30 know less than younger people once did, and they are less interested in what's happening in the larger world around them."[32] This decline, which has been re-emphasized in more recent surveys and will be discussed in more detail later in this chapter, has had its greatest impact on newspapers, but it also has implications for the broadcast media.

There are about 160 television stations in twenty markets in Texas, ranging in size from Dallas–Fort Worth and Houston, which ranked seventh and eleventh nationally in 2000, to Victoria, which ranked 204th. Some cable stations are now offering full-time news coverage. The first was established in Austin in 1999 by Time Warner Cable, which holds the cable TV franchise in Austin. Despite TV's emergence as Texans' primary news source, television coverage of state government and politics has become inconsistent in recent years, even in the larger cities. Only one TV station from outside Austin has a full-time bureau covering the state Capitol. Other stations sometimes will send news crews to Austin for special events, such as a gubernatorial inauguration or the opening day of a legislative session, but their overall coverage is spotty and inconsistent.

Even at its best, television is an inadequate substitute for newspaper coverage of government and politics. Most local television news programs provide only cursory reports on governmental issues and activities, and people who rely solely on television for news have little substantive information upon which to make critical and informed judgments. Television—which, of course, is visually oriented—is good at taping a protest demonstration on the Capitol steps, getting a sound bite from the governor, or gathering interviews with citizens outraged over a tax increase. But the limited air time given to even the most important stories makes it difficult to explain why the protesters marched on the Capitol or to explore the economic and political factors that produced the tax bill.

Most radio news also is of the headline variety, a quick summary of the day's news highlights. Many radio stations make no pretense of offering serious news coverage. Few have sufficient news staffs to cover major events or issues in Austin. They rely on wire stories or feeds from a news service such as the Texas State Network, which has an Austin bureau. A handful of news talk stations, however, offer more in-depth coverage and commentary on political events and public issues. This commentary includes talk show programs that offer primarily conservative viewpoints. Although a large part of the population regularly tunes in to radio, the medium runs a poor third as a primary source of state political news.

Television and radio often take their cues about what to cover from the print media. Most stations don't have large enough reporting staffs to do the extensive background work required to develop many complex stories. But once a story broken by a newspaper has grabbed attention, the electronic media usually will join in pursuit.

Growing Media Conglomerates and Technological Changes

Just as there is national concern about growing chain ownership of newspapers, there is also concern about ownership patterns in the television industry. As an unsettling precedent, some media watchers cite the 1985 purchase of the National Broadcasting Company (NBC) by General Electric, a nonjournalistic conglomerate whose primary business had been "neither news nor entertainment but household appliances, airplane engines, nuclear reactors, and arms."[33] General Electric extended its reach into the entertainment sector in 2003, when it agreed to merge NBC with Vivendi Universal Entertainment, owner of Universal Pictures, Universal Television and a number of cable TV systems. The new company, NBC Universal, was to be 80 percent owned by General Electric. "With this merger, NBC will stay in the forefront of the fundamental changes taking place in television and other media," said Jeffrey Immelt, GE's chairman and chief executive.[34]

Several national media chains own newspapers or broadcast properties in Texas. Texas-based A. H. Belo Corp., owner of the *Dallas Morning News,* also owns television stations in Dallas, Houston, San Antonio and Austin. San Antonio–based Clear Channel owned some 1,200 radio stations throughout the country in 2003 after an aggressive strategy of purchasing single stations and companies with several holdings.

Concerns over media ownership increased in 2003 after the Federal Communications Commission adopted new regulations to relax ownership restrictions on newspapers, TV affiliates and radio stations. The decision was so controversial that the Republican-controlled Senate voted 55–40 to reverse it, but the House leadership and the Bush administration supported the FCC. The rule change, unless reversed in court, would clear the way for greater market control by major media companies by allowing for more cross-ownership of broadcast outlets and newspapers in the same cities.[35]

There have been remarkable technological changes over the past decade, suggesting that we can anticipate a much greater range of news sources in the future. Most newspapers have their own websites on the Internet, making their stories accessible to millions of new readers well beyond their local or regional circulations. Some television stations also carry their newscasts and even live coverage of major courtroom trials on their websites. Newspapers and broadcasters also have expanded their use of the Internet to collect and analyze statistical data for news stories.

Traditional broadcast owners, meanwhile, are facing increasing challenges from cable and satellite television, the emerging digital broadcast system, and other technological advances. There is a high-stakes war among the traditional—or "old media"—outlets, cable television and telephone companies, and Internet providers for the huge profits to be made in the high technology information age. That war reached a new level in early 2000 with the multibillion-dollar merger of America Online, the number one Internet provider, with Time Warner, the media and cable television giant. The mega-deal and fallout from it seemed to promise not only to reshape competition within the communications industry, but also to open up new information sources for consumers.

The AOL-Time Warner merger also renewed debate over how much independence news outlets may be losing with corporate mergers, particularly since a relative handful of corporate owners with an array of business interests was now in ultimate control of most of those outlets. "The worry is not that there are fewer media outlets—the opposite is true—but that few people have ultimate control over them," the *New York Times* wrote. "Critics wonder if news judgments will be bent, with executives suppressing news deemed harmful to corporate interests. They wonder if companies will use their journalists to promote their other interests, be they movies, television shows or sports teams." Media experts interviewed by the newspaper, however, offered different opinions about those potential problems. "Defenders of the news divisions point out that plenty of media outlets would be eager to pick up on a story suppressed by a competitor. Top media executives also know and have argued to their corporate bosses that cheap or compromised journalism costs the enterprise both trust and profits," the newspaper noted.[36]

Three years after the merger, many questions still remained unanswered. The corporate board voted in 2003 to remove AOL from the company's name and revert to Time Warner. To many observers, the change signalled that America Online was merely one of many businesses—but not a dominant player—in the media giant. AOL had lost more than one million subscribers during the previous year because of faster Internet connections provided by cable TV and telephone companies.[37]

Many of the radio stations held by national conglomerates no longer provide local news. Some are basically remote facilities in which the programming is formatted in another city, and the reporters or disc jockeys are speaking from a studio miles away. Another potential source of local news is being lost to corporate consolidation. It is another step toward the homogenization of news.

Although it is difficult to foresee all the implications of the recent technological advances and high-stakes mergers, one can speculate that there will be major changes in the way the electorate receives information about politics and government—and the way the media will be exploited by officeholders and candidates.

THE CAPITOL PRESS CORPS

The state's major newspapers, the Associated Press, one television station, a radio network and an individual radio station are represented at the Capitol by reporters who cover state government and politics full time. The press corps has about forty permanent members and is larger during legislative sessions, when additional media organizations send representatives to Austin and some of the permanent bureaus add to their staffs. Several "insider" subscriber newsletters and Internet websites that focus on state government also have been launched in Austin. The muckraking *Texas Observer*, long a favorite of Texas liberals, is still published fortnightly and still has a faithful following. The slick magazine *Texas Monthly* offers limited coverage of state government, most notably its ranking of what it considers the ten best and ten worst legislators after each regular session. The *Texas Lawyer*, a weekly newspaper specializing in the activities of the courts and other news of interest to the legal profession, also has an Austin-based reporter. And several national news organizations have correspondents based in Austin, although they don't cover state government on a daily basis.

Individual news bureaus range in size from several staffers for the Associated Press and the larger newspapers to one-person operations for smaller organizations. Each multiperson bureau has a bureau chief who not only is a reporter but also makes assignments and handles administrative duties. Some newspaper bureaus also have columnists, and the larger bureaus have clerks and sometimes hire university journalism students as interns. The Associated Press is the only news organization with a full-time still photographer on its Capitol staff, although several freelance photographers are available to newspapers in Austin, and staff photographers are sent to the Capitol from home offices for special assignments.

The small newspaper bureaus usually give priority to covering members of their local legislative delegations and events of particular interest to their communities, while the large papers and the wire services provide more general coverage. But even the large papers find it impossible to cover the entire range of state government activities. Priorities are set, with the legislature, the governor, the attorney general, the comptroller, the appellate courts and the larger administrative agencies usually receiving the most attention.

The large dailies offer more investigative and interpretive reporting than do the wire services, television and radio. The large newspapers also are increasingly turning to specialty reporters based in their home offices, rather than at the Capitol, to cover all governmental aspects—state, local and federal—of such multifaceted issues as environmental protection, health care and transportation.

The statehouse bureaus are generally considered prestigious assignments and attract capable and aggressive reporters. Nevertheless, there has been considerable turnover on Capitol news staffs in recent years. Only a dozen or so of the reporters and columnists covering the legislature in 2003 had more than ten years of experience on the Capitol beat. This means many reporters have little historical perspective for comparing the administrations of different governors or the performance of the legislature over a sustained period. But most reporters successfully compensate for their limited institutional memories through research and interviews with long-time Capitol players.

There is no typical pattern to the careers of Capitol reporters. Some were promoted from their organizations' local staffs, while others were hired from competing bureaus or even from out-of-state newspapers. In recent years, relatively few Capitol reporters have chosen to retire in those jobs, but only a handful have gone on to become editors or news directors in their home offices. Some have moved to news bureaus in Washington and jobs in other media markets, while others have become press secretaries or information specialists for elected officeholders or state agencies. Some have even left the news business for unrelated occupations.

Most news bureaus lease private office space near the Capitol for their main offices and lease smaller, additional workspace from the state in an underground addition to the Capitol. With proper credentials, media representatives are granted access to the floors of the House and the Senate when the legislature is in session. Special worktables at the front of each chamber are provided for reporters, and the House and the Senate set standards for credentials under their respective rules.

Newspaper bureaus transmit their stories to their home offices via computer, and television correspondents use satellite transmissions. News organizations use the Internet and computerized databases to assist in researching and preparing stories, including, for example, articles detailing how many of a governor's appointees to state boards and commissions were political donors and how much money each gave.

But sound news judgment and perseverance are still the basic tools of the successful Capitol reporter, just as they are for thousands of news people elsewhere. Statehouse reporters usually have to dig out the best stories, frequently using confidential sources to develop tips or hunches. Legislators, other elected officials, members of their staffs, bureaucrats, and lobbyists love to tell secrets about each other. Such sources, of course, often have their own political or personal agendas, and the smart reporter is wary. Campaigns for state office are notorious for whispered accusations or innuendoes directed against opposing camps. Sometimes a legislator, without allowing his or her name to be used, will leak a controversial proposal to a reporter as a trial balloon to see how other lawmakers and the general public react to the idea before deciding whether to actively promote it. Similar anonymous leaks, cast in a negative light, can be used to kill someone else's proposal before he or she has had a chance to gather support for it. Although reporters run the risk of being used in such situations, they also can be put on the trail of significant stories. A newsperson has to evaluate each tip on its own merits, although he or she often is pressured by the knowledge that competitors also are getting similar tips.

GOVERNMENTAL PUBLIC RELATIONS

Most of the state's top elected officials and administrators of major agencies spend thousands of tax dollars each year on press secretaries and public relations operations to help disseminate public information and to promote themselves and their agencies. News releases, websites, press conferences, background briefings, slick reports, and videotapes are designed to maintain the visibility of state agencies, cultivate general goodwill, announce new programs, and anticipate budgetary attacks or program changes. In a dispute with the legislature or another state agency, a public official's media specialists often try to put a **"spin"** on a story that presents information in the best possible light for their boss.

The House and the Senate also provide media services for their members. Taxpayers pay for written news releases, newsletters, and radio and television feeds to local stations. These resources can be used by a legislator to maintain a flow of information to constituents that, in effect, amounts to a continuous political campaign.

Some governors have used political funds to purchase statewide television satellite time to communicate directly with the public on major policy issues or proposals. And websites give governors and other officeholders an excellent opportunity—unfiltered by the media's critical eye—to promote their proposals directly to the public and tout what they claim to be their accomplishments.

Most of the Austin-based trade associations and other special interest groups have public relations specialists to promote their causes and keep their members informed of developments at the Capitol. Interest groups are at the center of the policymaking process, and their proposals and efforts to get them enacted are inherently newsworthy. Lobbyists also provide a wealth of insider information to reporters, but news people must carefully evaluate it because of the large stakes that special interests have in the workings of state government.

MEDIA AND PACK JOURNALISM

To visitors in the House or the Senate gallery, the Capitol press corps must often resemble a pack of predators intent on devouring the governor or legislative leaders. Sometimes, state officials also may feel they won't escape with their lives when two dozen news people chase them down a Capitol hallway and thrust cameras and microphones into their faces. Capitol reporters and the organizations they represent are very competitive, and reporters prefer to operate independently of each other. But the size of the press corps, the logistics of covering major, breaking news events, and the fear of missing a big story to a competitor often force journalists into a pack, both physically and mentally.

Any reporter can break a major story on any given day, sending competitors scrambling to produce follow-up stories. But more often than not, the large daily newspapers determine which stories will get the most attention from the wire services, the broadcast media, and other members of the pack. The large papers generally have the most experienced reporters in the statehouse, and their large circulations make them attractive outlets for a bureaucrat, a lobbyist, a legislator, or a concerned citizen who wants to offer a proposal, try to kill a piece of legislation, or expose wrongdoing.

There are pluses and minuses to **pack journalism.** The pack often is at its best when devouring a story of major proportions. Media competition on such a story helps uncover details that one newspaper or one television station alone may not have enough resources to do. It serves to call the attention of more readers and viewers to a problem and increase pressure on public officials to correct it. A potential drawback is the possibility that reporters, under pressure to beat competitors to a new lead on the story, may not take enough time to double-check their facts and may report erroneous information. Another significant problem is that the pack mentality often causes journalists to focus their attention on a limited number of spectacular stories while ignoring other important issues. In this respect, pack journalism limits the agenda for public debate and discussion.

The fear of being beaten on new developments in major, running stories can also discourage reporters from sitting back and taking a more contemplative look at the implications behind the headlines. During two summer special sessions in 1991,

Capitol reporters gave extensive coverage to lottery and tax issues and proposals for government reorganization, including Governor Ann Richards's proposal for increased appointment powers over the state bureaucracy (see Chapter 9). But there were virtually no stories attempting to examine whether or how such restructuring of state agencies would improve the administration of public programs and the delivery of services. In their haste to be first with breaking news, media outlets often neglect a thorough examination of the complexities of governance.

Pack journalism in the Austin press corps pales significantly compared to coverage of major events or scandals in Washington. President Bill Clinton's relationship with White House intern Monica Lewinsky touched off one of the largest excesses of pack journalism ever.

HOW WELL INFORMED ARE TEXAS CITIZENS?

Despite the media's efforts, only a small percentage of Texans attempt to keep up with what their elected officials in Austin are doing. A few high-profile issues, such as taxes or the lottery, attract a lot of attention. But many taxpayers, particularly those who live in metropolitan areas that have numerous legislators, don't even know who their state representatives or state senators are, much less how they have voted on significant issues.

This may partly be the media's fault. Many small newspapers carry only brief wire service stories about news events in Austin, while others give an incomplete picture by concentrating primarily on issues of local interest. The major newspapers provide more complete coverage, but they seldom publish record votes of legislators within their readership areas. Most radio stations carry only cursory headline versions of statehouse news, and most television stations, through which most Texans get their news, don't do much better than that. Reporters don't always tell their readers and viewers how the actions of the legislature, the governor, the bureaucracy, and the courts are relevant to their lives and their futures.

But the uninformed and under-informed state of many Texas citizens is only partly the media's fault. There are ample information sources by which anyone, with minimal effort, can stay informed of major developments in state government. The distractions and demands on a person's time are great in today's fast-paced world, and a person who wants to know what's going on in the governmental and political arena often has to juggle priorities. But the opportunities are there. It is up to the individual to make the time and the effort.

Ignorance among the general electorate plays right into the hands of the special interests, who not only stay abreast of developments in Austin, but also spend millions of dollars on political donations and legislative lobbying to influence those developments to their advantage, not to the benefit of the general public. Most governmental actions, whether taken by the legislature or a state regulatory board, eventually will affect the pocketbooks or quality of life of thousands, perhaps millions, of Texans, most of whom will be caught by surprise. If recent indications are correct, the influence of special interests over the public's business will become even greater in the future.

In one of the greatest ironies of the so-called "information age," Americans are consuming less news now than they did forty years ago. The continued decline over the past ten years is reflected in Table 5–1. Technology, of course, has changed media sources. Online news, for example, developed with the Internet and is now widely accessible. But its use is limited. Surveys link news consumption patterns to political information

TABLE 5–1   Trends in Regular News Consumption (In Percent of Respondents)

	May 1993	April 1996	April 1998	April 2000	April 2002
Local TV News	77	65	64	56	57
Cable TV News	—	—	—	—	33
Nightly Network News	60	42	38	30	32
Network TV Magazines	52	36	37	31	24
Network Morning News	—	—	23	20	22
Radio[a]	47[b]	44	49	43	41
Call-in Radio Shows	23[c]	13	13	14	17
National Public Radio	15	13	15	15	16
Newspaper[a]	58[b]	50	48	47	41
Online News[d]	—	2[e]	13	23	25

[a]Newspaper and Radio figures based on use "yesterday."
[b]From 2/1994.
[c]From 4/1993.
[d]Online news at least 3 days per week.
[e]From 6/1995.

Source: The Pew Research Center for the People and the Press, "Americans Lack Background to Follow International News: Public's News Habits Little Changed by Sept. 11," June 9, 2002.

and make it clear that there are large numbers of citizens who have limited knowledge for making informed judgments about politics and public policy. Moreover, one suspects that this political ignorance translates into a decline in political participation.

The Pew Research Center for the People and the Press has regularly surveyed news consumption patterns in the United States. A study conducted in 1990, *The Age of Indifference,* indicated that newspapers, which have suffered an overall decline in regular readership since the 1960s, have been affected more adversely than the electronic media. When surveyed in 2002, only 26 percent of the national sample of people younger than thirty said they had read a newspaper the previous day, compared to 37 percent of those 30–49 years of age and 52 percent of those 50 to 64.

But researchers also found growing disinterest among the young in other media venues. As age increases, news consumption increases across almost every news source, with the exceptions of call-in radio shows and online news (see Table 5–2). "The gap between younger and older Americans is apparent for all types of television news, but is most noticeable when it comes to network news broadcasts," the Pew Center reported in its 2002 survey. It found that only 25 percent of Americans went online for news at least three times a week but noted that online news had a larger following than any other format except local TV news for people younger than 30.[38]

Earlier studies had determined that young Americans were less able than their parents to identify major newsmakers—except, perhaps, for sports figures—were much less critical of political leaders, and were less likely to vote. Only in coverage of sports and the abortion issue—which could directly affect the lives of many young persons—did young people match their parents' interest in news. "Abortion notwithstanding, an overall examination of the surveys conducted by Times Mirror (the predecessor to the Pew Center) reveals a younger generation with less curiosity about news of all sorts, and one with an especially small appetite for the most serious and complicated of issues," the survey concluded.[39]

TABLE 5–2   The News Generation Gap (In Percent of Respondents)

	18–29	30–49	50–64	65+
Did Yesterday				
Watched TV News	40	52	62	73
Local TV News	28	41	49	52
Network Evening	17	25	38	46
Cable TV News	16	23	30	35
Morning News	11	16	21	27
Read a Newspaper	26	37	52	59
Listened to Radio News	34	49	42	29
No News Yesterday	33	19	15	12
Watch/Listen/Read/Regularly				
Local TV News	46	54	64	69
Cable TV News	23	31	42	38
Nightly Network News	19	23	45	53
Network TV Magazines	15	22	30	33
Network Morning News	16	22	23	31
Call-in Radio Shows	16	19	20	10
National Public Radio	14	18	15	11
Time/Newsweek/U.S. News	12	13	15	13
Online News 3+ Times/Week	31	30	24	7

Source: The Pew Research Center for the People and the Press, June 9, 2002.

Researchers have suggested that the Vietnam conflict and the Watergate scandal, both of which damaged Americans' confidence in their government, may be partly to blame for such a large amount of indifference now. They also cite serious problems in public education—longtime classroom deficiencies that restrict young people's views of the world—which Texas and other states are still trying to resolve.[40] The increased number of entertainment alternatives now competing for young people's time is also a likely factor. Moreover, it has been suggested that many people believe that they can't make a difference. If so, many citizens have tuned out the political processes.

Whatever the reason, the prospects for a quality state government sensitive to the public interest in the next generation are discouraging. If the surveys accurately reflect the attitudes of the young, state government will be controlled for years to come by special interests, perhaps to a greater extent than ever before.

SUMMARY AND CONCLUSIONS

1. The news media is the primary information link between those who govern and those who are governed. It affects the development of public policy by influencing the election of policymakers and informing and educating the public on policy alternatives. It can make the causes of a few individuals the concerns of many. This role has remained basically un-changed in this country since the adoption of the First Amendment to the U.S. Constitution more than 200 years ago, but vast changes in technology have transformed the media's preparation and transmission of information.

2. Texas newspapers, much improved in recent years, offer the most complete, thoughtful coverage of state government and politics, but

most Texans now prefer the more abbreviated news summaries that television provides. Television has had a particularly strong impact on the elections process, in which wealthy or well-funded candidates can practically buy their elections through well-produced and highly effective paid advertising.

3. Thanks to major government scandals and the passing of former publishers who had helped run the conservative Texas establishment, the media today is much more independent of officialdom, and much more eager to challenge those in power, than it was only a generation ago. Despite its greater independence, the media still must fight charges of bias in its presentation of the news, in part because the subtle, subjective decisions of a relatively few reporters, editors, and news directors have a major impact on which stories are covered and how prominently they are presented. Ironically,

the fierce competition among media outlets has contributed to a "pack" mentality among reporters, who often pursue the same developments in the same major stories to avoid being beaten by a competitor.

4. Media organizations are persistent guardians of the public's access to governmental business through the state's Open Meetings and Public Information acts, but the fight against government secrecy is a never-ending battle.

5. One of the greatest ironies of the so-called "information age" is that young people apparently are paying less attention than their parents to governmental news and other substantive events occurring in the world around them. This dims the prospects for a quality state government in the next generation because ignorance among the general public plays right into the hands of the special interests who make it their business to influence public policy.

KEY TERMS

Information age
Agenda setting
Agenda building
Issue-attention cycle
Sound bite

Negative television ads
Open Meetings and Public
  Information acts
Media bias
Editorial autonomy

Shield law
Capitol press corps
Spin
Pack journalism

FURTHER READING

Articles

Denison, Dave, "Prime-Time Politics: Why TV News Doesn't Get the Picture," *The Texas Observer,* December 21, 1990, pp. 4–8.

Glendening, Parris N., "The Public's Perception of State Government and Governors," *State Government* 53 (Summer 1980), pp. 115–20.

Wolbrueck, David J., "Curtains for the Editor: Freedom of the Press Under Fire in Round Rock," *The Texas Observer,* April 19, 1991, pp. 22–23.

Books

Abramson, Jeffrey B., F. Christopher Arterton, and Gary R. Orren, *The Electronic Commonwealth.* New York: Basic Books, Inc., 1988.

Alger, Dean, *The Media and Politics.* Englewood Cliffs, NJ: Prentice Hall, 1988.

Ansolabehere, Stephen, and Shanto Iyengar, *Going Negative: How Political Advertisements Shrink and Polarize the Electorate.* New York: The Free Press, 1995.

Arterton, F. Christopher, *Media Politics.* Lexington, MA: Lexington Books, 1984.

Bennett, W. Lance, *News: The Politics of Illusion,* 2nd ed. New York: Longman, 1988.

Berkman, Ronald, and Laura W. Kitch, *Politics in the Media Age.* New York: McGraw-Hill Book Company, 1986.

Christ, W. G., Harry Haines, and Robert Huesca, "Remember the Alamo: Late Night Local Newscasts in San Antonio, Texas," in *The Electronic Election: Perspectives on the 1996 Campaign Communication,*

Vol. 1, eds., L. Kaid and D. Bystrom. Mahwah, NJ: Lawrence Erlbaum Associates, Inc., 1998.

Graber, Doris A., *Mass Media and American Politics,* 3rd ed. Washington, DC: Congressional Quarterly Press, 1989.

Jamieson, Kathleen Hall, *Packaging the Presidency.* New York: Oxford University Press, 1984.

Jamieson, Kathleen Hall, *Eloquence in an Electronic Age.* New York: Oxford University Press, 1988.

Joslyn, Richard, *Mass Media and Elections.* Reading, MA: Addison-Wesley Publishing Company, 1984.

Krasnow, Erwin G., Lawrence D. Longley, and Herbert A. Terry, *The Politics of Broadcast Regulation.* New York: St. Martin's Press, 1982.

Nimmo, Dan, and James E. Combs, *Mediated Political Realities.* New York: Longman, 1983.

Parenti, Michael, *Inventing Reality: The Politics of the Mass Media.* New York: St. Martin's Press, 1986.

Ranney, Austin, *Channels of Power: The Impact of Television on American Politics.* New York: Basic Books, Inc., 1983.

Websites

Freedom of Information Foundation of Texas http://www.foift.org   This organization "provides the leadership to ensure that the public's business is conducted in public and to protect individual liberties guaranteed by the First Amendment." It provides a range of services to its members in an effort to gain access to public information.

Stateline.org   http://www.stateline.org   Daily surveys more than 140 online newspapers and broadcast sites to point readers to the best coverage on state government policy and politics.

Texas Association of Broadcasters   http://www.tab.org   In addition to providing information about careers and jobs in the media, this site provides links to radio and television stations in Texas.

Texas Daily Newspaper Association.   http://www.tdna.org   This organization serves the interests of Texas newspapers. This site provides access to papers across the state, including university daily newspapers, and the organization's university journalism program.

Texas Press Association   http://www.texaspress.org   The Texas Press Association provides a range of services to Texas newspapers, many of which require authorization to access. Internships and job opportunities in the print media can be found at this site.

The Pew Research Center for the People and the Press   www.people-press.org   This research center focuses on the media habits of Americans. Periodic surveys are conducted on a wide range of policy issues.

ENDNOTES

1. Maxwell E. McCombs and Donald L. Shaw, "The Agenda-Setting Function of the Press," in *Media Power in Politics,* 2nd ed., ed. Doris A. Graber (Washington, DC: Congressional Quarterly Press, 1990), p. 75.
2. Doris A. Graber, *Mass Media and American Politics,* 2nd ed. (Washington, DC: Congressional Quarterly Press, 1984), pp. 78–79.
3. Ibid., pp. 268–69.
4. Gladys Engel Lang and Kurt Lang, *The Battle for Public Opinion: The President, the Press, and the Polls during Watergate* (New York: Columbia University Press, 1983), p. 58.
5. Larry N. Gerston, *Making Public Policy: From Conflict to Resolution* (Glenview, IL: Scott, Foresman and Company, 1983), pp. 55–56.
6. Personal interview with Bo Byers, Austin, Texas, July 12, 1990.
7. Anthony Downs, "Up and Down with Ecology—The Issue Attention Cycle," *Public Interest* 32 (Summer 1972), pp. 38–50.
8. See Barbara J. Nelson, *Making an Issue of Child Abuse: Political Agenda Setting for Social Problems* (Chicago: University of Chicago Press, 1984), pp. 51–75.
9. Times Mirror Center for the People and the Press, *The Age of Indifference: A Study of Young Americans and How They View the News* (Washington, DC: Times Mirror Center for the People and the Press, 1990), p. 28.
10. Walter Cronkite and Paul Taylor, "To Lift Politics Out of TV Swamp," *Houston Chronicle,* March 10, 1996, p. 1E.
11. "Alliance for Better Campaigns," *The Political Standard,* Vol. 3, No. 5, July 2000, p. 1.
12. Alliance for Better Campaigns press release, October 8, 2003.
13. Interview with Ann Arnold, July 13, 2000.
14. *Houston Chronicle,* November 3, 2002, p. 1A.
15. *Houston Chronicle,* September 12, 1990.
16. "Jim Hightower: The Media and the Message," *The Texas Observer,* December 21, 1990, p. 8.
17. *Houston Chronicle,* January 6, 1991.

18. *Houston Chronicle,* January 8, 1991.

19. *Dallas Morning News,* February 13, 1994.

20. *Public Opinion* (August/September 1985), p. 7.

21. Edward Jay Epstein, *News from Nowhere* (New York: Random House/Vintage Books), pp. 13–14.

22. Graber, Mass Media and American Politics, pp. 71–74.

23. Michael Parenti, *Democracy for the Few,* 5th ed. (New York: St. Martin's Press, 1988), p. 170.

24. Archie P. McDonald, "Anglo-American Arrival in Texas," in *The Texas Heritage,* 2e, edited by Ben Proctor and Archie McDonald (Arlington Heights, IL: Harlan Davidson, Inc, 1992), p. 28.

25. T. R. Fehrenbach, *Lone Star: A History of Texas and the Texans* (New York: The Macmillan Company, 1968), p. 302.

26. Ibid., p. 303.

27. George Norris Green, *The Establishment in Texas Politics, 1938–1957* (Westport, CT: Greenwood Press, 1979), p. 10.

28. Ibid., p. 162.

29. *Houston Chronicle,* January 28, 1993.

30. Vittorio Zucconi, "America's Media Empires," *World Press Review* (May 1986), p. 21. Excerpted from "La Republica" of Rome.

31. Scripps Howard, Inc., *The Scripps Howard Texas Poll,* Fall 1999. Telephone survey of 1,000 adult Texans.

32. Times Mirror Center for the People and the Press, *The Age of Indifference,* p. 1.

33. Zucconi, "America's Media Empires," p. 19.

34. *Houston Chronicle,* October 9, 2003, p. 9C.

35. *Houston Chronicle,* September 17, 2003, p. 1A.

36. *New York Times,* January 11, 2000, p. C12.

37. *Houston Chronicle,* September 24, 2003, p. 1C.

38. "Public's News Habits Little Changed by September 11," The Pew Research Center for the People and the Press, June 9, 2002.

39. Times Mirror Center for the People and the Press, *The Age of Indifference,* p. 9.

40. Ibid., p. 21.

6

The Party System in Texas

> . . . political parties created democracy and . . . modern democracy is unthinkable save in terms of party.
>
> *E. E. Schattschneider[1]*

> . . . the common and continual mischiefs of the spirit of party are sufficient to make it the interest and duty of a wise people to discourage and restrain it.
>
> *George Washington,*
> *Farewell Address to the People of the*
> *United States, September 17, 1796*

> We have a two-party system and you have to work with them. It's going to be tough to get the legislature to change the system that put them in office.
>
> *Darby Riley, President of the*
> *Environmental Democrats[2]*

Much has been written in the media about recent Republican gains that have transformed Texas from a one-party Democratic state into a Republican-dominant state. But Democratic or Republican, political parties still do not get much respect, esteem or attention. In subtle and not-so-subtle ways, many Texans assert that there is not a "dime's worth of difference between the two political parties." Others consider them a joke, and many cannot link the political parties to specific policy positions. Parties have little relevance for many Texans, and media coverage of party-related activities often focuses on political patronage, questionable campaign contributions, negative campaigning, petty conflicts that lead to governmental deadlock, and instances of graft or corruption. Many people don't give thought to the role of parties in a democratic political system. They know little of the origins, history, or structure of the political parties. They don't identify parties with effective or responsive government. And many couldn't care less about the health or viability of the state's party system. In sum, there is a significant segment of the state's population which holds clearly defined antiparty attitudes that are often expressed in the simple statement, "I vote for the person and not the party."

Other people are ambivalent toward political parties. They don't know much about their functions or activities and may not even be able to distinguish between the two major parties. They do not hold contempt for political parties, nor do they regard them to be a significant factor in decisions of governments. All they know about parties is that they produce competition, and, if nothing else, the ability to "throw the rascals out" and replace them with another set of rascals.

But some voters are intensely interested in political parties and are convinced that parties are essential to developing and maintaining a democratic society. A political party, these individuals believe, is one of the few mechanisms available to the general public for reviewing and possibly repudiating the actions of governmental leaders. With all of their weaknesses, political parties provide a democratic process for choosing leaders. They bring large numbers of people under an umbrella with some degree of consensus, and they clarify policy alternatives.

For much of the century after the Civil War, Texas was a one-party Democratic state. There was no organized opposition party available to mobilize the interests of those who felt neglected or excluded from the Democratic party. Electoral politics were based on factions and personalities, and the interests of the lower socioeconomic classes, especially minorities, were blatantly neglected. Over the past thirty years, however, Texas has witnessed the emergence of a strong Republican party and the decline of the Democratic party. During this period of change, the electoral power of minorities also has increased dramatically, and minority groups that once were excluded now play a significant role in Democratic party politics.

POLITICAL PARTIES AND A DEMOCRATIC SOCIETY

As long as a society is ruled by a few individuals and the interests or concerns of the general population have no political significance or influence, leaders have little reason to be concerned with what the masses think or want. But democratic societies are based on the principle that those who rule have a fundamental obligation to consider the preferences, interests, and opinions of those who are governed. Since it is impossible for every individual to participate in every public policy decision, we have chosen to construct a representative government in the United States. We choose individuals to act on our behalf, which makes it necessary for us to find mechanisms to assure that these individuals are selected fairly and are responsive and responsible. We try to accomplish this objective through several means, including elections, interest groups, and political parties.[3]

Although political parties share their representative roles with other institutions, scholars tend to agree that parties perform critical functions that other institutions cannot. There is considerable debate about formal definitions of parties, their characteristics, organizational and membership criteria, and the relationship of the parties to the governing institutions and the social system.[4] Our purpose is to focus on that part of the debate that would help us understand the political parties in Texas.

POLITICAL PARTIES IN PERSPECTIVE

Political parties are complex structures that relate to most other facets of government and politics. V. O. Key suggested that parties are social structures that are best understood from three perspectives: the party in the electorate, the party as an organization, and the party in government (Figure 6–1). The party in the electorate involves the party's relationship to voters and election activities. The party organization includes a wide range of activities from the precinct to the state level that are necessary to support the party's structure. The party in government covers the activities of those elected individuals who take office and carry out the functions of government.

Definition of Political Parties

We find the party definition given by political scientist Leon D. Epstein to be best suited to Texas. A **political party** is "any group, however loosely organized, seeking to elect governmental officeholders under a given label."[5] Although we tend to think only in terms of Democrat and Republican, other political parties that meet this definition have emerged at both the state and local level in Texas history. While political parties share some characteristics of other groups that function in the political arena, they are distinguished from these organizations by their primary preoccupation with contesting elections and the fact that "it is only parties that run candidates on their own labels."[6]

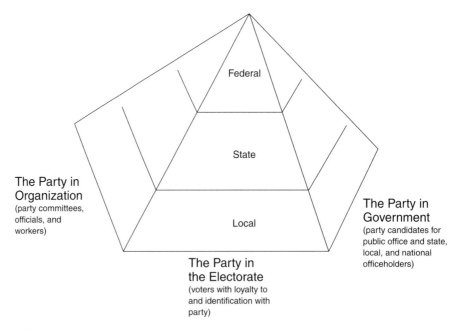

The Party in Organization
(party committees, officials, and workers)

The Party in Government
(party candidates for public office and state, local, and national officeholders)

The Party in the Electorate
(voters with loyalty to and identification with party)

Federal

State

Local

FIGURE 6–1   The Three Part Political Party.
Source: V. O. Key, *Politics, Parties, and Pressure Groups,* (New York: Cromwell, 1958) and Paul Allen Beck, *Party and Politics in America,* (New York: Longman, 1997).

Parties and Interest Groups

At first glance, political parties and interest groups often appear indistinguishable, but there are differences, which were partially addressed in the earlier chapter on interest groups. Interest groups are concerned with shaping public policy by influencing the actions and decisions of public officials, regardless of the officials' party affiliation. Political parties are structured under a "common label to recruit, nominate, and elect candidates for public office" under specific partisan labels.[7] An interest group usually focuses on a narrow range of policy issues. It can attempt to influence the outcome of elections, but it doesn't nominate candidates or take responsibility for the day-to-day management of government.[8] These are functions of the political parties and officials elected under their banners.

Studies conducted during the years of one-party Democratic domination in Texas concluded that the interest groups were especially powerful.[9] Some expect the relative power between interest groups and parties to change in two-party Texas, but that remains to be seen.

THE FUNCTIONS OF POLITICAL PARTIES

Intermediaries between the Electorate and Government

The twenty-two million people who live in Texas have a wide range of interests and needs that they expect their governments to fulfill. Samuel Huntington, a modernization theorist, noted that political parties, while sharing some characteristics with other social and political institutions, have a unique function in modern societies "to organize participation, to aggregate interests, and to serve as the link between social forces and the government."[10] Simply stated, the political parties link diverse segments of the population to government and thus contribute to the stability and legitimacy of the government.

Recruit and Nominate Candidates

There are thousands of partisan officeholders in Texas, ranging from constable to governor. And except for city, school board, and special district elections, which are nonpartisan, the parties have a virtual monopoly on nominating candidates. It is possible to get an independent on the ballot with no party affiliation, but an independent is not likely to get elected. Under Texas law, an individual who runs for an office in the primary election of one of the two major parties wins that party's nomination if he or she receives the majority vote in either the primary or a runoff.

Many local elected positions do not pay well and are not politically attractive and, in some areas of the state, it is difficult to get people to run for them. In some counties, the parties aggressively recruit candidates. In other counties, they don't. In some counties, one party may be nothing more than a shell or paper organization. In other counties, the parties are competitive, with very sophisticated organizations and paid professional staffs capable of providing prospective candidates with considerable campaign resources.

Parties have not always used the primary to nominate candidates. Prior to reforms enacted in the Terrell Election Laws of 1903 and 1905, candidates were nominated by party conventions, which were attended by the party faithful.

Contest Elections and Mobilize Voters

While candidate-centered campaigns built on modern media-oriented technology have reduced the role of the political parties in elections (see Chapter 7), parties are still the most important institutions for mobilizing voters for specific candidates. Although most Texans aren't active in party affairs, approximately 60 percent of Texas voters identify with either the Republican or Democratic party, which have a near monopoly on the votes cast. Given the size of the state, the number of people who participate in elections, the diversity of interests, and the variety of political subcultures within the state, the political parties have had considerable success in mobilizing voters in Texas.[11]

Organize and Manage the Government

Once elected, officeholders use their party affiliations in carrying out their public responsibilities, and with the development of a competitive party system in Texas, the parties have taken on a more significant role in the organization and management of government. Governor Ann Richards, a Democrat, appointed primarily Democrats to hundreds of positions on policymaking state boards and commissions and to vacancies on state courts. Her successors, Republicans George W. Bush and Rick Perry, appointed primarily Republicans.

After taking office in 1979 as Texas's first Republican governor in more than 100 years, Bill Clements appointed many Republicans to state boards, but he also named some Democrats, in part to encourage conservative Democrats to switch parties. His successful strategy was instrumental in adding to the strength and influence of the Republicans (often referred to as the Grand Old Party) in Texas.

Despite the growth of the Republican Party and increased GOP representation in the legislature—Republicans captured their first majority of modern times in the state Senate in 1997 and in the House of Representatives in 2003—the legislature's organizational structure in 2003 remained bipartisan. In the last quarter of the 20th century, Democratic leaders had made it a practice to build coalitions by appointing Republicans as well as Democrats to major chairmanships. Republican leaders of the House and the Senate continued this bipartisan approach. But the tradition was sorely tested in 2003 by the rancorous debate over redistricting, the state budget, and spending reductions in programs deemed critical to Democrats (see Chapter 8).

Party caucuses now appear to be more influential in defining policy positions and possibly legislative strategies. Although the regular session and three special sessions in 2003 were insufficient to declare a pattern, there was increased voting along party lines in both the House and the Senate. The ideological positions dividing the two parties in the legislature were sharper, and there was less willingness to compromise on selected, major issues. Legislative battles also became highly personalized in 2003. Trust that had crossed party lines consequently suffered. If partisanship continues to increase, the majority party in the legislature may begin to use its organizational powers to further reduce the influence of the minority party.

Mediating the Effects of Separation of Powers

The political parties also help to bridge the inherent conflicts between the executive and legislative branches of government. The governor needs legislative support for key programs and, in turn, legislators often need the governor's support and assistance to get their bills enacted. The chances of such cooperation are enhanced if the governor and a majority of the legislature are of the same party. Republican Governor George W. Bush usually worked well with Democratic lawmakers and shared many of their priorities. But not too many years earlier, Republican Governor Bill Clements often had a stormy relationship with Democratic legislators. Bush had a more accommodating style than Clements, but Bush also had the added advantage of being governor as Republicans were nearing a legislative majority. Republican Governor Rick Perry relied primarily on the leadership of his party to obtain approval for his legislative programs and found it possible to marginalize Democratic influence in the legislative process.

Provide Accountability

One of the fundamental problems of a democratic government is how to keep public officeholders responsive and accountable to the people. Elected officials can abuse power. They can engage in graft and corruption. They can pursue policies that conflict with the interests of most of their constituents or pursue foolish or shortsighted policies that produce adverse results. The political parties, in their criticisms of each other and their electoral competitiveness, serve to inform the voters of the shortcomings and failures of elected officials. This process provides alternatives for the voters and gives them an opportunity to "turn the rascals out."

Manage Conflict and Aggregate Interests

The United States generally has had a stable political system that manages conflict among competing groups and interests, and the political parties have played a major role in that process. A party tries to find common ground among varied interests within the electorate so that successful coalitions of voters can be put together to support that party's candidates on election day. The Texas Democratic party, for example, is built on a diverse coalition of African Americans, Hispanics, lower socioeconomic groups, labor, some professionals, and rural interests, to name a few. The Republican party's base is markedly different than that of the Democrats, but party leaders and candidates also work to build stable coalitions of voters. To build durable support for its candidates, the party must find common interests, structure compromises, and develop accommodations among groups of voters. As interests within the party agree to support a variety of programs and common principles, the party succeeds in resolving conflict.[12]

Agenda Setting

Public policy doesn't just happen. It is the result of groups organizing around issues and keeping pressure on elected officials to respond. Some issues are longstanding problems that have produced sharp differences of opinion and will take years to resolve. Others emerge rapidly, perhaps as a result of a catastrophic event. A deadly school bus accident in the Rio Grande Valley, for example, produced an immediate outcry for safety barriers between public roadways and open, water-filled gravel pits like the one in which many young bus passengers drowned. Groups seeking change often try to build support for their programs through the political parties.

The parties also play a role in establishing policy priorities. Candidates running for public office under a party's banner announce their support or opposition to specific policies and, once elected, are expected to use the resources of their offices to try to achieve those objectives. In anticipation of future elections, officeholders will spend much time and energy trying to carry out policies that will solidify their support among the voters.

THE PARTY IN THE ELECTORATE

The Texas party system has been restructured by the social and economic changes that the state has experienced over the past thirty years. Texas now has a strong Republican party, and while Democrats still hold on to many local offices, Republicans dominate statewide politics. But from the 1870s through the 1970s, Texas was a one-party Democratic state.

One-Party Politics

Texas's long domination by the Democratic party can be traced to the period immediately after the Civil War, when the Republican party was able to capture control of Texas government for a short period. Strong anti-Republican feelings were generated by the Reconstruction administration of Radical Republican Governor Edmund J. Davis, and the Republican party was perceived by most Texans of that era to be the party of conquest and occupation. By the time the Constitution of 1876 was approved, the Republican party's influence in state politics was negligible. From 1874 to 1961, no Republican won a statewide office in Texas, and in only a few scattered areas were Republicans elected to local offices.

The state voted for Herbert Hoover, the Republican presidential candidate, in 1928. But for many Texans the key issue in that election was the fact that Al Smith, the Democratic nominee from New York, was a Catholic and favored the repeal of Prohibition. Anti-Catholicism and support for Prohibition had deep roots among many fundamentalist religious groups in Texas during that period.

The anti-Republicanism that evolved from the Civil War and Reconstruction, however, is only a partial explanation for the Democratic party's longtime domination of Texas politics. V. O. Key, in his classic study, *Southern Politics,* presents the provocative thesis that Texas politics might be better understood in terms of "modified class politics."[13]

As Texas's conservative agricultural leaders attempted to regain control over the state's political system after Reconstruction, the postwar economic devastation divided Texas along class lines. Small farmers, African Americans, and an emerging urban labor class suffered disproportionately from the depression of this period. They turned their discontent into support for agrarian third parties, particularly the Populist party, which began to threaten the monopoly of the traditional Texas power structure.

To protect their political power, the established agricultural leaders moved to divide the lower social groups by directing the discontent of the lower-income whites against the African Americans. The rural elites, who manifested traditionalistic political values and wanted to consolidate power in the hands of the privileged few, also created alliances with the mercantile, banking, and emerging industrial leaders, who reflected the individualistic view of a limited government that served to protect their interests. These two dominant forces consolidated political power and merged the politics of race with the politics of economics. Then, for more than 80 years, the conservative Texas establishment pursued policies that best served its interests rather than those of the general population.

The elites were able to institutionalize their control through the adoption of constitutional restrictions and the enactment of legislation designed to reduce the number of voters. The effect of these actions was to reduce the potential of a popular challenge to the establishment's political monopoly.[14] Segregation legislation, called **Jim Crow laws,** stripped African Americans of many economic, social, and political rights and eliminated most of them from the political process. Restrictive voter-registration laws, including a poll tax, which also were designed to exclude African Americans, reduced the participation of low-income whites in the political process as well. And the costs of statewide political campaigns boosted the electoral prospects of candidates financed by the establishment.[15] The result of all this was a one-party Democratic system, dominated by influential conservatives.

The Texas Democratic party, however, was not homogeneous. It was split by factions, regional differences, and personal political rivalries. Initially, there were no sustained, identifiable factions, as voting coalitions changed from election to election through much of the first third of the twentieth century. But the onset of the Great Depression in 1929, the election of President Franklin Roosevelt in 1932, and the policies of the New Deal reshaped Texas politics in the 1930s.

State party systems are linked to the national party system, and developments in the Texas party system must be understood as part of this relationship. During the period from the Civil War to Franklin Roosevelt's election, the national party system was dominated by the Republican party. The elections from 1928 to 1936, however, produced a major national party realignment, and the Democratic party, capitalizing on the devastation of the Great Depression, replaced the Republicans as the dominant national party.

Roosevelt's administrations articulated and developed a radically different policy agenda than that of the Republican party. Government was to become a buffer against economic downturns as well as a positive force for change. Under Roosevelt, the regulatory function of the federal government was expanded to exercise control and authority over much of the nation's economy. The federal government also enacted programs such as Social Security, public housing, and labor legislation to benefit lower socioeconomic groups.

These national policies had a direct impact on many Texans and produced an active philosophical split within the Texas Democratic party that was to characterize Texas politics for the next two generations. A majority of Texas voters supported Roosevelt in his four elections, and the Democratic party maintained its monopoly over Texas politics. But competing economic interests clearly—and often bitterly—divided Texas Democrats along liberal and conservative lines.

A strong Republican party didn't emerge at this time in Texas or any other southern state because "southern conservative Democratic politicians, who would have been expected to lead such a realignment, or any politicians for that matter, did not relish jumping from a majority-status party to one in the minority."[16] Furthermore, the restrictive voter-registration laws designed to reduce participation by minorities and poor whites continued to limit the electoral prospects of liberal Democrats and allowed conservatives to remain largely in control of the state party. "As long as the conservative Democrats remained dominant, they served as a check on the potential growth of the Republican party."[17] There also were residual feelings from the Civil War and an antipathy toward the Republican party that required generations to die off before new voters were willing to change party allegiances.

Despite some liberal successes under Governor James Allred, who was elected in 1934 and again in 1936, the conservative wing of the party prevailed in state elections from the 1940s to the late 1970s. Democratic presidential candidates carried Texas in 1944, 1948, 1960, 1964, 1968, and 1976, even though some of them were too liberal to suit the tastes of the state's conservative Democratic establishment.

By 1941, the conservative Democrats began to lay the groundwork for an all-out attack on the "New Deal," or liberal, Democrats in the 1944 presidential election. Roosevelt won the nomination and election for a fourth term, but in Texas there was a bitter intra-party battle between conservative Democrats and liberal Democrats (loyal to Roosevelt) for control of the party organization and delegates to the Democratic National Convention. This election was followed by three successive presidential elections in which conservative Democrats bolted the party to support either third-party candidates or the Republican nominee.[18]

The harbinger of this conservative-liberal split in a statewide political race was the 1946 Democratic gubernatorial race between Homer Rainey and Beauford Jester. Rainey, a former University of Texas president who had been fired after a bitter fight over the UT governing board's censorship of books and efforts to force him to dismiss liberal faculty members, ran as a liberal, or progressive, candidate supporting academic freedom, labor legislation, and civil rights.

He was challenged by four conservatives who attacked him on the university issue, suggested there was rampant atheism at the university, and unleashed anti-labor, anticommunist, and anti–African American attacks. Jester, in a well-financed campaign, eventually defeated Rainey 2 to 1 in a runoff. Many of the allegations raised against Rainey were designed to inject demagoguery into the race and divert attention from the substantive social and economic issues of importance to the lower economic classes. The tactics served the economic and political objectives of the state's corporate establishment.

Similar volatile allegations emerged during many subsequent state elections, and the conservative Democrats were able to capitalize on them. In 1944, the U.S. Supreme Court had declared the white primary—party elections in which only whites could vote—unconstitutional in *Smith v. Allwright*. Subsequently, a number of candidates appealed to the sentiments of white supremacy. Texas also had its own brand of "McCarthyism" initiated by right-wing groups that alleged communist conspiracies throughout the state.[19]

Modified One-Party Democratic Politics

At first glance, it might appear that the **bifactionalism** in the Democratic party partially compensated for the lack of a competitive two-party system in Texas. But in his study of southern politics, V. O. Key argued against that perception. He concluded that factionalism resulted in "no-party politics." Factionalism produces discontinuity in leadership and group support, so that the voter has no permanent reference point from which to judge the performance of the party or selected candidates. Since there are no clear distinctions between who holds power and who does not, the influence of pressure groups increases.[20] In one-party Democratic Texas, state government and public policy were conducive to control by wealthy and corporate interests.

This bifactional pattern of state Democratic politics was tested by a number of factors, including the national party's increased commitment after 1948 to civil rights and social welfare legislation. These liberal developments alienated segments of the white population and eventually prompted many voters to leave the Democratic party and align with the Republicans.

Efforts by Texas oil interests to reestablish state control over the oil-rich tidelands off the Texas coast also played a key role in the demise of one-party politics and the development of a two-party system. President Harry Truman, concerned about national security and federal access to these offshore oil resources, refused to accede to state demands and vetoed legislation favorable to Texas oil interests in 1952. That veto prompted a series of maneuvers orchestrated by Democratic Governor Allan Shivers to move the support of conservative Democrats to the Republican party.

While promising to support the Democratic party, Shivers and his allies captured control of the Texas delegation to the 1952 Democratic National Convention. The Democrats nominated Adlai Stevenson for president, and the Republicans in their convention, Dwight Eisenhower. When the Texas Democratic party convened its fall convention, Shivers succeeded in winning the party's endorsement of Eisenhower. The "Shivercrats," as they were called, were successful in carrying Texas for the Republican nominee. This election helped establish a pattern of Texas retaining its Democratic leanings at the state and local level but voting for Republicans for president.[21]

For years, the Republican party's limited presence in Texas had been basically a patronage base for leaders who were more interested in an occasional appointment than in winning elections.[22] But the 1952 election marked a change in the party's state leadership and led to efforts to create a party capable of winning local and statewide elections.[23] It took years to develop the necessary organization, but the process would accelerate after the 1964 election.

In 1960, Democrat Lyndon B. Johnson ran both for vice president and for re-election to the U.S. Senate from Texas—a dual candidacy permitted under state law—and won both offices. His Republican opponent in the Senate race was John Tower, a relatively unknown college professor from Wichita Falls, who received 41 percent of the vote. After Johnson won the vice presidency and resigned from the Senate, a special election to fill the Senate seat was called in 1961. It attracted seventy-one candidates, including Tower, who defeated conservative Democrat William Blakely with 50.6 percent of the vote in a runoff.[24]

There is some evidence that liberal Democrats, in retaliation for having been locked out of the power centers of their party and in anticipation of an ideological realignment of the party system, supported Tower in this election.[25] The *Texas Observer*, an influential liberal publication, endorsed Tower with an argument for a two-party system. "How many liberals voted for Tower will never be known, nor will it be known how many 'went fishing,' " wrote Republican campaign consultant and author John R. Knaggs, who was a volunteer worker for Tower during the 1961 race. "But in reviewing Tower's razor-thin 10,343-vote margin out of 886,091 cast, it must be concluded that the liberal element was pivotal in electing the first Republican United States senator to represent Texas during the twentieth century."[26] Texas Republicans, incidentally, hadn't even held a primary in 1960.

Tower was reelected in 1966, 1972, and 1978, but no other Texas Republican won a statewide office until 1978, when Bill Clements was elected governor. Nevertheless, many students of Texas politics regard Tower's election in 1961 as a key factor in the development of the state's two-party system.[27]

Although Republicans made some gains in suburban congressional districts and local elections in the 1960s—including the election to Congress of a Houston Republican named George Herbert Walker Bush—the numbers were inconsequential. Most significant election battles continued to take place for a while longer within the Democratic party.

The only liberal Democratic candidate who was successful on a statewide basis during this period was Ralph Yarborough. After several losing campaigns, he was elected to the U.S. Senate in a special election in 1957 and held that office until his defeat in 1970 by conservative Democrat Lloyd Bentsen. Yarborough, who had a distinguished legislative career, was "the mainstay of the liberal wing until his primary defeat in 1970 and comeback failure in 1972."[28]

Despite some indications of an energized Republican party and the increased mobilization of minorities in support of the liberal wing of the Democratic party, conservative Democrats controlled state politics until 1978. Conservatives were able to dominate the nominating process in the Democratic primaries through well-financed and well-executed campaigns. In the general elections, liberal Democrats had little choice but to vote for a conservative Democrat against what was usually perceived to be an even more conservative Republican.[29]

During this period of Democratic factionalism, Texas Democrats played a major role in the U.S. Congress and national politics. Sam Rayburn, the longtime speaker of the U.S. House of Representatives and regarded as one of a handful of great speakers in U.S. history, came from a rural congressional district in northeast Texas. Before moving on to the vice presidency and then the White House, Lyndon B. Johnson was majority leader in the U.S. Senate. Other congressmen from Texas, as a result of the seniority system used in the selection of committee chairs in the U.S. Congress, had influential committee posts and used their positions to funnel large sums of federal dollars to the state.

Two-Party Politics in Texas

On the national level, **realignment** of political parties is often associated with a critical election in which economic or social issues cut across existing party allegiances and produce a dramatic, permanent shift in party support and identification.[30] Realignment did not occur in one single election in Texas, but over several decades. The early stages of this transformation are often hard to identify, but by the mid-1990s, it was clear that one-party politics had given way to a two-party system.

The civil rights movement was a major factor contributing to the transformation of the state's party system. African Americans and Hispanics went to federal court to attack state laws promoting segregation and restricting minority voting rights. Successful lawsuits were brought against the white primary, the preprimary endorsement, the poll tax, and racial gerrymandering of political districts (see Chapter 7). Then minorities turned to the U.S. Congress for civil rights legislation, a process that produced the 1965 Voting Rights Act, which Congress extended to Texas after 1975. African Americans and Hispanics challenged electoral systems throughout the state using federal law and a growing body of U.S. Supreme Court decisions prohibiting the dilution of minority voting power. Minorities were successful in their long, tortuous effort to increase electoral equity. But the creation of more political districts from which African Americans and Hispanics could win election also resulted in the creation of more districts from which Republicans could win public office. As the number of minority elected officials increased, the number of Republican elected officials also increased.

Economic factors also contributed to two-party development. African Americans and Hispanics are disproportionately low-income populations and generally support such governmental services as public housing, public health care, day care, and income support. These policies are associated by many with the liberal wing of the Democratic party. Minority organizations made concerted efforts to register, educate, and mobilize the people in their communities. Approximately 90 percent of the African American vote in Texas is Democratic, and while there is less cohesion among Hispanic voters, approximately 75 percent of the Hispanic vote goes to Democrats. As the numerical strength of minorities increased, conservative Anglo Democrats found their position within the party threatened and began to look to the Republican party as an alternative.

The large numbers of people who migrated to Texas from other states, particularly when the Sun Belt economy of the 1970s and early 1980s was booming and many northern industrial states were struggling, also contributed to the two-party system. Many of these new arrivals were Republicans from states with strong Republican parties, and many of them settled in high-income, suburban, Anglo areas in Texas.[31] Other significant factors were President Reagan's popularity in the 1980s and the 1978 election of Republican Governor Bill Clements, who encouraged many conservative Democratic officeholders to switch parties. Some scholars see an earlier outline of these changes in the so-called Southern strategy of Richard Nixon in 1968. Simply stated, the national Republican party made calculated efforts to peel off whites using wedge issues that were likely to resonate within the southern political culture.[32]

During the 1970s, the Texas Republican party had an organizational edge on the Democrats. As the minority party, the only way the GOP could successfully challenge the Democrats' numerical strength was to develop local party organizations capable of mobilizing membership, providing continuity between elections, and providing candidates with campaign resources. After the defeat of Republican presidential nominee Barry Goldwater in 1964, the national Republican party began rebuilding using modern campaign technology. The national party assisted state parties, and Texas Republicans applied the new campaign technology to state and local elections. Moreover, Republican candidates appeared to more readily adapt technology to their campaigns. For a short period in the late 1980s and early 1990s, Texas Democrats tried to catch up by using money provided by the national party organization, but the Democratic leadership seemed incapable of making maximum use of these resources to reenergize state and local party organizations.

Other events of the 1970s and the 1980s demonstrated that the transformation of the Texas party system was well on its way. After the Sharpstown scandal (see Chapter 8), the Texas House elected a liberal Democrat, Price Daniel Jr., as speaker in 1973. Three other moderate-to-liberal Democrats were elected to statewide office in the early 1970s: Bob Armstrong as land commissioner in 1970, John Hill as attorney general in 1972, and Bob Bullock as comptroller in 1974. These men initiated and carried out policies that were more equitable in the treatment of lower socioeconomic Texans.[33]

In 1978, John Hill defeated Governor Dolph Briscoe, a conservative, in the Democratic primary, and Bill Clements, then a political unknown, defeated Ray Hutchison, a former state legislator who had the endorsement of most Republican state leaders, in the Republican primary. Hill neglected to mend fences with conservative Democrats, and Clements, a multimillionaire, used much of his own money on an effective media campaign to defeat Hill for governor by 17,000 votes in the general election. Four years later, Clements lost to Democratic Attorney General Mark White, but in 1986 he returned to defeat White in an expensive, bitter campaign (see Chapter 9).

In the 1982 election, Democratic candidates who were considered liberal won additional statewide offices. Ann Richards was elected state treasurer; Jim Mattox, attorney general; Jim Hightower, agriculture commissioner; and Garry Mauro, land commissioner.

Party realignment also was reflected in the Texas Legislature. In 1971, Republicans held only 12 of the 181 legislative seats. But by 2003, Republicans held 88 of the 150 House seats and 19 of the 31 Senate seats.

The 1990 election further demonstrated how far the realignment process had gone. Democratic gubernatorial nominee Ann Richards defeated conservative businessman Clayton Williams, who had spent $6 million of his own money to win the Republican primary. But Republican Kay Bailey Hutchison was elected state treasurer, and Republican Rick Perry unseated Hightower to become agriculture commissioner. Republicans also retained one of the U.S. Senate seats from Texas when Phil Gramm easily won reelection to the seat once held by John Tower, and the GOP claimed eight of the 27 congressional seats from Texas. The 1990 census increased the number of congressional seats from Texas to 30, and Republicans had won 13 of them by 1996.

In a special election in 1993 to fill the U.S. Senate seat vacated by Democrat Lloyd Bentsen when he was appointed secretary of the treasury by President Bill Clinton, Kay Bailey Hutchison defeated Democrat Bob Krueger to give the Republicans both U.S. Senate seats from Texas. Hutchison easily won reelection in 1994, despite a political and legal controversy over her administration of the state treasurer's office.

Also in 1994, Governor Ann Richards was unseated by Republican nominee George W. Bush. Republicans that year also captured four other statewide offices that had been held by Democrats, marking the most statewide gains by Republicans in any single election since Reconstruction. They won two additional seats on the Texas Railroad Commission to give the party all three positions on that regulatory panel. They also captured a majority of the Texas Supreme Court and gained a seat on the Texas Court of Criminals Appeals. In the same election, Republicans posted sweeping victories across the country, cashing in on anger over President Bill Clinton's policies, and gained control of both houses of Congress and a majority of the nation's governorships.

Toward Republican Dominance

The political transformation of Texas accelerated even more in 1996, when Republicans swept all ten offices on the statewide general election ballot and captured a

GENE KELLY, DANCING ACROSS THE BALLOT

Gene Kelly, the famous Hollywood dancer, died some years ago, but his name continued to perform ballot magic in Texas for a while longer. Most recently, Gene Kelly handily defeated four unknown opponents for the Democratic nomination for the U.S. Senate in 2000.

The Gene Kelly from Texas is a retired Air Force lawyer from Universal City, in suburban San Antonio, and a perennial candidate for statewide office. Although he has never been elected—Republican incumbent Kay Bailey Hutchison defeated him in the 2000 general election—he has snatched Democratic nominations from more experienced and better funded candidates. And he has angered opponents and party officials, who contend he is an unqualified candidate simply trying to take advantage of his famous name. Most of Kelly's previous races had been for statewide judgeships.

Kelly's Senate nomination was made easier by the Texas Democratic party's failure to field a full slate of credible statewide candidates in 2000. Democrats didn't even contest six of the nine statewide offices on the ballot that year. Having lost all statewide races in 1996 and 1998, Texas Democrats were struggling, and party leaders believed they were better off concentrating their resources on legislative races in 2000. Hutchison's incumbency and strong fundraising capabilities also had scared off any major potential challengers. With five unknown, underfunded candidates running in the Democratic primary, it wasn't surprising that the candidate with the most familiar name would win. Following his normal pattern, Kelly, then 74, didn't campaign and rarely spoke to the news media. But he led the field in the primary and defeated Charles Gandy, a former state representative, in a runoff, even though Democratic party officials, who usually remain neutral in primary races, had endorsed Gandy.

majority of the state Senate for the first time since Reconstruction. Republican presidential nominee Bob Dole even carried the Lone Star State, despite a poor national showing against President Clinton. Republicans also increased their numbers in the Texas House and in the Texas congressional delegation. When the electoral dust had cleared, Republicans held twenty of Texas's twenty-nine statewide elected offices, including the top three. That number increased to twenty-one in 1997, when Presiding Judge Michael McCormick of the Texas Court of Criminal Appeals switched from the Democratic to the Republican party.

Lieutenant Governor Bob Bullock and Attorney General Dan Morales, both Democrats, chose not to seek reelection or any other office in 1998, and Republicans cashed in on the opportunity. With Governor Bush winning reelection in a landslide, Republicans again swept all statewide offices. And a few weeks after the 1998 election, the GOP secured all statewide offices in Texas for the first time since Reconstruction when Texas Supreme Court Justice Raul A. Gonzalez, a Democrat, retired in midterm and was replaced by a Republican appointee of Bush. Republicans did not capture control of the Texas House, but picked up four seats to narrow the Democratic margin to six seats. In the governor's race, Bush won 69 percent of the vote against Democratic challenger Garry Mauro, the longtime land commissioner.

Democrats fielded candidates for only three of the nine statewide offices up for election in 2000 (see "Gene Kelly, Dancing Across the Ballot"). One Democrat filed for each of two seats on the Texas Court of Criminal Appeals, and five Democrats, all minor candidates with little financial support, filed for Republican Kay Bailey

Hutchison's U.S. Senate seat. Only Republicans filed for a third Court of Criminal Appeals seat, three seats on the Texas Supreme Court, and two seats on the Texas Railroad Commission, the only other offices on the ballot. The Republican primary included some contested statewide campaigns. Democrats lost all their statewide races in 2000, but held their ground in state legislative races.

Republicans also swept all statewide races in 2002, including Gov. Rick Perry's victory over Democratic nominee Tony Sanchez and former Texas Attorney General John Cornyn's victory over former Dallas Mayor Ron Kirk in a race to succeed retiring U.S. Senator Phil Gramm. Republicans also finally gained control of the Texas House of Representatives in 2002, capturing 88 of the 150 seats after the Legislative Redistricting Board in 2001 had drawn new districts that favored Republicans (see Chapter 8). Additionally, the GOP increased its margin in the state Senate by winning 19 of the 31 seats. All statewide elected officials remained Republican.

Since the mid-1990s, Republicans also have made significant gains across Texas at the county level. In 1974, Republicans held 53 county offices but had captured 547 by 1990. Republicans claimed 1,443 county offices by 2002 (Table 6–1), paralleling the dramatic statewide realignment that was occurring. Democrats still held most county offices, but Republicans were battling for dominance as local voting patterns began to reflect those for statewide offices.

Changing Party Identification

The transformation of the state's party system from a one-party Democratic state to Republican dominance is also reflected in changes in party identification over the past forty years. Belden Associates of Dallas reported in a 1952 survey that 66 percent of Texans called themselves Democrats, and only 6 percent claimed to be Republicans.[34] There was little change in party identification from 1952 to 1964, but during

TABLE 6–1   Growth of Republican Officeholders in Texas, 1974–2002

Year	U.S. Senate	Other Statewide	U.S. Congress	Texas Senate	Texas House	County Offices	Total
1974	1	0	2	3	16	53	75
1976	1	0	2	3	19	67	92
1978	1	1	4	4	22	87	119
1980	1	1	5	7	35	166	215
1982	1	0	5	5	36	191	238
1984	1	0	10	6	52	287	356
1986	1	1	10	6	56	410	484
1988	1	5	8	8	57	485	564
1990	1	6	8	8	57	547	627
1992	1	8	9	13	58	634	723
1994	2	13	11	14	61	734	835
1996	2	18	13	17	68	938	1056
1998	2	27	13	16	72	1108	1238
2000	2	27	13	16	72	1299	1429
2002	2	27	15	19	88	1443	1594

Source: Republican Party of Texas.

the next decade, Republican party identification increased to 16 percent and Democratic party identification declined to 59 percent (Figure 6–2).

Between 1975 and 1984, there was a dramatic decline in voter identification with the Democratic party and a significant increase in Republican party identification. By 2002, approximately 36 percent of Texas voters called themselves Republicans, and 24 percent identified themselves as Democrats. The remainder of those surveyed called themselves independents (26 percent), third party affiliates or undecided (14 percent). This shift in party identification is further proof that Texas is now a Republican-dominant state.

As noted in Figure 6–2, a large number of voters identify themselves as independents. Independents don't have their own party, and their choices in most elections are limited to candidates from the two major parties. Further survey research, moreover, suggests that most self-proclaimed independents vote consistently for Republican candidates.

Ticket splitting, a practice associated with the realignment process, has been common in recent Texas elections. It explains, in part, why Democrats have still been able to keep most local offices despite Republican sweeps statewide. Many Texans cast their votes selectively as they go down the general election ballot. In 1990, for example, there were a number of Democratic votes cast for Republican U.S. Senator Phil Gramm and a sizable number of Republican defectors to Bob Bullock, the successful Democratic candidate for lieutenant governor.[35] Ticket splitting, however,

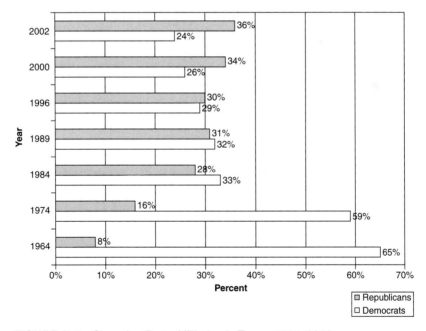

FIGURE 6–2 Changing Party Affiliation in Texas, 1964–2002.
Sources: The Texas Poll, Summer 1993, Fall 1993, Winter 1996, Spring 1996, Fall 1996, Spring 1999, Summer 1999, Fall 1999, Winter 2000, Spring 2001, Summer 2001, Fall 2001, Winter 2002.

WHERE HAVE ALL THE YELLOW DOGS GONE?

For a long-time Democrat (that is, a person 50 or older), there is a bit of nostalgia when someone asks, "Where have all the yellow dogs gone?" To a newcomer to the state, this probably conjures up an image of a mangy, brownish, yellow mutt that is used for coon hunting or running the dogs at night while their keepers drink hard liquor around the campfire. But to a real Democrat, it is a code word for those Democrats, often white conservatives, who swore by the phrase, "I'd vote for a yellow dog if he ran on the Democratic ticket." Moreover, those "yellow dogs" also would encourage voters to "pull one lever"—that is, vote straight Democratic.

Yellow-dog, one-party voters are a dying breed. Historically, there were counties in Texas that had never elected a Republican to local office. Some had never had a Republican party organization or seen a Republican challenge a Democrat in a local election. With the transformation of the state to one-party Republicanism, there are fewer and fewer yellow dogs. Franklin County, which is in deep East Texas, had not elected a member of the GOP from 1875 to 2000. But in 2002, three Republicans won elections to local offices.

So, where have all the yellow dogs gone? The answer is rather clear. Many of them have died and passed over. Many others have converted to the Republican party and are now voting the straight GOP ticket. Some of those yellow dogs have now become pedigree Republicans.

Source: John Williams, *The Houston Chronicle Online,* November 17, 2002.

---

is likely to decrease in the future as the new patterns of party affiliation solidify with a further increase of elected Republican officials and a reduction in the number of Democratic candidates in areas where Republicans dominate.

Voting differences and party identification sometimes are based on gender. Nationally, differences in the voting patterns of men and women have been significant. These differences are not as pronounced in Texas politics, but on occasions, there have been sharp differences between men and women. The gubernatorial election of 1990 produced one of the largest gaps between women and men in recent Texas political history. According to surveys of voters leaving the polls, Democrat Ann Richards enjoyed a lead of as much as 20 percent among women voters in some precincts in her defeat of Republican Clayton Williams. Part of that difference was believed to have been attributable to Williams's clumsy outspokenness, including a rape joke gaffe (see Chapter 5), which prompted a negative reaction among women across the state. Voter polls in the 1994 gubernatorial race indicated Richards held a more modest lead over Republican George W. Bush among women voters. Bush, who unseated Richards, obviously was more acceptable to women than Williams had been.[36]

There also is evidence suggesting that older and younger voters view the world in markedly different ways, a difference reflected in how people vote. Based on survey data, younger voters, for example, are more tolerant of candidates who have experienced problems with alcohol or drug abuse. Many younger voters also are more tolerant of lifestyles, which can create problems for conservatives who campaign against homosexuality and gay rights. Unlike older voters, fewer 18–29 year olds express any party identification. Moreover, younger people vote at much lower rates than older citizens.

In 1992, Republican President George H. W. Bush carried Texas while losing his reelection bid to Democrat Bill Clinton. That election marked the first time a Democratic candidate won the White House without winning Texas's electoral votes, a feat that Clinton repeated in 1996. The 1992 and 1996 elections also included the independent candidacy of Ross Perot, a billionaire computer magnate from Dallas, who attracted a lot of attention but finished third in Texas each time, as he did nationwide.

Differences Between Republicans and Democrats

There are marked differences in the social and economic characteristics of party identifiers. From studies, analysts have made the following generalizations:

The Texas Republican party is composed disproportionately of people who are:

- College educated
- Newcomers to Texas
- Anglos
- Large metropolitan area residents
- Earning higher incomes
- Middle age

Democrats are strongly represented among:

- Minorities
- Older residents
- Native Texans
- Those with lower income levels
- Those with less education.[37]

Data from the *Texas Poll* conducted in 2001–2002 provide a more detailed demographic profile of voters now identifying themselves as Democrats, Republicans, or independents (Table 6–2).

A Caveat to Realignment

Although the party system has been transformed in Texas, there is considerable disagreement about what these changes will mean in the long run.

V. O. Key, writing in the 1940s, concluded that race was becoming less important and the electorate was dividing along liberal and conservative lines. He concluded that a "modified class politics seems to be evolving."[38] More than a half century later, the parties appear, in part, to be aligning around economic issues that are manifested in liberal and conservative philosophies, but issues involving race continue to shape attitudes.

Chandler Davidson argues that "the Republican party's hard-line racial policy" attracted large numbers of conservative Democrats as well as supporters of George Wallace, the conservative American Independent party's 1968 presidential nominee, and "strengthened the commitment of African Americans and Mexican Americans to the Democratic Party."[39] Some Texas African Americans and Hispanics, primarily well-educated, well-to-do individuals, have become Republicans. But the vast majority

TABLE 6–2   Party Identification of Texas Voters by Social Groups, 2002

All Responding	Republican 36%	Democrat 24%	Independent 26%	Other 8%	Don't Know 6%
Age					
18–29	30	22	30	10	8
30–39	42	23	21	10	4
40–49	37	22	30	7	4
50–59	33	28	28	8	3
60 and Older	37	27	24	8	4
Education					
Some High School	28	23	35	8	6
High School Grad	31	30	24	9	6
Some College	35	26	29	8	2
College Grad	49	15	21	9	6
Graduate Work	39	26	30	3	2
Gender					
Male	36	23	28	10	3
Female	36	26	25	7	6
Income					
Less than $10,000	20	33	33	8	6
$10,001–$20,000	30	28	25	12	5
$20,001–$30,000	24	30	31	8	7
$30,001–$40,000	31	27	27	11	4
$40,001–$50,000	30	30	27	11	2
$50,001–$60,000	35	24	31	9	1
$60,001 and above	51	18	24	4	3
Race/Ethnicity					
Hispanic	22	29	27	13	9
Anglo	45	18	26	8	3
Black	3	61	24	3	9
Religion					
Protestant	43	24	23	7	3
Catholic	28	27	28	11	6

Source: Scripps Howard *Texas Poll,* Spring 2001, Summer 2001, Fall 2001, Winter 2002. A total of 4,000 Texans were surveyed in these polls.

remain Democrats, and Sunday morning visits to African-American churches in Houston and Dallas and appearances at south Texas *pachangas* (cookouts) are practically mandatory for Democratic candidates serious about winning statewide office.

Seeking to expand the Republican party's base, Governor George W. Bush made a strong appeal to Hispanics during his 1998 reelection campaign and, according to some estimates, was rewarded with about 40 percent of the Hispanic vote. Republicans in 2000 and 2002 also used campaign strategies aimed at peeling off Hispanic voters from the Democratic party. Some Republican strategists have been arguing for years that the GOP must strengthen its appeal to the growing Hispanic population—and chip away at Hispanics' traditional support for the Democratic party—if the GOP is to continue to maintain its control over state politics. White Anglo-Saxon Protestants who form the core of the Republican party are declining in proportion to the increased number of Hispanics in Texas. To maintain dominance, it has been argued, Republicans must embrace issues, such as improved health care and educational opportunities, which are central to Hispanic voting interests. It is premature to conclude that there will be an erosion of Hispanic support from the Democratic party, but both parties will be battling for the Hispanic vote over the next two decades. Republicans also have spoken about the need to appeal to African American Texans who share their core values, but the GOP has had little success attracting African Americans from the Democratic party.

An alternative view to realignment is that the party system is undergoing disintegration or **dealignment.**[40] This view is supported by the decline of the parties' electoral functions, their general organizational weaknesses, and voter indifference toward partisan labels, as manifested in ticket splitting and the increasing numbers of people calling themselves independents. Approximately 40 percent of voters in 2002 did not identify themselves as either Democrats or Republicans. According to this argument, political parties no longer perform their traditional functions because other institutions—including interest groups, the media, and the candidates themselves—control the political process, and the number of persons who identify with neither party will continue to grow.

A well-financed candidate, for example, can ignore party leaders and still win a party's nomination by using effective campaign and media tactics in the primary. Interest groups, which offer sophisticated organizations to shape public policy, may provide more access to policymakers than do the parties. And the media play a much greater role in screening candidates and shaping public opinion. The dealignment arguments, however, were more prominent in the last two decades of the 20th century. And although they may still have some validity, other evidence suggests that the party doomsayers were somewhat premature.

A contrary view in Texas is that the parties are undergoing a process of revitalization, attempting to reclaim basic party functions, especially in the areas of elections and campaigns.[41] Party activists are attempting to adapt modern campaign technology to the party organization. If the parties are able to provide strong support in fundraising, campaign advertising, phone banks, and other campaign functions, some candidates will likely become more dependent on the party organization. The massive infusion of "soft money" from corporations, labor unions, and other interest groups into the state and local party organizations by the national parties was one factor in this new vitality of state political parties. There also has been considerable collaboration between the state parties and the national parties in voter identification, voter mobilization, funding of campaigns, and organizational development. But campaign finance reforms enacted by Congress in 2002 restricted the use of soft money, and it is unclear what effects those changes will have on the Texas party system.

THE PARTY ORGANIZATION

To carry out their functions, the two major parties in Texas have developed permanent and temporary organizations, structured by state law, state and national party rules, and a series of court decisions protecting voters' rights.

Party organizations are built around geographic election districts, starting with the **precinct.**[42] There is, however, no hierarchical arrangement to party organization. V. O. Key described the party structure as a "system of layers of organization," with each level—county, state, and federal—concentrating on the elections within its jurisdiction.[43] There is a great deal of autonomy at each party level, based on the limited sanctions that one level can impose on another, and the fact that each level of the party needs the others to carry out electoral functions.[44]

There are no membership requirements for either the Democratic or the Republican party. Party members do not have to pay dues, attend meetings, campaign for candidates, or make contributions. When people register to vote in Texas, they are not required to state their party preference as they do in many other states. The right to participate in a party's electoral and nominating activities is based simply on voting in that party's primary election. When a person votes in one of the major party primaries, his or her voter registration card is stamped "Democrat" or "Republican."

The Permanent Organization

Election precincts—there were an estimated 8,500 in Texas in 2002—are created by the county commissioners of each of Texas's 254 counties. Population, political boundaries, and available voting sites help determine the number of precincts within a county. Voters in each precinct elect a **precinct chair** in the party primary (Figure 6–3). Any eligible voter within the precinct can file for this position, and the names of write-in candidates can be added to the ballot. (One of this book's authors was elected a precinct chair with two write-in votes.) Although there are many contested precinct chair elections, often no one runs for the office, leaving many precinct vacancies throughout the state. This problem has contributed to the parties' organizational decline. The chair calls the precinct convention (which will be discussed below) to order and serves as a member of the **county executive committee.** Precinct chairs also can mobilize party supporters to vote. Many people do absolutely nothing with the position, while others contribute much time and energy and have successfully delivered the precinct for their party's candidates in the general election. In some counties, the precinct chair is responsible for staffing the polling places on election day, but increasingly this is done by the county election administrator.

The second level of the party organization is the county executive committee, which includes each precinct chair and the **county chair,** who is elected to a two-year term by primary voters countywide. A major responsibility of the county chair and the executive committee is the organization and management of the primary election in their county. The county executive committee accepts filings by candidates for local offices and is also responsible for planning the county or district conventions. Funds for the management of primary elections are provided to the county party by the state through the secretary of state's office.

County committees may be well organized and actively work to carry out a wide range of organizational and electoral activities, or they may meet irregularly and have difficulty getting a quorum of members to attend. The county chair is an unpaid position. But party organizations in some counties have successful fundraising operations, and they support a party headquarters, retain professional staff, and are engaged in various party activities between elections.

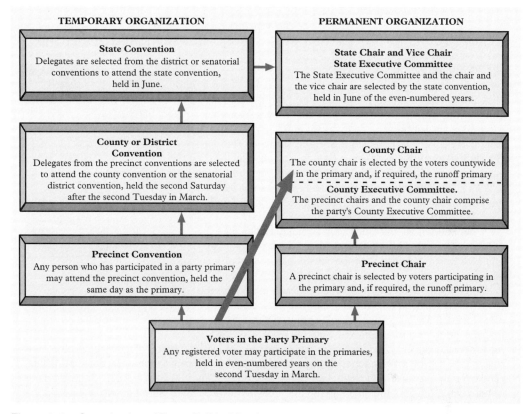

TEMPORARY ORGANIZATION

State Convention
Delegates are selected from the district or senatorial conventions to attend the state convention, held in June.

County or District Convention
Delegates from the precinct conventions are selected to attend the county convention or the senatorial district convention, held the second Saturday after the second Tuesday in March.

Precinct Convention
Any person who has participated in a party primary may attend the precinct convention, held the same day as the primary.

PERMANENT ORGANIZATION

State Chair and Vice Chair
State Executive Committee
The State Executive Committee and the chair and the vice chair are selected by the state convention, held in June of the even-numbered years.

County Chair
The county chair is elected by the voters countywide in the primary and, if required, the runoff primary
County Executive Committee.
The precinct chairs and the county chair comprise the party's County Executive Committee.

Precinct Chair
A precinct chair is selected by voters participating in the primary and, if required, the runoff primary.

Voters in the Party Primary
Any registered voter may participate in the primaries, held in even-numbered years on the second Tuesday in March.

Figure 6–3   Organization of Texas Political Parties.

The Texas Election Code provides for other district committees that correspond to a state senatorial, state representative, judicial, or congressional district. District committees that are solely within a county include precinct chairs, while multicounty district committees include representatives of all affected counties. These committees select candidates for vacancies in local and district offices if they occur between the primary and general election.

At the state level, a party's permanent organization is the **state executive committee,** which has sixty-four members, including the party's **state chair** and **vice chair.** When the parties meet in their biennial state conventions, two committee members—a man and a woman—are selected by delegation caucuses from each of the thirty-one state senatorial districts. The state chair and the vice chair, one of whom must be a woman, are also selected by the convention. The two top state party leaders and other executive committee members serve two-year terms and are unpaid.

Statewide candidates file for office with the executive committee, which also is responsible for planning and organizing the party's state convention and helps raise funds for the ongoing operations of the party. The committee serves to establish party policy, but day-to-day party operations are entrusted to the party's executive director and professional staff. The Texas Democratic party and the Texas Republican party have permanent staffs and headquarters in Austin.

— HOW I SEE IT —
CAMPUS CONUNDRUM: POLITICS, STUDENT ORGANIZATIONS, AND LEADERSHIP

Rick Schroeder

Rick Schroeder, a native San Antonian, graduated from Trinity University with a major in political science. He was a "campus activist," serving as the president of the College Republicans. He interned with U.S. Representative Henry Bonilla (R-TX) and worked with a trade association on legislative issues. He was instrumental in mobilizing students to work in the 2000 and 2004 Republican presidential campaigns. Subsequent to his undergraduate work, he pursued graduate studies in public affairs.

As I began my freshman year at Trinity University in 2000, I was excited about the infinite possibilities that lay ahead. It was an election year, political debates were alive all around the campus, and I resided on the first politically themed dorm floor on campus. Whether I was in my dorm room or in the classroom, political controversy surrounded me. I loved it! My conservative philosophy ran counter to many of the liberal professors and students I met, which led me to seek shelter in a conservative organization on campus. Although College Republicans were registered as an officially recognized organization, I could not locate the chapter president. In fact, I could hardly locate a Republican! I was extremely disappointed. My dreams of a great semester of hard work, grassroots campaigning, and conservative debates were squashed. Luckily, the resident assistant of my floor made sure that we, as a dorm floor, were exposed to a wide variety of political debates and events. Undoubtedly, the 2000 election year would have been a complete failure had my resident assistant not encouraged me to participate in these activities.

My quest to find active college Republicans did not end, however. Through a series of e-mails to students, I finally found the "acting" president. Not only did it take several e-mails to

Sometimes, the state committees are highly effective with strong, energetic leadership that carries over into the development and retention of a competent professional staff. At other times, however, the state committees have been divided along ideological, factional, or personal lines, producing conflict that sometimes has become open warfare. In those instances, a party finds it difficult to raise funds, maintain a highly qualified staff, and carry out its electoral functions.

Temporary Organization

The temporary organizations of the political parties are the series of conventions that are held every two years, beginning on the day of the party primaries. They are particularly significant in presidential election years because they—together with the presidential preference primary—help select the state's delegates to the national party conventions, which nominate the presidential candidates. The conventions finally receive one of his, I soon learned that he and the rest of the "acting" officers were paper tigers—all talk and no show. Their "senioritis" and lack of demographic diversity caused the organization to produce mediocre, if any, politically productive results for the campus or the surrounding community. From these initial observations, I learned one of the biggest lessons of my college career—for a membership organization to succeed, it must be headed by a demographically diverse leadership whose workload is sufficiently differentiated so that every officer has a clear set of expectations and goals.

All students, regardless of their ideological proclivity, have their own interests and natural abilities that they are interested in or good at. Leaders of political organizations should use this natural occurrence of ability. Place the student with computer skill competencies in charge of web mastering, communication majors in charge of public relations, and accounting majors in charge of the finances. You get the idea. Creating differentiated officer positions with clear responsibilities and goals allows an oftentimes burdened president to delegate authority and better choreograph the events of the entire organization. Moreover, such differentiation allows organizational officers to focus on their talents and stay away from activities they find boring or know nothing about. The social chair would probably find accounting tedious and boring, for example. Further, creating differentiated leadership positions allows an organization to focus on membership retention—a common problem of campus political organizations during nonelection years. Membership and social chairs permit campus clubs to focus on the ongoing social needs of their members and create a fun, inviting environment for political discourse.

Such demographic diversity should not end here. Leaders should take into account the long-term transfer of organizational leadership from one generation of student leaders to another. A political organization must differentiate the classes of its leadership or face a situation where the campus organization fades away as graduation day nears. Leadership drawn from a pool consisting of freshmen, sophomores, and juniors allows an organization to maintain its political programs, organizational activities, and political goals for the future despite the graduation of a handful of seniors. Moreover, this method of selecting officers allows an organization to maintain its viability during nonelection years, as underclassman officers are more likely to maintain their stake in an organization and its political mission. They, after all, are still going to be around during the next election cycle.

system also helps organize the permanent party structure and brings party activists together to share common political concerns and shape party policies. Most Texans, however, have little knowledge of the convention system, and few participate in it.

The Precinct Convention

Anyone who votes in a party primary, held on the second Tuesday in March of even-numbered years, is eligible to participate in that party's precinct convention, normally held in the same place as the primary after voting stops at 7 P.M. After the convention is organized and selects its permanent officers—chair, vice chair, and secretary—it begins its real business, the selection of delegates and alternate delegates to the county or senatorial district convention. Each precinct is assigned a specific number of delegates, based on the party's voting strength. Since 1972, the Democrats have used complex procedures designed to assure broad-based delegate representation by ethnicity, gender, and age. A precinct convention also can adopt resolutions to be submitted at the county or district conventions for possible inclusion in the party's **platform.**

In presidential election years, the presidential preference primary and the precinct conventions are the first steps in the selection of delegates to the national conventions. Before 1988, when Texas's participation in the first regional "Super Tuesday" presidential preference primary changed the delegate selection process, the precinct conventions were extremely crucial to presidential candidates because a candidate had to have strong support among delegates at the precinct level to ultimately capture a significant number of Texas delegates to the national convention. Now, much of that luster has been stolen by the primary, although the conventions still play a role in the Democratic party's presidential nominating process.

Precinct conventions held in nonpresidential election years are often poorly attended and, in many precincts, no one shows up. The precinct meeting may last 15 minutes, and those attending may not be able to get enough people to volunteer to be delegates to the upcoming county or senatorial convention. Such low participation rates are cited by those who conclude that the political parties are in decline.

In the past, highly motivated political and ideological movements have been able to capture precinct conventions and advance candidates who had little in common with mainstream party voters. Supporters of Barry Goldwater used this strategy in 1964 to help win the Republican presidential nomination for their candidate, as did supporters of Democrat George McGovern in 1972. But both men were soundly defeated in the general election. In recent years, the **Religious Right** has used a similar strategy to extend its influence in the Republican party and was successful for the first time in Texas in 1994. (See "The Religious Right and the Republican Party.")

THE PARTY ACTIVISTS

Texans who participate in the organizational activities of the political parties have characteristics that vary, to some extent, from other voters who support their respective political parties.

In a study of Republican and Democratic county and precinct chairs, Frank B. Feigert and Nancy L. McWilliams concluded that "they can be fairly described, for the most part, as white, Protestant, well-educated, of high income and holding high-status jobs." The Republican party has far fewer minority activists than does the Democratic party. More than 70 percent of Democratic and Republican activists were raised mainly in Texas, 80 percent lived in the state more than 20 years, 70 percent had been active in Texas politics for more than 10 years, but more than 50 percent had served in their positions less than 5 years. Self-recruitment was the most frequently given reason for involvement in the party organization.

The Republican leadership is highly conservative, while Democrats are more ideologically dispersed. Democratic activists are primarily moderate to liberal but include some conservatives. Democratic leaders are more supportive of social welfare and domestic programs than are Republicans, while Republicans are more conservative on taxing and spending issues.

Source: Frank B. Feigert and Nancy L. McWilliams, "Texas Party Activists: Yaller Dogs and Yuppies," a revised version of a paper originally prepared for delivery at the 1992 Citadel Symposium on Southern Politics, Charleston, SC, March 3–5, 1992.

THE RELIGIOUS RIGHT AND THE REPUBLICAN PARTY

As the Republican party expanded its support among Texas voters, it experienced sharp, often bitter, philosophical and ideological differences among its members. Overwhelmingly conservative, Republicans were split along lines of economic conservatism and the lifestyle conservatism advocated by the Religious Right. Conflict among Republicans over the abortion issue was a manifestation of the party's internal tension.

The Religious Right has long been part of the Texas political landscape.* While its influence was occasionally manifested in conservative Democratic politics, it has found far greater potential in the Republican party for shaping electoral politics. It has strong religious overtones and draws considerable support from evangelical groups across the state. Some scholars attribute much of its success to its ability to mobilize voters who have traditionally been inactive and bring them into the Republican party. The Republicans' difficulty in attracting minority groups gave the social conservative wing greater influence in the party.

Chandler Davidson concluded in 1990 that the Religious Right had not taken over the Republican party, "but its influence is significant and gives the Texas Republicans their particular stridency and, at times, their appearance of a Know-Nothing movement."** By 1994, however, the Religious Right was instrumental in a takeover by social conservatives of the Republican state convention and the party leadership.

Low voter turnout in the Republican primary had enabled well-organized social conservatives to gain control of the party's precinct conventions and elect a majority of delegates to the June state convention. Sensing defeat, Fred Meyer of Dallas, a traditional Republican who had guided the state party for six years during a period of growth and electoral success, stepped down as state GOP chairman and was replaced by Tom Pauken, a Dallas lawyer and former Reagan administration official who courted Christian activists. Delegates elected a new state party vice chair, Christian activist Susan Weddington of San Antonio, and put other members of the Religious Right on the State Republican Executive Committee.

The Religious Right also was instrumental in the election of Republican George W. Bush over Democrat Ann Richards in the 1994 gubernatorial race. According to a survey of voters as they left the polls, 20 percent of the 4.4 million Texans who voted in that election identified themselves as white Christian fundamentalists. Of those, 84 percent said they voted for Bush. They also voted heavily for other Republican candidates.***

Social and religious conservatives also took control of the 1996 Republican state convention and dominated the Texas delegation to the Republican National Convention. Some social conservatives, insisting the party retain its strong antiabortion policy, tried to deny U.S. Senator Kay Bailey Hutchison a delegate's slot to the national convention because she favored abortion rights with some restrictions. Such a move would have been an unheard-of snub for a high-ranking officeholder from the party. Hutchison finally got on the delegate list with the help of Governor Bush, U.S. Senator Phil Gramm, and Republican presidential nominee Bob Dole.

The State Republican Executive Committee elected Susan Weddington state party chair after Pauken resigned in 1997 to run unsuccessfully for state attorney general. Weddington served in that post and was an outspoken advocate for social conservative causes until 2003, when she resigned to take a job directing a new state charitable foundation. The State Republican Executive Committee elected party activist Tina Benkiser, an attorney from Houston, to succeed Weddington.

---

*George Norris Green, *The Establishment in Texas Politics,* 1938–1957 (Westport, CT: Greenwood Press, 1979), Chap. 5; Chandler Davidson, *Race and Class in Texas Politics* (Princeton: Princeton University Press, 1990), Chap. 10.

** Davidson, *Race and Class in Texas Politics,* p. 206.

*** *Dallas Morning News,* November 11, 1994.

The County or Senatorial District Conventions

County or senatorial district conventions are held two weeks after the precinct conventions. District conventions are held in the larger urban counties, such as Harris, Dallas, Tarrant, and Bexar, which include more than one state senatorial district. Delegates elected at the precinct conventions constitute the membership of this second level of the convention process, which, in turn, elects delegates to the state convention.

Conventions are about politics, selection of candidates, and control of the party apparatus. There have been intermittent periods of lackluster conventions. But during Texas's one-party, Democratic era, there were frequent, bitter convention fights between conservatives and liberals for control of the Democratic party. And although those fights were most evident at the state convention, they also permeated the precinct, county, and district conventions. As Texas Republicans have increased in number and developed more diversified interests, similar intraparty struggles have surfaced.

State Conventions

The two major parties hold their state conventions in June of even-numbered years. Convention delegates certify to the secretary of state the names of those individuals who were nominated to statewide offices in the March primaries, adopt a party platform, and elect the state party chair, the vice chair, and the state executive committee.

In presidential election years, the state conventions also select delegates to their respective parties' national nominating conventions, elect members to their parties' national committees, and choose presidential electors. Electors from the party that carries Texas in the presidential race will formally cast the state's electoral votes for that party's candidate in December after the general election.

The allocation among the candidates of Texas delegates to the Republican National Convention is determined by the presidential primary, but the actual delegates are selected at the state convention. Texas delegates to the Democratic National Convention are determined through a more complicated process, based both on the primary vote and on candidate support from attendees at the series of party conventions, beginning at the precinct level.

THE PARTY IN GOVERNMENT

As part of V. O. Key's three-part perspective on political parties, we have begun our discussion of the political party in the electorate. In the next chapter, we will expand on this analysis by looking more closely at voting behavior, partisan attitudes, and the party activists. We also have presented a brief summary of the party organization. We will discuss the party in government in later chapters on the legislature, the executive branch, the bureaucracy, and the judiciary.

Political parties in Texas, however, do not produce cohesive, policy-oriented coalitions in government and have been unable to hold their elected officials accountable or responsive to those supporting the party. Under ideal circumstances, some students of government believe, the two major parties would lay out clearly defined political philosophies and policies they would pursue if their candidates were elected. Once elected, persons supported by the party would be committed to these programs, giving the voters a clear standard by which to evaluate their performance in office. This perspective is often referred to as the "responsible party model."

There are several reasons why Texas parties are incapable of functioning in this manner, none of which lessen the disenchantment and disgust that many voters have felt toward political parties and politicians. First, the political parties in Texas are highly decentralized and unable to discipline members who pursue goals that conflict with the parties' stated objectives. The large number of elected officials at both the state and the local level serves to diffuse party leadership. Moreover, the coalitions that parties form with groups harboring different objectives, interests, and agendas make it next to impossible to develop clearly stated positions that would always differentiate one party from another. Philosophical, ideological, and programmatic differences among members and supporters of the same party result, for example, in ideological voting patterns in the legislature that cross party lines.

Another explanation for the lack of partisan accountability is the longstanding antiparty tradition of American politics. Many voters are ambivalent, even outright hostile, toward political parties and make little, if any, effort to become informed on political and public issues. And the parties make only limited efforts to include a large number of individuals in their organizational activities.

THIRD PARTIES IN TEXAS

There has been a tradition of **third parties** in Texas, including Grangers, Populists, Progressives, Socialists, Dixiecrats, the American Independent party, La Raza Unida, the Natural Law party and Libertarians. None has had statewide electoral success. But both the Populists in the 1890s and La Raza Unida in the early 1970s were perceived to be a significant threat to the established state party structure and those who controlled political and economic power.

Major third-party movements surfaced when Texas was still a one-party Democratic state and, in some respects, they suggested an alternative to the then-weak Republican party. But both from a state and a national perspective, they were movements of crisis or discontent.[45] The Democratic party, particularly its conservative wing, either co-opted these movements by making minor public policy concessions to them or by getting restrictive legislation, such as the poll tax, enacted to reduce their electoral base. In some instances, economic recriminations were the price individuals paid for participating in these third-party movements.[46]

La Raza Unida raised a particularly interesting prospect of a political party built upon an ethnic group. In the 1960s, young Hispanic leaders began to develop student organizations across the state that became the organizational framework on which this party was developed.[47] Low-income Hispanics historically had been excluded from any major role in the Democratic party by restrictive voter registration laws, at-large elections, and racial gerrymandering designed to minimize Hispanic voting strength. An even more fundamental problem was the fact that state public policy was not responsive to the educational and economic needs of Hispanics because conservative Democrats refused to enact legislation that would benefit that major part of the population.

La Raza Unida (People United), led by Jose Angel Gutierrez and Mario Compean, began in 1969 to organize in Crystal City in Zavala County and then extended its efforts to Dimmit, La Salle, and Hildago counties.[48] Overwhelmingly Hispanic and poor, these counties were characteristic of many South Texas counties, in which the Anglo minority controlled both the political and economic institutions and showed little sensitivity to the needs of low-income residents.

The struggle for access to the ballot box and fair elections in Zavala County parallels the experience of African Americans throughout the South. Manipulation of the election laws, economic reprisals, and intimidation by the police and Texas Rangers were used by the Anglo minority to try to retain control. La Raza Unida, however, won control of local and county offices in Crystal City and Zavala County in 1972, the same year that Ramsey Muniz ran as the party's gubernatorial candidate. During the general election campaign, there was considerable speculation in the press and apprehension among conservative Democrats that La Raza would drain a sufficient number of votes away from Dolph Briscoe, the Democratic nominee, to give Henry (Hank) Grover, a right-wing Republican, the governorship. Briscoe won the election, but without a majority of the votes.

The subsequent growth of liberal and minority influence within the Democratic party, internal dissension within La Raza Unida, and legal problems encountered by Muniz contributed to the demise of this third party after 1978.

The most successful third party in Texas in recent years has been the Libertarian party. Libertarians have qualified for a place on the ballot in every Texas general election since 1986 because the party has succeeded in winning at least 5 percent of the vote in at least one statewide race during each election year. But the party has never won an elected office in Texas.

In addition to statewide third parties, local political organizations connected to neither the Democratic nor the Republican party have been influential in some cities. Elections for city offices are nonpartisan, and most are held during odd-numbered years when there are no state offices on the ballot. Cities such as San Antonio and Dallas developed citizens' associations, which had all of the characteristics of political parties. Many of these local organizations controlled city governments for decades and maintained a virtual monopoly over city elections, but these groups have disappeared in recent years.

WHY A TWO-PARTY SYSTEM?

Why are there only two major political parties in Texas and the United States? Many other democratic countries have multiparty systems that function quite well. And, given the economic, regional, and social diversification of this nation and this state, one might conclude that multiple parties would be more capable of translating the interests of their members and supporters into public policy. Yet, the United States has a 200-year history of two-party politics.

By historical accident and certainly not by design, the first national party system in this country was configured around two identifiable coalitions of interests who articulated two alternative views of American government. Some have suggested that there was a natural dualism in American politics and parties aligned along these fundamental differences. By itself, that is not a very convincing argument, but subsequent generations have been politically socialized or educated to think that two parties are inevitable and preferred over any alternatives. Democrats and Republicans can fight over a wide variety of issues, but one will hear spokespersons of both parties extolling the virtues of two-party politics. Democrats and Republicans just don't talk about multiparty politics.

State election laws, which are written by Democratic and Republican legislators, also contribute to the persistence of a two-party system. Unlike the party primaries, where runoffs are held—if necessary—to select a nominee by majority vote, general elections are won by a simple plurality. The candidate who gets more votes than any other candidate, regardless of how many are in the race, is elected. There are no runoffs. That was how Dolph Briscoe won election with less than a majority of the vote in 1972, when La Raza Unida candidate Ramsey Muniz siphoned off traditional Democratic votes. Without a runoff, third-party candidates have little chance of winning office over major party nominees. Election laws also impose specific requirements that make it difficult for third parties to get their candidates listed on the ballot.

Some advocates of third parties argue that they are necessary to revitalize American politics and remove the "virtual monopoly" that the Democratic and Republican parties exercise over the American political process. The two major parties "own the keys to the castle; they control the power," wrote Robert Roth, press secretary of the Natural Law party. "The downside for the country is that they have closed themselves off to the infusion of new ideas; they exist in isolation. With few exceptions, both parties are starting to look and sound much the same, like two sides of the same coin."[49]

But most Texans do not have the intense ideological positions that may prompt the formation of a third party. Winning elections takes precedence over ideological purity, and only a relatively few individuals are "true believers" with a highly cohesive, systematic set of beliefs shaping their political behavior.[50] A conservative Republican may support marketplace economics and deregulation but oppose a ban on abortion. A liberal Democrat who is a Catholic may favor greater economic regulation and expanded social services but oppose government programs subsidizing family planning or sex education.

Although class and race shape politics and public policy debates, other issues and concerns cut across these groupings. While we can talk about the tendency of one party to attract more of one group of citizens than the other party, no party has a monopoly on key segments of the electorate. There are Hispanics, Anglos, and African Americans in both major parties. Labor divides its support between the two parties, as do religious, economic, and educational groups. The multiclass and heterogeneous base of support for the two major parties minimizes the potential for third parties.[51]

SUMMARY AND CONCLUSIONS

1. Historically, Texans, along with most other Americans, have been indifferent toward political parties, giving little respect to the basic roles that parties play in a democratic society.

2. Political parties build electoral coalitions and serve as intermediaries between the voters and the government. They recruit and nominate candidates, attempt to mobilize voters, resolve conflicts among diverse groups, and set the political agenda.

3. Weak political parties allow special interest groups to play a more prominent role in policy making. During much of its history, Texas had a weak one-party system, characterized by two competing factions within the Democratic party. This weak party system, based in part on the systematic exclusion of many citizens through discriminatory election laws, contributed to a powerful interest group system. In Austin, as well as at the local level, the power of interest groups is still seen in most aspects of the decision-making process, often to the detriment of the general public. It remains to be seen whether Texas's new two-party system will change the relative power between the political parties and interest groups.

4. Over the past thirty years, there have been significant changes in the state's party structure. One-party Democratic control has been transformed by complex economic, social, and political changes, and Texas is now a two-party state dominated by the Republican party. Texas voters are divided among Democrats, Republicans, and independents, but the GOP has an edge. While some of these changes are appropriately discussed in terms of realignment, another view is that the state has finally become more integrated into the national party system, thus closely approximating the political alignments that exist outside the South. Historically, politics in Texas were configured around class and race, and, despite all of the partisan changes, these two factors are still significant in party alliances.

5. Some scholars argue that partisan realignment in Texas has been offset by the organizational weaknesses of the political parties and a decline in party identification among voters. The more pessimistic scholars believe that the parties are dealigning or disintegrating, with some of their primary functions being assumed by other institutions, including the media and interest groups.

6. A competitive, viable two-party system is directly related to the responsiveness of public officials and governing institutions. Public policy can be shaped through responsible and competitive political parties. But the continued neglect of the needs and interests of large segments of the state's population challenges the very premises upon which a democratic society is based. Moreover, the parties have rarely functioned as highly cohesive, disciplined organizations in the government. With candidate-centered campaigns, the parties have lost much of their control over those elected under party labels. Legislators and other elected officials are somewhat like free agents, taking sides on issues with little concern of recrimination from their political parties.

7. State laws outline the formal party structure, but the vitality and strength of local party organizations vary widely from one area of the state to another.

KEY TERMS

Political party	Ticket splitting	State chair and vice chair
Jim Crow laws	Realignment	Platform
One-party system	Precinct chair	Party activist
Bifactionalism	County executive committee	Precinct
Two-party system	County chair	Religious Right
Dealignment	State executive committee	Third party

FURTHER READING

Articles

Bauer, John R., "Partisan Realignment and the Changing Political Geography of Texas," *Journal of Political Studies,* 12 (Spring/Summer 1990), pp. 41–66.

Champagne, Anthony, and Rick Collis, "Texas," in *The Political Life of the American States,* eds. Alan Rosenthal and Maureen Moakley. New York: Praeger, 1984.

Dyer, James A., Arnold Vedlitz, and David B. Hill, "New Voters, Switchers, and Political Party Realignment in Texas," *Western Political Quarterly,* 41 (March 1988), pp. 155–67.

Stanley, Jeanie R., "Party Realignment and the 1986 Texas Election," *Texas Journal of Political Studies,* 9 (Spring/Summer 1987), pp. 3–13.

Stanley-Coleman, Jeanie R., and Candace Windel, "Gender Politics in the 1994 Elections," *Texas Journal of Political Studies* 18 (Fall/Winter 1995/96), pp. 5–31.

Books

Anders, Evan, *Boss Rule in South Texas: The Progressive Era.* Austin: University of Texas Press, 1982.

Anderson, James E., Richard W. Murray, and Edward L. Farley, *Texas Politics,* 6th ed. New York: Harper-Collins Publishers, Inc., 1992.

Beck, Paul Allen, *Party Politics in America,* 8th ed. New York: Longman, 1997.

Black, Earl and Merle Black, *The Rise of Southern Republicans.* Boston: Harvard University Press, 2002.

Davidson, Chandler, *Race and Class in Texas Politics.* Princeton: Princeton University Press, 1990.

———, and Bernard Grofman, eds. *Quiet Revolution in the South: The Impact of the Voting Rights Act, 1965–1990.* Princeton, NJ: Princeton University Press, 1994.

Dyer, James, and Don Haynes, *Social, Economic and Political Change According to the Texas Poll.* Austin: College of Communication, University of Texas at Austin, 1987.

Erikson, Robert S., Gerald C. Wright, and John P. McIver, *Statehouse Democracy: Public Opinion and Policy in the American States.* New York: Cambridge University Press, 1993.

Frantaich, Stephen E., *Political Parties in the Technological Age.* New York: Longman, 1989.

Garcia, Ignacio, *United We Win: The Rise and Fall of La Raza Unida Party.* Tucson: Mexican American Studies and Research Center at the University of Arizona, 1989.

———. *Viva Kennedy Clubs: Mexican Americans in Search of Camelot.* College Station: Texas A&M University Press, 2000.

Grantham, Dewey W., *The Life and Death of the Solid South: A Political History.* Lexington, KY: University Press of Kentucky, 1988.

Green, George Norris, *The Establishment in Texas Politics, 1938–1957.* Westport, CT: Greenwood Press, 1979.

Hodges, Ed, *The Wins of Change: The Republican Tide in Texas.* Dallas: Pinnacle Press, 1999.

Ivins, Molly, *Molly Ivins Can't Say That, Can She?* New York: Random House, 1991.

Jewell, Malcolm E., and David M. Olson, *American State Political Parties and Elections,* rev. ed. Homewood, IL: The Dorsey Press, 1982.

Key, V. O., *Southern Politics.* New York: Vintage Books, 1949.

Knaggs, John R., *Two Party Texas: The John Tower Era, 1961–1984.* Austin: Eakin Press, 1986.

Maisel, L. Sandy, ed., *The Parties Respond,* 3rd ed. Boulder, CO: Westview Press, 1998.

Morehead, Richard, *50 Years in Texas Politics: From Roosevelt to Reagan, From the Fergusons to Clements.* Burnet, TX: Eakin Press, 1982.

Quinones, Juan Gomez, *Chicano Politics.* Albuquerque: University of New Mexico Press, 1990.

Sabato, Larry J., *The Party's Just Begun: Shaping Political Parties for America's Future.* Glenview, IL: Scott Foresman/Little, Brown College Division, 1988.

Smith, Oron. *The Rise of Baptist Republicanism.* New York: New York University Press, 1997.

Sundquist, James, *Dynamics of the Party System,* rev. ed. Washington, DC: The Brookings Institution, 1983.

Tower, John G., *Consequences: A Personal and Political Memoir.* New York: Little, Brown, 1991.

Websites

Green Party of Texas http://www.txgreens.org A third party committed to social justice, nonviolence, ecology, and grass-roots democracy, Greens have had limited impact on the state's electoral politics.

Libertarian Party of Texas http://www.lptexas.org Libertarians tend to advocate a very limited role of governments, and they are particularly vocal in supporting "the right of individuals to live in whatever manner they choose, so long as they do not interfere with the rights of others."

Texas Democratic Party http://www.txdemocrats.org This site provides a range of information on state party organization, county chairs, affiliate organizations, candidates, and policy issues.

Republican Party of Texas http://www.texasgop.org In addition to information about the Republican party and links to other state party organizations, this site provides information about Republican candidates, the party platform, and a calendar of party events.

ENDNOTES

1. E. E. Schattschneider, *Semisovereign People* (New York: Holt, Rinehart and Winston, 1960).
2. Lisa Song, "Politics on the Not-so Fringe," *San Antonio Current,* October 31, 2002.
3. Dennis S. Ippolito and Thomas G. Walker, *Political Parties, Interest Groups, and Public Policy: Group Influence in American Politics* (Englewood Cliffs, NJ: Prentice Hall, Inc., 1980), p. 2.
4. John F. Bibby, *Politics, Parties and Elections in America* (Chicago: Nelson-Hall, 1987), pp. 3–4.
5. Leon Epstein, *Political Parties in Western Democracies* (New York: Praeger, 1967), p. 9.
6. Bibby, *Politics, Parties, and Elections in America,* p. 15.
7. Sarah McCally Morehouse, *State Politics, Parties and Policy* (New York: Holt, Rinehart and Winston, 1981), p. 118.
8. Ibid., pp. 118–19.
9. Ibid., p. 117.
10. Samuel Huntington, *Political Order in Changing Societies* (New Haven, CT: Yale University Press, 1980), p. 91.

11. Robert J. Huckshorn, *Political Parties in America,* 2nd ed. (Monterey, CA: Brooks/Cole Publishing Company, 1981), p. 23.
12. Bibby, *Politics, Parties and Elections in America,* p. 12.
13. V. O. Key, *Southern Politics* (New York: Vintage Books, 1949), p. 225.
14. Chandler Davidson, *Race and Class in Texas Politics* (Princeton: Princeton University Press, 1990), p. 21.
15. Ibid., p. 6.
16. Alexander P. Lamis, *The Two-Party South,* expanded edition (New York: Oxford University Press, 1988), p. 23.
17. Ibid., p. 194.
18. George Norris Green, *The Establishment in Texas Politics, 1938–1957* (Westport, CT: Greenwood Press, 1979), p. 57
19. Ibid., pp. 121–34.
20. Key, *Southern Politics,* pp. 302–10.
21. Green, *The Establishment in Texas Politics,* pp. 142–48.
22. Key, *Southern Politics,* pp. 294–97.
23. Green, *The Establishment in Texas Politics,* p. 148.
24. Lamis, *The Two-Party South,* p. 195.
25. Ibid., p. 195; Davidson, *Race and Class in Texas Politics,* p. 201.
26. John R. Knaggs, *Two-Party Texas: The John Tower Era, 1961–1984* (Austin: Eakin Press, 1986), p. 15.
27. Davidson, *Race and Class in Texas Politics,* p. 199.
28. Lamis, *The Two-Party South,* p. 194.
29. Ibid., pp. 196–97.
30. For an excellent summary of realignment theory and conditions under which realignment is likely to take place, see James L. Sundquist, *Dynamics of the Party System,* rev. ed. (Washington, DC: The Brookings Institution, 1983).
31. James A. Dyer, Arnold Vedlitz, and David B. Hill, "New Voters, Switchers, and Political Party Realignment in Texas," *Western Political Quarterly,* 41 (March 1988), p. 164.
32. See Kevin P. Phillips, *The Emerging Republican Majority* (New Rochelle, NY: Arlington House, 1969) and Richard M. Scammon and Ben J. Wattenberg, *The Real Majority* (New York: Coward-McCann, 1970).
33. Green, *The Establishment in Texas Politics,* p. 208.
34. Dyer and Vedlitz, "New Voters, Switchers, and Political Party Realignment in Texas," p. 156.
35. *Texas Poll,* 7 (Spring 1990), p. 4.
36. *Dallas Morning News,* November 9, 1994.
37. Dyer and Vedlitz, "New Voters, Switchers, and Political Party Realignment in Texas," pp. 165–66.
38. Key, *Southern Politics,* p. 255.
39. Davidson, *Race and Class in Texas Politics,* p. 238.
40. Walter Dean Burnham, *Critical Elections and the Mainsprings of American Politics* (New York: Norton, 1970), Chap. 5; Walter Dean Burnham, *The Current Crisis in American Politics* (Oxford: Oxford University Press, 1982).
41. See Robert Huckshorn, *Political Parties in America,* pp. 358–60.
42. John F. Bibby, "State Party Organizations: Coping and Adapting to Candidate-Centered Politics and Nationalization," in *The Parties Respond: Changes in American Parties and Campaigns,* 3rd ed., ed. L. Sandy Maisel (Boulder, CO: Westview Press, 1998), pp. 23–49.
43. V. O. Key Jr., *Parties, Politics and Pressure Groups,* 4th ed. (New York: Thomas Y. Crowell Company, 1958), p. 347.
44. Bibby, *Politics, Parties, and Elections in America,* p. 82.
45. Daniel Mazmanian, *Third Parties in Presidential Elections* (Washington, D.C.: The Brookings Institute, 1974), p. 5.
46. George Rivera, "Building a Chicano Party in South Texas," *New South,* 26 (Spring 1971), pp. 75–78.
47. Ibid.
48. Juan Gomez Quinones, *Chicano Politics* (Albuquerque: University of New Mexico Press, 1990), pp. 128–31.
49. Robert Roth, *The Natural Law Party: A Reason to Vote* (New York: St. Martin's Press, 1998), p. 19.
50. John Crittenden, *Parties and Elections in the United States* (Englewood Cliffs, NJ: Prentice Hall, Inc., 1982), p. 11.
51. Huckshorn, *Political Parties in America,* p. 11

Elections, Campaigns, and Political Behavior

> If the gods had meant us to vote, they would have given us candidates.
>
> *Jim Hightower,*
> *former commissioner of agriculture,*
> *author, and columnist*[1]

> Politics is show business for ugly people.
>
> *Bill Miller, political consultant*[2]

At a time when millions of people around the world have eliminated authoritarian political systems and made great sacrifices to win free and open elections, Texans congratulate themselves if one-third of the eligible population votes. Such a poor turnout cannot be blamed on a lack of opportunity. After decades of denying voting rights to large parts of the population, Texas now has one of the most progressive voter registration laws in the United States. Contemporary political campaigns, especially those for national and statewide offices, have high media visibility. People are bombarded by sophisticated television advertising campaigns, direct mail, e-mail, phone bank solicitations for candidates, and daily news coverage. Yet something fundamental is disturbing Texas voters, as well as voters across the nation. Statewide election turnout rates in Texas are consistently low, and turnout rates in many local elections are downright appalling.

Some suggest that Texans do not care about what happens in government as long as their own selfish interests are being met. Other people argue that there is a sense of disenchantment, disillusionment, or alienation among Texas voters. Voters, they believe, feel disconnected from government and elected officeholders. They don't trust public officials to do what they said they were going to do in their election bids, and they believe politicians are using their offices to line their own pockets.

Other Texans care about politics, government, and public policy but believe that a single vote will make no difference.

Elected officials, moreover, are perceived to be increasingly insulated from the popular will. Although they articulate a commitment to elections and political participation, many are not really interested in cultivating an electorate that is actively involved in the decisions of government. Some observers also have argued that elections staggered throughout the year, as they are in Texas and other states, are designed to reduce voter participation. The real brokers of politics and public policy are the interest groups, lobbyists, and political action committees. And, with the decline of the political parties, many candidates become free agents who seem to sell their services to the highest bidders. When voters read or hear that candidates are taking hundreds of thousands of dollars from political action committees or individual donors, it is difficult to convince people that politicians aren't on the take.

Much has been written indicting contemporary elections in Texas and the United States. Elections were designed to give the people the opportunity to direct public policy through chosen officials who would then be held accountable at the next election, but the system will not work properly if people will not vote. Elections are clearly imperfect instruments, but we have found no other vehicle for translating the needs, interests, and expectations of the public into public policy.

THE FUNCTIONS OF ELECTIONS

For more than 200 years, we in the United States have been debating electoral issues. Who should participate? Should individuals who cannot read very well be permitted to vote? When should elections be held? What percentage of the popular vote is required to win an election—a majority or a plurality? What are the policy consequences of elections? Does it really make any difference who gets elected? Although these questions are significant, the most important issue is the relationship of elections to our definition of a democratic society. In the most fundamental terms, "elections are used to assure popular support and legitimacy for those who make governmental decisions."[3] A stable political system depends on popular support, and people freely participating in the process of choosing those who make public policy are more likely to accept and support policy without coercion or force.

While elections provide broad statements of the voters' expectations for future public policy and a prospective judgment on the performance of elected officials, they seldom articulate or direct precise programs. Successful political parties and candidates build broad-based campaign coalitions, and the competing demands of the diverse groups courted by candidates make it difficult for candidates to specify in detail the policies they plan to pursue once elected. Most people seeking public office, therefore, prefer to speak in general concepts and try to avoid answering hypothetical "what if" questions posed by reporters, such as "What if there isn't enough money in the budget to raise teachers' pay or improve health care? Will you support a tax increase or cut back on other programs?"

Nevertheless, after an election, a successful candidate is likely to indicate that the people have spoken and claim a mandate to pursue specific public policies of his or her choosing. If there is a mandate, it is for the person elected, not for a specific program.[4]

Elections enable voters to replace public officials or force officeholders to change their policies.[5] They are, in effect, the one institution that a democratic society can use to control its leaders and provide a retrospective judgment of the past actions of elected officials. But this role is based on the assumptions that (1) there is universal **suffrage,** (2) voters are offered clear alternatives, (3) large segments of the population are informed about those aspiring to public office and public policy, and (4) there is significant voter participation. Throughout Texas history, elections often have been manipulated for the advantage and interests of the few.

Texas's political culture has unwritten rules as to how elections should be conducted and what candidates should and should not do. For example, we expect a candidate to shake the hand of his or her opponent even after a bitter defeat or attack. That is why Republican Clayton Williams's snub of the handshake offered by Democrat Ann Richards during one joint appearance in the 1990 gubernatorial campaign received much media attention. Candidates can attack, counterattack, make charges and counter-charges against each other, and still be considered politically acceptable and civilized. Such election rituals are manifestations of the way in which we have institutionalized conflict.

Some would argue that elections and election rituals have only a symbolic function that serves to "quiet resentments and doubts about particular political acts, reaffirm belief in the fundamental rationality and democratic character of the system, and thus fix conforming habits of future behavior."[6] While this position may be extreme, there is an implicit warning in the author's conclusions. The trivialization of elections may ultimately result in even more disenchantment, disdain, and disgust with politics and government. If the electorate is "fed a steady diet of buncombe, the people may come to expect and to respond with the highest predictability to buncombe."[7]

CHARACTERISTICS OF TEXAS ELECTIONS

Texans have numerous opportunities to vote, often as many as three or four times a year, in a variety of elections. Voters in Texas and other states, in fact, get to vote on more candidates and issues than citizens of any other democracy.[8] Turnout and interest is highest in the general election in presidential election years, but can be abysmally low in elections for **constitutional amendments,** school boards and the governing bodies of single-purpose districts, such as hospital and water districts.

Election Cycles

Except for some constitutional amendment elections, which are set by the legislature, and emergency elections set by the governor to fill vacancies in specific offices, elections are held at regular, predictable intervals mandated by state law. There has been a systematic effort to separate elections and thereby minimize the convergence of issues in state and local races.[9] Most city and school board elections are held in May of odd-numbered years to separate them from party primaries held in March of even-numbered years and general elections held in November. Many constitutional amendment elections are scheduled on the same day as the general election, but they can be held separately (see Chapter 2). There are all kinds of explanations and justifications for this election scheduling, but there is evidence to suggest that it contributes to "voter fatigue," reduced voter turnout, and the disproportionate influence of a few individuals in many of the local and special elections where voter turnout usually is the lowest. Some experts believe that many voters have tired of elections and tuned them out.

These election cycles also shape the policymaking process. A tax increase, for example, is likely to take place soon after an election, not immediately prior to one. Voter dissatisfaction, officeholders hope, would be dissipated by the time an election takes place after their tax vote. This is a double-edged sword. It insulates public officials from immediate public discontent when hard and unpopular decisions must be made. It also makes it difficult to punish elected officials for pursuing questionable or highly unpopular programs.

Primary Elections

Texas and most other states use the direct **primary election** to nominate major party candidates for public office. Prior to the adoption of the primary in 1903, the political parties used the party conventions to nominate their candidates, but changes were made for two basic reasons. Throughout the country during that era, a Progressive reform movement criticized the conventions as undemocratic, corrupt, and dominated by a few of the party elites. That movement advocated the party primary as an alternative. Second, the personal rivalries and factional disputes that erupted at nominating conventions threatened the monopoly that the Democratic party had over Texas politics during that era, and the primary elections were a solution to excessive intraparty conflict. Under current law, any party that received 20 percent of the vote in the last gubernatorial election is required to nominate candidates by the primary. Other parties can continue to use the nominating convention.

Primaries are now held on the second Tuesday in March in even-numbered years, a change that was made in 1988 as part of the strategy of southern states to increase the region's influence in the presidential nominating process.

For practical purposes, the primaries in Texas are open because no party membership is designated on an individual's voter registration card. A voter does not register as a Republican or a Democrat. Only after a person has voted in a party's primary is the party's name stamped on the card, and that restricts a person to voting only in that party's runoff, if there is one.

Some students of Texas politics suggest that the structure of the state's primary delayed the development of the two-party system and contributed to the conservative establishment's long domination of state politics. Comparisons between earlier primary elections and general elections suggest that Republicans voted in the Democratic primaries and then voted for Republicans in the general election. Conservative candidates were usually nominated by both parties, so it was assured that conservatives would be elected in the general election.[10]

Voter turnout in the primary elections is traditionally lower than in the general election, but the emergence of a two-party system is producing appreciable changes in participation patterns in the Democratic and Republican primaries. During the period of one-party Democratic politics, the person who won the Democratic primary usually won the general election.

From the 1920s through 1970, the rate of turnout for the Democratic primary never exceeded 35 percent of the voting-age population. Over the past thirty years, it has eroded further, reflecting the realignment of the state's party system (see Chapter 6). About 28 percent of the voting-age population (persons 18 or older) voted in the hotly contested Democratic gubernatorial primary in 1972. Since then, turnout in Democratic primaries has fallen below 20 percent (see Table 7–1).[11] Less

TABLE 7–1   Turnout in Party Primaries, 1970–2002

	Democrats			Republicans		
Year	Total Votes Cast	Percent of Registered Voters	Percent of Voting Age Population	Total Votes Cast	Percent of Registered Voters	Percent of Voting Age Population
1970	1,011,300	24.37	14.07	109,021	2.63	1.52
1972	2,192,903	58.63	28.36	114,007	2.94	1.47
1974	1,521,306	28.44	18.38	69,101	1.29	.83
1976	1,529,168	28.47	17.33	356,307	6.63	4.04
1978	1,812,896	35.76	19.35	158,403	3.12	1.69
1980	1,377,767	25.67	13.82	526,769	9.81	5.28
1982	1,318,663	21.64	12.32	265,794	4.36	2.48
1984	1,463,449	21.34	12.89	336,814	4.91	2.97
1986	1,096,552	13.79	9.26	544,719	6.85	4.60
1988	1,767,045	22.78	14.44	1,014,956	13.08	8.29
1990	1,487,260	17.95	11.87	855,231	10.32	6.83
1992	1,482,075	18.56	11.47	797,146	9.98	6.17
1994	1,036,944	11.47	7.93	557,340	6.16	4.26
1996	921,256	9.50	6.73	1,019,803	10.52	7.44
1998	664,532	5.95	4.72	596,839	5.35	4.24
2000	786,890	6.78	5.43	1,126,757	9.70	7.78
2002	1,024,814	8.39	6.61	622,423	5.09	4.01

Source: Secretary of State, Elections Division.

than 6 percent of the voting-age population voted in the 2000 Democratic presidential primary and less than 7 percent in the 2002 gubernatorial primary.[12]

Prior to 1980, participation in the Republican primaries never exceeded 5 percent of the voting-age population.[13] That rate has increased somewhat since then, but the percentage of Texans voting in a Republican primary has never reached the level of participation that the Democratic party experienced when it dominated state politics. One million voters, or 8.3 percent of voting-age Texans, cast ballots in the 1988 Republican presidential primary, when Texan George Bush was on the ballot. That is the highest turnout percentage in a Republican primary in Texas so far. Approximately 1,126,000 voters cast ballots in the 2000 Republican presidential primary, when Bush's son, George W. Bush, was a candidate, but they accounted for only 7.8 percent of the voting-age population.[14] Only 4 percent of Texans old enough to vote participated in the 2002 Republican gubernatorial primary.

The above data mean that a smaller percentage of the population is now involved in selecting political nominees throughout the state. And, those who participate in party primaries tend to be more ideological in their political orientation than the general population.

A candidate must receive an absolute majority of votes cast for a specific office in a primary to receive a party's nomination. If no candidate receives a majority in multi-candidate races, the two top vote getters must face each other in a **runoff election.** Voter turnout rates for runoffs are consistently lower than those for the first primary.

Minority groups have argued that the absolute majority requirement discriminates against African American and Hispanic candidates. Although there has been no successful challenge to the requirement in the party primaries, it has been successfully challenged under the **Voting Rights Act** in many school district elections, where candidates usually are elected on a nonpartisan ballot. In cases where challenges have been successful, candidates receiving a plurality of votes (more votes than any other candidate) are elected.

Texas and a handful of other states give the political parties the responsibility of administering the primary elections. A party's county chairman and the county executive committee are responsible for printing the ballots, locating polling places, providing for voting machines, hiring the election judges and clerks, and canvassing the election returns. In recent years, however, the parties have had increasing difficulty managing their elections, prompting some joint administration of the primaries and contracts with counties for operating some elections.

Before 1972, the costs of the primaries were borne by the political parties, which paid for them primarily with filing fees paid by candidates running for office. Those fees could be extremely high. This system was perceived by many as a way of eliminating potential candidates from running for public office, and the system was successfully challenged in the federal courts in 1970.[15] Under current law, modest filing fees are still permitted, and the parties still conduct the primaries, but the state picks up most of the cost. Administrative costs for the 2002 primaries were more than $15.7 million, including about $2.1 million in Harris County (Houston) and $1.9 million in Dallas County.[16] A person can win a place on the primary ballot without paying a filing fee by submitting a designated number of registered voters' signatures on petitions to party officials.

While the primary has helped make the nominating process more democratic than the party conventions, some scholars and party advocates argue that the primary has contributed to the decline of the political parties. The parties no longer control the nomination process because any eligible individual can get on a primary ballot by paying the required filing fee or submitting the required petitions. Also, potential officeholders, organizing and funding their own campaigns, have little allegiance to the parties. A person who is even hostile toward the party's leadership, the party's platform, or its traditional public policy positions can win the party's nomination. A supporter of political extremist Lyndon LaRouche, for example, was elected chair of the Harris County Democratic party in 1988. Not only was this person an embarrassment to the party, but the party regulars had to pass rules to bypass his authority in order to minimize potential political damage.

Parties function primarily to win elections, but the primaries may result in an unbalanced ticket and minimize the party's electoral strength. Bitter primary battles also can increase conflict within a party, and an expensive primary race can leave a candidate under-funded for a general election campaign. Moreover, a primary can nominate a weak candidate who will fare poorly in the general election.[17]

General Elections

General elections for state and federal offices are held on the first Tuesday after the first Monday in November in even-numbered years. Unlike the primaries, the administration and costs of the general election are the responsibility of the county.

The names of the candidates nominated in the primaries by the two major parties are placed on a ballot along with the names of third-party candidates who have submitted petitions bearing the names of registered voters equal to 1 percent of the vote in the last gubernatorial election. While some areas still use paper ballots and mechanical voting machines, many counties use punch cards, mark-sense ballots, or touch-screen voting that permit the election returns to be counted by computer. The ballot is styled in such a way as to permit straight party voting by pulling one lever, marking one block, punching one hole, or selecting the straight party ticket option.[18] In campaigns, candidates and political leaders often urge voters to "pull one lever" in support of one party's entire slate of candidates.

In the election of 1896, the turnout rate was more than 80 percent of the eligible voting-age population, but only twelve years later in 1908, four years after the effective date of the poll tax, turnout had fallen to approximately 35 percent. During much of the period from 1910 to 1958, turnout rates in non-presidential, general elections were less than 20 percent, mainly because the outcome already had been determined in the Democratic primaries. Presidential elections generated a somewhat higher turnout, but in very few instances did the turnout rate exceed 40 percent of eligible voters.[19]

Forty-seven percent of Texas's voting-age population cast general-election ballots in the 1984 presidential race, 44 percent in the 1988 presidential election, approximately 50 percent in the spirited three-way presidential election of 1992, some 41 percent in 1996, and 44 percent in 2000. But only 29 percent of the voting-age population cast general-election ballots in the 1986 gubernatorial race, 31 percent in the 1990 race, 34 percent in the 1994 election, 27 percent in 1998, and 29 percent in 2002.[20]

State officials quoted in the news media often will refer to the voter turnout in terms of a percentage of registered voters. It sounds better than percentage of the voting-age population, but it is misleading. The 2000 general election turnout, for example, was 52 percent of the registered voters. But one-third of Texans of voting age had not even bothered to register.

City, School Board, Single-Purpose Districts

Elections for most city councils, school boards, and single-purpose districts are conducted in May in odd-numbered years. These are nonpartisan elections in which no candidate is identified by party label. Across the state, there are wide variations in the competitiveness of these elections, campaign costs, and turnout.

While turnout rates in **local elections** rarely match those in the general elections, competition for control of local governments became more intense in the 1970s and 1980s, partly because of the increased political mobilization of minority voters. More recently, however, participation seems to have declined. Contested local campaigns in large urban areas can be as expensive as state legislative and congressional races.

Most school board and single-purpose district elections, however, have abysmally low rates of voter participation. It is not uncommon for many seats to go uncontested, and turnout rates can be as low as 2 percent to 5 percent. Candidates often spend little, if any, money on these elections, and their campaigns are usually informal. Recent legislation permits local governments to cancel an election if no offices are contested, and numerous communities in recent years canceled their elections due to no contested offices.

Special Elections

The legislature can submit constitutional amendments to the voters in a general election or schedule them in a special statewide election, in which voter turnout is usually much lower.

Two amendments, one pertaining to public school finance reforms and the other to college student loan bonds, were submitted in a special election in August 1991, which attracted a statewide turnout of 11.4 percent of eligible voters. Thirteen constitutional amendments, including a proposal legalizing a state lottery, were submitted in a November 1991 election, which had a turnout rate of 26.4 percent. The student loan bonds were the only issue on both ballots. They were rejected in August but were approved only three months later by the larger number of voters.

Although there were no state or federal offices on the November 1991 ballot, there was greater voter participation than in most constitutional amendment elections because of high interest in the lottery, which won easy approval, and mayoral and city council races in Houston and Dallas, the state's two largest cities. Houston is an exception to most cities in that its city elections are held in November, rather than April, of odd-numbered years. The Dallas elections had been postponed from the previous spring by a federal court order in a dispute over city council districts.

In constitutional amendment elections held since 1991, average turnout of registered voters has been 11.5 percent, but this was only 8.2 percent of the voting-age population. A few of those were special elections. Most, however, were held on the general election date in November of odd-numbered years, when the only other significant races on the ballot were races for mayor and city council in Houston. Consequently, the turnout in Houston is heavier than the rest of the state in constitutional amendment elections and usually is a major factor in determining the outcome. It is somewhat disturbing that, in most years, less than 10 percent of Texas citizens care enough to vote for constitutional amendments (see Chapter 2). The low turnout also means that special interest groups can mount well-organized campaigns to place provisions favoring them into the constitution with little public scrutiny or interest.

Local governments also conduct special elections for bond issues, local initiatives and referenda, and the recall of public officials. While there are occasional high-interest, emotionally charged elections, turnout rates in these elections tend to be extremely low. People who do vote tend to be those with higher incomes and educational levels.

The governor also can call **special elections** to fill vacancies in certain offices, including legislative and congressional seats.

Extended Absentee Balloting

In 1988, Texas made a major change in the requirements for absentee voting. Prior to that time, if a voter was not going to be in the county on Election Day or was incapacitated, he or she could vote absentee in person at a designated polling place or by mail before Election Day. Now, anyone can vote early without having to state an excuse during an extended period for **absentee (or early) voting.** Urban counties, in particular, now maintain multiple voting places, including stations conveniently located in shopping malls, during the extended voting period, which runs from the twentieth day to the fourth day before the scheduled Election Day. Consequently, there has been a notable increase in the number of votes cast early—20 percent to 30 percent of all votes in some areas.

The extended early voting has radically changed campaign strategies and tactics. A candidate now has to communicate earlier to that part of the population that has a high likelihood of voting prior to Election Day. With a large portion of the vote cast early, a candidate might well carry the Election Day totals but lose the early vote and lose the election. A candidate also has to mobilize those voters who cast their votes on Election Day. Thus, a campaign must "peak" twice.

POLITICAL SUFFRAGE IN TEXAS: A STRUGGLE FOR MINORITIES AND WOMEN

Despite the rhetoric of democratic theory in the state's constitution and the somewhat venerable view people have of elections and voting, Texas has a dark history of voter disfranchisement. For many years, African Americans, Hispanics, and low-income whites were systematically excluded from the political process. Texas had a political system in which the interests of a few could prevail over the interests of the majority. Many people paid a high price for this early legacy of discrimination.

After the Civil War, the state initiated efforts to organize a civilian government that would reestablish Texas's full statehood in the Union. The Constitutional Convention of 1866 accepted the supremacy of the national government and eliminated slavery, but it refused to adopt the Thirteenth Amendment, which gave African Americans the right to vote and hold public office.[21] This constitution was rejected by the Radical Reconstructionists in Congress in 1867, and subsequent Texas constitutions extended full voting rights to African Americans. Forty-one African Americans served in the Texas Legislature from 1868 to 1894.[22] But while the Texas Constitution extended political rights to them, African Americans were threatened with physical violence and economic recriminations that reduced their political participation well into the twentieth century. In addition, several state laws were enacted to block their access to the ballot.

The Poll Tax

The conservative Texas establishment's reaction to the Populist movement and its potential for building a coalition between African Americans and low-income whites resulted in the legislature's adoption of a **poll tax,** which went into effect in 1904.[23] It was a tax of $1.50 to $1.75 that had to be paid each year before a person could vote. In the early 1900s, that was a large sum of money for low-income people. It was to be paid between October 1 and January 31, three months before the primaries were then held and nine months before the general elections, long before most people even began to think about voting. Consequently, the tax eliminated large numbers of voters who were likely to support the Populist Party and undermine the political establishment.[24]

The poll tax was in effect for more than sixty years in Texas. It was outlawed for federal elections by the Twenty-fourth Amendment to the U.S. Constitution, adopted in 1964, but Texas retained the poll tax for state and local elections, thus requiring two sets of registered voters and separate ballots. In November 1966, Texas voters approved an amendment to the state constitution eliminating the poll tax for state elections and implementing annual voter registration. By that time, the U.S. Supreme Court had already ruled that the state poll tax was unconstitutional.[25]

The White Primary

Texas, along with several other southern states, also implemented the **white primary,** which was designed to eliminate African American participation in the elections that really counted.[26] Initially, the Texas legislature in 1923 enacted a law that denied African Americans the right to vote in the Democratic primary. That law was declared unconstitutional by the U.S. Supreme Court in 1927 on the basis of the Fourteenth Amendment.[27] But, almost immediately, the legislature authorized the state party executive committee to establish the qualifications for voting in the primaries, and the Democratic party adopted a resolution that only whites could vote. This was challenged in the federal courts, and again, in 1932, the Supreme Court declared the white primary unconstitutional.[28]

Acting through its state convention and without legislative authorization, the Democratic party then proceeded in May 1932 to exclude African Americans from the primary again. The issue was taken a third time to the Supreme Court, which this time ruled that the party, as a voluntary organization, had the authority to determine membership and the right of participation.[29] But African Americans continued to use the courts to attack the white primary, and, finally, in the case of *Smith v. Allwright* in 1944, the Supreme Court reversed its earlier decision and declared the white primary unconstitutional.[30]

But those who insisted on excluding African Americans from participation were extremely imaginative in their efforts to circumvent the court's decisions. They substituted a restrictive, preprimary selection process to choose candidates, who then were formally nominated in the Democratic primary and subsequently elected in the general election. Finally, in 1953, the U.S. Supreme Court also declared this arrangement unconstitutional.[31]

Restrictive Registration Law

Until 1971, Texas had one of the most restrictive voter-registration systems in the nation. Voters had to register annually between October 1 and January 31. For voters who did not register in person at the county courthouse, deputy registrars could deliver or mail in only one registration form at a time, thus minimizing the possibilities of coordinated voter-registration drives. These restrictions discouraged voter registration across the state, especially among the African-American, Hispanic, and low-income populations.[32]

More court intervention forced major changes in the voter-registration law in 1971.[33] The highly restrictive system was transformed, in a relatively short time, into one of the most progressive systems in the country. Annual registration was replaced with permanent registration. An individual now can register by mail or in person up to thirty days prior to an election. Persons working individually or with a political campaign can be deputized to register voters, and large voter-registration drives are encouraged. County voter registration officials now must send out cards to voters, automatically renewing their registrations, every two years. And there are restrictions on how soon officials can remove the names of voters who have moved from registration lists.

Property Ownership and the Right to Vote

From colonial times, one requirement for the right to vote was property ownership, a practice that continued in modified form through the 1970s in many states, including Texas. Property ownership was not required to vote in primaries and most other elections, but it was required in bond elections that were used by local governments to win financing of new buildings, roads, sewer systems, and other infrastructure needs. The exclusion of nonproperty owners from these elections was based on the argument that revenue from property taxes was used to repay these bonds, and if a person did not own property on which to pay a tax, he or she should not have the right to vote for the bonds.

Landlords, however, passed through their property taxes to renters, and many renters, therefore, had a direct interest in the outcome of bond elections. Many urban areas, moreover, had large amounts of rental property and many residents who were barred from participating in those elections. Eventually, the federal courts declared property ownership as a requirement for voting in bond elections unconstitutional.

Women and the Right to Vote

The national movement for women's suffrage, or the right to vote, was a long struggle fought in the state capitals as well as in Washington. In 1915, the Texas legislature considered a constitutional amendment extending the right to vote to women, but rejected it. In 1918, women were given the right to vote in primary elections and party conventions. Then, in 1919, Texas became the first southern state to approve the Nineteenth Amendment to the U.S. Constitution, which, by late 1920, was approved by the required number of states to grant women's suffrage in all elections.[34]

Extension of the Vote to Those Eighteen Years of Age and Older

A long-standing debate over the age at which a person should be permitted to vote became more intense during the Vietnam War. Many people believed that individuals who were required to comply with the draft and risk death in battle should no longer be denied the right to vote. The Twenty-sixth Amendment, which lowered the voting age from twenty-one to eighteen, was adopted in 1971, and the first election in which eighteen-year-olds could vote was in 1972. Perhaps because of the political activism of many college students during the Vietnam era, there were expectations that young people would vote at higher rates than older adults, but this has never materialized. The lowest voter turnout rates, in fact, are among voters eighteen to twenty-nine years old.

Other Discriminatory Aspects of Election Systems

Even after the most obvious discriminatory practices against minorities were eliminated, there were more subtle, but just as pervasive, techniques for reducing the political power and influence of these same groups.

One technique is racial **gerrymandering** of political boundaries. State legislators and many city council members are elected from **single-member districts,** each of which represents a specific number of people in a designated area. After the 2000 census, for example, each member of the Texas House ideally represented 139,012 people, and each member of the state Senate, 672,639 people. To minimize the possibilities of minority candidates being elected, policymakers could divide minority communities and attach them to predominantly nonminority communities. This tactic is called *cracking.* Or, the minority communities could be consolidated into one district, a tactic called *packing,* with an 80 to 90 percent minority population, which would reduce the number of other districts in which minorities might have a chance of winning office. The federal Voting Rights Act forbids such practices, but minority groups continue to go to court to challenge redistricting plans.

At-large elections also have been used to reduce minority representation. At one time, members of the Texas House who came from urban counties were elected in multimember districts, which required candidates to win election in countywide races, a very difficult prospect for many minority candidates. The practice was eliminated in legislative races in the 1970s as a result of federal lawsuits. But many cities, school districts, and special districts across Texas continue to use at-large elections, requiring candidates to run for office citywide or districtwide. This system dilutes minority representation in most communities in which it is used. In addition to the increased costs of running in at-large elections, which discourage minority candidates, a minority group that may account for 60 percent of a city's total population and 52 percent of the voting-age population may account for only 45 percent of the registered voters. And, with the possibility of polarized voting, where minorities vote for the minority candidates and the nonminorities vote for the white candidates, there is a high likelihood that no minority could get elected in many at-large systems. At-large elections have come under increasing attack under the Voting Rights Act, and many local governments have adopted some form of single-member districting.

The Voting Rights Act

In 1965, the U.S. Congress passed the Voting Rights Act, which was extended to Texas in 1975. This law has been central to strategies by minorities in challenging discriminatory election systems and practices. Under the Voting Rights Act, minority groups can challenge state and local election systems in the federal courts. The burden of proof in such challenges is on the government. An election system that dilutes minority voting strength is illegal, even if there is no clear intent to discriminate against minorities. Furthermore, any changes in the election systems of state or local governments, including redistricting plans, must be reviewed and precleared by the U.S. Department of Justice or must be approved by the U.S. District Court in Washington, D.C. This legislation has produced changes in election systems across the state and has helped increase minority representation in the Texas legislature and on local governing bodies.

By the mid-1990s, however, the Voting Rights Act was under attack by conservatives. And the U.S. Supreme Court, in "reverse discrimination" cases from Texas and Georgia, ruled that some congressional districts had been illegally gerrymandered to elect minority candidates. In the Texas case, three federal judges held that the Texas legislature had violated the U.S. Constitution by designing two districts in Houston and one in the Dallas area to favor the election of African-American or

Hispanic candidates. The court redrew thirteen congressional districts in Texas—the three minority districts and ten districts adjoining them—and ordered special elections to fill the seats. Despite the redrawn boundaries, two incumbent African-American congresswomen in the affected districts were reelected. In effect, recent court cases have held that race or ethnicity can be considered in drawing legislative boundaries but cannot be the predominant factor. Representatives of minority groups fear that these recent cases will reduce the number of potentially winnable legislative districts for African-American and Hispanic candidates. They also are concerned that the Voting Rights Act will be significantly modified when temporary sections (4 and 5) expire in 2007.

Motor Voter Registration

The **"motor voter" registration** law was passed by the U.S. Congress in 1993 and signed by President Bill Clinton, despite the opposition of Republicans, who apparently feared it would benefit the Democratic party. An earlier version of the bill had been vetoed by President George Bush in 1992. The federal law, similar to a 1991 Texas law, requires states to provide eligible citizens the opportunity to register to vote when they apply for or renew a driver's license. The law also requires states to make voter registration forms available at certain agencies that provide welfare benefits or assist the disabled.[35]

POLITICAL GAINS BY MINORITIES AND WOMEN

Over the past thirty years, African Americans and Hispanics have made substantial gains in the electoral process. Elimination of restrictive voting laws and adoption of a liberal voter registration system have contributed to an increase in minority voters across the state, as have voter registration and mobilization drives coordinated by groups such as the National Association for the Advancement of Colored People and the Southwest Voter Registration Education Project. But as recent attacks on the Voting Rights Act indicate, the fight continues.

Hispanics

According to the 2000 census, Hispanics made up 32 percent of Texas's population. But the Hispanic population is younger than the Anglo and African-American populations, and Hispanics accounted for only 28.6 percent of Texans of voting age (Table 7–2).

Hispanics also include a significant number of immigrants (an estimated one out of seven) not eligible to vote, thus reducing Hispanic voters to approximately 25 percent of eligible adult citizens. Approximately 17 percent, or 2,121,962, of the 12,455,503 Texas voters registered in February 2002 had Hispanic surnames, compared to an estimated 9.1 percent in 1976.[36] (These figures under-represent Hispanic registered voters because Hispanic women married to non-Hispanics cannot be identified with counting methods used by the secretary of state.) But in recent general elections, Hispanics were only 12 to 15 percent of Texas voters participating. Voter turnout rates among Hispanics are lower, in part, because of the lower education and income levels of many Hispanics.

TABLE 7–2   2000 Population and Voting Age Population

	Total Population	Percent of Total	Population of Voting Age	Percent of Total
Hispanic/Latino (any race)	6,669,666	32.0%	4,282,901	28.6%
Not Hispanic/Latino	14,128,154	67.8%	10,682,160	71.4%
One Race	13,951,587	66.9%	10,543,445	70.5%
White	10,933,313	52.4%	8,426,166	56.3%
African American	2,364,255	11.3%	1,631,448	10.9%
Native American	68,859	0.3%	51,540	0.3%
Asian	554,445	2.7%	415,219	2.8%
Pacific Islander	10,757	0.1%	7,575	0.1%
Some Other Race	19,958	0.1%	11,497	0.1%
Two or More Races	230,567	1.1%	138,715	0.9%
Total	20,851,820		14,965,061	

Source: U.S. Census, 2000; Texas State Data Center.

Approximately 29 percent of Hispanic adults interviewed in the 2001–2002 *Texas Poll* identified with the Democratic party, but this percentage tells only part of the story.[37] Until Governor George W. Bush made substantial inroads into the Hispanic vote in 1998, Democratic candidates for president and governor consistently received more than 70 percent of the Hispanic vote in Texas.[38]

Hispanic voters dominated the 2002 Democratic primary, which for the first time featured two Hispanic gubernatorial candidates, Laredo businessman Tony Sanchez and former Attorney General Dan Morales. One of the three major candidates for the party's U.S. Senate nomination also was Hispanic—Victor Morales, a schoolteacher who had shocked party leaders in 1996 by winning the party's nomination for an unsuccessful race against U.S. Senator Phil Gramm. The William C. Velasquez Institute, which specializes in Hispanic-related voting activity, reported that preliminary figures indicated that Hispanics cast a record 33 percent of the Democratic primary votes.[39] Spending heavily from his wealth on television advertising, Sanchez easily defeated Dan Morales for the gubernatorial nomination. And tapping into the Hispanic vote, Victor Morales got into a runoff for the Senate nomination with former Dallas Mayor Ron Kirk, an African American. Each received about one-third of the vote. But Kirk, who was supported by most party leaders, swamped Victor Morales in fund raising and won the Senate runoff, when Hispanic voter turnout had fallen off. Both Sanchez and Kirk later lost their general election races to Republicans.

The increased electoral strength of the Hispanic population is borne out in Table 7–3, which compares the number of elected Hispanic officials in Texas in 1974 to those holding office in 2003. Some 540 Hispanics held elected office in 1974. By 2003, there were 1,965 Hispanic elected officials, the highest in any state. The marked increase can be attributed to a more equitable apportionment of city, county, and school district political boundaries, the growth of the Hispanic population, and increased organizational efforts among Hispanics.

Only four Hispanics—Texas Supreme Court Justices Raul A. Gonzalez and Alberto R. Gonzales, Attorney General Dan Morales, and Texas Railroad

TABLE 7–3   Latino Elected Officials in Texas, 1974–2003

	1974	1996	2001	2003
Federal	2	5	6	6
State	13	35	36	38
County	102	203	213	236
Municipal	251	536	555	565
Judicial/Law Enforcement	172	323	280	338
School Board	—	536	701	736
Special District	—	51	37	46
Total	540	1689	1828	1965

Sources: Juan A. Sepulveda, Jr., *The Question of Representative Responsiveness for Hispanics,* Cambridge, MA: Harvard College, honors thesis, March 1985; National Association of Latino Elected and Appointed Officials, *National Roster of Hispanic Elected Officials,* 1996, 2001, 2003.

Commissioner Tony Garza—have been elected to statewide office in Texas. There have been other Hispanic candidates, such as Victor Morales and Tony Sanchez, who have made serious statewide races. With changing demographics and the increased political sophistication of the Hispanic population, there is evidence to suggest that Hispanics will win additional statewide as well as local offices in the future.

African Americans

African Americans constitute approximately 11.3 percent of the state's population, 11 percent of the voting-age population, and 9 percent to 10 percent of those who vote. Approximately 61 percent of Texas African Americans call themselves Democrats, but 80 percent to 90 percent of the African American vote is normally cast for Democratic candidates. Voting cohesively as a group, African Americans, like Hispanics, have considerable potential to influence the outcome of both primaries and general elections.

The increased political clout of the African American population is also manifested in the number of African American elected officials (Table 7–4). In 1970, there were only twenty-nine African Americans elected to public office in Texas. The number increased to 196 in 1980 and 460 in 2001. Only two African Americans, former Texas Court of Criminal Appeals Judge Morris Overstreet, a Democrat, and Railroad Commissioner Michael Williams, a Republican, had been elected to statewide office before 2002. Two other African Americans—Republicans Wallace Jefferson and Dale Wainwright—won statewide races for the Texas Supreme Court in 2002. As noted earlier, former Dallas Mayor Ron Kirk, an African American, won the Democratic nomination for the U.S. Senate that year but lost to Republican John Cornyn in the general election.

Women

Historically, the world of Texas politics has been dominated by men, but that is beginning to change. Prior to Ann Richards's election as state treasurer in 1982, there had been only two women elected to statewide office. Richards was elected governor

TABLE 7–4   African American Elected Officials in Texas, 1970–2000

	1970	1980	2001
Federal	—	1	2
State	3	14	17
County	—	5	20
Municipal	16	75	282
Judicial/Law Enforcement	—	21	44
School Board	10	78	95
Special District	—	2	—
Total	29	196	460

Sources: Metropolitan Applied Research Center, Inc. and Voter Regional Council, Inc., *National Roster of Black Elected Officials;* Joint Center for Political Studies, *National Roster of Black Elected Officials,* 1980, 1998, 2001.

in 1990, and Kay Bailey Hutchison, who had succeeded Richards as state treasurer, was elected to the U.S. Senate in 1993. As governor, Richards also appointed more women to key positions on state boards and commissions than her predecessors.

By 2003, nine women were holding statewide offices in Texas, including Hutchison, who was still in the U.S. Senate; state Comptroller Carole Keeton Strayhorn; state Agriculture Commissioner Susan Combs; two members of the Texas Supreme Court, and four members of the Texas Court of Criminal Appeals. That same year, there were four women in the state Senate and thirty-one in the Texas House, a significant increase over 1981, when the legislature included only one woman in the Senate and eleven in the House.

Women are playing an increased role in local government as well, and this pattern can be expected to continue. Over the past three decades, the state's three largest cities—Houston, Dallas, and San Antonio—had women mayors. A 2004 survey by the Texas Municipal League counted 204 women mayors (or 17 percent) in the state's 1,211 cities. The 5,971 council members in the cities included 1,535 women, or 26 percent of the total.[40] Of the 254 county judges in 2002, 26 (10 percent) were women, and women held 67 (or 6.6 percent) of 1,016 county commissioner posts.[41]

THE NEW CAMPAIGN TECHNOLOGY

In the previous chapter on political parties, we discussed the long history of one-party Democratic politics in Texas. The only elections that counted then were the Democratic primaries, and they would often include five or six candidates for a single office. In statewide or local campaigns, candidates seldom ran as a ticket or coalition. Each candidate developed his or her own campaign organization, thus precluding the development of party campaign organizations. Individuals who became involved in a campaign were primarily motivated by their personal loyalties to a candidate and not to the political party.

With low rates of voter participation in the primaries and the absence of viable Republican challenges in the general elections, Democratic candidates were able to stumble through the election process with loose coalitions that often disintegrated

---

KARL ROVE: AN ADVISER IN HIGH PLACES

Probably the best-known Republican consultant from Texas is Karl Rove, a strategist and direct-mail specialist who worked for most major GOP officeholders in Texas in the 1980s and 1990s and, in the process, hitched his career to a future president. Rove first met George W. Bush in 1973 and supervised his first political campaign, an unsuccessful race for Congress in West Texas in 1978. Rove later managed Bush's successful races for governor in 1994 and 1998 and was a key adviser in his presidential campaign in 2000. In the White House, Rove remained Bush's chief political adviser, working out of an office in the West Wing.

Rove is a master of details and a consummate "spinner" of the political views he and Bush espouse. Rove's career hasn't been without controversy, mainly because he developed a reputation, early on, for winning at any cost. But the personal, as well as professional, bond between the president and his long-time adviser remained strong through Bush's governorship and his early months in the Oval Office.

"Rove is, quite simply, the most influential presidential aide in two decades," correspondent Howard Fineman wrote in *Newsweek* magazine in 2001. "He's in charge of legislative and political strategy, and outreach to citizen groups. He doesn't decide whether to fire on a Chinese fighter jet, but he does figure out how Bush's decision will 'play' in the country," Fineman added.

Source: "Washington Memo: Political Soul Mates Since 1973," *Newsweek,* April 18, 2001.

---

after Election Day. Although there was competition in the Democratic primaries, conservative candidates, tied to the establishment, generally prevailed. Despite differences in personality and style, these conservative candidates were fundamentally committed to the policy agendas of the economic elites of the state.

By today's standards, political campaigns through the 1950s were amateurish and unsophisticated. Modern political campaigns have been reshaped by a number of factors, including an expanded electorate that is highly mobile, the growing dominance of the Republican party, the organizational weaknesses of both political parties, the continuation of the candidate-centered campaign, and the increased reliance on the electronic media for news and political information.[42] Today's successful campaigns rely on sophisticated public opinion polling, slick campaign ads contrived by media experts, analyses of demographics, and targeting of selected populations through direct mail and phone banks—all orchestrated by professional **campaign consultants.**

Such consultants have been around in Texas in some form or another for a long time. W. Lee "Pappy" O'Daniel, the owner of a flourmill that produced Hillbilly Flour and master of ceremonies of a daily radio talk show, ran for governor in 1938, exploiting a rustic image couched in religious, evangelical language that had a wide appeal in the rural areas of the state. His speeches were designed to create an identification with the "common folks," but he was a wealthy businessman who had ties to Texas's corporate leaders. His homespun style was contrived, and O'Daniel relied heavily throughout his campaign on public relations expert Phil Fox of Dallas.[43] What is different about contemporary campaign consulting is that it is an identifiable industry with diversified expertise. More significantly, few candidates for statewide office or major local offices now run without utilizing the services of campaign consultants (see "Karl Rove: An Adviser in High Places).

Public Opinion Polling

In a society based on mass consumption, it is no wonder that techniques were developed to measure public attitudes and opinions. The origins of the industry are usually linked to George Gallup, who conducted a statewide poll in 1932 for his mother-in-law, who ran for secretary of state in Iowa. Survey research or public opinion polling has a variety of applications, most of which are nonpolitical; market research is now a multibillion-dollar industry.

Public opinion polling is used in political campaigns for a number of purposes (see "Who Am I?"). As would-be candidates consider running for office, they will often hire pollsters to conduct benchmark surveys of people who are likely to vote in the upcoming election. Using well-tested sampling techniques, the pollster will conduct either a telephone survey or a face-to-face survey of a representative sample of voters. The length and type of the survey usually is determined by available funds and the information desired by the candidate and those developing the campaign. Surveys are expensive. If the required number of completed interviews is 1,200 for a statewide race at a cost of $40–$50 each, it is clear that polling can consume a hefty chunk of the campaign budget.

Surveys also are used to develop campaign strategy, monitor or track the progress of the campaign, and modify the campaign as changes take place in the attitudes, perceptions, or mood of the electorate. The benchmark survey, often taken some time before the official campaign gets underway, is rather lengthy and attempts to assess public opinion relating to the office a candidate is seeking. Issues are identified, perceptions of candidates are probed, and trial heats with potential opponents are tested. A wide range of demographic questions are included to permit the

---

WHO AM I?

Statewide political candidates and officeholders often spend millions of dollars getting elected and reelected, but it seems that most of their constituents just are not paying any attention. According to a 1997 *Texas Poll,* most Texans—82 percent of those surveyed—knew then that George W. Bush was the governor. But after that there was a huge drop off in the public's ability to match the names of high-ranking state and federal officials with the offices they held.

The attorney general could be identified by name by only 30 percent; the comptroller and the land commissioner by 17 percent; the lieutenant governor by 16 percent; and the agriculture commissioner by 9 percent. Only 22 percent of the respondents could correctly name both U.S. senators from Texas.

Other, more recent surveys have indicated a similar lack of political awareness among the public.

Source: Texas Poll, Fall 1997, conducted for Scripps Howard by the Office of Survey Research of the University of Texas.

segmentation of the electorate into small groups whose specific interests or concerns can be identified and targeted.

As the campaign proceeds, tracking surveys are used to determine shifts in attitudes, perceptions, and support for the candidate. Does the candidate now have greater name identification? Do more people perceive the candidate positively and express their support with greater intensity? Is there a particular event or emerging campaign issue that might spell defeat? This information is used to adjust the campaign to changing conditions. Toward the end of the campaign, surveys are often taken nightly to permit further fine-tuning of the campaign in the final days.

A variation on the survey is the use of a focus group. As television advertisements are developed, the campaign staff may choose to test them before they are aired. A series of focus groups, each including eight to twelve persons recruited for specific demographic characteristics, will be asked to review these ads and provide their impressions and reactions. An experienced staff will watch these proceedings to identify subtle responses to the ads, the theme, or the message. On the basis of these qualitative assessments, the media consultants will decide which ads should be used and which should be discarded.

Segmentation and Targeting of the Electorate

A political campaign is fundamentally an organized effort to communicate with the electorate with the goal of convincing a majority of those who participate to vote for a specific candidate. But effective communication is difficult for a number of reasons. One is the low voter turnout in most elections. Voter turnout rates also vary among different ethnic, income, and education-level groups, and some of these voters will not support a particular candidate no matter what he or she says or does. In a partisan election, many people will vote for or against a candidate strictly on the basis of party identification. Obviously, not every voter shares a candidate's concerns and priorities.

Candidates use census data, surveys, and previous election returns with turnout and party voting patterns to divide voters into segments. Some research specialists are able to organize this information to permit the campaign to target its messages to small, well-defined populations. Psychodemographics, a technique used by some opinion specialists, combines survey and census data to divide populations by lifestyles rather than party identification. Whether direct mail, television, radio, newspapers, phone banks, or block walking is used to reach its audience, the modern campaign will direct a specific, relevant message to these segmented populations based on sophisticated market research.

For example, survey data may suggest that a disproportionate number of women between the ages of forty-five and fifty-four have not heard of the candidate but are concerned about health care and medical insurance. Based on demographic data and television program ratings, the media specialist knows that a large number of these women watch daytime television programs. To get a specific message to these voters, television spots with a health care message oriented to the specific concerns of women from forty-five to fifty-four will be developed and aired during these times of the day. Most populations can be identified and targeted in this manner, increasing the likelihood that a desired message gets to the specific voters whose perceptions and attitudes the consultant wants to influence.

The segmentation of the electorate may well lead to a fracturing of the political debate. Various segments of voters are exposed to narrow slices of the candidate's image, personality, and concerns. The campaign hopes that each group of voters will respond favorably to its own limited knowledge of the candidate, but some critics argue that this segmentation "further diminishes the importance of language, logic, and reason in the articulation of campaign issues."[44]

MEDIA AND ADVERTISING

It is easy to assume that a campaign can market a candidate much like a pack of cigarettes or a box of soap, and our increasing cynicism often leads to this facile conclusion. But voter response to candidates, the progress of the campaign, and the various ads and messages that voters receive form an extremely complex decision-making process. Scholars in various disciplines have attempted to unravel the effects of news reports, campaign advertising and campaign strategies and tactics on voter behavior. But the conclusions are only tentative because it is very difficult to demonstrate that a specific event, news story, or campaign ad results in the final decision of a voter.

Controlled Media

There are numerous media through which candidates can communicate their messages to the voters, and for those that can be purchased commercially, the only limitations are availability and finances. The media that is purchased by the candidate is often referred to as the **controlled media.** The decisions concerning which media to use, when to purchase advertisements, and what message to convey are under the candidate's control. There are some technical and legal questions pertaining to campaign advertising, but the candidate has a wide range of options.

Billboards, bench signs, advertisements on buses and cabs, and electronic signs can be purchased to establish voter awareness and name identification. Although such ads are not likely to convert or mobilize voters, they establish the candidate's visibility.

Although candidates talk about "pressing the flesh" and making direct contacts with the voters, it is simply impossible to talk personally to the number of people necessary to win an election, particularly in a statewide or urban race. Candidates stage block walks and rallies in which they personally participate and meet with supporters, but many of these are **media events** they hope will be covered by the press. Campaigns still rely on block walking and phone banks, but in a sophisticated campaign these tactics are coordinated with the media blitz and direct mail.

In many local elections across Texas, it is too costly or inefficient to use radio and television advertising. But it is almost impossible to run a viable statewide campaign without the use of the electronic media. Texas is large and diverse and has about twenty separate media markets. Candidates often spend half of the campaign budget for television and radio advertising, and the media specialists—ranging from the creative staff to the time buyers—have taken on increased importance in modern campaigns.

The thirty-second spot is now the standard for television advertising, and the candidate's consultants attempt to carefully craft advertisements that address concerns, perceptions, and expectations of varied segments of the electorate.[45] The media blitz usually picks up steam as the campaign moves closer to Election Day, because it is assumed that it takes several exposures to a given ad for a voter to respond and, in many cases, allegations raised in an opponent's advertisements must be addressed.

Campaign advertising became an issue in the 1990 gubernatorial race, which was marked with what seemed to be an endless series of negative campaign ads and related tactics (see Chapter 5). "Gay-bashing" advertisements were used against Democratic nominee Ann Richards when she received the endorsement of groups alleged to be linked to lesbian rights, and a fundraising letter from the national Democratic chairman attempted to link Republican nominee Clayton Williams with neo-Nazism and racism.[46]

The negative advertisement wasn't new to Texas politics, but most observers agreed that advertisements in the 1990 gubernatorial race were more vitriolic, aired with more frequency, and were seemingly more irrelevant to the issues facing the state than most ads had been in the past. As the advertisements continued, newspapers began to analyze their themes and veracity, and voters indicated that they were displeased with them. But consultants continued to convince their clients that negative attacks worked and that people, while objecting to negative ads, had higher recall of them than many other television spots.

The 2002 gubernatorial race, in which Republican Rick Perry and Democrat Tony Sanchez spent almost $100 million, much of it bashing each other over the airwaves, was equally vicious. Sanchez tried to blame Perry for high electric bills and homeowners insurance rates. And Perry tried to link Sanchez, a wealthy Laredo businessman, to drug dealers. Perry's allegation was based on a federal investigation that had determined that a savings and loan owned by Sanchez in the 1980s had unwittingly been used to launder drug money. Sanchez never was implicated in any wrongdoing, and he and other officials of the savings and loan, which later folded, said they didn't know the depositors were connected to the illegal drug trade.

The computer is becoming a major vehicle for communicating with voters, reflecting a further extension of the controlled media. In addition to communicating with volunteers, supporters, and the news media through e-mail, many candidates and officeholders now maintain websites, which provide an additional tool for communicating large amounts of information to voters. Candidates also use e-mail to raise campaign funds and quickly respond to speeches or allegations raised by political opponents.

Uncontrolled Media

Positive news stories about the candidate and campaign are potentially more valuable than paid advertising and don't cost the campaign money. Candidates and their handlers thus attempt to exploit the press by getting positive coverage and reducing as much as possible any negative slants in campaign stories. But the relationship between political candidates and the press is adversarial. The news media, ever alert for weaknesses in a candidate and tips spread by political opponents, can make or break a candidate by the coverage and slant given to the candidate's personality, reputation, view of the issues, and campaign activities.

Many campaigns hire press secretaries who specialize in media relations. One author has suggested that a successful media strategy entails the following: "Keeping the candidate away from the press; feeding the press a simple, telegenic political line of the day; and making sure the daily news line echoes ["magnify" may be the better word] the images from the campaign ads, thus blurring the distinction between commercials and 'reality.'"[47] It is common to hear consultants speak of "staying on message" as they attempt to influence media coverage.

Members of the press are keenly aware of these efforts to manipulate them, and the best reporters are usually able to resist. But the hectic, irrational nature of statewide campaigns, the pressure of news deadlines, the propensity for pack journalism, and the fear of being beaten to a major story by a competitor often work against a reporter's sincere efforts to get the "straight skinny" on the candidate's abilities, leadership potential, and his or her stand on the issues.

Clayton Williams used his millions to win the 1990 Republican gubernatorial nomination with an effective paid television campaign that portrayed an attractive image of an independent, can-do, cost-conscious businessman. But he lost the general election to Democrat Ann Richards after the uncontrolled news media painted a less attractive picture: that of a coarse, chauvinistic individual who had only the vaguest notion of what he would do as governor.

Direct Mail and Fundraising

People like to receive mail. Some people even like to receive junk mail, experts say, and direct mail has become a highly sophisticated component of modern campaigns. Direct-mail specialists provide campaigns with a technique for "persuasion and fundraising."[48] As a further refinement of the segmentation and targeting of voters, this technique permits the campaign to craft a specific message for a narrowly defined population and assure, with high probability, that households with the specified demographic or psychographic characteristics will receive the campaign message. In a sense, it is "narrow casting" a specific message to an identifiable audience.

Direct mail is big business in the United States, and it has been easily adapted to political campaigns. In many instances, the campaign messages and appeals are very emotional, designed to push the voters' "hot buttons" on specific issues. They are crafted by specialists who have studied the emotional appeals of such communications, and the attention to detail often astonishes the uninitiated. The length of a letter, the color of the paper on which it is printed, the underlining and highlighting of specific words or phrases, and teasers on the envelope to get the recipient to open the letter receive critical attention by the specialist. Evidence indicates that people respond to direct-mail appeals, and, if the technique is integrated with phone banks, block walks, and the media campaign, it becomes an extremely valuable campaign tool.

Direct mail also has become a major tool in campaign fundraising. Massive mailing lists targeting virtually every population group in the state have been developed, and names of persons with probable political attitudes and beliefs are easily extracted from these files by computer. Successive mailings to probable supporters have a high likelihood of producing campaign dollars. The continued use and refinement of these lists increase the rate of return, and while campaigns still rely on large contributions, the more modest contributions received from direct-mail solicitation have taken on increased importance.

Grassroots Tactics

The mass media in political races is increasingly replacing traditional grassroots tactics, such as door-to-door campaigning (or block walking), neighborhood gatherings, and phone banks operated by volunteers who call individuals in their neighborhoods or clubs on behalf of a candidate. Many campaigns use paid phone banks that may be located in another part of the state or in another area of the country, but voters often react negatively to these tactics. A call, letter, postcard, personal e-mail or visit from a neighbor who demonstrates an intense commitment to a candidate can still have a strong impact on voters. It takes a great deal of planning and resources to develop a grassroots campaign, but there is empirical evidence that such tactics can make a difference in the outcome of closely contested elections.

MONEY AND CAMPAIGNS

Campaign Costs

No one knows precisely how much is spent on political campaigns in Texas because there is no single place where all this information is collected. Candidates for state office file campaign finance reports with the state Ethics Commission, but candidates for city councils, county offices, and school boards file reports with the jurisdictions in which they are running. Costs vary across the more than 2,000 governmental units, but modern campaign technology and paid media are extremely expensive, even on the local level. A few recent examples of campaign costs in selected races are illuminating.

City council races in major cities such as San Antonio, Houston, Fort Worth, and Dallas can easily cost $50,000 to $100,000. Bob Lanier spent $3 million getting elected mayor of Houston in 1991, and eight candidates spent more than $6.6 million in the 1997 race to succeed him. The 1997 winner, Lee Brown, spent more than $2.1 million alone, and the second-place finisher, businessman Rob Mosbacher, spent more than $3.5 million.[49] Those earlier figures, however, paled in comparison to the nearly $9 million that businessman Bill White spent to win the 2003 Houston mayor's race.[50] There have been reports of candidates for county commissioner spending $100,000 and of district judges in metropolitan counties spending more than $150,000. Historically, school board elections have been low budget, but it is not uncommon for slates of candidates in large urban school districts to spend $10,000 to $15,000 in low-turnout elections.

Many people believe that campaign expenditures in statewide races in Texas, particularly gubernatorial races, are excessive. But fueled by the rising costs of television advertising and other modern campaign techniques—and two-party competition—expenditures continue to increase.

Republican Rick Perry and Democrat Tony Sanchez spent almost $100 million in the 2002 governor's race. Sanchez's expenditures included more than $50 million from his own pocket. He won a hard-fought victory over former Attorney General Dan Morales in the Democratic primary before losing to Perry in the general election.

Candidates for lieutenant governor in 2002 raised more than $25 million. Republican David Dewhurst, the victor, raised $16.3 million, including $11.3 million of his own money. Candidates for other statewide executive offices that year raised $24.9 million combined, with Republican candidates raising much more than Democrats.[51]

Following redistricting, all 31 of the Texas Senate seats were up for election in 2002. Approximately $21.5 million was raised by candidates competing for those seats, with more than 70 percent of the money coming from sources outside of the contested districts. Twenty-three of the 31 senators elected had no opposition in their party primaries, and nine had no opposition in the general election. The 31 winners raised an average of $587,000, and six senators raised more than $1 million apiece. Winning Democrats raised about $100,000 less, on average, than Republicans.

Contributions to all candidates in the 150 races for the Texas House in 2002 totaled $33.2 million. More than 70 percent of the contributions came from outside the candidates' districts. Ninety-seven House members elected that year had no opposition in their primary races, and sixty-two had no opposition in the general election. The smallest amount received by any candidate was $11,550, and the largest was $1,095,536, which was raised by Republican Tom Craddick of Midland, who had no opposition in the primary or general election but was running for speaker and was actively supporting other Republican candidates in a successful campaign to win a GOP majority in the House. The average amount raised by House members elected in 2002 was $165,000.

Unspent funds raised for a campaign can be carried over as a "war chest" for the successful candidate's next election. Even unopposed officeholders will attempt to raise large amounts of money to discourage potential opponents in the future. A significant question arising from a discussion of fund raising for the state Senate and the Texas House is why a person would go to such lengths to raise such huge sums of money to win an office that pays only $7,200 a year.

More than $10 million was spent on six races for the Texas Supreme Court in 1988, making them the most expensive judicial races in Texas history. Philosophical control of the court (see Chapter 11) was at stake, and the business and medical community battled the trial lawyers in a feeding frenzy.[52] The fourteen major-party candidates for five Supreme Court seats in 2002 raised $6.75 million. The Republican candidates who won all five seats spent $3.2 million.

Table 7–5 summarizes fundraising for state offices during the 2002 election cycle. If you eliminate Democrat Tony Sanchez, who largely funded his own unsuccessful gubernatorial race, it is evident that Republicans, who won all the statewide races and majorities in both the Texas House and the state Senate that year, had a clear advantage in fundraising.

Campaign Contributions

The growth of campaign fundraising and contributions has raised concerns that elections are being bought and that major campaign donors are purchasing influence in the policymaking process. Some critics argue that current practices are a form of legalized bribery, implying that public officials are available to the highest bidder. Money is critical to most successful campaigns for public office because it permits the candidate to purchase advertising and other resources for communicating to the

TABLE 7–5   Contributions by Type of State Office, 2001–2002

Office	Totals for Winner in General Election	Totals for Loser in General Election	Totals for Primary Losers
Governor	$20,469,556	$62,373,012	$ 132,797
Lt. Governor	16,347,728	8,703,573	—
Comptroller	4,996,428	825,059	—
Attorney General	7,803,818	5,250,157	—
Land Commissioner	1,399,122	1,308,427	—
Railroad Commissioner	1,198,258	202,742	671,375
Agriculture Commissioner	1,744,202	233,249	—
Supreme Court	3,229,026	1,866,737	1,657,643
Court of Criminal Appeals	13,103	5,450	110,321
House	24,664,676	5,504,926	2,914,705
Senate	17,735,122	1,886,165	1,845,598
Totals	$99,587,936	$88,159,496	$7,332,439

Source: Texans for Public Justice, *Money in Politex: A Guide to Money in the 2002 Texas Elections,* November 2003.

voters. But money is not the only factor affecting an election. Incumbency, existing party loyalties, the availability of party or campaign activists, the public's perceptions of a candidate, and a candidate's campaign skills or expertise also help determine electoral success. In numerous elections, well-financed candidates have been defeated by opponents with far fewer dollars. This may suggest that "there are genuine limits" on what money can accomplish in a campaign.[53]

Contributions are made to influence the outcome of an election and, subsequently, to shape public policy by electing persons who share similar political views with or who will be sympathetic or accessible to those making the contributions. Reports of large campaign contributions often prompt remarks that Texas has the "best Supreme Court that money can buy" or the "best legislature that money can buy." These remarks are given credence if key policy votes seem to be influenced by an officeholder's relationship to his or her political contributors.

Some people undoubtedly make contributions to candidates out of a sense of civic duty, general concern for good public policy, partisan loyalty, or personal friendship. But contributions of hundreds of thousands of dollars, either from individuals or political action committees, raise different questions about intent and purpose.

Rarely will anyone admit publicly that he or she is attempting to buy a candidate. Individuals and PACs making large political contributions usually say they are doing so for the purpose of "gaining access" to elected officials.[54] Since officeholders have limited time to consider and assess competing interests, lobbyists representing interest groups and their PACs contend that campaign contributions are necessary to facilitate access and give them an opportunity to present their cases on specific legislation.

Political scientists and others have attempted to prove that there is a relationship between campaign contributions and public policy, but so far the research is inconclusive. Multiple factors shape the decisions of public policymakers, including an officeholder's personal views, the views of his or her constituents, legal and technical issues, and the merits of the requests made by specific individuals or groups.[55] Yet, the strong appearance of a relationship between money and public policy is there, and advocates of campaign finance reform can make strong arguments for change.

The Fat Cats, PACs and the Really Big Money

During the 2002 election cycle, candidates running for state offices raised $195 million. Of the total, $126.9 million came from individual donors, PACs, and party committees. Some $68.1 million came from the candidates themselves, either in personal contributions or loans. Five percent of the money was contributed by sources from outside the state, but approximately $50 million came from individuals or organizations located in 19 zip codes in Texas. Two-thirds of the $126 million came from five cities—Austin, Houston, Dallas, San Antonio and Fort Worth.[56]

Unlike the federal government, Texas places no limits on the amount of money an individual or political action committee can contribute to most political candidates. And there are no limits on how much a candidate can contribute to his or her own campaign. The only exceptions in Texas are campaign contribution limits in judicial races, which were imposed by the legislature in 1995. Large contributions have long played a role in Texas politics and, over the years, most large contributions have gone to the conservative candidates, both Democrat and Republican. The use of direct mail to solicit small campaign donations may begin to partially offset some of the large campaign contributions, but large donors, sometimes called "fat cats," are still prominent in Texas political campaigns (see "Bob Perry: Homebuilder and Big Donor").

Forty-one individuals made contributions to candidates and PACs of $200,000 or more during the 2002 election cycle. The 50 top individual contributors to candidates in 2002 gave $14.3 million, or 11 percent of the total contributions. By contrast, 35,000 people who made contributions between $100 and $500 gave a total of $6.2 million, or only five percent of all contributions.[57]

Political action committees, as we discussed in Chapter 4, are an extension of interest groups. These committees, which collect money from their members for redistribution to candidates, have increased their importance at the state and local levels by bringing sophisticated fundraising skills to political campaigns. PACs are in the business of influencing elections, and they are key players in the fundraising game. Unlike PACs that are organized under federal law and contribute to national elections, PACs organized to influence state elections have few limitations on what they can contribute. Many PACs are organized by corporations and are a major source of business funding to political candidates in Texas. Corporations also can influence elections by spending money on issue advertising, provided they don't endorse a specific candidate. Many company executives also make individual contributions to candidates.

PACs and businesses contributed more than $50 million during the 2002 campaign season in Texas. The top 50 PACs/businesses contributed $47,586,261 to candidates and the political parties. One of the biggest contributors was Texans for Lawsuit Reform, which gave almost $2 million and played a leading role in a successful lobbying effort that produced more restrictions during the 2003 legislative session on damage lawsuits filed against doctors and businesses. Other major donors

---

BOB PERRY: HOMEBUILDER AND BIG DONOR

Houston homebuilder Bob Perry tries to maintain a low public profile, but in recent years he has received significant publicity for emerging as one of Texas's most generous political contributors. In 2002, he was the biggest donor to state political candidates and causes, contributing at least $3.8 million during that election cycle, mostly to Republicans. Texas Land Commissioner Jerry Patterson, a former state senator and one of many candidates backed by Perry, said the homebuilder had never asked for favors. "He's a reserved, serious and principled guy who has never tried to influence my vote. He truly is a philosophical contributor, who wants to improve the Republican party," Patterson said.#

But Perry's voice obviously is heard. He was believed to be influential in the legislature's creation in 2003 of a new state agency, the Residential Construction Commission, to develop performance standards for builders and discourage lawsuits against builders by unhappy homebuyers. Governor Rick Perry (who isn't related to the homebuilder) appointed an executive of Bob Perry's company to the new agency's board, less than one month after the governor had received a $100,000 contribution from Bob Perry. The homebuilder had contributed more than $500,000 to Rick Perry since 1997. The governor's office said the appointment wasn't influenced by the contributions, but by the appointee's experience in the homebuilding industry.*

Sources: #*Houston Chronicle,* December 22, 2002, p. 1A.
   *Houston Chronicle, September 30, 2003, p. 15A.

---

included the Texas Association of Realtors, the Texas Trial Lawyers Association, the Texas Medical Association, the Texas Dental Association, and the Texas State Teachers Association.

The fight over civil justice restrictions, or tort reform, has been a divisive issue—and a major source of campaign contributions—in the Texas legislature for years. Several major PAC contributors have been involved in the controversy. The trial lawyers were a major opponent of further restrictions, while the Texas Medical Association was a major ally of Texans for Lawsuit Reform in winning the new limits in 2003 (see Chapters 2 and 11).

Since money is the mother's milk of politics, the above data suggest a disturbing pattern. The really big money stands out. Moreover, it is often hard to trace the movement of money from a corporation to a PAC to a party committee and then to a candidate. Campaign costs are not likely to be reduced, nor are Texans likely to support public financing of campaigns. What is needed, though, is more information to make it easier to identify the trail of funds to elected officials.

Attempts at Reforms

On the heels of the Sharpstown scandal (see Chapter 8), the legislature enacted a major campaign finance reporting law in 1973 that, with some changes, is now administered by the state Ethics Commission. Although the law did not limit the size of political contributions, for the first time it required candidates to list the addresses as well as the names of donors and the amounts and dates of contributions. It also required political action committees contributing to candidates or officeholders to report the sources of their donations, which in the past had usually been hidden. For the first time, officeholders were required to file annual reports of their political contributions and expenses—even during years when they were not seeking reelection—and candidates were required to report contributions and other financial activity that occurred after an election. A candidate also had to formally designate a campaign treasurer before he or she could legally accept political contributions. Campaign finance reform, however, remains a difficult and seemingly endless struggle.

POLITICAL PARTICIPATION

Several years ago, a small group of protesters pitched tents and erected a series of crude displays outside the offices of what then was known as the Texas Water Commission in Austin. They came from a small town south of Dallas where, they claimed, a plant was polluting the environment with cancer-producing agents. People living in the community had experienced disproportionately high cancer rates and immunity and respiratory problems. These were middle-aged Texans who had never before participated in, much less organized, a demonstration. They appeared to be uncomfortable, but there was a sense of desperation as they talked about their families and friends.

A month or so later in San Antonio, several thousand antiabortionists organized a three-mile-long demonstration along a major highway. The demonstration took place after church on a Sunday, and many of the well-groomed protesters carried Bibles and had their young children in tow. Waving placards, singing songs, and praying, they used tactics that have been used across the nation by other antiabortion groups.

On any given day, Texas newspapers publish hundreds of "letters to the editor" addressing a wide range of state and local political issues. People contact public officials every day about stop signs, public facilities, garbage collection, and a multitude of governmental functions and responsibilities. Thousands of people are involved in politics as they attempt to shape the actions of public officials.

Voting or running for office are the first two activities that may come to mind when we think of political participation. But they are just a small part of the ongoing process necessary to sustain a democratic political system, translate the interests and demands of the public into specific policies, and assure governmental responsiveness.

Most people who participate in politics engage in what scholars call conventional political behavior. This includes voting, running for office, contributing to and campaigning for candidates, writing letters, gathering petitions, participating in other **grassroots** activities, and lobbying.

Fewer individuals participate in what is considered unconventional political behavior. These are acts that are likely to offend large segments of the population. In the view of some people, they can include boycotts, protest marches, and other nonviolent demonstrations, although many individuals consider any lawful, peaceful demonstration a very conventional means of exercising their constitutional rights. To virtually everyone, however, destruction of property, personal injury, assassination, and other forms of violence are totally unacceptable forms of political behavior.[58]

Not everyone, of course, participates in politics at the same level. Why some people get actively involved in politics and public life while others seem totally uninterested in government, current events, or public policy is a question that has challenged scholars, candidates, journalists, and reform groups for years. And it has generated much research.

From the day a person is born, he or she is subject to a socialization or learning process. The process is complex, lifelong, and structured by the interaction of the individual with the environment in which he or she lives. As the person approaches adulthood, the process includes the shaping of political attitudes, beliefs, and behavior.

Political socialization, the process by which people learn to behave politically, "transmits a broad array of values and opinions, from general feelings about trust in government to specific opinions" about the economy, political leaders, and institutions.[59] The agents of political socialization include the family, where the young child first learns of the views and attitudes of parents and relatives toward government, the political process, and leaders. The process is expanded through the schools, where children are exposed to national and state history, government, heroes, and values. Civics lessons and courses are taught to further shape commitment to the dominant values of the society. Other institutions, such as the church and the mass media, also contribute to this molding process. So do a person's peers and life experiences. Individuals tend to validate their perceptions and attitudes through the opinions of friends and acquaintances, and a major life experience, such as a tour of duty in the military or extended unemployment, has a potential effect on one's political behavior.

Political behavior is complex and changes over time. The limited space dedicated to this topic here is insufficient to flesh out its nuances and complexities, and we warn you to avoid drawing hard-and-fast conclusions. But a few broad generalizations about political behavior are in order.

A number of scholars have developed classifications of political behavior that run from high levels of involvement in a wide range of activities to virtual passivity. Sidney Verba and Norman H. Nie, well-known American political scientists specializing in political socialization, identified six categories of political participation detailed below:

> At one end of the spectrum are the complete **activists** (approximately 11 percent of the population), who are engaged in all types of political activity. Not only are these individuals involved in political campaigns, but they also participate in almost every other arena of community life. At the other end are the *inactives* (22 percent), who participate rarely, if at all, in the political life of the community. Some scholars refer to the first group as *political gladiators* and the second group as *apathetics.*
>
> Another group that is relatively inactive and shares many of the characteristics of the inactives are the *voting specialists* (21 percent). These individuals vote regularly in presidential and local elections but seldom engage in other organizational activities or attempt to contact policy makers personally.
>
> There are a small number of *parochial participants* (4 percent) who vote but do not engage in collective activity or campaigns. Nevertheless, they do contact policymakers over specific issues that affect their personal lives.
>
> Another group, the *communalists* (20 percent), demonstrates a high rate of participation in community life but a low level of campaign activity. These people participate in community activities such as church, PTA, and neighborhood associations but rarely engage in the high-conflict game of political campaigns.

The *campaigners* (15 percent) are just the opposite. They participate regularly in political campaigns but rarely in community activities. This group appears to be attracted to the conflict of campaigns.[60]

Although we have limited survey data for Texas, some generalizations emerge from national studies to provide insights into the patterns of political participation in the state:

1. **Income.** Individuals with higher income levels are more likely to be active participants in a wider range of political activities than those with low incomes. Affluent people have more time and resources to engage in political activities. They have a better understanding of the process, and they are acquainted with other participants and public officials.
2. **Education.** Participation increases as the level of education increases. People with college degrees are more likely to participate in politics than those less educated. Education also is correlated with income. Knowledge of political issues, public policies, the political process, and public officials makes a person aware of the importance and potential benefits of political participation.
3. **Sex.** Historically, men had participated in politics at higher rates than women. But in recent years women and men have been participating at comparable levels, and in some areas of the country, women now participate at higher rates than men. More women are now running for and winning public office. In recent years, there has been evidence of differences between men and women in support of the major political parties, which is often referred to as the "gender gap."
4. **Age.** Young people are far less likely to engage in politics than older people. The highest rates of participation are among middle-aged people. Younger adults tend to be in a transitory stage of their lives in which they don't identify with the issues or politics of the communities in which they live. Younger voters are engaged in a wide range of volunteer activities, but these tend not to be political.
5. **Race and ethnicity.** Rates of participation among Anglos are highest. But African Americans, despite historical patterns of discrimination, are now moving toward the Anglo level of participation. Hispanics tend to participate at much lower rates than either Anglos or African Americans. Explanations for these variations include educational and income differences, citizenship status, and the degree to which Hispanics have been assimilated into the political culture.
6. **Political efficacy.** Complex psychological attributes contribute to one's sense of having an impact on others or on political events. Political activists believe that they can influence the outcome of events. The more intense this sense of efficacy, the more likely one is to become involved politically.

In Texas and elsewhere, there is a great deal of concern about decreased political participation. Election turnout has declined, and it is often difficult to get strong candidates to run for public office. Public discourse has lost its civility, and citizens do not seem to have learned the lessons of the benefits and "logic of collective action." Surveys indicate much distrust of elected officials, and many people believe that government is for sale to the highest bidder. Moreover, some people just don't care. These findings lead many to conclude that there has been an erosion of democratic practices in the state and the nation.

SUMMARY AND CONCLUSIONS

1. Elections provide the general population with an opportunity to shape public policy indirectly, through the selection of leaders. For elections to achieve their ideal purpose under democratic theory, voters must be well informed, attentive to the actions of their leaders, and care about the outcome of elections.

2. One of the most disturbing aspects of the contemporary Texas political system is the low voter turnout in most elections, despite the elimination of discriminatory election laws, the creation of an extended voting period, and easy voter registration. Many people apparently are too uninformed about governmental actions to care to vote. Other people may be turned off by a feeling that public officials put their own interests and special interests before the public interest. Stories of governmental corruption and negative advertising in many political campaigns also disillusion voters. And frequent elections may contribute to voter fatigue.

3. Historically, political parties played a central role in elections, but now candidates increasingly rely on paid campaign consultants, who have taken over many of the traditional party functions. The consultants' primary objective

is to win campaigns, and they appear to give little consideration to the subsequent effects of campaigns on governance and policymaking.

4. The costs of statewide campaigns, as well as many regional and local campaigns, have escalated over the past three decades. Candidates receive much of their money in large campaign contributions from political action committees and wealthy individuals. Although money may not buy public officials, it certainly buys access to them, and it creates the impression that well-organized interests, corporations, or wealthy individuals have a disproportionate influence on policymakers.

5. Political participation includes a number of activities in addition to elections. People in the higher socioeconomic groups are more likely to participate in a wider range of political activities and have more influence on the policymaking process than people in the lower socioeconomic groups.

6. Over the past thirty years, Hispanics and African Americans have realized substantial gains in the electoral process and increased success in winning election to public office. There also has been a dramatic increase in the number of women elected to public office.

KEY TERMS

Suffrage	Absentee (or early) voting	Public opinion polling
Constitutional amendments	Poll tax	Controlled media
Primary election	White primary	Media event
Runoff election	Gerrymandering	Fat cat
Voting Rights Act	Single-member districts	Political action committee
General election	At-large election	Grassroots
Local election	Motor voter registration	Political socialization
Special election	Campaign consultant	Activists

FURTHER READING

Articles

Beiler, David, "The Eyes of America Were Upon Him," *Campaigns and Elections,* July, 1999, pp. 48–53.

Carrington, Paul O., "Big Money in Texas Judicial Elections: The Sickness and Its Remedies," *SMU Law Review,* 53 (Winter 2000), pp. 263–75.

Garcia, John A., "The Voting Rights Act and Hispanic Political Representation in the Southwest," *Publius* 16 (Fall 1986), pp. 49–66.

Lozano, Vince, "Endorsements and the Paper Chase," *The Texas Observer,* November 22, 1990, pp. 21–22.

Scripps Howard, *Texas Poll.* This quarterly survey is conducted by the Office of Survey Research at the University of Texas at Austin.

Books

Ansolabehere, Stephen, and Shanto Ivengar, *Going Negative: How Political Advertisements Shrink and Polarize the Electorate.* New York: The Free Press, 1997.

Baker, Ray J., *I Wouldn't Do It Any Other Way: Lessons I Learned from Vote Getting' Texas Style for the High and Mighty.* Wilsonville, Oregon: Book Partners, 1998.

Bennett, W. Lance, *The Governing Crisis: Media, Money, and Marketing in American Elections.* New York: St. Martin's Press, 1992.

Bryson, Conrey, *Dr. Lawrence A. Nixon and the White Primary,* rev. ed. El Paso, TX: Texas Western Press, 1992.

David, Chandler, and Bernard Grofman, eds., *Quiet Revolution in the South: The Impact of the Voting Rights Act, 1965–1990.* Princeton, NJ: Princeton University Press, 1994.

Diamond, Edwin, and Stephen Bates, *The Spot: The Rise of Political Advertising on Television,* rev. ed. Cambridge, MA: The MIT Press, 1988.

Dunham, Pat, *Electoral Behavior in the United States.* Englewood Cliffs, NJ: Prentice Hall, Inc., 1991.

Erikson, Robert S., Norman R. Luttberg, and Kent L. Tedin, *American Public Opinion,* 4th ed. New York: Macmillan Publishing Company, 1991.

Godwin, R. Kenneth, *One Billion Dollars of Influence.* Chatham, NJ: Chatham House Publishers, Inc., 1988.

Hershey, Marjorie Randon, *Running for Office.* Chatham, NJ: Chatham House Publishers, Inc., 1984.

Maisel, L. Sandy, *Parties and Elections in America,* 2nd ed. New York: McGraw-Hill, Inc., 1993.

Martel, Myles, *Political Campaign Debates.* New York: Longman, 1983.

Olien, Roger M., *From Token to Triumph: The Texas Republicans Since 1920.* Dallas: SMU Press, 1982.

Rosenstone, Steven J., *Mobilization, Participation, and Democracy in America.* New York: Macmillan Publishing Company, 1993.

Scher, Richard K., *The Modern Political Campaign.* Armonk, NY: M. E. Sharpe, 1997.

Sorauf, Frank J., *Money in American Elections.* Glenview, IL: Scott, Foresman and Company, 1988.

Traugott, Michael W., and Paul J. Lavrakas, *The Voter's Guide to Election Polls.* Chatham, NJ: Chatham House Publishers, Inc., 1996.

Wattenberg, Martin P., *The Rise of Candidate-Centered Politics.* Cambridge, MA: Harvard University Press, 1991.

Yeric, Jerry L., and John R. Todd, *Public Opinion: The Visible Politics.* Itasca, IL: F. E. Peacock Publishers, Inc.

Websites

Project Vote Smart   http://www.vote-smart.org Project Vote Smart is a national nonpartisan organization that tracks the performance of approximately 40,000 national and state elected officials and candidates. Information on policy positions, campaign finances and expenditures, and job performance is provided about the governor and state legislators.

Secretary of State   http://www.sos.state.tx.us   In addition to compiling county election data for state offices, this office provides information on election law, election procedures, county officials, and a program for voter education (Project V.O.T.E.).

League of Women Voters   http://www.lwvtexas.org The Texas League of Women Voters is a nonpartisan organization committed to increasing political participation, improving state and local government, and increasing public understanding of major policy issues.

ENDNOTES

1. Jim Hightower, *If the Gods Had Meant Us to Vote, They Would Have Given Us Candidates* (New York: HarperCollins, 2000).

2. These quotes were reported in Sam Attlesey, "Politicians Sometimes Say the Funniest Things," *Dallas Morning News,* October 13, 1991, p. 44A.

3. L. Sandy Maisel, *Parties and Elections in America* (New York: Random House, 1987), p. 1.

4. Gerald Pomper, *Elections in America* (New York: Dodd, Mead and Company, 1968), p. 12.

5. Herman Finer, *The Theory and Practice of Modern Government* (New York: Holt, 1949), p. 219.

6. Murray Edelman, *The Symbolic Uses of Politics* (Urbana, IL: University of Illinois Press, 1964), p. 17.

7. V. O. Key Jr., with the assistance of Milton C. Cummings Jr., *The Responsible Electorate* (Cambridge, MA: Harvard University Press, 1965), p. 7.

8. Maisel, *Parties and Elections in America*, p. 1.

9. Ibid., p. 3.

10. Frank J. Sorauf, *Party Politics in America*, 5th ed. (Boston: Little, Brown, 1984), p. 213; George Norris Green, *The Establishment in Texas Politics* (Westport, CT: Greenwood Press, 1979), p. 164.

11. Chandler Davidson, *Race and Class in Texas Politics* (Princeton, NJ: Princeton University Press, 1990), p. 24.

12. Secretary of State, Elections Division.

13. Davidson, *Race and Class in Texas Politics*, p. 24.

14. Secretary of State, Elections Division.

15. *Carter v. Dies*, 321 F. Supp. 1358, 1970.

16. Secretary of State, Elections Division, phone conversation on November 26, 2003.

17. Frank Sorauf, *Party Politics in America*, p. 220.

18. Robert S. Lorch, *State and Local Politics*, 3rd ed. (Englewood Cliffs, NJ: Prentice Hall, Inc., 1989), p. 63; Bexar County Elections Administration, phone conversation, December 19, 2003.

19. Davidson, *Race and Class in Texas Politics*, p. 24.

20. Secretary of State, Elections Division.

21. Rupert Richardson, Ernest Wallace, and Adrian Anderson, *Texas: The Lone Star State*, 5th ed. (Englewood Cliffs, NJ: Prentice Hall, Inc., 1988), p. 231.

22. See Merline Pitre, *Through Many Danders, Toils and Snares: Black Leadership in Texas, 1868–1890* (Austin: Eakin Press, 1985).

23. Richardson, et al., *Texas: The Lone Star State*, p. 312.

24. Wilbourn E. Benton, *Texas Politics: Constraints and Opportunities*, 5th ed. (Chicago: Nelson-Hall Publishers, 1984), pp. 72–73.

25. *Harper v. Virginia State Board of Elections*, 86 S. Ct. 1079 (1966).

26. Benton, *Texas Politics*, pp. 67–72.

27. *Nixon v. Herndon*, et al., 273 U.S. 536 (1927).

28. *Nixon v. Condon*, 286 U.S. 73 (1932).

29. *Grovey v. Townsend*, 295 U.S. 45 (1935).

30. *Smith v. Allwright*, 321 U.S. 649 (1944).

31. *John Terry, et al., Petitioners v. A. J. Adams, et al.*, 345 U.S. 461.

32. Beryl E. Pettus and Randall W. Bland, *Texas Government Today: Structures, Functions, Political Processes*, 3rd ed. (Homewood, IL: The Dorsey Press, 1984), pp. 85–86.

33. *Beare, et al. v. Preston Smith, Governor of Texas*, 321 F. Supp. 1100 (1971).

34. Benton, *Texas Politics*, p. 65.

35. *Congressional Quarterly Weekly Report* 51 (September 1993), p. 2318.

36. Robert R. Brischetto, *The Political Empowerment of Texas Mexicans, 1974–1988* (San Antonio, TX: Southwest Voter Research Institute, Inc., Latino Electorate Series, 1988), p. 5; Robert R. Brischetto, Unpublished Report (San Antonio, TX.: Southwest Voter Research Institute, Inc., 1993); Secretary of State, Elections Division.

37. *Texas Poll*, Spring 2001, Summer 2001, Fall 2001, Winter 2002 (Austin: Scripps Howard, 2002).

38. Robert Brischetto, Southwest Voter Research Institute, Inc., San Antonio, telephone conversations, November 1, 1991.

39. William C. Valasquez Institute, news release, March 13, 2002.

40. Texas Municipal League, *Texas Municipal League Directory of City Officials, 2004* (Austin: Texas Municipal League, 2004).

41. Based on a survey conducted by the V. G. Young Institute of County Government, Texas A & M University, 2002.

42. For an excellent analysis of the development of campaign professionals, see Larry J. Sabato, *The Rise of the Political Consultants* (New York: Basic Books, Inc., 1981).

43. Norris, *The Establishment in Texas Politics*, pp. 24–25.

44. W. Lance Bennett, *The Governing Crisis: Media, Money and Marketing in American Elections* (New York: St. Martin's Press, 1992), p. 32.

45. See Edwin Diamond and Stephen Bates, *The Spot: The Rise of Political Advertising on Television*, rev. ed. (Cambridge, MA: The MIT Press, 1988).

46. *Texas Observer*, September 28, 1990, p. 8.

47. Bennett, *The Governing Crisis*, pp. 33–34.

48. Sabato, *The Rise of the Political Consultants*, p. 220.

49. *Houston Chronicle*, December 2, 1997.

50. Associated Press, December 7, 2003.

51. Texans for Public Justice, *Money in Politex: A Guide to Money in the 2002 Texas Elections*, November 2003. Much of the data in the following analysis came from this report.

52. Anthony Champagne, "Campaign Contributions in Texas Supreme Court Races," *Crime, Law and Social Change* 17 (1992), pp. 91–106.

53. Sorauf, *Money in American Elections*, pp. 298–307.

54. Larry Sabato, *PAC Power* (New York: W. W. Norton, Inc., 1985), pp. 126–28.

55. Sorauf, *Money in American Elections*, pp. 306–17.

56. Texans for Public Justice, pp. 7, 10, 11.

57. Ibid., pp. 9, 17.

58. Samuel H. Barnes and Max Kaase, *Political Action* (Beverly Hills, CA: Sage, 1979), Chap. 2.

59. Lance T. LeLoup, *Politics in America*, 2nd ed. (St. Paul, MN: West Publishing Co., 1989), p. 156.

60. Sidney Verba and Norman H. Nie, *Participation in America* (New York: Harper and Row, 1972) pp. 79–80, 118–19. Seven percent of the sample was not classified.

8

The Texas
Legislature

"We've seen a huge philosophical change in the House from last session to this session."

Speaker Tom Craddick, 2003.[1]

Craddick's comment may have been an understatement. The Republican takeover of the Texas House of Representatives in 2003 was a watershed event in state politics. It marked the first GOP majority of that body since the 1870s and assured Craddick's election as the first Republican House speaker since Reconstruction. Moreover, it gave Republicans control of all major power points in the statehouse because they also maintained their majority in the state Senate and their hold on the governor's office. The conservative GOP agenda dominated legislative deliberations, including the crucial balancing of a new state budget. Despite a $10 billion revenue shortfall, Republican leaders held the line against higher state taxes, drawing applause from many middle-income and wealthy Texans. But lawmakers imposed spending cuts that reduced the availability of health care and other services for low-income and disadvantaged Texans and further widened the divide between the privileged and the unfortunate.

Legislative partisanship also increased in 2003, thanks primarily to a bitter fight over congressional redistricting that took the regular session and three special sessions to resolve. The effort was orchestrated by U.S. House Majority Leader Tom DeLay of Texas to give Republicans a majority of the Texas congressional delegation and help the GOP maintain control of the U.S. Congress. Until that point, Democrats held a 17–15 majority of the congressional seats from Texas, despite widespread Republican gains in other state offices. The battle to redraw the district lines to favor more Republican candidates focused national attention on the legislature when Democratic lawmakers, on two separate occasions, fled to neighboring states to block action on redistricting bills. More than 50 Democrats fled to Ardmore, Oklahoma, for four days that spring to deprive the House of a quorum and kill a redistricting bill in the regular session. And 11 Democratic state senators spent more than a month in Albuquerque, N.M., to shut down the Senate for an entire special session that summer. Eventually, the Republicans prevailed—pending federal court review of the new map—but the experience left behind a bitter, partisan taste in Austin that could affect future legislative deliberations.

The legislative experiences of 2003 reflected some of the enormous social, political, and economic changes that have occurred in Texas during the past generation. Forty years ago, a rural-dominated legislature showed little concern for the problems of urban areas and minority groups. Operating within the context of one-party Democratic control and an interest group system dominated by oil, finance, and agriculture, legislative leaders tied to conservative factions in the Democratic party pursued selected policies that benefited those sectors of the Texas economy.

Today, Texas is the country's second most populous state and is more than 80 percent urban. The ethnic and racial characteristics of its population have changed, and still more changes are projected in its social composition. Texas is now dominated by the Republican party, its economy is diversifying, and there are more demands today on the legislature than in the past. The issues and policy questions that confront lawmakers are more complex, and the special interests demanding attention are more numerous and diverse.

Demographically and politically, the legislature has undergone major changes. But lawmakers still have to operate under outdated constitutional restrictions—including strict limits on when they can meet—that were written for a rural state in a bygone era.

LEGISLATIVE FUNCTIONS

The legislature, whose members are elected from districts throughout Texas, is the chief policymaking branch of state government. Its basic role is similar to that of Congress at the federal level, though there are major differences between the two institutions. The Texas legislature performs a variety of functions, but its primary task is to decide how conflicts between competing groups and interests are to be resolved. Although often taken for granted, this orderly, institutionalized process of conflict management and resolution is critical to a stable political system.[2]

Enacting Laws

Every two years, the legislature enacts several hundred laws governing our behavior; allocating resources, benefits, and costs; and defining the duties of those institutions and bureaucrats responsible for putting these laws into effect. From local legislation that affects one city or county to general statewide policies and proposals for constitutional amendments, there are literally thousands of ideas advanced for new laws every legislative session. The legislative arena includes a wide range of players in addition to legislators, and lawmaking requires compromise and accommodation of competing ideas and interests.

Budgets and Taxes

The legislature establishes programs providing a variety of public services and sets priorities through the budgetary process. It sets the budgets for the governor, the bureaucracy, and the state courts. It decides whether state taxes should be increased, how high they should be increased, and how the tax burden should be distributed. Indirectly, its actions affect local tax rates as well.

Overseeing State Agencies

Hundreds of laws are passed each legislative session, and the legislature assigns specific state agencies and local governments the responsibility of carrying out the laws on a day-to-day basis. It is ultimately the legislature's responsibility to make sure agencies and bureaucrats are doing what they are charged with by law, and this review, or "oversight," process is achieved through legislative budget hearings, other committee investigations, and program audits.

The Senate further influences policy by confirming or rejecting the governor's appointees to hundreds of state boards and commissions that administer public programs.

Educating the Public

The 181 members of the Texas legislature certainly do not speak with one voice, and on major policy issues, it is inevitable that there will be a variety of opinions and proposed solutions. Individual lawmakers try to inform the public about their own actions and the collective actions of the legislature. They use speeches, letters to constituents, news releases, telephone calls, newsletters, websites, e-mails, and other techniques to explain the legislative process and substantive policy issues.

Representing the Public

The legislature is a representative body whose members are chosen in free elections. This process provides legitimacy to legislative actions and decisions. People may disagree over how "representative" the legislature is in terms of race, ethnicity, gender, or class. And many Texans may be indifferent toward or ignorant about public policy. But successful lawmakers must demonstrate concern for the attitudes and demands of their constituents. Legislators use many methods to learn how their constituents feel, including public opinion polls, questionnaires, phone calls, town hall meetings, and personal visits.

INSTITUTIONALIZATION OF THE TEXAS LEGISLATURE

The Texas legislature has undergone significant institutional changes over the past 125 years. Some of these changes were due to external factors, such as the development of a two-party system in Texas, changes in interest groups, and complex social and economic problems. Other changes were internal. They included the increased tenure of the legislative membership, changing career and leadership patterns, expanded workload and length of sessions, the development and enforcement of complex rules and procedures, the evolution of professional staffs, and the emergence of partisan divisions.[3] Political scientists describe these developments as **institutionalization.**

Institutionalization varies throughout the fifty states. Some state legislatures are highly professional, while others are not.[4] In some states, salaries are high, turnover is limited, and legislators think in terms of legislative careers. Similarly, some legislatures have developed sophisticated staff and support services. By contrast, in other legislatures, members are poorly paid, turnover is high, legislative service is regarded as a part-time activity, and support services are limited. The Texas legislature falls somewhere between those state legislatures that can be classified as highly professional and those that can be classified as amateur or citizen lawmaking bodies (see Table 8–1). The institutionalization process has produced a more professional legislature in Texas, and this development is likely to continue in the future.

Although it is generally assumed that a "professional" state legislature is a more effective policymaking body, there are some indications that this is not always true. In recent years, California, Pennsylvania, New York, and Illinois—states with professional legislatures—have witnessed ugly partisan confrontations, ethical violations, and the decline of civility among legislators.

TABLE 8–1   Professionalism in State Legislatures

Professional—Full-Time, Large Staff, High Pay, Low Turnover

California	Michigan	Ohio
Illinois	New Jersey	Pennsylvania
Massachusetts	New York	Wisconsin

Professional–Citizen—Moderate Pay, Staff, Turnover, and Time

Alabama	Indiana	North Carolina
Alaska	Iowa	Oklahoma
Arizona	Kansas	Oregon
Colorado	Kentucky	South Carolina
Connecticut	Maryland	Tennessee
Delaware	Minnesota	Texas
Florida	Mississippi	Virginia
Georgia	Missouri	Washington
Hawaii	Nebraska	

Citizen—Part-Time, Low Pay, Small Staff, High Turnover

Arkansas	Nevada	South Dakota
Idaho	New Hampshire	Utah
Louisiana	New Mexico	Vermont
Maine	North Dakota	West Virginia
Montana	Rhode Island	Wyoming

Source: National Conference of State Legislatures, *State Legislatures,* 20 (November, 1994) 5; cited in Thomas R. Dye, *Politics in States and Communities,* 10th ed. Upper Saddle River, NJ: Prentice Hall, 2000, p. 183.

THE ORGANIZATION AND COMPOSITION OF THE TEXAS LEGISLATURE

Following the oppressive efforts of Governor Edmund J. Davis and the Radical Reconstructionists to centralize power and authority in Texas after the Civil War, the rural delegates who dominated the constitutional convention in 1875 were distrustful, even fearful, of the excesses and abuses of big government. They created a part-time, **bicameral legislature** that included a 31-member Senate and a 150-member House of Representatives. All other states also have bicameral legislatures, except Nebraska, which has a unicameral system with only one lawmaking body of forty-nine members. The sizes of other state senates range from twenty in Alaska to sixty-seven in Minnesota, while houses of representatives vary in size from forty in Alaska to 400 in New Hampshire.[5]

Legislative Sessions

To curb lawmakers' power, the Texas constitutional framers limited the **regular legislative session** to a maximum of 140 days every two years but gave the governor the authority to call special sessions when necessary. Lawmakers convene in regular session on the second Tuesday of January in odd-numbered years. **Special sessions** are limited to thirty days each and to subjects submitted by the governor, but there is no limit on the number of special sessions that a governor can call.

From midsummer of 1986 through midsummer of 1987, for example, during a lingering budgetary crisis spawned by a depressed oil industry, the legislature convened for its regular 140-day session and four special sessions. Two of those special sessions lasted the maximum thirty days. The seventy-first legislature in 1989–1990 held six special sessions to deal with equalization of school funding and the provision of medical expenses and other compensation for workers injured on the job. The seventy-second legislature had two special sessions in the summer of 1991 to write a new budget, pass a tax bill, make changes in the criminal justice system, and redraw the boundaries of congressional districts. And, as noted earlier, the seventy-eighth legislature had three special sessions in the summer and early fall of 2003 in a protracted, partisan fight over congressional redistricting.

Some state officials and government experts believe the Texas legislature should have annual regular sessions, at least for budgetary purposes (see Chapter 13). Only six other state legislatures do not. But the change would require a constitutional amendment.

Terms of Office and Qualifications

Representatives serve two-year terms, while senators are elected to four-year, staggered terms. A senator has to be a qualified voter, at least twenty-six years old, a resident of Texas for five years preceding his or her election, and a resident of the district from which elected for at least one year. A representative must be a qualified voter, at least twenty-one years old, a Texas resident for two years, and a resident of the district represented for one year.[6] There is no limit on the number of terms an individual can serve in the legislature (see "The Move for Term Limits").

THE MOVE FOR TERM LIMITS

In 1991, a bipartisan group of influential Texans began lobbying for term limits for legislators and most other state officials to rid state government of "professional politicians" and, they argued, to make it easier to elect officeholders who would be more responsive to the public. But term limits for state officials would require a constitutional amendment, which must be initiated by the legislature.

Term limitation proposals have died during recent legislative sessions. Opponents argued that the forced retirement of the most experienced legislators would increase the power of the bureaucracy, the non-elected agency heads and staffs who have no direct accountability to the voters. They also argued that term limits would interfere with an individual's right to vote by unfairly restricting the number of eligible candidates for office. The only term limits, opponents said, should be imposed at the ballot box on election day.

State Senator Ken Armbrister, a Democrat from Victoria, joined a number of other lawmakers in sponsoring a term limits measure in 1995. Armbrister said he was responding to public opinion polls that indicated most Texans wanted term limits for their elected officials. Nevertheless, Armbrister said he had received only about ten letters from constituents urging him to support term limits. And after serving four years in the Texas House and eight years in the Senate, he was still popular enough with the voters in his district to have been reelected the previous year without drawing an opponent.

The Senate approved a constitutional amendment in 1995 to limit legislators and other elected state officials, except judges, to twelve years in any one office. But the proposal died in the House. Interestingly, only twenty-six of the 150 members of the Texas House in 1995 and seven of the thirty-one senators had been in office for twelve years or longer. Only one statewide elected official had exceeded the proposed limit. Turnover among Texas legislators, who are paid only part-time salaries, has traditionally been higher than in the U.S. Congress, which pays full-time salaries.

Pay and Compensation

Members of both the House and the Senate and their presiding officers have a base pay of $7,200 per year. This figure is set by the state constitution and can be raised only with voter approval. This is one of the lowest legislative pay levels in the country and was last increased in 1975 by a constitutional amendment that also set lawmakers' per diem, or personal expense allowance, at $30 a day while the legislature is in session.

Legislators proposed a constitutional amendment in 1989 to increase their salaries to more than $20,000 a year, but the voters turned the proposal down by a 2 to 1 margin. The amendment also would have removed voter control over legislative pay and given lawmakers the power to give themselves raises by setting their pay at one-fourth the governor's salary, which the legislature sets and regularly increases.

In 1991, Texas voters approved a constitutional amendment creating a state Ethics Commission that could recommend legislative pay raises to the voters and change per diem on its own. The commission set per diem at $125 per day for the 2003 legislative sessions.

By 2002, only Alabama, Texas, New Hampshire and Rhode Island had limits on legislative pay that could be changed only by constitutional amendment. Compensation commissions now recommend legislative pay levels in some states, while legislatures in other states set their own salaries, often with the approval of the voters. In 2000, legislative pay ranged from a high of $99,000 a year in California, where lawmakers set their own salaries and are considered a full-time legislature, to a low of $100 a year in New Hampshire, which has annual sessions but a constitutional limit on salaries.[7]

Supporters of higher legislative pay in Texas say it is only fair because legislative service has become much more than a part-time job for many lawmakers, particularly during periods of frequent special sessions. They argue that the present low compensation level restricts legislative service to wealthy individuals or those who have law practices or own businesses in which partners or employees can help take up the slack while they are in Austin. They believe higher pay would broaden the potential pool from which legislators are drawn—and perhaps improve the prospects for quality—by encouraging more salaried working people to run for legislative office. A broader pool of candidates also could broaden the perspectives from which policy issues are viewed and addressed.

The outside personal income of many legislators obviously does suffer while they are in office, but legislative service can also enhance business and professional connections. Critics of higher legislative pay also note that candidates, many of whom spend thousands of dollars to get elected to the legislature, know the pay level before they run for the office. Texas lawmakers also have provided themselves one of the best legislative retirement plans in the country. And they can increase their retirement benefits without voter approval.

Retirement benefits are computed on the basis of state district judges' salaries, which legislators raise during most regular sessions, thereby increasing their own retirement benefits as well. Many former legislators receive pensions that are much larger than their paychecks were while they were in office. In 1991, legislators sweetened their retirement plan even more by quietly amending a state employee retirement bill to allow former legislators to receive full retirement benefits at age fifty instead of fifty-five, as set in earlier law, and reduce the required time for service in office. The sponsor of the amendment, Representative Nolan "Buzz" Robnett, a Republican from Lubbock, who, incidentally, was fifty at the time, helped make himself eligible for $1,780 a month in retirement pay, almost triple his legislative salary.[8]

Physical Facilities

The House chamber and representatives' offices have been traditionally located in the west wing of the state Capitol, and the Senate chamber and senators' offices are in the east wing. The pink granite building was completed in 1888, but the growth of state government and periodic renovations created a hodgepodge of cramped legislative offices. After one visitor died in a fire behind the Senate chamber in 1983, it also became obvious that the building had become a firetrap. So the state launched a $187 million Capitol restoration and expansion project in 1990 that included a four-story underground addition to the building. Legislative committee hearing rooms and many lawmakers' offices were relocated from the main building to the underground extension, which is connected to the original Capitol and nearby office buildings by tunnels.

Completed in 1888 and recently renovated, the Texas Capitol in downtown Austin houses the governor's office and meeting chambers for the House of Representatives and the Senate.

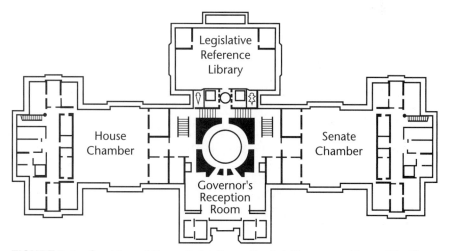

FIGURE 8–1 Corridors of Power in the Texas Capitol. *The second floor of the Texas Capitol, shown here, houses the Senate and House chambers, the Legislative Reference Library, and the Governor's Reception Room.*

When the legislature is in session, access to the floor of each chamber on the second floor of the Capitol is restricted to lawmakers, certain other state officials, some staff members, and accredited media representatives. The galleries, to which the public is admitted, overlook the chambers from the third floor of the Capitol.

In both the House and Senate chambers, members have desks facing the presiding officer's podium, which is flanked by desks of the clerical staff. Unlike the U.S. Congress, where seating is arranged by party affiliation, seats are assigned to state legislators by seniority.

Membership

In 1971, the Texas legislature was overwhelmingly white, male, and Democratic. There were two African Americans in the 150-member House and one in the thirty-one-member Senate. The one African-American senator was also the only woman in the Senate. She was Barbara Jordan of Houston who, two years later, would begin a distinguished career in Congress. Frances Farenthold of Corpus Christi was the only woman in the House. She was a reform-minded lawmaker who was often referred to as the "Den Mother of the Dirty Thirty," a coalition of liberal Democrats and conservative Republicans who challenged the power of House Speaker Gus Mutscher while a major stock fraud scandal involving the speaker was unfolding. In 1972, Farenthold ran a strong race for governor in the Democratic primary but lost a runoff election to Uvalde rancher Dolph Briscoe. There was only one Hispanic senator and eleven Hispanic members of the House. Only twelve legislators were Republicans—ten in the House and two in the Senate.

By 2003, changing political patterns and attitudes, redrawn political boundaries, and court-ordered single-member districts for urban House members had significantly altered the composition of the legislature (see Table 8–2). During the regular and special sessions that year, Republicans had a 19–12 majority in the Senate. The Senate also had two African-American members, seven Hispanics, and four women.

The House in 2003 had an 88–62 Republican majority, its first Republican majority of modern times. The 150 House members included fourteen African

TABLE 8–2   Comparative Profile of Texas Legislators, 1971–2003

	House			Senate		
	1971	1981	2003	1971	1981	2003
Democrats	140	112	62	29	24	12
Republicans	10	38	88	2	7	19
Males	149	139	119	30	30	27
Females	1	11	31	1	1	4
Hispanics	11	17	30	1	4	7
African Americans	2	13	14	1	0	2
Anglos	137	120	105[†]	29	27	22

Source: Texas House and Senate Rosters 1971, 1981, 2003.

[†]House also included one Asian American in 2003.

Americans, thirty Hispanics, one Asian American and thirty-one women. Representation from the urban and suburban areas of the state had grown, reflecting the population shifts accommodated by **redistricting.**

Business has been the dominant occupation of legislators serving in recent years, followed by law. Most of the thirty-one senators and more than sixty of the 150 House members in 2003 had a business background. Eight senators and forty-seven House members were attorneys, although not all of them made their living practicing law. The House included one chiropractor, one pharmacist, one automobile dealer, a drive-in restaurant owner and a flight instructor. Two senators were physicians, one was a consulting engineer and one was a retired firefighter.

Senators' ages ranged from thirty-nine to sixty-eight, with an average age of fifty-four. The age range for members of the House was twenty-four to seventy-eight, with an average age of forty-nine.

Legislative Careers

Various career patterns lead to election to the Texas legislature.[9] Lawmakers include former members of city councils and school boards, former prosecutors, former legislative aides, and long-time Democratic and Republican party activists. Twenty of the thirty-one senators in 2003 had previously served in the House. Many first-term legislators, however, arrive in Austin with relatively little political experience.

Legislative Turnover

Compared to other states, turnover in the Texas legislature is moderate. Relatively few individuals who serve can be considered career legislators. Only four senators and ten House members entered the 2003 regular session with twenty or more years of legislative service. The average legislative experience in the Senate was thirteen years, while House members had served an average of seven years.

In addition to the effects of redistricting of legislative seats every ten years, turnover is due primarily to the low pay and the personal costs involved in running for public office. When the legislature is in session, many legislators lose income from their regular sources of employment. Political ambition also is a factor. Many lawmakers who want to move up the political ladder serve only a few terms in the Texas House before running for the Texas Senate, the U.S. Congress, or other state or local offices. Other legislators quit after a few sessions to become lobbyists.

REPRESENTATION AND REDISTRICTING

Many European legislatures use a system called proportional representation, in which legislative seats are allocated on the basis of each party's vote. By contrast, the Texas legislature and most other American legislatures allocate seats geographically on the basis of single-member districts. The long legal and political battles over apportionment and redistricting address some of the fundamental questions of who should be represented and how they should be represented.

The Texas Constitution of 1876 provided that the legislature redraw state representative and senatorial districts every ten years, "at its first session after the publication of each United States decennial census," to reflect changing population patterns. Despite this requirement, members of earlier rural-dominated legislatures were reluctant to apportion the legislative seats equitably to reflect the increased urbanization of the state, and inequities grew. In 1948, Texas voters approved a constitutional amendment creating the Legislative Redistricting Board to carry out redistricting responsibilities if the legislature failed to do so during the required session. The board includes the lieutenant governor, the speaker of the House, the attorney general, the comptroller, and the commissioner of the General Land Office.

But for many more years, the urban areas of the state still were denied equality in representation, and rural legislators tended to neglect urban problems. After the 1960 census, it was possible for approximately 33 percent of the state's population to elect a majority of both the House and the Senate.

Court Intervention in Redistricting

Equality in redistricting finally came to Texas as a result of federal court intervention. In 1962, the U.S. Supreme Court, in the case of *Baker v. Carr,* applied the principle of equality to congressional redistricting. Then, in the case of *Reynolds v. Sims,* the court held that state legislative districts had to be apportioned on the "one person, one vote" principle. Litigation in 1965 (*Kilgarin v. Martin*) extended this ruling to Texas, and the "reapportionment revolution" produced dramatic changes in the composition of the Texas legislature.[10] To a large degree, the increased representation of minorities and Republicans in Texas's lawmaking body is a result of the legal and political redistricting battles.

The state Senate has always been elected by single-member districts, and after the 1970 census, the application of the equality principle to the Senate resulted in districts that were comparable in size. The issues of racial and partisan gerrymandering—the practice of drawing lines to favor a particular individual or group—were still to be resolved through subsequent litigation and federal legislation.

Rural members of the Texas House also were elected from single-member districts, but in the urban counties that had been allocated more than one representative, the elections were held in multimember districts. Each candidate for a House seat in an urban area had to run for election countywide, a practice that put ethnic and political minorities at a disadvantage because their votes were diluted by the dominant Anglo and Democratic populations.

In 1972, a three-judge federal court ruled that multimember districts in Dallas and Bexar Counties were unconstitutional because they diluted the voting strength of African Americans in Dallas and Hispanics in Bexar. Coincidentally, they also diluted the voting strength of Republicans in both counties.

Despite the fact that 50 percent of Bexar County's population was Hispanic, under the countywide, or at-large, election system only one Hispanic from Bexar had served in the Texas House in 1971. Dallas County, which had a large African-American population, had only one African-American House member. Single-member districts in Harris County had been drawn by the Legislative Redistricting Board in 1971, and after the U.S. Supreme Court upheld the lower court's decision regarding Dallas and Bexar Counties, multimember legislative districts were soon eliminated in all other urban counties.

After 1975, Congress put Texas under the provisions of the federal Voting Rights Act, which prohibits the dilution of minority voting strength, requires preclearance of redistricting plans by the Department of Justice, and gives African Americans and Hispanics a strong weapon to use in challenging a redistricting plan in court.

At the beginning of the twenty-first century, however, minorities believed their fight for equal representation was still far from over because the Voting Rights Act was under attack by conservatives. The U.S. Supreme Court, in "reverse discrimination" cases from Texas and Georgia, had ruled that some congressional districts had been illegally gerrymandered to elect minority candidates. And, in another case from Georgia, the high court held in 2003 that states have the right to determine how best to draw legislative and congressional districts to protect minority voters.[11]

Texas Republicans scored huge redistricting victories in 2001, after the legislature failed to redraw its own districts during that year's regular session. Under the state constitution, the task then fell to the five statewide elected officials, four of whom were Republicans, on the Legislative Redistricting Board. The panel drew new legislative maps that helped increase Republican strength in the thirty-one-member Senate to nineteen GOP senators. It also enabled Republicans to capture their first majority of modern times in the 150-member Texas House. With legislative candidates running under the new plan in the 2002 elections, the GOP increased its strength in the House from 72 seats to 88 seats, a margin that cleared the way for state Representative Tom Craddick of Midland, a Republican, to be elected speaker after the regular session convened in 2003. The GOP takeover of the Texas House also gave Republicans the opportunity to redraw the lines for Texas's congressional districts later that year. Republicans prevailed after a protracted partisan fight that included two walkouts by Democratic legislators. Unless reversed in court, the new congressional map was expected to give Republicans a strong majority among members of the U.S. Congress elected from Texas (see "Redistricting: A Partisan Drama).

REDISTRICTING: A PARTISAN DRAMA

The contentious, nationally publicized fight over congressional redistricting in 2003 was not the Texas Legislature's finest hour. But the drama of Democratic lawmakers fleeing across state lines to shut down legislative business in Austin, the bitter partisan rhetoric, and the persistence of the eventual Republican victors vividly illustrated the huge political stakes that were involved.

The Republican takeover of the Texas House in 2003 gave the GOP control of state government, but Democrats still held a 17–15 edge among members of the U.S. Congress elected from Texas. The lines for congressional districts had been redrawn to reflect new census data in 2001 by a federal court, not by the legislature, because the Texas House, which still had a Democratic majority in 2001, couldn't agree on a new map with the Republican-dominated Senate. Once Republicans had control of both legislative chambers, the Republican leader of the U.S. House, Congressman Tom DeLay, began urging Texas Republican leaders to redraw the congressional lines to favor more Republican candidates and help their party maintain its narrow majority of the U.S. House. But a redistricting bill died late in the regular legislative session that spring when more than 50 Democratic members of the Texas House fled to Ardmore, Okla., to break a House quorum and prevent the body from conducting business for four days—long enough to miss a deadline for action on the redistricting measure. The Democrats, outnumbered 88–62, didn't have enough votes in the House to defeat the bill outright, but they had enough members to shut down work because a quorum required two-thirds of the members to be present. The Democrats left the state in order to avoid being arrested by state troopers and forced to return to the Capitol. In their absence, Speaker Tom Craddick and the remaining members had placed a "call" on the House, authorizing the sergeant-at-arms to enlist the aid of law enforcement officers to round up the missing members.

But Republican leaders, most notably DeLay and Governor Rick Perry, didn't give up. Perry called the legislature back into a 30-day special session in June to tackle redistricting again. This time, Democrats didn't bolt, and the House easily approved the bill. But the measure died in the Senate, where Democratic senators used the "two-thirds rule" to block action on it. That traditional procedure required two-thirds of the senators to approve debate on any legislation, and Republicans, although they were in the majority, didn't constitute two-thirds of the body. At the end of the first special session, Lieutenant Governor David Dewhurst, a Republican who earlier had been reluctant to force a vote on redistricting, announced that he would bypass the two-thirds rule during a second special session. That prompted eleven Democratic senators to fly to Albuquerque, N.M., breaking a Senate quorum, only minutes before Perry issued a proclamation calling the second special session. The Democrats remained holed up in New Mexico for more than a month, outlasting the entire second session. The only Democratic senator who didn't flee was Ken Armbrister of Victoria, who represented a strongly Republican district.

While the national media listened and watched, the Democrats in Albuquerque and the Republicans in Austin exchanged a barrage of partisan charges and countercharges. The dissident Democrats—who included nine minorities and two Anglos who represented predominantly minority districts—accused the Republicans of trying to redraw congressional districts to dilute the voting strength of Hispanics and African Americans. "This is a shameful return to the days of the Jim Crow laws designed to prevent electoral participation of minorities in the South," said state Senator Leticia Van de Putte of San Antonio, chair of the Senate Democratic Caucus. Dewhurst and the Republican senators denied the charges. They said redistricting would enhance minority voting strength. And they argued that Republicans, with a majority in Texas, were entitled to a majority of congressional seats from the state. Republican senators also took the unusual step of imposing sanctions—including thousands of dollars in fines—on the absentees.

The stalemate finally ended when one of the Democrats, state Senator John Whitmire of Houston, returned to Texas, announcing that he would continue the fight on the Senate floor. Because Whitmire's return restored the Senate's two-thirds quorum, the remaining dissidents returned as well. Perry called a third special session in September, and Republican majorities in the House and the Senate approved different versions of a redistricting map. Final approval, however, was delayed for several days because House and Senate Republicans, ironically, continued to fight among themselves over a handful of districts. The main hangup was over West Texas, where Craddick insisted that his hometown, Midland, get a congressional district it could dominate. In the end, Craddick got his wish, but not before DeLay visited Austin to personally help negotiate between House and Senate members of the conference committee that drew the final map.

The third special session ended on October 12, and Perry quickly signed the new redistricting plan, which was expected to give Republicans as many as twenty-two of Texas's thirty-two congressional seats, if not overturned in court. Democrats filed suit in federal court, which they lost, to block the plan, or at least keep it from going into effect for the 2004 congressional elections. Republican state senators, meanwhile, didn't enforce the fines they had imposed on the dissident Democrats, but no one could predict how long the partisan ill will would linger—or what other issues it could infect.

Source: Houston Chronicle, August 14, 2003, p. 25A.

LEGISLATIVE LEADERSHIP

The highly institutionalized leadership structure found in the U.S. Congress is only now beginning to emerge in the Texas legislature—and only to a limited extent. The Texas legislature is a part-time institution that, until recently, was dominated by a small group of Democratic lawmakers. With no significant party opposition or minority representation until recent years, legislative leadership was highly personalistic and dependent on the political relationships between the presiding officers and key legislators.

House Leadership

The presiding officer of the House of Representatives is the **speaker,** who is elected by the House from among its membership. With the long tenures of Gib Lewis and his immediate predecessor in the speaker's office, Bill Clayton, there wasn't a contested speaker's race between 1975 and 1991 (see Table 8–3). Lewis's decision not to seek reelection in 1992 prompted several House members to announce for the post.

TABLE 8–3   Recent Presiding Officers of the Texas Legislature

Lieutenant Governors	When Served	Home	Party
Ben Ramsey	1951–1961*	San Augustine	Democrat
Preston Smith	1963–1969	Lubbock	Democrat
Ben Barnes	1969–1973	DeLeon	Democrat
Bill Hobby, Jr.	1973–1991	Houston	Democrat
Bob Bullock	1991–1999	Hillsboro	Democrat
Rick Perry	1999–2000	Haskell	Republican
Bill Ratliff	2000–2003	Mt. Pleasant	Republican
David Dewhurst	2003–	Houston	Republican

Speakers	When Served	Home	Party
Reuben Senterfitt	1951–1955	San Saba	Democrat
Jim T. Lindsey	1955–1957	Texarkana	Democrat
Waggoner Carr	1957–1961	Lubbock	Democrat
James A. Turman	1961–1963	Gober	Democrat
Bryon M. Tunnell	1963–1965	Tyler	Democrat
Ben Barnes	1965–1969	DeLeon	Democrat
Gus Mutscher	1969–1972	Brenham	Democrat
Rayford Price	1972–1973	Palestine	Democrat
Price Daniel, Jr.	1973–1975	Liberty	Democrat
Bill Clayton	1975–1983	Springlake	Democrat
Gib Lewis	1983–1993	Fort Worth	Democrat
James E. "Pete" Laney	1993–2003	Hale Center	Democrat
Tom Craddick	2003–	Midland	Republican

*Ben Ramsey resigned as lieutenant governor on September 18, 1961, upon his appointment to the Railroad Commission. The office was vacant until Preston Smith took office in 1963.

Source: Texas Legislative Council, *Presiding Officers of the Texas Legislature,* 1846–1982 (Austin: Texas Legislative Council, 1982).

But veteran Democratic Representative James E. "Pete" Laney, a farmer-businessman from Hale Center, secured the support of the necessary majority of House members several weeks before the 1993 legislature convened, and his election on the opening day of the session was unopposed.

Laney served five terms as speaker and, although he was a Democrat, enjoyed the support of many Republican House members. Continuing a bipartisan tradition, he appointed several Republicans to chair House committees. But Republicans, after winning a strong majority of House seats in the 2002 elections, elected state Representative Tom Craddick, a Republican from Midland, to succeed Laney as presiding officer in 2003. Craddick, a House member since 1969, became the first Republican speaker of modern times. Laney, who had won re-election to his West Texas district in 2002, remained in the House, becoming the first former speaker in years to return to a seat on the House floor after serving as presiding officer.

It is illegal for a speaker candidate to make outright promises in return for members' support, but, continuing a tradition, Craddick's key supporters won choice leadership positions when the new speaker exercised one of his most significant formal powers and made his committee assignments. Legislators know that the earlier they hop onto a winning bandwagon in a speaker's race, the better chance they probably will have at getting their preferred committee assignments and support for their legislative programs. Sometimes, however, choosing the winning candidate is difficult because the campaigning is largely conducted behind the scenes with candidates making personal pleas to individual House members.

Until the 1950s, it was unusual for a speaker to serve more than one two-year term. The position was circulated among a small group of legislators who dominated the House. Clayton, a lawmaker from Springlake in West Texas, set what was then a record by serving four consecutive terms before retiring in 1983. Lewis of Fort Worth and Laney each surpassed Clayton's record by serving five terms.

Unlike most of their predecessors, Clayton, Lewis, Laney, and Craddick devoted long hours to the job and kept large full-time staffs. With the complexities of a growing state putting more demands on the legislative leadership, recent Senate leaders (lieutenant governors) also have made their jobs virtually full time and also have hired large staffs of specialists to research issues and help develop legislation. The presiding officers also depend on key committee chairmen to take the lead in pushing through their legislative priorities.

During Laney's speakership, the state completed a multibillion-dollar expansion of its prison system, overhauled criminal justice laws and enacted a school finance law that addressed a Texas Supreme Court order for more equity in education spending. In a bipartisan endeavor, Laney actively supported then-Gov. George W. Bush's unsuccessful effort to replace a large chunk of local school property taxes with higher state taxes in 1997. He also encouraged opposing sides to find common ground on other major issues, but one of his own priorities was to improve the way the House conducted its business. Laney won significant changes in House rules that produced, in the view of many House members, a more democratic lawmaking process than under previous speakers.

Backed by a strong Republican majority, Craddick was a key figure in the legislature's tight-fisted approach to drafting the new state budget in 2003, which cut spending in many areas to bridge a $10 billion revenue shortfall. He was a strong opponent of raising state taxes, although he insisted the legislature enact a separate law allowing university governing boards to raise college tuition. Craddick also was

Speaker Tom Craddick (R-Midland) was elected speaker, the first Republican since Reconstruction, in 2003.

a key figure in the legislature's enactment of the redistricting bill to increase the number of Republicans elected to Congress from Texas. He was a consistently tough negotiator. "He's the toughest, hardest trader I've ever met. When you start trading with the speaker, it's tough trading," said state Senator Steve Ogden, a Republican from Bryan and a longtime friend of Craddick's.[12]

The speaker appoints a speaker pro tempore, or assistant presiding officer, who is usually a close ally. In 1981, Speaker Clayton named the first African American, Representative Craig Washington of Houston, to the post. Although Clayton was a rural conservative and Washington was an urban liberal, Washington was a critical member of the speaker's team. He also exercised considerable influence in the House on a wide range of issues of importance to minorities. Ten years later, Gib Lewis named another African-American legislator, Representative Wilhelmina Delco of Austin, as the first woman speaker pro temore.

The membership of most House committees is determined partly by seniority. The speaker has total discretion, however, in naming committee chairs and vice chairs and in appointing all the members of procedural committees, including the influential Calendars Committee, which will be described in more detail later in this chapter. Under a rules change in 2003, Craddick also had total discretion—without regard for seniority—in appointing the budget-writing House Appropriations Committee. The new speaker bumped some senior Democratic members from the panel.

The Lieutenant Governor

The lieutenant governor is chosen by the voters in a statewide election to serve a four-year term as presiding officer of the Senate. Unlike the vice president of the United States—the counterpart in the federal government, who has only limited legislative functions—the lieutenant governor has traditionally been the Senate's legislative leader. This office, elected independently of the governor, has often been called the most powerful office in state government because of the lieutenant governor's opportunity to merge a statewide electoral base into a dominant legislative role.[13] Lieutenant governors, however, get most of their power from rules set by the senators, not from the constitution.

The lieutenant governor's power is based in part on the same coalitional strategies that are used by the speaker through committee assignments and relationships with interest groups. But the lieutenant governor has traditionally had more direct control over the Senate's agenda than the speaker has over the House's. Under longstanding Senate rules, the lieutenant governor determines when—and if—a committee-approved bill will be brought up for a vote by the full Senate. In the House, the order of floor debate is determined by the Calendars Committee. Although that key panel is appointed by the speaker and is sensitive to the speaker's wishes, it represents an intermediate step that the lieutenant governor doesn't have to encounter.

The lieutenant governor also has had more formal control over the membership of Senate committees than the speaker has over House panels. Under longstanding rules, the Senate has allowed the lieutenant governor to appoint members of all standing committees without restrictions.

The Senate has a president pro tempore, or assistant presiding officer, who is chosen by senators from among their membership. This position is rotated among the senators on a seniority basis. It is held for a limited period, and the holder of the position is third in line of succession to the governorship. There is a tradition that the governor and the lieutenant governor both allegedly "leave" the state on the same day so that the president pro tempore can serve as "governor for a day" at one point during his or her term.

Bill Hobby, a quiet-spoken media executive who served a record eighteen years as lieutenant governor before voluntarily leaving the office in January 1991, patiently sought consensus among senators on most major issues and rarely took the lead in promoting specific legislative proposals. One notable exception occurred in 1979, when Hobby tried to force Senate approval of a presidential primary bill opposed by most Democratic senators. After Hobby served notice that he would alter the Senate's traditional operating procedure to give the bill special consideration, twelve Democratic senators, dubbed the "Killer Bees," hid out for several days to break a quorum and keep the Senate from conducting business. They succeeded in killing the bill and reminding Hobby that the senators set the rules.

Hobby's successor, Bob Bullock, had demonstrated strong leadership and a mercurial personality during sixteen years as state comptroller. Upon taking office as lieutenant governor, he had major policy changes in mind for state government and was impatient to see them carried out by the legislature. Unlike Hobby, Bullock took the lead in making proposals and then actively lobbying for them. During his first session in 1991, he reportedly had shouting matches with some lawmakers behind closed doors and one day abruptly and angrily adjourned the Senate when not enough members were present for a quorum at the scheduled starting time. But his experience and knowledge of state government and his tireless work habits won the respect of most senators and their support for most of his proposals.

Bullock, a Democrat, strengthened his leadership role during the 1993 and 1995 sessions and was actively involved in every major issue that the Senate addressed. Recognizing that increases in Republican strength after the 1992 and 1994 elections made the Senate more conservative than it had been in several years, and eager to strengthen his support in the business community, Bullock saw to it that compromises on major issues—including some long sought by business—were reached behind closed doors before they were made public. This approach kept controversy to a minimum and defused partisanship, but it distressed consumer advocates and environmentalists, who felt excluded from the process. It also prompted remarks that the Senate had abandoned democracy. There were so many unanimous or near-unanimous votes in the Senate in 1993 that some House members joked that senators who wanted to show dissent voted "aye" with their eyes closed.[14]

Bullock played a less active role during the 1997 session, after Republicans, for the first time this century, had won a majority of Senate seats. He was strongly supportive of some key legislation, including a statewide water conservation and management plan, but he did little to promote a property tax relief effort that Governor Bush had made his highest priority for the session. One key element of Bush's proposal, an increase in state taxes as a partial tradeoff for lower school district taxes, died primarily because of strong Senate opposition, which Bullock didn't try to defuse.

A few days after the 1997 session ended, Bullock surprised the Texas political community by announcing that he would not seek reelection in 1998. The former state leader, who had a history of health problems, was later diagnosed with lung cancer, and he died in June 1999.

After defeating Democrat John Sharp in a hard-fought race in 1998, former Agriculture Commissioner Rick Perry became Texas's first Republican lieutenant governor of modern times in 1999. Perry not only had to follow in Bullock's legendary footsteps, he also had to preside over the Senate during a session overshadowed by Governor George W. Bush's anticipated presidential race. The new lieutenant governor had the advantage, though, of entering the 1999 session with a $6 billion state budgetary surplus and a rare absence of emergencies. Perry lost one of his top priorities, a pilot project to allow students in low-performing public schools to use state-paid vouchers to transfer to private schools. But he generally received high marks for his performance during the session, from both Democrats and Republicans. Perry was more low key than Bullock, perhaps choosing to learn more about the Senate and its members before plunging into potential controversies. Nevertheless, he was credited with helping Republican and Democratic lawmakers negotiate a compromise on one of the key legislative packages of the session—a series of tax cuts, teacher pay raises, and other increased education spending.

Perry was elected to a lieutenant governor's term that wasn't to expire until January 2003. But in anticipation of Governor Bush's presidential race, the legislature in 1999 approved a constitutional amendment—which Texas voters later endorsed—to make it clear that Perry would have to give up the lieutenant governor's job in midterm if he were promoted to fill a vacancy in the governor's office. After Bush resigned the governorship in December 2000 to become president, Perry was promoted to governor. And, acting under the new constitutional amendment, senators elected state Senator Bill Ratliff, R-Mount Pleasant, to serve as lieutenant governor during the 2001 session.

Ratliff, a former chairman of the Senate Education and Finance committees, was businesslike in his role as presiding officer, and he generally received favorable reviews. He appointed the first African American, state Senator Rodney Ellis, D-Houston, to chair the budget-writing Finance Committee. He also parted ways with most Republican senators and supported Ellis's bill to strengthen the state law against hate crimes, which passed that session. And Ratliff blocked a bill that would have removed state

— HOW I SEE IT —
GET INVOLVED IN POLITICS

Mireya Zapata

A native of Puerto Rico, Mireya Zapata graduated from high school in Frankfurt, Germany, and holds a bachelor's degree in journalism from the University of Texas at Austin. Her first job in politics, while she was still a university student, was as a press aide in Democrat Garry Mauro's unsuccessful gubernatorial race in 1998. She also worked in two other statewide campaigns and as an assistant clerk for a committee of the Texas House before becoming chief of staff for state Representative Patrick Rose of Dripping Springs in 2003. She was interviewed for this book by one of the authors.

Q: Did you grow up around politics?

A: My late grandfather helped found the Democratic Party in Puerto Rico. And, I remember as a kid going to political rallies with my dad and waving signs. It was just something that was always there, that was always part of our dinner conversation.

Q: What do you like about working in politics?

A: I think it's rewarding in a unique way. You see results of what you do in such a personal manner. A woman calls because she's having problems getting her child support payments, and you can help by calling the attorney general's office. You're helping that woman in a very personal way. If a senior citizen is having problems with his property taxes, or whatever it may be, it's so real, and it hits home in day-to-day life. You can actually go home and think about what you did today and see that you've made an impact in your community. Also, people talk about how we young people are the future. I'm kind of helping pave the way for my generation's future.

Q: What do you not like, if anything, about campaigns and the governmental process?

A: I've worked for some people who had some very admirable qualities. But I think it's disappointing sometimes to see their strengths, their passion, and their commitment to the state be less important than their financial resources. I dislike the role that money plays in the political process. Sometimes the amount of money a candidate has ends up being more important than whether that person has the right qualities to be an elected official.

Q: Would you advise other young people to get involved in politics?

A: Yes. Even if they don't plan on it being their career, I think being involved in any capacity— whether it's working during a legislative session or volunteering in a campaign—broadens your view of the world. You're exposed to so many different issues. You meet such a wide variety of people that it really can change the kind of person that you are. You also should experience state government because whether you are a part of it or not, it affects your life.

Q: Would you like to run for an elected office someday?

A: That's not something I'm working towards. But I'm addicted. I really am. I'm addicted to politics.

Q: What other lessons have you learned from your involvement in government and politics?

A: You should look beyond the partisanship. Most of the people I've worked for have been Democrats. But I would rather see an 18-year-old vote for a Republican in an election than not vote at all. Participation is the most important thing.

legal restrictions against Native Americans operating casinos on their reservations in Texas. At the end of the 2001 session, Ratliff announced that he would seek election to the lieutenant governor's post in 2002. But several days later, admitting he didn't have the stomach for the compromises often involved in a statewide race, he announced that he had changed his mind and would seek reelection to his Senate seat instead. "I do love policy-making, but I do not love politics," he said.[15] Republican David Dewhurst won the 2002 lieutenant governor's race over Democrat John Sharp, who had narrowly lost the same office to Rick Perry in 1998.

Dewhurst, a wealthy businessman, had no legislative experience when he became the Senate's presiding officer in January 2003. His only experience in elected office had been his four previous years as state land commissioner, but he moved quickly to establish credibility as a leader. He appointed respected legislative insiders to key staff positions and spent many hours studying issues and meeting with individual senators. Although Republicans held a 19–12 Senate majority, he continued the tradition of appointing both Republicans and Democrats to leadership positions.

Dewhurst agreed with Gov. Rick Perry and Speaker Tom Craddick that the legislature would bridge a $10 billion revenue shortfall and write a new state budget without increasing state taxes. But he and the Senate helped to minimize some of the spending cuts by insisting that lawmakers tap into non-tax revenue, such as the state's Rainy Day savings account. On such budgetary details and other matters, including how quickly the legislature should move to improve the school finance system, Dewhurst sometimes differed with Perry and Craddick. Their differences stemmed partly from Dewhurst's independent nature, which was bolstered by the fact that he—not special interest groups—had largely funded his election to the state's powerful No. 2 office. The Senate's rules also required the lieutenant governor to seek more consensus among senators than the speaker normally has to do in the House. Legislation traditionally wasn't approved in the Senate without the consent of

David Dewhurst became Lt. Governor in 2003.

two-thirds of the senators, which meant that the 12 Democratic senators had enough clout to force some budgetary concessions.

Dewhurst orchestrated the Senate's biggest show of independence during the 2003 regular session by hammering out in a series of private meetings a new public education funding plan that would have raised the state sales tax in exchange for sharp reductions in local property taxes, which were increasingly under fire, particularly in many suburban and heavily Republican school districts. Dewhurst won unanimous Senate approval of the proposal, but the House never acted on it. Craddick and Perry insisted instead that lawmakers conduct another study of school finance, which already had been studied several times in recent years, and attempt to tackle the issue later, perhaps in a special session.

Senate unanimity disappeared—and Dewhurst's leadership was severely challenged—during the bitter partisan fight over congressional redistricting that took three special sessions in the summer and fall of 2003 to resolve. Democratic senators blocked a House-passed redistricting bill during the first special session by using a Senate tradition that required two-thirds of the senators to approve debate on any legislation. After Dewhurst announced that he would bypass that procedure—known as the "two-thirds rule"—to allow a redistricting bill to be passed on a simple majority vote during the second special session, eleven of the Senate's twelve Democrats fled to Albuquerque, N.M., where they remained for more than a month. Their flight, which received national media coverage, deprived the Senate of a quorum and the ability to conduct any business during the entire, 30-day second special session. It also severely damaged the Senate's tradition of personal and partisan cooperation. Democratic and Republican senators exchanged verbal attacks across state lines, with Dewhurst also catching much of the Democrats' anger. The ill feelings increased when Republican senators voted to impose sanctions, including thousands of dollars in fines, on the absentee Democrats. The boycotting senators eventually returned to Austin, and the legislature approved a congressional redistricting bill favoring Republicans during a third special session. The Republicans waived the fines but put the Democrats on probation, which meant the fines would be imposed if Democrats broke a quorum again. Dewhurst immediately began working behind the scenes to try to restore the Senate's ability to conduct business in a civil fashion, and he had his work cut out for him.

Influence and Control over the Legislative Process

The power of each presiding officer to appoint committees and determine which committee will have jurisdiction over a specific bill gives the speaker and the lieutenant governor tremendous influence over the lawmaking process.

The speaker and the lieutenant governor control the legislative process through the application of rules, including those set in the state constitution and those adopted by the House and the Senate. Each presiding officer is advised on procedures by a parliamentarian. The speaker and the lieutenant governor do not participate in House or Senate debate on bills and usually attempt to present an image of neutral presiding officers. Their formal powers, however, are further strengthened by their informal relationships with their committee leaders and interest groups. And, with the notable exceptions of the separate walkouts by House and Senate Democrats during the 2003 redistricting battle, the speaker and the lieutenant governor rarely lose control of the process.

In the Senate, the lieutenant governor can vote only to break a tie. The speaker can vote on any issue in the House but normally abstains from voting except to break a tie or to send a signal to encourage reluctant or wavering House members to vote a particular way on an issue.

The Leadership Teams

Traditionally, there has been no formal division along party lines or a formal system of floor leaders in either the Texas House or the Senate. The long-time, Democratic-dominated legislative system with the speaker's and lieutenant governor's control of committee appointments did not produce a leadership structure comparable to that of the U.S. Congress. The committee chairs constitute the speaker's and lieutenant governor's teams and usually act as their unofficial floor leaders in developing and building support for the leadership's legislative priorities. Most chairs are philosophically, if not always politically, aligned with the presiding officers.

THE COMMITTEE SYSTEM

The committee system is the backbone of the legislative process, and it is molded by the lieutenant governor and the speaker.[16] It is a screening process that decides the fate of most legislation.

The committee is where technical drafting errors and oversights in bills can be corrected and where compromise can begin to work for those bills that do eventually become law. Only 1,405 of the 5,753 bills and constitutional amendments introduced in the 2003 regular session won final legislative approval. Most of those that didn't make it died in a Senate or a House committee, many without ever being heard. Rarely does a committee kill a bill on an outright vote, because there are less obvious ways to scuttle legislation. A bill can be gutted, or so drastically amended or weakened that even its sponsor can hardly recognize it. Or it can simply be ignored.

Committee chairs have considerable power over legislation that comes to their committees. They may kill bills by simply refusing to schedule them for a hearing. Or, after a hearing, a chair may send a bill to a subcommittee that he or she stacks with members opposed to the legislation, thus allowing the bill to die slowly and quietly in the legislative deep freeze. Even if a majority of committee members want to approve a bill, the chair can simply refuse to recognize such a motion. Most chairs, however, are sensitive to the wishes of the presiding officers. If the speaker or the lieutenant governor wants a bill to win committee approval or another measure to die in committee, a chair usually will comply.

Referral to a subcommittee doesn't always mean the death of a bill. Subcommittees also help committees distribute the workload. They work out compromises, correct technical problems in bills, or draft substitute legislation to accommodate competing interest groups.

Standing Committees

The number and names of committees are periodically revised under House and Senate rules, but there have been relatively few major changes in the basic committee structure in recent years. During the 2003 sessions, the Senate had fifteen **standing committees,** varying in membership from five to fifteen.

There were forty-two standing committees in the House, with memberships ranging from five to twenty-nine (see Table 8–4). Most of these committees are substantive. That is, they hold public hearings and evaluate bills related to their particular subject areas, such as higher education, natural resources, or public health. A few committees are procedural, such as the Rules and Resolutions Committee, which handles many routine congratulatory resolutions, and the Calendars Committee, which schedules bills for debate by the full House.

TABLE 8–4   Senate and House Standing Committees: 78th Legislature, 2003

Senate Committee	Number of Members
Administration	7
Business and Commerce	9
Criminal Justice	7
Education	9
Finance	15
Government Organization	7
Health and Human Services	9
Infrastructure Development and Security	9
Intergovernmental Relations	5
International Relations and Trade	7
Jurisprudence	7
Natural Resources	11
Nominations	7
State Affairs	9
Veterans Affairs and Military Installations	5

House Committee	Number of Members
Agriculture and Livestock	7
Appropriations	29
Border and International Affairs	7
Business and Industry	9
Calendars	11
Civil Practices	9
Corrections	7
County Affairs	9
Criminal Jurisprudence	9
Defense Affairs and State-Federal Relations	9
Economic Development	7
Elections	7
Energy Resources	7
Environmental Regulation	7
Financial Institutions	7
General Investigating	5
Government Reform	7
Higher Education	9
House Administration	11

TABLE 8–4 (Continued)

House Committee	Number of Members
Human Services	9
Insurance	9
Judicial Affairs	9
Juvenile Justice and Family Issues	9
Land and Resource Management	9
Law Enforcement	7
Licensing and Administrative Procedures	9
Local and Consent Calendars	11
Local Government Ways and Means	7
Natural Resources	9
Pensions and Investments	7
Public Education	9
Public Health	9
Redistricting	15
Regulated Industries	7
Rules and Resolutions	11
Select Committee on Ethics	7
Select Committee on State Health Care Expenditures	11
State Affairs	9
State Cultural and Recreational Resources	7
Transportation	9
Urban Affairs	7
Ways and Means	9

Source: Texas House and Senate.

Some committees play more dominant roles in the lawmaking process than others, particularly in the House. The House State Affairs Committee, for example, handles many more major statewide bills than the Committee on State Cultural and Recreational Resources or the Committee on Agriculture and Livestock. The House Urban Affairs and County Affairs committees handle several hundred bills of importance to local governments each session. The importance of a committee is determined by the area of public policy over which it has jurisdiction or by its role in the House's operating procedure.

The House **Calendars Committee** historically has had more life-and-death power over legislation than any other committee because it sets the order of debate on the House floor. During each regular session, it kills hundreds of bills that have been approved by various substantive committees by refusing to set them for debate by the full House or scheduling them so late in the session they don't have time to win Senate approval. This committee traditionally works closely with the speaker and is one means by which the speaker and his team control the House. Although many legislators complain about the committee killing their priority bills, some lawmakers defend the panel as a means of keeping controversial legislation—on which many members would rather not have to cast votes—from reaching the House floor. "You have to realize that all bills do not get to the floor," then-Speaker Gib Lewis said in 1991. "You have to realize also that a lot of committee chairmen who have taken a great deal of heat over a long period of time—from authors or special interest groups—they'll finally pass a bill out and say, 'I hope we can kill it in Calendars.'"[17]

The state budget is the single most important bill enacted by the legislature because, through it, lawmakers determine how much money is spent on the state's public programs and services. In the House, the Appropriations Committee takes the lead in drafting state budgets, while the House Ways and Means Committee normally is responsible for producing any tax or revenue measures necessary to balance the budget.

The two most important committees in the Senate are the Finance Committee, which handles the budget and, usually, tax bills, and the State Affairs Committee, which, like its House counterpart, handles a variety of legislation of major, statewide importance.

Although committees have general subject areas of responsibility, legislative rules allow the lieutenant governor and the speaker some latitude in assigning bills. The presiding officer can assure the death of a bill by sending it to a committee known to oppose it or can guarantee quick approval of a measure by referring it to a receptive, or friendly, panel.

Standing Subcommittees

The U.S. Congress has developed a highly diversified subcommittee system.[18] Standing committees are divided into standing subcommittees that operate from one session to the next. These standing subcommittees are defined by the rules and have jurisdiction over specific legislative matters. There are only a few standing subcommittees in the Texas legislature. Most committee chairs in the legislature have traditionally appointed subcommittees of three to five members, as needed, to handle specific bills.

Conference Committees

Legislation must be passed in exactly the same form by the House and the Senate. If one chamber refuses to accept the other's version of a bill, a **conference committee** can be requested to try to resolve the differences. Conference committees of five senators and five representatives are appointed by the presiding officers. A compromise bill has to be approved by at least three senators and three House members who serve on the conference committee before it is sent back to the full House and the full Senate for subsequent approval or rejection. Over the years, conference committees have drafted legislation in forms dramatically different from earlier versions approved by the House or the Senate. But since a conference panel is supposed to do no more than adjust the differences between the House and the Senate versions of a bill, both chambers have to pass a concurrent resolution to allow a conference committee to add significant new language.

Special Committees

Special or **select committees** are occasionally appointed by the governor, the lieutenant governor, and the speaker to study major policy issues, such as tax equity or school finance. Select panels often include private citizens as well as legislators, and they usually recommend legislation. Standing legislative committees also study issues in their assigned areas during the interims between sessions, and the presiding officers can ask them to conduct special investigations or inquiries pertaining to governmental matters.

RULES AND PROCEDURES

Laws are made in Texas according to the same basic process followed by the U.S. Congress and other state legislatures.[19] But, as the discussion of the committee system already has indicated, the rules that determine how and when legislation is considered are complex and loaded with traps where legislation can be killed (Figure 8–2). One often hears the remark around the Capitol that "there are a lot more ways to kill a bill than to pass one." Legislators and lobbyists who master the rules can wield a

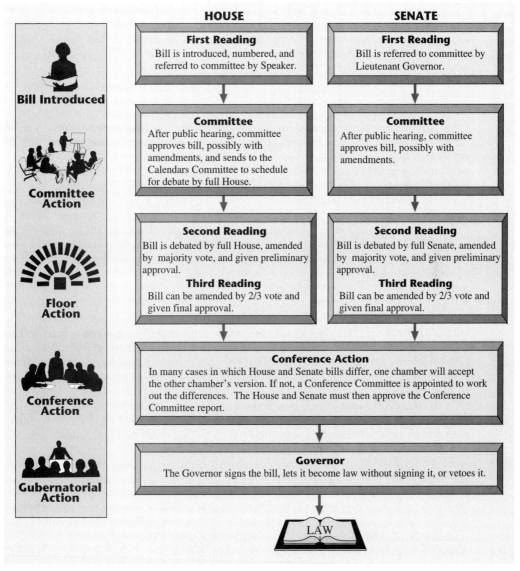

Bill Introduced	**HOUSE**	**SENATE**
	First Reading Bill is introduced, numbered, and referred to committee by Speaker.	**First Reading** Bill is referred to committee by Lieutenant Governor.
Committee Action	**Committee** After public hearing, committee approves bill, possibly with amendments, and sends to the Calendars Committee to schedule for debate by full House.	**Committee** After public hearing, committee approves bill, possibly with amendments.
Floor Action	**Second Reading** Bill is debated by full House, amended by majority vote, and given preliminary approval. **Third Reading** Bill can be amended by 2/3 vote and given final approval.	**Second Reading** Bill is debated by full Senate, amended by majority vote, and given preliminary approval. **Third Reading** Bill can be amended by 2/3 vote and given final approval.
Conference Action	**Conference Action** In many cases in which House and Senate bills differ, one chamber will accept the other chamber's version. If not, a Conference Committee is appointed to work out the differences. The House and Senate must then approve the Conference Committee report.	
Gubernatorial Action	**Governor** The Governor signs the bill, lets it become law without signing it, or vetoes it.	

LAW

FIGURE 8–2   Basic Steps in the Texas Legislative Process.

tremendous amount of influence over the lawmaking process. The House and the Senate each has a detailed set of rules governing the disposition of legislation, and each has a parliamentarian to help interpret them.

The simplified outline of the process by which a bill becomes a law starts with the introduction of a bill in the House or the Senate and its referral to a committee by the presiding officer, which constitutes first **reading.** That is the only reading that most bills will ever get.

A bill that wins committee approval can be considered on second reading by the full House or Senate, where it is debated and often amended. Some amendments are designed to improve a bill, while others are designed to kill it by loading it down with controversial or objectionable provisions that will prompt legislators to vote against it. Still other amendments that may be punitive toward particular individuals or groups are sometimes offered. Such an amendment, which may be temporarily added to a bill only to be removed before the measure becomes law, is designed to give a group or perhaps a local official a message that the sponsoring legislator expects his or her wishes to be heeded on a particular issue. Lawmakers also may offer amendments that they know have little chance of being approved merely to make favorable political points with constituents or interest groups.

If a bill is approved on second reading, it has to win one more vote on **third reading** before it goes to the other chamber for the same process, beginning with its referral to a committee.

If the second chamber approves the bill without any changes, or amendments, it then goes to the governor for signature into law or **veto.** The governor also can allow a bill to become law without his or her signature. This procedure is just the opposite of the pocket veto power afforded the president of the United States. If the president doesn't sign a bill approved by Congress by a certain deadline, it is automatically vetoed. If the governor of Texas doesn't sign or veto a bill by a certain deadline, it becomes law. A veto can be overridden and the bill allowed to become law by a two-thirds vote of both houses, although this process is rarely attempted.

The governor has to accept or reject a bill in its entirety, except for the general **appropriations bill,** or state budget, from which the governor can delete specific spending proposals. This power is called a **line-item veto.** The budget and any other bill approved by the legislature that appropriates money has to be certified by the comptroller before it is sent to the governor. Texas has a pay-as-you-go state government, and the comptroller has to certify that there will be enough available revenue to fund the bill.

If the second chamber amends the bill, the originating house has to approve, or concur in, the changes or request a conference committee. Any compromise worked out by a conference committee has to be approved by both houses, without further changes, before it is sent to the governor.

All bills except revenue-raising measures can originate in either the House or the Senate. Tax bills must originate in the House, although the legislative leadership severely bent that rule to win approval in a special session in 1991 of a tax bill necessary to balance a new state budget. After the House had dismantled a $3.3 billion revenue bill recommended by its Ways and Means Committee and sent the Senate nothing but a $30 million shell, Lieutenant Governor Bullock and the Senate, in consultation with lobbyists, took over the writing of a new tax bill, which the House later approved.

Other Procedural Obstacles to Legislation

Pieces of legislation also encounter other significant procedural obstacles. In the House, there is the Calendars Committee, which was discussed earlier in this chapter. In the Senate, there is the two-thirds rule.

The **two-thirds rule** for debating bills on the Senate floor has been a strong obstacle to controversial bills because it means that only eleven senators, if they are determined enough and one isn't absent at the wrong time, can keep any proposal from becoming law. This rule also is a source of the lieutenant governor's power. After a bill is approved by a committee, its sponsor can have it placed on the daily intent calendar. If the sponsor is recognized by the lieutenant governor, he or she will seek Senate permission to consider the bill. A sponsor can have majority Senate support for a measure but will watch it die if he or she cannot convince two-thirds of the senators to let the body formally debate it.

The two-thirds rule also gives a senator the opportunity to vote on both sides of an issue. Sometimes a senator will vote to bring up a bill and then vote against the measure when it is actually passed and only a majority vote is required for approval. This enables the senator to please the bill's supporters, give the sponsor a favor that can be repaid later, and, at the same time, tell the bill's opponents that he or she voted against the measure.

As noted earlier in this chapter, Lieutenant Governor David Dewhurst suspended the two-thirds rule to break a partisan impasse and win Senate approval of

State Senator Gonzalo Barrientos of Austin puts on comfortable shoes in anticipation of a lengthy filibuster.

a Republican-backed congressional redistricting bill during a special session in 2003. But the procedure still enjoyed strong support among senators. Any attempt to permanently repeal it would have to be made at the beginning of a legislative session, when the Senate adopts its procedural rules.

The Senate rules also provide for **tags** and **filibusters,** both of which can be effective in killing bills near the end of a legislative session. A tag allows an individual senator to postpone a committee hearing on any bill for at least forty-eight hours, a delay that is often fatal in the crush of unfinished business during a session's closing days. The filibuster, a procedure that allows a senator to speak against a bill for as long as he or she can stand and talk, is usually little more than a nuisance to a bill's supporters early in a session, but it also can become a potent and ever-present threat against controversial legislation near the end of a session. Sometimes several senators will engage in a tag-team filibuster, taking turns speaking against a bill. Often, the mere likelihood of a senator speaking against a bill is sufficient to kill a measure. Late in a session, the lieutenant governor may refuse to recognize the sponsor of a controversial bill for fear a filibuster will fatally delay other major legislative proposals. State Senator Bill Meier of Euless spoke for forty-three hours in 1977 against a bill dealing with the public reporting of on-the-job accidents. In so doing, he captured the world's record for the longest filibuster, which he held for years.

Shortcuts, Obfuscation, and Confusion

Sponsors of legislation languishing in an unfriendly committee or subcommittee often try to resurrect their proposals by attaching them as amendments to related bills being debated on the House or Senate floor. Such maneuvers often are successful, particularly if opponents are absent or if the sponsor succeeds in "mumbling" his amendment through without challenge. But the speaker or the lieutenant governor must find that such amendments are germane to the pending bill if an alert opponent raises a point of order against them.

To facilitate the passage of noncontroversial and local pieces of legislation, the House and the Senate have periodic local and consent or local and uncontested **calendars,** which are conducted under special rules that enable scores of bills to be routinely and quickly approved by the full House or Senate without debate. Bills of major statewide significance, even controversial measures, sometimes get placed on these calendars, but it takes only one senator or three representatives to have any bill struck. Legislators will sometimes knowingly let a controversial bill slip by on a local calendar without moving to strike it so as not to offend the sponsor or the presiding officer. But to protect themselves politically, should the bill become an issue later, they will quietly register a vote against the measure in the House or Senate journal.

Compromises on controversial legislation often are worked out behind closed doors long before a bill is debated on the House or Senate floor or even afforded a public committee hearing. It can be argued that this approach to consensus building is an efficient, businesslike way to enact legislation. But it also serves to discourage the free and open debate that is so important to the democratic process.

Recent speakers also have discouraged the taking of **record votes** during House floor debate on most bills. Many important issues are decided with "division" votes, which are taken on the computerized voting machine but leave no formal record of

---

VOTING FOR A DEAD MAN

When record votes are taken, House rules prohibit members from punching the voting buttons on other members' desks, but the practice occurs regularly. Sometimes members will instruct their desk mates or other legislators to cast specific votes for them if they expect to be absent when the votes are called for. Other legislators make a habit of punching the voting buttons at all the empty desks within easy reach. This practice is normally challenged only in cases of close votes, when members of the losing side request a roll-call verification of the computerized vote, and the votes of members who do not answer the roll call are struck.

The House was embarrassed in 1991 when a dead lawmaker was recorded as answering the daily roll call and voting on several record votes. The legislator had died in his Austin apartment, but his body wasn't discovered for several hours. Meanwhile, colleagues had been pushing his voting button. This practice is not a problem in the Senate, where the secretary of the Senate orally calls the roll on record votes.

---

how individual legislators have voted once the voting boards are cleared (see "Voting for a Dead Man"). This approach saves the taxpayers some printing costs and can give lawmakers some respite from lobby pressure. But it also serves to keep the taxpaying public back home in the dark about significant decisions made by their elected representatives. The fewer the record votes legislators have to make, the more easily they can dodge accountability to their constituents.

Often, legislators have their minds made up on an issue before the matter is debated on the floor. But there are many bills during each legislative session that most lawmakers will have little or no interest in and won't bother to study. When legislators are not familiar with a bill, they often simply vote the way the sponsor votes or the way the House or Senate leadership wants them to vote. Despite what tourists in the gallery may think, legislators who raise their fingers above their heads when a vote is taken are not asking the presiding officer for a rest break. They are signaling the way they are voting and encouraging other lawmakers to vote the same way. One finger means yes; two fingers mean no.

Partly because of the rules under which the legislature operates, partly because of the heavy volume of legislation, and partly because of political maneuvering, the closing weeks of a regular session are hectic. Legislators in both houses are asked to vote on dozens of conference committee reports they do not have time to read. With hundreds of bills being rushed through the legislature to the governor's desk, mistakes occur. Deliberate attempts are also made—often successfully—to slip in major changes in law through the confusion. For every surprise bill or special interest amendment that is caught, dozens slip through and become law.

THE EMERGING PARTY SYSTEM

Unlike the U.S. Congress, the Texas legislature is not organized along party lines, with rules that automatically give leadership positions to members of the majority party. The arrangement in Texas is due primarily to the absence of Republican legislators for many years and the more recent practice—before Republicans gained a

House majority in 2003—of rural Democrats aligning themselves with a Republican minority to produce a conservative coalition. As recently as 1971, the year before a federal court declared urban, countywide House districts unconstitutional, there were only ten Republicans in the House and two in the Senate. As Republicans increased their numbers, they aligned themselves with conservative Democrats to attempt to control the policymaking process. This ideological coalition became increasingly important as single-member districts boosted not only the number of Republican lawmakers but also the number of moderate and liberal Democratic legislators elected from urban areas. It became a means of maintaining some legislative control for conservative Democrats as the base of power shifted in their own party.

Republicans and conservative Democrats formally organized the Texas Conservative Coalition in the House in the 1980s. The coalition remained a strong force in the 1990s, chaired for several years by Representative Warren Chisum of Pampa, who switched from the Democratic to the Republican party in 1995. Chisum's mastery of the rules blocked many pieces of legislation on technicalities.

On occasion, liberal Democrats and conservative Republicans have formed "unholy alliances," but these coalitions were usually short-lived. During the controversy over the Sharpstown stock fraud scandal in 1971, liberal Democrats and Republicans formed a loose coalition called the "Dirty Thirty" that continually harassed House Speaker Gus Mutscher, who not only was a key figure in the scandal but also epitomized the rural conservative Democratic tradition of the statehouse.

The Growth of Partisanship

With the growth of the Republican party in Texas in the 1980s, Speaker Gib Lewis, a conservative urban Democrat, appointed Republicans to major committee chairs in the House. But partisan divisions increased in 1987 when Lewis, Democratic Lieutenant Governor Bill Hobby, and Republican Governor Bill Clements fought over a new state budget in the face of a huge revenue shortfall. On one side of the debate were moderate and liberal Democratic legislators, including inner city and South Texas minorities whose constituents had the most to gain from a tax increase and the most to lose from deep cuts in spending on human services and educational programs. On the other side were a handful of conservative, primarily rural Democrats and a number of Republicans with middle- and upper-middle-class suburban constituents who insisted on fiscal restraint. Clements eventually gave in and supported a tax increase, but most of the House Republicans continued to fight the measure until it was approved in a summer special session.

In 1989, Republicans formed their first caucus in the House, and soon both parties had active caucuses in both the House and the Senate, which began to play key roles in marshaling legislative support on selected issues. They also became active in legislative races as Republicans began to mount aggressive, well-financed challenges of Democratic incumbents.

During the 1995 legislative session, when Democrats still held a majority of House and Senate seats, Lieutenant Governor Bob Bullock and Speaker Pete Laney, both Democrats, continued the practice of naming Republicans, as well as Democrats, to committee chairs. Bullock and Laney also were strongly supportive of Republican Governor George W. Bush's legislative priorities. All three leaders cooperated in making major changes in public education and juvenile justice and setting limits on civil liability lawsuits.

After many bitterly contested legislative races, Republicans won their first majority of the Senate in modern times during the 1996 elections and gained four seats in the House to narrow the Democratic majority in that body to 82–68. Nonpartisanship, however, still prevailed for the most part in the 1997 session. Bullock, the Democratic lieutenant governor, gave Republicans some new leadership positions in the Senate but named Democrats to chair most committees. The Senate, which had a 17–14 Republican majority, slammed the door on an attempt by Bush to trade higher state taxes for major cuts in local school taxes, and opposition came from both Democratic and Republican senators. Special interests who did not want to pay the higher taxes were a more significant factor than partisanship in the death of the tax bill. The House had approved the tax tradeoff, with Bush persuading many Republicans in the House to vote for the measure. But legislative fights with strong partisan overtones increased in 1997 and subsequent sessions over such issues as abortion, gay rights, and whether tax dollars should be spent to pay for private school tuition for some students (see "The 'Memorial Day Massacre'").

Another partisan-charged issue in 1999 and 2001 was an attempt by some Democrats to strengthen the state law against hate crimes, after three white men in East Texas were accused—and later convicted—of dragging an African-American man, James Byrd Jr., to death behind a pickup truck. Most of the Republican opposition to the bill was because it increased penalties for crimes motivated by prejudice against homosexuals as well as prejudice over race or religion. That provision was opposed by social conservatives, and in 1999 Governor George W. Bush—who did not want to anger conservatives on the eve of his race for the Republican presidential nomination—called the bill unnecessary. The measure, which sponsors named for Byrd, died in the Senate in 1999 but was passed in 2001.

Republicans Take Control

Aided by the redrawn legislative districts discussed earlier in this chapter, Republicans made major gains in the 2002 elections. They increased their majority in the state Senate to 19–12, captured an 88–62 majority in the Texas House, their first since Reconstruction, and elected Republican Tom Craddick of Midland as speaker. Those victories, plus Gov. Rick Perry's election, gave Republicans control of all the points of power in the statehouse. They controlled the budget-setting process, making significant cuts in services to close a $10 billion revenue shortfall, enacted significant new restrictions on civil lawsuits and won the contentious fight over congressional redistricting. Throughout the year, partisanship was stronger than it had been since the GOP became a competitive party in Texas.

Craddick and David Dewhurst, the new Republican lieutenant governor, both appointed Democrats, as well as Republicans, to chair committees and serve in other leadership positions. Democrats chaired six of the Senate's fifteen standing committees and thirteen of the forty-two committees in the House. Craddick also appointed a Democrat, state Representative Sylvester Turner of Houston, as speaker pro tempore. But Craddick stacked the key chairmanships and the membership of the budget-writing House Appropriations Committee with Republicans who clearly reflected his conservative viewpoint. After winning a change in House rules that

THE "MEMORIAL DAY MASSACRE"

Partisan differences, which were building in the years leading up to the Republican takeover of the Texas House in 2003, erupted on the evening of Memorial Day in 1997, one week before the regular legislative session ended. They were ignited by fights over a bill to require parents to be notified before their minor daughters could receive abortions and a measure that would have prohibited the recognition of gay marriages in Texas. Both measures were to be approved in later years, but they died in the 1997 session, despite the strong support of social conservatives, who formed a significant bloc among Republicans in the House.

After abortion rights supporters and other Democratic House members used parliamentary maneuvers to block debate on both bills, Representative Arlene Wohlgemuth, a Republican from Burleson, used a technical procedural point to block consideration of fifty-two other bills remaining on the House's Memorial Day calendar. Wohlgemuth's move effectively killed most of the bills because that day was the deadline for the House to consider any legislation on second reading. Sponsors managed to save only a few of the measures, including an education bill strongly supported by then-Governor George W. Bush, by tagging them on as amendments to related bills that had already won House approval.

Wohlgemuth said she was simply retaliating against House members who killed the bills on abortion restrictions and same-sex marriages, which social conservatives believed would have passed had they been able to vote on them. "I think that a statement needs to be made about why measures that are important to families, important to the people of this state, have not been heard, have not been voted on," she said.

Wohlgemuth's action was not entirely partisan because some of the bills that she killed or jeopardized, including Bush's education priority, were sponsored by other Republican legislators. But the action had strong partisan overtones and was a preview of future legislative sessions.

Representative Kent Grusendorf of Arlington, an outspoken Republican critic of then-Democratic Speaker Pete Laney, supported Wohlgemuth. He said committees controlled by Democrats had stalled bills that were important to Republicans and had majority support in the House.

But long-time Democratic Representative Dan Kubiak of Rockdale, in a speech on the House floor, strongly criticized Wohlgemuth's tactic. Kubiak said the incident—which he dubbed the "Memorial Day Massacre"—"was only the latest outbreak of the cancer that threatens not only this body, but the democratic process itself."

Kubiak died the next year, and the voters in his central Texas district replaced him with a Republican. Partisanship remained a threat in the statehouse.

_____

Source: Dallas Morning News, May 28, 1997.

removed seniority as a factor in appropriations appointments, the new speaker bumped from the panel three outspoken Democrats who opposed budget cuts.

Partisanship will remain part of the legislative process for the foreseeable future. Before too many more years, the legislature may even organize itself along the same partisan lines as the U.S. Congress—with distinct party positions, such as floor leaders, caucus leaders, and whips. If this were to happen, the legislative rules and powers of the presiding officers discussed earlier in this chapter would be significantly changed. But this development will depend on how long Republicans continue to dominate the statehouse, on how Democrats continue to react and on the future leadership personalities that emerge in both parties. Another factor will be how well the two factions in the Republican party—the traditional fiscal conservatives and the social conservatives—are able to accommodate each other's interests.

OTHER LEGISLATIVE CAUCUSES

Hispanic- and African-American House members formed their own **caucuses** as their numbers began to increase in the 1970s in the wake of redistricting and creation of urban single-member districts. Their cohesive blocs of votes have proved influential in speaker elections and the resolution of major statewide issues, such as health care for the poor, public school finance, and taxation. Their ability to broker votes has won committee chairs and other concessions they may not otherwise have received (see "Gregory Luna and Irma Rangel, Champions of Education").

Some urban delegations, such as the group of legislators representing Harris County, the state's most populous county, have formed their own caucuses to discuss and seek consensus on issues of local importance. In Harris County's case, however, consensus is rarely found on major local controversies because of the political, ethnic, and urban-suburban diversity within the delegation. Twenty-five House members—one-sixth of the body's membership—represent various parts of Houston and Harris County, and seven senators have districts that are wholly within or include part of the county. On many occasions, debate in committees and on the House or Senate floor has bogged down into Houston fights over mass transportation, annexation, or fire and police civil service.

LEGISLATORS AND THEIR CONSTITUENTS

Although representative government is an essential component of American society, there are continued debates as to how people elected to public office should identify the interests and preferences of the people they represent.[20] Political theorists as well as legislators struggle with the problem of translating the will of the people into public policy. Most legislators represent diverse groups and interests in their districts. During a normal legislative session, there are thousands of proposed laws to consider, and legislators must constantly make decisions that will benefit or harm specific constituents.

Except for an occasional controversial issue—such as whether motorcycle riders should have to wear safety helmets or whether private citizens should be allowed to carry pistols—most Texans pay little attention to what the legislature is doing. That is why they often are surprised to discover they have to pay a few extra dollars to register their cars or learn that the fee for camping in a state park has suddenly been increased. Very few Texans—particularly in the large cities that are divided up among numerous lawmakers—can identify their state representatives or senators by name, and far fewer can tell you what their legislators have voted for or against. This public inattention gives a legislator great latitude when voting on public policies. It also is a major reason why most incumbent lawmakers who seek reelection are successful. Most legislative turnover is the result of voluntary retirements, not voter retribution. Several Democratic incumbents, however, fell victim to redistricting that

GREGORY LUNA AND IRMA RANGEL, CHAMPIONS OF EDUCATION

Gregory Luna and Irma Rangel made important contributions to young people, particularly minorities, in the legislature and other public forums.

Luna, whose father died when he was an infant, knew firsthand the difficulties that many Texas children faced in securing an education and a chance at a better life. He was only 11 when he got his first job as a busboy in a restaurant. After working as a police officer to help put himself through college and law school, Luna then devoted much of his adult life to improving civil rights and educational opportunities for Hispanics and all Texans.

As an attorney in San Antonio in 1968, Luna helped found the Mexican American Legal Defense and Educational Fund (MALDEF), which has waged successful courtroom fights for civil rights. MALDEF has forced school boards and other governments to redraw political boundaries to assure minority representation on governing bodies. And in the 1980s, MALDEF filed a landmark lawsuit against the state that forced the Texas legislature to more equitably distribute state education dollars among wealthy and poor school districts.

Luna served in the Texas House from 1985 to 1992 and in the state Senate from 1993 until illness forced his resignation in September 1999. He died only a few weeks later of complications related to diabetes. He was 66.

Luna was chair of the Senate Hispanic Caucus and vice chair of the Senate Education Committee, and throughout his legislative career he fought for further reforms of school funding and for improved educational opportunities. His legislative style was usually low key, but he was effective. He knew what he had to do to accomplish a goal and quietly went about doing it.

"He was a monument of many, many people who were able to benefit from his efforts for a better education system for everyone," said the Rev. Virgil Elizondo. "He was in the ministry of public service."[†]

Rangel, a Democrat from Kingsville, was a schoolteacher and a prosecutor before becoming, in 1976, the first Hispanic woman elected to the Texas House. She chaired the House Higher Education Committee for several years and sponsored a state law to boost affirmative action by requiring Texas colleges and universities to automatically admit students who graduated in the top 10 percent of their high school classes. She also was instrumental in boosting state funding for higher education institutions along the border with Mexico.

Rangel was still a member of the House—its fifth most senior member—when she died of cancer in March 2003 at age 71. State Representative Pete Gallego, D-Alpine, chairman of the Mexican-American Legislative Caucus, called Rangel's life a "testament to everything that is good about public service."[*]

Sources: [†]The Associated Press, as published in the *Houston Chronicle,* November 10, 1999.

[*]*Houston Chronicle,* March 19, 2003, p. 25A.

---

favored Republican challengers in 2002. Some were unseated at the polls, and others didn't seek reelection because of the redrawn district lines.

Media coverage of the legislature is uneven. The large daily newspapers with reporters in Austin make commendable efforts to cover the major legislative issues and players and provide both spot news accounts and in-depth interpretation of the legislature's actions. All too frequently, however, they are limited by insufficient space, and they rarely publish individual voting records or attempt to evaluate the performances of individual legislators. Most television and radio news shows provide only cursory legislative coverage.

Although legislators are aware of latent public opinion, they tend to be more responsive to the interest groups, or attentive publics, that operate in their individual districts or statewide.[21] People who are well-informed and attentive to public policy issues are a small portion of the total population, but they can be mobilized for or against an individual legislator. In some instances, these are community opinion leaders who, directly or indirectly, are able to communicate information to other individuals about a legislator's performance. Or they may belong to public interest and special interest groups that compile legislative voting records on selected issues of importance to their memberships. Although these records are only sporadically disseminated by the news media to the general public, they are mailed to the sponsoring groups' members.

Many special interest groups contribute thousands of dollars to a legislator's reelection campaign or to the campaign of an opponent. But politically astute legislators duly take note of all the letters, phone calls, petitions, e-mail messages, and visits by their constituents—plus media coverage—lest they lose touch with a significant number of voters with different views on the issues and thus become politically vulnerable.

A favorite voter-contact tool of many legislators is a newsletter they can mail to households in their districts at state expense. These mailings usually include photos of the lawmaker plus articles summarizing, in the best possible light, his or her accomplishments in Austin. Sometimes, legislators also include a public opinion survey seeking constituent responses on a number of issues.

LEGISLATIVE DECISION-MAKING

In addition to the formal rules of each legislative body, there are unwritten rules, or **norms,** that shape the behavior of legislators and other actors in the lawmaking process.[22] The legislature is like most other social institutions in that its members have perceptions of the institution and the process as well as the way they are expected to behave or carry out their responsibilities. Other participants also impose their views and expectations on lawmakers.

The legislative process is designed to institutionalize conflict, and the rules and norms of the legislature are designed to give this conflict an element of civility. Debate is often intense and vigorous, and it may be difficult for some lawmakers to separate attacks on their positions from attacks on their personalities. But most legislators have learned the necessity of decorum and courtesy. Even if lawmakers believe some of their opponents in the House and Senate are deceitful, personal attacks on other legislators are considered unacceptable. Personal attacks, even to the point of fistfights, occasionally occur, but they are rare (see "How Legislators Are Supposed to Act").

With about 5,700 pieces of legislation introduced during a regular session—the level reached in 2003—no legislator could possibly read and understand each bill, much less the hundreds of amendments offered during floor debate. And while there are moments of high drama when issues of major, statewide importance are being debated, most of the legislative workload is tedious and dull and produces little direct political benefit for most senators and representatives. But many of those bills

---

HOW LEGISLATORS ARE SUPPOSED TO ACT

Legislative "folkways," or legislative norms, refer to lawmakers' shared standards of conduct—what is regarded as appropriate behavior or what is expected of a legislator. Although they may be more important in some states than in others, most of the standards listed here are honored as part of the professionalism in nearly every state legislature. Mavericks occasionally violate the "rules of the game," but most newcomers to the legislature soon discover these and similar norms and honor them.

- Treat your colleagues with respect. Do not make personal attacks on them or harass them.
- Serve an apprenticeship. Take some time to do your homework and go through a learning process before charging around acting like a "know-it-all."
- Don't be a publicity hound. Stay away from the microphone unless you really have something to say.
- Don't conceal the real purpose of a bill or purposely overlook some portion of it in order to assure its passage.
- Don't make a commitment on a vote until you are ready to be bound by it. Keep your word. Be reliable when you have made a commitment.
- Committee work is your punishment for getting elected. Effective legislators specialize enough in their subject areas to be able to advise their colleagues, especially those not on their committees.
- Reciprocate when you can. Support your friends and colleagues whenever possible so that they will support you whenever they can.
- Defend the legislature when it comes under attack from the press, the governor, or other critics. Institutional patriotism is much admired by your colleagues.
- Don't burn your bridges. Learn to get along with others. Remember, today's foe may be tomorrow's ally in a crucially close vote on some new matter. A policy of "no permanent enemies" usually works best.

Source: James MacGregor Burns, J. W. Peltason, Thomas E. Cronin, David B. Magleby, L. Tucker Gibson Jr., and Clay Robison, *Government by the People: Texas Version,* 2nd ed. (Upper Saddle River, NJ: Prentice Hall, 1998), p. 670.

---

contain hidden traps and potential controversies that can haunt a legislator later, often during a reelection campaign. So legislators use numerous information sources and rely on the norms of the process to assist them in decision-making.

To make the process work, legislators must accommodate the competing interests they represent and achieve reciprocity with their fellow legislators. An individual legislator will usually have no direct political or personal interest in most bills because much legislation is local in nature and affects only a limited number of lawmakers and constituents. A legislator accumulates obligations as he or she supports another lawmaker's bill, with the full expectation that the action will be returned in kind.

A number of other factors, however, help shape lawmakers' decisions on major legislation.[23] The wishes of constituents are considered, particularly if there is a groundswell of dominant opinion coming from a legislator's district. Legislators also exchange information with other lawmakers, particularly with members of the same caucus, members who share the same political philosophy, and colleagues from the same counties or regions of the state. Lawmakers often take their cues from the sponsors of a bill or the speaker's and lieutenant governor's leadership teams. As the political parties develop more formal legislative structures, identifiable patterns of giving and taking cues are likely to emerge along party lines. That process already has begun to a significant extent on budgetary, taxation, and redistricting issues, as was demonstrated during the 2003 sessions.

A legislator's staff also assists in the decision-making process, not only by evaluating the substantive merits of legislation but also by assessing the political implications of a lawmaker's decisions. The Legislative Budget Board and the Legislative Council provide technical information and expertise that also can be weighed by legislators.

Interest groups are major sources of information and influence. Although an individual legislator will occasionally rail against a specific group, most lawmakers consider interest groups absolutely essential to the legislative process. Through their lobbyists, interest groups provide a vast amount of technical information and can signal the level of constituency interest, support, or opposition to proposed laws. A senator or representative can use interest groups to establish coalitions of support for a bill, and some legislators become closely identified with powerful interest groups.

The governor can also influence the legislature in several ways. He or she can raise the public's consciousness of an issue or need and can promote solutions through speeches and through the media. Governors can communicate indirectly to individual lawmakers through the governor's staff, party leaders, and influential persons in a lawmaker's district. Governors can also appeal personally to lawmakers in one-on-one meetings or in meetings with groups of legislators.

At the beginning of each regular session, the governor outlines his or her legislative priorities in a "state of the state" address to a joint session of the House and the Senate and usually has frequent meetings with the lieutenant governor and the speaker throughout a session. The governor may also visit the House or the Senate chamber in a personal show of support when legislation that he or she strongly advocates is being debated. Unlike most recent governors, Governor Ann Richards personally testified before legislative committees on several of her priorities, including ethics reform and government reorganization, during her first year in office.

The severity of a governor's arm-twisting is often in the arm of the beholder, but it can include appeals to a lawmaker's reason or conscience, threats of retaliation, appeals for party support, and promises of a quid pro quo. The greatest threat that a governor can hang over a legislator is the possible veto of legislation or a budget item of importance to the lawmaker. In a special session, the governor also can negotiate with a lawmaker over whether to add a bill that is important to the legislator to the special session's agenda, which is controlled by the governor.

Legislators also get information and support from other elected statewide officeholders, such as the attorney general, the comptroller, or the land commissioner. These officials and lawmakers can assist each other in achieving political agendas.

The news media provides information and perspective on issues in broader political terms. In part, the policy agenda is established by those issues the media perceives to be important.

The relative importance of any groups or actors on decision-making is difficult to measure and varies from lawmaker to lawmaker and from issue to issue (see "Some Influences on Legislators' Votes"). Outside influences can be tempered by a legislator's own attitude and opinion. On many issues, legislators get competing advice and

---

SOME INFLUENCES ON LEGISLATORS' VOTES

- Personal political philosophies
- Other legislators
- Their staffs
- Interest groups and lobbyists
- The governor
- Other elected administrators and state agency heads
- Legislative leaders
- Party leaders
- Local elected officials
- The media
- Court decisions
- Regional blocs within the state
- Legislative caucuses
- National trends
- Programs that have worked in other states

Source: Burns et al., p. 675.

---

pressure. As much as a lawmaker may like to be all things to all people, that cannot be. She cannot please a chemical lobbyist, who is seeking a tax break for a new plant on the Gulf Coast and also happens to be a large campaign contributor, and environmentalists, who fear the facility would spoil a nearby wildlife habitat. He cannot please the governor, who is promoting casino gambling as a new state revenue source, and most of the voters in his district, who have consistently voted against gambling. The ultimate decision and its eventual political consequences are the legislator's.

Should lawmakers cast votes on the basis of the specific concerns of their districts, their personal convictions, the position of political parties, or the wishes of the special interest groups that helped fund their campaigns? These criteria reflect complex relationships between the legislator and the people represented. And since the overriding consideration for most lawmakers is to get reelected, the legislator must balance them carefully.

LEGISLATIVE STYLES

Some legislators become known for their commitment to producing good legislation. These workhorses spend endless hours developing programs. They seem to overload themselves with legislation and are repeatedly turned to by the presiding officers to handle tough policy issues. Other lawmakers tend to defer to their leadership, direction, and cues, and their influence is essential to a productive legislative session.

Other legislators earn reputations as grandstanders. Almost every legislator has shown off for the media or the spectators in the gallery at one time or another, but there are a number who develop a distinct reputation for this style of behavior. They appear to be more interested in scoring political points with their constituents or interest groups—with the objective of being reelected or seeking higher office—than with mastering the substance of legislation. Many of these lawmakers are lightweights who contribute little to the legislature's product. And, while they may introduce many bills during a session, they are not interested in the details of the lawmaking process and are unable to influence other legislators to support their legislation.

The legislature also has a number of opportunists, including members who pursue issues to produce personal or political benefits for themselves. They may sponsor legislation or take a position on an issue to curry favor with a special interest group or bring benefit to their personal businesses or professions. Legislative rules prohibit legislators from voting on issues in which they have a personal monetary interest, but individual lawmakers can interpret that prohibition as they see fit. Many lawmakers will try to cash in on their legislative experience by becoming lobbyists after they leave office at considerably higher pay than they received as legislators.

Still other legislators appear to be little more than spectators. They enjoy the receptions and other perks of the office much more than the drudgery of committee hearings, research, and floor debate. Some quickly become weary of the legislative process and, after a few sessions, decide against seeking reelection.[24]

THE DEVELOPMENT OF LEGISLATIVE STAFF

The quality of a legislator's staff can help determine his or her success, and both the quality and quantity of legislative staffs have been significantly enhanced since the early 1970s.[25] This growth reflects an emerging professional approach to lawmaking and meeting the needs of an increasingly complex, urban state. During recent regular sessions, the House has had about 900 employees, including part-time workers, and the Senate about 800. These figures included Capitol and district office staff for individual senators and representatives, the committee staffs, assistants to the lieutenant governor and the speaker, and other support staff hired directly by the House and the Senate.

Additionally, there are permanent staff members assigned to the Legislative Budget Board, the legislature's financial research arm; the Legislative Council, which researches issues and drafts bills and resolutions for introduction by legislators; and the Legislative Reference Library, which provides resource materials for lawmakers, their staffs, and the general public. Other support staff are assigned to the Sunset Advisory Commission, which assists the legislature in periodic reviews of state agencies, and the state auditor, who is chosen by and reports to the legislative leadership.

Legislative staffers range from part-time secretaries and clerks to lawyers and other professionals who draft bills and provide research that results in major state laws. There are limits on the number of staff members and funds allocated for legislators' personal staffs. As a general rule, senators have larger staffs than House members. Staffing levels are usually reduced between sessions, and some members shut down their Capitol offices entirely. Most lawmakers, however, maintain offices both in Austin and in their home districts, even if their staffs function only to answer the phone.

A key support group in the House is the House Research Organization, which was organized as the House Study Group in the 1970s by a handful of primarily liberal lawmakers. The group's name was later changed, and its structure was reorganized to represent the entire House, but it still fills a strong research role. It is

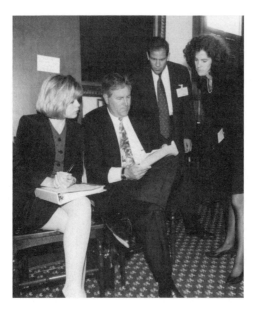

State Senator Ken Armbrister of Victoria talking with staff.

supported by funds from the House budget and is governed by a steering committee that represents a cross section of Democratic and Republican House members. During legislative sessions, its staff provides detailed analyses, including pro and con arguments, of many bills on the daily House calendar. During interims between sessions, it provides periodic analyses of proposed constitutional amendments and other issues. In 1991, the Senate formed a similar organization, the Senate Research Center, that performs similar functions.

The quality of other resources available to lawmakers also has improved in recent years. Legislators and their staffs can routinely check the status or texts of bills online, and so can the public. The Legislative Council maintains a website on the Internet that includes committee schedules, bill texts and analyses, and other legislative information. Private citizens also can use the website to identify their state representatives and senators.

LEGISLATIVE ETHICS AND REFORM

The vast majority of legislators are honest, hard-working individuals. But the weaknesses of a few and the millions of dollars spent by special interests to influence the lawmaking process serve to undermine Texans' confidence in their legislature and their entire state government (see "A Dubious Distinction"). Although most of us will always view the actions of our public officials with a certain degree of skepticism—for that is an integral part of our system—a lack of confidence in our elected officials can promote disrespect for our governmental institutions, deepen apathy toward the political process and, in turn, strengthen the influence of the special interests.

Legislators cannot pass laws guaranteeing ethical behavior, but they can set strong standards for themselves, other public officials, and lobbyists and provide stiff

---

A DUBIOUS DISTINCTION

Senator Drew Nixon, R-Carthage, made history the hard way when he was sentenced to six months in the Travis County jail in 1997 for unlawfully carrying a weapon. He became the first Texas legislator to ever serve a jail sentence while in office. Nixon's sentence stemmed from his arrest during a prostitution sting in Austin during the 1997 legislative session. According to police, he was arrested for agreeing to pay a female undercover officer $35 for sex. A loaded pistol, which he was not licensed to carry, also was found under his car seat.

Nixon pleaded guilty to both charges but asked a Travis County jury for probation. He got probation and a $2,000 fine on the prostitution conviction. But jurors sentenced him to jail on the weapons violation because he had pleaded no contest to a similar charge in Dallas and got probation four years earlier, before he was elected to the Senate. Nixon served his sentence on weekends after the legislative session ended. He didn't seek reelection in 2000.

---

penalties for those who fail to comply. Such reform efforts are periodically attempted, but, unfortunately, they usually are the result of scandals and fall short of creating an ideal ethical climate.

The **Sharpstown stock fraud scandal** rocked the Capitol in 1971 and 1972 and helped produce some far-reaching legislative and political changes.[26] It involved banking legislation sought by Houston banker-developer Frank Sharp that was approved by the legislature in a special session in 1969, only to be vetoed by Governor Preston Smith. A lawsuit filed in 1971 by the federal Securities and Exchange Commission broke the news that Smith, House Speaker Gus Mutscher, Representative Tommy Shannon of Fort Worth, who had sponsored the bills, and others had profited from stock deals involving Sharp's National Bankers Life Insurance Company. Much of their stock was purchased with unsecured loans from Sharp's Sharpstown State Bank.

Mutscher, Shannon, and an aide to the speaker were convicted of conspiracy to accept bribes. Mutscher, who had consolidated power in the House and was often regarded as ironhanded and arbitrary, was forced to resign. Later, the House moved to limit the speaker's power through a modified seniority system for committee appointments. Subsequent speakers still exercised a great deal of power, but it was constrained by expectations that the speaker would be more responsive to the membership. The media also started giving greater scrutiny and coverage to the activities of the speaker.

Fallout from the Sharpstown scandal helped an outsider, Uvalde rancher Dolph Briscoe, win the 1972 gubernatorial race and helped produce a large turnover in legislative elections. In 1973, the legislature responded with a series of ethics reform laws, including requirements that lobbyists register with the secretary of state and report their total expenditures in trying to influence legislation. State officials were required to file public reports identifying their sources of income, although not specific amounts.

Weaknesses in those laws, however, were vividly demonstrated in 1989, when wealthy East Texas poultry producer Lonnie "Bo" Pilgrim distributed $10,000 checks to several senators in the Capitol while lobbying them on workers' compensation reform, and the Travis County district attorney could find no law under which to prosecute him. There also were published reports that lobbyists had spent nearly $2 million entertaining lawmakers during the 1989 regular session without having to specify which legislators received the "freebies," thanks to a large loophole in the lobby registration law. The revelations—including frequent news stories about lobbyists treating lawmakers to golf tournaments, ski trips, a junket to Las Vegas for a boxing match, and limousine service to a Cher concert—created an uproar.

Some senators had angrily rejected Pilgrim's checks on the spot, while others returned them after the media pounced on the story. But the very next year, Pilgrim—a long-time political contributor—again contributed thousands of dollars to several statewide officeholders and candidates. This time, the checks were not offered under the Capitol dome but were more traditionally sent through the mail, and they were gratefully accepted. Only one officeholder, who was passed over by Pilgrim in favor of his opponent, tried to make a campaign issue of the new contributions.

Despite all the headlines over ethical problems, legislative turnover was minimal in 1990. But in early December, about a month after the general election, a Travis County grand jury began investigating Speaker Gib Lewis's ties to a San Antonio law firm, Heard, Goggan, Blair, and Williams. The firm had made large profits collecting delinquent taxes for local governments throughout Texas under a law that allowed it to collect an extra 15 percent from the taxpayers as its fee. For several years, it had successfully defeated legislation that would have hurt its business. The *Fort Worth Star-Telegram* reported that Heard Goggan had paid about half of a $10,000-tax bill owed to Tarrant County by a business that Lewis partly owned.[27] And the *Houston Chronicle* reported that the grand jury was also looking into a trip that Lewis had taken to a Mexican resort during the 1987 legislative session with four Heard Goggan partners and a lobbyist (all males) and six women (including a waitress from a topless nightclub in Houston).[28] The trip had been taken while a bill opposed by Heard Goggan was dying in a House committee.

On December 28, only twelve days before the 1991 regular legislative session was to convene and Lewis was to be reelected to a record fifth term as the House's presiding officer, grand jurors indicted Lewis on two misdemeanor ethics charges. He was accused of soliciting, accepting, and failing to report an illegal gift from Heard Goggan—the partial payment of the tax bill. Lewis insisted he was innocent and vowed to fight the charges. He said the tax payment was the settlement of a legal dispute. And he angrily accused Travis County District Attorney Ronnie Earle, who headed the prosecution and had been publicly advocating stronger ethics laws, of using the grand jury to "influence the speaker's election." Lewis said Earle was guilty of "unethical and reprehensible behavior."[29]

Lewis won a postponement of his trial under a law that automatically grants continuances to legislators when they are in session. The grand jury investigation, which prosecutors said would include other legislators or former legislators, continued for several more weeks, but no more indictments were issued.

Meanwhile, considerable attention was focused on an ethics reform bill. Governor Ann Richards, who had campaigned for reform, personally testified before House and Senate committees for tougher ethical requirements for state officials and lobbyists. The Senate approved an ethics bill fairly early in the session, but the House did not act on its version of the bill until late in the session. The final bill was produced by a conference committee on the last night of the session in a private meeting and was approved by the House and the Senate only a few minutes before the legislature adjourned at midnight. There wasn't time to print and distribute copies, and very few legislators knew for sure what was in the bill.

This performance and the bill itself left a bad taste all around. Despite complaints that the measure wasn't strong enough and the controversy over the secretive way in which the final compromise had been written, Richards signed the bill. But she did so in the privacy of her office, not in the public ceremony that governors usually hold for their priority pieces of legislation. Ronnie Earle, the Travis County district attorney, was among those displeased with the legislation, and the best that former Congresswoman Barbara Jordan, the governor's ethics adviser, could say about the measure was that it was a "worthy effort." But Richards called the new law a "very strong step in the direction of openness and ethics reform in this state." The new law required more reporting of lobby expenditures and conflicts of interest between lobbyists and state officials, prohibited special interests from treating legislators to pleasure trips, prohibited lawmakers from accepting honoraria—or fees—for speaking before special interest groups, and created a new state Ethics Commission to review complaints about public officials.

But the measure did not put any limits on financial contributions to political campaigns, nor did it prohibit legislator-attorneys from representing clients before state agencies for pay. Moreover, it authorized the Ethics Commission to slap a bigger fine ($10,000) on someone who filed a frivolous complaint against a public official than the maximum fine ($5,000) that could be levied on an officeholder for violating the ethics law. That latter provision was viewed by many critics as an unreasonable effort to discourage citizen complaints. The new law also provided that complaints filed with the Ethics Commission would remain confidential unless the commission took action, a provision that would allow the commission to dismiss or sit on legitimate complaints without any public accounting.

In January 1992, Lewis announced that he wouldn't seek reelection to another term in the House. In a plea bargain later the same month, prosecutors dropped the two ethics indictments against Lewis in return for the speaker's "no contest" plea to two minor, unrelated charges. Lewis paid a $2,000 fine for failing to publicly disclose a business holding in 1988 and 1989, for which he had already paid a minor civil penalty to the secretary of state.

Lewis's decision to retire set off the first speaker's race in the House since 1975, and many House members, including most of the first-term legislators, used the campaign to bargain for reforms in the way the House conducted its business. As noted earlier, some of those reforms were adopted in 1993 with the support of the new speaker, Pete Laney, who, ironically, had been a long-time member of Lewis's team. The first-term legislators, in particular, had complained in 1991 that the House rules had been used to create an undemocratic process that catered to special interests and favored an inner circle of legislators close to the speaker.

The legislature enacted other significant changes in ethics laws in 2003. The new provisions required officeholders and candidates to identify the occupations and employers of people who contribute more than $500, required financial reports to be filed with the Ethics Commission electronically, increased penalties for people who filed their reports late, restricted—but didn't prohibit—legislators from representing clients before state agencies, and required—for the first time—officeholders and candidates for municipal offices in the large cities to file personal financial disclosure statements.

SUMMARY AND CONCLUSIONS

1. Texas, the nation's second most populous state, has a part-time, low-paid legislature that operates under restrictions drafted by nineteenth-century Texans in the wake of the repressive Reconstruction era. There are serious questions about the legislature's ability to respond readily to modern needs and crises. Because lawmakers meet in regular session only every other year, emergencies sometimes require special legislative sessions.

2. On a continuum from a highly professional legislature to a citizen or amateur lawmaking body, the Texas legislature is somewhere in between. Turnover is moderate.

3. As recently as 1971, there were only a handful of African Americans, Hispanics, Republicans, and women in the 150-member House of Representatives and the thirty-one-member Senate. But political realignment and federal court intervention in redistricting, particularly the ordering of single-member House districts for urban counties in 1972, have significantly increased the number of women, ethnic minorities, and Republicans in the legislature. Republicans now have a majority of both the Texas House and the state Senate.

4. Unlike the U.S. Congress, the Texas legislature is not organized along party lines and has only the tentative beginnings of an institutionalized leadership structure. The presiding officer of the House is the speaker, who is elected by the other House members. The presiding officer of the Senate is the lieutenant governor, who is elected by the voters statewide. Leadership in both the House and the Senate has been highly personalistic, centering on the presiding officers and their legislative teams.

5. The most significant powers of the speaker and the lieutenant governor are the appointment of House and Senate committees that screen and draft legislation and the assignment of bills to committees. The fate of most pieces of legislation is decided at the committee level. The presiding officers also play key roles in the development of major legislative proposals and, to a great extent, depend on their hand-picked committee chairs to sell their legislative programs to House and Senate colleagues.

6. To be sent to the governor for signature into law, a bill must be approved on three readings in both the House and the Senate. Referral to committee is first reading, and that is as far as most bills get. Many are never scheduled for a hearing by the chairs of the committees to which they are assigned. Many others die in subcommittees.

7. Other hurdles to legislation are the Calendars Committee in the House and the two-thirds rule in the Senate. The Calendars Committee, composed entirely of speaker appointees, sets the schedule for floor debate in the House, and the two-thirds rule prohibits any bill from being debated on the Senate floor without the approval of two-thirds of the senators.

8. For those bills that survive the committee process, second reading is a crucial step. This is where most floor debate on legislation occurs and where many bills are further amended. If a bill is approved on second reading, it advances to third reading and, if approved again, then to the other legislative chamber, where it is referred to committee and has to repeat the process.

9. To become law, a bill has to be approved in exactly the same form by both chambers. A conference committee of House and Senate members often has to work out a compromise when the versions passed by the two chambers differ.

10. The governor can sign a bill, veto it, or let it become law without his or her signature. The governor can use the line-item veto to delete specific spending provisions from the general appropriations bill, or state budget. But all other bills have to be accepted or rejected in their entirety.

11. Tax bills must originate in the House. All other bills can originate in either chamber.

12. The legislative rules and heavy volume of bills considered sometimes enable lawmakers to sneak major, controversial proposals into law by adding little-noticed amendments to other bills.

13. The growth of Republican strength has increased partisan activity in the legislature and fueled speculation that, sooner or later, attempts may be made to organize the

legislature along the partisan lines of the U.S. Congress. Both major parties already have active legislative caucuses.

14. There is considerable diversity among legislators in style and work habits. Their decisions are influenced by a number of factors, including constituents, interest groups, colleagues, staff, the governor, and the media.

15. Although most legislators are honest, hardworking individuals, the weaknesses of a few and the millions of dollars spent by special interests to influence the lawmaking process serve to undermine Texans' confidence in state government. Lawmakers make periodic efforts to strengthen their ethical standards, but usually only after well-publicized scandals.

KEY TERMS

Institutionalization
Bicameral legislature
Regular session
Special session
Redistricting
Speaker
Standing committee
Calendars Committee

Conference committee
Select committee
Reading
Third reading
Veto
Appropriations bill
Line-item veto
Two-thirds rule

Tag
Filibuster
Calendar
Record vote
Caucus
Norms
Sharpstown stock fraud scandal

FURTHER READING

Articles

Anderson, Arthur J., "Texas Legislative Redistricting: Proposed Constitutional and Statutory Amendments for an Improved Process," *Southwestern Law Journal* 43 (October 1989), pp. 719–57.

Bickerstaff, Steve, "State Legislative and Congressional Reapportionment in Texas: A Historical Perspective," *Public Affairs Comment* 37 (Winter 1991), pp. 1–13.

Boulard, Garry, "Lobbyists as Outlaws," *State Legislatures* 22 (January 1996), pp. 20–25.

Edwards, Julie, "The Right to Vote and Reapportionment in the Texas Legislature," *Baylor Law Review* 41 (December 1989), pp. 689–730.

Freeman, Patricia K., "A Comparative Analysis of Speakers' Career Patterns in U.S. State Legislatures," *Legislative Studies Quarterly* 20 (August 1995), pp. 365–76.

Hamm, Robert, and Robert Harmel, "Legislative Party Development and the Speaker System: The Case of the Texas House," *Journal of Politics* 55 (November 1993), pp. 1140–51.

King, James D., "Changes in Professionalism in U.S. State Legislatures," *Legislative Studies Quarterly* XXV (May 2000), pp. 327–43.

Kubin, Jeffrey C., "The Case for Redistricting Commissions," *Texas Law Review* 75 (March 1997), pp. 837–872.

Moncrief, Gary F., Joel A. Thompson, and Karl T. Kurtz, "The Old Statehouse, It Ain't What It Used to Be," *Legislative Studies Quarterly* 21 (February 1996), pp. 57–72.

Mooney, Christopher Z., "Citizens, Structures and Sister States: Influences on State Legislative Professionalism," *Legislative Studies Quarterly* 20 (February 1995), pp. 47–67.

Thielemann, Gregory S., "Committee Leadership and Power in the Texas Legislature," in *Texas Politics: A Reader*, eds. Anthony Champagne and Edward J. Harpham. New York: W. W. Norton, 1997.

Thorburn, Wayne, "The Growth of Republican Representation in the Texas Legislature: Coattails, Incumbency, Special Elections, and Urbanization," *Texas Journal of Political Studies* 11 Spring/Summer 1989), pp. 16–28.

Books

Barber, James David, *The Lawmakers*. New Haven, CT: Yale University Press, 1965.

Blondel, J., *Comparative Legislatures*. Englewood Cliffs, NJ: Prentice Hall, Inc., 1973.

Deaton, Charles, *The Year They Threw the Rascals Out*. Austin, Shoal Creek Press, 1973.

Fenno, Richard F., *Home Style: House Members in Their Districts*. Boston: Little, Brown, 1978.

Herskowitz, Mickey, *Sharpstown Revisited: Frank Sharp and a Tale of Dirty Politics in Texas.* Austin: Eakin Press, 1994.

House Research Organization, *Term Limits: Tenure or Turnover,* No. 186 (February 4, 1994).

Jewell, Malcolm E., and Samuel C. Patterson, *The Legislative Process in the United States,* 4th ed. New York: Random House, 1986.

Jones, Nancy Baker, and Ruthie Winegarten, *Capitol Women: Texas Female Legislators, 1923–1999.* Austin: University of Texas Press, 2000.

Keefe, William J., and Morris S. Ogul, *The American Legislative Process: Congress and the States,* 8th ed. Englewood Cliffs, NJ: Prentice Hall, Inc., 1993.

Kingdon, John W., *Congressmen's Voting Decisions,* 2nd ed. New York: Harper & Row, Publishers, 1981.

Mayhew, David, *Congress: The Electoral Connection.* New Haven, CT: Yale University Press, 1974.

Rosenthal, Alan, *Legislative Life: People, Process and Performance in the States.* New York: Harper & Row, Publishers, 1981.

———, *Governors and Legislatures: Contending Powers.* Washington, DC: Congressional Quarterly Books, 1990.

———, *The Decline of Representative Democracy: Process, Participation and Power in State Legislatures.* Washington, DC: CQ Press, 1998.

Texas Legislative Council, *Presiding Officers of the Texas Legislature, 1946–1982.* Austin: Texas Legislative Council, 1982.

Websites

Texas Legislature On-Line   http://www.capitol.state.tx.us   In addition to providing links to other legislative websites such as the House, Senate, Legislative Budget Board, State Auditor, and the Sunset Commission, TLOL provides legislative histories, access to bills, amendments, and statutes affected by proposed legislation.

Texas Senate   http://www.senate.state.tx.us   In addition to information from the lieutenant governor's office, biographical information, committee assignments, district data, and addresses are provided for each member of the Senate.

Texas House of Representatives   http://www.house.state.tx.us   This site provides direct access to live broadcasts of legislative proceedings, information pertaining to the legislative process in the House, information from the speaker's office, and general information about the Capitol complex. Biographical information, committee assignments, district data, and addresses are provided for each member of the House.

Texas Legislative Council   http://www.tlc.state.tx.us   The Texas Legislative Council (TLC) is a state agency within the legislative branch. The TLC drafts bills and other legislative documents, conducts legal and public policy research, and produces informational publications for the Senate and the House.

ENDNOTES

1. *Houston Chronicle,* October 12, 2003, p. 33A.
2. For an extended discussion of legislative functions, see William J. Keefe and Morris S. Ogul, *The American Legislative Process,* 8th ed. (Upper Saddle River, NJ: Prentice Hall, 1993), pp. 16–37.
3. On the general concept of legislative institutionalization, see Nelson W. Polsby, "The Institutionalization of the U.S. House of Representatives," *American Political Science Review* 62 (March 1968), pp. 144–68. For a discussion of the emergence of the modern Congress, see Randall B. Ripley, *Congress: Process and Policy,* 4th ed. (New York: W.W. Norton and Company, 1988), pp. 48–67.
4. Thomas R. Dye, *Politics in States and Communities,* 8th ed. (Englewood Cliffs, NJ: Prentice Hall, Inc., 1994), pp. 179–83.
5. Council of State Governments, *Book of the States,* 1998–1999 (Lexington, KY: The Council of State Governments, 1996), p. 68.
6. See Article 3 of the Texas Constitutions for the constitutional provisions pertaining to the structure, membership, and selection of the Texas Legislature.
7. Council of State Governments, *Book of the States,* 2003, vol. 35 (Lexington, KY: The Council of State Governments, 2003), pp. 127–131.
8. *Austin American-Statesman,* June 11, 1991.
9. For a comprehensive analysis of the literature on legislative recruitment and careers, see Donald R. Matthews, "Legislative Recruitment Careers," *Legislative Studies Quarterly* IX (November 1984), pp. 547–85.
10. *Baker v. Carr,* 369 U.S. 186 (1962); *Reynolds v. Sims,* 337 U.S. 533 (1964); *Kilgarlin v. Martin,* 252 F. Supp 404 (S.D. Tex 1966).
11. *Georgia v. Ashcroft,* 539 U.S. _____ (2003).
12. *Houston Chronicle,* October 12, 2003, p. 33A.
13. Fred Gantt, *The Chief Executive in Texas: A Study of Gubernatorial Leadership* (Austin: University of Texas Press, 1964), p. 238.
14. *Houston Chronicle,* June 6, 1993.
15. *Houston Chronicle,* June 6, 2001, p. 1A.

16. For a good summary of the scholarly work on legislative committees, see Heinz Eulau and Vera McCluggage, "Standing Committees in Legislatures: Three Decades of Research," *Legislative Studies Quarterly* IX (May 1984), pp. 195–270.

17. *Austin American-Statesman,* May 13, 1991.

18. See Steven H. Haeberle, "The Institutionalization of the Subcommittee in the United States House of Representatives," *Journal of Politics* XL (November 1978), pp. 1054–65.

19. See Malcolm E. Jewell and Samuel C. Patterson, *The Legislative Process in the United States* (New York: Random House, 1966), Chap. 11, for a summary of the function of legislative rules and procedures.

20. For a brief overview of the representative problem, see Neal Riemer, ed., *The Representative: Trustee? Delegate? Partisan? Politico?* (Boston: D.C. Heath and Company, 1967). For a more comprehensive treatment of the subject, see Hanna F. Pitkin, *The Concept of Representation* (Berkeley: University of California Press, 1967).

21. For an excellent treatment of the relationship of U.S. legislators to their districts and constituencies, see Richard F. Fenno, Jr., *Home Style: House Members in Their Districts* (Boston: Little Brown, 1978).

22. There have been a number of studies of these informal norms within the legislative process. One is Donald R. Matthews, *U.S. Senators and Their World* (New York: Vintage Books, 1960). For the adaptation of this concept to state legislatures, see Alan Rosenthal, *Legislative Life: People, Process, and Performance of the States* (New York: Harper & Row, 1981).

23. The general concepts for this discussion are based on John W. Kingdon, *Congressmen's Voting* Decisions, 2nd ed. (New York: Harper & Row, Publishers, 1981).

24. These legislative styles are similar to those developed by James David Barber, *The Lawmakers* (New Haven, CT: Yale University Press, 1965), Chaps. 2–5.

25. For a general discussion of staff in state legislatures, see Rosenthal, *Legislative Life,* Chap. 10.

26. Richard Morehead, *50 Years in Texas Politics* (Burnet, TX: Eakin Press, 1982), pp. 236–37.

27. *Fort Worth Star-Telegram,* Dec. 4, 1990.

28. *Houston Chronicle,* Dec. 12, 1990.

29. *Houston Chronicle,* Jan. 1, 1991.

CHAPTER 9

The Texas Executive

I just love this job.

Governor Ann Richards,
on more than one occasion soon after taking office.

The Governor's office is not the primrose path of pleasure. Every time you throw yourself in opposition to what somebody wants, you immediately become the target for many a poisoned arrow.

Governor Pat M. Neff[1]

The salary isn't bad, the fringe benefits are pretty good, and the job is very prestigious. One might definitely get a sense of power and influence from holding the position. And, if you thrive on publicity, it may be satisfying to have a pack of journalists following your every move and hanging on your every word. But sooner or later, the reporters will become a pain in the neck. It will be hard to get time to yourself, and, if you are not careful, your efforts to relax may be subject to criticism. You will be authorized a large staff, but it will attempt to structure most of your waking hours. You can easily spend $30 million or $40 million—or even more—and a year's worth of sixteen-hour days winning the job and, in the process, be subjected to all kinds of ridicule and personal attacks. Once elected, you may catch all kinds of flak for developments over which you have little, if any, control. Finally, eight or ten other people will want your job and will be eager to make you look bad so they can challenge you when your term is up.

The office that usually comes to mind when people think of state government is the office of governor. It clearly is the most visible office in the state. But while the popular image of the office is one of power, those elected to it discover that the office is institutionally weak. The term "chief executive" is almost a misnomer, thanks to constitutional restrictions meant to ensure that no governor can repeat the oppressive abuses of the Reconstruction administration of Governor Edmund J. Davis.

Unlike the president of the United States, the governor of Texas has no formal appointive cabinet through which to impose policy on the governmental bureaucracy. Several other major state agencies are headed by independently elected officers, including such key players as the attorney general and the comptroller. The governor appoints hundreds of members of boards and commissions that set policy for numerous other state agencies. But most of those boards are structured in such a way that a new governor has to wait until halfway through his or her first term to appoint a majority of panel members.

All of this is not to suggest that the governor is merely a figurehead. The governor can veto legislation and has the exclusive authority to schedule special sessions of the legislature and set their agendas. Despite its limitations, the appointments power offers the opportunity to make a strong mark on state government. The high visibility of the office also offers a governor a ready-made public forum. So, while the state constitution limits the formal powers of the office, a governor's influence is shaped by his or her personality, political adroitness, staff appointments, and ability to define and sell an agenda that addresses broad needs and interests.

A HISTORICAL PERSPECTIVE ON THE EXECUTIVE FUNCTION IN TEXAS

The top executive officeholder in Texas has not always had such limited authority. In the 1836 Constitution of the Republic, the powers of the president of Texas "closely resembled the powers of the American president, except he was forbidden to lead armies without the consent of Congress."[2] The constitution adopted after Texas was annexed to the United States in 1845 continued the office of a strong single executive and gave the governor significant powers, including the appointment of other executive officials.[3] When Texas adopted a revised constitution upon joining the Confederacy in 1861, there were only some minor reductions in the powers of the governor. The new charter called for the election of two other executive officeholders: the state treasurer and the comptroller of public accounts.[4]

The governor also retained extensive powers under the Constitution of 1866, written at the end of the Civil War. Although the treasurer and the comptroller remained elected, the legislative power of the governor was expanded through the line-item veto over budget bills, a power still retained today. The Constitution of 1866 was short-lived and replaced by the Constitution of 1869 to bring the state into compliance with the Reconstruction policies of the Radical Republicans who had taken over the U.S. Congress. The Constitution of 1869 was influenced by Jacksonian democracy, which led to the diffusion of the executive function among eight officeholders, six of whom were to be elected statewide.[5]

But Radical Reconstruction policies and the abuses of the Davis administration prompted Texans to put strict limits on the power of the governor in the Constitution of 1876, which still forms the basic framework of state government. The new constitution retained the **plural executive** structure of independently elected officeholders. The only executive officer the governor was given the power to appoint was the secretary of state. Terms of the governor and other elected members of the executive branch were limited to two years, their salaries were defined by the constitution, and the duties of each office were specified in great detail, thus limiting their discretionary powers. Restrictions also were placed on outside employment and holding any other office or commission.[6]

A few of the restrictions on the executive branch have been loosened over the years through constitutional amendments, but the changes have not significantly enhanced the governor's authority. In 1954, voters approved an amendment giving the legislature the authority to raise the governor's salary.[7] Another amendment, in 1972, expanded the term of office for the governor and most other statewide executive officeholders to four years. In 1980, the governor was given the power, with the approval of the state Senate, to remove persons from boards and commissions whom the governor had personally appointed.[8] But when Governor Ann Richards in 1991 tried to revive interest in giving the governor cabinet-style appointment powers over major state agencies, she met with only limited success.

THE STRUCTURE OF THE PLURAL EXECUTIVE

Article 4, Section 1 of the 1876 Constitution created the executive branch, which "shall consist of a Governor, who shall be the Chief Executive Officer of the State, a Lieutenant Governor, Secretary of State, Comptroller of Public Accounts, Treasurer, Commissioner of the General Land Office, and Attorney General." Later added to the executive branch were the Agriculture Commissioner, the three-member Railroad Commission, and the fifteen-member State Board of Education. Only the secretary of state is appointed by the governor (Figure 9–1). Members of the education board are elected from districts, while the other officeholders are elected statewide. The constitution requires most of these officials to be at least thirty years old and a resident of Texas for at least five years.[9]

Agencies headed by these officials are autonomous and—except for limited budgetary review—independent of the governor. In a confrontation with the governor over policy, agency heads can claim their own electoral mandates. Writing in 1964, Fred Gantt concluded that there had been only "scattered incidents of hostility within the executive branch" and said that generally "elected officials have cooperated remarkably well with their chief executives."[10] Gantt's observations were based on a period in which Texas was a one-party Democratic state. Party politics were dominated by conservatives, and their interests were generally reflected by statewide elected officials, who believed it was in their own best political interests to cooperate with each other.

But the potential for conflict between the governor and other executive officials increased as Texas became a two-party state, and conflict is likely to become more common in the future, even between officials within the same party. During Republican Governor Bill Clements's first term (1979–1983), the other elected officers in the executive branch were Democrats, including Attorney General Mark White, who frequently feuded with the governor and jockeyed for the political advantage that allowed him to unseat Clements in 1983. In 2003, budgetary differences erupted between Republican Comptroller Carole Keeton Strayhorn and other Republican officeholders, including Governor Rick Perry. They resulted in the legislature's approval of a bill, signed by Perry, that transferred two key programs from the comptroller's office to the Legislative Budget Board. (This dispute will be discussed in more detail in the section on the comptroller of public accounts later in this chapter.)

There can be conflict between any members of the executive branch. In 1994, for example, a coastal management plan promoted by Democratic Land Commissioner Garry Mauro was actively opposed by Perry, who was then agriculture commissioner.

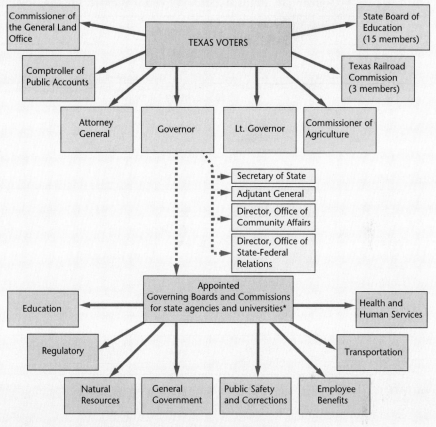

FIGURE 9–1 The executive branch in Texas is a combination of elected and appointed officials who administer more than two hundred state agencies. *Source:* Comptroller of Public Accounts, *Breaking the Mold: A Report of the Texas Performance Review,* Vol. 1, p. 13.

One may argue that the effect of the plural executive on state politics and the governor's control of the executive branch is minimal because, for the most part, rancorous conflict among these elected officials still appears to be infrequent. But one may also argue that the governor, in an effort to avoid conflict with officials over whom he or she has no control, pursues policies that are not likely to be disruptive, innovative, or responsive to pressing contemporary issues.

It is difficult to develop coordinated policies if those holding office in a plural executive system have sharply different or competing agendas. But proponents of the plural executive contend that it does what it was intended to do: control and constrain the governor. While collegial or collective decision-making is often

TABLE 9–1   Ranking of States According to Formal Powers of the Governor

Strong

Alaska	Minnesota	Utah	West Virginia
Illinois	New York		

Moderately Strong

Colorado	Maryland	New Jersey	Pennsylvania
Connecticut	Michigan	New Mexico	South Dakota
Hawaii	Montana	North Dakota	Tennessee
Iowa	Nebraska	Ohio	Wisconsin
Maine			

Moderate

Arkansas	Kansas	Missouri	South Carolina
California	Kentucky	Nevada	Texas
Delaware	Louisiana	New Hampshire	Virginia
Florida	Massachusetts	Oklahoma	Washington
Idaho	Mississippi	Oregon	Wyoming
Indiana			

Weak

Alabama	Georgia	Rhode Island	Vermont
Arizona	North Carolina		

Source: Thad Beyle, "The Governors," at http://www.unc.edu/~beyle/tab7.5-InstPowers03A.doc.

inefficient and potentially leads to deadlock, the advocates of the plural executive contend that democracy, in most instances, is to be preferred over efficiency.

The Governor of Texas in a Comparative Perspective

For more than thirty years, scholars have ranked the various state governors on their formal constitutional and legal powers, such as budgetary authority, appointment and veto powers, and term limitations.[11] And, from the earliest to the latest studies, the governor of Texas has ranked consistently with the weaker state governors (Table 9–1).

THE QUALIFICATIONS OF THE GOVERNOR

The Texas Constitution has few requirements for a person who desires to run for governor. A **governor** must be at least thirty years old, a U.S. citizen, and a resident of Texas for at least five years. There also is a vague requirement that no individual can be excluded from office for religious beliefs, "provided he acknowledges the existence of a Supreme Being."[12] The constitution, however, doesn't spell out all the roadblocks to winning the office.

Until the election of Bill Clements in 1978, every governor since 1874 had been a Democrat (Table 9–2). Clements served two terms (1979–1983 and 1987–1991). Republican George W. Bush was elected to the office in 1994 and again in 1998, and Republican Rick Perry was elected in 2002, as Republican strength increased in Texas.

Most governors have been well-educated, middle-aged, and affluent white male Protestants. In many cases, their families were active in public life and helped shape their careers. No minorities and only two women have been elected to the office. Miriam A. "Ma" Ferguson, whose husband, James E. "Pa" Ferguson, had earlier been governor, served two terms (1925–1927 and 1933–1935), and Ann Richards served

TABLE 9–2   Governors of Texas Since 1870

Edmund J. Davis	1870–1874
Richard Coke	1874–1876
Richard B. Hubbard	1876–1879
Oran M. Roberts	1879–1883
John Ireland	1883–1887
Lawrence Sullivan Ross	1887–1891
James Stephen Hogg	1891–1895
Charles A. Culberson	1895–1899
Joseph D. Sayers	1899–1903
Samuel W.T. Lanham	1903–1907
Thomas Mitchell Campbell	1907–1911
Oscar Branch Colquitt	1911–1915
James E. Ferguson*	1915–1917
William Pettus Hobby	1917–1921
Pat Morris Neff	1921–1925
Miriam A. Ferguson	1925–1927
Dan Moody	1927–1931
Ross S. Sterling	1931–1933
Miriam A. Ferguson	1933–1935
James V. Allred	1935–1939
W. Lee O'Daniel	1939–1941
Coke R. Stevenson	1941–1947
Beauford H. Jester	1947–1949
Allan Shivers	1949–1957
Price Daniel	1957–1963
John Connally	1963–1969
Preston Smith	1969–1973
Dolph Briscoe, Jr.**	1973–1979
Williams P. Clements, Jr.	1979–1983
Mark White	1983–1987
William P. Clements, Jr.	1987–1991
Ann Richards	1991–1995
George W. Bush	1995–2000
Rick Perry	2000–

*Only governor of Texas to be impeached and convicted.

**Prior to 1974, governors were elected for two-year terms of office.

Source: Texas Almanac, 1996–1997 (Dallas: The Dallas Morning News, Inc., 1995).

one term (1991–1995). By the time Richards became governor, only three women had ever been elected to any other statewide executive office in Texas. Richards, a Democrat, served two terms as state treasurer before being elected governor and was succeeded as treasurer by Republican Kay Bailey Hutchison. From 1919 to 1923, Annie Webb Blanton was state superintendent of schools, an elective office that no longer exists.

With the rising costs of statewide political campaigns, a candidate's personal wealth or ability to raise large sums of money has taken on increased importance (see Chapter 7). Otherwise qualified prospects are dissuaded from running for governor and other offices because of the difficult burden of fundraising. Former Governor Bill Clements and fellow Republican Clayton Williams, a Midland businessman who lost the 1990 gubernatorial race to Richards, spent millions of dollars out of their own pockets in gubernatorial races that were their first bids for elective office. Similarly, Democrat Tony Sanchez, a wealthy Laredo businessman, spent more than $60 million of his personal fortune in an unsuccessful race for governor in 2002. Their experience raises the possibility that personal wealth and the willingness to spend it on one's own election campaign will take on more importance in future races.

Modern campaigns are increasingly shaped by the mass media, particularly television, and media-driven campaigns usually are concerned more with image than substance. Several candidates have had difficulty utilizing or exploiting the mass media to their advantage. Candidates—no matter how qualified—who do not understand the electronic media are likely to be rebuffed in their efforts to win major statewide office.

Previous public service has provided gubernatorial aspirants with public visibility and linkages to party leaders, interest groups, and public officials around the state. Such relationships help candidates develop broad electoral support. Texas governors have previously served in local and statewide offices, the legislature, and Congress. Preston Smith (1969–1973) was a legislator and lieutenant governor prior to being elected governor. Dolph Briscoe (1973–1979) also served in the legislature. Mark White (1983–1987) served as secretary of state and then as attorney general. Ann Richards was a county commissioner and then state treasurer. Although he had never previously held elective office, Clements was a deputy U.S. secretary of defense prior to winning his first gubernatorial race. George W. Bush was elected governor in 1994 without any previous formal government experience. He had been an unofficial adviser to his father, former President George Bush. Rick Perry was a state representative, agriculture commissioner, and lieutenant governor before becoming governor.

IMPEACHMENT AND INCAPACITATION

A governor can be removed from office through **impeachment** proceedings initiated in the House of Representatives and conviction by the Senate in a trial of the impeachment charges (see "Impeaching a Governor"). Other states such as California can remove a governor through recall as well as impeachment. Through a process initiated by a petition of a defined number of voters, a special election is held on the question of the removal of the governor. If the governor is removed by popular vote, a new governor is then elected. This is occurred in late 2003 when Democrat Gray Davis was recalled as governor, and voters, in the same election, selected Arnold Schwarzenegger, a Republican, to replace him.

If the governor dies, is incapacitated, is impeached and convicted, or voluntarily leaves office in midterm, the lieutenant governor replaces the governor until the next general election. In instances when the governor leaves the state, the lieutenant governor serves as acting governor.

IMPEACHING A GOVERNOR

Texas is one of only a few states that have removed a governor by impeachment. In 1917, a controversy erupted over Governor James E. "Pa" Ferguson's efforts to remove five University of Texas faculty members. The governor vetoed the university's appropriations, and when he called a special legislative session to consider other funding, he was immediately faced with articles of impeachment based primarily on the misuse of public funds. He ultimately was convicted and removed from office. But for two more decades, the husband-and-wife team of Ma and Pa Ferguson and the controversy that continued to surround them dominated a great deal of Texas politics.

Governor James E. "Pa" Ferguson was the only Texas governor to be removed from office through the impeachment process.

Miriam A. "Ma" Ferguson was the first woman to serve as governor of Texas (1925–1927 and 1933–1935).

Source: Fred Gantt Jr., *The Chief Executive in Texas* (Austin: University of Texas Press, 1964), pp. 229–30.

THE SALARY AND "PERKS" OF THE OFFICE

In 2003, the governor of Texas was paid $115,345. The state also provides the governor with a mansion and staff to maintain it, a security detail, travel expenses, and access to state-owned planes and cars.

THE POWERS OF THE GOVERNOR

There are competing views of the chief executive's functions, which have changed over time. Early state constitutions limited gubernatorial powers, and governors in many states found themselves in a subordinate position to their legislatures. Throughout the nineteenth century, those relationships were often redefined. At times, the governors' powers were increased and those of the legislatures reduced. During other periods, such as the era of Jacksonian democracy, the powers of both institutions were subjected to strong restrictions to assure greater responsiveness to the public. Reform movements of the early twentieth century, responding to political corruption, focused on management and efficiency in the governors' offices. In some states, the office of governor was restructured around the organizational principles of an executive cabinet. Events such as the Great Depression contributed to a further redefinition of executive leadership, with an emphasis in some states on policy initiatives, administrative control and coordination, and expanded political leadership.[13] The Texas Constitution of 1845, adopted when the state was admitted to the Union, modeled the governor's authority on the strong executive principle found in the U.S. Constitution. Later Texas constitutions reduced the powers of the office, however, reflecting apprehension of strong executive and political authority.

Texans, nonetheless, appear to have high expectations of their governor. Governors are evaluated in terms of their policy agendas and the leadership they exercise in achieving those goals. But how does a governor meet such expectations when the formal powers of the office are limited? The following discussion analyzes the formal powers and reviews the informal resources that the governor can use to complement them.

Legislative Powers

The governor has the opportunity to outline his or her legislative priorities at the beginning of each regular biennial session through the traditional "state of the state" address to the legislature. The governor also can communicate with lawmakers—collectively or individually—throughout the session. In this fashion, the governor can establish a policy agenda, recommend specific legislation, and set the stage for negotiations with legislative leaders, other state officials, and interest groups. The governor's addresses and other formal messages to the legislature are well covered by the media. They give the governor the opportunity to mobilize the public support that may be essential to the success of his or her initiatives.

The governor's effectiveness can be enhanced by the office's two major constitutional powers over the legislature—the veto and the authority to call and set the agenda for special legislative sessions.

The governor can call any number of special sessions, which can last as long as thirty days each, and designate the subjects to be considered during the session.

Sometimes, the mere threat of a special session can be enough to convince reluctant lawmakers to approve a priority program of the governor or reach an acceptable compromise during a regular session. Most legislators, who are paid only part-time salaries by the state, dread special sessions because they interfere with their regular occupations and disrupt their personal lives. Governor Bill Clements, who called two special sessions on workers' compensation reform in 1989, used the threat of a third to convince a handful of senators to break a year-long impasse and approve legislation backed by the governor, a majority of the House, and the business community. Governor Rick Perry called three special sessions in 2003 to win approval of a congressional redistricting bill that favored Republican candidates. The bill wouldn't have been passed without Perry's persistence (see Chapter 8).

There also are risks in calling special sessions. The governor's influence and reputation are on the line, and further inaction by the legislature can become a political liability. In some instances, the legislative leadership has liberally interpreted the subject matter of a governor's special session proclamation and considered bills not sought by the governor. Since the speaker and the lieutenant governor make the parliamentary rulings that determine whether a specific piece of legislation falls within the governor's call, the governor has to draft a proclamation setting a special session's agenda very carefully. Once a special session is called, the governor can increase his or her bargaining power by adding legislators' pet bills to the agenda in exchange for the lawmakers' support of the governor's program.

The governor of Texas has one of the strongest veto powers of any governor. While the legislature is in session, the governor has ten days to veto a bill or let it become law without his or her signature. A veto can be overridden by a two-thirds vote of both the House and the Senate. During the past fifty years, Governor Clements was the only governor to have a veto overridden. It was a local bill related to game management that the Democrat-dominated legislature voted to override during the Republican governor's first term. The governor has twenty days after the legislature adjourns to veto bills passed in the closing days of a session. Such vetoes are absolute because the only way the legislature can respond is to have the bill reintroduced in the next session.

The governor also has line-item veto authority over the state budget. That is, the governor can strike specific spending items without vetoing the entire bill. All other bills have to be accepted or rejected in their entirety. A governor may veto a bill for a number of reasons, including doubts about its constitutionality, objections to its wording, concerns that it duplicates existing law, or substantive differences with its policy. A governor's threat of a veto often is as effective as an actual veto because such threats can prompt legislators to make changes in their bills to meet a governor's objections.

Historic records on gubernatorial vetoes are not complete, but Governor Dan Moody apparently was one of the more frequent veto users. He vetoed 117 bills and resolutions during his four years in office from 1927 to 1931. Governor Richards vetoed thirty-six bills and resolutions in one regular and two special sessions in 1991 and allowed 228 bills to become law without her signature. Richards vetoed twenty-six bills and let another nineteen become law without her signature in 1993. Governor Bush vetoed twenty-four bills in 1995, his first year in office. Bush vetoed thirty-seven bills in 1997 and thirty-one in 1999. Perry vetoed eighty-two bills in 2001 and forty-eight in 2003 (see "The Governor's Leadership Resources").

THE GOVERNOR'S LEADERSHIP RESOURCES

Formal Constitutional Powers

- Veto legislation
- Exercise a line-item veto over the state budget
- Call and set the agenda for special legislative sessions
- Make recommendations on the budget
- Propose emergency budgetary transfers when the legislature is not in session
- Appoint hundreds of members of policymaking boards and commissions, subject to Senate confirmation
- Remove his or her own appointees from boards, with Senate approval
- Fill vacancies in U.S. Senate seats and certain elective state offices
- Proclaim acts of executive clemency, including stays of execution, for convicted criminals
- Mobilize the Texas National Guard to protect lives and property during natural disasters and other emergencies

Informal Resources

- A large staff to help develop and sell policy proposals
- The attention of the mass media
- The political party, whose potential support is growing with the new two-party system in Texas
- Support and mobilization of interest groups

Budgetary Powers

The governor of Texas has weaker budgetary authority than the governors of most states and the president of the United States. These budgetary constraints limit the governor's ability to develop a comprehensive legislative program. The budgetary process will be discussed in more detail in Chapter 13, but the legislature has the lead in budget-setting, with a major role played by the Legislative Budget Board (LBB), a ten-member panel that includes the lieutenant governor, the speaker, and eight key lawmakers. The LBB and the governor both make budgetary recommendations to the legislature, but lawmakers usually give greater attention to the LBB's product.

To meet emergencies between legislative sessions, the governor can propose the transfer of funds between programs or agencies, with the approval of the LBB. Or the LBB can recommend a funds transfer, subject to the governor's approval.

Appointive Powers

One indication of a strong governor is the power to hire and fire the persons responsible for implementing public policy. But as we discussed earlier in this chapter, the Texas governor's administrative authority is severely limited by the plural executive structure under which independently elected officeholders head several major state agencies.

Most of the remainder of the state bureaucracy falls under more than 200 boards and commissions that oversee various agencies created by state law. Most of these are part-time, unpaid positions whose occupants are heavily dependent on agency staffs and constituents for guidance. Although members of these boards are appointed by the governor and confirmed by the Senate, the structure creates the potential for boards and commissions to become captives of the narrow constituencies they are serving or regulating and reduces their accountability to both the governor and the legislature.

Most board members serve six-year **staggered terms.** That means it takes a new governor at least two years to get majorities favoring his or her policies on most boards. Resignations or deaths of board members may speed up the process, but a governor cannot remove a predecessor's appointees. A governor, with the approval of two-thirds of the Senate, can fire only his or her own appointees.

During her first year in office in 1991, Governor Ann Richards pressed for more "accountability" over the bureaucracy by asking the legislature to give her the power to directly appoint the executive directors of state agencies. These officials historically had been hired by the various boards and commissions. The legislature gave the governor a small taste of the cabinet-style authority she had sought, but it didn't change the system. The governor was given the authority to appoint a new commissioner to oversee several health and human service agencies, a new executive director of the Department of Commerce, and an executive director of a new Department of Housing and Community Affairs. The governor retained her previous authority to appoint the secretary of state, the adjutant general, and the director of the Office of State-Federal Relations.

The governor appoints individuals to boards and commissions with approval of two-thirds of the Senate. **Senatorial courtesy,** an unwritten norm of the Senate, permits a senator to block the governor's nomination of a person who lives in that senator's district. The governor and staff members involved in appointments spend considerable time clearing potential nominees with senators, because political considerations are as important in the confirmation process as a nominee's qualifications.

Individuals seek gubernatorial appointments for a variety of reasons, and the appointments process can be hectic, particularly at the beginning of a new governor's administration. Potential nominees are screened by the governor's staff to determine their availability and competence, political acceptability, and support by key interest groups. Although most governors would deny it, campaign contributions are also a significant factor. A number of Governor Clements' appointees had made substantial contributions to his campaign.[14] Governors Richards, Bush and Perry also appointed major contributors to important posts. Governor Perry made the most controversial appointment of his first year in office, former Enron Corporation executive Max Yzaguirre as chairman of the Public Utility Commission, one day before receiving a $25,000 political donation from then-Enron Chairman Ken Lay in 2001. Perry insisted the timing was coincidental, but it generated much controversy after Enron filed for bankruptcy a few months later, prompting Yzaguirre's resignation from the post. Then, in 2003, less than one month after receiving a $100,000 contribution from homebuilder Bob Perry of Houston, Governor Perry appointed a top executive of the homebuilder's company to a new state commission charged with developing building performance standards. The commission had been created by the legislature to reduce consumer lawsuits against builders. Since June 1997,

Bob Perry, who wasn't related to the governor, had contributed $580,000 to Rick Perry.[15] The governor appoints individuals to fill vacancies on all courts at the district level or above. If a U.S. senator dies or resigns, the governor appoints a replacement. When a vacancy occurs in another statewide office, except for the lieutenant governor, the governor also appoints a replacement. All of these appointees must later win election to keep their seats.

Governor Richards was particularly sensitive to constituencies that historically have been excluded from full participation in the governmental process and appointed a record number of women and minorities to state posts. About 41 percent of Richards' appointees during her four-year term were women, and about 33 percent were minorities. Her successor, Governor Bush, appointed women to 37 percent and minorities to 24 percent of the posts he filled during his first five years in office.[16] Bush appointed the first African American, Michael Williams, to the Texas Railroad Commission, and, at different times during his administration, appointed two Hispanics—Tony Garza and Alberto R. Gonzales—secretary of state. Bush later appointed Gonzales to fill a vacancy on the Texas Supreme Court. After Bush was elected president, he appointed Garza as U.S. ambassador to Mexico and Gonzales as White House counsel. Governor Perry appointed the first African American, Wallace Jefferson, to the Texas Supreme Court.

Judicial Powers

Texas has a seven-member Board of Pardons and Paroles, appointed by the governor. This panel, which was reduced from eighteen members by a 2003 law, decides when prisoners can be released early, and its decisions do not require action by the governor. The governor, however, can influence the board's overall approach to paroles, as Governor Richards did when she convinced her appointees to sharply curtail the parole rate. This was done in response to citizen outrage over crimes committed by parolees (see Chapter 13).

The governor has the authority to grant executive clemency—acts of leniency or mercy—toward convicted criminals. One is a thirty-day stay of execution for a condemned murderer, which a governor can grant without a recommendation of the parole board. The governor, on recommendation of the board, can grant a full pardon to a criminal, a conditional pardon, or the commutation of a death sentence to life imprisonment.[17]

If a person flees a state to avoid prosecution or a prison term, the U.S. Constitution, under the extradition clause, requires that person, upon arrest in another state, to be returned to the state from which he or she fled. The governor is legally responsible for ordering state officials to carry out such extradition requests.[18]

Military Powers

The Texas Constitution authorizes the governor to function as the "commander-in-chief of the military force of the state, except when they are called into actual service of the United States."[19] The governor appoints the adjutant general to carry out this duty. Texas cannot declare war on another country, and the president of the United States has the primary responsibility for national defense. But when riots or natural disasters occur within the state, the governor can mobilize the Texas National Guard to protect lives and property and keep the peace. Should the United States go to war, the National Guard can be mobilized by the president as part of the national military forces. After the September 11, 2001, terrorist attacks on the World Trade Center and the Pentagon, some National Guard members from Texas were activated to temporarily bolster security at airports. Others went overseas to assist in the military operations in Afghanistan and Iraq.

INFORMAL RESOURCES OF THE GOVERNOR

Governors can compensate for the constitutional limitations on their office with their articulation of problems and issues, leadership capabilities, personalities, work habits, and administrative styles. Some governors want to get involved in the minutiae of building policy coalitions and give much of their personal time to effecting compromises and agreements. Other governors find such hands-on involvement distasteful, inefficient, and time-consuming and leave such detail work to subordinates.

As the most visible state official, the governor sometimes gets the credit that belongs to others but can just as readily be blamed for problems beyond his or her control. For example, a major factor in Governor Mark White's loss of his 1986 reelection bid was falling oil prices that had devastated the state's economy. White had no choice but to call the legislature into special session only a few months before the November election. Under the circumstances, he probably exercised the best leadership that he could in convincing lawmakers to cut the budget and raise taxes. But it wasn't the type of leadership appreciated by most voters.

The Governor's Staff

Nineteenth-century governors had only three or four individuals to assist them, but staffs have grown with the increased complexity of state government and the increased demands on the governor's time. By 1963, under John Connally, the governor's staff had grown to sixty-eight full-time and twelve part-time employees.[20] Under the administration of Dolph Briscoe in the 1970s, the staff expanded to more than 300, but staff sizes were smaller in most subsequent administrations. At one point in her term, Ann Richards had almost 300 people on her staff. The number decreased to about 200 under George W. Bush, but Bush approved higher salaries for some of his key staffers. In 2002, Governor Perry had about 200 employees.

The staff's organization reflects the governor's leadership style (see Figure 9–2). Some governors create a highly centralized office with a chief of staff who functions to screen contacts and information going to the governor. Other governors want greater personal contacts with numerous staff members. But the critical question is whether the governor is getting sufficient information with which to make decisions that produce good public policy and minimize the potential for controversy, conflict, or embarrassment. Under ideal circumstances, the staff enhances the governor's political, administrative, and policymaking capabilities. There have been instances, however, when a governor has permitted his staff to insulate him by denying access to persons with significant information or recommendations.

Governors generally choose staffers who are loyal and share their basic political attitudes. Since communication with the governor's various constituencies is fundamental to success, some staffers are chosen for their skills in mass communications and public relations. Others are hired for their expertise in specific policy areas.[21] In

The Office of the Governor

April 2003

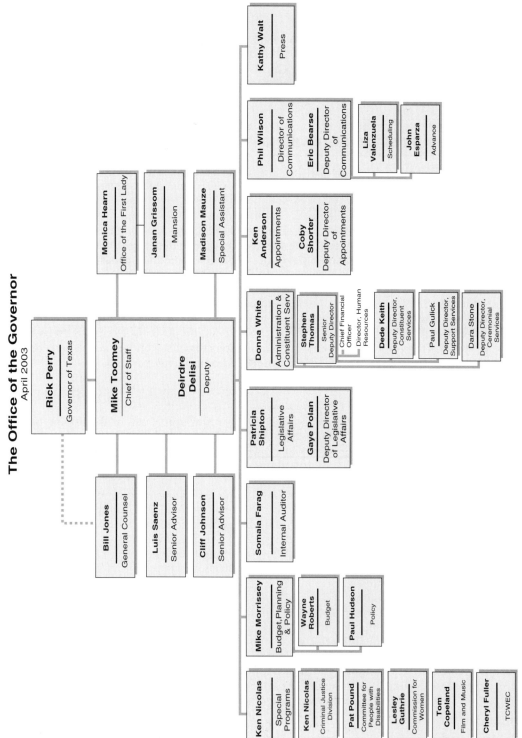

FIGURE 9–2 The Office of the Governor, April 2003. *Source:* The Office of the Governor.

many respects, staff members function as the governor's surrogates. Thus, if one makes a mistake, particularly a serious mistake, the public will perceive it as the governor's error.

The staff collects, organizes, and screens information, helps decide who sees the governor, and otherwise schedules the governor's time. Staffers also work on strategies to garner support for the governor's proposals from legislators, agencies, interest groups, and the public. Because the governor often lacks the time to conduct discussions and negotiations personally, key staff members often represent the governor in meetings and in lobbying lawmakers. Sometimes the governor gets involved personally, particularly if his or her participation is needed to break an impasse and effect a solution.[22]

The Governor and the Mass Media

The mass media help shape the political and policy options of the governor. Governors who have failed to understand the impact of the mass media often have courted disaster. A governor who is readily accessible to the media and understands the constraints under which the media operate is likely to develop a good working relationship with the press. But success with the media is more than being accessible and friendly.

Governors call press conferences to announce new policies or explain their positions on pending issues. They stage pseudo "news events," such as visiting a classroom to emphasize concern for educational quality or a high-tech facility to demonstrate a commitment to economic development. They or their staffers sometimes leak information to selected reporters to embarrass the opposition, put an action of the administration in the best possible light, or float a trial balloon to gauge legislative or public reaction to a proposal. Some governors spend political funds to purchase radio or television time to try to mobilize public opinion in support of pet proposals before the legislature. Overall, the timely use of the media can contribute significantly to the power and influence of a governor.

Periodic statewide public opinion polls commissioned by media organizations often include questions about the governor's performance. Those ratings are widely monitored by players in the political arena.

The Governor and the Political Party

Historically, the political factions within one-party Democratic Texas were somewhat ill-defined. Factionalism was often described in terms of liberal or conservative, but there were also complex urban-rural, regional, and economic differences. Democratic governors built policy coalitions around these factions, but there was little stability or continuity, and most governors derived only limited power from their position as party leader.

Under the two-party system, however, the political party is taking on more importance and may provide greater resources to the governor. During his second term in the late 1980s, Bill Clements often had enough Republican votes in the House to thwart the will of the Democratic majority. After Republicans had gained legislative control, Rick Perry had strong support from Republican lawmakers and party officials during the budgetary and redistricting battles of 2003 (see Chapter 8).

Upon taking office in 1995, Republican Governor George W. Bush enjoyed the support of party leaders for his own priorities—efforts to improve education, restrict civil lawsuits, reform juvenile justice, and change the welfare system. Initially, he kept his distance from much of the agenda advocated by the social conservatives who had taken control of leadership positions in the Texas Republican party in 1994. But in 1999, when he was preparing for a presidential race, Bush strengthened his anti-abortion credentials with social conservatives by helping to convince the legislature to enact one of their major priorities—a law requiring parents to be notified before their minor daughters could have abortions.

The Governor and Interest Groups

Successful governors must be consummate political animals who continually nurture relationships throughout the political system. A gubernatorial candidate aggressively solicits the endorsements and contributions of various groups. These groups, in turn, develop stakes in gubernatorial elections and usually assume that the candidates they support will be responsive to their interests. A governor's policy initiatives often include legislation of benefit to key support groups, which maintain active roles throughout the policy process. Business groups, for example, were major contributors to Gov. Rick Perry's successful election race in 2002, and the governor strongly supported their priorities, including additional limits on civil lawsuits, during the 2003 regular legislative session.

LEADERSHIP STYLES OF RECENT TEXAS GOVERNORS

Gubernatorial leadership styles have been as varied as the personalities that molded the chief executives' approaches to their jobs. Some governors have come to the office with well-defined policy agendas and attempted to exploit every resource available to them. Other governors have taken a more limited view of the office. They adopted an administrative or managerial posture and left policy initiatives to other institutions or elected officials. New programs, especially those with far-reaching tax or social implications, were pursued with considerable caution.

Some governors have thrived on the constant attention and political and social interactions that go with the office. They have worked long hours, continually engaged in public relations and coalition building. Strange as it may seem, however, there have been other governors who were introverted and apparently found many aspects of the office distasteful. They often insulated themselves from the public and other political officials through their staffs and seemed detached from the activities necessary to influence public policy.[23]

Bill Clements (1979–1983, 1987–1991)

Clements, a self-made multimillionaire who had founded an international oil-drilling firm, personally funded much of his first campaign in 1978, effectively using a sophisticated media strategy. The man who shocked the Democratic establishment by defeating John Hill by 17,000 votes had held no previous elected office. His only governmental experience had been as deputy secretary of defense under Presidents Richard Nixon and Gerald Ford. He was an outsider, a Republican, highly opinionated and blunt, and had a reputation for solid management skills. All the other elected statewide officials were Democrats, as were the vast majority of legislators, although many lawmakers shared his conservative views.

Governor Bill Clements (1979–1983, 1987–1991).

Upon arriving in Austin, Clements did not understand the limitations of the powers of the governor.[24] In his election campaign, he had tapped a rather widely held view that state government was wasteful and had proposed that 25,000 state jobs be eliminated. He also appealed to popular notions of limited government and proposed that the Texas Constitution be amended to allow private citizens to propose laws through the initiative and referendum process. But he gradually learned that he couldn't singlehandedly run the statehouse and the bureaucracy the way he had the corporate boardroom, and he didn't accomplish either of those goals.

In an interview years later, Clements admitted that he didn't fully understand how state government worked when he first took office. "Until I came to Austin and until I actually was in office and everything, I really didn't understand the detailed nuance of how the state government really functioned. I'd say it took me at least through that first legislative session. And, by the time that was over, well, I began to understand exactly how the state government works."[25]

Clements eagerly exercised his veto power. During his first legislative session in 1979, he vetoed a near-record fifty-one bills.[26] He also struck $252 million from the $20.7 billion state budget for 1980–1981.[27]

Clements generally received high marks for the quality of his staff and board appointments during his first term. Republicans, who for years had been shut out of appointments to boards and commissions, were appointed by the Republican governor. Yet Clements also appointed many conservative Democrats. In part, his appointment strategies were designed to convert conservative Democrats to the Republican party, thus extending and consolidating Republican gains across the state. Clements made many judicial appointments during his two terms, including the first two women to the Texas Supreme Court and the first African American to the Court of Criminal Appeals.

But Clements never developed effective public relations with the legislature, the news media, and the general public, and he often found himself at odds with other elected officials and interest groups, primarily because of his outspokenness. He was often portrayed as insensitive, as someone inclined to "shoot from the lip" and worry about the consequences later. After learning at a meeting at Texas A & M University that scuba diving by a pregnant woman could damage a fetus, he angered many women by saying, in jest, that diving could serve as a form of birth control. After an offshore Mexican oil well blew out and threatened Texas beaches in 1979, Clements advised coastal residents against "crying over spilt milk." The insensitive remark was compounded by revelations that SEDCO, the drilling firm he had founded, had leased the drilling equipment used on the blown-out well.

At the end of his first term in 1982, Clements's job performance rating had dropped, his image had suffered, and the Texas economy had begun to show signs of weakness. A revitalized Democratic statewide political effort helped Mark White unseat Clements in a bitterly fought campaign that Clements wasn't soon to forget.

In 1986, Clements became only the second person in Texas history to regain the governor's office after losing it. And, while his motivations for staging a comeback effort weren't totally clear, it was widely believed that his main interest was revenge. His hostility toward White remained so intense that he snubbed White's offer of a handshake on Inauguration Day, a clear violation of the unwritten rules of American politics.

A major distraction at the beginning of Clements's second term was the governor's admission of his involvement in a "pay-for-play" football scandal at Southern Methodist University that prompted the National Collegiate Athletic Association to suspend SMU's intercollegiate football program for two years. Clements didn't initiate the illicit payments to athletes but admitted that, as chairman of SMU's governing board during the period between his two terms as governor, he participated in a decision to let previously approved payments continue.

Clements also spent his first six months back in Austin battling Lieutenant Governor Bill Hobby and Democratic legislators over the state budget. Clements insisted on deep service cuts that would have enabled him to keep a 1986 campaign promise against higher taxes, but he finally gave in during a summer special session in 1987 and signed a record $5.6 billion tax increase.

The public's opinion of Clements, meanwhile, was plummeting. Two-thirds of the respondents to the *Texas Poll* that summer said they disapproved of the governor's job performance.[28] Clements's negative ratings remained high throughout the remainder of his term. By the time he left the governor's office the second time, in 1991, he was widely viewed more as an obstructionist who would rather fight the Democratic majority in the legislature than as a leader who was ready to seek solutions to significant state problems.

After another standoff with the legislature over taxes in 1990, Clements again gave in and signed a $512 million tax increase. The revenue helped pay for a new school finance bill—which, ironically, was struck down as unconstitutional by the Supreme Court the next year—and met funding shortfalls in the Texas Department of Human Services and the Texas Department of Health.

Clements, an avowed fiscal conservative, signed $6.1 billion in tax increases during his second term—more than any other governor in Texas history. The Texas economy was undergoing a painful transition in the wake of the oil bust, and state government's existing tax base was strained at a time of increasing budgetary demands. Those factors weren't the governor's fault, but Clements had eroded the credibility of public officials by making antitax campaign promises he couldn't keep.

Clements counted an overhaul of the workers' compensation system a major victory during his second term. At his insistence, the legislature in 1989 created a new state agency and established new legal standards under which workers injured on the job could seek compensation from their employers or insurance companies. But it took two special sessions after lawmakers failed to resolve an impasse over the issue in the 1989 regular session. Clements never presented the legislature with a specific proposal of his own. He left that to legislative leaders. His role was to hold a gun to the legislature's head by threatening to keep lawmakers in Austin as long as it took to get a bill that he would accept. It was an effective exercise of the governor's power to call and set the agenda for special sessions.

Clements's two terms converged with the emergence of a two-party system in Texas, and his candidacy and elections contributed significantly to this historic development. By proving that a Republican could win the governorship, Clements made the Republican party attractive to many conservative Democrats, and many switched to the GOP.

There were only a handful of Republicans in the legislature and none in any other elected state offices when Clements was elected to his first term. After Clements had completed his second term in January 1991, Republicans held four of the nine seats on the Texas Supreme Court, two other statewide offices (in addition to a U.S. Senate seat), and more than one-third of the seats in the Texas House. They also had made major inroads in county and other local offices throughout the state.

In an interview in late 1990, Clements assessed his contribution to the development of a two-party system: "The electorate out there breaks down into about one-third Democrats, one-third Republicans, and one-third independents. Well, that is a significant change in the political profile of Texas. That's a historic change, and I guess I'd like to say that I put a brick in place to bring that about."[29]

Ann Richards (1991–1995)

Taking her oath in January 1991, Governor Ann Richards attempted to convince the public that her election marked the emergence of a "New Texas." She invited supporters to join her in a march up Congress Avenue to symbolically retake the Capitol for "the people." Emphasizing the progressive Democratic themes of her campaign, she promised in her inaugural address a user-friendly, compassionate state government that would expand opportunities for everyone, particularly minorities and women. She promised to clean up the environment, improve education, attack crime, cut red tape, and boost ethical standards for public officeholders.

But the euphoria of the day was tempered by the reality of a $4 billion-plus potential deficit, a court order for school finance reform that could make the shortfall even greater, and a grand-jury investigation into legislative behavior that had further eroded public confidence in state government.

Richards moved quickly to establish herself as an activist governor. The day after her inauguration, she continued a campaign assault against high insurance rates by marching over to a meeting of the State Board of Insurance to speak against a proposed increase in auto insurance premiums. Unlike her recent predecessors, she also testified before House and Senate committees, ensuring that her legislative priorities would receive maximum media coverage. She also used the media to attack the state bureaucracy.

Richards quickly fulfilled a campaign promise to appoint more women and minorities to key positions in state government. She appointed the first African American to the University of Texas System Board of Regents, the first African-American

Governor Ann Richards (1991–1995).

woman to the Texas A & M University governing board, and the first Hispanic to the Texas Court of Criminal Appeals. Twenty-five percent of the appointees during her first three months in office were Hispanic, 21 percent were African American, and 49 percent were women. Richards also named a disabled person to the Board of Human Services and a crime victim to the Board of Criminal Justice.[30]

With the state facing a revenue crunch, Richards took the lead in lobbying legislators for a constitutional amendment to create a state lottery. She failed to muster the necessary two-thirds vote in the House during the 1991 regular session, but finally prevailed in winning legislative approval in a special session that summer. The lottery was a relatively safe issue on which to stake a leadership claim because polls indicated it had the strong support of most Texans as a new source of revenue for state government.

Most other major issues before the legislature during Richards's first year in office, however, weren't so simple, and the new governor was less willing to strike specific policy positions on them. She preferred to support the initiatives of Democratic legislative leaders, or take the best bill they were willing to give her, rather than demand that legislators enact a specific plan. Richards, for example, outlined strong provisions for a new ethics law for legislators and other public officials, but ended up signing a much weaker bill rather than trying to force a showdown. She also accepted a watered-down version of a bill creating a new, consolidated environmental protection agency. She had little input in the budget- and tax-writing process, which Lieutenant Governor Bob Bullock dominated. Detractors would say Richards's leadership wilted in the heat of legislative battle. Supporters would say she was a pragmatist who knew the limits of her office and recognized the necessity of political compromise.

Richards's early leadership experiences in office were not unlike those encountered by other newly elected governors. When issues are articulated during a campaign, the substantive details of a legislative package are generally not considered. After the election, the most pressing issue is recruiting staff and getting organized to take office. The transition from election day to inauguration day is only about two months, which leaves little time to develop a comprehensive legislative package. A new governor thus is often forced to take the best bill available.

The progressive goals that Richards had outlined in her campaign were also tempered by the reality that Texas was a predominantly conservative state. Despite promoting a vision of a "New Texas" that offered more compassion for the poor, improved health care for the sick, and greater educational opportunity for all, Richards took pains to establish credentials for fiscal restraint. She opposed a proposal for a personal income tax, even though it could have provided a big boost in health and human services programs and education spending. And she eagerly embraced a thorough review of state spending practices that helped reduce the size of the revenue and tax bill that she eventually signed during her first year in office.

Frustrated over a new governor's limited ability to influence the decisions of policymaking boards loaded with holdover appointees from a previous administration, Richards in 1991 proposed that the legislature give the governor the authority to directly appoint state agency heads. Richards believed that a new governor whose proposals presumably were endorsed by most voters shouldn't have to wait through most of her first term to begin implementing new policies. "The public views the governor as head of the executive branch and holds her responsible," said Paul Williams, who at the time was Richards' executive assistant. "This (proposal) actually gives governors the power the public perceives them to have."[31]

The cabinet concept was not new, and neither was legislators' reluctance to fully embrace it for fear of tipping the balance of governmental power away from the legislature. Lawmakers gave Richards some additional appointment powers over selected agencies, most notably in the health and human services area. But the governor's limited power over the bureaucracy remained virtually unchanged.

Although Richards entered the 1993 legislative session with one of the highest public approval ratings of any governor in Texas history, she remained cautious during the entire session, apparently to save political capital for a 1994 reelection race. She joined Lieutenant Governor Bob Bullock and Speaker Pete Laney in insisting that a new state budget be written without an increase in state taxes. There was no tax bill, but the new budget didn't enable the legislature to give teachers a pay raise, which had been a Richards priority, and it didn't keep up with growing caseloads in health and human services.

In one of the most emotional issues of the session, Richards sided with police chiefs, mayors, physicians, and members of the clergy—and against a majority of the legislature—in killing a proposal to allow private citizens to legally carry handguns. (It was revived and approved under Governor George W. Bush two years later.) She successfully advocated an immunization program for children and actively promoted the legislature's efforts to meet a Texas Supreme Court order for a constitutional school finance system, but didn't propose a plan of her own.

Richards staked out a strong anticrime position early in her term. In 1991, she ordered her appointees to the Board of Pardons and Paroles to sharply curtail a high rate of releases from state prisons, and she supported a huge prison expansion program. Richards also made economic development a major goal. She actively recruited companies to locate or expand in Texas and was instrumental in lobbying the U.S. Congress for approval of the North American Free Trade Agreement (NAFTA), even though NAFTA was bitterly opposed by organized labor, one of her long-time, key supporters.

Richards was a national figure who was readily welcomed on Wall Street, at Hollywood parties, and in corporate boardrooms throughout the country. Many analysts believed her role as Texas's chief ambassador was her greatest contribution, along with the appointments that opened up the state policymaking process to a record number of women, Hispanics, and African Americans.

Richards, who had no legislative experience, didn't seem to relish the often bloody give-and-take of the legislative process but obviously enjoyed her celebrity role as governor. During the 1993 session, Richards told reporters she wasn't the kind of leader who could force results. Instead, she said, she tried to contribute to "an atmosphere in which good things can happen."[32]

Although Richards was unseated by Republican George W. Bush in 1994, polls indicated she remained personally popular with her constituents. But most conservative, independent voters had never been comfortable with Richards politically. Her defeat coincided with voter discontent with the Democratic party that swept the country that year. A number of other Democratic governors were also defeated, and Republicans captured control of both houses of the U.S. Congress. Richards's opposition to the handgun bill during the 1993 legislative session was another factor, particularly in key conservative areas of the state.

George W. Bush (1995–2000)

George W. Bush, son of former President George Bush, had never held public office before being elected governor, but he had gained valuable political experience campaigning for and serving as an unofficial adviser to his father. The younger Bush became Texas's second Republican governor in modern times by conducting an effective campaign for improvements in the public schools, tougher penalties for juvenile offenders, and reform of the welfare and civil justice systems. He succeeded in winning legislative approval of all four programs during the 1995 legislative session, the first of his term.

Governor George W. Bush (1995–2000).

Bush's public style was low key. He seemed to go out of his way to avoid controversy during his first year in office. But he remained focused on his four primary goals, and he was assisted by conservative, Democratic legislative leaders who shared his views and sensed that public sentiment was on the governor's side. Although Democrats had majorities in both the House and the Senate in 1995, the Texas legislature was dominated by conservatives of both major parties, and work on some of the reforms the new governor wanted had already been initiated by Democratic officials.

While keeping a low public profile during his first legislative session, Bush actively worked with legislators behind the scenes, making minor compromises when necessary on his policy priorities. The governor had frequent private meetings with House and Senate members and would sometimes drop by their Capitol offices unannounced. He had weekly breakfast meetings with Lieutenant Governor Bob Bullock and Speaker Pete Laney, two Democrats whose work was crucial to the governor's program. "We disagree, but you'll never read about it," Bush said of his meetings with the two legislative leaders. "The way to forge good public policy amongst the leadership of the legislative branch and executive branch is to air our differences in private meetings that happen all the time. The way to ruin a relationship is to leak things [to the media] and to be disrespectful of meeting in private."[33]

Bush also believed his decisive victory in the 1994 election helped his cause in the legislature. "I won by 352,000 votes," he told reporters the day after the 1995 session adjourned. "And when you stand up in front of the legislature and outline a legislative agenda that was endorsed by the will of the people, that helps remind people that this is what Texans want."[34]

Unlike Governors White, Clements, and Richards before him, Bush did not face budgetary problems in state government that could have distracted lawmakers' attention from his priorities. Unlike Richards, Bush supported legislation that gave adult Texans the right to carry concealed handguns. The gun bill was not one of Bush's major priorities, but it had been an issue in his victory over Richards. Bush signed the gun bill approved by lawmakers in 1995.

Bush faced a tougher challenge during the 1997 legislative session, when he made school property tax reform a major goal. He proposed that state government assume a larger share of the cost of funding the public schools by lowering local school taxes by about $3 billion a year. To replace the lost revenue, he proposed an increase in the state sales tax, the enactment of a new business tax, and the transfer of $1 billion in state budgetary savings to the public schools. The House rejected most of Bush's proposal and approved a controversial tax tradeoff that would have increased numerous state taxes in exchange for major cuts in local school taxes. Bush lobbied Republican legislators for the House plan and helped convince about half of the sixty-eight Republicans in the House to vote for it. Assured that Bush was actively backing the plan, Speaker Laney helped persuade a large number of Democratic House members to vote for it. The bipartisan balancing act was necessary because many Republican legislators had campaigned against higher taxes of any kind, and many Democratic lawmakers had previously been targeted by Republicans over the tax issue.

Despite the success in the House, the Senate, which had a Republican majority, refused to approve a large increase in state taxes. Bush remained mostly in the background while the Senate debated the issue. After it became obvious the House and the Senate were in a stalemate, legislative negotiators requested the governor's active participation once again. But Bush was unable to forge any compromise that raised state taxes. The governor managed to salvage only a modest amount of property tax relief—about $150 a year for the average homeowner—by convincing the legislature to increase homestead exemptions, a form of tax break that homeowners get on their school taxes. The legislature used $1 billion in state budgetary savings to repay school districts for the revenue they lost from the higher exemptions.

In failing to win more substantial property tax relief, Bush couldn't overcome two major obstacles. One was strong opposition from business lobbyists to the proposed state tax increases. The other was the absence of a state budgetary crisis that would have forced the legislature to increase taxes. "We have a budget surplus. How do you start with a surplus and turn that into a tax bill? It's pretty hard to explain," said state Senator John Whitmire, a Democrat from Houston.[35]

Bush said he wanted to lower property taxes because they had become so high they were making home ownership difficult for many Texans. Some Democrats said Bush had failed as a leader because he had been unable to convince the legislature to enact a more substantial property tax cut package, but the governor dismissed the criticism. "I think people are going to say this is a man who set a very bold agenda and acted boldly," he said.[36] He said the higher homestead exemption that the legislature did pass was important.

Bush easily won reelection over Democratic challenger Garry Mauro in 1998 and entered the 1999 legislative session amidst widespread speculation that he was preparing for a presidential race. With his pending White House campaign obviously on his mind, he convinced the legislature to enact some additional tax cuts and increase education spending. And he accepted a priority of Democratic lawmakers to give school teachers a $3,000-a-year pay raise. Bush's biggest legislative defeat in 1999 was the rejection of a pilot program to allow students from low-performing public schools to use tax-backed vouchers to attend private schools. But, in an effort to shore up support among religious and social conservatives in the Republican party, Bush won approval of a law to require parents to be notified before their minor daughters could receive abortions. It was the most significant piece of abortion-control legislation to be passed by Texas lawmakers since the U.S. Supreme Court had legalized abortion 26 years earlier.

Bush officially launched a campaign for the 2000 Republican presidential nomination in June 1999. He was elected president in the 2000 election, resigned as governor in December and was succeeded by Rick Perry, the lieutenant governor.

Rick Perry (2000–)

Republican Rick Perry came to the governor's office with much more governmental experience than his immediate and more famous predecessor, George W. Bush. He had served six years as a state representative, eight years as state agriculture commissioner, and almost two years as lieutenant governor before succeeding Bush as governor in December 2000, after Bush had resigned to become president. But Perry wasn't blessed with Bush's politically powerful name or his popularity, and he hadn't been elected governor. He had inherited the job. Moreover, the 2001 legislative session, with which Perry immediately had to deal, promised to be contentious because of political redistricting and a worrisome budgetary outlook.

Perry, however, survived his first session mostly unscarred. He didn't have to sign or veto any redistricting bills because Republicans and Democrats in the legislature were unable to agree on new political boundaries for themselves or

Governor Rick Perry served first as lieutenant governor and assumed the governorship in 2000 when George W. Bush resigned the governorship to become the President of the United States. He was elected to a full term in 2002.

Texas's congressional delegation. The legislative impasse put legislative redistricting in the hands of the Legislative Redistricting Board and deferred congressional redistricting—for the time being, anyway—to a federal court. Lawmakers wrote a new state budget without having to raise taxes and, at Perry's urging, even found enough money to triple funding for a grant program to help thousands of young Texans from low-income families attend college.

The legislature enacted one of Perry's criminal justice priorities, a law to give prison inmates the ability to obtain court-ordered DNA testing if they can demonstrate that there is a substantial possibility that the results will prove them innocent. But the governor didn't get his way on another criminal justice issue with significant political overtones. In one of the most emotional and partisan issues of the session, the legislature approved a bill, backed by most Democrats and opposed by most Republicans, to strengthen penalties for crimes motivated by hate or prejudice. It was a fight that had begun in earnest two years earlier, after three white assailants had dragged an African American, James Byrd, Jr., to death behind a pickup in East Texas. At one point, Perry convinced a Republican senator to help delay action on the bill because he opposed a provision that listed protected classes of people, including homosexuals, which was strongly opposed by social conservatives in the Republican Party. But after the measure won final legislative approval, Perry signed it within a few hours after it reached his desk. He said he still had doubts about it. "But I also believe that as governor, and as a Texan, I have an obligation to see issues from another person's perspective, to walk in another person's shoes," he said.[37]

Some legislators criticized Perry's mostly low-key style during the legislative session and complained that he didn't let them know early enough and clearly enough what he wanted. Shortly after the legislative session had ended, however, Perry flexed his muscles and vetoed a record eighty-two bills, including a measure that would have banned the execution of mentally retarded convicts in Texas. Aware that international attention was focused on his decision, Perry invited relatives of murder victims to join him at a state Capitol news conference announcing the veto. Crime victims' advocates praised the veto, but death penalty opponents criticized it. A year later, the United States Supreme Court, acting in a case from another state, prohibited the execution of mentally retarded inmates throughout the country.

Other vetoes drew sharp criticism from a range of people. Among the loudest complaints came from doctors over the governor's veto of a bill that would have required insurance companies to promptly pay health care providers for their services. Physicians and hospitals complained that health maintenance organizations and other insurers were dragging their feet in paying valid claims, often creating financial hardships for providers. Perry vetoed the bill at the urging of business groups that argued that it would have removed arbitration as an option for settling health insurance claims and would have encouraged lawsuits. A similar prompt-pay bill was enacted by the legislature in 2003—without the provision that offended the business groups—and Perry signed it.

During his first year as governor, Perry also had to dodge political fallout from the spectacular collapse of Enron Corporation, the Houston-based energy-trading giant, which had been a major source of political donations during his public career. Soon after Enron filed for bankruptcy in late 2001, throwing thousands of employees out of work and costing investors and retirees millions of dollars, controversy erupted over Perry's appointment of a former Enron executive, Max Yzaguirre, to chair the Texas Public Utility Commission. Perry had appointed Yzaguirre in June 2001, several months before most people even suspected that Enron was in financial trouble. But after the Enron story exploded, Democrats started questioning Yzaguirre's eligibility for the regulatory post and the timing of his appointment. Perry had received a $25,000 political donation from then-Enron Chairman Ken Lay the day after appointing Yzaguirre. Perry insisted Yzaguirre was legally qualified and that the timing of the contribution was coincidental. But after the controversy had raged for several weeks, Yzaguirre resigned. It wasn't clear whether he chose to step down on his own or was quietly encouraged to do so by the governor.

Despite his rural roots—Perry grew up in Paint Creek, a tiny town in West Texas—the governor was acutely aware of the clogged freeways that plagued the daily lives of urban and suburban Texans and, early on, sought to make improved transportation a signature issue of his administration. He actively campaigned for a constitutional amendment, which voters approved in November 2001, creating the Texas Mobility Fund, a revolving fund against which bonds could be pledged for highway construction. It was a significant departure from the state's traditional pay-as-you-go method of paying for highways. Then, in early 2002, Perry proposed a massive $175 billion transportation network for Texas, which would include toll roads, railroads, and underground utility tunnels grouped in corridors stretching across the state. The plan, which Perry called the Trans Texas Corridor, would take an estimated fifty years to complete.

Perry defeated Democratic nominee Tony Sanchez, a multimillionaire Laredo businessman, in a bruising campaign to win a full term in the governor's office in 2002. Perry's victory and the first Republican takeover of the Texas House in modern times put the GOP in undisputed control of state government, and Perry acted accordingly. The governor joined Republican legislative leaders in demanding that a $10 billion revenue shortfall be bridged by cutting spending, not raising state taxes, and Republicans prevailed. Advocates of health care programs and other services protested the spending reductions, and many of the state's daily newspapers editorialized for limited tax increases to help minimize the cuts in services. The legislature raised some state fees and enacted legislation to allow university governing boards to increase tuition, but Perry refused to budge on taxes, apparently convinced that most middle class Texans agreed with him. He also argued that the state's relatively low tax burden had to be protected to keep the state attractive to businesses looking for places to expand. Perry also won from the legislature a special economic development fund that could be used to provide economic incentives for business recruitment.

The governor also advocated and won significant new restrictions on medical malpractice claims and other civil lawsuits. He said the so-called "tort reform" changes were essential to easing a crisis in health care, particularly in rural areas, and improving the state's business climate, although opponents argued that they put unnecessary, new restrictions on consumers' access to the courts.

As was more fully discussed in Chapter 8, Perry also played a dominant role in a bitter, partisan fight over congressional redistricting in 2003. Perry fully supported an effort, initiated by U.S. House Majority Leader Tom DeLay of Sugar Land, to increase the number of Republicans elected to the U.S. House from Texas. Under a 2001 redistricting plan drawn by a federal court, Democrats still held a 17–15 majority in the Texas congressional delegation, despite recent Republican sweeps of all statewide offices and Republican majorities in both the Texas House and the state Senate. DeLay, Perry, and other GOP leaders argued that the congressional delegation should more accurately reflect the state's Republican strength. A bill that would have redrawn the congressional districts to favor more Republican candidates died during the 2003 regular session after more than 50 Democratic members of the Texas House fled to Ardmore, Oklahoma, to break a quorum and keep the House from acting on the measure. Using one of his strongest constitutional powers, Perry then called the legislature back into special session that summer to try again. Eventually it took three special sessions to complete the task, but Perry was persistent. He even waited out a second Democratic boycott, when eleven Democratic senators flew to Albuquerque, N.M., to hold out for more than a month and shut down the Senate during the entire second special session. A redistricting bill that the Republican-dominated legislature finally passed during the third special session, unless overturned in court, was expected to increase the number of Republicans elected to Congress from Texas by as many as seven, all at the expense of incumbent Democrats. Texas Democrats and others, including minority groups, quickly filed federal lawsuits against the plan, which were pending at the end of 2003.

For a while, at least, the redistricting dispute may have put a dent in Perry's public popularity. A Scripps Howard *Texas Poll* taken at the height of the controversy in August 2003, while the Democratic senators were still in New Mexico, indicated that Perry's job approval rating was at his lowest, 44 percent, since he had become governor. It had fallen 6 percentage points since June. The same poll showed that Texans by a narrow margin (46 percent to 40 percent) opposed congressional redistricting but strongly disagreed (62 percent to 29 percent) with the Democratic walkout. Perry said he wasn't worried. "I get up every day and try to do what's right for the people of Texas," he said. "I don't wake up and fret about what a particular poll at a particular point in time says."[38]

OTHER OFFICES OF THE EXECUTIVE BRANCH

Lieutenant Governor

The **lieutenant governor** is the second highest-ranking official in the state, but the executive powers of this office are limited. Were the governor to die, be incapacitated, removed from office, or voluntarily leave office in midterm, the lieutenant governor would become governor. That eventuality has occurred only four times. In

1917, William P. Hobby replaced James E. Ferguson, who was impeached. Governor W. Lee O'Daniel resigned in 1941 to enter the U.S. Senate and was succeeded by Coke Stevenson. Governor Beauford Jester died in office in 1949 and was replaced by Allan Shivers. And, George W. Bush resigned in December 2000 after being elected president and was succeeded by Rick Perry.

In Texas, the office of lieutenant governor is primarily a legislative office. Because of the lieutenant governor's key legislative role and statewide constituency, many experts consider this position the most powerful office in state government. The lieutenant governor, who need not belong to the same party as the governor and is elected independently of the governor, is the presiding officer of the Senate and traditionally has been given enormous power over the legislative process by the Senate rules. The legislative powers and prerogatives of the office far exceed those of the vice president on the federal level. The lieutenant governor also chairs the Legislative Budget Board, which plays a key role in the state budgetary process.

Democrat Bill Hobby, son of the former governor, served a record eighteen years as lieutenant governor before retiring in 1991. He was succeeded by Bob Bullock, a former state comptroller and one of the most influential state officials in recent history. Bullock, who chose not to seek reelection in 1998 and died the next year, was succeeded by Republican Rick Perry, a former state agriculture commissioner.

Perry presided over the Senate for only one session, 1999, before succeeding Bush as governor after the 2000 presidential election. State senators then elected state Senator Bill Ratliff, R-Mt. Pleasant, to complete Perry's term as lieutenant governor and preside over the Senate during the 2001 session. Republican David Dewhurst was elected lieutenant governor in 2002. The former state land commissioner had no legislative experience but made a quick, yet thorough, study of major issues and legislative procedures (see Chapter 8).

David Dewhurst assumed the office of lieutenant governor in 2003, after serving one term as Texas Land Commissioner.

Attorney General

As the state's chief legal officer, the **attorney general** is called upon to defend state laws enacted by the legislature and orders adopted by regulatory agencies. The office also enforces the state's antitrust and consumer protection laws and helps collect child-support payments from delinquent noncustodial parents. Recent attorneys general have been kept busy defending the state or negotiating settlements in federal and state court actions challenging the constitutionality of state prisons, the public school finance system, the method of selecting state judges, and other major policies.

Unlike counterparts in the federal government and some other states, the Texas attorney general is primarily a civil lawyer. Except for representing the state in the appeals of death penalty cases and assisting local prosecutors, the position has relatively little responsibility for criminal law enforcement. Many candidates for the office like to campaign on tough law-and-order platforms, but responsibilities for criminal prosecution are vested in locally elected county and district attorneys (see Chapter 12). The attorney general also gives opinions on the legality of actions of other state and local officials and is at the center of the policymaking process.[39]

Dan Morales, a former Democratic state representative from San Antonio, was elected attorney general in 1990, becoming the second Hispanic elected to statewide office in Texas. He won reelection in 1994 but chose not to run for a third term in 1998. He was succeeded by former Texas Supreme Court Justice John Cornyn, Texas's first Republican attorney general in modern times. Cornyn was elected to the U.S. Senate in 2002 and was succeeded by Republican Greg Abbott, another former Texas Supreme Court justice.

In a major policy decision made independently of the governor, the legislature, and other state officials, Morales in 1996 filed a multibillion-dollar damage suit against tobacco companies, seeking reimbursement for public health care costs associated with smoking (see Chapter 13). Some other state officials supported Morales' decision, although others had reservations about the state jumping into the tobacco controversy. But Morales acted within his authority as the state's chief legal officer. The decision was his alone to make, and it resulted in a $17.3 billion settlement for the state. The tobacco suit also sparked a controversy over legal fees that, several years after Morales had left office, resulted in him being sentenced to federal prison for four years for mail fraud and filing a false income tax return (see "Dan Morales: A Spectacular Rise and Fall").

Comptroller of Public Accounts

The comptroller is the state's primary tax administrator, accounting officer, and revenue estimator. Texas functions under a **pay-as-you-go** principle, which means that the state cannot adopt an operating budget that exceeds anticipated revenue. The comptroller is responsible for providing the revenue estimates on which biennial state budgets are drafted by the legislature. A budget cannot become law without the comptroller's certification that it falls within the official revenue projection. The comptroller's office produces a revenue estimate of all projected state income for the two-year budget period by using sophisticated models of the state's economy.[40] If the revenue estimate is below the legislature's budget proposals, appropriations must be reduced or taxes must be raised. In a volatile, changing economy, it is difficult to accurately project revenues two years in the future. In the mid-1980s, then-Comptroller

DAN MORALES: A SPECTACULAR RISE AND FALL

Dan Morales was one of state government's biggest vote getters during two terms as attorney general and, as only the second Hispanic ever elected to statewide office in Texas, was considered a rising star of the Democratic Party. He chose not to seek reelection in 1998. But before leaving office, he sued the tobacco industry over smoking-related health care costs and won a $17.3 billion settlement for the state from cigarette manufacturers. The settlement, to be paid out over many years, would generate huge amounts of revenue for health care or any other programs the legislature chose.

The settlement was clearly the highlight of Morales' political career, but, ironically, it also contributed to his eventual downfall. The settlement sparked much controversy over $3.3 billion in legal fees awarded to five private lawyers whom Morales had hired under a contingency contract to represent the state in the litigation. Although tobacco companies agreed to pay the lawyers' fees, Attorney General John Cornyn, Morales' Republican successor, called the payments excessive. He also questioned the legality of the outside lawyers' agreement with Morales and spent much of his first year in office investigating the lawyers' work. The legal fees also were attacked by business groups seeking limits on civil court judgments and lawyers' payments. These same groups—so-called "tort reformers"—had contributed heavily to Cornyn's election campaign.

Neither Cornyn nor federal prosecutors found any illegalities in Morales' dealings with the five lawyers or in the outside lawyers' work for the state. But Morales' attempt to steer as much as $520 million in legal fees to a sixth lawyer, Marc Murr of Houston, resulted in a lengthy federal investigation. Morales said Murr, a personal friend, was an important part of his anti-tobacco legal team, but other lawyers said Murr did little, if any, work on the case.

While the investigation, which stretched over four years, was still pending, Morales attempted a political comeback by running for governor in the 2002 Democratic primary. He lost to Laredo businessman Tony Sanchez and later crossed party lines to endorse Republican Governor Rick Perry, who defeated Sanchez in the general election.

Finally, in March 2003, a federal grand jury indicted Morales, accusing him of trying to improperly steer millions of dollars in legal fees from the tobacco settlement to Murr. The indictment also charged the former attorney general with misappropriating campaign money to make a down payment on a $775,000 house while he was still in office, lying on a loan application for a $600,000 mortgage and filing a false income tax return for 1998, his last year in office. Seven months later, Morales was sentenced to four years in federal prison after pleading guilty to mail fraud and filing a false income tax return. He admitted backdating a government contract and forging government records related to the tobacco suit. In a separate deal with prosecutors, Murr pleaded guilty to one count of mail fraud.

Morales expressed "sincere regret and remorse" at his sentencing before U.S. District Judge Sam Sparks of Austin. But he said that the "vast majority of misdeeds" he had been accused of where untrue. Most political observers were left scratching their heads.

Source: Houston Chronicle, November 1, 2003, 29A.

Bob Bullock had to adjust his revenue estimate downward several times to account for plunging oil prices.

The comptroller's powerful role in budgetary affairs was enhanced by the legislature in 1990 with the additional authority to conduct management audits of local school districts, and again in 1991 with similar oversight authority over other state

Carole Keeton Strayhorn, the first Republican elected Comptroller of Public Accounts, announces a Public Integrity Task Force charged with the responsibility of investigating alleged cheating on statewide student tests and inaccurate reporting by local school districts.

agencies. Through this process, Comptroller John Sharp and his successor, Republican Carole Keeton Strayhorn, identified billions of dollars' worth of potential savings for legislative budget writers and local school boards.

Strayhorn, who changed her name from Rylander after marrying in early 2003, was a strong supporter of—and reaped favorable publicity from—the management audits. But the legislature, in a 2003 special session, transferred those programs to the Legislative Budget Board after the comptroller had become involved in a series of budgetary disputes with legislators and other Republican leaders. Always outspoken and widely viewed as politically ambitious, Strayhorn had surprised the governor and the Legislature with a larger-than-anticipated revenue shortfall of $10 billion at the beginning of the 2003 regular session. Strayhorn later threatened—but only briefly—not to certify the new state budget drafted by lawmakers. And, finally, to make matters worse, she announced that the no-new-taxes budget about which the governor and Republican lawmakers had bragged actually included $2.7 billion in higher fees to be paid by millions of Texans. Strayhorn blamed Governor Rick Perry for the decision to strip the management audit programs from her agency. The governor's office denied the allegation, but Perry had signed the bill. Strayhorn was so angry that she strongly hinted that she might challenge Perry in the 2006 Republican gubernatorial primary.

Commissioner of the General Land Office

Texas retains ownership, including mineral rights, to approximately 22 million acres of public lands, which are managed by the state **land commissioner.** Revenues generated by mineral leases and other land uses are earmarked for education through the Permanent University Fund and the Permanent School Fund. This agency also is responsible for the Veterans Land Program, which provides low interest loans to veterans for the purchase of land and houses.

During sixteen years in office, Land Commissioner Garry Mauro, a Democrat, developed several environmental initiatives, including beach cleanup efforts and a program for cleaning up oil spills off the Texas coast. Mauro also took the lead in developing a coastal zone management plan to coordinate environmental protection efforts along the coast. After Mauro unsuccessfully ran for governor in 1998, the next land commissioner, Republican David Dewhurst, a businessman from Houston, continued the beach cleanup efforts. Dewhurst also won legislative approval of a program to replenish beaches and protect them from erosion. Dewhurst was elected lieutenant governor in 2002 and was succeeded as land commissioner by Jerry Patterson, a former state senator from Harris County. Patterson's priorities included development of new nursing homes for veterans and new veterans' cemeteries.

Commissioner of Agriculture

This office, created by statute rather than by the constitution, is responsible for carrying out laws regulating and benefiting the agricultural sector of the state's economy. In addition to providing support for agricultural research and education, the agency is responsible for the administration of consumer protection laws in the areas of weights and measures, packaging and labeling, and marketing. Republican Rick Perry aggressively promoted Texas agricultural products during two terms as commissioner. Republican Susan Combs, a former state representative from Austin, was elected to the office in 1998 after Perry ran for lieutenant governor. She also urged Texans to buy more produce grown in the Lone Star State.

Secretary of State

The **secretary of state,** the only constitutional official appointed by the governor, has a variety of duties, including granting charters to corporations and processing the extradition of prisoners to other states. The primary function of this office, however, is to administer state election laws. That responsibility includes reviewing county and local election procedures, developing statewide policy for voter registration, and receiving and tabulating election returns.

State Treasurer

The Constitution of 1876 created a **state treasurer** to be the custodian of state funds. Shortly after taking office in 1993, however, Treasurer Martha Whitehead came to believe the office was no longer needed. She convinced the legislature and the voters to abolish it with a constitutional amendment, which was adopted in 1995. The

Republican Susan Combs, addressing staff members about drought conditions in Texas, was elected state agriculture commissioner in 1998.

agency's duties were transferred to the comptroller's office (see "She Campaigned to End Her Own Job").

Elected Boards and Commissions

Texas Railroad Commission.   This body was originally designed to regulate intrastate (within Texas) operations of railroads. It also regulated intrastate trucking for many years, but it lost its trucking responsibilities and most of its railroad regulation to the federal government. It still has some oversight over rail safety and regulates oil and natural gas production and lignite mining in Texas.

The commission includes three elected members who serve six-year, staggered terms and rotate the position of chair among themselves. The oil and gas industry has historically focused much attention on this agency and made large campaign contributions to commission members. Many critics claim the commission is a prime example of a regulatory body that has been co-opted by those interests it was created to regulate.

And, in recent years, it has become a staging area for opportunistic politicians who seek election to the commission primarily as a stepping-stone to higher office. A commissioner doesn't have to resign in the middle of his or her six-year term to seek another office and, as an incumbent regulator, has little trouble collecting large

---

SHE CAMPAIGNED TO END HER OWN JOB

State Treasurer Martha Whitehead was a rarity in Texas politics—an officeholder who campaigned to abolish her own job. The treasurer's post was created by the Constitution of 1876 to manage the state's money, but by the 1990s it had become a relatively minor office overshadowed by the much larger fiscal operations of the state comptroller. It nevertheless still offered some political benefits for its occupants. Democrat Ann Richards, who was state treasurer for eight years, used the office to launch a successful race for governor. Republican Kay Bailey Hutchison was elected to the U.S. Senate from the treasurer's office. But Whitehead, who was appointed to the office by Richards in 1993 after Hutchison won the Senate seat in a special election, held the office for only a few months before deciding it was wasting taxpayers' money and needed to be abolished.

Pledging to lead a campaign to wipe the office off the books, Whitehead was elected to a new term in 1994 over a Republican opponent, Austin banker David Hartman, who argued that the treasurer's office should remain an independent agency to assure adequate checks and balances on state finances. The legislature placed a constitutional amendment on the November 1995 ballot to abolish the office and transfer its duties to the comptroller. The amendment was opposed by Texas Republican party leaders but was overwhelmingly approved by voters. The elimination of the elected treasurer's post was effective on September 1, 1996. Some of the agency's 200 employees were transferred to the comptroller's office, but other jobs were phased out.

---

contributions from the oil and gas industry that can be used to further political ambitions. Both Democrat John Sharp and Republican Carole Keeton Strayhorn (formerly Rylander) used seats on the commission to strengthen their political bases for successful races for state comptroller in 1990 and 1998, respectively. Other recent commission members haven't been as successful, but not because they didn't try. Between 1980 and 2002, fifteen people served on the three-member commission, and only four actually completed a full six-year term. One recent commissioner, Tony Garza, resigned in midterm to accept President George W. Bush's appointment as ambassador to Mexico.

The game of musical chairs has prompted calls in recent years for the commission to be abolished and its duties transferred to other agencies appointed by the governor, including the Public Utility Commission, which already has oversight over electric utilities, and the Texas Commission on Environmental Quality, the state's main environmental protection agency. Democrat Hector Uribe, a former state senator, ran for the commission in 1996, promising to work to abolish it. But Strayhorn, his Republican opponent, argued that the agency was important and needed to be retained. Strayhorn defeated Uribe for a six-year term on the commission, but two years later she ran for and won election to the comptroller's office.

State Board of Education. Since the early settlers declared their independence from Mexico, public education has been a major policy issue in Texas. In recent years it probably has attracted more attention than ever before. The debate has focused not only on educational quality and financing, but also on how best to carry out and manage public education programs. The state has bounced back and forth between an elected state education board and an appointed one.

Prior to educational reforms enacted in 1984, the **State Board of Education** was made up of twenty-seven members elected from congressional districts across the state. At the urging of reformers dissatisfied with student performance, the legislature provided for a new education board of fifteen members to be appointed by the governor and confirmed by the Senate. The idea was to reduce the board's independence while new education reforms ordered by the legislature were being carried out. But the law also provided that the board would again become an elected body within a few years. Some state leaders later proposed that the board remain appointive and put the question to the voters, who opted for an elected board in 1986. The present board has fifteen members elected from districts established by the legislature.

Philosophical and partisan bickering on the board in recent years prompted the legislature to reduce its powers. The panel's main remaining duties include investment of education dollars in the Permanent School Fund and some oversight over textbook selection and curriculum standards.

But the day-to-day administration of the Texas Education Agency, the agency responsible for public education, is under the direction of the commissioner of education, who is appointed by the governor.

SUMMARY AND CONCLUSIONS

1. Although it is the most visible office in state government and the public believes it has considerable power, the office of governor is weak in formal powers. Unlike the president of the United States, the governor of Texas has no formal cabinet that serves at his or her pleasure. Texas has a "plural executive," which includes several independently elected statewide officeholders. This arrangement was a reaction to the abuses of the Davis administration during the Reconstruction era, but reform advocates argue that it diminishes the ability of the executive branch to respond to modern problems.

2. Administrative responsibilities are further fragmented through 200-plus boards and commissions authorized by statutory law. Although the governor appoints individuals to these boards, the governor's control is diluted by board members' staggered terms, the need for senatorial approval of the governor's appointments, and legal requirements relating to the composition of these boards.

3. A governor's cabinet has long been advocated by some critics of state government as a solution to the fragmentation of the executive branch. But the legislature has been reluctant to expand the governor's power in this fashion.

4. Besides appointments, the governor's main formal powers are the veto of legislation, line-item veto authority over the budget, and the authority to call and set the agenda for special legislative sessions.

5. Potentially, the governor has a number of informal resources that can be used to shape public policy. Governors have used their staffs, their access to the mass media, their party roles, and their relationships to key interest groups to influence the legislature and other elected officials.

6. Other elected officeholders in the executive branch are the lieutenant governor, the attorney general, the comptroller, the land commissioner, the agriculture commissioner, the three members of the Texas Railroad Commission, and the fifteen members of the State Board of Education. The top appointed official in the executive branch is the secretary of state. Although the lieutenant governor is part of the executive branch, the duties of that office are primarily legislative.

KEY TERMS

Plural executive

Governor

Staggered terms

Senatorial courtesy

Lieutenant governor

Attorney general

Comptroller of Public Accounts

Pay-as-you-go

Land commissioner

Agriculture commissioner

Secretary of state

State treasurer

Railroad Commission

State Board of Education

FURTHER READING

Articles

Fairbanks, James David, "The Textbook Governor," *Texas Journal of Political Studies* 6 (Fall/Winter 1983), pp. 54–63.

Thompson, Pat, and Steven R. Boyd, "Use of the Line Item Veto in Texas, 1940–1990," *State and Local Government Review* 26 (Winter 1994), pp. 38–45.

Books

Anderson, Ken. *You Can't Do That, Dan Moody: The Klan Fighting Governor of Texas.* Austin: Eakin Press, 1998.

Beyle, Thad L., "Being Governor," in *The State of the States,* 3rd ed., ed. Carl E. Van Horn. Washington, DC: Congressional Quarterly Press, 1996, pp. 77–107.

Beyle, Thad L., "Governors: The Middlemen and Women in Our Political System," in *Politics in the American States: A Comparative Analysis,* 6th ed., eds. Virginia Gray and Herbert Jacob. Washington, DC: Congressional Quarterly Press, 1996, pp. 207–52.

Beyle, Thad L., and J. Oliver Williams, *The American Governor in Behavioral Perspective.* New York: Harper & Row, Publishers, 1972.

Davis, J. William, *There Shall Also Be a Lieutenant Governor.* Austin: Institute of Public Affairs, University of Texas, 1967.

Dickson, James D., *Law and Politics: The Office of Attorney General in Texas.* Austin: Sterling Swift, 1976.

Frederick, Douglas W., "Reexamining the Texas Railroad Commission," in *Texas Politics: A Reader,* ed. by Anthony Champagne and Edward J. Harpham. New York: W.W. Norton, 1997, pp. 67–76.

Gantt, Fred, Jr., *The Chief Executive in Texas: A Study of Gubernatorial Leadership.* Austin: University of Texas Press, 1964.

Ivans, Molly, and Lou Dubose. *Shrub: The Short but Happy Life of George W. Bush.* New York: Random House, 2000.

Lauderdale, Michael. *Reinventing State Government.* Austin: University of Texas Press, 1999.

Lipson, Leslie, with an introduction by Marshall E. Dimock, *The American Governor from Figurehead to Leader.* Chicago: University of Chicago Press, 1939.

Morris, Celia, *Storming the Statehouse: Running for Governor with Ann Richards and Dianne Feinstein.* New York: Charles Scribner's Sons, 1992.

Paulissen, May Nelson, and Carl McQueary. *Miriam: The Southern Belle Who Became the First Woman Governor of Texas.* Austin: Eakin Press, 1995.

Prindle, David, *Petroleum Politics and the Texas Railroad Commission.* Austin: University of Texas Press, 1981.

Reston, James, Jr., *The Lone Star State: The Life of John Connally.* New York: Harper & Row, Publishers, 1989.

Richards, Ann, Governor of the State of Texas, *Blueprint for the New Texas,* February 6, 1991.

Rosenthal, Alan, *The Governor and the Legislature.* Washington, DC: CQ Press, 1988.

Sabato, Larry, *Goodbye to Good-Time Charlie: The American Governorship Transformed,* 2nd ed. Washington, DC: Congressional Quarterly Press, Inc., 1983.

Shropshire, Mike, and Frank Schaeffer, *The Thorny Rose of Texas: An Intimate Portrait of Governor Ann Richards.* New York: Birch Lane Press, 1994.

Texas General Land Office, *The Land Commissioners of Texas.* Austin: Texas General Land Office, 1986.

Tolleson-Rinehart, Sue, and Jeanie R. Stanley, *Claytie and the Lady.* Austin: University of Texas Press, 1994.

Weaver, Jacqueline Lang, *Unitization of Oil and Gas Fields in Texas: A Study of Legislative, Administrative and Judicial Politics.* Washington, DC: Resources for the Future, Inc., 1986.

Welch, June R., *The Texas Governors.* Dallas: Yellow Rose Press, 1988.

Wiggins, Charles, Keith E. Hamm, and Howard Balanoff, "The Gubernatorial Transition in Texas: Bolt Cutters, Late Trains, Lame Ducks, and Bullock's Bullets," in *Gubernatorial Transitions: The 1982 Elections,* ed. Thad L. Beyle. Durham, NC: Duke University Press, 1985.

Websites

Governor of Texas   http://www.governor.state.tx.us The governor's website offers up-to-date and archived news releases and speeches, ongoing initiatives, and a detailed description of the structure and functions of the governor's office. Links are provided to the important divisions or sections of the governor's office as well as to other state agencies.

State of Texas   http://www.state.tx.us   The state's web page provides links to over 200 state agencies. Most of the state agencies have their own sites, with detailed information about their orga-nizational structure, programs, budgets, reports, and recent activities.

Office of the Comptroller   http://www.cpa.state.tx.gov   In addition to providing links to other state agencies, the comptroller's office provides a wide array of information pertaining to state taxes, management and accounting systems, and performance reviews of state operations and agencies.

National Governors Association (NGA)   http://www.nga.org   This bipartisan organization provides information on "Key State Issues" and monitors and analyzes the progress of important state policy issues. Information on the governors of all fifty states is also available.

ENDNOTES

1. Pat M. Neff, *Messages of Pat M. Neff* (Austin: A. C. Baldwin, 1921), pp. 34–35.
2. Fred Gantt Jr., *The Chief Executive in Texas* (Austin: The University of Texas Press, 1964), p. 24.
3. Ibid., pp. 24–25.
4. Ibid., p. 27.
5. Ibid., pp. 27–32.
6. Ibid., pp. 32–36.
7. Ibid., p. 37.
8. Charles F. Cnudde and Robert E. Crew, *Constitutional Democracy in Texas* (St. Paul, MN: West Publishing Co., 1989), p. 90.
9. Texas Constitution, Art. 4, Sec. 4.
10. Gantt, *The Chief Executive in Texas,* p. 116.
11. Joseph A. Schlesinger, "The Politics of the Executive" in *Politics in the American States,* 2nd ed., eds. Herbert Jacob and Kenneth N. Vines (Boston: Little, Brown, 1971), Chap. 6; Thad L. Beyle "The Governors, 1988–89," in *The Book of the States, 1990–1991* (Lexington, KY: The Council of State Governments, 1990), p. 54.
12. Texas Constitution, Art. 1, Sec. 4.
13. For an excellent treatment of the American governor through the Depression years, see Leslie Lipson, *The American Governor from Figurehead to Leader* (Chicago: University of Chicago Press, 1939).
14. *Dallas Morning News,* April 1987, p. H-2.
15. *Houston Chronicle,* September 30, 2003, page 15A.
16. Texas Constitution, Art. 4, Sec. 11.
17. Wilbourn E. Benton, *Texas Politics: Constraints and Opportunities,* 5th ed. (Chicago: Nelson-Hall Publishers, 1984), pp. 164–66.
18. Ibid., pp. 166–67.
19. Texas Constitution, Art. 4, Sec. 7.
20. Gantt, The Chief Executive in Texas, pp. 90–107.
21. Robert S. Lorch, *State and Local Politics,* 3rd ed. (Englewood Cliffs, NJ: Prentice Hall, Inc., 1989), pp. 115–16.
22. Ibid., pp. 116–19.
23. See James E. Anderson, Richard W. Murray, and Edward L. Farley, *Texas Politics,* 6th ed. (New York: HarperCollins Publishers) for an excellent analysis of the leadership styles of Governors Shivers, Daniel, Connally, Smith, and Briscoe.
24. *Fort Worth Star-Telegram,* January 1, 1980.
25. *Houston Chronicle,* December 2, 1990.
26. *Houston Post,* June 17, 1979.
27. Austin American-Statesman, June 16, 1979.
28. *Texas Poll,* Summer 1987, conducted for Harte-Hanks Communications, Inc., by the Public Policy Resources Laboratory at Texas A & M University.
29. *Houston Chronicle,* December 2, 1990.
30. *Texas Government Newsletter,* 19 (February 25, 1991).
31. *Austin American-Statesman,* July 4, 1991.
32. *Houston Chronicle,* June 2, 1993.
33. *Houston Chronicle,* April 15, 1995.
34. *Houston Chronicle,* May 31, 1995.
35. *Houston Chronicle,* May 27, 1997.
36. *Dallas Morning News,* June 4, 1997.
37. *Houston Chronicle,* May 12, 2001, page 1A.
38. *Houston Chronicle,* August 27, 2003, page 23A.
39. Daniel Elazar, "The Principles and Traditions Underlying State Constitutions," *Publius* 12 (Winter 1982), p. 17.
40. Texas Comptroller of Public Accounts, *Fiscal Notes* (December 1990), p. 9.

CHAPTER 10

The Bureaucracy and Policy Implementation

Government is going to be seen as bigger, dumber and slower than ever before if we don't become smaller, smarter and faster.
Carole Keeton Strayhorn, State Comptroller, 2003[1]

Citizens across Texas rely on the routine services public employees provide, often with little understanding or appreciation of the importance these people play in their daily lives. We take it for granted that the water that comes through our taps will not cause dysentery. The garbage is picked up regularly, with most of us giving little thought to what happens to it. But let a dump catch on fire, and it doesn't take long for someone to contact officials to see what will be done about containing the blaze. Most of us have no idea where sewerage goes or how it is treated. We have little sense of the complex administrative structures required to maintain streets, public libraries, transportation systems, and a host of other public services. Although most of us have attended public schools, we know little, or nothing, about the diverse workforce required to make them work.

Most of us know someone who works for a government in Texas. They are our neighbors, members of our churches, part of our circle of friends, and club members with whom we share common interests. We tend to have positive perceptions of public employees whom we know or with whom we interact. But we also have much ambivalence toward public employees and the agencies for which they work.

In a more general sense, bureaucrats and bureaucracies are even pejorative terms for many Texans. They convey an image of inefficiency, indifference or incompetence in the delivery of public services and are often associated with "red tape." Many people associate governmental agencies with waste or the irresponsible use of taxes, and some citizens believe that public agencies are undemocratic or unaccountable. Many candidates for elected office campaign on promises to reduce governmental waste and spending, streamline government, and reduce the number of people on public payrolls. Such bureaucrat bashing plays well with most voters, and it provides few liabilities for political candidates. But, once elected, public officials soon realize that governments do not run on rhetoric but on the work of the same public employees, or bureaucrats, against whom they campaigned.

Over the past two decades, the number of people working for the federal government has declined as many of their functions have been contracted out to private companies, without significant savings to taxpayers or evidence of improvement in services. The number of state and local employees, meanwhile, has increased to about one and one quarter million full-time workers alone. Some 270,000 people work full-time for the state, and about 950,000 for local governments in Texas. Several hundred thousand more work part-time.

But state agencies have an aging workforce with many workers nearing retirement, and the task of replacing them has been made more difficult by the bureaucrat bashing that has convinced many young people that a career in the public sector is undesirable. Effective administration of public services requires competent employees, but some scholars argue that we have created an environment in which governments at all levels will have a difficult time recruiting new employees who are the best and the brightest.

The sheer size of state government and the fragmented structure of the executive branch (see Chapter 9) also contribute to problems in the state bureaucracy. No single, elected official is ultimately responsible for the quality of public services performed by thousands of state workers. A loosely connected and often confusing network of more than 200 state agencies and universities is responsible for carrying out programs and policies approved and funded by the legislature and the governor. Programs often are developed and agencies established with little thought for policy coordination between departments. The organization of many agencies also is influenced by interest groups, which believe agencies should serve their needs, not those of the general public.

Fragmentation also extends to local governments. With thousands of school districts, cities, counties, and special districts in Texas—many with overlapping jurisdictions—people often are confused about where to turn for help with public services.

The legislature and the governor develop and enact the broad outlines of public policy, but the hundreds of state agencies and local governments must transform those policies into specific programs, based on standard operating procedures. As noted in previous chapters, the legislature meets in regular session only five months every other year; and the governor has only limited powers over the executive branch. The part-time boards and commissions that oversee most state agencies can exercise considerable independence in interpreting policies and determining the character and the quality of public services. Many boards, moreover, are heavily dependent on the guidance of veteran administrators and career bureaucrats within their agencies.

Bureaucracies and bureaucratic behavior have been debated intensely for more than 100 years. The debate has not been conclusive, but it has been instructive. There is general agreement that modern, interdependent societies require large bureaucracies to provide the range of services demanded by citizens. There are inherent nondemocratic aspects in the hierarchical structure of bureaucracies, but bureaucracies, through the uniform application of rules and procedures, contribute to the maintenance of a democratic society. Unlike people in other political systems in which bribery is widespread, we have come to expect that we have rights to public services without having to slide money under the table. The power and influence of bureaucrats must be checked by aggressive review and oversight by the legislature. There are examples of abuse and malfeasance in governmental agencies, but other agencies are effective in carrying out the policy mandates of legislative bodies.

DEFINING BUREAUCRACY

Max Weber, a German sociologist writing in the early part of the twentieth century, regarded bureaucracies as efficient means of organizing large numbers of people to carry out the required tasks for accomplishing specific goals.[2] Bureaucratic structures are inevitable in large, complex societies that have a great deal of individual and group interdependence. To a large extent, these complex organizations are "superior to other methods of organizing people to perform tasks."[3]

Scholars have identified a number of characteristics of bureaucracies, the first of which is size. Whether defined in terms of the number of employees, size of budgets, or number of programs administered, size suggests complex relationships among the people working for an organization. Employees of some large state agencies are scattered among many cities, and both the size and geographic dispersion of these agencies contribute to their organizational hierarchy.[4]

Within governmental organizations, specific positions are assigned specific responsibilities or given specific authority in a hierarchical arrangement. Most agency staffs have one individual at the top, with the organization divided into bureaus, divisions, field offices, or other units. The organization develops complex rules for supervision, management, and reporting of activities.

Bureaucracies require a division of labor among employees and encourage the development of expertise based on experience and education. State agencies break down the responsibilities given to them by the legislature into narrowly defined tasks for their employees. Thousands of workers become specialists in a limited number of activities.

The specialization and division of labor in large organizations require rules and procedures to coordinate the activities of many individuals. Rules reduce the need for continued supervision of employees, and they lay the foundation for standardized behavior.[5] Rules define how tasks are to be carried out, who is responsible for carrying them out, and who qualifies for the organization's, or agency's, services.

Contemporary bureaucracies also are characterized by impersonal relationships, which is why people often complain about having to deal with "faceless" bureaucrats. Responsibilities within an agency are assigned to positions, which can be held by several workers who are supposed to be able to provide the requested service. When you get a voter-registration card or have your driver's license renewed, the name of the person assisting you should make no difference. People come and go in large organizations, and the ongoing functions of organizations are not dependent on specific individuals.[6]

THE GROWTH OF GOVERNMENT IN TEXAS

In 1967, there were 388,000 full-time equivalent state and local government employees in Texas. Thirty years later, there were more than three times that many (see Table 10–1). By 1997, the latest year for which we have comprehensive data, Texas had 582 state and local government employees per 10,000 residents, making it eleventh highest in that category among the fifty states. Texas had only 137 state employees per 10,000 population, forty-fourth among the states. But its 447 local government workers per 10,000 population ranked sixth highest.[7] The number of employees has increased along with the state's population since the 1997 census of governments, but the rankings have remained much the same. Many public services performed by local governments—including public education, fire and police protection, and sanitation services—require large numbers of professionals and other workers.

There has been a substantial expansion of programs at all levels of government in recent years. State spending during the 1982–1983 biennium was $25.6 billion and, only twenty-two years later, the legislature appropriated $118 billion for the 2004–2005 biennium. Between 1990 and 2001 alone, state spending increased by 131 percent, while the population grew by 23 percent.[8] Although some argue that state spending is out of control, Texas still ranks low in per-capita government expenditures. Texas was 50th among the states in per-capita spending by state government alone—$2,611 per person—in 2000. When combined state and local spending was compared, Texas rose to 45th, thanks partly to the large share of public school costs borne by local taxpayers. In such key areas as per-capita state spending on public health, education, and welfare, Texas ranked behind most other states.[9] Efforts to curtail government growth and spending have met with only marginal success. Texas citizens have come to expect a wide range of public services, and these expectations increase as the population grows. The federal government also has imposed mandates on state and local governments that require additional expenditures and personnel. And the success of interest groups in winning approval of new

TABLE 10–1 Employment by Type of Government, 1967–1997

Unit of Government	Full-Time Equivalent Employees			
	1967	**1977**	**1987**	**1997**
State	88,734	163,870	198,769	261,975
Total Local	299,578	477,177	646,913	850,380
Counties	32,978	60,287	77,851	103,481
Municipalities	75,168	115,481	139,340	160,574
School Districts	177,734	282,492	400,035	539,530
Special District	13,698	18,917	29,687	46,795
Texas Total	388,312	641,047	845,682	1,112,355

Sources: U.S. Department of Commerce, Bureau of the Census, *Census of Governments,* 1967, Vol 3, No. 2, table 15; *Census of Governments,* 1977, Vol 3, No. 2, table 15; *Census of Governments,* 1987, Vol 3, No. 2, table 14; *Census of Governments,* 1997, Vol 1, table 12.

TABLE 10–2   State and Local Employment by General Functions, 1997

	State	Counties	Cities/ Towns	School Districts	Special Districts
Education	32.7%	0.8%	2.7%	100%	
Social Services*	30.1%	28.0%	7.5%	—	52.8%
Public Safety & Corrections	17.7%	33.6%	35.6%	—	0.2%
Transportation	5.4%	8.2%	8.6%	—	1.7%
Government Administration	6.5%	22.5%	9.4%	—	
Environment/Housing	5.1%	2.4%	18.5%	—	15.6%
Utilities	—	0.1%	11.8%	—	28.1%
All other	2.6%	4.4%	5.9%	—	1.5%
Total Employees	261,975	103,481	160,574	539,530	46,794

*Includes income maintenance.

Source: U.S. Department of Commerce, Bureau of the Census, *1997 Census of Governments,* Vol. 1, Table 13.

programs adds to the growth of public employment. The legislature reduced spending on many programs to help bridge a $10 billion revenue shortfall in 2003, but it remained to be seen how those cuts would affect overall state government employment.

Eighty percent of state government employees work in five areas: higher education, highways and public safety, corrections, public welfare, and health care.[10] Most employees of county governments work in social services, public safety and corrections, and general governmental administration. Approximately one-third of city employees are engaged in fire and police protection, while another 30 percent work for city utilities and in housing, sewerage, sanitation, parks and recreation, and natural resources departments (Table 10–2). Elementary and secondary school teachers are employees of local school districts. Although there is some overlap in governmental functions, the employment patterns also demonstrate clear differences among state and local governments.

BUREAUCRATS AND PUBLIC POLICY

The bureaucracy does more than carry out the policies set by the legislature. The bureaucracy is involved in virtually every stage of the policy-making process.

The legislature usually broadly defines a program and gives the affected agency the responsibility of filling in the details through the agency's rule-making process.[11] In their interpretations, administrative agencies sometimes change a vague law from its original legislative purpose. Although the legislature can use oversight committees and the budgetary process to control the bureaucracy, agencies often have resources and political influence that protect their prerogatives. Many appointed agency heads have political ties to interest groups affected by the work of their agencies, and these officials help develop policy alternatives and laws because legislators are dependent on their technical expertise.

Policy Implementation

Implementation is the conversion of policy plans into reality.[12] While one state agency may be primarily responsible for translating legislative intent into a specific program, other governmental bodies are also involved. The courts, for example, shape the actions of the bureaucrats through their interpretation of statutes and administrative rules. And there may be jurisdictional and political battles between different agencies over program objectives. Such conflicts often result from Texas's plural executive system of government, in which the governor and several other statewide officials are elected independently of each other and numerous other agencies are headed by appointed boards and commissions (see Chapter 9).

In some cases, a new agency may have to be organized and staffed to carry out the goals of a new law. More often, however, the new responsibilities are assigned by the legislature to an existing agency, which develops the necessary rules, procedures, and guidelines for operating the new program. Additional employees are hired if the legislature provides the necessary funding. If not, responsibilities are reassigned among existing personnel. Sometimes, tasks are coordinated with other agencies. Ultimately, all this activity translates into hundreds of thousands of daily transactions between governmental employees and the public.

Establishing rules and standards at the agency level for carrying out programs enacted by the legislature is a complex process that also involves the legislative sponsors, interest groups, sometimes specific businesses, and other interested parties. Rules and procedures are not just hatched in a vacuum. The task is highly political, subject to intense negotiations, and often contentious. It often requires a great deal of political adroitness by administrators to assure a program's success.

All of us have heard horror stories of persons who have suffered abuse, neglect, incompetence, or capriciousness at the hands of public employees and agencies. Whether it is an indigent family that fell through the cracks of the welfare system or a county jail prisoner who was lost in the administrative process of the judicial system, these stories tend to reinforce the suspicion and hostility that many people have toward bureaucracies and public employees. There is no question that these abuses deserve attention and demand correction. But thousands of governmental programs are successfully carried out with little or no fanfare and are consistent with the intent and purpose of the authorizing legislation.

Most public employees take pride in what they do and attempt to be conscientious in translating policy objectives into workable public services. They are citizens and taxpayers who also have to receive services from other state and local agencies. A complex, interdependent state with more than 22 million people depends on the effectiveness and efficiency of governmental agencies. And that activity appears, on the whole, to be mutually satisfactory or beneficial to most parties.

Obstacles to Policy Implementation

When things go wrong in state government and problems go unresolved, there is a tendency to blame the bureaucrats for excessive red tape, inefficiency, mismanagement, or incompetence. As we noted earlier, bureaucrat bashing plays well politically, and many candidates for public office run on such campaigns. But in many cases they are unfairly blaming government employees for complex problems that policymakers have been unable—or unwilling—to resolve. One high profile issue is the perennial struggle to improve the quality of the public education system. Some of the criticism directed at educational bureaucrats has been justified, but the legislature and the governor are ultimately responsible for the enactment of sound educational policies and the development of a sufficient and equitable system of paying for them.

Some legislative policies may be misdirected, with little potential for producing the intended results. Or economic and social conditions may change, making programs inappropriate. Administrators also may find that alternative approaches would have worked better than those ordered by the legislature, which also frequently fails to fund programs adequately. In some cases, those charged with carrying out a new policy may not have the know-how or the resources to make it work.[13] Finally, programs often produce unanticipated results.[14]

The accountability and responsiveness of state and local agencies are also affected by other factors, including the influence of special interests. Thanks to the clout of special interest lobbyists with the legislature, regulatory agencies are often headed by boards that include a majority of members from the professions or industries they are supposed to regulate. Many taxpayers may feel this system is merely a legalized way of letting the foxes guard the henhouse. It is an extension of the "iron triangles" concept (see Chapters 4 and 13), whereby special interests seek to influence not only the legislators responsible for enacting laws but also the agencies responsible for enforcing them.

Appointment to State Agencies

Business and professional groups argue that their professions can be effectively regulated only by individuals knowledgeable of them. Although that argument has some validity, it also increases the potential for incestuous relationships that mock the regulatory process. There is always the possibility—and often the likelihood—that industry representatives serving on boards or commissions will be inclined to protect their industries against the best interests of consumers. This pattern of influence and control is often referred to as **co-optation.** It speaks to the possibility that agencies are captured by the industries they are supposed to regulate. Licensing agencies also may seek to adopt unfair regulations designed to restrict new competitors from entering an industry.

Historically, many nine-member state regulatory boards included only industry representatives. But under the sunset review process, which will be discussed in more detail later in this chapter, laws have gradually been changed to turn over some positions on most of those boards to public members. The Sunset Advisory Commission has concluded: "Boards consisting only of members from a regulated profession or group affected by the activities of an agency may not respond adequately to broad public interests. This potential problem can be addressed by giving the general public a direct voice in the activities of the agency through representation on the board."[15]

The "fox and the henhouse" approach to state regulation was highlighted when Governor Ann Richards demanded that the Texas Department of Health crack down on deplorable conditions in some nursing homes. It was revealed that state inspectors had repeatedly found unsanitary conditions in three nursing homes partly owned by a member of the Texas Board of Health. The board member, an appointee of former Governor Bill Clements, denied any allegations of improper care but resigned after moving to another state.[16] Texas law then required that one member of the eighteen-member health board be involved in the nursing home industry, while other members included other health care professionals. The board has since been restructured.

POLITICAL CONTROL AND THE RESPONSIVENESS OF THE BUREAUCRACY

Legislative Budgetary Control

Every two years, the legislature has traditionally set the budgets for state agencies and then provided little scrutiny over how effectively the money was actually spent, unless there was a financial crisis that required a special legislative session or an emergency transfer of funds by the governor and the Legislative Budget Board. Perhaps the most control that lawmakers exercise over agency spending, besides setting the bottom line, is their approval of a number of line items in agency budgets that restrict portions of the budget to specific programs (see "How to Control Bureaucrats").

HOW TO CONTROL BUREAUCRATS

Taking a cue from political scientist Robert Lineberry, Texas policymakers can use several strategies to control bureaucracies and help ensure that policies are carried out as intended:

- **Change the law** or make legislation more detailed to reduce or eliminate the discretionary authority of an agency.
- **Overrule the bureaucracy** and reverse or rescind an action or decision of an agency. With the independence of many agencies, boards, and commissions at the state level, the governor can reverse few agency decisions. So this step often requires legislative action.
- **Transfer the responsibility for a program** to another agency through administrative reorganization.
- **Replace an agency head** who refuses to or is incapable of carrying out program objectives. But there are only a few agencies over which the governor can directly exercise such authority in Texas.
- **Cut or threaten to reduce the budget** of an agency to force compliance with policy objectives.
- **Abolish an agency or program** through sunset legislation.
- **Pressure** the bureaucracy to change, using legislative hearings and public disclosures of agency neglect or inadequacies.
- **Protect public employees** who reveal incompetence, mismanagement, and corruption through whistleblower legislation.
- **Enact revolving-door restrictions** to reduce or eliminate the movement of former state employees to industries over which they had regulatory authority.

Source: Robert Lineberry, *American Public Policy* (New York: Harper & Row, 1977), pp. 84–85.

Performance Reviews

Facing a large revenue shortfall in 1991, the legislature directed Comptroller John Sharp to conduct unprecedented performance reviews of all state agencies to determine ways to eliminate mismanagement and inefficiency and save tax dollars. Sharp recommended $4 billion worth of spending cuts, agency and funds consolidations, accounting changes, some minor tax increases, and increases in various state fees to more accurately reflect the costs of providing services. Pressure from special interests killed many of the recommendations, but the legislature adopted about $2.4 billion of them. Sharp produced follow-up reports in 1993, 1995, and 1997, and his successor, Carole Keeton Strayhorn, continued the performance reviews after she took office. At the beginning of the 2003 session of the legislature, she made 64 recommendations for further restructuring of state agencies and their operations, some of which were adopted by lawmakers. The comptroller also has similarly reviewed the operations of a significant number of local school districts.

The performance reviews generally have been considered instrumental in improving administrative practices. But after a series of budgetary disputes in 2003, the legislature, with Gov. Rick Perry's approval, transferred the work from the comptroller's office to the Legislative Budget Board (see Chapter 9). The move was criticized by those who believed the reviews should have remained under the oversight of an independently elected officeholder, but it remained to be seen what the ultimate effect of the transfer would be.

One of Sharp's proposals adopted by the legislature in 1993 created the Council on Competitive Government, which was designed to give Texas businesses more opportunities to bid on state contracts and provide some state services more efficiently. It also enabled state agencies to bid on services performed by other state agencies if the bidding agencies thought they could do the work more efficiently. The council, which evaluates the proposals, includes the governor, the lieutenant governor, the comptroller, the chair of the General Services Commission, and the employee representative on the Texas Workforce Commission.

Some state government functions had been privatized before the council was created. One of the best known was the state lottery, which was administered from the beginning by a private company under a state contract (see "The Politics of Privatization").

Sunset Legislation

Although Texas has been slow to modernize its budgetary process and other key functions of state government, it was one of the first states to require formal, exhaustive reviews of how effectively agencies are doing their jobs. The sunset process enacted in 1977 was so named because most agencies have to be periodically recreated by the legislature or automatically go out of business.[17] Relatively few agencies—except for a number of inactive ones like the Pink Bollworm Commission and the Stonewall Jackson Memorial Board—have been abolished. But the obligatory review has produced some significant structural and policy changes in the state bureaucracy that the legislature may not have otherwise ordered. It also has expanded employment opportunities for lobbyists, because special interest groups have much to win or lose in the sunset process. In many cases, special interests have succeeded in protecting the status quo.

THE POLITICS OF PRIVATIZATION

Privatization, the process of governments contracting with private companies to provide public services, has become increasingly popular in recent years. Advocates say privatization promotes efficiency and saves taxpayers money because private businesses know how to reduce waste to remain competitive. But, as a major controversy over the Texas Lottery demonstrated, privatization doesn't always remove politics from the delivery of public services.

From its beginning, the Texas Lottery was operated by a private, Rhode Island-based company, Gtech Corp. State officials said Gtech, which also operated lotteries in a number of other states and foreign countries, had the expertise necessary to ensure the successful administration of the game. The company beat out another competitor for its first Texas contract in 1992. Then, in 1996, the Texas Lottery Commission negotiated a new, five-year contract with Gtech without taking bids. The contract was worth $130 million a year to the company, which received a portion of the revenue from lottery ticket sales. Only a few months later, however, Gtech and the lottery were engulfed in controversy, and questions were being raised about Gtech's political connections.

The controversy erupted with a report that a close friend of Lottery Director Nora Linares had an undisclosed $30,000 contract with Gtech in 1992 and 1993. By the time news of the contract broke in late 1996, Linares' friend, Mike Moeller, was in federal prison on an unrelated bribery conviction stemming from his previous employment with the Texas Department of Agriculture. Linares said she hadn't known about the contract, but the controversy led to her firing by the Lottery Commission. It also sparked hundreds of news media stories about Gtech and its insider connections. The company had hired several influential Texas lobbyists, including former Lieutenant Governor Ben Barnes, to help get and keep its lucrative contract. Other people and companies with political connections, it was revealed, also had contracts of one kind or another with the lottery—from advertising the games to providing supplies.

Each agency is usually up for sunset review every twelve years under a rotating order set out in the sunset law. The review begins with the Sunset Advisory Commission, which includes four state representatives appointed by the speaker of the House, four senators appointed by the lieutenant governor, and two public members, one named by the speaker and the other by the lieutenant governor. The commission employs a staff that studies each agency up for review during the next regular, biennial legislative session and reports its findings to the panel, which makes recommendations to the legislature.

In a few cases, the commission will propose that an agency—usually a minor one—be terminated or consolidated with another agency. In most cases, however, the commission recommends the continuation of an agency but outlines suggested changes in its organizational structure and operations. The future of the agency is then debated by the full legislature. If lawmakers fail to approve a sunset bill for any agency by September 1 of the year the agency is scheduled for review, the agency will be phased out of existence over the next year. It will be terminated abruptly on September 1 if the legislature refuses to approve a new budget for the agency. In recent years, however, the legislature has postponed controversial sunset decisions by passing special laws to allow some agencies to stay open past their review dates.

TABLE 10–3   Sunset Action from 1979 to 2003, 66th to 78th Legislative Sessions

Actions Taken	Total	Percent
Agencies Reviewed	346*	
Agencies Continued	282	81%
Agencies Abolished Outright	31	9
Agencies Abolished and Functions Transferred	16	5
Agencies Combined	11	3
Agencies Separated	2	1

*Some agencies reviewed were not subject to continuation or abolishment.
Source: Texas Sunset Advisory Commission.

The Texas Higher Education Coordinating Board is subject to sunset review, but individual universities are not. Also exempted from sunset review are the courts and state agencies created by the constitution, such as the governor's office, the attorney general, the comptroller, and the General Land Office.

The sunset process hasn't reduced the size of the state bureaucracy. By 1997, there were more than 262,000 full-time state employees, compared to about 164,000 in 1977, the year the sunset law was approved. Although more than forty-five agencies have been terminated or merged, others have been created (Table 10–3). But Bill Wells, the Sunset Advisory Commission's former executive director, said the statistics didn't tell the full story. He believed the sunset process had served to slow down the creation of new agencies. "You can't say how many [new agencies] would have been created if sunset hadn't heightened the awareness of the fact that we've got maybe too many agencies now," he said. "There is a heightened awareness of the fact that you need to go a little slower, and you need to really have a problem before you create an agency."[18]

The sunset review process has helped rid state government of some deadwood, modernized some state laws and bureaucratic procedures, and made some agencies more responsive and accountable to the public. Under a sunset policy discussed earlier in this chapter, public members have been added to the boards of numerous small regulatory agencies that previously had included only representatives of the professions or industries that they regulated.

The largest agencies and those with influential constituencies are usually the most difficult to change because special interests are working overtime and making large political contributions to protect their turf. In 1993, for example, the insurance lobby succeeded in weakening some regulatory reforms in the Department of Insurance sunset bill. In another case that year, there was such a high-stakes battle involving telephone companies, newspaper publishers, electric utilities, and consumers over the Public Utility Commission sunset bill that the legislature postponed action on PUC sunset for two years. The lobby's influence over the 1993 sunset bills prompted Governor Ann Richards and some legislators to suggest that the sunset process should be changed or repealed because it was being abused by special interests. But consumer advocates, who value the sunset process, blamed the problem on legislators who had difficulty saying no to special interest lobbyists.

Since major state agencies have to be re-created in some form, they can be held hostage by legislators for any number of purposes during their review year. In 1989, Governor Bill Clements and other foes of Agriculture Commissioner Jim Hightower used the sunset process to trim Hightower's influence. Unlike most other statewide, elected offices, the agriculture commissioner's post wasn't created by the state constitution. It is statutory, which made it vulnerable when the Department of Agriculture had to pass sunset review. Hightower, a liberal Democrat, had cultivated the enmity of conservative agricultural producers and the chemical industry by, among other things, proposing tighter restrictions on the use of pesticides and more protection for agricultural workers. Clements, a Republican who opposed most of Hightower's politics, backed efforts to change the law to replace Hightower's job with a commissioner or multimember commission appointed by the governor. Hightower had strong support in the Senate, which then had a Democratic majority, for keeping his post elective. But he had trouble in the House, where one-third of the members were Republicans and many rural, conservative Democrats shared a dim view of his policies and politics. Hightower had survived attacks in previous legislative sessions, but this time, with the future of the agricultural agency at stake, he was forced to accept a compromise. His job remained elective, but he had to share his authority to regulate pesticides with a new, appointive board created in the sunset law. Hightower's political troubles were so deep that he was unseated the next year by Rick Perry, one of the legislative sponsors of the pesticide regulation compromise.

The Revolving Door

Over the years, many regulatory agencies had become training grounds for young attorneys and other professionals taking their first jobs out of college or law school. They would work for state agencies for a few years for relatively low pay while gaining valuable experience in a particular regulatory area and making influential contacts in the state bureaucracy. Then they would leave state employment for higher-paying jobs in the industries they had regulated and would represent their new employers before the state boards and commissions for which they had once worked. Or they would become consultants or join law firms representing regulatory clients. Former gubernatorial appointees to boards and commissions—not just hired staffers—also participated in this **revolving door** phenomenon, which raised ethical questions about possible insider advantages.

An early step in restricting the revolving door was part of the 1975 law that created the Public Utility Commission (PUC). This law prohibited PUC members and high-ranking staffers from going to work for regulated utilities immediately after leaving the agency. An ethics reform law in 1991 expanded the restrictions to other agencies.

WHISTLEBLOWING

Governmental agencies make mistakes that can be very costly to the public in terms of financial waste or regulatory neglect, which may endanger the public's health or safety. Since agencies spend huge sums of money for supplies, construction, and basic services, there also is the potential for public officials or employees to be offered kickbacks or bribes to influence decisions that would benefit particular vendors or contractors.

Texas has a **whistleblower** protection law, which is designed to protect public employees who report wrongdoing within their agencies to their supervisors. If an employee is subjected to retaliation after having come forward, the law permits the worker to file a lawsuit against the offending agency.

A major test of the law's effectiveness was brought by George Green, an architect for the Texas Department of Human Services. Green complained of shoddy construction on agency facilities, kickbacks, and noncompliance with contracts and said his supervisors refused to take action against the offending contractors. After he went public with his charges, Green was fired for allegedly abusing sick-leave time and making one unauthorized call on his state telephone—a 13-cent call to his father. Criminal charges were brought against him, and although they were eventually dropped, he spent $130,000 in legal fees, could not find a job, and depleted his personal assets.

Green sued the state under the whistleblower law and won a $13.6 million judgment from a Travis County jury in 1991. The amount included $3.6 million in actual damages that Green had suffered and $10 million in punitive damages to punish the state for the way he had been treated. The state appealed, dragging out a resolution of the case, until the judgment eventually was upheld by the Texas Supreme Court in 1994. But the legislature was not in session that year, and state leaders said there was no money in the state budget to pay Green. So he had to wait for the legislature to convene in 1995. Green, meanwhile, was still unemployed and living off the generosity of friends and family and a personal loan he had made against a portion of his judgment.

By the time the legislature convened in 1995, Green's judgment, with interest, had grown to almost $20 million, and interest continued to grow at the rate of more than $4,500 a day. The case was receiving considerable media attention nationally, as well as in Texas. But many legislators, particularly in the House, did not want to pay him the full amount, which they considered excessive. They particularly objected to the $10 million the jury had awarded as punitive damages and pointed out that taxpayers would ultimately have to pick up the tab. Green refused to accept an amount smaller than the judgment and interest, and the 1995 session ended in late May without Green receiving any payment.

Legislators, however, took steps to assure there never would be such a large whistleblower judgment again. They changed the law to limit all whistleblower suit damages against the state to $250,000. Critics of the change warned it would seriously curtail whistleblower suits and undermine an important taxpayer protection because the best lawyers, whose fees are based on the size of a judgment, would quit taking whistleblower cases.

Finally, in November 1995, Green reached a compromise with legislative leaders. The Legislative Budget Board (LBB), which can transfer funds when the full legislature is not in session, approved a $13.8 million settlement, which Green accepted. Part of the money went to lawyers and a lobbyist who had helped Green collect payment, and $1 million of the total went to an investor who had loaned Green money during his battle. Lieutenant Governor Bob Bullock, who chaired the LBB, apologized to Green and called his ordeal a "black mark on the history of Texas."[19]

Even then, Green's story continued. A former consultant sued Green for allegedly failing to pay him for helping Green collect the judgment from the state. In December 1996, another Travis County jury awarded the former consultant more than $600,000 in actual and punitive damages against Green.

Green's experience speaks to a major problem. Few public employees can afford to be subjected to this type of retaliation, and few have the resources to fight state government. Although the original intent of the law was to protect whistleblowers and to encourage their inside information, most state and local employees may have received a different message from the Green case and the legislature's decision to weaken the law.

Public employees appear to have five options when they encounter wrongdoing within their agencies:

1. They can simply remain silent and not rock the boat for fear of possible recriminations.
2. They can work through the normal operating procedures of the organization to try to influence or change the actions of other employees.
3. They can leak information to the news media and hope that external, public pressure will force changes.
4. Employees also can leave the organization and then attempt to go public to prompt changes.
5. Or they can simply go away and find employment elsewhere.

REGULATION

The legislature delegates a great deal of authority for carrying out state policy to regulatory agencies, and regulation, in turn, takes many forms. There is economic regulation, which affects the prices that some businesses can charge for their services. Major state regulators in this area include the Department of Insurance, which has oversight over rates that can be charged for automobile and homeowners insurance, and the Public Utility Commission, which has authority over rates charged for some telephone services and over electric rates charged by some utility companies. City governments regulate selected areas of the local economy (see "How We See It").

A second regulatory function is the **licensing** of professions and franchising of corporations. Under state law, some occupations require formal training, testing, and subsequent licensing from a state agency. These include doctors, nurses, accountants, lawyers, and a host of other professions. Individuals and companies also must have state charters or licenses to open a state bank, a funeral home, or a nursing home. Licensing implies regulation, and the acceptance of a license implies a willingness to comply with state controls. On the local level, contractors are required to meet building codes established by city councils.

State agencies also regulate the allocation of natural resources and safeguard their quality. The Texas Commission on Environmental Quality enforces state laws protecting air and water. Disputes over the use of water from the underground Edwards Aquifer in the San Antonio area prompted state intervention, and a drought in the mid-1990s convinced the legislature to order the development of a statewide water conservation and management plan (see Chapter 13). In another crucial conservation area, the Texas Railroad Commission establishes the rate at which a well can pump oil from the ground.

— HOW WE SEE IT —
NEGOTIATING BUREAUCRACIES

Despite all the rhetoric for shrinking government, historical evidence shows that state and local government has expanded in response to a growing population and increased demands for public services. Although some people promote privatization as a solution to big government, privatization simply replaces a public bureaucracy with a private bureaucracy. And, trying to resolve a problem by negotiating the complex administrative structures of private companies often is no less frustrating for the consumer or taxpayer than dealing with governmental red tape.

Both of this book's authors have studied the actions of bureaucracies for more than thirty years. And, like many other people, we have had to negotiate their complexities to resolve issues that personally affected us. In so doing, we have concluded that the best defense is a good offense. That is, learn how an agency works and then develop the appropriate strategy and tactics to achieve your objective. To this end, we have compiled some rules for "working the bureaucracy."

Remember you are dealing with people: Bureaucracies are comprised of individuals, most of whom want to do a good job. Many of them are overworked, but most take pride in what they do and strive to be successful in carrying out their tasks. Approach them in a cooperative spirit, not as if you are looking for a fight.

Find the right agency and the right person or persons authorized to provide solutions: Bureaucracies also operate under organizational structures that divide responsibilities among employees. Standard operating procedures describe what each person is authorized to do. The first person you call or meet in an agency may not be the person who can deal with your issue. You may feel you are "getting the run around" if you are transferred from person to person or agency to agency. But you can save yourself some time and frustration by making clear your needs or request in your first encounter with a governmental employee. That will enhance the chances of your request being assigned promptly to the right person or office.

Be patient: Employees of large organizations often don't know everything their agencies do. Most public workers are specialists. They have specific areas of responsibility and specific tasks and often know little about other offices or divisions within their agency.

Be tenacious: Dealing with bureaucracies can be frustrating, but persistence is imperative. The more questions you ask, the more you are going to understand the organization and the quicker you are going to find someone who can help you.

Know your rights and act on them: Governments exist for you. You do not exist for governments. The more you learn about governmental procedures, the more likely you are to be successful. If an employee of a state agency dismisses your inquiry or claim in a cavalier manner, go above that person's head to the next person in the chain of command. If the obstruction persists at the higher levels of the agency, call your legislator's office with a detailed summary of what occurred. (It also will help to know which state representative and which state senator represent you.) Not all legislators will respond to your complaint, particularly if you have dealt with the agency erratically. But many will, and agencies normally respond to inquiries from legislators, who set their budgets and pass the laws under which the agencies operate.

Occasionally, you may have to be adversarial: Sometimes, unfortunately, governmental agencies and their employees misinterpret the law or refuse to do what the law requires. If those cases, your only recourse may be filing a lawsuit against the agency. Corporations and well-organized interest groups usually have the financial resources for such a fight. Most citizens, however, don't. So, concentrate on the above steps, and do everything you can to avoid getting to this one.

State and local governments also can regulate by providing operating subsidies to businesses, including tax breaks that are subject to limitations imposed by the legislature. These incentives usually are offered for specified periods to encourage businesses to locate or expand in a specific community. In return, the businesses may agree to conditions imposed on them by the participating government. Cities grant franchises to cable television systems, which agree to provide a specific level of service in return for the operating rights.

State agencies also regulate companies for fairness and competition. Although there are many federal laws dealing with price fixing, monopolies, and unfair competition, there also are state statutes relating to the competitiveness of the state's economy. Additionally, the state is involved in what some writers call social regulation.[20] This type of regulation is much broader than the economic regulation just described. Social regulations affect "the conditions under which goods and services are produced and the physical characteristics of products that are manufactured."[21] While the federal government has preempted many state policies in these areas, there are state agencies involved in regulating workplace safety and consumer protection.

MERIT SYSTEMS AND PROFESSIONAL MANAGEMENT

Earlier in our history, public employees in Texas were hired on the basis of **political patronage,** or the personal relationships and friendships they had with elected or appointed public officials. Little consideration was given to their skills, competence, or expertise. There were few rules concerning terms of employment, advancement, or the rights or conduct of public employees, and there were wide variations in wages and salaries from agency to agency. There also were high rates of employee turnover.

To better serve the public and state workers, some reform advocates pushed for a **merit employment system** based, in part, on the Civil Service Commission created by the federal government for its workers in 1883. Although other states have developed comprehensive, statewide employment or personnel systems administered by a single agency, the reform movement in Texas has not been as successful. Improvements have been made, but state government in Texas continues to function under a decentralized personnel system.[22]

Merit-based public employment was inconsistent with the individualistic views of government, politics, and public administration evolving from the dominant political subcultures of Texas (see Chapter 1). The plural executive system worked against efforts to centralize and coordinate personnel policies because the various elected, executive officeholders jealously guarded their prerogatives to hire and fire the people who worked for them.

Governmental functions have expanded in modern times, and carrying out public policy has become more complex and technical.[23] Many programs require highly specialized skills, not political hacks who have no formal training or expertise for technical jobs. Furthermore, the public has gradually developed higher expectations of its government and reacts unfavorably to incompetent public workers. Additional pressure for merit employment has come from the federal government. Since the 1930s, numerous federal grants have required the state to enact a merit system for state employees administering them. In more recent years, federal laws prohibiting hiring discrimination on the basis of sex, age, disability, race, or ethnicity have been extended to state and local governments. These requirements, in turn, have forced Texas government to pay more attention to employment practices.[24]

Even so, politics has not been totally eliminated in the hiring and promotion of public employees. State government's personnel "system" is not a merit system but a highly fragmented system with different agencies assigned various personnel responsibilities. Ultimately, the legislature has the legal authority to define personnel practices, and the biennial budget is the major tool used by legislators to establish some 1,300 job classifications and corresponding salary schedules. The legislature also establishes policies on vacations, holidays, and retirement. But the primary responsibility for carrying out personnel policies is still delegated to the various state agencies. An administrator can develop specific policies for an agency as long as the agency works within the general framework defined by the legislature. Some agencies have developed modern personnel plans—including employee grievance procedures and competitive examinations for placement and advancement—while others have not.

All state job openings are required to be listed with the Texas Workforce Commission. Agencies also advertise for workers through the mass media and college placement centers. But many jobs still are filled as a result of friendships, personal contacts, and the influence of key political players.

Higher and public education employees are subject to different employment policies, which are determined by individual university governing boards and local school districts. Unlike state government, many cities across Texas have adopted centrally administered merit systems organized around the accepted principles of modern personnel management. Their personnel departments include independent civil service commissions that have some rule-making authority and hear appeals of personnel matters. These changes, which resulted from the urban reform movement (see Chapter 12), were designed to recruit quality employees and insulate them from external political pressures. They have led to a high level of professionalism in some cities. Large metropolitan counties also have tried to structure their employment systems on the basis of merit, but the partisan election of county officials thwarts the full implementation of merit systems.

SUMMARY AND CONCLUSIONS

1. Despite a historical ambivalence, if not animosity, toward government, Texans have come to expect good roads and schools, safe drinking water, and a host of other public programs to meet their needs and interests. Consequently, government has grown with the population. More than 1.3 million Texans are now employed by state and local governments. Collectively, we refer to them and the agencies for which they work as the bureaucracy.

2. The bureaucracy has the primary responsibility of carrying out public policies adopted by the legislature and local governing bodies. Administrative agencies are also involved in virtu-

ally every stage of the policymaking process. Legislators depend on administrative agencies for counsel and advice when they draft public policies, and they rely on them to help assess the success or failure of policies.

3. When things go wrong and problems go unresolved, there is a tendency to blame bureaucrats. But, often, government employees are unfairly blamed for complex problems that elected policymakers have been unwilling or unable to resolve. The fragmented structure of the executive branch of state government is, in itself, a major obstacle to the efficient, responsive delivery of public services. There also is the potential for

agencies headed by appointed boards to become unaccountable to the voters and susceptible to the influence of special interest groups.

4. Through sunset legislation, Texas became one of the first states to require formal reviews of how effectively state agencies are doing their jobs. Most agencies are subject to periodic review and reauthorization by the legislature. The process has not reduced the size of the bureaucracy, but it has helped rid state government of obsolete agencies and produced greater accountability. The legislature also has empowered the Legislative Budget Board to conduct performance reviews of state programs to promote efficiency and reduce waste. In addition, Texas has adopted revolving-door restrictions that prohibit former board members and key employees of regulatory agencies from going to work for regulated companies within a certain period after leaving their state posts.

5. Although many local governments have adopted merit employment systems, state government functions under a decentralized personnel system. It is highly fragmented, with each agency largely free to set its own personnel policies.

KEY TERMS

Bureaucracy	Revolving door	Political patronage
Co-optation	Whistleblower	Merit employment system
Sunset legislation	Licensing	

FURTHER READING

Articles

Barrett, Katherine, and Richard Greene, "Grading the States: A Management Report Card," *Governing* (February 1999), pp. 17–90.

Campbell, Brett, "Killing the Messenger: Did DHS Retaliate Against a Whistleblower?" *The Texas Observer,* July 12, 1991, pp. 8–11.

Curry, Landon, "Politics of Sunset Review in Texas," *Public Administration Review* 50 (January–February 1990), pp. 58–63.

Davis, Edwin S., "Rule-Making Activity of Selected Texas Regulatory Agencies," *Texas Journal of Political Studies* 8 (Fall/Winter 1986), pp. 26–36.

Frederick, Douglas W., "Reexamining the Texas Railroad Commission," in *Texas Politics: A Reader,* eds. Anthony Champagne and Edward J. Harpham. New York: W.W. Norton, 1997, pp. 67–76.

Gormley, William T., Jr., "Accountability Battles in State Administration," in *The State of the States,* 3rd ed., ed. by Carl E. Van Horn. Washington, DC: Congressional Quarterly Press, 1996, pp. 161–78.

Leon, Mark, "Watchdog or Lapdog?" *The Texas Observer,* April 5, 1991, pp. 6–7.

Slack, James D., "Bureaucracy and Bureaucrats in Texas," in *Texas Public Policy,* ed. Gerry Riposa. Dubuque, IA: Kendall/Hunt Publishing Company, 1987.

Slack, James D., "Representative Bureaucracy and Affirmative Action Policy in Texas Government: Implementing Federal Policy in the Lone Star State," in *Texas Public Policy,* ed. Gerry Riposa. Dubuque, IA: Kendall/Hunt Publishing Company, 1987.

Books

Beal, Ronald L. *Texas Administrative Practice and Procedure.* Charlottesville, VA: Michie, 1998.

Dubnick, Melvin J., and Barbara S. Romzek, *American Public Administration.* New York: Macmillan Publishing Company, 1991.

Gosling, James J., *Budgetary Politics,* 2nd ed. New York: Garland Publishing, Inc., 1997.

Knabe, Eileen, et al., *Guide to Texas State Agencies.* Austin: Lyndon B. Johnson School of Public Affairs, The University of Texas at Austin, 1990.

Meier, Kenneth J., *Regulation: Politics, Bureaucracy and Economics.* New York: St. Martin's Press, 1985.

Office of Governor, Division of Planning Coordination, *Quality Texas Government: People Make the Difference.* Study conducted by the Texas Research League, Austin, Texas, 1972.

Palumbo, Dennis, and Steven Maynard-Moody, *Contemporary Public Administration.* New York: Longman, 1991.

Ripley, Randall B., and Grace A. Franklin, *Policy Implementation and Bureaucracy,* 2nd ed. Chicago: The Dorsey Press, 1986.

Ripley, Randall B., and Grace A. Franklin, *Congress, the Bureaucracy, and Public Policy,* 3rd ed. Chicago: The Dorsey Press, 1984.

Schuman, David, and Dick W. Olufs, III, *Public Administration in the United States* Lexington, MA: D. C. Heath and Company, 1988.

Straussman, Jeffrey D., *Public Administration,* 2nd ed. New York: Longman, 1990.

Sunset Advisory Commission, *Guide to the Texas Sunset Process,* 2003. Austin: Sunset Advisory Commission, 2003.

Texas Comptroller of Public Accounts, *Breaking the Mold: A Report of the Texas Performance Review,* July 1991.

Ward, Peter M., *Colonias and Public Policy in Texas and Mexico.* College Station: Texas A & M University Press, 1999.

Websites

State of Texas http://www.state.tx.us The state's web page provides links to more than 200 state agencies. Most of the state agencies have their own sites with detailed information about their organizational structure, programs, budgets, reports, and recent activities.

Office of the Comptroller http://www.cpa.state.tx.us In addition to providing links to other state agencies, the comptroller's office provides a wide array of information pertaining to state taxes, management and accounting systems, and performance reviews of state operations and agencies.

ENDNOTES

1. Carole Keeton Strayhorn, Texas Comptroller of Public Accounts, "Limited Government, Unlimited Opportunity," January 2003.
2. See Max Weber, "Bureaucracy," in Max Weber *Essays in Sociology,* eds. H. H. Gerth and C. Wright Mills (New York: Oxford University Press, 1971), pp. 196–244.
3. Jeffrey D. Straussman, *Public Administration* (New York: Longman, 1990), p. 65.
4. The following discussion is based on Dennis Palumbo and Steven Maynard-Moody, *Contemporary Public Administration* (New York: Longman, 1991), pp. 26–31; and Straussman, *Public Administration,* pp. 63–64.
5. Melvin J. Dubnick and Barbara S. Romzek, *American Public Administration* (New York: Macmillan Publishing Company, 1991), p. 248.
6. Ibid, pp. 248–49.
7. U.S. Department of Commerce, Bureau of the Census, *Government Organizations, 1997,* Vol. 1 (Washington, DC: Government Printing Office, 1999), Table 9.
8. Strayhorn, "Limited Government, Unlimited Opportunity," January 2003, p. 1.
9. U.S. Bureau of the Census, *Statistical Abstract,* 2002, Tables 422 and 430; *Texas Factbook,* 2004.
10. Texas Legislative Budget Board, *Fiscal Size Up: 2000–2001 Biennium,* pp. 13–16.
11. Theodore J. Lowi, *The End of Liberalism,* 2nd ed. (New York: W. W. Norton, 1979), p. 274.
12. Larry N. Gerston, *Making Public Policy* (Glenview, IL: Scott, Foresman and Company, 1983), p. 95
13. Palumbo and Maynard-Moody, *Contemporary Public Administration,* p. 304.
14. Straussman, *Public Administration,* p. 246.
15. *Sunset Advisory Commission Report,* October 1991.
16. *Dallas Morning News,* October 24, 1991
17. Colorado was the first state to adopt sunset legislation in 1976. See Straussman, *Public Administration,* p. 39.
18. The Associated Press, as published in the *Dallas Times Herald,* August 14, 1983.
19. *Houston Chronicle,* November 16, 1995.
20. Straussman, *Public Administration,* p. 286.
21. William Lilley III and James C. Miller III, "The New Social Regulation," *The Public Interest,* 47 (Spring 1977), 53.
22. Council of State Governments, *The Book of the States, 1990–1991,* Vol. 28 (Lexington, KY: Council of State Governments, 1990), p. 346.
23. For an excellent summary of the merit system movement, see Dennis Palumbo and Steven Maynard-Moody, *Contemporary Public Administration* (New York: Longman, 1991), pp. 165–74.
24. Office of the Governor, Division of Planning Coordination, *Quality Texas Government, 1972.* Much of this discussion is based on this report.

11

The Judicial System in Texas

> The Texas (judicial) system is a hodgepodge of courts.[1]

> It is fair to suggest that Texas does not have a "court system" or "judicial system."[2]

In recent years, Texas courts have been beset by a series of controversies that have severely strained the principle of blind, impartial justice. Large campaign contributions to elected state judges from lawyers who practice before them and from other special interests have fueled a high-stakes war for philosophical and political control of the judiciary. The practice has drawn frequent criticism and even raised questions in the national media about whether Texas courtrooms are "for sale."

Minorities and women, meanwhile, remain grossly underrepresented among the ranks of Texas judges. Even the basic structure of the judicial system—an assortment of about 2,600 courts of various, often overlapping, jurisdictions—is so outdated that many experts believe it should be overhauled. But change doesn't come easily.

State courts resolve civil disputes over property rights and personal injuries. They also determine guilt or innocence and set punishment in criminal cases involving offenses against people, property, and public institutions. And to a more limited extent than the federal judiciary, they help set policy by reviewing the actions of the executive and legislative branches of government. Civil disputes may stem from something as simple as a tenant breaking an apartment lease to something as complex and potentially expensive as a manufacturer's liability for defective tires that contribute to the deaths or injuries of dozens of motorists. Criminal cases range from traffic offenses, punishable by fines, to capital murder, for which the death penalty can be imposed.

Some streamlining of Texas's judicial processes, especially at the appellate level, was accomplished in 1981. But the Texas judiciary, particularly in urban areas, has become overloaded by criminal cases and an increasingly litigious approach to civil disputes. It can take months to get a civil or a criminal case—one that isn't settled out of court or in a plea bargain with prosecutors—to trial.

STATE COURTS IN THE FEDERAL SYSTEM

Like people in every state, Texans are subject to the jurisdiction of both state and federal courts. The federal judiciary, created by Article III of the United States Constitution, has jurisdiction over violations of federal laws, including criminal offenses that occur across state lines, and over banking, securities, and other activities regulated by the federal government. Federal courts have also had major effects on state government policies and Texas's criminal justice system through interpretations and applications of the U.S. Constitution and federal laws, including the Bill of Rights.

Texas has a bill of rights in its constitution, but the federal courts have taken the lead in protecting many civil and political rights. The U.S. Supreme Court declared the white primary election unconstitutional in *Smith v. Allwright,* and federal court intervention continues in the redistricting of legislative and congressional district lines.[3] The federal judiciary also ordered far-reaching improvements in the state prison system (see Chapter 13). And when police officers read criminal suspects their rights, the officers are complying with constitutional requirements determined by the U.S. Supreme Court in the *Miranda* case.[4] Nevertheless, it is estimated that more than 97 percent of all litigation is based on state laws or local ordinances. Thus anyone involved in a lawsuit is likely to be found in a state rather than a federal court.

THE LEGAL FRAMEWORK FOR THE JUDICIAL SYSTEM

The United States and Texas constitutions form the basic legal framework of the Texas court system. Building on that framework, the Texas legislature has enacted codes of criminal and civil procedure to govern conduct in the courtroom and statutory laws for the courts to apply.

Most criminal activities are defined and their punishments established in the Texas **Penal Code.** In criminal cases the state initiates action against a person accused of a crime, often based on charges made by another individual. The most serious criminal offenses, for which prison sentences can be imposed, are called felonies. The most minor offenses, punishable by fines or short sentences in county jails, are called misdemeanors. Many property crimes and drug offenses are classified as state jail felonies and are punishable by community service work or time in a state jail, a prison-like facility operated by the state.

Civil lawsuits, which can be brought under numerous statutes, involve conflicts between two or more parties—individuals, corporations, governments, or other entities. Civil law governs contracts and property rights between private citizens, affords individuals an avenue for relief against corporate abuses, and determines liability for personal injuries. Administrative law includes government enforcement powers over many aspects of the state's economy.

An individual with a grievance has to take the initiative of going to court. A person can be having problems with a landlord who refuses to return a deposit, a dry cleaner who lost a suit, or a friend who borrowed and wrecked a car, but in a civil dispute, there is no legal issue to be resolved unless a lawsuit is filed. An injured person filing a lawsuit is a plaintiff. Since even the most minor disputes in the lowest courts can require professional assistance from a lawyer, plaintiffs soon discover that the pursuit of justice can be very costly and time consuming.

Statutes and constitutional laws are subject to change through legislative action and popular consent of the voters, and over the years there have been significant changes in what is legal or illegal, permissible or impermissible. At one time, for example, state law provided for a potential life prison sentence for the possession of a few ounces of marijuana. Small amounts are now considered a misdemeanor punishable by a fine. The legal drinking age was lowered to 18 for a few years but was reestablished at twenty-one after parents and school officials convinced the legislature that the younger age had helped increase alcohol abuse among teenagers.

THE STRUCTURE OF THE TEXAS COURT SYSTEM

There are five levels of Texas courts, but some courts at different levels have overlapping authority and jurisdiction (Figure 11–1). Some courts have only **original jurisdiction.** That is, they can only try or resolve cases being heard for the first time. They weigh the facts presented as evidence and apply the law in reaching a decision, or verdict. Other courts have only **appellate jurisdiction.** They review the decisions of lower courts to determine if constitutional and statutory principles and procedures were correctly interpreted and followed. Appellate courts are empowered to reverse the judgments of the lower courts and order cases retried if constitutional or procedural mistakes were made. Still other courts have both original and appellate jurisdiction.

At the highest appellate level, Texas has a **bifurcated court system** with the nine-member Texas Supreme Court serving as the court of last resort in civil cases and the nine-member Texas Court of Criminal Appeals functioning as the court of last resort in criminal cases. Only one other state, Oklahoma, has a similar structure.[5]

Unlike federal judges, who are appointed by the president to lifetime terms, state judges, except for those on municipal courts, are elected to limited terms in partisan elections. Midterm vacancies, however, are filled by appointment. Vacancies on the justice of the peace and county courts are filled by county commissioners courts, while vacancies on the district and appellate benches are filled by the governor.

Courts of Limited Jurisdiction

The lowest ranking courts in Texas are municipal courts and justice of the peace courts. There is a high probability that you or someone you know has appeared before a judge in one of these courts because both handle a large volume of traffic tickets. Some of these courts are big sources of revenue for local governments, and they are often accused of subordinating justice and fairness to financial considerations.

Some 882 **municipal courts** are established under state law, including some with multiple judges. The qualifications, terms of office, and method of selecting municipal judges are determined by the individual cities, but they are generally appointed by the city council. Municipal courts have original and exclusive jurisdiction over city ordinances, but most of these courts are not courts of record, where a word-for-word transcript is made of trial proceedings. Only very rudimentary

FIGURE 11–1 Court Structure of Texas September 1, 2003. *Source:* Office of Court Administration. Post Office Box 12066, Austin, Texas, 78711-2066.

information is officially recorded in most of these courts, and any appeal from them is heard *de novo* by the higher court. That means the second court has to conduct a new trial and hear the same witnesses and evidence all over again because no official record of the original proceedings was kept. The informality of these proceedings and the absence of a record add to the confusion and cost of using the system.[6] In response to these problems, the legislature in recent years has created municipal courts of record for some cities.

Each county in Texas is required to have one **justice of the peace court,** and each county government in the larger metropolitan areas may create sixteen. There are 835 of these courts in Texas. Justices of the peace are elected to four-year terms from precincts, or subdivisions of the county drawn by commissioners court, which also sets their salaries. Justices of the peace are not required to be licensed attorneys, a situation that has generated much criticism of these courts.

Although their duties vary from county to county, justice of the peace courts, with certain restrictions, have original jurisdiction in civil cases when the amount in dispute is $5,000 or less, and they have original jurisdiction over criminal offenses that are punishable by fines only. In some areas of criminal law, they have overlapping jurisdiction with municipal courts. Justices of the peace also sit as judges of small claims courts, and in many rural counties they serve as coroners. They also function as state magistrates with the authority to hold preliminary hearings to determine if there is probable cause to hold a criminal defendant.

These are not courts of record, and cases appealed from them are tried *de novo* in county courts, county courts-at-law, or district courts. Each justice court has an elected constable to serve warrants and perform other duties for the court.

County Courts

If there is confusion about the authority and jurisdiction of municipal and justice of the peace courts, it is compounded by the county courts. They were created by the Texas constitution to serve the needs of the sparsely populated, rural society that existed when the charter was written in 1875. But population growth and urbanization have placed enormous demands on the judicial system, and rather than modernize the system, the state has added courts while making only modest changes in the structure and jurisdiction of the existing courts.

Each county has a **constitutional county court.** The holder of this office, the county judge, is elected countywide to a four-year term. This individual is the chief executive officer of the county and presides over the county commissioners court, the policymaking body of county government. Most urban county judges don't perform judicial duties. But county judges in many rural counties perform both executive and judicial functions, a dual responsibility that some experts believe is inconsistent with the constitution's separation of powers doctrine. Although a large number of county judges are lawyers, they are not required to be. They are required only to be "well informed in the law" and to take appropriate courses in evidence and legal procedures.

The constitutional county court shares some original civil jurisdiction with both the justice of the peace and district courts. It has original criminal jurisdiction over misdemeanors punishable by fines of more than $500 and jail sentences of one year or less. These courts also probate wills and have appellate jurisdiction over cases tried originally in justice of the peace and municipal courts.

Over the years, the legislature also has created 226 **statutory county courts,** or county courts-at-law, in more than seventy counties. Some specialize in probate cases and are called probate courts. These courts were designed to deal with specific local problems and, consequently, have inconsistent jurisdictions. Judges on these courts are elected countywide and have to be lawyers, but the authority of a particular court is defined by the legislation creating it. Some cannot hear civil disputes involving more than $2,500, while others can hear disputes involving as much as $100,000. Drunken-driving cases are the primary criminal cases tried before these courts.

Courts of General Jurisdiction

The primary trial court in Texas is the **district court.** Although there is some overlapping jurisdiction with county courts, district courts have original jurisdiction over civil cases involving $200 or more in damages, divorce cases, contested elections, suits over land titles and liens, suits for slander or defamation, all criminal felony cases, and misdemeanors involving official misconduct. In recent years, the legislature has created district courts with specialized jurisdictions over criminal or civil law or over such specialties as family law—divorces and child custody cases. In some large metropolitan counties that have numerous district courts, the jurisdictions of the respective courts are determined by informal agreements among the judges. District court judges are elected to four-year terms, must be at least twenty-five years old, and must have practiced law or served as a judge of another court for four years prior to taking office.

The Texas Constitution gives the legislature the responsibility to define judicial districts, and as the expanding population produced greater caseloads, new district courts were created. In 1981, there were 328 district courts. In 2003, there were 420. A single county may be allocated more than one district court

Associate Judge Peter Sakai is seen presiding over the Child Abuse and Neglect Court in San Antonio.

with overlapping geographical jurisdiction. Harris County, the state's most populous county, has fifty-nine district courts, each covering the entire county. By contrast, one rural district court may include several counties. As these courts evolved, there was little systematic consideration of the respective workloads of individual courts, and there are now great disparities in the number of people that district courts serve.

Many urban counties suffer from a heavy backlog of cases that can delay a trial date in a civil lawsuit for months or years and has prompted a widespread use of plea bargains in criminal cases (see "How Long Is Too Long?"). In a **plea bargain,** a criminal defendant, through a lawyer, will negotiate a guilty plea with prosecutors that will result in a lesser sentence than could be expected from a trial conviction. The process saves the state the time-consuming expense of a full-blown trial and has become an essential tool in clearing urban court dockets.

Former District Attorney John B. Holmes Jr. estimated that 90 percent of the thousands of felony cases filed in Harris County (Houston) each year were disposed of through plea bargains. Without plea bargains, the caseload would simply overwhelm the twenty-two Harris County district courts that handle criminal cases.

Harris County's civil district courts disposed of more than 84,000 lawsuits—divorces, personal injuries, tax disputes, and others—in fiscal year 2002 but left more than 101,000 other cases pending. Many civil lawsuits are resolved through negotiations between the opposing parties, but those that are tried and appealed can take several years to be resolved.

The wide disparities in populations and caseloads of the various district courts prompted the adoption of a constitutional amendment in 1985 that created the Judicial Districts Board. That panel was responsible for redrawing judicial districts with an eye toward a more equitable distribution of the workload. But in 1994, yielding to pressure from incumbent judges who didn't want to lose their offices, it issued recommendations that primarily preserved the status quo. Extensive changes by the legislature were considered unlikely.

Although the district court is the state's primary trial court and the state pays the district judges' base salaries, the counties pick up virtually all the other district

---

HOW LONG IS TOO LONG?

Trial delays are bad enough for prosecutors and taxpayers, but they can be a nightmare for criminal defendants innocent of the charges against them, especially if they have to spend months in jail awaiting trial. The *Fort Worth Star-Telegram* reported the case of a twenty-three-year-old construction worker from Mexico who spent 575 days—more than a year and a half—in the Tarrant County Jail awaiting trial on charges of fondling a five-year-old girl. When his case finally reached the courtroom, it took a jury forty-two minutes to find him innocent and free him. His room and board in jail had cost Tarrant County taxpayers $23,000. But his ordeal had cost him much more, and his case should make all of us ask how long justice can be delayed before it is justice denied.

Source: Fort Worth Star-Telegram, April 23, 1993.

court expenses. The counties provide courtrooms, pay the courts' operating expenses, and supplement the judges' state pay.

Intermediate Courts of Appeals

There are fourteen intermediate **Courts of Appeals** covering thirteen multicounty regions that hear appeals of both civil and criminal cases from the district courts. Two courts, the First Court of Appeals and the Fourteenth Court of Appeals, are based in Houston and cover the same area. The Texas Constitution provides that each court shall have a chief justice and at least two other justices, but the legislature can add to that number and has done so for most courts. Each Houston court has nine judges, and the Fifth Court of Appeals in Dallas has thirteen judges. Five of these intermediate courts, however, have only three members. Appellate judges are elected to six-year terms. They must be at least thirty-five years old and have at least ten years of experience as an attorney or a judge on a court of record.

All Courts of Appeals combined disposed of more than 12,000 cases during fiscal 2002 but had almost 8,000 other cases pending on their dockets at the end of the year, with criminal cases accounting for more than half of the unfinished business. But there are disparities in the caseloads between individual courts, with those in Houston and Dallas handling the lion's share. The Texas Supreme Court partially balances the load by transferring cases among courts. The Courts of Appeals normally decide cases in panels of three judges, but an entire court can hear some appeals *en banc*.

The Highest Appellate Courts

The creation of separate courts of last resort for civil and criminal cases was part of the effort by the constitutional framers of 1875 to fragment political power and decentralize the structure of state and local government. It was also based on the rationale that criminal cases should be handled more expeditiously, and the way to accomplish this was through a separate appellate court.[7]

Although it decides only civil appeals, the **Texas Supreme Court** is probably viewed by most Texans as the titular head of the state judiciary, and it has been given some authority to coordinate the state judicial system.[8] The Supreme Court is charged with developing administrative procedures for the state courts and rules of civil procedure. It appoints the Board of Law Examiners, which is responsible for licensing attorneys, and has oversight of the State Bar, the professional organization to which all lawyers in Texas must belong. The Supreme Court also has disciplinary authority over state judges through recommendations of the State Commission on Judicial Conduct.

The Texas Supreme Court includes a chief justice and eight justices who serve staggered, six-year terms. Three members are up for election every two years on a statewide ballot (Table 11–1). Members must be at least thirty-five years old and must have been a practicing attorney, a judge of a court of record, or a combination of both for at least ten years.

The **Texas Court of Criminal Appeals,** which hears only criminal cases on appeal, includes a presiding judge and eight other judges elected statewide to staggered, six-year terms (Table 11–2). The qualifications for members of this court are the same as those for the Supreme Court.

TABLE 11–1 Chief Justices of the Texas Supreme Court, 1876–Present

Oran M. Roberts	1876–1878
George F. Moore	1878–1881
Robert S. Gould	1881–1882
Asa H. Willie	1882–1888
John W. Stayton	1888–1894
Reuben R. Gaines	1894–1911
Thomas J. Brown	1911–1915
Nelson Phillips	1915–1921
C. M. Cureton	1921–1940
W. F. Moore	1940–1941
James P. Alexander	1941–1948
J. E. Hickman	1948–1961
Robert W. Calvert	1961–1972
Joe R. Greenhill	1972–1982
Jack Pope	1982–1985
John L. Hill Jr.	1985–1988
Thomas R. Phillips	1988–2004

Source: Office of Chief Justice Thomas R. Phillips, Supreme Court of Texas.

TABLE 11–2 Presiding Judges, Court of Criminal Appeals, 1891*–Present

John P. White	1891–1892
James M. Hurt	1892–1898
W. L. Davidson	1899–1913
A. C. Prendergast	1913–1916
W. L. Davidson	1917–1921
Wright C. Morrow	1921–1939
Frank Lee Hawkins	1939–1951
Harry N. Graves	1951–1954
W. A. Morrison	1955–1961
Kenneth K. Woodley	1961–1965
W. T. McDonald	1965–1966
W. A. Morrison	1966–1967
Kenneth K. Woodley	1967–1971
John F. Onion Jr.	1971–1989
Michael J. McCormick	1989–2001
Sharon Keller	2001–

*Court was restructured in 1891 through a constitutional amendment.

Source: Texas Almanac, 1996–1997 (Dallas: The Dallas Morning News, Inc., 1995).

Under the federal system, some decisions of the Texas Supreme Court and the Texas Court of Criminal Appeals can be appealed to the U.S. Supreme Court. Those cases have to involve a federal question or a constitutional right assured under the U.S. Constitution.

JUDICIAL REFORM

Judicial reform has been a recurring issue in Texas politics. Small, incremental changes have been made since the 1970s, but many jurists and scholars continue to push for an overhaul of the state courts. In September 1989, Texas Supreme Court Chief Justice Thomas R. Phillips requested an in-depth study of the Texas judiciary by the Texas Research League, a privately financed, nonprofit organization specializing in studies of state government.

The League concluded that the court system was fundamentally flawed and sorely in need of an overhaul. It made twenty-seven recommendations, including one that the legislature rewrite the judiciary article of the state constitution to provide a fundamental framework for a unified court system.

Despite a series of similar studies and reports, however, reform of Texas courts has been difficult. The public may have a lot to gain from judicial restructuring, but the primary stakeholders—the judges, the attorneys, the court administrative personnel, and litigants who benefit from delays, confusion, and inefficiency—have resisted change. Unless there is a spontaneous popular demand for reform, there will be few structural changes in the judiciary until some or all of these participants perceive some advantages from reform.[9]

COURT PERSONNEL

Texas Judges

In 2002, the last year for which extensive data were available, about one-half of the members of the intermediate and highest appellate courts had come to the bench from private law practice. About one-third had previously served on lower courts. Most district judges had come to their offices from private law practice or from a prosecutor's office. There was greater diversity in career patterns for judges on the county courts, justice of the peace courts, and municipal courts, given the limited constitutional requirements for many of those positions.

The average length of service on the Supreme Court was seven years; on the Court of Criminal Appeals, four years, seven months; on the Courts of Appeals, seven years, two months; and on the district courts, nine years, seven months. At that time, the most experienced district judge had been in office for thirty-two years.[10]

The development of a two-party system in Texas has affected the partisan affiliation of state judges. Republicans have seen election gains and more appointments to judicial vacancies. A number of judges have switched from the Democratic party. Dallas County, in particular, has experienced considerable party switching by incumbent judges.[11] By 2003, almost two-thirds of the judges at the district court level and higher were Republicans.

Most Texas judges are white males. With increasing frequency, women, Hispanics, and African Americans are entering the legal profession and running for judicial offices, but they are still proportionately underrepresented in the judiciary. As will be discussed later in this chapter, minorities are pressing for changes in the judicial selection process to enhance their chances to serve on the bench.

Other Participants in the State Judiciary

County and district clerks, both elected offices, are custodians of court records. Bailiffs are peace officers assigned to the courts to help maintain order and protect judges and other parties. Other law enforcement officers play critical roles in the arrest, detention, and investigation of persons accused of crimes.

County attorneys and district attorneys are responsible for prosecuting criminal cases. Both positions are elected (see Chapter 12). Some counties don't have a county attorney. In those that do, the county attorney is the chief legal advisor to county commissioners, represents the county in civil lawsuits, and may prosecute misdemeanors. The district attorney prosecutes felonies and, in some counties, also handles misdemeanors. The district attorney exercises considerable power in the criminal justice process by deciding which cases to take to a **grand jury** for an indictment, whether to seek the maximum penalty for an offense, or whether to plea bargain with a defendant for a reduced sentence. The office represents one county in metropolitan areas and several counties in less populated areas of the state.

The Jury Systems

Other important players in the judicial process are the private citizens who serve on juries, of which there are two kinds—grand juries and trial, or petit, juries. Although

TULIA: A MISCARRIAGE OF JUSTICE

What began as a drug sting in Tulia, a small town in the Texas Panhandle, quickly escalated into one of the biggest miscarriages of justice in recent Texas history. After belated, but intense, media coverage, help finally arrived for 35 victims, but not before they had paid a high price.

In July 1999, 46 Tulia residents, including 39 African-Americans, were arrested on drug charges. Thirty-eight of the defendants were later convicted, all on the testimony of Tom Coleman, the sole undercover officer and only prosecution witness against them. After the *Texas Observer* newspaper, followed by other media, focused attention on the arrests and raised questions about whether they were racially motivated, special evidentiary hearings into the drug sting were convened in March 2003. Retired state District Judge Ron Chapman of Dallas presided over the hearings, during which Coleman's testimony was discredited, and recommended that the Texas Court of Criminal Appeals overturn all 38 convictions. In a separate proceeding, Coleman was later indicted on three counts of perjury stemming from his testimony before Chapman.

The Texas Legislature then stepped in, passing a law that allowed 14 Tulia defendants who were still in prison to be released on bond while the Court of Criminal Appeals considered their cases. And, finally, Gov. Rick Perry pardoned 35 of the defendants in August 2003, more than four years after the arrests. "Questions surrounding testimony from the key witnesses in these cases, coupled with recommendations from the Board of Pardons and Paroles, weighed heavily in my final decision," the governor said. "Texans demand a system that is tough but fair. I believe my decision to grant pardons in these cases is both appropriate and just," he added. Perry's office said three of the Tulia defendants weren't eligible for pardons.

Jeff Blackburn of Amarillo, an attorney for the Tulia defendants, also filed a civil lawsuit in federal court, seeking damages against a regional drug task force and several local government officials in Swisher County, where Tulia is located. Will Harrell, executive director for Texas of the American Civil Liberties Union, said systemic flaws in the criminal justice system, such as police misconduct, abuse of authority and inadequate legal representation of the poor, still needed to be addressed.

Source: Houston Chronicle, August 23, 2003, p. 1A.

there is some debate about the competency of a jury of ordinary citizens to make reasonable decisions on complex and technical civil and criminal matters, no acceptable alternatives have been found.

In theory, the grand jury functions to ensure that the government has sufficient reason to proceed with a criminal **prosecution** against an individual. It includes twelve persons selected by a district judge from a list proposed by a jury commission appointed by the local district judge or judges. Although the grand jury evolved to protect the individual against arbitrary and capricious behavior by governmental officials, a district attorney can exercise great control over a grand jury through deciding which evidence and which witnesses jurors will hear. There have been allegations over the years that grand juries overrepresent the interests of upper social and economic groups and underrepresent minorities. Grand jury meetings and deliberations are conducted in private, and the accused is not allowed to have an attorney present during grand jury questioning.

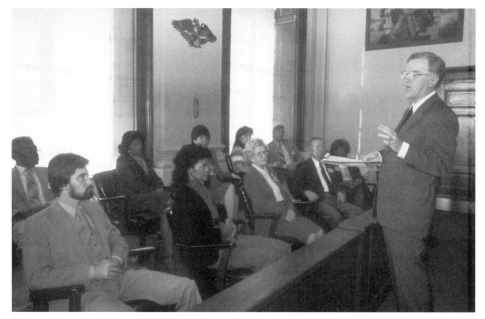

An attorney addressing a jury in a state court in Dallas.

A grand jury usually meets on specified days of the week and serves for the duration of the district court's term, usually from three to six months. If at least nine grand jurors believe there is enough evidence to warrant a trial in a case under investigation, they will issue an **indictment,** or a "true bill," a written statement charging a person or persons with a crime. A grand jury investigation also may result in no indictment, or a "no bill."

In some cases, grand juries will issue indictments alleging misdemeanors. That often happens after an investigation fails to produce a strong enough case for a felony indictment. Most misdemeanors, however, aren't handled by grand juries. They are handled by the district or county attorney, who prepares an information—a document formally charging an individual with a misdemeanor—on the basis of a complaint filed by a private citizen.

The jury on which most people are likely to be called to serve is the trial, or **petit, jury.** Citizens who are at least eighteen years old and meet other minimal requirements are eligible for jury duty, and anyone refusing to comply with a jury summons can be fined for contempt of court (see "Rounding up a Jury"). Persons older than seventy, individuals with legal custody of young children, and full-time students are exempted from jury duty.

The legislature in 1991 increased the likelihood of an individual's being called to jury duty by providing that county and district clerks prepare jury summonses from lists of Texans holding driver's licenses or Department of Public Safety identification cards. Previously, prospective jurors were chosen from voter registration lists, and it was believed that some Texans had not been registering to vote in order to avoid jury duty.

ROUNDING UP A JURY

Some people called it "street justice." Others said it was bad public relations. It was probably both, and it was certainly unusual.

Justice of the Peace Mark Fury had scheduled a night jury trial for a minor traffic case in his southwest Houston courtroom but, at the last minute, discovered he didn't have enough jurors. So he issued a writ, ordering deputy constables to go across the street and round up some shoppers in a grocery store parking lot.

Nineteen people soon found themselves unexpectedly pressed into jury duty. Not all were chosen for the jury, but all had to report to the courtroom and had their evening plans disrupted. Several weren't too happy about it.

"It just seemed everybody was a little crusty toward everybody. They were just all mad," one draftee said.

Lisa Sedgwick, who had planned to go to a soccer game that night, ended up being the jury foreman instead.

The jury roundup, although rare, was legal. But people caught in the judge's net couldn't understand why he didn't just simply postpone the trial of such a minor case.

Fury said he believed the jurors had "a positive experience."

"I thought it went very smoothly. I expected there to be a larger number of acrimonious people," he said.

The jury convicted the defendant, a teenager, of speeding.

_____

Source: Houston Chronicle, August 22, 1997.

Six persons make up a jury in a justice of the peace or county court and in a misdemeanor trial in district court. Twelve persons sit on juries in felony trials in district court. Attorneys for both sides in a criminal or civil case screen the prospective jurors, known as veniremen, before a jury is seated. In major felony cases, such as capital murder, prosecutors and defense attorneys may take several days to select a jury from among hundreds of prospects.

Attorneys for each side in a criminal case are allowed a certain number of peremptory challenges, which allow them to dismiss a prospective juror without having to explain the reason, and an unlimited number of challenges for cause. In the latter case, the lawyer has to state why he or she believes a particular **venireman** wouldn't be able to evaluate the evidence in the case impartially. The judge decides whether to grant each challenge for cause but can rule against a peremptory challenge only if he or she believes the prosecutor is trying to exclude prospective jurors because of their race, such as keeping African Americans off a jury that is to try an African-American defendant. If that happens, the defendant is entitled to a new group, or panel, of prospective jurors.

In civil cases, attorneys for both sides determine whether any persons on the jury panel should be disqualified because they are related to one of the parties, have some other personal or business connection, or could otherwise be prejudiced. For example, a lawyer defending a doctor in a malpractice suit probably would not want to seat a prospective juror who had been dissatisfied with his own medical treatment.

Such potential conflicts are discovered by attorneys' careful screening and questioning of veniremen.

Unanimous jury verdicts are required to convict a defendant in a criminal case. Agreement of only ten of the twelve members of a district court jury and five of the six on a county court jury, however, are necessary to reach a verdict in a civil suit. In a criminal case, jurors have to be convinced "beyond a reasonable doubt" that a defendant is guilty before returning a guilty verdict.

JUDICIAL PROCEDURES AND DECISION-MAKING

Civil litigants and criminal defendants (except those charged with capital murder) can waive their right to a jury trial if they believe it would be to their advantage to have their cases decided by a judge. Following established procedures, which differ between civil and criminal cases and are enforced by the judge, the trial moves through the presentation of opening arguments by the opposing attorneys, examination and cross examination of witnesses, presentation of evidence, rebuttal, and summation. Some trials can be completed in a few hours, but the trial of a complex civil lawsuit or a sensational criminal case can take weeks or months. Convicted criminal defendants or parties dissatisfied with a judge or jury's verdict in a civil lawsuit can then appeal their case to higher courts.

The procedure in the appellate courts is markedly different from that in the trial courts. There is no jury at the appellate level to rehear evidence. Instead, judges review the decisions and the procedures of the lower court for conformance to constitutional and statutory requirements. The record of the trial court proceedings and legal briefs filed by attorneys are available for appellate judges to review.

Most civil and criminal appeals are initially made to one of the fourteen intermediate Courts of Appeals. Parties dissatisfied with decisions of the Courts of Appeals can appeal to the Texas Supreme Court or the Court of Criminal Appeals.

Cases reach the Texas Supreme Court primarily on **petitions for review,** usually filed by the losing parties, who claim that legal or procedural mistakes were made in the lower courts. The petitions are divided up among the nine justices for review. Then, meeting in private conference, the court decides which petitions to reject outright—thus upholding the lower court decisions—and which to schedule for attorneys' oral arguments. A case won't be heard without the approval of at least four of the nine justices.

Oral arguments, in which lawyers present their perspectives on the legal points that are at issue in their cases and answer questions from the justices, are presented in open court. The responsibility for writing the majority opinions that state the court's decisions is determined by lot among the justices. It often takes several months after oral arguments before a decision is issued. Differences over legal points and judicial philosophies are debated among the justices behind the closed doors of their conference room. But they sometimes spill out for public view through split votes and strongly worded dissenting opinions.

Most cases taken to the Texas Supreme Court on appeal are from one of the Courts of Appeals, but occasionally the Supreme Court receives a direct appeal from a district court. In 1980, the high court agreed to hear about one in every eight appeals that it received. It now hears only about one in every ten, partly because the court has changed its rules to increase from three to four the number of justices required to approve a hearing.

The Texas Supreme Court also acts on petitions for **writs of mandamus,** or orders directing a lower court or another public official to take a certain action. Many involve disputes over procedure or evidence in cases still pending in trial courts.

The Texas Court of Criminal Appeals has appellate jurisdiction in criminal cases that originate in the district and county courts. Death penalty cases are appealed directly to the Court of Criminal Appeals. Other criminal cases are appealed first to the intermediate Courts of Appeals. Either the defendant or the prosecution can appeal the Courts of Appeals' decisions to the Court of Criminal Appeals by filing petitions for discretionary review, which the high court may grant if at least four judges agree. The court sets one day a week aside for lawyers' oral arguments in the cases it agrees to review. The task of writing majority opinions is rotated among the nine judges.

A MIXED SELECTION SYSTEM

Most Texans apparently believe that the election of judges is the best way to keep the judiciary responsive to the public. Or so various surveys have indicated. But the election process has been diluted by a large number of appointments to judicial vacancies. District and appellate judges who resign or retire in midterm are replaced by gubernatorial appointees. County commissioners courts fill midterm vacancies in the county and justice of the peace courts. In reality, therefore, Texas has a mixed judicial selection system.

Eight of the nine judges on the Texas Court of Criminal Appeals in 2002 had initially been elected to their positions, but five of the nine members of the Texas Supreme Court had initially been appointed by a governor. About half of the Courts of Appeals and district court judges serving that year had initially been appointed.[12] Appointees are required to run for office in the next general election to keep their seats, but their incumbency can enhance their election chances.

JUDICIAL CONCERNS AND CONTROVERSIES

For more than twenty years, Texas courts have been at the center of conflict and controversy. Large campaign contributions from lawyers and other special interests to judges and judicial candidates have raised allegations that Texas has the best justice that money can buy. With billions of dollars at stake in crucial legal decisions, the Texas Supreme Court has been a philosophical and political battleground. Meanwhile, minorities, who hold a disproportionately small number of judicial offices, continue to press for greater influence in electing judges. And lengthy ballots, particularly in urban areas, make it increasingly difficult for most voters to choose intelligently among judicial candidates (see "Long Ballots Produce Election-Day Surprises").

Although these issues and concerns may seem unrelated, they all share one important characteristic: They cast a cloud over the Texas judiciary. Each, in its own way, undermines public confidence in the state courts and makes many Texans question how just their system of justice is.

LONG BALLOTS PRODUCE ELECTION-DAY SURPRISES

Like most other candidates for the Texas Court of Criminal Appeals, Houston attorney Steve Mansfield received little publicity when he began a campaign in 1994 to unseat Democratic Judge Charles Campbell, a twelve-year incumbent. Running as a crime victims' advocate, Mansfield first defeated an equally unknown attorney for the Republican nomination. He then got more publicity than he wanted—all of it negative. In the middle of his general election campaign, Mansfield was found to have lied about his personal and political background and exaggerated his legal experience. He was primarily an insurance lawyer with little experience in criminal law. Still, he unseated Campbell, thanks to heavy straight-ticket Republican voting in a GOP landslide.

Bad publicity continued to dog Mansfield, even after he took office. Texas Republican Party officials shunned him at a party fundraiser, and the Board of Law Examiners investigated the circumstances under which he had obtained a Texas law license, which he needed to serve on the court.

At his swearing-in ceremony in January 1995, Mansfield promised to be a hard-working judge, and he spent his first year in office living up to his promise by authoring thirty-three opinions, slightly more than the court average. It was unknown how much of the actual research and writing could be credited to Mansfield and how much to the experienced staff he inherited from Campbell and was wise enough to retain. But, as he had promised during his campaign, Mansfield usually sided with the prosecution.

Several months after Mansfield took office, the State Bar publicly reprimanded him for his campaign lies. But the Board of Law Examiners did not challenge his law license, which cleared the way for him to remain on the court for his full six-year term. Many judges, prosecutors, and other state officials considered Mansfield's election an embarrassment and a good argument for appointing, rather than electing, judges. Despite the controversy, Mansfield enjoyed his new job. "It's certainly been the greatest challenge I've ever faced. I've worked very hard to live up to the trust the people of Texas put in me," he said.

Mansfield didn't seek reelection in 2000 and left the court after six years. Attempting a comeback, he ran for another Court of Criminal Appeals seat in the 2002 Republican primary but lost. Unfortunately, Mansfield was not the first candidate of questionable qualifications to win election to a statewide court in Texas. The most infamous example was Donald B. Yarbrough. Yarbrough, also an unknown attorney from Houston, claimed that God had told him to run for the Texas Supreme Court. Yarbrough's name was similar to that of Don Yarborough, who had run unsuccessfully for governor two times in the 1960s, and that of former U.S. Senator Ralph Yarborough. Thanks to his familiar name, he upset a much more qualified candidate, Appellate Judge Charles Barrow, for a seat on the high court in 1976. Yarbrough spent approximately $350 campaigning, while Barrow had the endorsement of the legal establishment.

Yarbrough, a Democrat, served about six months on the Supreme Court, then became the target of a criminal investigation and resigned as the legislature was preparing to remove him. After he left the court, he was convicted of lying to a grand jury investigating allegations that he had plotted to have a banker killed. He was sentenced to five years in prison, but while free on bond during an appeal, he left the country to attend medical school in Grenada and refused to return when his appeal was denied. He finally was apprehended in the Caribbean, sentenced to two additional years for jumping bond, and imprisoned.

Texas voters are confronted with long ballots that in some counties may include forty or fifty names for judicial offices alone, making it virtually impossible for most voters to recognize the names of all the judges, much less weigh their qualifications. In such instances, people often vote for names with which they are vaguely familiar.

Source: Houston Chronicle, June 28, 1995.

Judicial Activism

In earlier chapters, we noted the historical domination of state politics and policies by the conservative, business-oriented establishment. That domination also applied to the judiciary, as insurance companies, banks, utilities, and other large corporate entities became accustomed to favorable rulings from a Democratic, but conservative, Texas Supreme Court.

Establishment-oriented justices, usually elected with the support of the state's largest law firms, tended to view their role as strict constructionists. They believed that the responsibility of the courts was to narrowly interpret and apply the law. The legislature had the authority to enact public policy. Judges were not to engage in setting policy but were to honor legal precedent and prior case law, which had generally favored the interests of corporations over those of consumers, laborers, and the lower social classes.

The establishment began to feel the first tremors of a philosophical earthquake in the 1970s. The Texas Trial Lawyers Association, whose members represent consumers in lawsuits against businesses, doctors, and insurance companies, increased its political activity. And, in 1973, the legislature, with increased minority and female membership from single-member House districts ordered by the federal courts, enacted the Deceptive Trade Practices–Consumer Protection Act, which encouraged injured parties to take their grievances to court. Among other things, the new law allowed consumers to sue for attorneys' fees as well as compensatory and punitive damages.

Trial, or plaintiffs', attorneys, who usually receive a healthy percentage of monetary damages awarded their clients, began contributing millions of dollars to successful Texas Supreme Court candidates, and judicial precedents started falling. A revamped court issued significant decisions that made it easier for consumers to win large judgments for medical malpractice, faulty products, and other complaints against businesses and their insurers. The new activist, liberal interpretation of the law contrasted sharply with the traditional record of the court. "All of a sudden, we have a magnificent Supreme Court, which is not controlled by a sinister, rich, opulent elite," trial attorney Pat Maloney of San Antonio, a major contributor to Supreme Court candidates, said in a 1983 interview with the *Fort Worth Star-Telegram.*[13]

The business community and defense lawyers accused the new court majority of exceeding its constitutional authority by trying to write its own laws. Some business leaders contended the court's activism endangered the state's economy by discouraging new businesses from moving to Texas, a fear that was soon to be put to partisan advantage by Republican leaders.

Judicial Impropriety

Controversy over the Texas Supreme Court escalated into a full-blown storm in 1986 when the Judicial Affairs Committee of the Texas House investigated two justices, Democrats C. L. Ray and William Kilgarlin, for alleged improper contact with attorneys practicing before the court. The two justices denied the allegations, made largely by former briefing attorneys, but never testified before the legislative panel. Both justices had consistently sided with plaintiffs' lawyers and had received considerable campaign support from them, and they contended the investigation was politically motivated and orchestrated by defense lawyers and corporate interests opposed to their judicial activism.

Chief Justice John L. Hill voluntarily testified before the committee and said he suspected but couldn't prove that information about the Supreme Court's deliberations on some cases had been improperly leaked to outsiders. Hill urged the committee to let the State Commission on Judicial Conduct, a state agency charged with investigating complaints of ethical violations by state judges, look into the allegations and "let the chips fall where they may."[14] The committee eventually concluded its investigation without recommending any action against the justices.

But in June 1987, the State Commission on Judicial Conduct issued public sanctions against both. Ray was reprimanded for seven violations of the Code of Judicial Conduct, including the acceptance of free airplane rides from attorneys practicing before the court and improper communication with lawyers about pending cases. Kilgarlin received a milder admonishment because two of his law clerks had accepted a weekend trip to Las Vegas from a law firm with cases pending before the court. Both justices were cited for soliciting funds from attorneys to help pay for litigation the justices had brought against the House Judicial Affairs Committee and a former briefing attorney who testified against them.

Later in 1987, the Texas judiciary, particularly the Texas Supreme Court, received negative publicity on a national scale when the high court upheld a record $11 billion judgment awarded Pennzoil Company in a dispute with Texaco Inc. Several members of the Texas Supreme Court were even featured on a network television program that questioned whether justice was "for sale" in Texas.

The record judgment was awarded to Pennzoil after a state district court jury in Houston had determined that Texaco had wrongfully interfered in Pennzoil's attempt to acquire Getty Oil Company in 1984. Texaco, which sought protection under federal bankruptcy laws, later reached a settlement with Pennzoil, but it also waged a massive public relations campaign against the Texas judiciary.

In a segment on CBS-TV's program, *60 Minutes,* correspondent Mike Wallace pointed out that plaintiff's attorney Joe Jamail of Houston, who represented Pennzoil, had contributed $10,000 to the original trial judge in the case and thousands of dollars more to Texas Supreme Court justices. The program also generally criticized the elective system that allowed Texas judges to legally accept large campaign contributions from lawyers who practiced before them. The program presented what already had been reported in the Texas media, but after the national exposure, Governor Bill Clements and other Republicans renewed attacks on the activist, Democratic justices. And some Texas newspapers published editorials calling for changes in the judicial selection process.

Campaign Contributions and Republican Gains

Chief Justice Hill, a former attorney general who had narrowly lost a gubernatorial race to Clements in 1978, had been a strong supporter of electing state judges and had spent more than $1 million winning the chief justice's seat in 1984. As did his colleagues on the court, he accepted many campaign contributions from lawyers. But in 1986, Hill announced that the "recent trend toward excessive political contributions in judicial races" had prompted him to change his mind.[15] He now advocated a so-called **merit selection** plan of gubernatorial appointments and periodic retention elections. But Hill was the only Supreme Court member to endorse such a change. The other eight justices—like Hill, all Democrats—still favored the elective system, and the legislature ignored pleas for change.

Hill resigned from the court on January 1, 1988, to return to private law practice and lobby as a private citizen for changing the judicial selection method. His resignation and the midterm resignations of two other Democratic justices before the 1988 elections gave Republicans a golden opportunity to make historic inroads on the high court. And they helped the business community regain control of the court from plaintiffs' attorneys.

Party realignment and midterm judicial appointments by Clements had already increased the number of Republican judges across the state, particularly on district court benches in urban areas. But only one Republican had ever served on the Texas Supreme Court in modern times. Will Garwood was appointed by Clements in 1979 to fill a vacancy on the court but was defeated by Democrat C. L. Ray in the 1980 election.

GOP leaders had already been planning to recruit a Republican slate of candidates for the three Supreme Court seats that normally would have been on the ballot in 1988. Now, six seats were contested, including those held by three new Republican justices appointed by Clements to fill the unexpected vacancies. Even though a full Supreme Court term is six years, the governor's judicial appointees have to run in the next election to keep their seats. Clements appointed Thomas R. Phillips, a state district judge from Houston, to succeed Hill and become the first Republican chief justice since Reconstruction.

The competing legal and financial interests in Texas understood that the six Texas Supreme Court races on the 1988 ballot would help set the philosophy of the court for years to come. Consequently, these were the most expensive court races in Texas history, with the twelve Republican and Democratic nominees raising $10 million in direct campaign contributions. Much of the money was spent on television advertising.

Contributions to the winners averaged $836,347. Phillips, one of three Republican winners, spent $2 million, the most by a winning candidate. The smallest amount spent by a winner was $449,290. Some individual donations to candidates were as large as $65,000.[16] Reformers argued that such large contributions created an appearance of impropriety and eroded public confidence in the judiciary's independence.

But the successes of Republicans and conservative Democrats in the 1988 races probably hindered, more than helped, the cause of reforming the judicial selection process. The business and medical communities, which had considerable success fighting the plaintiffs' lawyers under the existing rules with large campaign contributions of their own, were pleased with the election results. "I'm a happy camper today," said Kim Ross, lobbyist for the Texas Medical Association, whose political action committee had supported two conservative Democratic winners and the three Republican victors.[17] In several key liability cases over the next few years, the high court began to demonstrate a rediscovered philosophy favoring business defendants over plaintiffs.[18]

Republicans won a fourth seat on the Texas Supreme Court in 1990 and a fifth in 1994, to give the GOP a majority for the first time since Reconstruction. Republican challengers in 1994 also unseated nineteen incumbent Democratic district judges in Harris County in strong straight-party voting. Republicans picked up a sixth and a seventh seat on the Supreme Court after two Democratic justices resigned in midterm in 1995 and were replaced with Republican appointees of Governor George W. Bush. Republicans completed their sweep of the high court in 1998 when Justice Rose Spector, one of two remaining Democratic justices, was unseated by Republican Harriet O'Neill and Democrat Raul A. Gonzalez retired in midterm and was replaced by Bush appointee Alberto R. Gonzales. No Democratic challengers filed for the three Supreme Court seats that were on the 2000 ballot. Democrats ran for all five seats on the 2002 ballot but lost all five races.

Legislative Reaction to Judicial Activism

The business community had also moved its war against the trial lawyers to the legislature, which in 1987 enacted a so-called **"tort reform"** package that attempted to put some limits on personal injury lawsuits and damage judgments entered by the courts. (A tort is a wrongful act over which a lawsuit can be brought.) Insurance companies, which had been lobbying nationwide for states to set limits on jury awards in personal injury cases, were major proponents of the legislation. They were joined by the Texas Civil Justice League, an organization of trade and professional associations, cities, and businesses formed in 1986 to seek similar changes in Texas tort law. The high-stakes campaign for change was enthusiastically supported by Governor Bill Clements but was opposed by consumer groups and plaintiffs' lawyers, who had been making millions of dollars from the judiciary's new liberalism.

Cities, businesses, doctors, and even charitable organizations had been hit with tremendous increases in insurance premiums, which they blamed on greedy trial lawyers and large court awards in malpractice and personal injury lawsuits. Trial lawyers blamed the insurance industry, which, they said, had started raising premiums to recoup losses the companies had suffered in investment income after interest rates had fallen.

Among other things, the 1987 tort reform laws limited governmental liability, attempted to discourage frivolous lawsuits, and limited the ability of claimants to collect damages for injuries that were largely their own fault. They also set limits on punitive damages, which are designed to punish whoever caused an accident or an injury and are often awarded in addition to an injured party's compensation for actual losses.

Other limits on lawsuits were enacted in later legislative sessions, including 1995 and 2003. The 1995 changes, major priorities of then-Governor George W. Bush, imposed even stricter limits on punitive damages and limited the liability of a party who is only partially responsible for an injury. The 2003 legislation, actively sought by Gov. Rick Perry and a new Republican majority in the Texas House, set new restrictions on class action lawsuits and imposed new limits on money that could be awarded for non-economic damages—such as pain, suffering or disfigurement—in medical malpractice cases. Lawsuits—or the threat of lawsuits—had been blamed for rising pre-miums for medical malpractice insurance, which some doctors and other advocates of civil justice changes had characterized as a "crisis" in health care in Texas.

A leading proponent for the civil justice restrictions in 2003 was Texans for Law-suit Reform, a Houston-based business group whose political action committee gave more than $1 million to successful legislative candidates during the 2002 campaigns.[19]

Winners and Losers

In a study released in 1999, Texas Watch, a consumer advocacy group, said that doc-tors, hospitals, and other business-related litigants had been big winners before the Texas Supreme Court during the previous four years and that consumers had fared poorly. The group studied more than 625 cases in which the court had written opin-ions between January 1, 1995, and April 14, 1999. That was a period during which most court members had received substantial campaign funding from doctors, insurers, and other business interests. And most of the opinions were issued after the Texas leg-islature had enacted tort reform laws setting limits on civil lawsuits. The study deter-mined that physicians and hospitals had won 86 percent of their appeals, most of which involved medical malpractice claims brought by injured patients or their fam-ilies. Other consistent winners were insurance companies (73 percent), manufac-turers (72 percent), banks (67 percent), utilities (65 percent), and other businesses (68 percent). Insurance policyholders, injured workers, injured patients, and other individual litigants won only 36 percent of the time.[20] The report covered only cases in which the Supreme Court had written opinions. Hundreds of other cases in which the high court upheld lower courts without issuing its own opinions weren't studied. "Individuals are the lowest link in the legal food chain that ends in the Texas Supreme Court," said Walt Borges, who directed the study. "The study raises a question about the fairness of the Texas Supreme Court and state law," he added.[21]

CBS-TV's *60 Minutes,* which had turned the national spotlight on plaintiffs' lawyers and their political contributions to Texas judges in 1987, revisited the Texas judiciary in a followup program in 1998. Noting that the partisan system of electing judges had remained unchanged, the new *60 Minutes* segment suggested that justice might still be for sale in Texas, but with different people now wielding the influence. The Texas legislature in 1995 had imposed modest limits on campaign contributions to judges and judicial candidates and restricted the periods during which judges and their challengers could raise funds. But a judge could still receive as much as $30,000 from members of the same law firm and as much as $300,000 in total contributions from special interests through political action committees. The 1996 races for the Texas Supreme Court—the first conducted under the new law—demonstrated how weak the new reforms were. Four Republican incumbents, including Chief Justice Thomas R. Phillips, still raised a combined $4 million, easily swamping fundraising efforts by their unsuccessful challengers.

Some observers believed, nevertheless, that the Texas Supreme Court had begun moving toward the philosophical center by the end of the 1990s, thanks mainly to the moderating influence of Gov. Bush's appointees. By 1999, four of the nine Supreme Court justices had initially been appointed to the high court by Bush to fill midterm vacancies. A fifth, Harriet O'Neill, had been a Bush appointee to the Fourteenth Court of Appeals in Houston before she was elected to the Supreme Court. Attorney Doug Alexander of Austin, an appellate specialist, told the

Texas Lawyer newspaper that he thought the court had found a middle ground. "The weight of the full court now, while judicially conservative, is not agenda conservative," Alexander said. "It's a court that seems to be trying to apply the law as it sees it instead of changing the law to fit an agenda."[22]

In two cases often cited as significant consumer victories, the Texas Supreme Court sided with three women who sued their employer over a supervisor's harassment and with a woman seeking damages from a vacuum cleaner company after allegedly being raped by one of the company's independent salesmen. In the harassment case, the court ruled that the three women, who had been warehouse workers for GTE Southwest, Inc., were entitled to $275,000 in damages for emotional distress. The women alleged that they had been constantly harassed for two years, and that was a factor in the court's decision. The court wrote that the supervisor's "ongoing acts of harassment, intimidation and his daily obscene and vulgar behavior, which GTE defends as his 'management style,' went beyond the bounds of tolerable workplace conduct."[23] In the second case, the Supreme Court ruled that the Kirby Company should pay $160,000 in damages to a woman who said she was raped by a door-to-door vacuum cleaner salesman. Although the salesman was an independent contractor, the court ruled that Kirby should have required a criminal background check. The salesman had earlier been put on probation for indecency with a child.[24]

But the court began to demonstrate another philosophical shift against consumers after Bush left Texas to become president in 2001, according to consumer advocates. Justice Alberto R. Gonzales resigned in mid-term to accept Bush's appointment as White House counsel. Justices Greg Abbott and James Baker also stepped down in mid-term, and Justice Deborah Hankinson didn't seek re-election in 2002. Rick Perry, who succeeded Bush as governor, appointed two attorneys from San Antonio—Wallace Jefferson and Xavier Rodriguez—to the Gonzales and Abbott vacancies. In a report issued in September 2002, Texas Watch claimed that Jefferson and Rodriguez had helped the court re-establish a pro-business stance. The advocacy group said the court had ruled for business defendants and against workers and other consumers in about two-thirds of the cases it decided between August 2001 and August 2002. Perry's office, however, defended his appointees. "The governor's appointments to the Texas Supreme Court are well-qualified, well-respected individuals who make decisions based solely on the law," spokesman Gene Acuna said.[25] Jefferson, the first African-American to serve on the Texas Supreme Court, won election in 2002, but Rodriguez was unseated in the Republican primary that year.

Minorities Fight for Representation

As the high-stakes battles were being waged over the Texas Supreme Court's philosophical and political makeup, minorities were actively seeking more representation in the Texas judiciary. But instead of pouring millions of dollars into judicial races, Hispanics and African Americans filed lawsuits to try to force change through the federal courts.

Throughout Texas history, Hispanics and African Americans have had difficulty winning election to state courts. The high cost of judicial campaigns, polarized voting along ethnic lines in the statewide or countywide races that are required of most judges, and low rates of minority participation in elections have minimized their electoral successes. The first Hispanic was seated on the Texas Supreme Court in 1984 and on the Court of Criminal Appeals in 1991. The first African American was seated on the Texas Court of Criminal Appeals in 1990 and on the Texas Supreme Court in 2001.

Another factor limiting minority participation is a proportional shortage of minority attorneys, from whose ranks judges are drawn. State leaders' efforts to increase the number of minority lawyers were thwarted for several years by an antiaffirmative action federal court ruling in 1996 and a related state attorney general's opinion, which prohibited Texas law schools and universities from giving preferential treatment to minorities in admissions, student aid, and other programs. Those restrictions were eased in 2003, when the U.S. Supreme Court ruled that college admissions policies could include race as a factor, provided racial quotas weren't established.

As of February 1989, a few months before a major lawsuit went to trial over the issue, only 35 of 375 state district judges were Hispanic, and only seven were African American. There were only three Hispanics and no African Americans among the eighty judges on the fourteen intermediate Courts of Appeals. Although they constituted at least one-third of the Texas population, African Americans and Hispanics held only 11.2 percent of the district judgeships and less than 4 percent of the intermediate appellate seats.[26] African Americans sat on only three of the fifty-nine district court benches in Harris County (Houston), although they accounted for 20 percent of that county's population. African Americans held only two of 36 district judgeships in Dallas County, where they made up 18 percent of the population. Hispanics held three district court seats in Houston and one in Dallas. Three African American judges in Dallas, who had been appointed by Governor Mark White to fill judicial vacancies, had been unseated in countywide elections. One was Jesse Oliver, a former legislator who had won election to the Texas House from a subdistrict within Dallas County but couldn't win a 1988 judicial race countywide. Oliver, a Democrat, had overwhelming African American support but lost about 90 percent of Dallas's white precincts.[27]

In a lawsuit tried in September 1989 in federal district court in Midland, attorneys for the League of United Latin American Citizens (LULAC) and other minority plaintiffs argued that the countywide system of electing state district judges violated the federal Voting Rights Act by diluting the voting strength of minorities. This case, *League of United Latin American Citizens et al. v. Mattox et al.*, took almost five years and two appeals to the United States Supreme Court to resolve. It didn't change Texas's judicial selection system, but a summary of the case and its bumpy journey through the judicial process highlights the political stakes involved in the issue.

In November 1989, U.S. District Judge Lucius Bunton ruled that the countywide system was illegal in nine of the state's largest counties—Harris, Dallas, Tarrant, Bexar, Travis, Jefferson, Lubbock, Ector, and Midland. Those counties elected 172 district judges, almost half of the state's total, but had only a handful of minorities serving on the district courts. Bunton did not order an immediate remedy but strongly urged the legislature to address the issue in a special session. After the legislature failed to act, Bunton the next year ordered judges in the nine counties to run for election from districts in nonpartisan elections. But the state won a stay of Bunton's order from the Fifth U.S. Circuit Court of Appeals, and partisan, countywide judicial elections were held as scheduled in 1990.

Ironically, one minority judge was outspoken in his opposition to district elections. State District Judge Felix Salazar of Houston didn't seek reelection in 1990, at least in part because he disliked the prospect of having to run from a district rather than countywide. A Democrat, Salazar lived in a predominantly non-Hispanic white

Houston neighborhood and in previous elections had been endorsed by a diversity of groups. He claimed that small districts could work against the interests of minorities because a judge from a conservative Anglo district could feel political pressure to sentence minority criminal defendants more harshly than whites. "The judge will have to espouse the feeling of the community. His district may think that's all right, and it will be hell unseating him," he told the *Houston Chronicle*.[28]

Other opponents of district elections argued that districts could also put undue pressure from minority communities on judges. But Jesse Oliver, the former African-American legislator and judge who had been unseated in a countywide race in Dallas, didn't agree that judicial districts would distort the administration of justice any more than countywide elections. "For one thing, if the community does exert pressure, then the white community is exerting all the pressure now because they are electing the judges in Dallas County," he said.[29]

Ruling on the Texas case and on one from Louisiana in June 1991, the U.S. Supreme Court held that the Voting Rights Act applied to elections for the judiciary. But the high court didn't strike down the at-large election system. "We believe that the state's interest in maintaining an electoral system—in this case, Texas's interest in maintaining the link between a district judge's (countywide) jurisdiction and the area of residency of his or her voters—is a legitimate factor to be considered" in determining whether the Voting Rights Act has been violated, the court wrote. The court also emphasized that the state's interest was only one factor to be considered and didn't automatically outweigh proof of diluting minority votes.[30]

The U.S. Supreme Court returned the Texas lawsuit to the Fifth U.S. Circuit Court of Appeals for more deliberations, and, in January 1993, a three-judge panel of the Fifth Circuit ruled 2–1 that countywide elections illegally diluted the voting strength of minorities in eight counties—Harris, Dallas, Bexar, Tarrant, Jefferson, Lubbock, Ector, and Midland.

Under pressure from minority legislators, Attorney General Dan Morales agreed to a settlement with the plaintiffs that would have required district elections for most of the judges in those counties and a ninth, Travis County. The settlement was endorsed by Governor Ann Richards, Democratic legislative leaders, and Democratic majorities in the Texas House and Senate. But it was opposed by Texas Supreme Court Chief Justice Thomas R. Phillips and state District Judges Sharolyn Wood of Houston and Harold Entz of Dallas, Republican defendants in the lawsuit.

The full Fifth Circuit rejected the settlement in a 9–4 vote in August 1993, holding that the "evidence of any dilution of minority voting power (in countywide judicial elections) is marginal at best."[31] The Fifth Circuit said partisan affiliation was a more significant factor than ethnicity in judicial elections. Then in January 1994, the U.S. Supreme Court brought the lawsuit to an end by upholding the Fifth Circuit's opinion.

That left the issue of judicial selection in the hands of the Texas legislature, which for years had refused to change the elective system. State Senator Rodney Ellis, a Houston Democrat and a leading proponent of district elections, called the decision "devastating" and said it amounted to a "wholesale assault on civil rights." State District Judge Sharolyn Wood, a Houston Republican who had fought district elections, had a different reaction. "Hooray for Texas!" she said.[32]

By 1998, according to the most recent, complete data available, only 8 percent of the state judges at the county court level and higher were Hispanic and 2.5 percent were African American.[33]

MINORITY JUDICIAL APPOINTMENTS

Democratic Governor Mark White appointed the first Hispanic, Raul A. Gonzalez, the son of migrant workers, to the Texas Supreme Court in 1984 to fill a vacancy created by a resignation. Gonzalez made history a second time in 1986 by winning election to the seat and becoming the first Hispanic to win a statewide election in Texas. A native of Weslaco in the Rio Grande Valley, Gonzalez had been a state district judge in Brownsville and had been appointed to the Thirteenth Court of Appeals in Corpus Christi by Republican Governor Bill Clements in 1981.

Gonzalez, a Democrat, was one of the most conservative members of the Supreme Court during his tenure. Consequently, he came under frequent attack from trial lawyers and, ironically, from many of the constituent groups within his own party who advocated increasing the number of minority judges. Gonzalez's reelection race in 1994, one of the most bitterly contested Supreme Court races in recent memory, proved that ethnicity can quickly take a back seat to judicial philosophy and partisanship.

Gonzalez defeated a strong challenge in the Democratic primary from Corpus Christi attorney Rene Haas, who was supported by trial lawyers, women's groups, consumer advocates, several key Democratic legislators, and a number of African-American and Hispanic leaders in the Democratic party. Gonzalez drew heavy financial support from business interests, insurance companies, and defense attorneys.

Gonzalez had angered many Democrats by siding with the Republican justices in a 5–4 decision upholding a Senate redistricting plan that favored Republicans in the 1992 elections. And he angered many women and trial lawyers by voting with the court majority in two cases overturning damages awarded women who had complained of being emotionally and physically abused by men.

Raul Gonzalez resigned from the Supreme Court in midterm in late 1998 and was replaced by Alberto R. Gonzales, a Republican appointee of Governor George W. Bush and only the second Hispanic to serve on the high court. As had Raul Gonzalez, Alberto Gonzales came from a modest background. His parents were migrant workers when he was born in San Antonio, but they soon moved to Houston, where his father became a construction worker. The young Gonzales, one of eight children, joined the Air Force after graduating from high school, attended the Air Force Academy, and earned degrees from Rice University and Harvard Law School. He had never been a judge before Governor Bush named him to the Supreme Court. But he had been a partner in one of Houston's largest law firms, had been Bush's top staff lawyer, and had served under Bush as Texas secretary of state.

Alberto Gonzales's appointment came at a time when Governor Bush was actively trying to increase the Republican Party's appeal to Hispanics, and Bush acknowledged that it was important to him that Gonzales was Hispanic. "Of course, it mattered what his ethnicity is, but first and foremost what mattered is, I've got great confidence in Al. I know him well. He's a good friend. He'll do a fine job," Bush said.[34] Bush's confidence in Gonzales continued after Bush became president in 2001. He appointed Gonzales White House counsel. There also was considerable speculation that Bush was grooming Gonzales for an appointment to the United States Supreme Court, if a vacancy occurred during the Bush administration.

On succeeding Bush, Republican Governor Rick Perry named minorities to the first two vacancies he had the opportunity to fill on the Texas Supreme Court in

2001. One was Wallace Jefferson, an appellate lawyer from San Antonio who became the first African-American to serve on the high court. Perry named Jefferson to succeed Alberto Gonzales, who had resigned to take the White House job. Jefferson, a Republican, was the great-great-great grandson of a slave. Later the same year, Perry appointed Xavier Rodriguez, a San Antonio labor lawyer, to the Supreme Court to succeed former Justice Greg Abbott, who had resigned to run for Texas attorney general. Rodriguez became the third Hispanic to serve on the court, but he was unseated in the 2002 Republican primary by Austin lawyer Steven Wayne Smith, an Anglo. Jefferson was elected in 2002 to keep his seat on the high court, and a second African-American, Republican Dale Wainwright, a state district judge from Houston, was elected to an open Supreme Court seat the same year.

Governor Ann Richards appointed the first Hispanic, Fortunato P. Benavides, to the Texas Court of Criminal Appeals to fill a vacancy in 1991. Benavides had been a justice on the Thirteenth Court of Appeals and a district judge and a county court-at-law judge in Hidalgo County. But Benavides's tenure on the statewide court was short-lived. He was narrowly unseated in 1992 by Republican Lawrence Meyers of Fort Worth, an Anglo, who became the first Republican elected to the criminal court. Benavides later was appointed by President Clinton to the Fifth U.S. Circuit Court of Appeals.

Governor Bill Clements appointed the first African American, Louis Sturns, a Republican state district judge from Fort Worth, to the Texas Court of Criminal Appeals on March 16, 1990, to succeed Democratic Judge M. P. "Rusty" Duncan, who had died in an automobile crash. Since the vacancy had occurred after the filing deadline for the 1990 party primaries, the State Republican Executive Committee put Sturns on the general election ballot as the GOP nominee for the seat. The State Democratic Executive Committee nominated another African American, Morris Overstreet, a county court-at-law judge from Amarillo. Overstreet narrowly defeated Sturns in the November general election to become the first African American elected to a statewide office in Texas. Overstreet served on the court until 1998, when, instead of seeking reelection, he lost a race for the Democratic nomination for Texas attorney general.

WOMEN IN THE JUDICIARY

The first woman to serve as a state district judge in Texas was Sarah T. Hughes of Dallas, who was appointed to the bench in 1935 by Governor James V. Allred and served until 1961, when she resigned to accept an appointment by President John F. Kennedy to the federal district bench. Ironically, Hughes is best known for swearing a grim-faced Lyndon B. Johnson into office aboard Air Force One on November 22, 1963, following Kennedy's assassination in Dallas.

Ruby Sondock of Houston was the first woman to serve on the Texas Supreme Court. She had been a state district judge before Governor Bill Clements named her to the high court on June 25, 1982, to temporarily fill a vacancy. Sondock chose not to seek election to the seat and served only a few months. She later returned to the district bench. Barbara Culver, a state district judge from Midland, became the second female Supreme Court justice when Clements appointed her in February 1988 to fill another vacancy. Culver also served less than a year. She was unseated by Democrat Jack Hightower in the 1988 general election.

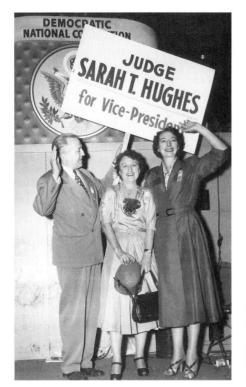

Sarah T. Hughes (center), the first woman to serve as a district court judge in Texas, in 1961 was appointed a federal district court judge and in 1963 swore in Lyndon Johnson as president after John F. Kennedy was assassinated in Dallas.

Democrat Rose Spector, a state district judge from San Antonio, became the first woman elected to the Texas Supreme Court when she defeated Republican Justice Eugene Cook in 1992. In 2003, there were two women on the Supreme Court, including Justice Harriet O'Neill, who unseated Spector in 1998.

In 1994, Republican Sharon Keller, a former Dallas County prosecutor, became the first woman elected to the Texas Court of Criminal Appeals, and she subsequently became the first female presiding judge of the court in 2001. By 2003, there were four women on the court. By 1998, more than 140 women were judges at the county court level or higher in Texas.[35]

THE DIFFICULT SEARCH FOR SOLUTIONS

The debates and lawsuits over judicial elections and representation in Texas emphasize the significant role of the courts in policymaking as well as day-to-day litigation. The composition of the courts makes a difference. Although some may argue that the role of a judge is simply to apply the law to the facts and issues of a specific case, judges bring to the courts their own values, philosophical views, and life experiences, and these factors serve to filter their interpretations of the law—and determine the shape of justice for millions of people.

There is no one simple solution to all the problems and inequities in the judicial system. Strict limits on the amount of campaign funds that judges and judicial candidates could raise from lawyers and other special interests, for example, could reduce the appearance of influence-peddling in the judiciary and temper the high-stakes war between the trial lawyers and the business community for philosophical control of the courts. Campaign finance reform also could help build or restore public confidence in the impartiality of the judiciary. Such reform, however, may not improve opportunities for more minorities to win election to the bench. Nor would it shorten the long election ballots that discourage Texans from casting informed votes in judicial races.

The same could be said of nonpartisan judicial elections or a merit selection system—two frequently mentioned alternatives to Texas's system of partisan judicial elections. In nonpartisan elections, judges and judicial candidates would not run under Democratic, Republican, or other party labels. This would guard against partisan bickering on the multimember appellate courts and eliminate the possibility that a poorly qualified candidate could be swept into office by one-party, straight-ticket voting.

Under the merit selection plan (sometimes referred to as the Missouri Plan), the governor would appoint judges from lists of nominees recommended by committees of experts. The appointed judges would have to run later in **retention elections** to keep their seats, but they wouldn't have opponents on the ballot. Voters would simply decide whether a judge should remain in office or be removed—to be replaced by another gubernatorial appointee.

Texas is one of only seven states with a partisan election system for judges. Other states have nonpartisan judicial elections or some sort of appointment or merit selection plan. Each alternative has its advantages, but none would necessarily eliminate undue political influences on the judiciary.

Under a merit selection system, interest groups could still apply pressure on the governor and the members of the committees making recommendations for appointments. Although a merit selection plan could be written to require the nominating panels to make ethnically diverse recommendations to the governor, that wouldn't answer the question of how to structure the retention elections. Minority appointees could still be at a disadvantage in retention elections if they have to run countywide, rather than in smaller geographic districts. Despite their popularity among minorities, district elections for judges are still viewed by many decision makers as a form of **ward politics** that may be appropriate or desirable for legislative seats but not for judges. Judges, they argue, don't represent a particular constituency.

Several unsuccessful attempts have been made in recent years to overhaul the judicial selection process. The only noteworthy change occurred in 1995, when, as discussed earlier in this chapter, lawmakers set modest limits on campaign contributions to judges and judicial candidates and restricted the periods during which judges and judicial candidates could accept political donations.

Frustrated by legislative stalemates, two public interest groups in early 2000 asked a federal court to strike down Texas's judicial election system and force the legislature to replace it. The lawsuit by Public Citizen, Inc., the Gray Panthers, and several individual Texas lawyers said that the millions of dollars that lawyers and other special interests gave to judges and judicial candidates during each election cycle violated due process because the money undermined the appearance of impartiality of Texas judges. The suit noted that, under Texas law, judges weren't even required to step down from cases involving their political contributors. "Texas has become notorious across the country as a state where 'justice is for sale,'" said Tom "Smitty" Smith, director of Public Citizen's Texas office.[36] But the suit was dismissed later that year by a federal judge, who ruled that political donations to state judges from lawyers who practiced before them didn't necessarily create a biased judicial system.

CRIME AND PUNISHMENT

Under both the United States Constitution and the Texas Constitution, a person charged with a crime is presumed innocent until the state can prove guilt beyond a reasonable doubt to a judge or a jury. The state also has the burden to prosecute fairly and to follow principles of procedural due process outlined in constitutional and statutory law and interpreted by the courts. Even persons charged with the most heinous crimes retain these fundamental rights. Although there is often a public outcry about "coddling" criminals, the process is designed to protect an individual from governmental abuses, to lessen the chance that an innocent person will be wrongly convicted of a crime.

A PATIENT'S RIGHTS CAN BE COSTLY

Freddy Ray Lilly, a Vietnam veteran under psychiatric treatment for being delusional and paranoid, fatally shot his stepfather, Henry Zezulka, because he believed Zezulka was going to burn down his mobile home. The family learned later that Lilly had told his psychiatrist, Dr. Renu K. Thapar of Houston, a month before the shooting that he felt like killing his stepfather. But, according to court records, Thapar had never warned any relatives or law enforcement officers about the threat or of Lilly's discharge from the hospital a few weeks before the shooting.

Lilly's mother, Lyndall Zezulka, sued the psychiatrist for negligence, contending that she should have been warned. A state district judge in Houston threw out the suit without a trial, but the First Court of Appeals ruled that Mrs. Zezulka was entitled to a trial.

The case finally reached the Texas Supreme Court, which in 1999 sided with the district judge and dismissed the suit. The high court unanimously held that mental health providers in Texas are prohibited by state confidentiality laws from warning a patient's family about a patient's threats. Thapar was required by the law to "closely guard a patient's communications," the court said. It noted that the psychiatrist could have told law enforcement officers of Lilly's threats but wasn't required to do so.

"The statute does not shield mental health professionals from civil liability for disclosing threats in good faith," Justice Craig Enoch wrote for the court. He said doctors could face a "Catch 22" if they were required to tell police of a patient's threats. "They either disclose a confidential communication that later proves to be an idle threat and incur liability to the patient, or they fail to disclose a confidential communication that later proves to be a truthful threat and incur liability to the victim and the victim's family."

Source: Thapar v. Zezulka, 994 S.W.2d 635 (1999).

In Texas, as well as in other states, these rights have sometimes been violated. But over the years the federal courts, in particular, have strengthened their enforcement. Through a case-by-case process, the U.S. Supreme Court has applied the Bill of Rights to the states by way of the "due process of law" and the "equal protection of law" clauses of the Fourteenth Amendment to the U.S. Constitution. The failure of police or prosecutors to comply with specific procedures for handling a person accused of a crime may result in charges against an individual being dropped or a conviction reversed on appeal.

Arrested suspects must be taken before a magistrate—usually a justice of the peace or a municipal court judge—to be formally informed of the offense or offenses with which they are charged and told their legal rights. Depending on the charges, a bond (bail) may be set to allow them to get out of jail and remain free pending their trials. They have the right to remain silent, to consult with an attorney and have an attorney present during questioning by law enforcement officers or prosecutors, and to be warned that any statement they make can be used against them in a trial. Defendants who cannot afford to hire a lawyer must be provided with court-appointed attorneys at taxpayer expense. Many of these protections were extended to the states by the U.S. Supreme Court in the landmark **Miranda ruling** in 1966.

All criminal defendants have the right to a trial by jury but—except in capital murder cases—may waive a jury trial and have their cases decided by a judge. Defendants may plead guilty, not guilty, or **nolo contendere** (no contest). Prosecutors and defense attorneys settle many cases through plea bargaining, a process described earlier in this chapter. The trial judge doesn't have to accept the plea bargain but usually does. When defendants choose to have their guilt or innocence determined by a judge, the judge also determines the punishment if they are convicted. A jury can return a guilty verdict only if all jurors agree that the defendant is guilty beyond a reasonable doubt. If the jury cannot reach a unanimous verdict—even after lengthy negotiations and prodding from the judge—the judge must declare a mistrial. In that case, the prosecution has to seek a new trial with another jury or drop the charges. In a jury trial, a defendant may choose to have the punishment set by the jury. If not, it is determined by the judge.

In 1991, the Texas Court of Criminal Appeals took the major step of ordering, for the first time, an official definition of "reasonable doubt" that was to be submitted to every jury deciding a criminal case. According to the definition, evidence against a criminal defendant must be so convincing that jurors would be willing to rely upon it "without hesitation" in the most important events in their own lives.[37]

Jury trials are required in **capital murder** cases, which are punishable by death or life in prison. Executions in Texas used to be carried out by electrocution at the state prison unit in downtown Huntsville. Some 361 individuals were executed in Texas from 1924 to 1964, when executions were suspended because of legal challenges. In 1972, the U.S. Supreme Court halted executions in all the states by striking down all the death penalty laws then on the books as unconstitutional. The high court held that capital punishment, as then practiced, violated the constitutional prohibition against cruel and unusual punishment because it could be applied in a discriminatory fashion. Not only could virtually any act of murder be punished by death under the old Texas law, but so could rape and certain other crimes.

In 1973, the Texas legislature rewrote the death penalty statute to try to meet the Supreme Court's standards by defining capital crimes as murder committed under specific circumstances. The list was expanded later and now includes the murder of a law enforcement officer or firefighter who is on duty, murder committed during the course of committing certain other major crimes, murder for hire, murdering more than one person, murder of a prison guard or employee, murder committed while escaping or attempting to escape from a penal institution, or murder of a child younger than six.

A jury that has found a person guilty of capital murder must answer certain questions about the defendant before choosing between death or life imprisonment, the only punishments available. Jurors are required to consider whether a convicted murderer will be a continuing danger to society as well as mitigating circumstances, including evidence of mental retardation, before deciding punishment.[38]

The first execution under the 1973 Texas law was carried out in 1982. By then the legislature, acting in 1977, had changed the method of execution from the electric chair to the intravenous injection of a lethal substance. By 2004, more than 300 men and two women had been executed in Texas by lethal injection. Karla Faye Tucker, the first woman executed in Texas since the Civil War, was put to death in 1998 for killing two people with a pickax almost fifteen years earlier. The second woman was executed in early 2000 for the murder of her husband.

After considerable controversy in Texas and other states, the U.S. Supreme Court in June 2002 banned the execution of mentally retarded convicts. Death penalty opponents had argued that before the high court ruling Texas had executed at least six inmates who were demonstrably retarded. The Texas Legislature, in its first session after the Supreme Court ban, failed to revise its death penalty **statute** to comply with the court's order, requiring defense attorneys to continue the battle, case by case. Some feared that, without new state guidelines for evaluating and trying convicts,

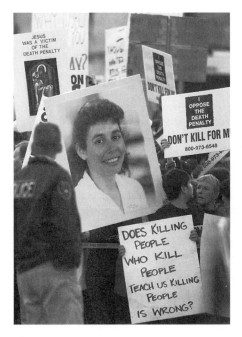

Death penalty protesters outside the Huntsville prison on the occasion of the execution of Karla Faye Tucker, the first woman to be put to death in Texas since the Civil War.

additional mentally retarded people would be executed in Texas, despite the Supreme Court's ban.[39]

After capital murder, the most serious criminal offense is a first degree **felony,** punishable by a prison sentence of 5 to 99 years or life. Second-degree felonies are punishable by two to twenty years in prison, and third-degree felonies by two to ten years in prison. A state jail felony, which includes many property crimes and drug offenses, is punishable by up to two years in a state-run jail or time in a community corrections program, each of which is supposed to emphasize rehabilitation as well as punishment (see "Why We Put People in Prison").

Aggravated sexual assault and noncapital murder are examples of first-degree felonies. Burglary of someone's home and bribery are second-degree felonies. Third-degree felonies include intentional bodily injury to a child and theft of trade secrets. Most nonviolent property crimes, including burglary of an office building, and minor drug cases are state jail felonies.

The most minor crimes are classified as Class A, B, or C **misdemeanors.** Crimes such as public lewdness and harboring a runaway child are examples of Class A misdemeanors and are punishable by a maximum $4,000 fine and one year in a county jail. The unauthorized use of television cable decoding equipment and falsely claiming to be a police officer are examples of Class B misdemeanors and carry a maximum sentence of 180 days in a county jail and a $2,000 fine. Class C misdemeanors include illegal gambling and the issuing of bad checks. They are punishable by a maximum $500 fine.

People convicted of crimes can be sentenced to **probation** (also called community supervision). That means they are not sent to prison but must meet certain conditions, such as restrictions on where they travel and with whom they associate. Except for those under the death penalty, convicted felons sentenced to prison can become eligible for **parole**—early release under supervisory restrictions—after serving a portion of their sentences. Capital murderers sentenced to life in prison can

---

WHY WE PUT PEOPLE IN PRISON

1. **Retribution.** Society is entitled to punish those who commit crimes. If the state does not do so, people will be tempted to take matters into their own hands.
2. **Deterrence.** Putting those who commit crimes in prison warns others and keeps some who might otherwise violate the law from doing so.
3. **Protection of society.** Some criminals are so dangerous to the lives and property of others that the only thing to do with them is to lock them in prison.
4. **Rehabilitation.** By placing convicted persons in a protected and controlled environment, some can be rehabilitated so that they will eventually become law-abiding and productive citizens.

Source: James MacGregor Burns, J.W. Peltason, Thomas E. Cronin, David W. Magleby, L. Tucker Gibson Jr., and Clay Robison, *Government by the People: Texas Version,* 2nd ed. (Upper Saddle River, NJ: Prentice Hall, 1998), p. 731.

be considered for parole after serving 40 years. Parole decisions are made by the Board of Pardons and Paroles, which is appointed by the governor.

A landmark federal court order in 1980 forced the state to spend billions of dollars expanding and improving its prison system and forced the legislature to reevaluate the punishment of some criminals (see Chapter 13).

THE POLITICS OF CRIMINAL JUSTICE

The Texas Court of Criminal Appeals must try to balance the constitutional rights of convicts against the public welfare—a role that puts the court at the center of major philosophical and political battles.

The combatants on one side of the debate are the prosecutors—the elected district and county attorneys—who don't like to see the convictions they have won reversed, partly because too many reversals could cost them reelection. Judges of the trial courts, who also must periodically face the voters, are also sensitive to reversals. So are the police and sheriff's departments that arrest the defendants and provide the evidence on which criminal convictions are based.

On the other side of the debate are defense attorneys, who have an obligation to protect the rights and interests of their clients and who in their appeals often attack procedures used by police, prosecutors, and trial judges. Also on this side are civil libertarians, who insist that a criminal defendant's every right—even the most technical—be protected, and minority groups, which have challenged the conduct of trials in which minorities have been excluded from juries weighing the fate of minority defendants (see "More Than Technicalities Were at Stake").

Throughout much of its early history, the Texas Court of Criminal Appeals was accused of excessive concern with legal technicalities that benefited convicted criminals.[40] The court reversed 42 percent of the cases appealed to it during the first quarter of the twentieth century, when Texas and many other states had a harsh

---

MORE THAN TECHNICALITIES WERE AT STAKE

Randall Dale Adams and Clarence Lee Brandley owe their lives to the appellate process. Both men came perilously close to being executed for murders they apparently didn't commit. Adams spent more than a decade behind bars before he was released in 1989 after a documentary film indicated he had been wrongfully convicted of the murder of a Dallas police officer. The Texas Court of Criminal Appeals ordered a new trial, but the Dallas County district attorney chose not to retry him.

Brandley, an African-American janitor at Conroe High School, was convicted by an all-white jury of the rape and murder of a sixteen-year-old girl. But the Texas Court of Criminal Appeals reversed the conviction after being presented with evidence that Brandley had not received a fair trial and had been a victim of racial prejudice.

Neither man would have lived long enough to win freedom had not the appellate process, which many prosecutors attack as too time consuming and too "technical," worked to delay their scheduled executions.

system of criminal justice that often reflected class and racial bias. By 1966, the reversal rate had dropped to 3 percent. But changes in the court's makeup and changes in political attitudes produced fluctuations in that record in subsequent years.

The court signalled a shift toward a conservative philosophy after the 1994 elections of Judges Sharon Keller and Steve Mansfield had increased the number of Republicans on the court to three. During the first thirteen months the new judges were in office, for example, the court ordered the reinstatement of two death sentences it had reversed before Keller's and Mansfield's arrival. The court's conservatism was solidified with a Republican sweep of all three court seats on the 1996 ballot. A 6–3 Democratic majority had become a 6–3 Republican majority, the first GOP majority on the court since Reconstruction. Republicans increased their majority to 7–2 in 1997, when long-time Presiding Judge Mike McCormick, one of the court's most conservative members, switched from the Democratic to the Republican party. The Republican takeover of the court was completed in 1998, when Democrats lost their last two seats on the panel. Republicans also swept all the court seats on the 2000 and 2002 ballots. McCormick did not seek reelection in 2000 and was replaced as presiding judge by Sharon Keller, a former prosecutor.

After the GOP takeover, the Court of Criminal Appeals quickly began compiling a strong, pro-prosecutorial record, particularly in death penalty cases. The court upheld a number of death sentences that later were overturned by federal courts. In one case, later reversed by a federal court, it affirmed a capital conviction even though the defendant's attorney had slept through part of his trial (see "Justice Dozes"). In another case, it upheld a death sentence despite the fact that a prosecution witness had argued improperly that the defendant was a future danger to society partly because he was Hispanic. That ruling prompted then–Texas Attorney General John Cornyn, a Republican and strong law-and-order advocate, to admit to the United States Supreme Court that the prosecution had committed reversible error in the case. Such rulings prompted defense lawyers and civil libertarians to heap much criticism upon the court. "They're so far gone they're barely even a court anymore," lawyer Jeff Blackburn of Amarillo said in an interview with the *Houston Chronicle*.[41]

JUSTICE DOZES

Justice is supposed to be blind, but it isn't supposed to be asleep. At least that was the conclusion of one of the more controversial death penalty convictions to emerge from Texas in recent years. Calvin Burdine was convicted and sentenced to death for the 1983 murder of his roommate, W.T. "Dub" Wise. His conviction was upheld by the Texas Court of Criminal Appeals, and he spent 18 years on death row before the Fifth U.S. Circuit Court of Appeals overturned the sentence because Burdine's defense attorney had slept through portions of his trial. In a plea bargain with prosecutors, Burdine then was sentenced to life in prison.

Source: Houston Chronicle, June 20, 2003, p. 29A.

INCREASED POLICY ROLE OF THE STATE COURTS

The federal judiciary has traditionally had more influence than the state courts in molding public policy. Over the years, it has been at the center of political debate over the proper role of the judiciary in the policy-making process. This debate, often framed in terms of judicial activism versus judicial restraint, attempts to address the question of where judicial interpretation of the law and the Constitution ends and legislating from the bench begins. It's a question often answered only in terms of subjective, political philosophy.

Much of the Texas Supreme Court's time is spent refereeing disputes between trial lawyers and insurance companies. But in recent years, this court has increasingly played an active role in shaping broader public policies and addressing significant constitutional issues (see "The Constitution Is for Everybody").

In one of its most significant and best-known rulings, the Texas Supreme Court, in the Edgewood school finance case in 1989, unanimously ordered major, basic changes in the financing of public education to provide more equity between rich and poor school districts (see Chapter 13). The lawsuit was brought against the state by poor districts after years of legislative inaction against a property tax–based finance system that had produced huge disparities in local resources and the quality of local schools.

The unanimity of the opinion, written by then-Justice Oscar Mauzy, a Democrat, surprised many legislators and school officials because two of the three Republican justices on the court at that time had been appointed by Governor Bill Clements, who had insisted that the courts had no business trying to tell the legislature what to do about school finance. The decision, which held that the school finance law violated a constitutional requirement for an efficient education system, obviously was the

---

THE CONSTITUTION IS FOR EVERYBODY

The Texas Supreme Court ruled in 1994 that a Ku Klux Klan leader had a constitutional right to keep Klan membership lists secret. The high court held that a state district judge had illegally jailed Michael Lowe for refusing to turn over KKK membership lists to state officials investigating the harassment and intimidation of African Americans attempting to desegregate a public housing project in Vidor. "The rights to form, discuss and express unpopular views are protected fundamental rights," the court said. "Where the organization advocates views which might subject members to ridicule . . . from the mere fact of membership, First Amendment associational rights are the basis for a qualified privilege against disclosure of membership lists."

In an unusual twist, the white supremacist Lowe was represented by an African-American civil liberties lawyer, Anthony Griffin of Galveston. The case, which Griffin took at the request of the American Civil Liberties Union, cost him another job as chief Texas attorney for the National Association for the Advancement of Colored People. Griffin said he was "ecstatic" about the court's ruling. "I think it's a wonderful opinion for the state Supreme Court to reaffirm the virtue of the First Amendment," he said.

Source: Houston Chronicle, June 8, 1994.

product of considerable compromise among the nine justices. Their deliberations were secret, but then-Justice Franklin Spears, a Democrat, told the *Fort Worth Star-Telegram:* "We wanted to speak with one voice. The opinion is a composite of many ideas, much brainstorming, much compromising."[42] Mark Yudof, then dean of the University of Texas School of Law, said the court may have been determined to offer a united front because it attached as much importance to the school finance case as a united U.S. Supreme Court had to the landmark *Brown v. Board of Education of Topeka* desegregation case in the 1950s.[43]

Compliance with the school finance order did not come easily, however. A 1990 school finance law failed to meet the court's standards. So the court issued another order in 1991 and a third order in 1992, after the legislature had again come up short. The court lost its unanimity on the third order, which struck down a 1991 law that had established special county education districts with a minimum property tax. In a challenge brought this time by wealthy school districts, a 7–2 court majority ruled that the tax was a statewide property tax prohibited by the Texas Constitution. Mauzy and fellow Democratic Justice Lloyd Doggett dissented sharply.

The legislature responded with still another school finance law in 1993. This law gave the wealthiest school districts several options for sharing revenue with poor districts, and it was challenged by both rich and poor districts. The rich districts objected to sharing their property wealth, while the poor districts argued that the new law was inadequately funded and did not sufficiently reduce the funding gap between rich and poor districts. The Texas Supreme Court upheld the law in a 5–4 decision in January 1995. By that time a majority of the court's members were Republicans. In the majority opinion, Justice John Cornyn, a Republican, wrote: "Children who live in property-poor districts and children who live in property-rich districts now have substantially equal access to the funds necessary for a general diffusion of knowledge. . . . It is apparent from the court's [previous] opinions that we have recognized that an efficient system does not require equality of access to revenue at all levels."[44]

But Republican Justice Craig Enoch, who dissented, wrote that the state had failed to adequately provide for the public schools. He said the new law contributed to further "constitutional tensions" by promoting continued use of local property taxes.

By 2003, the school finance law was under attack again, this time from school districts contending that the share-the-wealth requirement and inadequate state aid were forcing many districts to raise local school maintenance tax rates to the maximum $1.50 per $100 valuation. They argued that amounted to an unconstitutional statewide property tax.

In 1992, a state district judge in Brownsville ruled that the state's system of funding higher education was also unconstitutional because it shortchanged Hispanics in south Texas. But the Texas Supreme Court reversed that decision and upheld the higher education system.[45]

In another education case with major implications, the Texas Supreme Court in 1994 upheld the right of Texas parents to educate their own children. Ending a ten-year legal battle, the court overturned a Texas Education Agency ruling that home schools were illegal. The court held that a home school was legitimate if parents used books, workbooks, or other written materials and met "basic education goals" by teaching basic subjects.[46]

In 1998, dealing with another controversial issue, the Texas Supreme Court upheld $1.2 million in damages against antiabortion protesters who had staged massive demonstrations at Houston abortion clinics during the 1992 Republican National Convention. Some clinics had been vandalized and patients harassed. The high court also upheld most of the restrictions a lower court had set on demonstrations near the clinics and the homes of several doctors who performed abortions. The court said it was trying to balance free speech rights with the rights of the clinics to conduct business, the rights of women to have access to pregnancy counseling and abortion services, and privacy rights of physicians. The court prohibited demonstrators from blocking access to clinics, intimidating patients, and engaging in other forms of aggressive behavior.[47] In a case from Florida, the U.S. Supreme Court had ruled in 1994 that judges could limit demonstrations near abortion clinics but that restrictions on protestors had to be strictly limited.[48]

The Texas Supreme Court became embroiled in the abortion issue again in early 2000 after a state law went into effect requiring parents to be notified by the doctors before their minor daughters could have abortions. The law included a "judicial bypass" provision, giving a young woman who didn't want her parents to be told an opportunity to convince a judge that she was mature and well-informed enough to make an abortion decision by herself or that notifying her parents would be harmful. Acting on several early cases, the Texas Supreme Court set guidelines for district judges to follow in making bypass decisions.

In another abortion case, decided in 2002, the Texas Supreme Court held that the state's refusal to pay for medically necessary abortions for poor women didn't violate the Texas Constitution. The court ruled that the restriction on funding abortions for women on Medicaid didn't discriminate by gender and advanced a legitimate governmental interest of favoring childbirth over abortion.[49]

Deciding still another controversial issue, the Texas Supreme Court in 1996 ruled against the Log Cabin Republicans, a gay GOP group that had been denied a booth at the Republican State Convention in San Antonio. The court said the group had no grounds to sue for deprivation of rights under the Texas Constitution because the Republican party was not a governmental agency.[50]

SUMMARY AND CONCLUSIONS

1. Texas has a confusing array of courts, many with overlapping jurisdictions. It is one of only two states with a bifurcated court system at the highest appellate level. The Texas Supreme Court is the court of last resort in civil cases, and the Texas Court of Criminal Appeals in criminal cases.

2. This judicial system is particularly inadequate in urban counties, where thousands of criminal cases each year are disposed of through plea bargains negotiated by prosecutors and de-

fendants, and where it can take years to resolve civil disputes that aren't settled out of court.

3. State judges, except those on municipal court benches, are elected in partisan elections. But, in practice, Texas has a mixed judicial selection system because many judges quit or retire in midterm, allowing the governor or a county commissioners' court to appoint their successors.

4. Grand juries are supposed to ensure that the government has sufficient evidence to proceed

with a criminal prosecution against an individual. Petit, or trial, juries hear evidence and render verdicts in both civil and criminal cases. Litigants in civil cases and most criminal defendants can waive a jury trial and have their cases decided by a judge.

5. Cases can be appealed to appellate courts, where there are no juries. Appellate courts review the decisions and procedures of trial courts for conformity to constitutional and statutory requirements.

6. Judges who espouse strict construction believe they are supposed to narrowly interpret and apply the laws enacted by the legislature. Judicial activists take a more expansive view of the law and often offer broad policy interpretations in their decisions.

7. The Texas Supreme Court became a battleground in the 1980s between trial lawyers who represent injured parties—or plaintiffs—in damage lawsuits and the businesses, doctors, and insurance companies they sue. After trial lawyers began contributing millions of dollars to successful Supreme Court candidates, judicial precedents that had favored the corporate establishment began to fall, and it became easier for plaintiffs to win huge damage awards. The business and medical communities retaliated by winning some legislative changes in the procedures under which lawsuits are tried and by increasing their own contributions in judicial races.

8. Party realignment increased the number of Republican judges on trial courts in the 1980s and soon gave Republicans, with support from the business and medical communities, their first majority on the Texas Supreme Court in modern times.

9. Only a handful of women and minorities have ever served on the state's highest courts, and historically they have been underrepresented on the lower court benches as well. In a lawsuit in 1989, the countywide system of electing judges in nine of the state's largest counties was found to violate the Voting Rights Act by diluting the voting strength of minorities. That ruling was reversed by the U.S. Supreme Court in 1994.

10. The philosophical battles, the underrepresentation of minorities, and long ballots that discourage urban voters from learning the qualifications of judges and judicial candidates have increased pressure to reform the judicial selection process. But the legislature has been reluctant to change it. Possible alternatives are nonpartisan elections, elections from geographic districts, or a merit selection plan. Under the latter plan, the governor would appoint judges from lists of nominees recommended by experts. Judges would have to run later in retention elections to keep their seats, but they wouldn't have opponents on the ballot. Although each of these alternatives has supporters, none alone would resolve all the problems and controversies affecting the judiciary.

11. The Texas Court of Criminal Appeals is at the center of philosophical and political disputes as it weighs the constitutional rights of convicted criminals against the public's concern about crime. In recent years, the court has developed a strong record in support of prosecutors, particularly in death penalty cases.

12. The federal judiciary has traditionally had more influence than the state courts in molding public policy. But in recent years the Texas Supreme Court has increasingly played an active role in addressing significant constitutional issues, such as school funding and abortion.

KEY TERMS

Penal Code	Appellate jurisdiction	Justice of the peace court
Civil lawsuits	Bifurcated court system	Constitutional county court
Original jurisdiction	Municipal courts	Statutory county court

District court
Plea bargain
Court of Appeals
Texas Supreme Court
Texas Court of Criminal
   Appeals
Grand jury
Prosecution
Indictment

Petit jury
Venireman
Petition for review
Writ of mandamus
Merit selection
Tort reform
Retention elections
Ward politics
Miranda ruling

Nolo contendere
Capital murder
Felony
Misdemeanor
Probation
Parole
Statutes

FURTHER READING

Articles

Burka, Paul, "Trial by Technicality," *Texas Monthly*, April 1982, pp. 126–31, 210–18, 241.

Champagne, Anthony, and Greg Thielemann, "Awareness of Trial Court Judges," *Judicature*, 74 (February–March 1991), 271–76.

Champagne, Anthony, "Campaign Contributions in Texas Supreme Court Races," *Crime, Law and Social Change*, 17 (1992), pp. 91–106.

———, "Judicial Selection in Texas: Democracy's Deadlock," in *Texas Politics: A Reader*, eds. Anthony Champagne and Edward J. Harpham (New York: W. W. Norton, 1997).

———, "The Role of Personality in Judicial Reform," *State Constitutional Commentaries and Notes*, 2 (Winter 1991), 5–8.

———, "The Selection and Retention of Judges in Texas," *Southwestern Law Journal*, 40 (May 1986), 53, 95–99.

Chapman, Ronald W, "Judicial Roulette: Alternatives to Single-Member Districts as a Legal and Political Solution to Voting-Rights Challenges to At-Large Judicial Elections," *SMU Law Review* 48 (January/February 1995), pp. 457–84.

Cooper, Lance A., "A Historical Overview of Judicial Selection in Texas," *Texas Wesleyan Law Review*, 2 (Fall 1995), pp. 317–333.

Hardberger, Phil, "Juries Under Siege," *St. Mary's Law Journal*, 30 (1998), pp. 1–142.

Hill, John, "Taking Texas Judges Out of Politics: An Argument for Merit Election," *Baylor Law Review*, 40 (1988).

House Research Organization, *1988 Primary Referendum Proposals: Official English and Judicial Selection*, 141 (February 23, 1988).

Riddlesperger, James W., "Judicial Attitudes toward Judicial Selection in Texas," *Texas Journal of Political Studies*, 10 (Spring/Summer 1988), 3–18.

Schaefer, Roger C., "Implementing Criminal Justice Policy—Texas Style," in *Texas Public Policy*, ed. Gerry Riposa. Dubuque, IA: Kendall/Hunt, 1987.

———, "Texas Criminal Justice: The Policy Arena and Actors," in *Texas Public Policy*, ed. Gerry Riposa. Dubuque: IA: Kendall/Hunt, 1987.

Books

Horton, David M., and Ryan Kellus Turner. *Lone Star Justice: A Comprehensive Overview of the Texas Criminal Justice System*. Austin: Eakin Press, 1999.

Jacob, Herbert, *Justice in America: Courts, Lawyers, and the Judicial Process*, 3rd ed. Boston: Little, Brown, 1978.

Parrish, James R., *A Two-Headed Monster: Crimes and Texas Prisons*. Austin: Eakin Publications, 1989.

Reamy, Gerald S., *Criminal Offenses and Defenses in Texas*. Norcross, Georgia: Harrison, 1987.

Sharp, John, Comptroller of Public Accounts, *Texas Crime, Texas Justice*. Austin: Comptroller of Public Accounts, 1992.

Teske, H. C. Jr., ed., *Crime and Justice in Texas*. Huntsville: Criminal Justice Center, Sam Houston State University, 1988.

Texas Judicial Council, *Office of Court Administration, Texas Judicial System, 74th Annual Report*. Austin: Texas Judicial Council, 2003.

Texas Research League, *Texas Courts: A Proposal for Structural-Functional Reform*, Report 2. Austin: Texas Research League, 1991.

Texas Research League, *The Texas Judiciary: A Structural-Functional Overview*, Report 1. Austin: Texas Research League, 1990.

Websites

Office of Court Administration   http://www.courts. state.tx.us   This agency provides administrative support and technical assistance to all courts in Texas. Links to all state appellate courts are found here along with information about the state court system.

Texas Bar Association   www.texasbar.com   This site provides access to a wide range of information relevant to the legal profession.

Texas Department of Criminal Justice   http://www. tdcj.state.tx.us   This agency is responsible for the administration of the state's prison/jail system. Organizational data can be found at this site, along with statistics and reports on the prison population, prison sites, paroles, and programs designed to prevent recidivism.

Texas Juvenile Probation Commission   http://www. tjpc.state.tx.us   This agency works with local juvenile probation departments to rehabilitate juvenile offenders. This site provides information about state funding, standards, training, certification, and monitoring of caseworkers, and statistics on juvenile offenders.

Texas Youth Commission   http://www.tyc.state.tx.us   The Texas Youth Commission is responsible for "secure care, custody and control of juveniles who are committed to state custody" for criminal behavior. This site includes information on facilities, programs, correctional treatment, and juvenile crime in Texas.

Bureau of Justice Statistics   http://www.ojp.usdoj. gov/bjs   The Bureau of Justice Statistics is the primary source for criminal justice statistics in the United States.

ENDNOTES

1. Anthony Champagne, "Judicial Selection in Texas: Democracy's Deadlock," in *Texas Politics: A Reader,* eds. Anthony Champagne and Edward J. Harpham (New York: W. W. Norton, 1997), p. 97.
2. Texas Research League, *Texas Courts: A Proposal for Structural-Functional Reform,* Report 2, May 1991.
3. *Smith v. Allwright,* 321 U.S. 649 (1944).
4. *Miranda v. Arizona,* 384 U.S. 436 (1966).
5. Texas Research League, *The Texas Judiciary: A Structural-Functional Overview,* Report 1, August, 1990.
6. Allen E. Smith, *The Impact of the Texas Constitution on the Judiciary* (Houston: University of Houston, Institute for Urban Studies, 1973), p. 45.
7. Ibid., p. 28.
8. Ibid., p. 31.
9. Texas Research League, *Texas Courts: A Proposal for Structural-Functional Reform,* pp. 1–15.
10. Texas Judicial System, *Office of Court Administration, Texas Judicial System: 74th Annual Report* (Austin: Office of Court Administration, 2002).
11. Anthony Champagne, "The Selection and Retention of Judges in Texas," *Southwestern Law Journal,* 40 (May 1986), pp. 79–80.
12. Texas Judicial Council, *Texas Judicial System: 74th Annual Report* (Austin: Texas Office of Court Administration, 2002).
13. *Fort Worth Star-Telegram,* September 4, 1983.
14. *Houston Chronicle,* April 12, 1986.
15. *Houston Post,* May 18, 1986.
16. Anthony Champagne, "Campaign Contributions in Texas Supreme Court Races," *Crime, Law and Social Change,* 17 (1992), pp. 91–106.
17. *Houston Post,* November 10, 1988.
18. *Austin American-Statesman,* December 9, 1993.
19. *Houston Chronicle,* August 21, 2003, p. 24A.
20. Texas Watch, *The Food Chain: Winners and Losers in the Texas Supreme Court, 1995–1999.* Austin: Texas Watch, 1999.
21. Texas Watch press release, May 3, 1999.
22. *Texas Lawyer,* July 19, 1999, p. 1.
23. *GTE Southwest Inc. v. Bruce,* 998 S.W.2d 605 (1999).
24. *Scott Fetzer Co. dba The Kirby Co. v. Read,* 990 S.W.2d 732 (1998).
25. *Houston Chronicle,* September 18, 2002, p. 25A.
26. Samuel Issacharoff, *The Texas Judiciary and the Voting Rights Act: Background and Options* (Austin: Texas Policy Research Forum), pp. 2, 13.
27. *Texas Lawyer,* September 18, 1989.
28. *Houston Chronicle,* December 24, 1989.
29. *Texas Lawyer,* September 18, 1989.
30. *League of United Latin American Citizens, et al. v. Mattox, et al.,* 501 U.S. 419 (1991); *Chisom v. Roemer,* 501 U.S. 380 (1991).
31. *League of United Latin American Citizens v. Clements,* 999 F2d 831 (1993).
32. *Houston Chronicle,* January 19, 1994.
33. State Bar of Texas, Department of Research and Analysis, *A Statistical Profile of Texas Judges* (Austin: State Bar of Texas, 1998).
34. *Houston Chronicle,* November 13, 1998, p. 1A.
35. State Bar of Texas, Department of Research and Analysis, *A Statistical Profile of Texas Judges* (Austin: State Bar of Texas, 2003).
36. Public Citizen, Inc., press release, April 3, 2000.
37. *Texas Lawyer,* November 11, 1991.
38. *Texas Lawyer,* June 3, 1991.

39. *Houston Chronicle,* May 11, 2003, p. 1A.

40. Paul Burka, "Trial by Technicality," *Texas Monthly,* April, 1982, pp. 126–31, 210–18, 241.

41. *Houston Chronicle,* August 27, 2003, p. 23A.

42. *Fort Worth Star-Telegram,* October 4, 1989.

43. *Brown v. Board of Education of Topeka,* 347 U.S. 483 (1954).

44. *Edgewood v. Meno,* 893 S.W.2d 450 (1995).

45. *Richards v. LULAC,* 868 S.W.2d 306 (1993); *Houston Chronicle,* June 16, 1994.

46. *Texas Education Agency v. Leeper,* 893 S.W.2d 432 (1994).

47. *Operation Rescue—National v. Planned Parenthood of Houston and Southeast Texas, Inc.,* 975 S.W.2d 546 (1998). See also *Houston Chronicle,* July 4, 1998, p. 1A.

48. *Madsen v. Women's Health Clinic, Inc.,* 512 U.S. (1994).

49. *Charles E. Bell v. Low Income Women of Texas,* 95 S.W.3d 253 (2002).

50. *Republican Party of Texas v. Dietz,* 924 S.W.2d 932 (1996).

12

Local Government in Texas: Cities, Towns, Counties, and Special Districts

> . . . the best school of democracy and the best guarantee of its success is the practice of local self-government.
>
> *James Bryce[1]*

Texans have an affinity for local government. There are more than 4,700 local governments, of all sizes, across the state. Some operate with a handful of employees and budgets of one or two hundred thousand dollars a year, while others have tens of thousands of employees with billion dollar–plus budgets. Their governmental structures range from the simple to the complex. Some special districts perform one basic function, while others, such as large cities, perform any number of services that are limited only by budgetary and legal restraints. Some counties have fewer than 1,000 people, and others have more than two million residents. One school district in West Texas has only twenty students, while the Houston Independent School District has more than 200,000. Three of the ten largest cities in the United States are in Texas, but many cities across the state have fewer than 1,000 residents.

As we tackle the issues of local government, we can only scratch the surface. The key to understanding local governments in Texas is to understand what responsibilities have been assigned to them by the Texas constitution and statutory law. Once we have developed the institutional roadmap of local governments, we will turn our attention to a number of core problems confronting them and their political capacities to address these issues. Throughout this analysis will be two underlying dimensions—what changes can make local governments more effective, and is it possible or desirable to reduce the fragmentation in local governments?

A tradition of localism is rooted in the fabric of our political history. Since the founding of the nation, Americans have expressed a strong belief in the right to local self-government.[2] In many areas of the young country, local governments existed long before there was a viable state or federal government. Early communities had to fend for themselves and had limited expectations of services or protections to be provided by state or federal governments.

This history of local self-help has led to the popular notion that local governments have fundamental rights based on the concept of local sovereignty, or ultimate power. Thomas Jefferson, for example, developed a theory of local government, designed in part to strengthen the powers of the states, in which local sovereignty was rooted in the sovereignty of the individual. Local governments, which he termed wards, would have a wide range of responsibilities, including education, police, roads, caring for the poor, conducting elections, some minor judicial functions, and a semblance of a militia to maintain local defenses.[3]

In light of the expanded role of state and federal governments, we might find Jefferson's view rather romantic, outdated, and naive. Nonetheless, the concept has permeated American attitudes toward government and continues to shape citizen responses to government initiatives. Some people suggest that this cultural legacy persists in grass-roots politics, the flight to suburbia, the creation of neighborhood organizations, and the persistence of distrust of the national and state governments. Today, it is common to hear the argument that local government is closest to the people and best represents their interests and desires.[4]

Although this view is widely held, the prevailing constitutional theory on the relationship of local governments to the state is the unitary system that was discussed in Chapter 3. Simply stated, this theory holds that local governments are the creations of the state. The powers, functions, and responsibilities that they exercise have been delegated or granted to them by the state government, and no local government has sovereign powers. There have been numerous court cases enunciating this principle, which is referred to as the **Dillon rule,** but the best summary is derived from an Iowa case in which a court held the following:

> The true view is this: Municipal corporations owe their origin to, and derive their powers and rights wholly from, the legislature. It breathes into them the breath of life, without which they cannot exist. As it creates, so it may destroy. If it may destroy, it may abridge and control. Unless there is some constitutional limitation on the right, the legislature might by a single act, if we can suppose it capable of so great a folly and so great a wrong, sweep from its existence all of the municipal corporations in the State, and the corporations could not prevent it. We know of no limitation on this right so far as the corporations are concerned. . . . They are, so to phrase it, the mere tenants at will of the legislature.[5]

The Dillon rule is now the prevailing theory defining the relationships of states and local governments, and it is applicable to local governments in Texas. In short, local governments are fundamentally the administrative subdivisions of the state and have no rights except those granted to them by the state.

LOCAL GOVERNMENTS IN THE TEXAS POLITICAL SYSTEM

Local governments—counties, cities, school districts, and special districts—are created by the state and operate under limits set by the Texas Constitution and the legislature. They have found their capabilities and resources increasingly burdened by the pressing needs of a growing, urban state. Some of this pressure has come from the state and federal governments ordering significant improvements in environmental, educational, health, and other programs, but letting cities, counties, and school districts pick up much of the tab. Prior to the state's commitment to an extensive prison construction program in the 1990s, for example, the Texas government forced counties to spend millions of local taxpayer dollars to house state prisoners in county jails because it had failed to adequately address a criminal justice crisis. Local school districts and their property taxpayers also are at the mercy of the legislature, which has ordered expensive educational programs and has raised classroom standards without fully paying for them. Cities, too, find their budgetary problems exacerbated by state mandates. Local governments are the governments closest to the people, but they have to shoulder much of the responsibility—and often take much of the public outrage—for policy decisions made in Austin and Washington.

Although the legal position expressed by the Dillon rule subordinates local governments to the state, there are practical and political limitations on what the state can do with local governments.[6] More importantly, the state relies on local governments to carry out many of its responsibilities.

Texas granted cities home rule authority in 1912. Home rule cities, discussed in more detail below, have considerable authority and discretion over their own local policies, but within limits set by state law. Texas voters approved a constitutional amendment in 1933 that also gave counties home rule authority, but no county established home rule government before the amendment was repealed in 1969. In principle, the amendment was quite progressive, but it was subject to contradictory interpretations, and procedures for a county to adopt home rule were excessively restrictive and difficult to comply with.[7]

In a 1980 study, the Advisory Commission on Intergovernmental Relations ranked the states according to the discretionary authority they granted to their local governments. Texas ranked eleventh in a composite that included all local subdivisions—cities, counties, school districts, and other special districts. But Texas ranked forty-third in the discretionary authority given to its counties alone and first in the discretionary authority given to its cities.[8] There have been many changes in state constitutions and statutory laws over the past twenty-five years, and we would not expect the rankings to remain the same. But cities in Texas still exercise much more discretion in carrying out their functions than do county governments.

The states vary considerably in the major responsibilities assigned to different levels of government. Texas, like most other states, assigns the primary responsibility for public education to local school districts while retaining the primary responsibility for highways, public welfare, and public health at the state level. Police protection, sanitation services, parks, recreation, and libraries are the primary responsibility of city governments. Public hospitals are a shared function of the state, counties, and special districts.[9] Texas counties share with the state a primary responsibility for the courts and criminal justice system.

MUNICIPAL GOVERNMENT IN TEXAS

Despite popular images of wide-open spaces dotted with cattle and oil wells, Texas is an urban state. Some areas, particularly in West Texas, still have a lot of elbow room, but more than eighty percent of Texans live in cities or urbanized areas. First-time visitors to the state often express surprise at the size and diversity of Houston and Dallas and the more relaxed charm of San Antonio, whose riverwalk reminds many tourists of some European cities. Austin, the seat of state government and location of a world-class university, is highly attractive to young professionals and high-technology businesses.

When the Texas constitution was adopted in 1876, the state was rural and agrarian. Less than 10 percent of the population lived in cities. According to the 1880 census, Galveston was the largest city with a population of 22,248, followed by San Antonio with 20,550. Dallas, a relatively new settlement, had 10,358 residents, and Houston, 16,513. For most of the period from 1880 to 1920, San Antonio was Texas's largest city, but since the 1930 census, Houston has held that distinction.[10]

In 1940, only 45 percent of Texans lived in urban areas, but by 1960, some 60 percent of the population resided in cities. Since the 1970 census, eight of every ten Texans have been living in cities. More recent data indicate that approximately 83 percent of Texans live in urbanized areas.

Houston, San Antonio, and Dallas are among the ten largest cities in the United States. According to the 2000 census, Houston had a population of 1.95 million; Dallas, 1.2 million; and San Antonio, 1.14 million (Table 12–1). Five additional Texas cities—El Paso, Fort Worth, Austin, Corpus Christi, and Arlington—each had more than 250,000. But growth rates have varied widely from city to city, thanks to local differences in economic expansion, **annexation** policies, in-migration from other areas, and fertility and mortality rates. In some instances, the growth rate for the central city has been relatively modest, while growth in surrounding suburban areas has been quite high, reflecting continued urban sprawl.

Compared with many other parts of the country, Texas cities have a relatively low ratio of population to incorporated area. Texas cities are relatively young and had a lot of inexpensive land available to them during their early development. So, unlike older cities in other states, they tended to expand outward rather than upward. Texas cities also have used liberal annexation powers granted by the legislature to block the development of nearby, small municipalities that would block their

TABLE 12–1   Select Characteristics for the Ten Largest Cities in Texas, 2000

City	2000	Percent over 65	Percent under 18	Median Age	Percent African American	Percent Hispanic	Persons per Square Mile
Houston	1,953,631	8.4	27.5	30.9	25.3	37.4	3,372
Dallas	1,188,580	8.6	26.6	30.5	26.0	35.6	3,470
San Antonio	1,144,646	10.4	28.5	31.7	6.8	58.7	2,808
Austin	656,562	6.7	22.5	29.6	10.2	30.6	2,611
El Paso	563,662	10.7	31.0	31.1	3.0	76.6	2,263
Fort Worth	534,694	9.6	28.3	30.9	20.4	29.8	1,828
Arlington	332,969	6.1	28.3	30.7	14.1	18.3	3,476
Corpus Christi	277,454	11.1	28.1	33.2	4.7	54.3	1,795
Plano	222,030	4.9	28.7	31.1	5.2	10.1	3,101
Garland	215,768	7.1	29.8	31.7	12.1	25.6	3,779

Source: Texas State Data Center; U.S. Census 2000.

expansion. Houston covers approximately 540 square miles, the largest land mass of any city in the state, and has a **population density** of approximately 3,375 persons per square mile. Population density affects policy and budgetary issues relating to virtually every public service provided by the city. Land use, zoning laws, police and fire protection, the location of libraries and parks, and the development of water and sanitation systems are all related to the density of a city's population.

The racial and ethnic composition of Texas cities also is a major factor in urban diversity. Arlington, located between Dallas and Fort Worth, reported in the 2000 census a combined African American and Hispanic population of 32 percent. By contrast, El Paso had a combined minority population of approximately 80 percent, with 76.6 percent of the population identified as Hispanic. Five of Texas's ten largest cities—Houston, Dallas, San Antonio, El Paso, and Corpus Christi—have minority populations exceeding 50 percent (see "History-Making Mayors: Ron Kirk and Lee Brown"). Along the Texas-Mexico border, Laredo is 94 percent Hispanic; Brownsville, 91 percent; McAllen, 80 percent; and Harlingen, 73 percent. In 2000, the African-American population in Dallas was 26 percent. Houston's African-American population was 25 percent, and Fort Worth's, 20 percent. But the African-American population in El Paso was less than 3 percent; in Corpus Christi, 4.7 percent; and San Antonio, 6.8 percent.

The more than 1,200 incorporated municipalities in Texas are diverse, and urban life, politics, and government have developed different styles across the state. The basic forms of city government are defined by statutory and constitutional law, but cities vary in their demographic makeup, their economies, the historical experiences that shaped their development, and their quality of life. There are local differences in economic development, public safety, public education, health and environmental quality, housing, transportation, culture, recreation, and politics.[11]

THE CITIES AND THE STATE

Although Texas became an urban state in 1950, a rural-dominated legislature was slower in redrawing House and Senate districts to reflect the population changes. Urban areas did not receive a fair share of legislative seats until the 1970s, when the federal courts finally forced the state to redistrict using the principle of "one man, one vote." So, historically, state public policy and expenditures were tilted toward rural areas and interests, while urban areas were often neglected. The early neglect contributed to many of the problems now confronting cities, although recent policies enacted by a more urban-oriented legislature have been more responsive to cities' concerns.

The state has granted cities of Texas—unlike its counties and special districts— a wide range of discretionary power over organizational structure and local public policy. Texas, in fact, ranks high among the states in that regard, but cities still are strongly affected by state laws and policies.

Cities, therefore, actively lobby the legislature and other state officials on numerous issues. The Texas Municipal League (TML) is supported by member cities and maintains a full-time staff in Austin to monitor the activities of the legislature and state agencies. Many of the larger cities also designate staff members to serve as legislative liaisons, or they retain professional lobbyists. In the larger cities, there usually is a legislative committee of the city council that works with the city staff,

HISTORY-MAKING MAYORS: RON KIRK AND LEE BROWN

In one key respect, Ron Kirk's election as mayor of Dallas in 1995 wasn't all that unusual. He had the strong support of the city's business leaders, who liked his campaign pledge for more aggressive economic development. Kirk's election, however, made history. He was Dallas's first African-American mayor. In a city well known for its conservatism and recent racial divisions, Kirk attracted a broad base of support that included both establishment whites and African Americans who had long been unhappy with the city's power structures.

A former Texas secretary of state under Governor Ann Richards, Kirk was elected to head a city council that included four other African Americans, two Hispanics, and eight whites. Dallas has a council-manager form of government, and its mayor's office is weak in terms of formal powers. But the high-profile post offered Kirk the opportunity to use the skills of salesmanship and persuasion that had served him so well during his campaign. Successful economic development, which he viewed as essential to the city's future, would improve racial harmony in Dallas, he predicted. "It doesn't matter whether your ancestors came over on the *Mayflower* or a slave ship," he said, "we're all in the same boat now."* Kirk was reelected to a second four-year term in 1999 but resigned in late 2001 to make an unsuccessful bid for the U.S. Senate.

In 1997, Lee Brown scored a similar historical victory in Houston, when he was elected that city's first African-American mayor. Brown, who earlier had been Houston's first African-American police chief and had been drug policy director under President Bill Clinton, campaigned as a "mayor for all of Houston." Unlike Dallas, Houston has a strong mayoral office, giving Brown appointment powers over most city department heads and significant influence over city policies.

After taking 53 percent of the vote in a runoff against white businessman Rob Mosbacher, Brown told supporters at a victory celebration, "Another great barrier has fallen in the city of Houston—the doors of opportunity have opened wider for all of Houston's children."**

Brown received virtually all the African-American vote and almost 30 percent of the white vote in the runoff. He and Mosbacher split the Hispanic vote. Brown said race was not an issue in the campaign.

He was easily reelected to a second two-year term in 1999 and won a third term in 2001 after a hard-fought runoff against Houston City Council member Orlando Sanchez. Brown had to give up the mayor's office after his third term ended in 2003 because of Houston term limitations.

---

*Quoted in *Governing,* July 1995, p. 108.
**Quoted in *Houston Chronicle,* December 8, 1997.

community leaders, and civic organizations to establish a legislative agenda. Houston, Dallas, and San Antonio have the potential for considerable impact on the state legislature when their legislative delegations share common interest or goals. But often there are sharp differences among local delegations. Increasingly, state legislators from numerous central cities are collaborating on issues that affect them all.[12]

Hundreds of pieces of legislation that could affect cities are introduced during each legislative session. TML's highest priority is to block "bad legislation" that it believes is adverse to the interests of Texas cities.[13]

General Law and Home Rule Cities

The Texas constitution provides for two general categories of cities: general law and home rule. **General law cities** have fewer than 5,000 residents and have more restrictions in organizing their governments, setting taxes, and annexing territory than do home rule cities. They are allowed only those powers specifically granted to them by the legislature. Most Texas cities—approximately 885—are general law cities.[14]

A city with more than 5,000 inhabitants can adopt any form of government its residents choose, provided it does not conflict with the state constitution (Article XI, Sections 4, 5) or statutes. This option is called **home rule** and is formalized through the voters' adoption of a **charter,** which is the fundamental document—something like a constitution—under which a city operates. A charter establishes a city's governing body, the organization of its administrative agencies and municipal courts, its taxing authority, and procedures for conducting elections, annexing additional territory, and revising the charter (see "Is This Any Way to Change a City's Charter?"). As of 2002, there were 318 home rule cities in Texas.[15]

IS THIS ANY WAY TO CHANGE A CITY'S CHARTER?

Boerne, Tex., which is just northwest of San Antonio, held a special election in May 2002 to amend its charter to bring it in line with a law recently enacted by the Texas legislature. The new law permits local governments to purchase items valued at $25,000 or less without seeking bids. Prior to its enactment, the limit was $15,000, and the charter of Boerne included this figure. To permit the city to follow the state law and to anticipate future increases in the cap, a charter amendment would have permitted the city council to change spending caps each year as allowed by state law.

In a cliff-hanger election in which only 57 of 4,836 registered voters participated, the charter amendment was defeated, 29–28. The election occurred when there were no city or school board elections to draw voters to the polls. Few voters apparently were even aware the issue was on the ballot, and some just didn't care or believe the issue was important to them.

What happened in Boerne occurs throughout the state in charter elections. Just as is true for changes to the state constitution, all too often a small minority of a city's voters decide on changes in its fundamental law. While we have no empirical evidence, it might be argued that most changes are well-intentioned and necessary. But it is evident that a few individuals can use charter elections for their own self-interests.

Source: "Boerne Rejects Charter Change," *San Antonio Express-News,* May 2, 2002.

FORMS OF CITY GOVERNMENT IN TEXAS

Texas cities have experimented with three forms of government—the mayor-council, the council-manager, and the commission (see "Why Different Forms of City Government?"). According to the Texas Municipal League, there were 1,211 municipal governments in Texas in 2004. More than 900 cities operated with some variation of the mayor-council form; approximately 280 used some form of council-manager or commission-manager government; and only a handful used the commission form of government.[16]

Mayor-Council

The mayor-council, the most common form of municipal government in Texas, was derived from the English model of city government. The legislative function of the city lies with the city council, and the executive function is assigned to the mayor. This type of government is based on the separation of powers principle, which also characterizes the state and federal governments.

WHY DIFFERENT FORMS OF CITY GOVERNMENT?

Most major Texas cities have functioned under more than one form of government. Both Houston and San Antonio have functioned under all three primary forms described in this chapter. Changes in city charters often follow periods of intense political conflict, inertia, or an inability to respond to long-term problems. Proposed changes in governmental structures and election systems often threaten groups and interests that have a stake in the way business is currently being conducted, and charter revisions have a tendency to polarize a community.

Does the form of government under which a city operates make any significant difference? Political scientists have spent a lot of time trying to answer that question and, while there is some consensus on the general weaknesses of the city commission, opinions are divided on the other forms of local governments. The general public appears to pay little attention to city charters or governmental structures, but elected officials and other city leaders, public employees, special interest groups, minority leaders, and some reform-minded citizens consider the structure of city government a crucial issue.

A city charter spells out how a city chooses to run its affairs and helps determine which citizens will have access to policymaking and which citizens will find it difficult to influence governmental decisions. In part, a charter is an expression of a city's social, economic, and political structure. Some scholars refer to these complex relationships as a city's "regime." Other scholars have concluded that the urban reform movements that advocated nonpartisan elections, which often were tied to council-manager government, were advancing middle- and upper-middle-class views and interests. The original intent of these changes may have been to encourage managerial efficiencies, but many urban governments became less responsive to the needs and interests of the lower income groups and minority populations.

Sources: William Lyons, "Reform and Response in American Cities: Structure and Policy Reconsidered," *Social Science Quarterly* 59 (June 1978), p. 130; Robert Lineberry and Edmund Fowler, "Reformism and Public Policies in American Cities," *American Political Science Review* 61 (September 1967), pp. 701–17; Willis D. Hawley, *Nonpartisan Elections and the Case for Party Politics* (New York: John Wiley & Sons, 1973).

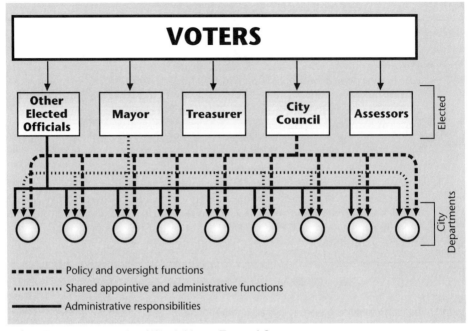

FIGURE 12–1   Example of Weak Mayor Form of Government.

In theory, the mayor, who is elected citywide, is the chief executive officer. In terms of power, however, there are two distinguishable forms of mayor—the **weak mayor** and the **strong mayor**—and in most Texas cities, the mayor is weak.

The city charter determines a mayor's strength. The weak mayor has little control over policy initiatives or implementation. The mayor's power may be constrained by one or more of the following: limited or no appointment or removal power over city offices, limited budgetary authority, and the election of other city administrators independently of the mayor (Figure 12–1). Under these circumstances, the mayor shares power with the city council over city administration and policy implementation, and "is the chief executive in name only."[17] These restrictions limit both the political and administrative leadership of the mayor. Although it is possible for a mayor to use personal or political resources to influence the city council and other administrators and to provide energetic leadership, there are formidable obstacles to overcome.[18]

A strong mayor has real power and authority, including appointive and removal powers over city agency heads (Figure 12–2). Such appointments often require city council approval, but the appointees are responsible to the mayor and serve at mayoral discretion. The mayor has control over budget preparation and exercises some veto authority over city council actions. This form of city government clearly distinguishes between executive and legislative functions (see "City Council Service, Often a Thankless Job").

The strong mayor form of government is found in many of the larger American cities, but it has been adopted by only two major cities in Texas—Houston and El Paso. This form may be unpopular in the state because the strong mayor often was associated with urban political machines, ward politics, and political corruption. Moreover, the fragmentation of authority and responsibility in local government parallels that found

Organizational Chart, City of El Paso

¹Governed by separate board with city county joint functions
² Governed by separate board

FIGURE 12–2 Example of Strong Mayor Form of Government.

in state government and is another reminder of the deep distrust of government that Reconstruction produced in Texas. Finally, the state's individualistic and traditionalistic subcultures (see Chapter 1) reinforce hostile attitudes toward governmental institutions that are potentially more responsive to lower socioeconomic groups.

As might be expected, the salaries of the mayors and council members of cities with the strong mayor system are generally higher than under other forms of city government. In many cities, mayors and council members receive no pay or only modest reimbursement for services. The mayor of Houston earned $165,817 in 2002, and council members, $44,218. El Paso's mayor earned $28,944, and council members, $17,364.[19]

CITY COUNCIL SERVICE, OFTEN A THANKLESS JOB

Regardless of the form of government, most city councils in Texas are small, with five to fifteen members elected for two-year terms. Most council seats are elected at large, or citywide, and council elections are nonpartisan. Council members in most cities can serve for an unlimited number of terms. Referenda on term limitations, however, have been held in several Texas cities, including San Antonio and Houston.

In most cities, a council office is part-time, with little or no compensation. The pay is nowhere near commensurate with the time spent on the job in most of the large cities. Council members in San Antonio are paid $20 per meeting; those in Dallas were paid $50 per meeting until voters authorized in 2001 a yearly salary of $37,500. Low salaries were part of the early urban reform tradition. The idea was that persons would run for office out of a sense of civic duty rather than to advance themselves financially.

The frequency of council meetings varies. In many small towns, councils may meet for only a few hours each month, but councils in large cities meet much more frequently, usually weekly, with meetings lasting for several hours. Cities are dealing with a wider range of complex issues than ever before, and demands on a council member's time are great. In addition to their policymaking roles, council members in large cities are faced with increased demands for constituent services.

Council members often complain that they had no idea how much time the public would demand of them and their families. The following commandments for surviving have been offered by Hal Conklin, a former mayor.

1. Make an honest inventory of the hours that your political commitment will take.
2. Establish a contract with your employer for the hours that you are going to spend in your political commitment.
3. Set office hours and stick to them.
4. Delegate and hold accountable staff members and volunteers.
5. Put unmonitored phone lines on answering machines, especially at home.
6. Distinguish between home hours and work hours.
7. Make a date with your spouse (or significant other) for the same time each week.
8. Exercise regularly each day; eat a stress-controlled diet.
9. Start and end your day with activities that soothe the soul.
10. Keep your sense of humor.

Source: Hal Conklin, "Ten Commandments for Surviving as a City Councilmember," *Texas Town and City* 83 (June 1995), pp. 12, 19.

City Commissions

The commission and council-manager forms of government are products of the twentieth century. Both reflect, in part, efforts to reform city governments through administrative efficiency, the reduction of partisan conflict, and the adaptation of a businesslike approach to running city government.

The origin of the **city commission** usually is traced to the Texas island city of Galveston. After a hurricane and subsequent flooding devastated most of the city in 1900, the government then in office proved incompetent and incapable of responding. The crisis prompted a group of citizens to win the legislature's approval of a new form of government designed to be more responsive by combining the city's legislative and administrative functions in the offices of five city commissioners. City commissions were soon adopted by other major Texas cities, including Dallas, Houston, and San Antonio. But with the subsequent development of council-manager government as an alternative, there has been a marked decline in the city commission's popularity. It has been replaced in Houston, Dallas, and San Antonio, and only a few small cities in Texas still have this form of government.

Initially, the commission was supported as a businesslike approach to running city government. By eliminating partisan elections and combining the executive, administrative, and legislative functions, it was argued, cities could provide services more efficiently. But critics have identified several problems. The commission minimizes the potential for effective political leadership because no single individual can be identified as the person in charge. Moreover, there is minimal oversight and review of policies and budgets. Commissioners are elected primarily as policymakers, not administrators, and there are downsides to electing amateurs to administer increasingly technical and complex city programs.

The few cities in Texas that use the pure form of commission government now generally have three members—a mayor and two commissioners—who are each assigned responsibilities for specific city functions, such as water, sanitation, and public safety. Some of the commission cities now use a city administrator or manager, hired by the commission, to run the daily affairs of the city.

Council-Manager Government

After enthusiasm for the city commission waned, urban reformers, both in Texas and nationally, looked to the **council-manager** form of government (Figure 12–3). Its specific origins are disputed, but it was influenced by the commission. The first cities in Texas to use council-manager government were Amarillo and Terrell in 1913, and it soon became popular among home rule cities. Dallas and San Antonio have been the largest cities in the state to adopt it. Its principal characteristics are a professional city management, nonpartisan city elections, and a clear distinction between policymaking and administration.

In some council-manager cities, the mayor is chosen by the city council from among its membership to preside over council meetings and fulfill a primarily symbolic role. But in other cities, the mayor is elected citywide, an arrangement that enhances the political position of the office without necessarily giving it formal legal authority. The mayor is usually a voting member of city council but has few other institutional powers. The mayor does, however, have the opportunity to become a

City of San Antonio

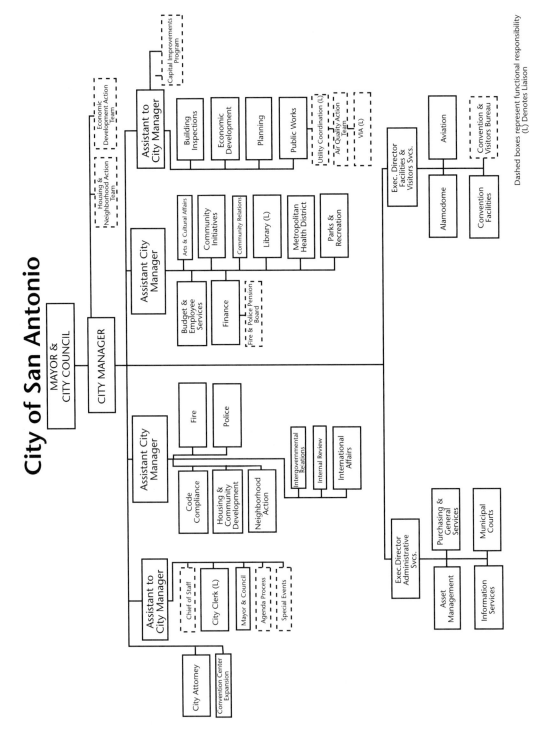

FIGURE 12–3 Example of Council-Manager Form of Government. (*Source:* City of San Antonio)

Mayor Ed Garza served four years on the city council prior to his election as mayor of San Antonio in 2001.

visible spokesperson for the city and has a forum from which to promote ideas and programs.

The city council is primarily responsible for developing public policy. It creates, organizes, and restructures city departments, approves the city budget, establishes the tax rate, authorizes the issuance of bonds (subject to voter approval), enacts local laws (ordinances), and conducts inquiries and investigations into the operations and functions of city agencies.[20]

The council hires a full-time city manager, who is responsible for administering city government on a day-to-day basis. The manager hires and fires assistants and department heads, supervises their activities, and translates the policy directives of the city council into concrete action by city employees. The city manager is also responsible for developing a city budget for council approval and then supervising its implementation. Professionalism is one of the key attributes of the council-manager form of government. Initially, many city managers were engineers, but in recent years there has been a tendency for managers to become generalists with expertise in public finance. City managers are fairly well paid. In 2002, the salary of the city manager of Dallas was $263,000. The city manager of San Antonio was paid $200,000, and the city manager of even a small city such as Seguin received $111,580.[21]

In the not too distant past, the salaries of mayors and council members serving in council-manager cities were very low, but there has been a trend in recent years to increase salaries in response to the expanded workload. Annual salaries of the mayor and city council members in Austin are $53,000 and $45,000, respectively. Until recently, the mayor and council members in Dallas received $50 per meeting, but voters approved a charter amendment in 2001 to raise the mayor's pay to $60,000 a year and council members to $37,500.[22] By contrast, San Antonio's council members currently earn $20 per meeting and the mayor, $50 per meeting. By late 2003, San Antonio was also considering a charter revision that would raise significantly the salaries of the mayor and members of the council as well as increase their terms of office.

There is a delicate line between policymaking and administration, and a city manager is, in principle, supposed to be politically neutral. The overall effectiveness of city managers depends on three main factors: their relationships with their city councils; their ability to develop support for their recommendations within the council and the community at large without appearing to have gone beyond the scope of their authority; and the overall perception of their financial and managerial skills. In the real world of municipal government, city managers play a central role in setting policy as well as carrying it out. Managers' adroit use of their resources and their sensitivity to political factions and the personal agendas of elected officials are key to determining their success.

MUNICIPAL ELECTION SYSTEMS

Nonpartisan City Elections

Virtually every city in Texas elects its council members in nonpartisan elections. Claiming that there was "no Democratic or Republican way to pave a street," city reformers who were part of the nonpartisan movement (1920s to 1950s) expressed a strong aversion to political parties and particularly to the urban political machines. To enforce separation of city elections from party politics, most municipal elections are held at times other than the party primaries or the general election.

The nonpartisan ballot—combined with at-large, citywide elections—has historically benefited higher social and economic groups. Parties and party labels normally serve as cues for voters. When they are eliminated in city elections, voters are forced to find alternative sources of information about candidates. Many local newspapers, which endorsed candidates and decided how much coverage to give them, had ties to the dominant urban elites. Candidates from lower socioeconomic groups had few contacts with the influential civic and business organizations that recruited, supported, and endorsed candidates. Although no longer in existence, San Antonio's Good Government League and Dallas's Citizens Charter Association controlled the recruitment and election of candidates in those two cities for several decades. Both organizations drew members from the Democratic and the Republican parties, but they reflected and pursued the interests of higher socioeconomic groups, often to the detriment of lower income and minority populations.

Despite the nonpartisan characteristics of city election systems, partisanship and party affiliation can play a role in city elections. Party labels are still excluded from the ballot, but some city council candidates are beginning to be identified by their party affiliations through news stories, endorsements by party organizations, and campaign advertisements. In the 2001 and 2003 city elections in Houston, for example, party affiliations of major candidates were widely known, and national party committees contributed money to some of the campaigns. Areas that are Republican in partisan orientation are likely to support individuals with Republican attributes, and, conversely, areas that vote Democratic in general elections are likely to support candidates with Democratic leanings. These developments clearly challenge the nonpartisan traditions of many cities throughout Texas.

— HOW I SEE IT —
LESSONS FOR LEADERSHIP

Nelson Wolff

Nelson Wolff, a native of San Antonio and lawyer by training, served as San Antonio's mayor from 1991 to 1995. He also has served as Bexar County judge, state representative, state senator and San Antonio city council member and has been involved in public affairs for most of his adult life. He has worked with a number of growth initiatives for the city and was chairman of the Greater San Antonio Chamber of Commerce in 1998. He serves on the boards of the International Bank of Commerce, Southwest Research Institute, Texas Public Radio, and City Public Service. Wolff's book, *Mayor,* which is his personal account of San Antonio politics during the 1970s and 1980s, was published in 1997. Wolff summarizes key lessons that he learned while serving in San Antonio politics.

County Judge Nelson Wolff presiding over a meeting of the Bexar County Commissioners Court.

1. **Catch the wave of changing political institutions.** Political institutions change, and a successful politician must recognize those changes and put them to use. When I ran for mayor in 1991, I tapped into the newly formed northside neighborhood associations, which eventually provided muscle to pass numerous issues.
2. **A council member must become the sorcerer's apprentice.** Since the first direct election of the mayor in 1975, all mayors of San Antonio have first served on the city council. Being a member of the council gives you a seat of power from which you can build political support. You learn where and how to use the levers of political power. Most importantly, it gives you the opportunity to closely study the mayor you serve with and to learn from the mistakes and right decisions that he or she may make.
3. **Setting an agenda is an officeholder's most powerful tool.** On my first day as councilman in 1987, as I listened to Mayor Henry Cisneros lay out a comprehensive agenda, I knew that I had observed Henry's most important tool to keep the council and the citizens focused on his priorities. Prior to laying out the agenda, he had gained political support for the major items from the media and key constituent groups. His agenda became the city's agenda.
4. **There are no permanent friends and enemies in politics.** Political friends must not be mistaken for true friends. Political friends come and go, and enemies accumulate. It's best to not burn bridges. Someone can be with you today on an issue and against you tomorrow on another issue. Take what you can get.
5. **It takes tension to create political progress.** I used tension to pass several initiatives. Many times during my term as mayor, community tensions created by environmental, neighborhood, and community activists led to progress.
6. **Sometimes you have to go out of town to find a friend.** Local legislative delegations do not fare well in the face of a heavily controversial local issue. I faced this problem

in 1992 in an effort to address our water problem through the creation of the Edwards Aquifer Authority. We had to create a political fund to support key legislative leaders from other areas of the state in order to get the bill passed because of our split local delegation.

7. **In politics as in boxing, a tie goes to the champion.** A challenger must move aggressively against an incumbent. If the challenger and the incumbent are perceived equal, or if the challenger has not shown strong reasons to remove the incumbent, the voters will stay with the incumbent.

8. **Balancing interests can lead to breakthroughs.** The committee that the council appointed to address urban scenic corridors, landscaping, tree preservation, and signs was balanced among business, environmentalists, and neighborhood leaders. By keeping pressure on them to compromise, we were able to pass groundbreaking ordinances.

At-Large Elections

Another notable feature of city politics in Texas is the general use of citywide or at-large elections. In 1992, the lastest year for which comprehensive data are available, there were 6,409 individuals elected to the governing bodies of 1,171 cities and towns in Texas. Some 5,649, or 88 percent, were elected at-large. Only 12 percent were elected from single-member districts, discussed in the following section.[23] Of the 1,204 Texas cities in 2002, some 207, or 14 percent, used single-member districts.[24]

In an at-large election, all of a city's voters participate in the selection of all the members of the city council. In a pure at-large system, every candidate runs against every other candidate. If there are eight candidates running for five positions on the city council, the candidates with the five highest vote totals are the winners.

A variation of the at-large system is the place system. Candidates file for a specific council seat and run citywide for places, or positions. Cities using the place system may require that the winning candidate receive a simple plurality of votes (more votes than any other candidate running for the same position) or an absolute majority of votes (more than half of the votes cast). If a city requires the latter and there are more than two persons in a race, runoff elections between the two highest vote getters are often required.

Single-Member Districts

An alternative to at-large elections is the single-member district, or ward. Under this system, a city is divided into separate geographic districts, each represented by a different council member. A candidate must live in and run for election from a specific district, and voters can cast a ballot only in the race for the council seat that represents their district. A person elected from a single-member district can, depending on the city's charter, be elected by a plurality or an absolute majority of votes.

Legal Attacks on At-Large Elections

Election systems are not politically neutral (see "The Debate over Electoral Systems"). At-large systems have historically benefited the nonminority, high-income areas of a

---

THE DEBATE OVER ELECTORAL SYSTEMS

There has been much debate over what is the most desirable form of city elections. Advocates of at-large, nonpartisan elections often warn of ward politics and the potential relationship of single-member districts to political machines, bosses, partisan conflict, corruption, and mismanagement. Even without corruption, they argue, council members elected from districts are concerned primarily with the interests of their own neighborhoods and may be more susceptible to trade-offs, swapping votes for programs and services that would benefit small segments of the community rather than benefiting the entire city. It also has been argued that district elections divide communities along racial, ethnic, or economic lines, resulting in high levels of political conflict. Moreover, proponents of at-large elections argue that their system produces higher caliber candidates, results in more media exposure for political campaigns, and permits a voter to participate in the selection of the entire city council rather than just one member.*

But, on the other hand, critics of the at-large system believe that single-member districts make elected officials more responsive to the needs and interests of specific constituencies. They also argue that at-large elections discriminate against African Americans and Hispanics because of racially polarized voting and the dilution of the impact of minority voting strength. Furthermore, citywide election campaigns, especially in the larger cities, are much more expensive than district campaigns, thus adversely affecting the electoral chances of candidates from low-income, often minority, areas. It has also been argued that single-member districts produce a more diverse group of elected officials and ensure that a city council considers more diverse views and interests. At-large elections, critics say, permit a small group of individuals—the city's elites—to control the electoral process and the council by recruiting and financially supporting candidates to protect their interests.

Many local governments across Texas now use single-member districts, which have resulted in a significant increase in the number of Hispanics and African Americans elected to office.

---

*Tom Albin, et al., *Local Government Election Systems* (Austin: Local Government Election Systems Policy Research Project, University of Texas, 1984), p. 2.

city, while single-member districts tend to be more inclusive of all groups and areas of a city.

Hispanics and African Americans, through various advocacy groups such as the National Association for the Advancement of Colored People, the Mexican American Legal Defense and Educational Fund, Texas Rural Legal Aid, the G.I. Forum, and the Southwest Voter Registration and Education Project, have challenged in federal courts the election systems used by numerous Texas cities. From the small East Texas town of Jefferson to El Paso, Houston, and Dallas, minority groups have, with considerable success, proved the inequities of at-large elections and forced city governments to adopt electoral plans with districts that give minorities a better chance of electing candidates to city councils. The ethnic and racial composition of city councils has changed dramatically over the past twenty years, with a marked increase in the number of Hispanics and African Americans elected to these governing bodies (see Chapter 7).

CITY REVENUES AND EXPENDITURES

Despite a growing number of expenses that they are expected to address, Texas cities have limited financial options. Unlike counties and school districts, they receive no state appropriations for any purpose. City governments are disproportionately dependent on **regressive taxes,** such as property and sales taxes and fees for services. Moreover, the state limits the property tax rate a city can impose and permits citizens to petition their city council for a **rollback election** to nullify any tax increase of more than 8 percent in a given year. Although there have been few rollback elections in recent years, the potential for such citizen initiatives serves to constrain policymakers.

When the Texas economy went sour in 1985 and 1986, cities experienced revenue shortfalls from a decline in sales tax revenues, reductions in the assessed value of property, and the elimination of many federal assistance programs. By 1993, however, the financial positions of most Texas cities improved, and throughout the last part of the 1990s, cities were able to expand municipal services, hire additional city employees, increase salaries, and limit tax and fee increases.[25]

The financial downturns that were experienced in the last half of 2001 once again imposed financial pressures on Texas cities. The sluggish economy and the decline in the state sales tax forced cities through 2003 to scramble to maintain services and minimize tax increases. A survey of Texas cities conducted by the Texas Municipal League in early 2003 led to the conclusion that fiscal conditions facing cities were worse than they had been in the past twelve years.[26] Over twenty-three percent of the cities responding to the survey anticipated lower tax revenues in 2003, but there was some optimism in that few city financial officers projected additional declines in 2004. Some 35 percent of the cities raised the nominal property taxes in 2003, and overall, some forty-six percent experienced an increase in the effective tax rate. Approximately 43 percent of the responding cities raised one or more fees on such services as water, wastewater, and solid waste disposal. Cities engaged in other cost reduction strategies such as hiring freezes, wage freezes, and laying off public employees. A significant number of Texas cities postponed capital spending as a major part of their efforts to balance their budgets.[27]

Although cities are required by law to balance their operating budgets, many municipal construction projects are financed by loans through the issuance of general obligation bonds, which are subject to voter approval. These bonds are secured by the city's taxing power. The city pledges its full faith and credit to the lender and, over a number of years, repays the bonds with tax revenue. Cities also fund various projects through revenue bonds that are payable solely from the revenues derived from an income-producing facility maintained by the city. The poor economy of the late 1980s made it more difficult for cities to borrow money. And with a significant pent-up demand for improving infrastructure (streets, waste disposal systems, libraries, and other facilities), cities entered an era of bond financing that had been radically altered by the performance of Wall Street and changes in state and federal tax laws.[28] Although city finances improved in the last decade of the 20th century, cities across the state continued to postpone capital spending for streets, roads, water systems, and a variety of other capital improvements.[29]

URBAN PROBLEMS IN TEXAS

During the 1970s and through the early 1980s, Texas cities were key participants in the dramatic economic growth of the state. Many of the older cities of the country—particularly in the East and the Midwest—"looked at their Texas counterparts and envied their capacity to attract population and business."[30] Texas cities had low taxes, a pro-business tradition, few labor unions with significant economic clout, an abundant work force, proximity to natural resources, and governing bodies that favored economic growth and development. At the beginning of the twenty-first century, however, many Texas cities are confronted with some of the problems associated with the older urban areas outside of Texas.

Graying of Texas Cities

The Texas population is aging, or graying. Americans are living longer, and older age groups are among the fastest growing segments of the population. As the population ages, additional pressures are placed on city governments for public services. The local property tax, a major source of revenue for city governments, is stretched almost to its limits. Moreover, many Texas cities have granted, in addition to the standard homestead exemption, additional property tax exemptions for individuals older than sixty-five. As more and more people become old enough to claim these exemptions, younger taxpayers will be called upon to shoulder the burden through higher tax rates. There is also the looming possibility that older citizens on fixed incomes will be much more reluctant to support bond issues if they result in significant property tax increases.

"White Flight"

The population characteristics of Texas cities change over time, and major metropolitan areas are experiencing a "white flight" to the suburbs, a dramatic increase in the growth rate of minority populations, and small growth rates among Anglos in the central cities.[31] Income levels for most minority Texans have always been lower than those of Anglos, and a larger proportion of the minority population falls below the poverty level (see Chapter 1). The increased concentration of lower income people in the central cities increases pressure for more public services, while a declining proportion of affluent property owners weakens the local tax structures that pay for the services.

Declining Infrastructures

There has been much concern across Texas and the United States about the declining infrastructures of local governments. Streets, bridges, water and sewer systems, libraries, and other facilities must be constantly maintained or expanded to support a growing population. Moreover, many Texas cities are out of compliance with federal standards for treating water and sewage and disposing solid waste and must spend millions of dollars on physical improvements to avoid or reduce fines for noncompliance. Some capital improvements are paid for out of current operating budgets, but a more common practice is for cities to borrow money to improve roads,

Poor neighborhoods stand in sharp contrast to the nearby high-rise office buildings of downtown Houston.

streets, water systems, and the like. These bonds are repaid from taxes on property. When property values decline—as they did in the late 1980s—cities are restrained by the constitution and statutes as to the indebtedness they can incur to support needed improvements.

By the end of the 1990s, property values were increasing across most of the state, and cities had more opportunities to borrow money for capital improvements. Nevertheless, most cities had a large backlog of proposed projects and were often forced to postpone needed construction.

Crime and Urban Violence

Crime is a major problem facing Texas cities and counties, just as it is in many other parts of the country. Although crime rates in most offense categories declined in the 1990s, there were still major problems with drug abuse, gang violence, and juvenile crime. Political candidates and elected officials often propose expansion of law enforcement, but many city and county budgets cannot absorb the costs.

State- and Federal-Mandated Programs

As we discussed in Chapter 3, both federal and state governments have increasingly used mandates in recent years to implement public policy. A mandate is a law or regulation enacted by a higher level of government that compels a lower level of government to carry out a specific action. In simpler terms, it is a form of "passing the buck." Federal mandates cover a wide range of governmental functions, including transportation, education for the disabled, water and air quality, and voter registration. States, meanwhile, have shifted much of the cost of public education to local governments.

Despite a decrease in federal funding for many urban problems since the 1980s, there has been an increase in federal mandates on the states, counties, and the cities and an increase in state mandates on local governments, often with no financial support. In some cases, the state simply passes the responsibility for—and the costs of—carrying out federal mandates to local governments. Congress enacted a law in 1995 to restrict unfunded mandates, but the law applied only to future, not existing, mandates. Such restrictions can still be circumvented if Congress chooses.

Although this practice may seem unfair and illogical, it is politically attractive to federal policymakers because they can "appease a large and vocal interest group which demands an extensive program without incurring the wrath of their constituents." While they get the credit for such programs, they do not get the blame for their costs.[32] Cities and other local governments across Texas claim that these unfunded requirements are excessively expensive, force them to rearrange their priorities, and limit local initiatives dealing with their most pressing issues. If local governments do not comply with mandates, they will be subject to litigation and face the prospects of losing federal or state funds. If they comply with mandates, they are then likely to reduce other services or seek alternative sources of funding now denied them.

COUNTY GOVERNMENT IN TEXAS

Prior to Texas independence, local government was organized both under Spanish and Mexican law around the municipality. This unit consisted of large land areas with "presidios for military protection, missions established by the Catholic church, and settlements established by various colonists and impresarios."[33] There were twenty-three such municipalities at the time of independence, and they became the first twenty-three counties organized under the Texas constitution of 1836.

Texas now has 254 counties, more than any other state. The constitution gives the legislature the power to create, abolish, or alter counties. But it prescribes certain requirements for a new county, including its size and the proximity of its boundaries to the county seat of the county from which it is created. The last county created was Kenedy in 1921.[34]

Counties are administrative sub-units of the state that were developed initially to serve a predominantly rural population. Created primarily to administer state law, they possess powers delegated to them by the state, but they have relatively few implied powers.[35] Unlike home rule cities, counties lack the basic legislative power of enacting ordinances. They can carry out only those administrative functions granted them by the state. Counties administer and collect some state taxes and enforce a variety of state laws and regulations. They also build roads and bridges, administer local welfare programs, aid in fire protection, and perform other functions primarily local in nature.[36] All Texas counties function under the same constitutional restrictions and basic organizational structure, despite wide variations in population, local characteristics, and public needs.

Real county jail, circa 1900.

The Diversity of Counties

According to the 2000 census, Loving County, the state's least populous, had only sixty-seven residents, compared to 3,400,578 in Harris County, the most populous (Table 12–2). Rockwall County includes only 147 square miles, while Brewster County covers 6,204 square miles. Fifty-five percent of Texas's residents live in the ten most populous counties.

Motley County with a population of about 1,400 had a 2003 budget of $666,747 and paid its county judge $14,501 a year and its commissioners $11,786. Loving County, which had only 67 residents counted in the 2000 census, had a budget of $1,264,209, while paying its county judge $34,138 a year and its commissioners $17,392. Dallas County had a $678 million budget and paid its county judge $130,262 and its commissioners $107,358 a year. Harris County's 2003 budget was $1.39 billion. Its county judge was paid $133,000, and each of its commissioners received $126,000.[37] Although there is an obvious relationship between the population of a county and salaries paid to its officials, the county's tax base is also a significant factor.

The Structure of County Government

The organizational structure of county government is highly fragmented, reflecting the principles of Jacksonian democracy and the reaction of late-nineteenth century Texans to Radical Reconstruction. The governing body of a county is the **commiss-ioners court,** but it shares administrative functions with other independently elected

TABLE 12–2   Ten Largest and Ten Smallest Texas Counties, 1980–2000

	1980 Population	1990 Population	2000 Population
Harris County	2,409,547	2,818,199	3,400,578
Dallas County	1,556,390	1,852,810	2,218,899
Tarrant County	860,880	1,170,103	1,446,219
Bexar County	988,800	1,185,394	1,392,391
Travis County	419,573	576,407	812,280
El Paso County	479,899	591,610	679,622
Hidalgo County	283,229	383,545	569,463
Collin County	144,576	264,036	491,675
Denton County	143,126	273,525	432,976
Fort Bend County	130,846	225,421	354,452
Glasscock County	1,304	1,447	1,406
Sterling County	1,206	1,438	1,393
Terrell County	1,595	1,410	1,081
Kent County	1,145	1,010	887
Roberts County	1,187	1,025	859
McMullen County	789	817	851
Borden County	859	799	729
Kenedy County	543	460	414
King County	425	354	356
Loving County	91	107	67

Source: U.S. Censuses, 1980, 1990, 2000.

officials (Figure 12–4). Moreover, the name "commissioners court" is somewhat misleading because that body has no judicial functions.

Commissioners Court and County Judge.   The commissioners court includes a county judge, who is elected countywide, and four county commissioners, who are elected from a county's four commissioners precincts. Like other elected county officials, the judge and the commissioners serve four-year terms and are elected in partisan elections.

Until recent years there were gross inequities in the population distributions among commissioners precincts in most counties. This issue of malapportionment came to a head in the 1968 case of *Avery v. Midland County*. Ninety-seven percent of the county's population, which lived in the city of Midland, elected only one commissioner, and the remaining three percent of the county's residents elected the other three. Similar inequities were prevalent all over the state, but the U.S. Supreme Court applied the "one man, one vote" principle to the counties and required that districts be equally apportioned.[38] Subsequently, Congress placed Texas under the Voting Rights Act in 1975, and counties were required to consider the interests of minority populations in drawing the boundaries for commissioners precincts. African Americans and Hispanics across the state have challenged county electoral systems and have increased minority representation on county commissioners courts. After the 2000 census, most Texas counties quickly redistricted their commissioner precincts in compliance with state and federal law.

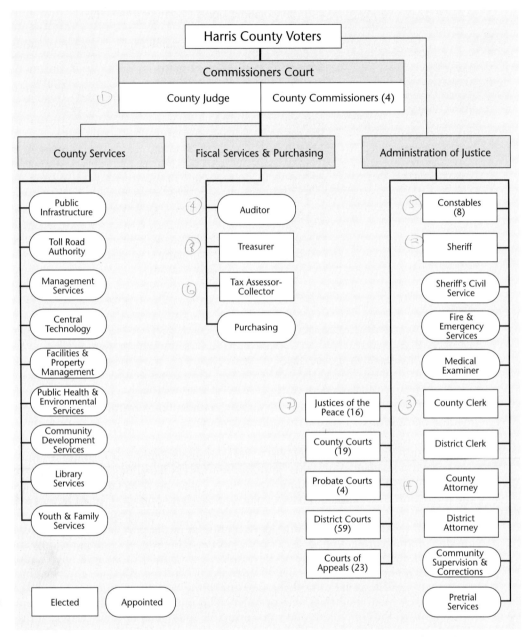

FIGURE 12–4   Example of County Government Organization. (*Source:* Harris County).

The **county judge** presides over commissioners court, participates in the court's deliberations, and votes on issues before it. If there is a vacancy among the commissioners, the county judge appoints a replacement. If the county judge vacates his or her office, the commissioners choose a replacement.

TABLE 12–3   Major Duties of the Commissioners Court

1. Set tax rate and adopt county budget.
2. Appoint county officials authorized under statutory law and hire personnel.
3. Fill county elective and appointive vacancies.
4. Administer elections, including the establishment of voting precincts, the appointment of an election administrator, the appointment of precinct judges, the calling of county bond elections, and the certification of election returns.
5. Let contracts and authorize payment of all county bills.
6. Build and maintain county roads and bridges.
7. Build, maintain and improve county facilities, including jails.
8. Provide for libraries, hospitals, and medical care for the indigent.
9. Provide for emergency relief and civil disaster assistance.
10. Provide for fire protection and sanitation.

Source: Texas Commission on Intergovernmental Relations: An Introduction to County Government (Austin: TCIR, 1985), p. 9.

The Texas Constitution also gives the county judge some judicial responsibilities, but does not require the officeholder to be a lawyer. Most urban counties have county courts-at-law that relieve the county judge of judicial duties. However, county judges in some rural counties perform a judicial as well as an executive role, combining two sets of duties in one office.

The commissioners court fills midterm vacancies in other county offices. It also has authority over the county budget, which permits the court to exercise some influence, if not control, over other elected officeholders.[39] The court sets the annual tax rate, which is limited by the Texas constitution, approves the tax roll, and supervises all expenditures of county money (Table 12–3). Other county officials must obtain the court's authorization for personnel positions, salaries, and office expenses. Consequently, the budgetary process often sparks political disputes and other conflicts.

Historically, county road construction and maintenance were primary functions of commissioners court. The Optional Road Law of 1947 gave counties the authority to create a consolidated road system under the supervision of a county engineer, who relieved commissioners of road maintenance and construction headaches. But the importance of roads to the commissioners and their constituents can still generate political disputes.

County Clerk.   The constitution provides for an elected **county clerk** to serve as the clerk of the commissioners court, the clerk of the county courts, and, in the smaller counties, the clerk of the district court. Over the years, the legislature has enacted hundreds of statutory provisions defining specific responsibilities of the office, prompting one writer to describe the office as the "dumping ground for miscellaneous functions" of the county.[40] The office is the depository of a county's vital statistics, such as birth and death records, and documents related to real estate transactions. It issues marriage licenses and various other licenses required by state law.[41] The county clerk also serves as a county's chief elections administrator if commissioners court has not created a separate elections administrator's office.[42]

District Clerk.   This position, also elected countywide, assists a county's district court or courts by maintaining custody of court documents and records.[43] In small counties, the county clerk is authorized to double as the district clerk, and fifty-three counties combined these two offices in 2003.[44]

County and District Attorneys.   The state's legal interests in both civil and criminal matters are represented at the local level by one of three officers—the **county attorney,** the **district attorney,** or the criminal district attorney. The legislature has enacted numerous provisions for legal departments that vary from county to county. Some counties have no county attorney but have a criminal district attorney. Under state law, others are authorized both a county attorney and a district attorney. Additionally, there are inconsistencies in the specific functions and responsibilities of the offices from county to county.[45] District attorneys prosecute the more serious cases, usually felonies, in the district courts, while the county attorneys prosecute lesser offenses, primarily misdemeanors, in the county courts.[46]

These officers can also provide legal advice and opinions to other county officials and give legal counsel to public officials or employees who have been sued for acts committed in carrying out their official duties. Upon request of the commissioners court, the district attorney or county attorney may initiate lawsuits on behalf of the county. Various other laws charge these attorneys with protecting the public health, assisting the attorney general in cases involving deceptive trade practices, enforcing the state's election laws, collecting delinquent taxes, and even enforcing the Texas Communist Control Act of 1951.[47]

Tax Assessor-Collector.   The property tax is the primary source of revenue for counties. Although the commissioners court sets property tax rates, the **county tax assessor-collector,** another elected officer, has the task of ascertaining who owns what property, how much tax is owed on that property, then collecting the tax. In counties with fewer than 10,000 people, these responsibilities are assigned to the sheriff, unless voters decide to create a separate tax assessor-collector office. Seventeen counties, mainly those below 5,000 in population, continue to let the sheriff handle the job.

Prior to reforms enacted in the 1970s, the tax assessor-collector also was responsible for appraising property or determining its value. This process was often steeped in politics because the higher the value of a piece of property, the more taxes its owner has to pay. Lowering property values for selected friends or supporters gave those holding this office considerable power, which often was abused. In an effort to move toward greater consistency across the state and to enhance the professionalism of tax appraisals, the legislature now requires each county to create an appraisal district that is separate from the tax office.[48] The appraisal district, whose members represent other local governmental units, now determines the value of all property in the county. The district also certifies the tax rolls, and other governmental units are required by law to use its appraisals.[49]

County Law Enforcement.   **Sheriffs** and **constables,** a county's law enforcement officers, are part of an old tradition under the Anglo-Saxon legal system. Each county has one sheriff with countywide jurisdiction, but the number of constables can vary. In counties with fewer than 18,000 residents, the commissioners court can designate the entire county as a single justice of the peace precinct or can create as many as four precincts, with each precinct assigned one constable. In the large counties, as many as eight justice of the peace precincts can be created with a constable assigned to each. Most larger counties have four constables.[50]

In a small rural county, the sheriff is the primary law enforcement officer for the entire county. But in the urban counties, city police departments generally assume exclusive jurisdiction in the incorporated municipal areas, leaving the sheriff jurisdiction over the unincorporated areas. Most sheriffs have considerable discretion in the hiring, promotion, and firing of deputies and other employees, although some counties have adopted a merit employment system for the sheriff's office. The sheriff also serves as the administrative officer for the district and county courts.

Constables are authorized to patrol their precincts, make arrests, and conduct criminal investigations, but their primary function is to serve as administrative officers of the justice of the peace courts. They are responsible for serving subpoenas, executing judgments of the court, and delivering other legal documents.[51]

County governments are responsible for constructing and staffing county jails, which are managed in most counties by the sheriff and in some counties by a jail administrator. During the late 1980s and early 1990s, counties across the state pursued an aggressive policy of jail construction in response to court decisions, increased crime rates, and a shortage of state prison space. Jail construction was a "growth" industry during this period, but by the mid-1990s some counties found that they had overextended their finances to construct these jails. They also were left with excess jail capacity after the state built new prisons. To compensate for these problems, several counties contracted with other states to house their prisoners in Texas jails.

All counties are authorized to create an office of medical examiner. This individual is appointed by commissioners court and determines the cause of death of murder victims or others who die under suspicious or unusual circumstances. In counties that do not have a medical examiner, the justice of the peace is charged with conducting an inquest to determine if there are conditions to merit an autopsy.

Counties, either individually or as part of multicounty judicial districts, are required to provide facilities for a criminal probation office. Probation standards are set by the state. Funded by the state, the chief adult probation officer of a county is chosen by the district judges, who supervise the office.

County Auditor.   All counties with 10,000 or more population are required to have a county auditor, and smaller counties may have one if the commissioners court chooses. Two counties with fewer than 25,000 residents may jointly agree to hire an auditor to serve both counties. The **county auditor** is appointed by the district judges of the county for a two-year term. He or she is primarily responsible for reviewing every bill and expenditure of a county to assure its correctness and legality. Such oversight can, in effect, impose budgetary restrictions on commissioners court and produce political conflict with other county officers.

The role of the auditor varies from county to county. In counties with more than 225,000 people, the auditor is the budget officer who prepares the county budget for submission to commissioners court unless an alternative has been authorized by the legislature.[52] In smaller counties, the commissioners court prepares the budget, based on estimates provided by the auditor.

County Treasurer.   This officer is responsible for receiving and disbursing county funds. Although this office has existed since 1846, its primary functions are now carried out by the county auditor, and constitutional amendments have permitted the elimination of this office in nine counties.

CRITICISMS OF COUNTY GOVERNMENT

The structure of county government in Texas, designed for a rural state, has inhibited efforts of urban counties to respond to growing needs for public services. The state has experimented with county home rule, but the provisions were so poorly written, confusing, and contradictory that local home-rule at the county level was never given a real chance. Efforts were made in the 1997 and 1999 sessions of the legislature to amend the constitution to once again allow counties to adopt home rule, but there was limited statewide support for this change.

Even though the county functions primarily as an extension, or administrative subdivision, of state government, there is little supervision of the counties by the state and wide disparity in the way counties interpret and administer their functions.

The fragmentation represented by several independently elected officers always poses the potential for jurisdictional conflict, administrative inefficiency, and even government deadlock.

Like other local governments in Texas, counties rely heavily on the property tax for revenue but cannot exceed tax rate limits set by the state constitution. Those limits reflected a general apprehension about government when they were initially set in 1876. They now further restrict the counties' ability to provide services.

Historically, county courthouses have been associated with political patronage and the spoils system. Victorious candidates have claimed the right to appoint personal and political friends to work for them, and state courts have held that elected county officials have wide discretion in the selection of their employees. Reformers have advocated a civil service system for county employees based on merit and competitive examinations and offering job security from one election to the next. A 1971 law allows counties with more than 200,000 population to create a civil service system, but it excludes several county offices, including the district attorney. An elected public official retains considerable control over the initial hiring of employees through a probationary period of six months.[53]

SPECIAL DISTRICTS IN TEXAS

Every day, Texans utilize the services of municipal utility districts (MUDs), water conservation and improvement districts (WCIDs), hospital districts, and a host of other local governments, which have been deemed by some as the "invisible governments" of the state.[54] There are approximately 3,300 such governmental units across Texas classified as **special districts,** and every year additional ones are created. These include drainage districts, navigation districts, fresh water supply districts, river authorities, underground water districts, sanitation districts, housing authorities, and soil conservation districts. School districts are also considered a form of special district.

Functions and Structures

Special districts are units of local government created by the state to perform specific functions. Wide variations in their functions, taxing and borrowing authority, governance, and performance limit generalizations about them. Most special districts are authorized to perform a single function and are designated single-purpose districts. But some are multipurpose districts because the laws creating them permit them to provide more than one service to constituents. For example, in addition to providing water to people in their service areas, MUDs may assume responsibility for drainage, solid waste collection, fire fighting, parks, and other recreational facilities.[55] Some districts, such as hospital districts, normally cover an entire county. Others, such as MUDs, cover part of one county, while still others, such as river authorities, cover a number of counties.

A special district is governed by a board, either appointed by other governmental units or elected in nonpartisan elections. The board members of hospital districts are appointed by county commissioners courts; city housing authority boards are appointed by mayors or city councils. Many of these districts have taxing and borrowing authority, but others have no taxing powers and are supported by user fees or funds dedicated to them by other governmental agencies. Many special districts are eligible for federal grants-in-aid.

Special districts exist for a variety of reasons. Independent school districts were created, in part, to depoliticize education and remove the responsibility for it from county and city governments. Reformers in the late nineteenth and early twentieth centuries argued that the governance of schools had to be autonomous and insulated from partisan politics. That goal could be accomplished only by the creation of districts that had their own governing bodies and tax bases. Similar arguments also have been made about other specialized governmental functions.[56]

In some cases, existing governments are unwilling or unable—because of state restrictions on their tax, debt, or jurisdictional authority—to provide essential services to developing communities. Counties are particularly limited by state law and the constitution and do not have the authority to provide many of the services now demanded by their citizens. So special districts were created to fill the gap. Since many districts can be created by statute, it has been far easier to create an additional layer of government than change the authority or powers of existing governments by constitutional amendment.[57]

The cost of providing a particular governmental service is another reason for the growth of special districts. By creating a special district that includes a number of governmental units and a larger population and tax base, the costs can be spread over a wider area. Special districts often are promoted by individuals, groups, or corporations for selfish gains. Builders, for example, sometimes develop plans for large tracts of land in the unincorporated areas of a county and then get local governments or the legislature to create municipal utility or water districts to provide water and sewer services.[58]

Some special districts have been designed to serve specific geographical areas. River basins that extend for thousands of square miles and cover ten or twenty counties have presented a particular problem. Because no existing governments had jurisdiction over the use of water resources in these basins, river authorities with multicounty jurisdictions were created.[59]

Consequences of Single-Purpose Districts

From one perspective, special districts compensate for the fragmentation and limited authority of local government that exists throughout Texas. But, ironically, these districts also contribute to further fragmentation and delay the more difficult development of comprehensive, multipurpose governmental units that could more efficiently provide public services.

A special district has been called a "halfway house between cityhood and noncityhood, between incorporation and nonincorporation."[60] Residents of a developing community or subdivision may not want to create a new city or become part of a nearby existing city, but they need certain basic services, such as water, electricity, and fire protection, some of which could be provided through the creation of special districts.

Many special districts are small operations with limited financial resources and few employees. Salaries often are low, and some districts have difficulty retaining the licensed technical people required to perform daily operations. In some cases, record keeping and management operations are shoddy and amateurish, and the costs of providing services by many of these operations may actually be higher than what similar services cost in larger governmental systems. Special districts may also use outside legal and professional assistance, which can be very costly, and many districts lack the expertise to maximize their investments or borrowing potential.[61]

Some special districts expand their functions beyond the original purpose for which they were created. The metropolitan transit authority in San Antonio, for example, authorized under state law to impose a 1 percent sales tax for public transportation, became involved in building the Alamodome, a multipurpose convention and sports facility. As governments expand their functions, there is a greater potential for intergovernmental rivalry, conflict, deadlock, and duplication of costs.

Except for the 1,000-plus independent school districts and a small number of other highly visible districts, such as river authorities, most special districts operate in anonymity. The public has only limited knowledge of their jurisdiction, management, operations, or performance. Many taxpayers may not even be aware they are paying taxes to some of these entities, nor do they have any concept of the districts' indebtedness. There is little media coverage of their work, few individuals attend their board meetings, and turnout for their elections is extremely low. In the case of the governing boards that are appointed by other governmental agencies, the appointment process is often dominated by a small number of individuals or groups who also dominate the activities of the special district. This domination is probably the most damning indictment of special districts.

INDEPENDENT SCHOOL DISTRICTS

The current controversies over educational quality and equity in Texas have roots in the early organization and governance of the public schools. Education was an issue in the Texas independence movement, but it was the Reconstruction period that set the stage for many of the long-term issues of school finance and governance. During Reconstruction, the Radical Republicans attempted to centralize the education system at the state level. But with the end of Republican control prior to the constitutional convention of 1875, the centralized system was eliminated and the control and financing of public education were transferred to the counties.

In place of an orderly, comprehensive system that assured public education to every child in the state, community schools were created. They could be formed by any group of parents petitioning the county judge, who had considerable influence and control over the schools. County judges could appoint trustees nominated by the organizing parents and distribute money from the state's Available School Fund to the organized schools within their respective counties. This produced marked differences in the availability, funding, and quality of public education across the state. Community schools also were self-selective. People who initiated the creation of a school could decide which children could attend. Consequently, there was racial and economic segregation, and the children of Texans with limited political clout were denied access to an adequate public education. These characteristics dominated public education in Texas at the end of the nineteenth century, and vestiges remained until 1909.

The **independent school district,** currently the basic organizational structure for public education in Texas, had its origins in the Constitution of 1876. Cities and towns were allowed to create independent school districts and to impose a tax to support them. Initially, the city government served as the school board, but in 1879 school districts were permitted to organize independently of the city or town, elect their own boards of trustees, and impose their own school tax. But residents of rural areas, where most nineteenth-century Texans lived, were denied these powers and had only the option of forming community schools. So, in effect, Texas operated under a dual school system, with the majority of students subject to the discretionary and often arbitrary powers of county governments.

Inequities in the Public Education System.   From the very beginning, the inequities in such a school system were clear to many parents, elected officials, and educators, and there were early efforts to reform and modernize public schools. Most were linked to national education reform movements. For example, the Peabody Education Board, a national organization, provided financial aid and technical support to leaders of the state reform movement during the early part of the twentieth century. More recently, national attention has been directed to the problems of public education through widely publicized studies, such as *A Nation at Risk: The Imperative for Educational Reform* (1983), which was conducted by the National Commission on Excellence in Education. Many national, state, and local organizations have attempted to identify and articulate the most serious problems with public education, develop alternatives for resolving these problems, and initiate litigation or legislative and administrative solutions. Although education is primarily a local responsibility, three recent presidents have made educational policy one of their top priorities.

Reformers have focused much of their attention on compulsory education laws, adequacy and equity in school funding, quality curricula, teacher preparation, and testing for progress and accountability. Some reform efforts also have been directed at the structure and governance of local school districts. The diverse and fragmented structure of Texas schools has been modified over the years through consolidation, greater uniformity in the organization of school districts, the extension of the independent school district to virtually every community in the state, and the expansion of the authority of the Texas Education Agency.

Local School Governance

Although regulation and coordination are provided on a statewide level through the State Board of Education (SBOE) and the Texas Education Agency (TEA), public education is now administered through approximately 1,050 local school districts, which include some 7,600 schools. In 2002, the smallest districts, the Divide Independent School District in Kerr County and the San Vicente ISD in far West Texas, each had twenty students. The largest, the Houston Independent School District, had 210,670 students. The thirteen largest districts, each of which had 50,000 students or more, enrolled more than one million of the 4.1 million students attending prekindergarten through grade 12 in Texas public schools during the 2001–2002 school year. By contrast, 502 districts had fewer than 500 students each, serving a total of only 115,000 students. By 2002, students from minority ethnic or racial groups constituted 59 percent of the public school population in Texas, and their numbers are projected to increase.[62]

School districts are governed by school boards, ranging in size from three to nine members; most have seven. Trustees are elected in nonpartisan elections for terms that vary from two to six years, with most serving three-year terms. In 2003, approximately 140 of the 1,050 school districts elected their boards from single-member districts.[63] School districts with significant minority populations have shifted from at-large elections to single-member districting, primarily as a consequence of lawsuits or the threats of lawsuits by minority plaintiffs under the Voting Rights Act.

Most school board elections are held on the first Saturday in May, the same day most cities hold their elections. School board election turnouts are low, usually less than 10 percent of registered voters. But turnout increases when there are highly visible issues, such as the firing of a superintendent or a dramatic increase in taxes. One unanticipated consequence of single-member districts has been a general decline in voter turnout for school board elections.

The Board of Trustees of the San Antonio Independent School District is composed of seven members elected from single-member districts. This body has the primary responsibility for setting school district policies.

Recruiting qualified candidates for school boards often is difficult, and many elections are uncontested. Individuals are asked to run by the superintendent, other members of the board, or key community leaders, many of whom point out that it is difficult to find people who are willing to give the required time and energy. Individuals often have little knowledge of what school board members do, and because many trustees serve for only one term, some boards have high turnover rates. Moreover, there is no way for a potential trustee to anticipate the amount of time it will take for briefings by the superintendent and staff, preparing for and participating in board meetings, and taking phone calls from parents and taxpayers. A board member must also deal with the political aspect of the job, including attendance at community functions and major school programs and meeting with teachers and taxpayer groups. Board members receive no salaries but are reimbursed for travel related to board business.

The most important decision that a school board makes is the hiring of a school superintendent. In organization and management structure, the school district is similar to the council-manager form of government used by many cities. The board hires a superintendent, who is in charge of the district's day-to-day operations. Although the board has the primary policymaking responsibility for a district, part-time board members are often dominated by the superintendent and the superintendent's staff. School trustees and superintendents tend to talk about "keeping politics out of education," and superintendents often attempt to convey the impression that they serve simply to carry out the will of their boards. In most instances, however, a school board's agenda is established by the superintendent, and the board members depend on the superintendent and other professional staff members for information and policy recommendations. Very few board members have much time to give to the district, and most have only limited knowledge of the many laws affecting education. State law, in fact, restricts the intrusion of board members into the daily management and administration of a district. An excessively politicized school board that becomes involved in day-to-day administration can be called to task by the Texas Education Agency. In an extreme case, the TEA can even take over the management of a school district.

COUNCILS OF GOVERNMENT

Councils of government (COGs), or regional planning commissions, were created under the Texas Regional Planning Act of 1965. That law was enacted, in part, to comply with federal regulations requiring local planning and review procedures.[64] The intent of these regional planning agencies was to coordinate planning efforts that crossed the boundaries of existing governments (Association of Texas Regional Councils). These organizations evolved over the years to take on additional duties, including comprehensive planning and services relating to employment and job training, criminal justice, economic development, health, aging, early childhood development, alcoholism, drug abuse, transportation, land resource management, environmental quality, and rural development.[65] In effect, through an incremental process, councils of government "have been asked increasingly to undertake implementation activities and direct services at the local level."[66]

Although councils of government are "defined by law as political subdivisions of the state, they have no regulatory power or other authority possessed by cities, counties, or other local governments."[67] Stated another way, they do not have jurisdictional authority with police and taxing powers. They cannot enact local legislation, nor do they have the power to force compliance. Decisions of the COGs are not binding on their members.[68]

The councils, instead, are support agencies designed to promote voluntary collaboration and coordination of public services among local governments. Their effectiveness varies across the state and appears to be partially related to the willingness of their members to engage in serious intergovernmental policy planning and implementation, the technical expertise of their staffs, and the political effectiveness of their leaders.

Twenty-four regional councils of government in Texas each serve a specific geographic area (Figure 12–5). Membership is voluntary. In 2002, more than 2,000 counties, cities, school districts, and other special districts were members of COGs.[69] Each COG decides the composition and structure of its governing body, so long as

01 Panhandle Regional Planning Commission
02 South Plains Association of Governments
03 Nortex Regional Planning Commission
04 North Central Texas Council of Governments
05 Ark-Tex Council of Governments
06 East Texas Council of Governments
07 West Central Texas Council of Governments
08 Rio Grande Council of Governments
09 Permian Basin Regional Planning Commission
10 Concho Valley Council of Governments
11 Heart of Texas Council of Governments
12 Capital Area Planning Commission
13 Brazos Valley Development Council
14 Deep East Texas Council of Governments
15 South East Texas Regional Planning Commission
16 Houston-Galveston Area Council
17 Golden Crescent Regional Planning Commission
18 Alamo Area Council of Governments
19 South Texas Development Council
20 Coastal Bend Council of Governments
21 Lower Rio Grande Valley Development Council
22 Texoma Council of Governments
23 Central Texas Council of Governments
24 Middle Rio Grande Valley Development Council

FIGURE 12–5   State Planning Regions. (*Source:* Office of the Governor).

two-thirds of its members are elected officials from counties or cities. Member governments pay dues, but the primary sources of funding for COGs have been the state and federal governments. The state pays a regional council a flat fee for each county that is a member and provides a per capita payment for each person residing in the COG. At one time, the regional councils relied extensively on federal grants-in-aid, but there was a 70 percent decrease in direct federal funding of the COGs during the 1980s. Indirect federal pass-through funds administered by state agencies also provide funds for the COGs.[70] Several COGs have expanded their technical support and some management services to offset these lost revenues.[71] At the end of the 2003 legislative sessions, COGs were reviewing the impact of budget cuts and administrative reorganization on their functions, programs, and staffs.

SOLUTIONS TO THE PROBLEMS OF LOCAL GOVERNMENTS

Privatization of Functions

As local governments attempt to juggle their financial problems with increased demands for public services, they have tended to contract out some services to private companies. Many governments believe **privatization** can reduce costs through businesslike efficiency, and they consider it an attractive alternative in the face of voter hostility toward higher taxes. Cities, for example, are contracting for garbage pickup, waste disposal, towing, food services, security, and a variety of other services. Privatization also provides a way for local governments that have reached their limit on bonded indebtedness to make new capital improvements by leasing a facility from a private contractor. A civic center or school facility can be constructed by a private contractor and leased back to the government for an extended period.

Annexation and Extraterritorial Jurisdiction

Population growth in the areas surrounding most large Texas cities has forced municipalities and counties to wrestle with urban sprawl. El Paso included 26 square miles in 1950 but had expanded to 250 square miles by 2000. Houston grew from 160 square miles in 1950 to 579 square miles in 2000, and similar expansions have been repeated in most of the state's other metropolitan areas.

The cities' ability to expand their boundaries beyond suburban development derives from their annexation powers and **extraterritorial jurisdiction** over neighboring areas (see "A Subdivision's Fight against Austin"). With the Municipal Annexation Act of 1963, the legislature granted cities considerable discretionary authority over nearby unincorporated areas. Specific annexation powers and extraterritorial jurisdiction vary with the size of a city and the charter under which it functions. Generally, cities have extraterritorial jurisdiction over unincorporated areas within one-half mile to five miles of the city limits, making development in those areas subject to the city's building codes, zoning and land use restrictions, utility easement requirements, and road and street specifications. This authority restricts the use of unincorporated land and requires those building outside of the city to build according to at least minimal standards. Later, when those areas are annexed by the city, they are less likely to quickly degenerate into suburban slums that will require a high infusion of city dollars for basic services.

A SUBDIVISIONS'S FIGHT AGAINST AUSTIN

For years, developers building subdivisions on the scenic western outskirts of Austin have been fighting environmentalists and Austin city officials over environmental restrictions. That war reached new intensity in 1995, when the developer of Circle C Ranch, a planned community in southwest Travis County, went to the Texas legislature to win unprecedented independence for his subdivision.

Houses in the Circle C Ranch development.

In a major departure from traditional public policy, which gave cities strong control over development around them, developer Gary Bradley convinced lawmakers to enact a special law freeing Circle C Ranch from Austin's control and future annexation, although the subdivision was within the city's extraterritorial jurisdiction. The law created a new super water district to govern Circle C development, subject to approval by state environmental officials. The district was headed by a nine-member board appointed by the governor.

Bradley and other supporters of the bill, including many Circle C residents, argued that the new law was necessary to allow for a more complete development of the community, which at the time was entirely residential. Construction of offices, retail stores, and apartment houses had been blocked by Austin's strict water and development regulations. Austin officials said that the regulations were necessary to control development in the environmentally sensitive area and protect the city's water supply and quality of life. But Bradley and his supporters argued that it was unfair for Austin to impose such restrictions on non-Austin residents, who could not participate in city council elections.

The bill was criticized as an anti-environmental, special interest piece of legislation, made all the more suspect by the fact that Bradley, according to an analysis by the *Austin American-Statesman,* had contributed $20,355 to twenty-one legislators. And although the state representative who represented Circle C cosponsored Bradley's bill, most other legislators from Austin and Travis County opposed it. State Senator Gonzalo Barrientos, who represented both Circle C and the city of Austin, filibustered for more than twenty-one hours on two occasions against it. "Sam Houston must be rolling over in his grave," Barrientos said. "We are creating a governmental body that is the antithesis of democracy. The board of this district is unelected."*

Over the objections of Austin officials, Governor George W. Bush let the bill become law without his signature and appointed nine people to the new Circle C board. But Austin challenged the new law in court, and in 1997 a state district judge declared the law unconstitutional because it was designed to benefit a special class of landowners. Austin annexed Circle C in December 1997.

In another challenge of city annexation powers, residents of suburban Kingwood asked the Texas legislature in 1997 to overturn their annexation by the city of Houston. The legislature refused to intervene, but the annexation disputes prompted a legislative study of cities' annexation powers and eventually led to changes in annexation laws.

---

*Quoted in the *Austin American-Statesman,* May 25, 1995.

Cities can annex areas equivalent to 10 percent of their existing territory in a given year, and if this authority is not exercised in one year, it can be carried over to subsequent years. Annexation usually does not require a vote of those people who are to be incorporated into the city. However, within two and a half years, a city is required to provide annexed areas with services comparable to those provided in its older neighborhoods. Otherwise, individuals living in these newly annexed areas can exercise an option to be de-annexed, a situation that rarely occurs.

Aggressive use of annexation has permitted several large cities to expand geographically with population growth, thus often limiting the development of small suburban towns that would potentially limit future expansion. Cities have even annexed thin strips of land, miles from urban development, along major roads and arteries leading into them. Since a city's extraterritorial jurisdiction extended as far as five miles on either side of the strip that was annexed, this practice has enabled a city to control future development in a large area. In San Antonio, these annexation policies have often been referred to as "spoke annexation," and it has taken more than thirty years for much of the territory brought under the city's jurisdiction to be developed and annexed by the city.[72]

In recent legislative sessions, many lawmakers have demonstrated an anticity sentiment with proposals that would have eroded municipal authority, reduced municipal revenues, and imposed costly new mandates. Of particular concern to cities were attacks on annexation powers. The legislature in 1999 enacted a major overhaul of annexation authority, including a provision that requires cities to outline their annexation plans three years in advance. But cities felt that they were able to obtain, through their lobbying efforts, a relatively "well-balanced" law.[73] The legislature in 2001 continued to reflect growing suburban-rural hostility toward the central cities. It enacted a law that modified the extraterritorial jurisdiction of cities by requiring city-county agreements on the regulation of subdivisions.[74]

Modernization of County Government

City governments provide most basic public services in urban areas, and as cities expand to county boundaries and beyond, there is increased overlapping jurisdiction of county and city governments and a reduction of county services in the annexed areas. Counties, nevertheless, still play an important role in Texas. Rural Texans, in particular, continue to rely on counties to provide a number of services, and demands on counties will increase. Recommendations to modernize county government include another attempt at county home rule, granting counties some legislative or ordinance-making authority, and creating an office of county administrator, appointed by commissioners court, to run the departments now assigned to commissioners. Another recommendation is to extend the civil service system to smaller counties and to all county employees.[75]

Economic Development

Historically, cities have collaborated with the private sector to stimulate local economies. Private sector initiatives have come from chambers of commerce or economic development foundations, corporations, other groups, or individuals, and city governments have participated. Cities also are using a variety of new financing techniques to assist in economic development, including development impact taxes and fees, user charges, creation of special district assessments, tax increment financing, and privatization of governmental functions.[76]

A state law was enacted in 1989 to permit cities, with the approval of local voters, to impose a 0.5 percent sales tax for local economic development. By late 1999, voters in more than 200 Texas cities had approved this tax option.[77]

Texas cities, as well as some counties, aggressively court American and foreign companies to relocate or develop new plants or operations in their communities. Cities and local chambers of commerce sponsor public relations campaigns touting local benefits and attractions. Local governments offer tax abatements—exemptions from property taxes on a business for a specified period—to encourage a company to locate or expand in a particular Texas city (see "Abatements: Expensive Tax Breaks"). Other financial incentives to companies being courted include lowered utility bills and assistance in obtaining housing for employees. Many cities have established relationships with "sister cities" in foreign countries, and state government has assisted cities by establishing trade and commerce offices in a few key foreign cities. The city of San Antonio aggressively wooed Toyota to locate a new manufacturing plant in South Texas, and the coordinated efforts of the city, the state, and the private sector resulted in a decision in 2003 to bring the new plant to the city. State and local officials predicted the facility would be a major economic generator and help transform the city's economy.

The legislature has permitted counties to form industrial development corporations or enterprise zones and to relax state regulatory policies to encourage the redevelopment of depressed areas. Portions of a county may be designated as reinvestment zones, in which tax abatements can be offered to attract new businesses. Counties also can create county boards of development, civic centers, foreign trade zones, and research and development authorities.[78]

ABATEMENTS: EXPENSIVE TAX BREAKS

As the Texas economy was diversifying in the 1990s, economic development was very important to many communities. Texas towns and cities competed with each other and with cities in other states for industries that would provide jobs and help their communities grow. They offered incentives for companies to build new plants or expand existing facilities. One popular incentive was a form of tax break called a tax abatement. Companies receiving tax abatements from local governments did not have to pay property taxes on their new facilities for a designated number of years. Proponents defended such breaks as an important economic development tool and argued that abatements eventually paid for themselves in the form of an expanded tax base. But some legislators and other critics believed school districts and other local governments were giving away too much potential tax revenue.

According to a staff report prepared for the Senate Economic Development Committee in 1996, 186 of the state's 1,050 school districts had given tax abatements since 1985. The state comptroller's office said those abatements had cost $480 million in lost property tax revenue. "Our children's future should not be traded for new jobs now," said state Senator David Sibley of Waco, the committee chairman. The lost money, he said, could have been spent on supplies, teachers' salaries, and other educational needs. The legislature, however, let tax abatements continue.

Source: Quoted in the _Austin American-Statesman,_ October 31, 1996.

Interlocal Contracting

Because many small governments have limited tax bases and staffs, they enter into contracts with larger governments for various public services. In 1971, the legislature, following a constitutional amendment, enacted the Interlocal Cooperation Act, which gave cities, counties, and other political subdivisions rather broad authority for such contracts.[79] The law has been amended several times to expand the scope of these agreements, and local governments are now contracting with each other for services in at least twenty-five functional areas, ranging from aviation to water and wastewater management.[80] Contracting is not an alternative to consolidation of local governments, but it does hold out some promise for improving the quality of local services and reducing their costs.

Metro Government and Consolidation

In the metropolitan areas of Houston, Dallas, and San Antonio, there are literally hundreds of cities and special districts providing public services. In Harris County (Houston) alone, there are about 498 separate governmental units (Table 12–4). Legislators, scholars, and reform groups have extensively studied the duplication and other problems produced by such proliferation and fragmentation and have made numerous recommendations over the years. There have been a variety of proposals designed to eliminate duplication and overlap, including city-county

TABLE 12–4 Local Governments in the Ten Largest and the Ten Smallest Texas Counties, 1997

	Total	County	Municipal	School Districts	Special Districts
State	4,700	254	1,177	1,087	2,182
Harris	498	1	28	24	445
Dallas	64	1	25	16	22
Tarrant	68	1	34	17	16
Bexar	51	1	22	16	12
Travis	94	1	14	8	71
El Paso	36	1	6	10	19
Hidalgo	77	1	21	16	39
Collin	50	1	24	15	10
Denton	62	1	33	11	17
Fort Bend	132	1	15	5	111
Motley	6	1	2	1	2
Glasscock	4	1	1	1	2
Terrell	4	1		1	2
Kent	5	1	1	1	2
Roberts	4	1	1	1	1
McMullen	5	1		1	3
Borden	2	1		1	
Kenedy	2	1		1	
King	3	1		1	1
Loving	2	1			1

consolidation and various forms of **metro government.** Efforts initiated by San Antonio and Bexar County to obtain constitutional authority to propose city-county consolidation to voters in the county failed in the 1997 legislative session. Other metropolitan areas joined Bexar County and San Antonio in an expanded effort to obtain this authority from the legislature in the 1999 session, but again it failed. Without such authority, county-city collaboration is more likely to take the form of increased intergovernmental contracting and the informal cooperation that local governments develop out of necessity and mutual self-interest.[81]

Public Improvement Districts

Under one state law, property owners in a specific area of a city or its extraterritorial jurisdiction can petition the city to create a special **public improvement district.** These districts can undertake a wide range of improvements—landscaping, lighting, signs, sidewalks, streets, pedestrian malls, libraries, parking, water, wastewater, and drainage facilities. Public improvement districts do not have the same autonomy as other special districts. They are created solely through the discretionary powers of the city and are funded by assessments on property within their boundaries.[82] Although their budgets and assessments must be approved by the city, they can be operated and managed by private management companies or by the citizens themselves. Fort Worth created a special improvement district for its downtown area in 1986, and other cities have considered the option.

SUMMARY AND CONCLUSIONS

1. Local governments in Texas are the creations of the state and have only those powers granted to them by the state constitution and statutes. With limited discretionary authority but a great deal of responsibility, local governments often find it difficult to respond effectively to the needs of their citizens.

2. More than 83 percent of the state's population lives in urban areas. Texas cities have highly diverse social structures, economies, and historical traditions and, subsequently, there are marked differences in urban politics across the state. Five of the ten largest cities have more than 50 percent minority populations, contributing to a long-standing controversy over urban electoral systems.

3. Texas cities smaller than 5,000 people are designated general law cities and are limited as to what form of government they can use. Cities larger than 5,000 can function as home rule cities, choosing a form of government that satisfies community needs as long as it does not conflict with the state constitution or statutes.

4. Texas cities have experimented with three forms of government—mayor-council, commission, and council-manager. The choices reflect complex political dynamics, and as social, economic, and political environments change, cities often change their form of government.

5. A notable feature of city politics in Texas is the widespread use of nonpartisan, at-large elections. In homogeneous communities, these election systems appear to work quite well. But in communities with highly diverse racial, economic, and social groups—in which voting is polarized—at-large elections adversely affect key segments of the population. Prompted by legal attacks on at-large elections under the Voting Rights Act, many cities, as well as special purpose districts, have adopted single-member districts, thus increasing minority representation on local governing bodies.

6. County governments, initially created to serve a rural population, function primarily as the administrative subdivisions of the state. Much like state government, county government is

highly fragmented with administrative powers shared by a variety of elected officials.

7. Hundreds of special-purpose districts provide numerous public services and add to the fragmentation of local government. Most people know little about their jurisdiction, structure, functions, and leadership, making them the "invisible governments" of Texas.

8. Texas has approximately 1,050 independent school districts, which are working to improve the quality of education against a backdrop of social, cultural, and financial problems.

9. Texas has twenty-four regional councils of government, which were created in compliance with federal law to coordinate policy planning efforts of governments in multicounty areas. Councils of government decide the composition and structure of their governing bodies, and they function primarily to serve the needs of their members.

10. Texas cities are now experiencing many of the same problems of the older cities of the East and Midwest. Populations are aging, and there is evidence of white flight from the core urban centers. A disproportionately larger share of the population in the central cities is low income and least able to pay taxes to support municipal services. Cities also are faced with significant problems of deteriorating infrastructures.

11. Federal and state governments have imposed additional requirements on the cities that are increasingly difficult to meet.

12. Local governments are experimenting with a variety of techniques to deal with their problems. Cities have used their annexation powers and extraterritorial jurisdiction to expand their tax bases and exercise limited controls over development in adjacent areas. Cities are also using public improvement districts to permit targeted areas to impose additional taxes for needed services. Both counties and cities are privatizing governmental functions to decrease costs and increase efficiency. Interlocal contracting permits governments to provide services to each other on a contractual basis, and many counties and cities are engaged in aggressive economic development programs. Some people advocate governmental consolidation, but there is limited support for this alternative in Texas.

KEY TERMS

Dillon rule	Regressive tax system	County auditor
Annexation	Rollback election	County treasurer
Population density	Commissioners court	Special district
General law city	County judge	Independent school district
Home rule city	County clerk	Councils of government
City charter	County attorney	Privatization
Weak mayor	District attorney	Extraterritorial jurisdiction
Strong mayor	County tax assessor-collector	Metro government
City commission	Sheriff	Public improvement district
Council-manager government	Constable	

FURTHER READING

Articles

Davidson, Chandler, and Luis Ricardo Fraga, "Slating Groups as Parties in a Nonpartisan Setting," *Western Political Quarterly* 41, (June 1988), pp. 373–90.

Jones, Laurence, Curtis Hawk, and Delbert A. Taebel, "Political Changes and Partisanship in Texas County Government," *Texas Journal of Political Studies* 11 (Spring/Summer 1989), pp. 28–42.

Murray, Richard W., "Power in the City: Patterns of Political Influence in Houston, Texas" in *Perspectives* on American and Texas Politics, eds. Donald S. Lutz and Kent L. Tedin. Dubuque, IA: Kendall/Hunt, 1987.

Thomas, Robert, "City Charters and Their Political Implications," in Perspectives on American and Texas Politics, eds. Donald S. Lutz and Kent L. Tedin. Dubuque, IA: Kendall/Hunt, 1987.

Reynolds, Morgan O., "General Ordinance-Making Powers for County Governments in Texas," Special Report, Texas Real Estate Research Center, College Station: College of Agriculture, Texas A & M University, August 1985.

Rice, Bradley R., "The Galveston Plan of City Government by Commission: The Birth of a Progressive Idea," Southwestern Historical Quarterly 78 (April 1975), pp. 36–48.

Zax, Jeffrey S., "Election Methods and Black and Hispanic City Council Membership," Social Science Quarterly 71 (June 1990), pp. 339–55.

Books

Bridges, Amy, Morning Glories: Municipal Reform in the Southwest. Princeton, NJ: Princeton University Press, 1997.

Bernard, Richard M., and Bradley R. Rice, eds., Sunbelt Cities: Politics and Growth since World War II. Austin: University of Texas Press, 1983.

Brooks, David B., Texas Practice: County and Special District Law, Vols. 35 and 36. St. Paul, MN: West Publishing Company, 1989.

Bullard, Robert D., Invisible Houston: The Black Experience in Boom and Bust. College Station: Texas A & M University Press, 1987.

Burns, Nancy, The Formation of American Local Governments. New York: Oxford University Press, 1994.

De Leon, Arnoldo, Ethnicity in the Sunbelt: A History of Mexican Americans in Houston. Houston: University of Houston Press, 1989.

Domhoff, G. William, Who Really Rules? New Haven and Community Power Reexamined. Santa Monica, CA: Goodyear Publishing Company, Inc., 1978.

Feagin, Joe R., Free Enterprise City: Houston in Political-Economic Perspective. New Brunswick, NJ: Rutgers University Press, 1988.

Goodall, Leonard E., ed., Urban Politics in the Southwest. Tempe: Arizona State University Institute of Public Administration, 1967.

Hanson, Russell L., ed., Governing Partners: State-Local Relations in the United States. Boulder, CO: Westview Press, 1998.

Harrigan, John J., Political Change in the Metropolis, 4th ed. Glenview, IL: Scott, Foresman, 1989.

Hawley, Willis D., Nonpartisan Elections and the Case for Party Politics. New York: John Wiley & Sons, 1973.

Herzog, Lawrence A., Where North Meets South: Cities, Space and Politics on the United States-Mexico Border. Austin: University of Texas Press, 1990.

Johnson, David R., John A. Booth, and Richard J. Harris, eds., The Politics of San Antonio: Community, Progress, and Power. Lincoln: University of Nebraska Press, 1983.

Lineberry, Robert L., Equality and Urban Policy: The Distribution of Urban Services. Newbury Park, CA: Sage 1977.

Lorch, Robert S., State and Local Politics: The Great Entanglement, 5th ed. Englewood Cliffs, NJ: Prentice Hall, Inc., 1989.

McComb, David G., Houston: A History. Austin: University of Texas Press, 1981.

Marando, Vincent L., and Robert D. Thomas, The Forgotten Governments: County Commissioners as Policy Makers. Gainesville: The University Presses of Florida, 1977.

Miller, Char, and Heywood T. Sanders, eds., Urban Texas. College Station: Texas A & M University Press, 1990.

Norwood, Robert E., and Sabrina Strawn, Texas County Government: Let the People Choose, 2nd ed. Austin: Texas Research League, 1984.

Orum, Anthony M., Power, Money and the People: The Making of Modern Austin. Austin: Texas Monthly Press, 1987.

Perrenod, Virginia Marion, Special Districts, Special Purposes: Fringe Governments and Urban Problems in the Houston Area. College Station: Texas A & M University Press, 1984.

Perry, David C., and Alfred J. Watkins, eds., The Rise of the Sunbelt Cities. Beverly Hills, CA: Sage Publications, 1977.

Polsby, Nelson, Community Power and Political Theory, 2nd ed. New Haven, CT: Yale University Press, 1980.

Syed, Anwar Hussain, The Political Theory of American Local Government. New York: Random House, 1966.

Tees, David W., Richard L. Cole, and Jay G. Stanford, eds., Interlocal Contract in Texas. Arlington, TX: Institute of Urban Studies, The University of Texas at Arlington, 1990.

Thometz, Carol Estes, The Decision-Makers: The Power Structure of Dallas. Dallas: Southern Methodist University Press, 1963.

Thrombley, Woodworth G., Special Districts and Authorities in Texas. Austin: The University of Texas, 1959.

Weaver, Robert R., and Sherman M. Wyman, Economic Development in Texas: New State and Local Initiatives. Arlington, TX: Institute of Urban Studies, The University of Texas at Arlington, 1988.

Wolff, Nelson W., *Mayor: An Inside View of San Antonio Politics, 1981–1985.* San Antonio: *San Antonio Express-News,* 1997.

Young, Roy E., *The Place System in Texas Elections.* Austin: Institute of Public Affairs, The University of Texas, 1965.

Websites

State Of Texas   http://www.state.tx.us   This site provides access to websites for all counties in Texas as well as the Councils of Government. Select cities have developed web pages that can also be accessed through this site. Information varies, with some sites providing more comprehensive information than others.

Texas Association of Counties   http://www.county.org This association serves county governments throughout the state. Links to related organizations can be found here, as well as information on recent legislation and laws pertaining to counties, support services, news releases, and educational programs for county officials.

Texas Municipal League   http://www.tml.org The purpose of this organization is to provide services to Texas cities. In addition to providing links to twenty-two affiliate organizations, this site provides information on the association's publications, programs, and services, including its legislative policy program.

Texas Association of School Boards   http:// www.tasb.org   The Texas Association of School Boards serves the 1,000-plus state school districts through policy advocacy and support services. This site includes links to many of the school districts as well as information pertaining to services, programs, and publications.

ENDNOTES

1. James Bryce, *Modern Democracies,* Vol. I (New York: Macmillan, 1921), p. 133.
2. Anwar Hussain Syed, *The Political Theory of American Local Government* (New York: Random House, 1966), p. 27.
3. Ibid., pp. 38–52. Syed presents a summary of Jefferson's theory of local government.
4. Roscoe C. Martin, *Grass Roots* (Tuscaloosa: University of Alabama Press, 1957), p. 5.; Robert C. Wood, *Suburbia* (Boston: Houghton Mifflin, 1958), p. 18.
5. *City of Clinton v. The Cedar Rapids and Missouri River Railroad Co.,* 24 Iowa 455 (1868).
6. Roscoe C. Martin, *The Cities in the Federal System* (New York: Atherton Press, 1965), pp. 28–35.
7. David B. Brooks, *Texas Practice: County and Special District Law,* Vol. 35 (St. Paul, MN: West Publishing Company, 1989), pp. 41–46. A good part of the materials presented on county government rely on this comprehensive work.
8. Advisory Commission on Intergovernmental Relations, *Measuring Local Government Discretionary Authority,* Report M–131 (Washington, DC: ACIR, 1981).
9. Advisory Commission on Intergovernmental Relations, *State and Local Roles in the Federal System* (Washington, DC: ACIR, 1982), pp. 32–33.
10. For an excellent overview of urban development in Texas, see Char Miller and David R. Johnson, "The Rise of Urban Texas," in Char Miller and Heywood T. Sanders, eds., *Urban Texas: Politics and Development* (College Station: Texas A & M University Press, 1990).
11. See Richard L. Cole, Ann Crowley Smith, and Delbert A. Taebel, with a foreword by Marlan Blissett, *Urban Life in Texas: A Statistical Profile and Assessment of the Largest Cities* (Austin: University of Texas Press, 1986), for an example of rankings of larger Texas cities on various dimensions measuring aspects of urban quality of life.
12. Randy Cain, "TML and Large Cities Approach Legislature Together," *Texas Town and City,* LXXIX (January 1991), pp. 18–19.
13. "Seventy-fifth Texas Legislature Adjourns," *Texas Town and City,* LXXXIV (June 1997), p. 10; "Texas Legislature Adjourns," *Texas Town and City,* LXXXVIII (June 1999), p. LVI.
14. Texas Municipal League, telephone conversation with research staff, May 2002, Austin, Texas.
15. Ibid.
16. Texas Municipal League, June 2004.
17. Murray S. Stedman, *Urban Politics,* 2nd ed. (Cambridge, MA: Winthrop Publishers, Inc., 1975), p. 51.
18. Beryl E. Pettus and Randall W. Bland, *Texas Government Today,* 3rd ed. (Homewood, IL: The Dorsey Press, 1984), p. 347.
19. Telephone calls to budget staff in El Paso and Houston, Texas, Dec. 30, 2003.
20. Wilbourn E. Benton, *Texas Politics,* 5th ed. (Chicago: Nelson-Hall Publishers, 1984), p. 260.
21. Telephone calls to budget staff in Dallas, San Antonio, and Seguin, Texas, Dec. 30, 2003.
22. Telephone calls to budget staffs in Austin and Dallas, Texas, Dec. 30, 2003.
23. Bureau of the Census, *1992 Census of Government,* Table 11.
24. Texas Municipal League, telephone conversation with research staff, May 2002, Austin, Texas.
25. Frank J. Sturzl, "Good Times Keep Getting Better," *Texas Town and City,* 86 (March 1999), pp. 18–21.

26. Frank Sturzl, "Fiscal Conditions Survey Shows that Municipal Revenue is Declining," *Texas Town and City*, LXXXX (March 2003) p. 10.
27. Ibid., pp. 11–12.
28. Lawrence E. Jordan, "Municipal Bond Issuance in Texas: The New Realities," *Texas Town and City*, LXXIX (December 1991), pp. 12, 25.
29. Sturzl, "Good Times Keep Getting Better," p. 21.
30. Miller and Sanders, *Urban Texas: Politics and Development*, p. xiv.
31. *Texas Almanac, 1992–1993* (Dallas: A. H. Belo Corp., 1991), pp. 137–38, U.S. Census, 2000.
32. Frank Sturzl, "The Tyranny of Environmental Mandates," *Texas Town and City*, LXXIX (September 1991).
33. Brooks, *Texas Practice: County and Special District Law*, Vol. 35, p. 2.
34. Ibid., p. 14.
35. For a sample of Texas court decisions that affirm the general principle of the Dillon rule, that the county can only perform those functions allocated to it by law, see Robert E. Norwood and Sabrina Strawn, *Texas County Government: Let the People Choose*, 2nd ed. (Austin: The Texas Research League, 1984), pp. 11–12.
36. Ibid., p. 9.
37. Texas Association of Counties, *2003 Salary Survey* (Austin: Texas Association of Counties, 2003); phone conversion with Office of Budget Management, Harris County, December 5, 2003.
38. *Avery v. Midland County*, 88 S. Ct. 1114 (1968).
39. Norwood and Strawn, *Texas County Government*, p. 22.
40. Brooks, *Texas Practice: County and Special District Law*, Vol. 35, p. 331.
41. Texas Commission on Intergovernmental Relations, *An Introduction to Texas County Government* (Austin: TCIR, 1980), p. 10.
42. Brooks, *Texas Practice: County and Special District Law*, Vol. 35, pp. 392–93.
43. Brooks, *Texas Practice: County and Special District Law*, Vol. 36 (St. Paul, MN: West Publishing Company, 1989), pp. 104–5.
44. Texas Association of Counties, *2003 Salary Survey*.
45. Brooks, *Texas Practice: County and Special District Law*, Vol. 36, pp. 4–8.
46. Ibid., pp. 49–50.
47. Ibid., pp. 18–49.
48. Norwood and Strawn, *Texas County Government*, p. 24.
49. Brooks, *Texas Practice: County and Special District Law*, Vol. 35, p. 495.
50. Brooks, *Texas Practice: County and Special District Law*, Vol. 36, pp. 122–23.
51. TCIR, *An Introduction to County Government*, p. 22.
52. Norwood and Strawn, *Texas County Government*, p. 27.
53. Brooks, *Texas Practice: County and Special District Law*, Vol. 35, pp. 273–74.
54. Virginia Marion Perrenod, *Special Districts, Special Purposes: Fringe Governments and Urban Problems in the Houston Area* (College Station: Texas A & M University Press, 1984), p. 4.
55. Ibid., p. 4.
56. Woodworth G. Thrombley, *Special Districts and Authorities in Texas* (Austin: Institute of Public Affairs, The University of Texas, 1959), pp. 17–18.
57. Benton, *Texas Politics: Constraints and Opportunities*, p. 282.
58. Perrenod, *Special Districts, Special Purposes*, p. 18.
59. Thrombley, *Special Districts and Authorities in Texas*, p. 13.
60. Robert S. Lorch, *State and Local Politics*, 3rd ed. (Englewood Cliffs, NJ: Prentice Hall, Inc., 1989), p. 246.
61. Ibid., p. 247.
62. Texas Education Agency, *Snapshot 2002:2001–2002 School District Profiles* (Austin: Texas Education Agency, 2002).
63. Texas Association of School Boards, *Special Tabulation of Election Systems Used by Texas Public Schools*, August 22, 1997.
64. Governor's Planning and Budget Office, *Regional Councils in Texas: A Status Report and Directory, 1980–1981*, p. 9.
65. Governor's Budget and Planning Office, *Regional Councils in Texas: Annual Report and Directory, 1990–1991*, p. 8.
66. Texas Association of Regional Councils, "What is a COG?", www.txregionalcouncil.org.
67. Ibid.
68. Governor's Budget and Planning Office, *Texas Regional Councils: Annual Report and Directory, 1992–1993*.
69. Texas Association of Regional Councils, "What is a COG?"
70. Telephone interview by author on March 21, 2000 with governor's office.
71. Brooks, *Texas Practice: County and Special District Law*, Vol. 36, pp. 380–84.
72. For a more detailed discussion of annexation authority, see Wilbourn E. Benton, *Texas Politics*, pp. 264–66.
73. "Texas Legislature Adjourns," *Texas Town and City*, 86 (July 1999), p. 10.
74. "Texas Legislature Adjourns," *Texas Town and City*, 89 (July 2001), p. 11.
75. Norwood and Strawn, *Texas County Government*, pp. 75–81.
76. Joel B. Goldsteen and Russell Fricano, *Municipal Finance Practices and Preferences for New Development: Survey of Texas Cities* (Arlington, TX: Institute of Urban Studies, The University of Texas at Arlington, 1988), pp. 3–11.
77. Bill R. Shelton, Bob Bolen, and Ray Perryman, "Passing a Sales Tax Referendum for Economic Development," *Texas Town and City*, LXXIX (September 1991), 10.

78. Brooks, *Texas Practice: County and Special District Law,* Vol. 36, pp. 229–42.

79. Tom Adams, "Introduction and Recent Experience with the Interlocal Contract," in *Interlocal Contract in Texas,* eds. Richard W. Tees, Richard L. Cole, and Jay G. Stanford (Arlington, TX: Institute of Urban Studies, University of Arlington, 1990), p. 1.

80. Tees, et al., *Interlocal Contract in Texas,* pp. B1–B7.

81. Vincent Ostrom, *The Meaning of American Federalism* (San Francisco: Institute for Contemporary Studies, 1991), p. 161. Ostrom suggests that advocates of metropolitan government often overlook the "rich and intricate framework for negotiating, adjudicating, and deciding questions" that are now in place in many urbanized areas with multiple governmental units.

82. Ann Long Diveley and Dwight A. Shupe, "Public Improvement Districts: An Alternative for Financing Public Improvements and Services," *Texas Town and City,* LXXIX (September 1991).

Contemporary Public Policy Issues in Texas

> It's as big as the House and Senate want to make it, and it's as big as the needs of Texas are. I mean, goodness gracious, how long is a piece of string? How do we rank (in spending)? How do we look, compared to other states throughout the country?
>
> *Lieutenant Governor Bob Bullock[1]*

At the beginning of the twenty-first century, Texas's problems with poverty, pollution, crime, education, a clogged transportation system and an outdated tax structure were similar to challenges faced by other states. And in Texas, as elsewhere, identifying a policy problem was easier than forging a political solution, as the state's new Republican leadership was learning. With much difficulty, Texas had survived the collapse of its traditional oil-based economy and then the collapse of its real estate industry in the 1980s. As the economy diversified, state government also had spent billions of taxpayer dollars on major improvements in prisons and mental health facilities and a more equitable distribution of public education dollars. But the work of addressing public needs is never completed, and the political controversy involved in setting policy is never stilled, as our discussion of selected, major issues in this chapter will demonstrate. These issues represent enduring problems, and the policy decisions made in recent years are part of a long sequence of actions and inactions by state officials.

THE POLICY PROCESS

Political scientists and policy analysts spend a lot of time defining public policy and all its critical elements. But we will use the definition developed by Thomas Dye, who defined public policy as "whatever governments choose to do or not to do."[2]

Except for an occasional federal judge, individuals acting alone haven't forced many changes in public policy. The political power necessary to shape policy is exercised through groups and, as we have pointed out throughout this book, some groups or interests have been more influential than others. Before we discuss specific policy changes, we will attempt to outline the concepts involved in the process.

The Elements of Public Policy

Setting public policy usually involves questions of costs and benefits. The ultimate political problems to resolve are who will benefit from specific policy decisions and who will pay the bill.[3] Certain groups, businesses, or individuals receive direct benefits from governmental decisions—benefits that are paid for by other individuals through taxes. In this process there is, in effect, a transfer of money from one segment of the population to another. Critical decisions must be made on the allocation of the tax burden, which will inevitably produce intense political conflict.

Public policies also provide indirect benefits. Although low-income Texans may receive the direct benefits of welfare assistance, job training programs, and subsidized housing and health care, the entire population eventually stands to gain if the poverty cycle is interrupted. Similar arguments can be made for funding equity between poor and rich school districts. The state's economic growth and future prosperity will be adversely affected and its crime rate will rise if serious problems of illiteracy and school dropouts aren't successfully addressed now.

Public policy also includes regulation of the private sector. Indiscriminate use of land, water, and other natural resources has been curtailed by environmental policies seeking to protect the best interests of the state as a whole. But those policies often conflict with property rights and spark angry responses from some businesses and private property owners, who threaten political retaliation against public officeholders.

Additionally, public policy affects the governmental process itself. Decisions on political redistricting, revisions in election laws, and changes in the structure and organization of state and local governments ultimately address the issue of how power is distributed. They help determine how many people will be able to achieve their personal and collective objectives and improve their lives.

Another dimension of public policy is rooted in the notion of the general good of the community. Related to the concept of indirect benefits, it reflects the values upon which a political culture is based. Whether defined in terms of "it's the right thing to do" or a more systematic theory of the bonds that create the political community, there are elements of public policy that reflect the common needs or interests of those who live in the state.

The Stages of the Policy Process

There are many activities in the private sector that bear on public policy, such as a decision by a large corporation to close its operations in a city. But the following discussion focuses on the governmental institutions that make binding and enforceable decisions affecting all those who live in the state.[4]

A number of scholars have approached policymaking as a sequential process (Table 13–1). Although this approach may suggest artificial start and stop points, the process is dynamic and continuous.

TABLE 13–1   Stages of the Policy Process

Stages	Actions Taken
Identification and Formation of an Issue	Defining a common problem and building coalitions to force the issue on the public agenda.
Access and Representation	Gaining access to elected or administrative officials and getting them to see the problem.
Formulation	Getting those in government to initiate action on the problem by sifting through alternative solutions.
Adoption or Legitimation	The government's specific solution to the problem, including the authorization of programs and allocation of funds.
Implementation	The application of the government's policy to the problem.
Evaluation	Assessing the effects of the policy and determining if its objectives were achieved.

Sources: Charles O. Jones, *An Introduction to the Study of Public Policy,* 2nd ed. (North Scituate, MA: Duxbury Press, 1977), and James E. Anderson, David W. Brady, Charles S. Bullock III, and Joseph Stewart Jr., *Public Policy and Politics in America,* 2nd ed. (Monterey, CA: Brooks/Cole Publishing Company, 1984).

People have to identify a problem before they can expect the government's help in resolving it.[5] Subsequent steps in the policymaking process include gaining access to public officials, getting a solution drawn up and adopted, seeing it carried out, and evaluating its effectiveness.

People in a particular neighborhood, for example, may experience an increase in respiratory problems. Right away, they suspect a nearby chemical plant, and their suspicions are reinforced every time winds blow across the neighborhood from the direction of the plant. After complaints to the plant manager bring no satisfaction—or relief—the unhappy neighbors turn to government. To make sure they are heard, they identify others affected by the same problem and join forces in a citizens' group. Such groups are central to the policymaking process. By banding together, people increase their financial resources, leadership capabilities, and political strength.

Their next step is to find the governmental body or agency that can address the problem and then convince it to do so. They may first approach the city council, only to learn that state laws and regulations govern emissions from the plant. They may then turn to the Texas Commission on Environmental Quality, which may determine that the plant is violating its state permit and may impose an administrative fine or seek legal action by the attorney general. Or the commission may find its hands tied by a loophole in the state's anti-pollution laws. In that case, the concerned citizens need help from the legislature, where they have to convince their elected representatives to translate their concerns into a change in policy.

Simply identifying a problem and getting a large number of other people to share your concerns is not a solution. Solutions must be developed and enacted through specific laws, regulations, or other policy changes. Philosophically, there is little disagreement that every child in Texas should have access to a quality education.

But what does that mean in practical political terms? Proposed solutions have been extremely diverse. Legislative staffs, blue ribbon committees, independent research organizations, academicians, and consultants from various points on the political spectrum have all contributed studies and opinions. The resolution of their differences is essentially a political process. In the final analysis, "successful policy formulations must deal with the question of selecting courses of action that can actually be adopted."[6]

The legislature is primarily responsible for sifting through proposed alternatives and setting policy at the state level. But the separation of powers doctrine under which our government operates gives the judiciary important scrutiny over legislative action—or inaction. In recent years, several major federal and state court decisions have forced the legislature to make far-reaching changes in education, criminal justice, and mental health and mental retardation programs. Those court orders have prompted some lawmakers and other critics to complain that the judiciary overstepped its authority and was attempting to preempt the legislature. Others believe, however, that the legislature had neglected its responsibilities and needed some prodding.

Virtually every public policy has a cost. It is not enough for the legislature to create a program. Programs have to be funded, or they are meaningless. Sometimes, the legislature requires local governments to pick up the tab, but most programs have to compete with hundreds of other programs for a limited number of state tax dollars. Thus, the state's complex budgetary process is at the heart of policymaking and is closely monitored by individuals and organizations interested in policy development. Conflicts over the budgetary process can be very intense.

Once legislation has been enacted and funded, its specific provisions must be implemented, or carried out. Much of this activity is the responsibility of state and local agencies that have been created to carry "a program to the problem."[7] Earlier political scientists referred to this stage of the policy process as public administration, and much of it falls within the domain of administrative agencies and departments. But government bureaucrats aren't the only ones involved in carrying out policy. So are legislators, judges, interest groups and non-profit organizations. The activities in this implementation phase include:

Interpretation—the translation of program language into acceptable and feasible directives;

Organization—the establishment of organizational units and standard operating procedures for putting a program into effect; and

Application—the routine provision of services, payments, or other agreed-upon program objectives or instruments.[8]

Governments spend a lot of time evaluating the effects of public policy. An enormous amount of information is gathered to determine if programs have met stated goals and, if not, what changes or adjustments are required. Legislative committees, in their oversight function, demand information from agencies to help determine whether to continue to fund programs, expand them, or change them. With an eye on future funding, agencies also spend considerable resources assessing the impact of their own activities and performance. Program evaluation also is part of the broader issue of accountability of public officials and their responsiveness to the needs, demands, and expectations of their constituents. Interest groups, think tanks, scholars, and the news media also actively participate in this phase of the policy process.

Program assessment and evaluation become the basis for future policy and funding decisions. We have found some comprehensive solutions to a limited number of problems, including some diseases, but most governmental policy produces only limited or partial solutions. Problems and issues are ongoing, and policymakers often have to adjust or redirect their efforts at problem-solving. A solution enacted today can produce additional problems requiring further attention tomorrow. As we will discuss later in this chapter, for example, recent changes in public education policies and funding are part of a long history of efforts to improve the quality of education in Texas.

Iron Triangles and Issue Networks

There are thousands of players in the policy arenas of state and local governments, including bureaucrats, the courts, interest groups, businesses, the news media, and policy specialists. Although some of these have a broad perspective on state policy and a wide range of policy interests, most have narrow and highly specialized interests. One way to think about the relationships among policy participants is to "identify the clusters of individuals that effectively make most of the routine decisions in a given substantive area of policy."[9]

At the state level, these clusters—sometimes referred to as iron triangles of government—include members of the House and the Senate, their staffs, high-level bureaucrats, and representatives of interest groups. Both houses of the legislature are divided into standing committees, which have jurisdiction over specific policy areas, and key committee members usually form one leg of each triangle. There are hundreds of these subsystems in state government, although the use of this concept to explain policy development does not always identify all of the critical players or explain the complexity of the process.

Political scientist Hugh Heclo argues that "the iron triangle concept is not so much wrong as it is disastrously incomplete," and he offers a more complex model—**issue networks**—for mapping out the relationships inherent in the policy process.[10] This concept acknowledges the key roles of the iron triangle players but also takes into account other factors, including the increased interdependence of state and local governments on the federal government. Specialists from all three levels of government are frequently involved in developing specific policies. And, groups such as the National Governors' Association, the Council of State Governments, and the U.S. Conference of Mayors actively seek to influence federal policies that affect state and local governments.

The policy process also is increasingly dominated by specialists who may be identified with interest groups, corporations, legislative committees, or administrative agencies. These experts, or "technopols," understand the technical nature of a problem and, more importantly, the institutional, political, and personal relationships of those involved in trying to solve it.[11]

The number of actual participants in policy development will vary, of course, from issue to issue. Sometimes, only a few individuals are involved in shaping a specific policy. But on other occasions, when changes are being considered in tax law, health care, or public education, for example, there is a "kaleidoscopic interaction of changing issue networks."[12]

In the following discussion of contemporary state policies, you will see some practical applications of these concepts.

THE BUDGETARY PROCESS

Balancing a new state budget in the face of a $10 billion revenue shortfall was the legislature's most difficult task in 2003, and that regular session of the legislature was the most difficult budgetary session in a dozen years. With Republicans in charge of the statehouse, the new budget was written without increasing state taxes, but fees for numerous state services were increased and funding was cut for health care and many other important programs. The Republican approach to bridging the revenue shortfall differed from how the legislature had resolved the most significant, previous budgetary crisis in 1991, when Democrats still held the governor's office and a majority of both legislative houses. The legislature balanced the 1991 budget with some cuts and other cost-savings steps plus a $2.7 billion package of tax and fee increases. The legislature, with voter approval, also created the Texas lottery that year as a future revenue source. Texas lawmakers wrote state budgets in 1993, 1995, 1997, 1999, and 2001 without raising state taxes, but they put more stress on an already strained budget and tax system.

Like most other states and unlike the federal government, Texas operates on a pay-as-you-go basis that prohibits **deficit financing.** The comptroller must certify that each budget can be paid for with anticipated revenue from taxes, fees, and other sources. And, like other states, Texas greatly increased its spending on state government programs in the 1970s, 1980s, and 1990s. Population growth and inflation were major factors, in addition to federal mandates and court orders for prison and education reforms.

The biggest share of state expenditures (including federal funds appropriated by the legislature) is for education, which accounted for approximately 42 percent of the 2004–2005 budget. Health and human services, which has seen a significant boost in recent years from increased Medicaid spending but suffered other cuts in the 2003 session, was second at 34 percent. Business and economic development accounted for 12 percent.

The two-year 2004–2005 state budget totaled $118 billion, an increase of about $67.4 billion over the 1990–1991 budget. The 2002–2003 budget was approximately $111 billion. Legislative budget experts said increases in federal programs and mandates and federal court orders accounted for much of the increase. Federally driven programs and mandates accounted for 49 percent of the 1994–1995 Texas budget, up from 41 percent in 1990–1991, according to one state study.[13]

Two-Year Budgets

The Texas legislature's budget-writing problems are compounded by the length of the budget period and the structure of the budget itself. Since the Texas Constitution provides that the legislature meet in regular session only every other year, lawmakers must write two-year, or biennial, budgets for state government. That means state agencies, which begin preparing their budget requests several months before a session convenes, have to anticipate some of their spending needs three years in advance. Critics, including many legislators and agency directors, say two-year budgets require too much guesswork and cause inadequate funding of some programs and wasteful spending in other areas. They believe that Texas, which is the nation's second most populous state and has a wide diversity of needs in a changing economy, should have annual budget sessions of the legislature, a change that would require a constitutional amendment.

The governor and legislative leaders have the authority between legislative sessions to transfer funds between programs and agencies to meet some emergencies. The governor proposes transfers to the Legislative Budget Board (LBB), a ten-member panel that includes the lieutenant governor, the speaker, and eight key legislators. The LBB can accept, reject, or modify the governor's proposal and can propose budgetary changes to the governor.

Agencies submit their biennial appropriations, or spending, requests to the Legislative Budget Board. After its staff reviews the requests, the LBB normally recommends a budget that the full legislature uses as a starting point in its budgetary deliberations.

Dedicated Funds

The legislature's control over the budget-setting process is further restricted by legal requirements that dedicate or set aside a major portion of state revenue for specific purposes, leaving legislators with discretion over only about one-half of total appropriations. The remainder includes federal funds earmarked for specific purposes by the federal government or monies dedicated to specific uses by the state constitution or state law. The state treasury has more than 500 separate funds, including many that are dedicated to highways, education, parks, teacher retirement, and dozens of other specific purposes. These restrictions hamper the legislature, particularly during lean periods. But the dedicated funds are jealously guarded by the interest groups that benefit from them, and many funds have become "sacred cows" that most legislators dare not try to change.

One of the major **dedicated funds** is the Highway Trust Fund, which automatically gets three-fourths of the revenue from the motor fuels tax. Under the Texas Constitution, revenue in that fund can be spent only to purchase right of way for highways or to construct, maintain, and police highways. The remainder of the motor fuels tax revenue goes to public education. Any legislative proposal to tap into the highway fund for other state needs would be fought by a strong lobbying effort from highway contractors as well as business leaders, mayors, and county judges with local road projects they wanted completed.

Other major dedicated funds include the Permanent School Fund and the Permanent University Fund, land- and mineral-rich endowments that help support the public schools and boost funding for the University of Texas and Texas A & M University systems. In 1991, the legislature, working with the comptroller, began consolidating and eliminating many funds, but constitutionally dedicated funds cannot be changed without voter approval.

STATE TAXES

The legislature enacted a hybrid corporate income tax in 1991, but Texas entered the twenty-first century as one of only nine states without a personal income tax, and public and political opposition to that revenue source remained high. Each budgetary crisis had seemingly stretched the existing tax structure to the breaking point, only to see the legislature come up with another patch. Critics compared the tax structure to an ugly patchwork quilt that had been stitched together over the years to accommodate various special interest groups and cover an assortment of emergencies. Senator Carl Parker, a Port Arthur Democrat, argued in Senate floor debate in 1991: "They (existing taxes) hit the poor people worse than they do rich folks. They let some people off scot-free, while they tax others heavily. And the direction we seem to be going is worse, not better."[14]

The Regressive Tax System

A 2003 study by Citizens for Tax Justice and the Institute on Taxation & Economic Policy ranked Texas's tax system among the ten most regressive in the country. Texas's system is based largely on the sales tax, the local property tax, and fees that consume a larger portion of the incomes of the poor and the middle classes than the upper class (Table 13–2). Based on this study's calculations, state and local governments in Texas taxed poor families at 11.4 percent of their incomes and middle-class families at 8.4 percent. By contrast, the wealthiest Texans (the richest 1 percent of the families) paid only 3.5 percent of their incomes in state and local taxes. Political leaders have long touted Texas as a low-tax state, but, according to this study, that is only from the perspective of wealthy Texans.[15]

Sales Taxes

The last major change in Texas's general tax policy occurred in 1961, when the legislature, over the objections of then-Governor Price Daniel, enacted the state's first **sales tax.** Its initial rate was 2 percent of the cost of purchased goods. The rate has since been increased several times, and the tax now produces about one-fourth of all state revenue. In 2003, the statewide sales tax rate of 6.25 percent was tied with Illinois for seventh highest in the nation. The 8.25 percent rate charged in most Texas metropolitan areas, where city and mass transportation authority taxes of 1 percent each are added to the state tax, ranked fifteenth among the states. The sales tax generated $14.5 billion in 2002, which was 26 percent of the state's revenue.[16]

TABLE 13–2   Ten Most Regressive State Tax Systems

"The Terrible Ten"	Taxes as a Percentage of Income		
	Poorest 20%	Middle 60%	Top 1%
Washington	17.6	11.2	3.3
Florida	14.4	7.7	3.0
Tennessee	11.7	8.9	3.4
South Dakota	10.0	8.4	2.3
Texas	11.4	8.4	3.5
Illinois	13.1	10.5	5.8
Michigan	13.3	11.2	6.7
Pennsylvania	11.4	9.0	4.9
Alabama	10.6	9.0	4.9
Nevada	8.3	6.5	2.0

Source: Citizens for Tax Justice, *Who Pays?: A Distributional Analysis of the Tax System in All 50 States, 2nd edition* (Washington, DC: Institute on Taxation and Economic Policy, January 2003), p. 9.

With each financial crisis, it becomes more difficult politically for the legislature to raise the sales tax rate. And even though groceries and medicine are tax exempt, critics charge that the sales tax is regressive because it affects low-income Texans disproportionately more than wealthier citizens. Moreover, the sales tax is heavily weighted toward products and leaves many services—including legal and medical fees and advertising—untaxed. Thus sales tax revenue doesn't automatically grow with the state's economy because the Texas economy is becoming more and more service-oriented.

Franchise Taxes

The **franchise tax,** which was overhauled in 1991 and is now a hybrid corporate income tax, is the state's major business tax. It accounts for three percent of total state revenue and six percent of tax revenue. But it applies only to corporations, which are taxed on their income or assets, whichever is greater. The tax doesn't cover partnerships or sole proprietorships and is paid by fewer than 200,000 of the state's 2.5 million businesses. Still, it is a broader based tax than it was before the 1991 changes were made. Previously, the tax was based primarily on assets, rather than assets or income. That meant service corporations, which didn't require much equipment or capital expenditures, were much more lightly taxed than petrochemical or manufacturing firms. By adding service corporations to the tax base, the state was able to tap into revenue from some of Texas's fastest growing industries. In 1997, Governor George W. Bush proposed that the franchise tax be replaced with a broader based business activity tax, which would have applied to all forms of businesses, including corporations, partnerships, and sole proprietorships. He said a business activity tax—part of a plan to lower school property taxes—was fairer to businesses. But the legislature rejected his proposal.

Property Taxes

The biggest source of taxpayer dissatisfaction and anger in Texas in recent years has been the local **property,** or ad valorem, **tax,** the major source of revenue for cities, counties, and school districts. Total property tax levies nearly doubled between 1993 and 2002, from $14.7 billion to $27.3 billion, according to the state comptroller's office.[17] The heaviest increases have been in local school taxes, which have been significantly raised to pay for state-mandated education reforms and school finance requirements, including a law ordering the transfer of millions of dollars from wealthy to poor school districts (see later section in this chapter).

Severance Taxes

Oil and gas severance taxes helped the legislature balance the budget with relative ease when oil prices were high in the 1970s. But energy-tax revenue slowed considerably after the energy industry crashed in the 1980s. Severance taxes accounted for 28 percent of state tax revenue in 1981, but only 5 percent in 2003.[18]

Other Taxes

State government also has several volume-based taxes, such as taxes on cigarettes, alcoholic beverages, and motor fuels. They have set rates per pack or per gallon and don't produce more revenue when inflation raises the price of the product. These taxes, particularly the so-called **"sin taxes"** on cigarettes and alcohol, have been raised frequently over the years. In 2003, Texas's cigarette tax ranked 36th in the country at 41 cents per pack, up from 18.5 cents per pack in 1982.[19]

Gambling on New Revenue

For years, Texas government maintained a strong moralistic opposition to gambling. Charitable bingo games were tolerated and eventually legalized. But the state constitution prohibited lotteries, and horse race betting was outlawed in the 1930s. After the oil bust in the 1980s, however, many legislators began to view gambling as a financial opportunity rather than a moral evil, and in key elections most Texas voters indicated they agreed.

In a special session in 1986, when spending was cut and taxes were raised to compensate for lost revenue from plummeting oil prices, the legislature legalized local option, parimutuel betting on horse and dog races. Voters approved the measure the next year. In 1991, under strong pressure from Governor Ann Richards, the legislature approved a constitutional amendment to legalize a state **lottery,** which voters also endorsed that year. Limited casino gambling on cruise ships operating off the Texas coast also has been legalized by the legislature.

Gambling, however, has not been a panacea for the state's financial needs. Years after parimutuel betting had been approved, the horse and dog racing tracks still had not produced any significant revenue for the state treasury.

The lottery jumped off to a much more impressive start. It became the first lottery in the United States to sell more than $4 billion worth of tickets in its first two years of operation, and it reached that milestone in twenty-two months. By late 1997, however, lottery sales had begun to lag behind projections, and even supporters of the game warned that the lottery couldn't necessarily be depended upon as a reliable, long-term revenue source. Lawmakers for the first time in 1997 dedicated lottery revenue to public education but also ordered that shortfalls in school funding from the lottery be made up with tax dollars.[20] The lottery generated $888 million for the Foundation School Program in 2003. In an effort to boost lottery sales and state revenue, the legislature that year also approved Texas's entry for the first time in a multistate lottery offering occasional jackpots of $100 million or more.[21]

Texas isn't the only state banking on gambling enterprises to help ease financial problems. Several other states also have recently approved lotteries or begun to experiment with casino-style gambling, and some businesspeople have lobbied to bring casino gambling to Texas. At least two Indian tribes—the Tiguas in West Texas and the Alabama-Coushatta in East Texas—operated casinos on their reservations for several years under federal law. But Texas Attorney General John Cornyn went to court to shut them down, arguing that the tribes had illegally offered forms of gambling not allowed in the rest of the state.

Bonds: Build Now, Pay Later

Although the Texas Constitution has a general prohibition against state government going into debt, the state had about $17.3 billion in state bonds outstanding in 2002. About $3.4 billion of the total would have to be paid off with tax dollars spread over the next generation.[22] Taxpayer-supported debt ballooned during tight budgetary periods when the legislature, prompted by federal court orders, used **general obligation,** or tax-backed, **bonds** to finance the construction of prisons and mental health and mental retardation facilities. These expenses were submitted to the voters for approval in the form of constitutional amendments.

Some legislators have become increasingly uneasy about loading up the additional tax liability on future taxpayers. Interest on bonds can double the cost of a construction project, experts say. Debt service paid from taxes totaled $374 million in 2002, according to the state comptroller's office.[23] Bond issues, however, have been widely supported by Democrats and Republicans, liberals and conservatives alike. In promoting a prison bond issue in 1989, then-Governor Bill Clements said, "If there ever was anything that was proper for us to bond, it's our prison system, where those facilities will be on line and in use for a twenty-five or thirty-year period."[24]

Over the years, the state also has issued hundreds of millions of dollars in bonds for such self-supporting programs as water development and veterans' assistance. Those programs use the state's credit to borrow money at favorable interest rates. The state lends that money to a local government to help construct a water treatment plant or to a veteran to help purchase a house, and the debt is repaid by the loan recipients, not by the state's taxpayers.

Alternatives to Finding New Revenues

State leaders throughout the country have been reexamining their delivery of public services to assure taxpayers they were getting the best possible return on their dollars. Texas was in the forefront of these efforts.

In 1991, the Texas legislature, facing a large revenue shortfall, instructed the state comptroller to supervise periodic performance reviews of all state agencies and programs with an eye toward eliminating inefficiency and mismanagement and producing savings. The comptroller also reviewed the budgets and operations of some local school districts. Billions of dollars in potential savings were identified over the next several years, and a number of the comptroller's recommendations were adopted by the legislature and school boards.

The legislature transferred those programs from the comptroller's office to the Legislative Budget Board in 2003 after a series of budgetary disputes with Comptroller Carole Keeton Strayhorn (see Chapter 9).

The Income Tax: An Alternative to a Regressive Tax System?

Various liberal legislators and groups seeking more funding for state services have long advocated a state **income tax.** But until fairly recently no major officeholder or serious candidate for a major office dared even hint at support for such a politically taboo alternative. Finally, in late 1989, then–Lieutenant Governor Bill Hobby broke the ice for serious discussion of the issue in a speech to the Texas Association of Taxpayers, whose members included executives of many of the major businesses in Texas. Hobby, who had already announced that he wouldn't seek reelection in 1990, proposed that a personal and corporate income tax be enacted, coupled with abolition of the corporate franchise tax and reductions in property and sales taxes. Hobby also told his audience that it would take the business community to convince the legislature to pass an income tax.

Lieutenant Governor Bob Bullock then shocked much of the political establishment by announcing in March 1991, less than two months after succeeding Hobby, that he would actively campaign for a state income tax. Bullock, a former state comptroller, said it was the only way to meet the state's present and future needs fairly and adequately while also providing relief from existing unpopular taxes. Bullock proposed making local school property taxes deductible from the income tax, and he recommended the repeal of the franchise tax. "I personally dislike—and I imagine most Texans do—any type of new taxes. But I also know deep down in my heart, deep down in my heart, that it's the right thing to do for Texas," he said.[25]

Although other surveys indicated there was still widespread opposition to an income tax among Texans, the *Texas Poll* published that spring signaled that Bullock had struck a favorable chord with many property taxpayers. Half of the poll's 1,003 respondents said they would favor a 5 percent state income tax if it enabled local property taxes to be cut in half, and 54 percent said they would support an income tax to pay for public schools if property taxes were greatly reduced.[26]

But Bullock didn't receive much support from lobby groups. And the Texas House, which must initiate legislative action on tax bills, remained strongly opposed to an income tax, as did the governor, Democrat Ann Richards.

Eventually, the legislature that year changed the corporate franchise tax to include the hybrid corporate income tax described earlier in this chapter, while holding the line against a personal income tax. A blue-ribbon task force appointed by the governor and legislative leaders to study revenue options recommended that the legislature enact both corporate and personal income taxes in 1993. The recommendation, believed to have been engineered behind the scenes by Bullock, came over the objections of the task force chairman, former Governor John Connally. Connally argued that an income tax would raise too much money and encourage excessive spending by the legislature. And, he added, "The people don't want it."[27]

During the 1993 legislative session, Bullock pulled another surprise and proposed a constitutional amendment, which won easy legislative approval, to ban a personal income tax unless the voters approved one. Bullock probably had more than one reason for his apparent about-face. One obvious factor was that his 1994 reelection date was approaching, and he needed to defuse any political problems caused by his endorsement of an income tax two years earlier. Moreover, Governor Richards and most legislators still strongly opposed an income tax. Some observers also believed that Bullock viewed his new proposal as a way to eventually win Texans' approval of a personal income tax. His constitutional amendment provided that an income tax would have to help fund public education and be accompanied by a reduction in unpopular school property taxes, provisions similar to his 1991 income tax plan.

Whatever Bullock's motivations, the amendment was overwhelmingly approved by Texas voters in November 1993, leaving many people convinced that a major revenue option had been removed from the state's budget picture for years to come.

As of 2003, Texas was one of only nine states without a personal income tax. And whenever the legislature does decide to try to sell one to voters, support from the business community will be crucial. The sales tax was first adopted after the business lobby got behind it, and business interests remain influential today. State government's ability to provide quality education, highways, and other public support systems is essential to the business community's long-term success. A personal income tax also would offer businesses the opportunity to transfer more of their tax load to consumers. That, ironically, could produce a conflict with some of the more liberal, long-time supporters of an income tax. A likely solution would be the enactment of generous tax exemptions for low-income Texans.

EDUCATIONAL POLICIES AND POLITICS

Public Education: A Struggle for Equity and Quality

More tax dollars are spent on education than any other governmental program in Texas. In 1949, the legislature enacted the Gilmer-Aikin law, which made major improvements in the administration of public education and significantly boosted funding for public schools, but it was soon outdated. By the 1970s, it was obvious that quality and equity were lacking in many classrooms. Thousands of functional illiterates were being graduated from high school each year, and thousands of children in poor school districts were being shortchanged with substandard facilities and educational aids.

Public elementary and secondary education in Texas is financed by a combination of state and local revenue, a system that produced wide disparities in education spending among the state's approximately 1,050 school districts. The only local source of operating revenue for school districts is the property tax. Districts with a wealth of oil production or expensive commercial property had high tax bases that enabled them to raise large amounts of money with relatively low tax rates. Poor districts with low tax bases, on the other hand, had to impose higher tax rates to raise only a fraction of the money that the wealthy districts could spend on education.

While poor districts had to struggle to maintain minimal educational programs, rich districts could attract the best teachers with higher pay, build more classrooms, purchase more books and computers, and, in some cases, have enough money left over to put AstroTurf® in their football stadiums and construct indoor swimming pools. The glaring inequities didn't exist only between different counties or regions of the state. In many cases, educational resources varied greatly between districts within the same county (see "School Consolidations versus Community Identity"). But many of the poorest districts were in heavily Hispanic south Texas, and ethnicity became a significant factor in a protracted struggle between the haves and the have-nots. Hispanic leaders played major roles in the fight to improve the futures of their children.

In 1968, a group of parents led by Demetrio P. Rodriguez, a San Antonio sheet metal worker and high school dropout, filed a federal lawsuit (*Rodriguez v. San Antonio Independent School District*) challenging the system. The plaintiffs had children in the Edgewood Independent School District, one of the state's poorest. A three-judge federal panel agreed with the parents and ruled in 1971 that the school finance system was unconstitutional. But the state appealed, and the U.S. Supreme Court in 1973 reversed the lower court decision. The high court said that the Texas system of financing public education was unfair but held that it didn't violate the U.S. Constitution. Its consciousness raised, the legislature started pumping hundreds of millions of dollars in so-called "equalization" aid into the poorer school districts. But lawmakers didn't change the system, and the inequities persisted and worsened.

SCHOOL CONSOLIDATIONS VERSUS COMMUNITY IDENTITY

There were more than 5,000 school districts in Texas in 1947, and that number was greatly reduced over the next several years. But despite potential savings, efficiency in school administration, and more equitable distribution of tax dollars, consolidations have been relatively rare in recent years, with districts now numbering approximately 1,050. In many small towns, the school district is not only a major employer; it is also the center of social activities and the heart of the community itself. And, be it rich or poor, local residents don't want to give up the hometown school.

The *Houston Chronicle* vividly illustrated that point at the beginning of the 1990–1991 school year with a visit to sparsely populated Cochran County in west Texas. The Whiteface Consolidated School District, which sits atop an oil field, had a tax base of $1.3 million per student and a tax rate of only 46 cents per $100 valuation. It had an indoor swimming pool that the entire community of 450 people shared, and it paid its teachers, on the average, about $3,500 a year more than the neighboring Morton Independent School District did. Morton, the county seat, is a slightly larger town only twelve miles away, but the oil field ends somewhere between the two communities. With a tax base of only $73,400 per student, Morton was one of the state's poorest school districts, and its tax rate was 96.5 cents per $100 valuation. But Morton Superintendent Charles Skeen said consolidation was no more popular with the people of Morton than it was with their neighbors in Whiteface.

"When you have two communities and you take the school out of one of them, the people fear they will lose their town," Skeen said. Whiteface Superintendent David Foote said virtually the same thing: "A lot of people live in this town so their children can go to a small school. They know that if a community loses its school, where the school is the center of the community, the community dies.*

Houston Chronicle, August 19, 1990.

By the early 1980s, there was a growing concern among Texas leaders over not just the financing of public education but also the quality of education. Their concerns were shared by leaders in other states in the wake of a national study called *A Nation at Risk* that had sharply criticized the nation's educational systems as inadequate. In 1983, newly elected Governor Mark White tried to raise schoolteachers' salaries to keep a campaign promise to the thousands of teachers who had been instrumental in his election. When the legislature refused to increase taxes for higher teacher pay without first studying the educational system with an eye toward reform, White joined Lieutenant Governor Bill Hobby and House Speaker Gib Lewis in appointing the Select Committee on Public Education. Computer magnate Ross Perot of Dallas—who several years later would become better known as an independent candidate for president—was selected to chair it. In an exhaustive study, the panel found that high schools were graduating many students who could barely read and write and concluded that major reforms were necessary if the state's young people were to be able to compete for jobs in a changing and highly competitive state and international economy.

With Perot spending some of his own personal wealth on a strong lobbying campaign, the legislature in a special session in 1984 enacted many educational reforms in a landmark piece of legislation known as **House Bill 72** and raised taxes to boost education spending. The bill raised teacher pay, limited class sizes, required prekindergarten classes for disadvantaged four-year-olds, required students to pass a basic skills test before graduating from high school, and required school districts to provide tutorials for failing students. It also replaced the elected State Board of Education, viewed as antireform by state leaders, with a new panel appointed by the governor. The new board became an elected body four years later, after the appointed panel had time to oversee the initial implementation of the new law.

The two most controversial provisions in the 1984 education reform law, however, were a literacy test for teachers and the so-called **no pass, no play** rule, both of which were to contribute to White's reelection defeat in 1986. Most teachers easily passed the one-time literacy—or competency—test, a requirement for keeping their jobs, but many resented it as an insult to their abilities and professionalism. The no-pass, no-play rule, which prohibited students who failed any course from participating in athletics and other extracurricular activities for six weeks, infuriated many coaches, students, parents, and school administrators, particularly in the hundreds of small Texas towns where Friday night football was a major social activity and an important source of community pride. Education reformers, however, viewed the restriction as an important statement that the first emphasis of education should be on the classroom, not on the football field or the band hall.

The 1984 law, however, still didn't change the basic, inequitable finance system, and the state was soon back in court over that issue. This lawsuit (*Edgewood v. Kirby*) was filed in state district court in Austin, and it contended the inequities violated the Texas Constitution. It was initially filed in 1984, shortly before the enactment of House Bill 72, by the Edgewood Independent School District, twelve other poor districts, and a number of families represented by the Mexican American Legal Defense and Educational Fund (MALDEF). Dozens of other districts and individuals joined the case as plaintiff-intervenors, and, in 1987, state District Judge Harley Clark of Austin ruled the school finance system violated the state constitution.

The Third Court of Appeals reversed Clark in December 1988. But the Texas Supreme Court, in a unanimous, landmark decision in October 1989, struck down the finance system and ordered lawmakers to replace it by May 1, 1990, with a new law that gave public school children an equal opportunity at a quality education. The bipartisan opinion, written by Democratic Justice Oscar Mauzy, a former chairman of the Senate Education Committee, didn't outline a specific solution. In an obvious effort to reach consensus among all nine justices, it was purposefully vague in some areas. But the court said the existing finance system violated a state constitutional requirement for an efficient system of public education. It warned the legislature that merely increasing the amount of state education aid wasn't enough. The decision concluded that "a Band-Aid will not suffice; the system itself must be changed."[28]

The Texas Supreme Court cited glaring disparities among school districts' abilities to raise revenue from property taxes because of wide differences in taxable wealth. "The amount of money spent on a student's education has a real and meaningful impact on the educational opportunity offered that student," the court wrote. "High-wealth districts are able to provide for their students broader educational experiences including more extensive curricula, more up-to-date technological equipment, better libraries and library personnel, teacher aides, counseling services, lower student–teacher ratios, better facilities, parental involvement programs, and dropout prevention programs. They are also better able to attract and retain experienced teachers and administrators."[29]

Funding Problems Persist

Governor Bill Clements called the legislature into special session in February 1990 to address the Texas Supreme Court order. But the issue was so divisive it took four special sessions and an extension of the court's deadline for the governor and the legislature to agree on a new finance plan, which included a small increase in the state sales tax to boost funding to poor districts. But the Edgewood plaintiffs called the new law inadequate and promptly took the state back to court.

After a trial on the new law, state District Judge Scott McCown of Austin, who had taken over jurisdiction of the lawsuit after Harley Clark retired, agreed. Although he allowed the new law to remain in effect for the 1990–1991 school year, McCown ruled in September 1990 that the plan was, like its predecessor, unconstitutional because it didn't narrow the huge gap in wealth between rich and poor school districts. The Texas Supreme Court agreed.

A legislative solution still remained difficult, and lawmakers had to enact two more school finance plans before finally meeting the Supreme Court's approval. Acting in 1993, the legislature approved a law, signed by Governor Ann Richards, that gave wealthy school districts several options for sharing revenue with poor districts. It was challenged both by rich districts, which objected to the requirement that they share their property wealth, and by poor districts, which argued that the new law was inadequately funded and didn't sufficiently reduce the funding gap between rich and poor districts.

The Texas Supreme Court upheld the 1993 law in a 5–4 decision in January 1995. In the majority opinion, Justice John Cornyn, a Republican, wrote that children from poor and wealthy school districts "now have substantially equal access to the funds necessary for a general diffusion of knowledge." But Republican Justice Craig Enoch, who dissented, said the state had failed to adequately provide for public education and warned of more funding problems because of the continued heavy reliance on local property taxes.[30]

In the late 1990s, the legislature increased funding for public education but failed to keep up with the increasing needs of a growing school enrollment. The property tax burden continued to increase, and by 2003, local property taxes were paying for about sixty percent of public education costs (see Table 13–3). The school finance system also was under attack again in court. A number of school districts had joined a suit in state district court, arguing that the 1993 law was unconstitutional because many districts had been forced to raise their property tax rates to or near the limit allowed by the state for school operations, $1.50 per $100 valuation. The districts argued that the situation amounted to, in effect, a state property tax, which was prohibited by the Texas Constitution. The districts also were seeking more state aid.

The Texas Supreme Court ruled in May 2003 that the districts were entitled to a trial of their suit, putting more pressure, some people believed, on the legislature to once again write a new school finance law. As the suit prepared to go to trial, legislative committees were studying school finance and other potential education changes.

TABLE 13–3   Sources of Funding for Public Education in Texas, 2002–2003

Originating Source	Receipts	Percent of Total
Local	$15,224,658,397	49.96
State	11,874,718,623	38.97
Federal	1,013,068,998	3.32
Other Local and Intermediate*	1,277,976,328	4.19
Total Revenue	**$29,390,422,346**	**96.45**
Equity Transfers	962,384,447	3.16
Other Resources	120,700,865	0.40
Total Receipts	**$30,473,507,658**	**100.0**

*Education Service Center and County.

Source: Texas Education Agency, *2002–2003 Budgeted Financial Data.*

Other Issues Affecting the Public Schools

Teacher Pay and Working Conditions.   The school districts' financial problems and other work-related stresses were taking their toll on schoolteachers. Thirty-eight percent of teachers were seriously considering quitting the profession in 1994, according to a survey by the Texas State Teachers Association (TSTA). Teachers complained of low pay, excessive paperwork and other administrative hassles, and poor student discipline.[31] The legislature raised the minimum teacher salary in 1995 and gave teachers an across-the-board pay increase in 1999. But according to the National Education Association, Texas still ranked only thirty-second in the country, with average teacher pay of $39,232 in 2001–2002.[32] The legislature in 2001 gave teachers a $1,000 annual allotment for health care insurance but cut that payment in half two years later to help balance a new state budget without raising state taxes.

Charter Schools.   Upon taking office in 1995, Governor George W. Bush advocated more innovation for local schools and less red tape for teachers and administrators. The legislature responded with a major rewrite of the education law to allow school districts and other groups to create charter schools that would be free of some state regulations. The charter school movement got off to a mixed start. Several had financial problems or were mismanaged and had to shut down after only brief periods of operation. But others flourished, strongly supported by parents and students who believed their innovative techniques enhanced the learning experience. Within a few years, some 260 charter schools were operating in Texas.

Virtual Charter Schools.   The growth of Internet use sparked interest in putting schools online, but the concept encountered strong opposition in Texas from teachers' groups, who argued that the state should raise teacher pay and make other improvements in public school classrooms before diverting tax dollars for programs that, at least initially, would benefit only a limited number of students. Legislation that would have authorized a pilot online education program was defeated by Texas lawmakers in 2003. That same year, more than 120 virtual schools were operating in other states.[33]

Private School Vouchers.   For several years, a number of legislators, primarily Republicans, have advocated a voucher program that would allow some public school children to attend private schools at state expense. The idea, supporters say, is to allow disadvantaged children from failing schools to have a chance at a quality education. But opponents, including public education groups, say such a program would unfairly divert money from the public schools at a time when public classrooms need more funding. Voucher bills have failed during several recent legislative sessions.

Social Promotions.   Governor Bush won legislative approval in 1999 of a requirement designed to end co-called "social promotions," the practice of promoting a child to a higher grade to keep up with other children of the same age. For the first time, public school students, beginning in the third grade, had to pass a standardized state test to be promoted. Previously, such a test had to be passed only as a condition for graduating from high school. The first group of third-graders affected by the new law did well when they took the test in 2003. Eighty-nine percent passed on the first administration of the test. Those who failed were given two other chances, and eventually 96 percent made the grade.

Home Schools.   In 1994, the Texas Supreme Court upheld the right of parents to educate their own children at home, ending a 10-year legal battle over the home school issue in Texas. The court said a home school was legitimate if parents met "basic education goals" and used a curriculum based on books, workbooks, or other written materials. It was reported at the time that nearly one million American families, including 100,000 in Texas, educated their children at home.[34]

Higher Education: The Quest for Excellence and Equity Continues

Texas has thirty-five state-supported, general academic universities; eight medical schools and health science centers; four public law schools; fifty community (or junior) college districts; and four campuses of the Texas State Technical College System. These institutions of higher learning serve more than one million students. They are governed by numerous policy-setting boards appointed by the governor or, in the case of community colleges, elected by local voters. The Texas Higher Education Coordinating Board, which is appointed by the governor, has oversight over university construction and degree programs.

The state makes no pretense that all its universities were created equal. The University of Texas at Austin and Texas A & M University at College Station are the state's largest universities, have higher entrance requirements than other schools, fulfill important research functions and, thanks to a constitutional endowment, have some of the state's best educational facilities. They receive revenue generated by the land- and mineral-rich **Permanent University Fund (PUF).** The University of Texas receives two-thirds of the money in the Available University Fund, which includes dividends, interest, and other income earned by the PUF, and Texas A & M receives one-third. University of Texas and Texas A & M regents can also pledge revenue to back bonds issued for land acquisition, construction, building repairs, purchase of capital equipment, and purchase of library materials for other campuses within the two university systems. Universities outside the two largest systems share in a separate building fund to which the legislature appropriates about $175 million a year.

Responding to a federal desegregation lawsuit, the state in the 1980s made a commitment to improve higher educational opportunities for minority students and employment opportunities for minority faculty members. More funding was provided for predominantly African-American Texas Southern University in Houston and Prairie View A & M University in nearby Waller County. Prairie View, which is part of the Texas A & M System, was guaranteed a special share of Available University Fund revenue in a constitutional amendment adopted in 1984. Texas agreed to a five-year desegregation plan with the U.S. Department of Education in 1983 and subsequently created the Texas Educational Opportunity Plan, under which traditionally Anglo schools, including the University of Texas at Austin and Texas A & M, increased minority recruitment efforts.

Residents of heavily Hispanic south Texas, however, challenged the state's distribution of higher education dollars. In a lawsuit filed in state district court in Brownsville in 1987, several Hispanic groups and individuals represented by the Mexican American Legal Defense and Educational Fund contended the state's higher education system discriminated against Mexican-American students by spending less on universities in the border area. The plaintiffs pointed out that there were no state-supported professional schools south of San Antonio and only one doctoral program—in bilingual education at Texas A & I University in Kingsville.

After the lawsuit was filed, Texas A & I, Laredo State University, and Corpus Christi State University were made part of the Texas A & M System, and Pan American University campuses in Edinburg and Brownsville were added to the University of Texas System. But efforts to negotiate a settlement of the suit failed, and it went to trial in late 1991 as a class action on behalf of all Mexican Americans who allegedly suffered or stood to suffer discrimination in higher education in the Mexican border area of Texas. In January 1992, state District Judge Benjamin Euresti Jr. of Brownsville ruled the higher education funding system unconstitutional because it discriminated against South Texas, but his ruling later was overturned by the Texas Supreme Court.[35]

Hopwood: A Temporary Setback to Affirmative Action

Texas's efforts to increase minority enrollments in its universities suffered a setback in 1996 when the Fifth U.S. Circuit Court of Appeals in New Orleans ruled that a race-based admissions policy previously used by the University of Texas School of Law was unconstitutional. The U.S. Supreme Court refused to grant the state's appeal and let the appellate court's decision stand. The so-called Hopwood case was named after lead plaintiff Cheryl Hopwood, one of four white students who sued after not being admitted into the law school.[36]

Then–Texas Attorney General Dan Morales held in 1997 that the Hopwood ruling went beyond the law school and prohibited all universities in Texas from using race or ethnicity as a preferential factor in admissions, scholarships, and other student programs. Morales's opinion was attacked as overly broad by many civil rights leaders and minority legislators, but it had the force of law.[37] The Texas legislature, meeting in 1997, attempted to soften the blow to affirmative action by enacting a new law that guaranteed automatic admissions to state universities for high school graduates who finished in the top 10 percent of their classes, regardless of their scores on college entrance examinations. The law was designed to give the best students from poor and predominantly minority school districts an equal footing in university admissions with better prepared graduates of wealthier school districts. The new law also allowed university officials to consider other admissions criteria, including a student's family income and parents' education level.

There was little change in minority enrollments at many Texas universities after the Hopwood decision because many universities hadn't used race as a factor in admissions anyway. But the two largest—the University of Texas at Austin and Texas A & M University—did. The drop-off in minority enrollment was particularly troubling at the UT law school the first year after the Hopwood restrictions went into effect. The first-year law class of almost 500 students in the fall of 1997 included only four African Americans and twenty-five Hispanics. There had been thirty-one African Americans and forty-two Hispanics in the previous year's entering class. And the more flexible admissions standards set by the legislature applied only to entering undergraduate students, not to those seeking admission to law school and other professional schools.[38]

Many higher education administrators and civil rights leaders said it was wrong to dismantle affirmative action programs that had been designed to improve educational and professional opportunities for minorities, who had historically suffered from segregation and were still overrepresented among the nation's poor. They said it was particularly shortsighted to de-emphasize minority recruitment efforts at a time when Hispanics and African Americans were only a few years away from making up a majority of the Texas population.

But Morales urged university officials to redouble their efforts to recruit disadvantaged students of all races. "We must express to young Texans the reality that in this country one is capable of rising as high as his or her individual talents, ability, and hard work will allow," he said.[39]

Finally, in 2003, the U.S. Supreme Court, ruling in a case from Michigan, effectively repealed Hopwood by holding that universities can use affirmative action programs to give minority students help in admissions, provided that racial quotas weren't used. The University of Texas, among other institutions, then began steps to develop new, race-based admissions criteria. Some legislators, meanwhile, wanted to put limits on the number of students who could be admitted to a university under the 10 percent law because it was restricting admissions options at the state's most desirable schools, including the University of Texas at Austin.

Tuition Deregulation: The Price of Admission Goes Up

With tax dollars becoming increasingly tight, University of Texas officials successfully lobbied the legislature in 2003 for a new law that, for the first time, gave individual university governing boards the freedom to set tuition rates independently of legislative action. Armed with the new tuition deregulation law, University of Texas regents approved a $360 a semester increase for fulltime UT-Austin students for the spring 2004 semester and, by varying amounts, also increased tuition at the UT system's other campuses. The increase raised the total bill, including fees, for an average fulltime undergraduate student from Texas attending UT-Austin to $2,595 a semester, and further increases were likely. But UT-Austin President Larry Faulkner said the higher tuition was still a bargain, compared to many other major universities around the country. "If you were to line up name-brand public institutions nationally, we're less expensive than they are by something like a thousand dollars a year," he said.[40] Other universities also began considering tuition increases.

CRIMINAL JUSTICE

Texas did away with public hangings on the courthouse square years ago but retained a frontier attitude toward crime and criminals, an attitude that produced a criminal justice system based more on revenge than rehabilitation (see "Witnessing Executions"). Politicians were elected to the legislature on tough, anticrime promises to "lock 'em up and throw away the key." Once in office, they passed laws providing long sentences for more and more offenses and built more prisons. Eventually, the system was overwhelmed by sheer numbers, and crime became a bigger problem than ever.

Legislators and most other state policymakers ignored deteriorating prison conditions until U.S. District Judge William Wayne Justice of Tyler declared the prison system unconstitutional in 1980 in a landmark lawsuit brought by inmates (***Ruiz v. Estelle***). He cited numerous problems, including overcrowded conditions, poor staffing levels, inadequate medical and psychiatric care for prisoners, and the use of so-called "building tenders"—inmates who were given positions of authority over other prisoners, whom they frequently abused. Justice ordered extensive reforms with which the state agreed to comply, and he appointed a monitor to help him supervise what was then known as the Texas Department of Corrections and is now the institutional division of the Texas Department of Criminal Justice.[41]

WITNESSING EXECUTIONS

After executions were resumed in Texas in 1982, they were witnessed by only a limited number of public officials plus as many as five people designated by the condemned, if he wished to have family members or friends present. Lobbying by crime victims' advocates convinced the Texas Board of Criminal Justice in 1995 to expand the witness list to include as many as five relatives or friends of the condemned's murder victim or victims. Survivors said watching their loved ones' killers be put to death could help bring "closure" to their ordeal. The witness viewing area in the small death chamber in Huntsville was partitioned to separate the condemned's witnesses from those of the victim.

The first execution to be witnessed by the victims' loved ones was that of Leo Ernest Jenkins on February 9, 1996. Jenkins had been sentenced to die by lethal injection for the August 1988 murders of Mark Brandon Kelley, 26, and his sister, Kara Denise Kelley Voss, 20, during a robbery of their family's pawn shop in Houston. The execution was witnessed by the victims' parents, Linda and Jim Kelley; their sister, Robin Amanda Kelley; their grandmother, Angie Kelley; and Mark Kelley's widow, Lisa.

"This is justice in a big way. Believe me, justice was served tonight," Linda Kelley, the victims' mother, said. "I was angry. I was angry at him [Jenkins] when he died."*

Dallas Morning News, February 10, 1996.

One key order by Justice limited the population of prison units to 95 percent of capacity to guard against a recurrence of overcrowding and to allow for the housing of inmates according to their classifications, which were designed to separate youthful, first-time offenders from more hardened criminals and those with special needs from the general prison population.

Crowded Prisons Prompt Reforms

The prison population limit and an increase in violent crimes in the 1980s helped produce a criminal justice crisis that lasted for several years. By the time the Ruiz lawsuit was settled in 1992 and the state given more flexibility over its prison operations, Texas had spent hundreds of millions of dollars building new prisons but still couldn't accommodate all the offenders flooding the system. Thousands of convicted felons were backlogged in overcrowded county jails because there wasn't enough room in the prisons. And hundreds of dangerous criminals were being paroled early to endanger and outrage law-abiding Texans.

Many of the convicts overloading the system were nonviolent, repeat offenders—among them alcoholics and drug addicts who continued to get in trouble because they were unable to function in the free world. Experts believed that alcoholism, drug addiction, or drug-related crimes were responsible for about 85 percent of the prison population.[42] At the urging of Governor Ann Richards in 1991, the legislature created a new alcoholism and drug abuse treatment program within the prison system, which planners hoped would reduce that recidivism.

In settling the *Ruiz* lawsuit in 1992, the state agreed to maintain safe prisons, and the federal court's active supervision of the prison system ended. Then, in 1993, the legislature enacted a major package of criminal justice reforms, including the first overhaul of the penal code in twenty years. The plan doubled the minimum time that violent felons would have to serve in prison—from one-fourth to one-half of their sentences—before becoming eligible for parole. To reserve more prison space for the most dangerous criminals, however, the legislature lowered the penalties for most property crimes and drug offenses. These nonviolent offenders were diverted to community corrections programs or a new system of state-run jails, to which they could be sentenced for a maximum of two years. To build 20,000 new state jail beds and additional prison units, the legislature and Texas voters also approved a $1 billion bond proposal in 1993. It was the fourth bond authorization, for a total of $3 billion, mostly for prison construction, that voters had approved in six years.

Senator John Whitmire of Houston, then-chairman of the Senate Criminal Justice Committee and an architect of the changes, said the new plan would not only be tough but also "smart" against crime. The changes were supported by some district attorneys, but other prosecutors and some law enforcement officers feared that the lighter penalties for many drug dealers and property criminals would boost the crime rate and make their jobs more difficult.

After taking office in 1991, Governor Richards directed her appointees to the Board of Pardons and Paroles to sharply curtail a parole rate that had been releasing several hundred inmates a week, including murderers and other violent offenders who might kill and rape again. Richards credited the reduction in paroles with a drop in the state's crime rate, but it also increased the backlog of convicted felons in many county jails to dangerously high levels. By early 1994, there were 30,000 state convicts packed into county jails because there was no room for them in state prisons, and several jails had erupted in prisoner disturbances.

The legislature authorized doubling the size of the prison system during the 1994–1995 budget period, and a construction boom was soon underway. Although prisons had traditionally been located in east Texas, new prisons were built throughout the state. Small cities and rural counties, seeking to recover from the recession of the 1980s and eager for the new jobs that prisons would provide, offered the state free land and other considerations in an intense lobbying frenzy. Private contractors also lobbied the Board of Criminal Justice, which chose the sites and granted the contracts.

More Trouble Ahead?

By the late 1990s, Texas had room for more than 150,000 inmates in its prisons, state jails, and substance abuse facilities, and the backlog of convicted felons in county jails was temporarily eliminated. But criminal justice experts warned the state would soon need even more prison space if the legislature didn't enact additional sentencing and parole reforms and attack crime among juveniles. And, sure enough, within a few years the prisons were full again. To partially address the problem, the State Board of Pardons and Paroles relaxed its rules to speed up the release of convicts who had been returned to prison for minor violations of their paroles, such as not reporting to their parole officers on time.

Fighting Juvenile Crime

Although the overall crime rate in Texas decreased in the early and mid-1990s, crime committed by juveniles increased. Republican George W. Bush, who unseated Richards in the 1994 gubernatorial election, made juvenile justice reform a campaign issue.

The legislature responded in 1995 with a far-reaching law that cracked down on juvenile offenders and offered some prevention programs to divert troubled children from lives of crime. The law lowered from fifteen to fourteen the age at which violent offenders could be tried as adults, and it expanded the list of offenses for which delinquents could receive fixed sentences in state facilities—up to forty years for the most violent. The measure also required any child expelled from school to be referred to juvenile court, encouraged local governments to enact more curfews for teenagers, and beefed up programs for runaway youths and other disadvantaged children.

By the late 1990s, the juvenile crime rate had started to drop, and the 1995 crackdown may have been a factor. But in the long run, many experts believed, the success or failure of public programs in education, health care, and welfare reform would be the determining factors in Texas's war on crime because many criminal offenders, in addition to being substance abusers, are poor and high school dropouts.

The Death Penalty: Still Popular in Texas

Texas continues to lead the nation in executions. More than 300 men and two women have been put to death in Texas since executions resumed in 1982 (see "A Woman's

A WOMAN'S EXECUTION

Most of the more than 300 executions that have been carried out in Texas since executions were resumed in 1982 have received only routine attention in the news media. But the scheduled execution of the 145th inmate—a woman and professed born-again Christian—attracted worldwide attention and renewed debate over the death penalty.

Karla Faye Tucker, 38, was sentenced to die for her role in the pickax murders of two Houstonians in 1983, two of the most gruesome murders in the city's history. As her execution date approached, she appealed for clemency on the basis that she had undergone a religious conversion and been rehabilitated while in prison. She won support from influential religious leaders and even from a former prosecutor involved in her case. But crime victims' advocates strongly supported her execution. The courts rejected her appeals, and the Texas Board of Pardons and Paroles refused her plea to have her death sentence commuted to life in prison. The particularly horrible nature of her crime apparently was a factor in the board's decision.

Tucker was put to death by lethal injection on February 3, 1998, in Huntsville. She was the first woman executed in Texas since the Civil War and only the second woman put to death in the United States since the resumption of the death penalty.

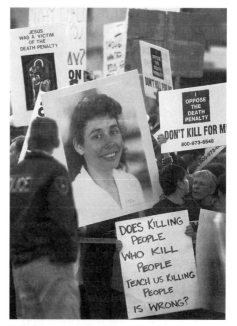

Death penalty protestors outside the Huntsville prison on the occasion of the execution of Karla Faye Tucker, the first woman to be put to death in Texas since the Civil War.

Another woman, Betty Lou Beets, a 62-year-old great-grandmother, was executed in Texas on February 24, 2000. She was put to death for the 1983 murder of Dallas firefighter Jimmy Don Beets, her fifth husband. Prosecutors said she shot him to death to collect his $110,000 pension and life insurance package.

Execution"). Death penalty opponents took advantage of Governor George W. Bush's presidential race in 2000 to focus international attention on the issue, but most Texans continued to support capital punishment.

According to a Scripps Howard *Texas Poll* conducted during the presidential race, 73 percent of Texans supported the death penalty, even though 57 percent of the respondents said they believed that innocent people had been executed. Nearly nine out of ten respondents said that death row inmates should have the right to obtain free DNA testing to try to prove their innocence.[43]

HEALTH AND HUMAN SERVICES

This area is where state government weighs compassion against the cold realities of its budget, and Texas has historically been stingy. Texas has traditionally spent less money per capita on health and welfare than most states. Even in the 1970s, when the oil industry was still pumping a healthy amount of tax revenue into the state treasury, Texas was slapped with two federal court orders for providing inadequate care to the mentally ill and the mentally retarded in state institutions. Perhaps the tight-fisted attitude springs from the legacy of frontier colonists standing on their own two feet to fight adversity and win a better life. This view has been perpetuated by countless politicians claiming that Texans could prevail in hard times by pulling up their bootstraps and hanging tough. But this perception ignores the reality that many people in modern Texas cannot pull their bootstraps because they don't have any boots. According to the 2000 census, approximately 15.4 percent of Texans—more than one of every seven—lived in poverty. Particularly hard hit were children, the elderly, and minorities (see Chapter 1).

Welfare Reform: The Jury Is Still Out

By the late 1990s, welfare changes designed to break the cycle of poverty were major priorities of both state and federal governments. New laws emphasized education and job training for welfare recipients and put limits on how long they could collect benefits. The Texas legislature in 1995 enacted a law that required recipients of public assistance to sign responsibility agreements and participate in educational or job training programs in order to receive benefits. It also imposed limits of one to three years on the time a person could collect welfare. The federal government enacted a more sweeping welfare reform law in 1996 that put a five-year lifetime limit on welfare benefits for most recipients and required able-bodied adults to go to work within two years of receiving assistance. The U.S. Congress abolished the Aid to Families with Dependent Children (AFDC) program, which had provided federal funds for every eligible welfare recipient since the 1930s. In its place, the states were given broad authority to design their own welfare programs with fixed amounts of federal money. The new federal law also gave the states quotas to meet in finding jobs for welfare recipients and eliminated most welfare benefits for immigrants.

It will take years to fully evaluate the effectiveness of the welfare changes, but early results in Texas were mixed. State officials reported that more than 100,000 people left Texas's welfare rolls during the first half of 1997 alone. But most of them were children, and not all of the adults quickly found jobs—or at least the kind of employment that would remove them from poverty. About half of the adults who left the welfare rolls had found new jobs, while 10 percent were earning more money from existing jobs, according to an October 1997 survey by the Texas Legislative Council. The legislative researchers said that state and federal welfare reforms had helped, but they concluded that the state's strong economy was the main reason former welfare recipients were finding jobs.[44]

The state agency primarily responsible for moving people from welfare to work was the Texas Workforce Commission, which coordinated job training programs for low-income Texans. Supporters credited the agency with helping reduce the state's welfare rolls by thousands of people. But critics said the agency was training too many people for menial, minimum-wage jobs that didn't pay enough to permanently remove them from poverty. They said the commission needed to offer more training for higher paying jobs that offered a more secure future. But state officials said the economy and private employers—not the government—determined the type of jobs available.[45]

The state's welfare reform law also required poor people to attend state-run classes on how to get a job before they could receive welfare payments. "The class had no textbook and no test," wrote a newspaper reporter who attended one of the early classes conducted by state work counselors in Austin. "But the lesson was clear: Texas expects you to try to get a job before asking for welfare."[46]

More than 275,000 Texas families had left the welfare rolls by 2000. But health care coverage had become a major problem for many of them, a study released that year indicated. The report by Families USA, a Washington-based advocacy group that supports universal health coverage, determined that 100,000 low-income Texas parents had lost Medicaid coverage since 1996. That was a 46 percent drop in adult Medicaid enrollees in Texas and the second-largest decline among the fifteen states that account for most of the country's uninsured people. Medicaid is a government-sponsored health insurance program for the poor. Although the study didn't determine whether people who left Medicaid had other health insurance, advocates for the poor said many of the people who left Medicaid were probably former welfare recipients who had taken low-paying jobs that didn't offer health insurance. "Only a small minority are lucky enough to land jobs that include an employer-paid health benefit," said Anne Dunkelberg, a health policy analyst at the Center for Public Policy Priorities, an Austin-based advocacy group for low- and middle-income people. "It's an unfortunate shortcoming of welfare reform that we can't guarantee folks that full-time work will get them access to health insurance."[47] State officials said some former welfare recipients could still be eligible for Medicaid but didn't know how many.

Health Insurance for Children

Another critical health care need in Texas is insurance coverage for children. Nearly one-fourth of Texas's 5.8 million children in 1999 didn't have health insurance, ranking Texas next to last among the states in that category. The legislature responded that year by creating the Children's Health Insurance Program, or CHIP, to provide low-cost health coverage to children of the working poor, those families who earned too much to qualify for Medicaid but couldn't afford insurance on their own. The program was open to children younger than nineteen whose families' annual income was no more than twice the poverty level, or $34,100 a year for a family of four. Legislators budgeted $179.6 million for the program in the 2000–2001 state budget, with each dollar the state spent drawing as much as $3 in federal matching funds.[48] In the 2001 legislative session, $122 million was appropriated to simplify and facilitate coverage of children eligible for Medicaid.

But thousands of children lost health insurance after the legislature in 2003 reversed course and imposed stricter rules for CHIP coverage to help close a $10 billion shortfall in the state budget. Within only a few months, enrollment had dropped by about 50,000. Average CHIP enrollment was expected to be about 347,000 in 2005, a one-third reduction from 2003.[49] Also by 2003, Texas led the nation in the percentage of uninsured residents, with one in four people, children and adults, lacking health insurance.[50] Critics said state legislators, in cutting back on CHIP coverage, were short-sighted because many children unable to receive preventive health care will end up in the emergency rooms of public hospitals, where treatment for serious, but preventable, illnesses will cost taxpayers even more.

Reorganizing Health and Human Services

The legislature in 2003 also ordered a major reorganization of the state's health and human services agencies. The goal of the most sweeping overhaul of social services in modern Texas history was to make state government smaller and save tax dollars through administrative changes and some privatization. Republican leaders who backed the changes predicted they would benefit both the needy recipients of state services and the taxpayers footing the bill. But advocates for the poor were skeptical. It would take several years to complete the consolidation of twelve agencies into five and assess the results, but the reorganization caught the immediate attention of the business community. Several dozen companies submitted bids for consulting contracts to help the state carry out the effort.

A Big Payoff from Tobacco

In a major health-related initiative, then–Texas Attorney General Dan Morales sued the tobacco industry in 1996, seeking billions of dollars in reimbursement for tax money spent to treat smoking-related illnesses. The suit also sought restrictions on tobacco companies' marketing and advertising that Morales said were targeting children.

Shortly before Texas's suit was scheduled to go to trial in early 1998, Morales and the tobacco industry negotiated a $17.3 billion settlement. Tobacco companies agreed to pay Texas and its county hospitals the huge sum over twenty-five years and end all their advertising on billboards and public transportation facilities in the state. The agreement called for Texas's first-year proceeds from the settlement, or about $1.2 billion, to be spent on antismoking and health care programs, mostly for children. Morales believed those expenditures were particularly important because health care had traditionally been underfunded in Texas and he considered the antitobacco suit a health care issue. The legislature agreed. Part of the money was used to fund the new Children's Health Insurance Program, described earlier in this section, and most of the remaining funds were used to create numerous health care–related endowments for medical schools and to establish an antismoking education program at the Texas Department of Health.

The way the legislature structured the antismoking education program, however, was controversial. Lawmakers put $200 million of the tobacco funds into an endowment, which budget writers said would ensure the most effective use of the money for years to come. Most health care providers and advocates supported that approach. But the American Cancer Society of Texas, the American Lung Association's Texas division, and the Campaign for Tobacco Free Kids objected because the $200 million endowment initially would generate only about $10 million a year that could actually be spent. The dissenting groups said that amount was woefully inadequate for developing effective antismoking programs in a state as large as Texas.

An even larger controversy, meanwhile, raged over $3.3 billion in legal fees awarded to a team of private plaintiffs' lawyers that Morales had hired on a contingency contract to represent the state in the tobacco suit. The fees were to be paid by tobacco companies, not by the state, over an undetermined number of years. And Morales insisted that the state couldn't have won the huge settlement without the lawyers' help. But then-Governor George W. Bush and other critics complained that the legal fees were excessive (see "Dan Morales: A Spectacular Rise and Fall" in Chapter 9).

Texas wasn't the only state to sue tobacco companies. Mississippi, Florida, and Minnesota also negotiated separate out-of-court settlements with the industry. And after Texas reached its settlement in 1998, cigarette companies negotiated a national $246 billion settlement with the remaining states.

ENVIRONMENTAL PROBLEMS AND POLICIES

Texas is blessed with an abundance of fragile natural resources that can no longer be taken for granted. But efforts to impose environmental regulations are difficult for a number of reasons. For one, Texas still has a large share of the nation's oil refining and chemical manufacturing industries, despite the 1980s oil bust. And while efforts have been made to reduce environmental risks, state policymakers are influenced by economic considerations because those same industries employ thousands of people and pump billions of dollars into the economy and the state treasury. Compounding the problem are the desire to attract new industries, a legacy that emphasizes individual property rights, and Texans' love for their automobiles, pickups, and sport utility vehicles.

Dirty Air

In a national environmental survey in 1992, *City & State* magazine ranked Texas forty-eighth of the fifty states in the quality of governmental programs protecting natural resources. "This is a state that will do what it can to attract and keep business, even if that means a price must be paid with increased pollution," the magazine said.[51] Texas received some additional notoriety in 1999 when Houston beat out Los Angeles for the unwanted title of the nation's "dirtiest air" city. Specifically, the Houston metropolitan area led the nation that year in the number of days—fifty-two—in which the city's air violated the national health standard for ozone, the main ingredient in smog. Los Angeles ended the year with forty-two violation days. Ozone, which contributes to respiratory health problems, is formed when various pollutants in the air mix in sunlight, and it can be a major problem on sunny, summer days.

Some progress has been made since then. For one thing, Los Angeles reclaimed its "dirtiest air" standing. Los Angeles recorded 49 days of smog reaching unhealthy levels in 2002, compared to 26 in Houston, that city's fewest number of days in 15 years.[52] But problems persist.

Unlike large cities in many other states, Texas cities have been slow to develop local rail transportation systems. Dallas only recently built one, and Houston is just getting started. Meanwhile, automobiles have increasingly clogged streets and freeways and spewed tons of pollutants into the air (see "Big Enough to Drive an SUV Through"). State officials responded with antipollution restrictions only after being forced to do so by the federal government. To meet federal Clean Air Act standards for smog reduction, the state now requires motorists in the Houston, Dallas-Fort Worth and certain other metropolitan areas to have special emissions inspections of their cars. And, speed limits on freeways and highways in metropolitan areas have been lowered to 55 miles per hour. In 2003, the legislature—to avoid losing millions

---

BIG ENOUGH TO DRIVE AN SUV THROUGH

The sport utility vehicles opposed by some environmentalists as fuel-guzzlers but popular, nevertheless, with many drivers may become even more commonplace on Texas's crowded roads and highways under a provision in the 2003 federal tax reduction law. That provision increased to $100,000 the tax deduction that small businesses could take for investments in new equipment, such as computers, photocopiers—or SUVs. The idea was to boost the economy with new equipment purchases, and auto dealers were certainly ready to help out. "It's a loophole, and this weekend we can show you how to make that loophole big enough to drive a fleet of trucks and sport utility vehicles through," invited one dealer's ads.

Source: Houston Chronicle, November 7, 2003, p. 8C.

---

of dollars in federal highway funding—also enacted a plan for raising state funds to pay for the emission reduction effort. The plan, among other things, increased the costs of auto title transfers and imposed surcharges on some large diesel equipment.

Many state political leaders also have preferred to encourage industries to voluntarily reduce pollution, rather than impose strict cleanup requirements. Then–Governor George W. Bush, for example, convinced the legislature in 1999 to enact a voluntary cleanup program for many of the old industrial facilities in Texas that still hadn't been brought into compliance with federal clean air standards. These facilities had been built before 1971 and had initially been "grandfathered" by lawmakers that year from the higher emission-control standards placed on new industrial plants. Environmentalists complained that many of the old facilities were major polluters and urged the legislature to require them to upgrade their equipment. But state lawmakers required only "grandfathered" power plants operated by utility companies to be upgraded while continuing voluntary compliance for the older plants in other industries. Legislators raised state emissions fees on the biggest polluters as an incentive for them to comply, but environmentalists complained that the higher fees would apply to only a handful of plants.[53]

An Endangered Water Supply

Population growth and a drought in the mid-1990s increased public concern over Texas's water supply. Much of the attention of environmentalists, farmers, ranchers, and government officials initially was focused on the underground Edwards Aquifer, the sole source of water for San Antonio and its rural neighbors. A major legal battle began in 1991, when the Sierra Club sued the federal government, contending the U.S. Interior Department had violated the Endangered Species Act. The environmentalists said the department had failed to guard against excessive pumping from the underground reservoir, which could endanger salamanders that live in the aquifer or aquifer-fed springs.

The lawsuit angered many San Antonians and farmers and ranchers. But U.S. District Judge Lucius Bunton of Midland ruled in favor of the Sierra Club,

SONGBIRDS IN DANGER

Virtually every elected statewide official, including some avowed environmentalists, protested strongly upon learning in 1994 that the U.S. Fish and Wildlife Service was considering setting aside parts of thirty-three central Texas counties as a protected habitat for the golden-cheeked warbler, an endangered songbird. The politicians were reacting to angry farmers and ranchers, who feared restrictions under the Endangered Species Act would limit their operations, and other concerned landowners, who were convinced their property values would plummet.

Several hundred Texans rallied at the state Capitol to demand legislation protecting private property rights. The issue was not new, but 1994 was an election year, and most state officials were on the ballot. Then–Lieutenant Governor Bob Bullock, who owned land in Llano County, one of the affected areas, purchased ads in local newspapers, siding with other landowners against "federal intrusion and regulatory overkill."

Environmentalists said state leaders were shortsighted. "The Endangered Species Act's protections actually enhance private property values by conserving the natural ecosystems and scenic beauty in our communities," said National Wildlife Federation president Jay D. Hair.* But Texas is a state in which many political candidates believe bird hunting (for doves) is a mandatory campaign activity. And, as one reporter noted in an article in the *Houston Chronicle:* "Golden-cheeked warblers can't vote. Even if they could, there are only a few thousand of the endangered birds left, not enough to make much of an impression on people running for statewide office in Texas."**

---

*Lone Star Chapter, Sierra Club, *State Capitol Report* 2, No. 16 (September 2, 1994), p. 5.
***Houston Chronicle*, August 28, 1994.

warning that overpumping not only threatened endangered species but also posed a contamination threat to the aquifer itself (see "Songbirds in Danger"). Bunton eventually ordered San Antonio and several smaller cities to reduce pumping from the aquifer, but his order was blocked in 1996 by the Fifth U.S. Circuit Court of Appeals in New Orleans.[54] In 1993, the Texas legislature created the regional Edwards Aquifer Authority with the power to regulate pumping from the aquifer and to protect the reservoir from pollution. The Texas Supreme Court upheld the state law in 1996, despite the objections of landowners who contended the state was ignoring their rights.[55]

Advocates of landowners' rights argued that any pumping limitations could damage the livelihoods of farmers and ranchers and adversely affect the San Antonio economy. Emotions ran high. Maurice Rimkus, a Uvalde County farmer, said of the Sierra Club: "It's a loose nut that's been cross-threaded on the bolt. They're a bunch of idealists living in a dream world."[56]

But environmentalists argued that more than salamanders were at stake. The future of San Antonio and the entire region was dependent on protecting water levels in the aquifer, they said. "San Antonio and the agricultural users have been in a state of denial for a number of years about the seriousness of the situation," said Ken Kramer, director of the Lone Star Chapter of the Sierra Club.[57] After the drought worsened in 1996, the legislature approved a comprehensive, statewide water conservation plan in 1997.

By 2003, the controversy over the Edwards Aquifer Authority was threatening to erupt anew. Just as the regional board was preparing to write regulations to protect water quality, developers began lobbying legislators to restrict its powers.[58] Another water issue also was beginning to attract attention. State Land Commissioner Jerry Patterson proposed leasing state lands to private companies, which would pump groundwater for sale to cities or other entities that needed it. Patterson said such leases could raise more money for public education, but critics questioned how much water a growing state could afford to sell.

Centralized Regulation

The legislature in 1993 centralized most of state government's environmental protection efforts into one agency, the Texas Natural Resource Conservation Commission, which consolidated separate agencies that had specialized in protecting water, air, and other selected resources. Both industrial interests and environmentalists generally preferred the new commission, later renamed the Texas Commission on Environmental Quality, over the fragmented regulatory system that it replaced. But some environmental leaders complained that the agency, in deciding the fate of new industrial permits, all too often favored economic development over environmental protection. "I do think that overall the agency tries to be balanced, but almost inevitably they really end up leaning a little too close to industry, in part because it has the [money] to plead its case day in and day out," said Sierra Club leader Ken Kramer. But Texas Chemical Council spokesman Jon Fisher believed the agency was fair. "The bottom line in an environmental regulatory agency is one that recognizes that their job is to protect the environment and not to harass business. Likewise you don't have to hurt the environment to protect business," Fisher said.[59]

SUMMARY AND CONCLUSIONS

1. The political power necessary to shape policy is exercised through groups, and some groups are more influential than others. Setting public policy also usually involves questions of costs and benefits. The ultimate political problem is who will benefit from specific policy decisions and who will pay the bill.

2. "Iron triangles" of state government—key legislators and their staffs, high-level bureaucrats, and interest group lobbyists—are at the center of the policymaking process. They also can be part of larger "issue networks" that reflect the increased interdependence of state and local governments on the federal government and the heightened role of issue specialists.

3. The legislature is primarily responsible for setting policy at the state level, but the separation of powers doctrine gives the judiciary important scrutiny over legislative action—or inaction. In recent years, federal and state court decisions have forced the legislature to make major changes in education, criminal justice, and mental health and mental retardation programs. These developments have compounded a state budgetary process already made difficult by a two-year budget cycle, a changing economy, and outdated tax and budgetary structures.

4. Although Texas recently spent billions of dollars on an unprecedented prison expansion program, most state leaders realize that new prisons alone won't solve the crime problem. More crucial in the long run will be the state's efforts to improve quality in the public schools and develop equity in school financing, because

many failures in the public school system soon enter the criminal justice system. State officials also recognize the importance of alcohol and drug abuse treatment programs in fighting criminal behavior.

5. Texas historically has been stingy in spending on health and human services programs, reflecting the individualistic political view that has long been dominant in the state. New federal and state laws require state officials to move thousands of poor people off the welfare rolls and into jobs, but welfare reform is a difficult task.

KEY TERMS

Issues networks

Deficit financing

Dedicated funds

Sales tax

Franchise tax

Property tax

Sin tax

Lottery

General obligation bond

Income tax

House Bill 72

No pass, no play

Edgewood v. Kirby

Permanent University Fund (PUF)

Ruiz v. Estelle

FURTHER READING

Articles

Burka, Paul, "You Lose Again!" *Texas Monthly* 26 (March 1998), pp. 108, 114–117.

Eckl, Corina, "The Cost of Corrections," *State Legislatures* 24 (February 1998), pp. 30–33.

King, Michael, "Who's Poisoning Texas: Part I?" *Texas Observer* 90 (April 24, 1998), pp. 8–12.

———, "Who's Poisoning Texas: Part II?" *Texas Observer* 90 (May 8, 1998), pp. 8–13.

Mandell, Jeff, "Privatizing Hopwood," *Texas Observer* 90 (January 16, 1998).

Somma, Mark, "Institutions, Ideology, and the Tragedy of the Commons: West Texas Groundwater Policy," *Publius* 27 (Winter 1997), pp. 1–13.

Texas Comptroller of Public Accounts, "School Daze: Finding the Right Equation," *Fiscal Notes,* March 1991, pp. 1–12.

Walters, Jonathan, "Did Somebody Say Downsizing?" *Governing* 11 (February 1998), pp. 17–20.

Books

Anton, Thomas J., *Federalism and Public Policy: How the System Works.* New York: Random House, 1989.

Cochran, Clarke E., Lawrence C. Mayer, T. R. Carr, and N. Joseph Cayer, *American Public Policy: An Introduction,* 5th ed. New York: St. Martin's Press, 1996.

Dye, Thomas R., *Understanding Public Policy,* 9th ed. Upper Saddle River, NJ: Prentice Hall, 1998.

Heclo, Hugh, "Issue Networks and the Executive Establishment," in *The New American Political System,* ed. Anthony King. Washington, DC: American Enterprise Institute, 1978.

Harpham, Edward J., "Welfare Reform and the New Paternalism in Texas," in *Texas Politics: A Reader,* ed. Anthony Champagne and Edward J. Harpham. New York: W.W. Norton, 1997.

Sharp, John, Texas Comptroller of Public Accounts, *A Report from the Texas Performance Review: Behind the Walls—The Price and Performance of the Texas Department of Criminal Justice.* Austin: Texas Comptroller of Public Accounts, 1994.

———, Texas Comptroller of Public Accounts, *Breaking the Mold: New Ways to Govern Texas: A Report from the Texas Performance Review,* 2 vols. Austin: Texas Comptroller of Public Accounts, 1991.

Thomas, Clark D., "Education Reform in Texas," in *Texas Politics: A Reader,* ed. Anthony Champagne and Edward J. Harpham. New York: W.W. Norton, 1997.

Weinstein, Bernard L., "Taxes in Texas," in *Texas Politics: A Reader,* ed. Anthony Champagne and Edward J. Harpham. New York: W. W. Norton, 1997.

Websites

Center for Public Policy Priorities   http://www. cppp.org   The center focuses on public policies affecting low- and middle-income people, including health care, child care, human services funding, welfare reform, and nutrition.

Common Cause of Texas http://www.ccsi.com/~comcause Common Cause is a nonpartisan, nonprofit citizens organization committed to "honest and accountable government." Reports, policy positions, and legislative alerts can be found at this site.

Consumers Union http://www.consumersunion.org This is an independent, nonprofit "testing and information organization serving only consumers." The organization's advocates testify before federal and state legislative and regulatory bodies on policies affecting consumers. The organization's communications and policy positions can be found at this site.

Sierra Club http://sierraclub.org/chapters/tx The Sierra Club has been actively involved in a number of statewide environmental issues. In addition to providing links to other sites, this site has policy reports and action alerts.

Texas Association of Business http://www.tabcc.org Committed to serving business interests in Texas, this site provides information on the organization's legislative program, legislative updates, and links to other legislative sources.

Texas Taxpayers and Research Association http://www.ttara.org This is an association of businesses and individuals interested in state fiscal policy and other public policy issues.

ENDNOTES

1. Lieutenant Governor Bob Bullock, January 31, 1991, responding to a reporter's question about how big a tax bill he believed the legislature would have to enact that year.
2. Thomas R. Dye, *Understanding Public Policy,* 8th edition (Upper Saddle River, NJ: Prentice Hall, 1998), p. 2.
3. This section draws primarily from L. L. Wade and R. L. Curry, Jr., *A Logic of Public Policy: Aspects of Political Economy* (Belmont, Calif.: Wadsworth Publishing Company, Inc., 1970), Chap. 1.
4. Ibid. See Chapter 1 for an excellent introduction to the definitional issues and approaches to public policy analysis.
5. The following discussion is organized around the general stages presented by James E. Anderson, David W. Brady, Charles S. Bullock, III, and Joseph Stewart, Jr., *Public Policy and Politics in America,* 2nd ed. (Monterey, CA: Brooks/Cole Publishing Company, 1984) and Charles O. Jones, *An Introduction to the Study of Public Policy,* 2nd ed. (North Scituate, MA: Duxbury Press, 1977).
6. James Anderson, et al., *Public Policy and Politics in America,* p. 8.
7. Jones, *An Introduction to the Study of Public Policy,* pp. 138–39.
8. Ibid., p. 139.
9. Randall B. Ripley and Grace A. Franklin, *Congress, the Bureaucracy, and Public Policy,* 3rd ed. (Homewood, IL: The Dorsey Press, 1984), p. 10.
10. Hugh Heclo, "Issue Networks and the Executive Establishment," in *The New American Political System,* ed. Anthony King (Washington, DC: American Enterprise Institute, 1978), p. 88. Much of this section is based on this article.
11. Ibid., p. 107.
12. Ibid., p. 104.
13. State of Texas, Legislative Budget Board, *Analysis of Federal Initiatives and State Expenditures,* June 15, 1994.
14. *Houston Chronicle,* April 22, 1991.
15. Michael P. Ettlinger, Robert S. McIntyre, Elizabeth A. Fray, John F. O'Hare, Julie King, and Neil Miransky, *Who Pays? A Distributional Analysis of the Tax Systems in All 50 States,* 2nd ed. (Washington, DC: Citizens for Tax Justice and the Institute on Taxation and Economic Policy, 2003), p. 9.
16. Texas Comptroller of Public Accounts, Texas Revenue History by Source, 1978–2002.
17. Ibid.
18. Interview with Texas Comptroller of Public Accounts' Office, November, 2003.
19. Ibid.
20. *Houston Chronicle,* December 17, 1997.
21. Interview with Texas Comptroller of Public Accounts' Office, November, 2003.
22. Ibid.
23. Ibid.
24. *Houston Chronicle,* January 16, 1989.
25. *Houston Chronicle,* March 7, 1991.
26. *The Texas Poll,* April 21, 1991, conducted for Harte-Hanks Communications, Inc., by the Public Policy Resources Laboratory of Texas A & M University.
27. *Houston Chronicle,* June 30, 1991.
28. *Edgewood Independent School District, et al. v. William Kirby, et al.,* 777 S.W. 2d 391 (1989).
29. Ibid.
30. *Edgewood Independent School District, et al. v. Lionel Meno, et al.,* 893 S.W. 2d 450 (1995).
31. Associated Press, *Houston Chronicle,* April 30, 1994.
32. National Education Association, news release, May 21, 2003.
33. Associated Press, November 4, 2003.
34. *Houston Chronicle,* June 16, 1994.

35. *Ann Richards, et al. v. League of United Latin American Citizens, et al.,* S.W. 2d 306 (1993).

36. *Hopwood, et al., v. State of Texas, et al.,* 78 F.3d 932 (1996).

37. *Houston Chronicle,* February 7, 1997.

38. *Houston Chronicle,* August 25, 1997.

39. *Houston Chronicle,* February 7, 1997.

40. *Austin American-Statesman,* October 18, 2003, p. B1.

41. *Ruiz v. Estelle,* 503 F.Sup. 1265 (1980).

42. *Houston Chronicle,* September 8, 1991.

43. The Scripps Howard *Texas Poll,* The Scripps Howard Data Center, June 2000.

44. *Houston Chronicle,* October 19, 1997.

45. *Dallas Morning News,* December 14, 1997.

46. *Austin American-Statesman,* December 6, 1997.

47. *Dallas Morning News,* June 20, 2000, p. 1A.

48. *Dallas Morning News,* April 8, 2000, p. 1A.

49. Center for Public Policy Priorities, "The Policy Page," Austin: Texas, November 9, 2003.

50. *Houston Chronicle,* November 12, 2003, p. 1A.

51. *City & State,* July 13, 1993, pp. SG2, SG6.

52. *Houston Chronicle,* September 24, 2003, p. 23A.

53. *Houston Chronicle,* May 31, 1999, p. 26A.

54. *Austin American-Statesman,* September 11, 1996.

55. Associated Press, *Dallas Morning News,* June 29, 1996.

56. *Austin American-Statesman,* June 13, 1994.

57. Ibid.

58. *San Antonio Express-News,* November 17, 2003, p. 6B.

59. *Austin American-Statesman,* September 9, 1996.

Glossary

Absentee (or early) voting A period before the regularly scheduled election date during which voters are allowed to cast ballots. With recent changes in election law, a person does not have to offer a reason for voting absentee.

Activists A small segment of the population that is engaged in various political activities.

Agenda building The process of groups or individuals identifying problems or issues that affect them and keeping pressure on policymakers to develop and implement public policy solutions.

Agenda setting A theory that the media's choice of which news events and issues to cover helps define what is important for the public to know and what issues to think about.

Age of Indifference A study published in 1990 by the Times-Mirror Center for the People and the Press, which concluded that young people are paying less attention to what's going on in the world than their parents did at their age. These findings are particularly ironic and disturbing since they come during the middle of the so-called "information age," when information is so readily available.

Agriculture commissioner An elected state official responsible for administering laws and programs that benefit agriculture.

Annexation The authority of cities to add territory, subject to restrictions set by state law.

Appellate jurisdiction The authority of a court to review the decisions of lower courts to determine if the law was correctly interpreted and legal procedures were correctly followed.

Appropriations bill A legislative action authorizing the expenditure of money for a public program or purpose. A general appropriations bill approved by the legislature every two years is the state budget.

At-large election A system under which city council members or other officeholders are elected by voters in the entire city, school district, or single-purpose district. Many of these election systems have been struck down by the federal courts or by the U.S. Justice Department under the Voting Rights Act as discriminatory against minorities.

Attorney general The state's chief legal officer. He or she represents the state in lawsuits, is responsible for enforcing the state's antitrust, consumer protection, and other civil laws, and issues advisory opinions on legal questions to state and local officeholders. This elected official has little responsibility for criminal law enforcement.

Bicameral legislature A law-making body, such as the Texas legislature, that includes two chambers.

Bifactionalism The presence of two dominant factions organized around regional, economic, or ideological differences within a single political party. For much of the twentieth century, Texas functioned as a one-party system with two dominant factions.

Bifurcated court system Existence of two courts at the highest level of the state judiciary. The Texas Supreme Court is the court of last resort in civil cases, and the Court of Criminal Appeals has the final authority to review criminal cases. Texas and Oklahoma are the only two states that use this system.

Block grants Federal grants of money to states and local governments for broad programs or services rather than narrowly defined programs. These grants give state and local governments more discretion over the use of the funds.

Bureaucracy The agencies of government and their employees responsible for carrying out policies and providing public services approved by elected officials.

Calendar The agenda or the list of bills to be considered by the House or the Senate on a given day.

Campaign consultant A professional expert who helps political candidates plan, organize, and run their campaigns.

Capital murder Murder committed under certain circumstances for which the death penalty or life in prison must be imposed.

Capitol press corps Representatives of Texas newspapers, television and radio stations, and wire services who are assigned to Austin full time to report on state government and politics.

Categorical grants-in-aid Grants of federal money that can be spent only for specific programs or purposes. This is the source of most federal assistance to state and local governments.

Caucus A group of legislators who band together for common political or partisan goals or along ethnic or geographic lines.

City charter A document, defined or authorized by state law, under which a city operates. In Texas home rule cities, local voters may choose among several forms of city government.

City commission A form of city government in which elected commissioners collectively serve as a city's policy-making body and individually serve as administrative heads of different city departments. Although once popular, this form of government is rarely used in Texas today.

City, general law Texas cities with fewer than 5,000 residents are allowed to exercise only those powers specifically granted to them by the legislature. Most cities in Texas are classified as general law cities.

City, home rule Texas cities with more than 5,000 residents can adopt any form of government residents choose, provided it does not conflict with the state constitution or statutes. Home rule powers are formalized through local voters' adoption of a city charter spelling out how the city is to be governed.

Civil lawsuit A noncriminal legal dispute between two or more individuals, businesses, governments, or other entities.

Commissioners court The principal policy-making body for county government. It sets the county tax rate and supervises expenditures.

Committee A group of legislators who review and hold public hearings on issues or bills they are assigned by the presiding officer in the House or Senate. Committees normally specialize in bills by subject matter and are designated standing committees. A bill has to win committee approval before it can be considered by the full House or Senate. Most bills die in committee, which serves as a legislative screening process.

Committee, Calendars A special procedural committee in the Texas House of Representatives that schedules bills that already have been approved by other committees for floor debate.

Committee, conference A panel of House members and senators appointed to work out a compromise on a bill if different versions of the legislation were passed by the House and the Senate.

Committee, select A special committee—usually appointed by the governor, the lieutenant governor, and the speaker—that studies a specific issue and makes recommendations to the legislature. This panel usually includes private citizens as well as legislators.

Committee, standing A legislative committee that specializes in bills by subject matter. A bill has to win committee approval before it can be considered by the full House or Senate.

Compact theory The view that governments originated from the general agreement among and consent of members of the public to address common interests and needs.

Comptroller of Public Accounts The state's primary tax administrator and revenue estimator. It is an elective position.

Confederation A system in which each member government is considered sovereign, and the national government is limited to powers delegated to it by its member governments.

Constable An elected law enforcement officer assigned as an administrative officer in a justice of the peace precinct. He or she is responsible primarily for executing court judgments, serving subpoenas, and delivering other legal documents. Constables also are authorized to patrol their precincts, make arrests, and conduct criminal investigations.

Constitution Legal structure of a political system, establishing government bodies and defining their powers.

Constitution, Civil War The constitution adopted by Texans after the state seceded from the Union and joined the Confederacy in 1861.

Constitution of Coahuila y Tejas The first of seven constitutions under which Texas has been governed. Adopted in 1824 and implemented in 1827 by the Republic of Mexico, it recognized Texas, then being colonized by Anglo settlers under Stephen F. Austin, as a Mexican state with Coahuila, its neighbor south of the Rio Grande.

Constitution of 1845 The constitution under which Texas was admitted to the United States.

Constitution of 1866 The short-lived constitution under which Texas sought to be readmitted to the Union after the Civil War and before the Radical Reconstructionists took control of Congress.

Constitution of 1876 The Texas constitution adopted at the end of Reconstruction, while Texas was still a rural, frontier state. Amended many times since, it remains in effect today. It is a highly restrictive, anti-government document drafted by Texans reacting to the abuses of the Radical Reconstructionists and the oppressive administration of Governor Edmund J. Davis. Tight restrictions placed on the governor, the legislature, and other state officials inhibit the ability of state government to respond to the complex needs of what is now a growing, urban state.

Constitution of the Republic The constitution adopted March 16, 1836 by Texas colonists declaring independence from Mexico and its military dictator, Santa Anna. It was the same charter under which Texas functioned as an independent republic for nine years.

Constitution, Reconstruction Drafted in 1869, this constitution centralized power in state government while weakening local governments. It didn't reflect the sentiments of most Texans, but it conformed to the wishes of the Radical Reconstructionists.

Constitutional amendments A change in the constitution that is proposed by the legislature and subject to vote approval.

Constitutional Convention of 1974 The last major attempt to write a new Texas constitution. Members of the legislature served as delegates and failed to overcome political differences and the influence of special interests.

Constitutional county courts The Texas Constitution provides for 254 courts with limited jurisdiction and held by an elected county judge.

Cooperative federalism Policies emphasizing cooperative efforts among the federal, state, and local governments to address common problems and provide public services to the citizens.

Co-optation Influence over state regulatory boards by the industries they are supposed to regulate, often to the detriment of the general public.

Council-manager government A form of city government in which policy is set by an elected city council, which hires a professional city manager to head the daily administration of city government.

Council of government A council comprising representatives of other governments in a defined region of the state. There are twenty-four of these regions in Texas, and these councils serve to encourage cooperation, coordination, and planning among local governments and to provide services to the participating governments.

County attorney An elected official who is the chief legal officer of some counties. He or she also prosecutes lesser criminal offenses, primarily misdemeanors, in county courts.

County auditor An officer appointed by the district judges of the county. This person is primarily responsible for reviewing every bill and expenditure of a county to assure it is correct and legal. All counties with 10,000 or more residents are required to have an auditor, and smaller counties may have one if commissioners court chooses. In counties with more than 225,000 people, the auditor is also the budget officer who prepares the county budget for consideration by commissioners court.

County chair The presiding officer of a political party's county executive committee. He or she is elected countywide by voters in the party primary.

County clerk The chief record-keeping officer of a county.

County court, constitutional (*See* County judge.)

County court-at-law, statutory A court created by the legislature that exercises limited jurisdiction over criminal and/or civil cases. The jurisdiction of these courts varies from county to county.

County executive committee A panel responsible on the local level for the organization and management of a political party's primary election. It includes the party's county chair and each precinct chair.

County judge The presiding officer of a county commissioners court. This office also has some judicial authority, which is assumed by separate county courts-at-law in most urban counties.

County tax assessor-collector An elected official who determines how much property tax is owed on the different pieces of property within a county and then collects the tax. This officeholder acts on the basis of property values determined by the county appraisal district and a tax rate set by county commissioners court.

County treasurer An elected officer who is responsible for receiving and disbursing county funds. The office's primary functions are now carried out by the county auditor, and the office has been eliminated in a number of counties.

Court of Appeals An intermediate level court that reviews civil and criminal cases from the district courts.

Court of Criminal Appeals A Texas nine-member court with final appellate jurisdiction over criminal cases.

Dealignment A view that the party system is breaking up and the electoral influence of political parties is being replaced by interest groups, the media, and well financed candidates who use their own media campaigns to dominate the nomination and election process.

Dedicated funds   Constitutional or statutory requirements that restrict some state tax or fee revenues to spending on specific programs.

Deficit financing   Borrowing money to meet operating expenses. It is prohibited by the Texas constitution, which provides that state government operate on a pay-as-you-go basis.

Delegated powers   These are powers specifically assigned to the national, or federal, government by the U.S. Constitution, including powers to tax, borrow and coin money, declare war, and regulate interstate and foreign commerce.

Denied powers   Powers that are denied to both the states and national government. The best known restrictions are listed in the Bill of Rights.

Devolution   Return of powers assumed by the federal government to the states.

Dillon rule   A principle holding that local governments are creations of state government and their powers and responsibilities are defined by the state.

District attorney   An elected official who prosecutes the more serious criminal offenses, usually felonies, before state district courts.

District court   Court with general jurisdiction over criminal felony cases and civil disputes.

Economic diversification   The development of new and varied business activities. New businesses were encouraged to relocate or expand in Texas after the oil and gas industry, which had been the base of the state's economy, suffered a major recession in the 1980s.

Edgewood v. Kirby   A lawsuit in which the Texas Supreme Court in 1989 declared the Texas school finance system unconstitutional because of wide disparities in property wealth and educational opportunities between school districts.

Editorial autonomy   The freedom of a local newspaper or television station to set its own news policies independently of absentee owners who may run a chain of media outlets throughout the country.

Election, general   An election for state, federal, and county offices held in November of even-numbered years. The ballot includes nominees of the two major political parties plus other candidates who meet certain legal requirements.

Election, local   An election for city council, the school board, and certain other local offices. Most of these are nonpartisan.

Election, primary   An election in which the Democratic or Republican party chooses its nominees for public offices. In presidential election years, the primary also plays a key role in selecting Texas delegates to the parties' national nominating conventions.

Election, retention   Elections in which judges run on their own records rather than against other candidates. Voters cast their ballots on the question of whether the incumbent judge should stay in office.

Election, rollback   An election in which local voters can nullify a property tax increase that exceeds 8 percent in a given year.

Election, runoff   This is required if no candidate receives an absolute majority of the votes cast in a primary race. The runoff is between the top two vote-getters.

Election, special   An election set by the legislature or called by the governor for a specific purpose, such as voting on constitutional amendments or filling a vacancy in a legislative office. Local governments can also call special elections.

Elitism   The view that political power is primarily held by a few individuals who derive power from leadership positions in large business, civic, or governmental institutions.

Establishment, The   In the days of one-party Democratic politics in Texas, it was a loosely knit coalition of Anglo businessmen, oilmen, bankers, and lawyers who controlled state policymaking through the dominant, conservative wing of the Democratic party.

Extradition   A process by which a person in one state can be returned to another state to face criminal charges.

Extraterritorial jurisdiction   The power of an incorporated city to control development within nearby unincorporated areas.

Fat cat   An individual who contributes a large amount of money to political candidates.

Federalism   A system that balances the power and sovereignty of state governments with the national government. Both the states and the national government derive their authority directly from the people, and the states have considerable autonomy within their areas of responsibility.

Felony   A criminal offense that can be punished by imprisonment and/or a fine. This is a more serious offense than a misdemeanor.

Filibuster   A procedure that allows a senator to speak against a bill for as long as he or she can stand and talk. It can become a formidable obstacle or threat against controversial bills near the end of a legislative session.

Full faith and credit   A provision in the U.S. Constitution (Article IV, Section 1) that requires states to recognize civil judgments and official documents rendered by the courts of other states.

General obligation bonds   A method of borrowing money to pay for new construction projects, such as prisons or mental hospitals. Interest on these bonds, which require voter approval in the form of constitutional amendments, is paid with tax revenue.

Gerrymandering   The drawing of political districts in such a way as to reduce the effect of voting by members of an ethnic or political minority.

Globalization of the economy   Increased interdependence in trade, manufacturing, and commerce between the United States and other countries.

Governor   The state's top executive officeholder.

Governor E. J. Davis   The Reconstruction era governor of Texas who was alleged by his opponents and many historians to have been one of the most abusive governors in American history. After his election in 1869, he convinced a Radical majority in the legislature to impose a series of authoritarian laws, including measures to create an oppressive state police force and give the governor the power to declare martial law. He was defeated by Texas voters in 1873 but left office only after armed militia marched on the Capitol.

Grand jury   Panel that reviews evidence submitted by prosecutors to determine whether to indict, or charge, an individual with a criminal offense. A grand jury can hear witnesses, but all its meetings are in private.

Grange   An organization formed in the late nineteenth century to improve the lot of farmers. Its influence in Texas after Reconstruction was felt in constitutional provisions limiting taxes and government spending and restricting banks, railroads, and other big businesses.

Grant, formula   A federal grant based on specific criteria such as income levels or population.

Grant, project   A federal grant for a defined project.

Grassroots   A term used to describe a wide range of political activities designed to organize and mobilize the electorate at the local level. While modern campaigns are increasingly dominated by the campaign consultants, such support can prove crucial for political candidates, particularly for those with limited financial resources.

House Bill 72   A landmark school reform law enacted in 1984. Among other things, it reduced class sizes, required teachers to pass a literacy test to keep their jobs, and imposed the no pass, no play rule, which restricts failing students from participating in extracurricular activities.

Hyperpluralism   The rapid expansion of interest groups that serves to disrupt and potentially deadlock the policy-making process.

Impeachment   A procedure by which the legislature can remove a governor or certain other public officials from office for misconduct. It is the first of two stages of the removal process and is essentially the political equivalent of an indictment.

Implied powers Although not specifically defined by the U.S. Constitution, these are powers assumed by the national government as necessary in carrying out its responsibilities.

Independent school district A specific form of special district that administers the public schools in a designated area. It is governed by an elected board of trustees empowered to levy local property taxes, establish local school policies, and employ a school superintendent as its chief administrator.

Indictment A written statement issued by a grand jury, charging a person or persons with a crime or crimes.

Individualism An attitude, rooted in classical liberal theory and reinforced by the frontier tradition, that citizens are capable of taking care of themselves with minimal governmental assistance.

Individualistic subculture A view that government should interfere as little as possible in the private activities of its citizens while assuring that adequate public facilities and a favorable business climate are available to permit individuals to pursue their self interests.

Influence-peddling The abuse of public office by elected or appointed officials who bend the rules or provide special treatment for certain individuals or groups in return for bribes or favors.

Information age A reference to the contemporary era where there has been an explosion of information available through new information technologies.

Initiative A petition and election process where voters propose laws or constitutional amendments for adoption by a popular vote.

Institutionalization The complex process of institutional change and adaptation in the organization and operations of the legislature.

Interest group A group of people with common goals who are organized to seek political

results they are unable to achieve by themselves.

Interstate compacts Formal, long-term cooperative agreements among the states dealing with common problems or issues and subject to approval of the U.S. Congress.

Iron rule of oligarchy A theory developed by Robert Michels, a European sociologist, that all organizations inevitably are dominated by a few individuals.

Iron triangles Relationships among the interest groups, the administrative agencies, and the legislative committees involved in drafting the laws and regulations affecting a particular area of the economy or a specific segment of the population.

Issue networks Term coined by Hugh Heclo to describe the complex institutional and political relationships in the policy-making process.

Issue-attention cycle A pattern in which public interest in an issue or problem is heightened by intensive media coverage. Media attention and public interest will wane after government takes steps to address their concerns, but most issues or problems are never permanently resolved. Another crisis, perhaps years later, will restart the cycle.

Jim Crow laws Legislation enacted by many states after the Civil War to limit the rights and power of African Americans.

Justice of the peace court A low-ranking court with jurisdiction over minor civil disputes and criminal cases.

Land commissioner An elected official who manages the state's public lands and administers the Veterans Land Program, which provides low interest loans to veterans for the purchase of land and houses.

Legislative norms Unwritten rules of the legislature that define roles and behaviors of lawmakers.

Legislature The lawmaking branch of state government. In Texas, it includes a 150-member House of Representatives and a 31-member Senate elected from districts throughout the state.

Licensing A key regulatory function of government that seeks to ensure that individuals and companies providing critical professional services to the public are properly trained or qualified.

Lieutenant governor The presiding officer of the Senate. This officeholder also becomes governor if the governor dies, becomes incapacitated, or is removed from office.

Limited government The constitutional principle restricting governmental authority and spelling out personal rights.

Lobbying An effort, usually organized and using a variety of strategies and techniques, to influence the making of laws or public policy.

Lottery A form of gambling, conducted by many states, in which participants purchase tickets that offer an opportunity to cash in on a winning number or set of winning numbers. Voters legalized a state lottery in Texas in 1991.

Mandamus, writ of A court order directing a lower court or another public official to take a certain action.

Mandates Federal laws or regulations that require state or local governments to take certain actions, often at costs that the federal government doesn't reimburse. The state government also imposes mandates on local governments.

Maquiladora Program Economic program initiated by Mexico to increase manufacturing and the assembly of goods.

Matching funds Money that states or local governments have to provide to qualify for certain federal grants.

Mayor, strong A form of city government that gives the mayor considerable power, including budgetary control and appointment and removal authority over city department heads.

Mayor, weak A form of city government in which the mayor shares authority with the city council and other elected officials but has little independent control over city policy or city administration.

Media bias A perception—sometimes real, sometimes imagined—that reporters and news organizations slant their news coverage to favor one side or the other in particular issues or disputes.

Media, controlled Paid advertising in the media whose content and presentation are determined by a political candidate or campaign.

Media event An event staged by an officeholder or political candidate that is designed to attract media—especially television coverage.

Media, uncontrolled Media coverage by newspaper, magazine, television, and radio reporters over which a political candidate or campaign has no control.

Merit selection A proposal under which the governor would appoint state judges from lists of potential nominees recommended by committees of experts. Appointed judges would have to run later in retention elections to keep their seats but wouldn't have opponents on the ballot. Voters would simply decide whether a judge should remain in office or be replaced by another gubernatorial appointee.

Merit system A personnel system under which public employees are selected for government jobs through competitive examinations and the systematic evaluation of job performance.

Metro government Consolidation of city and county governments to avoid duplication of public services. This approach has been tried in several other parts of the country but so far has attracted little interest in Texas.

***Miranda* ruling** A far-reaching decision of the U.S. Supreme Court that requires law enforcement officers to warn a criminal suspect of his right to remain silent and have an attorney present during questioning.

Mischief of factions Term coined by James Madison to describe the complex relationships among groups and interests within the American political system and the institutional arrangements that potentially balance the power of groups.

Misdemeanor A minor criminal offense punishable by a fine or a short sentence in the county jail.

Moralistic subculture   A view that government's primary responsibility is to promote the public welfare and should actively use its authority and power to improve the social and economic well-being of its citizens.

Motor voter registration   Term referring to federal and state laws that allow people to register to vote at offices where they receive their driver's licenses.

Municipal court   Court of limited jurisdiction that hears cases involving city ordinances and primarily handles traffic tickets.

Myths   Stories, narratives, or phrases used to describe past events, explain their significance, and help provide an understanding of a society's culture, its political history, and institutional arrangements.

Negative television advertisements   Television commercials in which political candidates attack their opponents, sometimes over a legitimate issue, but more often over an alleged flaw in their opponent's character or ability to hold office. Many such ads are deliberately misleading or outright false.

New federalism   A term used to describe recent changes in federal-state relationships. Used primarily by conservative presidents, it suggests a devolution or return of power to the states and a decreased role of the federal government in domestic policy.

Nolo contendere   A plea of no contest to a criminal charge.

No pass, no play rule   A student failing a course is restricted from participating in extracurricular activities.

Norms   Unwritten rules of institutional behavior that are critical to its stability and effectiveness.

North American Free Trade Agreement   Treaty signed in 1993 to lower trade barriers among the United States, Mexico, and Canada and to create a common economic market. It is widely referred to as NAFTA.

Ombudsman   A special assistant to an elected official or designated employee in a state agency who handles citizen complaints about government.

One-party system   The domination of elections and governmental processes by a single party, which may be split into different ideological, economic, or regional factions. In Texas, the phrase is used to describe the period from the late 1870s to the late 1970s, when the Democratic party claimed virtually all elected, partisan offices.

Open meetings-open records acts   Laws that require state and local governmental bodies to conduct most of their actions in public and maintain records for public inspection.

Original jurisdiction   The authority of a court to try or resolve a civil lawsuit or a criminal prosecution being heard for the first time.

Pack journalism   The tendency of news organizations to cover the same elements of major stories and issues and of reporters to swarm key figures when major news is breaking.

Parole   The early release of an inmate from prison, subject to certain conditions.

Party activist   Member of a political party involved in organizational and electoral activities.

Pay-as-you-go principle   A constitutional prohibition against state government borrowing money for its operating budget.

Penal code   A body of law that defines most criminal offenses and sets a range of punishments that can be assessed.

Permanent University Fund   A land- and mineral-rich endowment that benefits the University of Texas and Texas A & M University systems, particularly the flagship universities in Austin and College Station.

Petition for review   Petition to Texas Supreme Court that legal or procedural mistakes were made in the lower court, thus meriting a hearing before the court.

Petit jury   A panel of citizens that hears evidence in a civil lawsuit or a criminal prosecution and decides the outcome by issuing a verdict.

Platform   A set of principles or positions on various issues adopted by a political party at its state or national convention.

Plea bargain   A procedure that allows a person charged with a crime to negotiate a guilty plea with prosecutors in exchange for a lighter sentence than he or she would expect to receive if convicted in a trial.

Plural executive A fragmented system of authority under which most statewide, executive officeholders are elected independently of the governor. This arrangement, which is used in Texas, places severe limitations on the governor's power.

Pluralism Theories holding that a diversity of groups—and people—are instrumental in the policy-making process, and no one group is able to dominate the decisions of government.

Political action committee Often referred to as a PAC, this is a committee representing a specific interest group or including employees of a specific company that raises money from its members for distribution to selected officeholders and political candidates.

Political culture A widely shared set of views, attitudes, beliefs, and customs of a people as to how their government should be organized and run.

Political myths Generally held views rooted in the political culture that are used to explain the common historical and cultural experiences.

Political party A group that seeks to elect public officeholders under its own name.

Political patronage The hiring of government employees on the basis of personal friendships or favors rather than ability or merit.

Political socialization The process that begins in early childhood whereby a person assimilates the beliefs, attitudes, and behaviors of society and acquires views toward the political system and government.

Poll tax A tax that Texas and some other states used to require people to pay before allowing them to vote. The purpose was to discourage minorities and poor whites from participating in the political process. The tax was declared unconstitutional in the 1960s.

Popular sovereignty The constitutional principle of self-government; the belief that the people control their government and governments are subject to limitations and constraints.

Population density Number of persons residing within a square mile.

Precinct A specific, local voting area created by county commissioners court. The state election code outlines detailed requirements for drawing up these election units.

Precinct chair A local officer in a political party who presides over the precinct convention and serves on the party's county executive committee. Voters in each precinct elect a chair in the party's primary election.

Precinct convention A meeting held by a political party in each precinct on the same day as the party primary. In presidential election years, the precinct conventions and the primaries are the first steps in the selection of delegates to the major parties' national nominating conventions.

Preemptions Federal laws that limit the authority or powers of state and local governments.

Privatization Government contracting with private companies to provide some public services.

Privileges and immunities The right of a resident of one state to be protected by the laws and afforded the legal opportunities in any other state he or she visits. Certain exceptions, however, have been allowed by the courts, including the right of states to charge nonresidents higher college tuition or higher hunting and fishing license fees.

Probation A procedure under which a convicted criminal isn't sent to prison if he or she meets certain conditions, such as restrictions on travel and with whom he or she associates.

Prosecution The conduct of legal proceedings against an individual charged with a crime.

Public Improvement District Specific area of a city in which property owners pay special taxes in return for improvements to streets and other public facilities in their neighborhood.

Public interest groups Groups that are primarily concerned with consumer or environmental protection, the promotion of strong ethical standards for public officials, or increased funding for health and human services programs. Since they often are poorly funded, grassroots, volunteer efforts are crucial to their success.

Public opinion polling   The scientific compiling of people's attitudes toward business products, public issues, public officeholders, or political candidates. It has become a key ingredient of statewide political campaigns and is usually conducted by telephone using a representative sample of voters.

Radical Reconstructionists   The group of Republicans who took control of Congress in 1866 and imposed hated military governments on the former Confederate states after the Civil War.

Radical right   Extreme philosophical right that is often characterized by its position on market economics and social or "life-style" issues.

Railroad Commission   A three-member, elected body that regulates oil and natural gas production and lignite mining in Texas.

Reading, first   The introduction of a bill in the House or the Senate and its referral to a committee by the presiding officer.

Reading, second   Initial debate by the full House or Senate on a bill that has been approved by a committee.

Reading, third   Final presentation of a bill before the full House or Senate.

Realignment   A major shift in political party support or identification, which usually occurs around a critical election. In Texas, this was a gradual transformation from a one-party system dominated by Democrats to a two-party system in which Republicans became the dominant party statewide.

Record vote   A vote taken in the House or the Senate of which a permanent record is kept, listing how individual legislators voted. By contrast, there are voice votes where legislators simply voice ayes or nays on an issue without being permanently recorded.

Redistricting   The process of redrawing legislative and other political district boundaries to reflect changing population patterns. Districts for the Texas House, state Senate,

and U.S. Congress are redrawn every ten years by the legislature.

Referendum   An election, usually initiated by a petition of voters, where an action of a legislative body is submitted for approval by the voters.

Regressive tax system   A tax system that imposes a disproportionately heavier burden on low-income people than on the more affluent.

Regular session   The 140-day period in odd-numbered years in which the legislature meets and can consider laws on any issue or subject.

Religious Right   An ultraconservative political faction that draws considerable support from fundamentalist religious groups and economic conservatives.

Republic   A political system in which sovereign power resides in the citizenry and is exercised by representatives elected by and responsible to them.

Reserved powers   Powers given state governments by the Tenth Amendment. These are powers not delegated to the national government nor otherwise prohibited to the states by the Constitution.

Revenue sharing   A program begun under President Nixon and later repealed in which state and local governments received federal aid that could be used for virtually any purpose the recipient government wanted.

Revolving door   The practice of former members of state boards and commissions or key employees of agencies leaving state government for more lucrative jobs with the industries they used to regulate. It raises questions of undue industry influence over regulatory agencies.

Right-to-work law   Law prohibiting the requirements of union membership in order to get or hold a job.

Ruiz* v. *Estelle   A lawsuit in which a federal judge in 1980 declared the Texas prison system unconstitutional and ordered sweeping, expensive reforms.

Secretary of state   Administers state election laws, grants charters to corporations, and processes the extradition of prisoners to other states. This officeholder is appointed by the governor.

Senatorial courtesy An unwritten policy that permits a senator to block the confirmation of a gubernatorial appointee who lives in the senator's district.

Separation of powers The division of authority among three distinct branches of government—the legislative, the executive, and the judicial—which serves as checks and balances on each other's power.

Session, regular This is the 140-day period in odd-numbered years in which the legislature meets and can consider and pass laws on any issue or subject.

Session, special A legislative session that can be called at any other time by the governor. It is limited to thirty days and can consider only subjects or issues designated by the governor.

Sharpstown stock fraud scandal After rocking state government in 1971 and 1972, it helped produce some far-reaching legislative and political changes. It involved the passage of banking legislation sought by Houston financier Frank Sharp and quick profits that some state officials made on stock purchased in an insurance company owned by Sharp with unsecured loans from Sharp's Sharpstown State Bank.

Sheriff An elected official who is the chief law enforcement officer of a county. In urban areas, his or her jurisdiction usually is limited to the unincorporated areas of a county, while local police departments have jurisdiction over incorporated cities.

Shield law A law that protects a news reporter from having to disclose confidential sources of information to a court. A number of states have such laws, and some media representatives were lobbying for a similar law in Texas.

Single-issue group A single purpose or highly ideological group that promotes a single issue or cause with only limited regard for the views or interests of other groups. Such groups often are reluctant to compromise.

Single-member district A system in which a legislator, city council member, or other public official is elected from a specific geographic area.

Sound bite A short, quotable phrase by a public official or political candidate that may sound good on television or radio but lacks depth and is often meaningless.

Speaker The presiding officer of the House of Representatives.

Special district A unit of local government created by the state to perform a specific function or functions not met by cities or counties, including the provision of public services to unincorporated areas.

Spin The presentation of information in the best possible light for a public official or political candidate. It usually is provided by a press secretary, campaign consultant, or other individual representing the officeholder or candidate.

Staggered terms A requirement that members of state boards and commissions appointed by the governor serve terms that begin on different dates. This is to assure that a board maintains a level of experience by guarding against situations where all board members leave office at the same time.

State Board of Education A fifteen-member body, whose members are elected by districts, that oversees the administration of public education in Texas.

State chair and vice chair The two top state leaders of a political party, one of whom must be a woman. They are selected every two years by delegates to the party's state convention.

State convention A meeting held in June of even-numbered years by each of the two major political parties. Delegates to this convention elect the party's state leadership and adopt a party platform. In presidential election years, it selects the delegates to the party's national nominating convention.

State executive committee The statewide governing board of a political party. It includes a man and a woman elected by party members from each of the thirty-one state senatorial districts and the state chair and vice chair.

State treasurer This elected office, which administered state funds, was abolished in

1995. Its duties were transferred to the comptroller's office.

Statutes   Laws enacted by a legislative body.

Subcommittee   A few members of a larger committee appointed to review legislation and make recommendations to the committee on the disposition of a bill.

Suffrage   The right to vote.

Sunset legislation   The process under which most state agencies have to be periodically reviewed and re-created by the legislature or go out of business.

Supremacy clause   A provision of the U.S. Constitution that says federal law prevails in conflicts between the powers of the states and the national government.

Supreme Court, Texas   A nine-member court with final appellate jurisdiction over civil lawsuits.

Tag   A rule that allows an individual senator to postpone a committee hearing on any bill for at least 48 hours, a delay that can be fatal to a bill during the closing days of a legislative session.

Tax, franchise   The state's major business tax. It is applied only to corporations and, until changed by the legislature in 1991, was based on a business's assets. Now it is a hybrid corporate income tax that is based on a corporation's income or assets, whichever would produce the highest payment to the state.

Tax, income   A tax based on a corporation's or an individual's income. Texas has a hybrid corporate income tax but is one of only a few states without a personal income tax.

Tax, property   A tax on homes, businesses, and certain other forms of property that is the main source of revenue for local governments. The tax is based on the assessed value of the property.

Tax, sales   A tax charged as a set percentage of most retail purchases and many services. It is the main source of tax revenue for state government and an important source of revenue for many cities and metropolitan transit authorities.

Tax, sin   A common nickname for a tax on tobacco or alcoholic beverages.

Third party   A minor political party. There have been many in Texas over the years, but none has had significant success on a statewide level.

Ticket splitting   The decisions of voters to divide their votes among candidates of more than one political party in the same election.

Tort reform   Changes in state law to put limits on personal injury lawsuits and damage judgments entered by the courts.

Traditionalistic subculture   A view that political power should be concentrated in the hands of a few elite citizens who belong to established families or influential social groups. Public policy basically serves the interests of this small group.

Transnational regionalism   The expanding economic and social interdependence of South Texas and Mexico.

Two-party system   A political system that has two dominant parties, such as that of the United States.

Two-thirds rule   A rule under which the Texas Senate has traditionally operated that requires approval of at least two-thirds of senators before a bill can be debated on the Senate floor. It allows a minority of senators to block controversial legislation.

Unitary system   A system in which ultimate power is vested in a central or national government and local governments have only those powers granted them by the central government. This principle describes the relationship between the state and local governments in Texas.

Unicameral   A single-body legislature.

Urbanization   The process by which a predominantly rural society or area becomes urban.

Venireman   A person who has been called for a jury panel.

Veto   The power of the governor to reject, or kill, a bill passed by the legislature.

Veto, line-item   The power of the governor to reject certain parts of an appropriations, or spending, bill without killing the entire measure.

Voting Rights Act   A federal law designed to protect the voting rights of minorities by requiring the Justice Department's approval of changes in political districts and certain other electoral procedures. The act, as amended, has eliminated most of the more restrictive state laws that limited minority political participation.

Ward politics   Term, often with negative connotations, that refers to partisan politics linked to political favoritism.

Whistleblower   A government employee who publicly reports wrongdoing or unethical conduct within a government agency.

White primary   A series of state laws and party rules that denied African Americans the right to vote in the Democratic primary in Texas in the first half of the twentieth century.

Writ of mandamus   Court order directing a lower court or another public official to take a certain action.

Photo Credits

Chapter 1 Page 6: Culver Pictures, Inc.; page 7: Texas State Library, Archives Division, Austin Texas, No. ITC-73-79; page 8: Courtesy of T. R. Fehrenbach; page 9: Bob Daemmrich/ Bob Daemmrich Photography, Inc.; page 10: Bob Daemmrich/Bob Daemmrich Photography, Inc.; page 13: Joel Salcido/Bob Daemmrich Photography, Inc.; page 18: Reuters/ Camilla McElligott/Hulton/Archives; page 26: CORBIS.

Chapter 2 Page 43: The University of Texas Institute of Texan Cultures at San Antonio, No. ITC-73-79; page 47: Texas State Library & Archives Commission; page 49: Texas State Library & Archives Commission; page 57: The University of Texas Institute of Texan Cultures at San Antonio, No. 74-804.

Chapter 4 Page 101: Bob Daemmrich/Bob Daemmrich Photography, Inc.; page 118: Courtesy of Jack Gullahorn.

Chapter 5 Page 140: Houston Chronicle Library.

Chapter 6 Page 182: L. Tucker Gibson, Jr.

Chapter 8 Page 233: Stock Boston; page 241: Courtesy of the Office of Tom Craddick; page 245: Courtesy of the Office of David Dewhurst; page 253: The Senate of the State of Texas/Senate Media Services; page 266: The Senate of the State of Texas/Senate Media Services.

Chapter 9 Page 281 (left): Texas State Library & Archives Commission; page 281(right): CORBIS; page 291: Bob Daemmrich Photography, Inc.; page 294: Pete Souza/Liaison Agency,

Inc.; page 296: Bob Daemmrich/Boston Stock; page 299: Courtesy of the Governor's Office; page 302: Jerry H. Hoefer/AP/Wide World Photos; page 305: David J. Phillip/AP/Wide World Photos; page 307: Harry Cabluck/AP/Wide World Photos.

Chapter 11 Page 336: L. Tucker Gibson, Jr./Thomas R. Dye; page 342: David Woo/Stock Boston; page 346: Houston Chronicle. Copyright 1994 Houston Chronicle Publishing Company. Reprinted with permission. All rights reserved.; page 357: Harvey Georges/AP/Wide World Photos; page 361: Eric Gay/AP/Wide World Photos.

Chapter 12 Page 377 (top): Paul Buck/Bob Daemmrich Photography, Inc.; page 377 (bottom): Tim Johnson/AP/Wide World Photos; page 385: Overstreet Studios; page 387: L. Tucker Gibson, Jr./Thomas R. Dye; page 392: Peter Vadnai/Corbis/Stock Market; page 394: L. Tucker Gibson, Jr.; page 404: San Antonio ISD; page 408: Michael Patrick Photography/ Bradley Development.

Chapter 13 Page 441: Eric Gay/AP/Wide World Photos.

Index